A SEAPORT LEGACY

The Story of St. John's, Newfoundland

PRESS PORCÉPIC

A SEAPORT LEGACY

The Story of St. John's, Newfoundland

by

Paul O'Neill

Published by Press Porcepic, 70 Main Street, Erin, Ontario, N0B 1T0, in November of 1976 with the assistance of the Canada Council and the Ontario Arts Council.

Printed in Canada by
John Deyell Company

Endpaper photo—St. John's harbour from the Southside Hills, circa 1880. Photo by S.H. Parsons.
Reproduced from a cracked glass plate in the possession of St. John's City Hall.

Dust Jacket photo—St. John's harbour looking down Long's Hill, 1831, drawn by Lt. Col. Oldfield, courtesy of St. John's City Hall.

Distribution:

CANADA	U.S.A.	U.K.
Musson Book Company	Books Canada Inc.	Books Canada Ltd.
30 Lesmill Road	33 East Tupper Street	1 Bedford Road
Don Mills, Ontario	Buffalo, New York	London N2
M3B 2T6	14203	England

Canadian Shared Cataloguing in Publication Data

O'Neill, Paul, 1928—
A seaport legacy

Continues the author's The oldest city,
with index covering both vols.
1. St. John's, Nfld. — History. I. Title. II. Title:
    The story of St. John's, Newfoundland.

FC2196.4.0542   971.8   C76-017156-4
F1124.5.S140542
ISBN 0-88878-110-5

For Margaret
Who Shared with John
My Youth, My Affection and My City

BOOKS BY PAUL O'NEILL

Spindrift and Morning Light
The City in Your Pocket
Legends of a Lost Tribe
The Oldest City, The Story of St. John's Newfoundland, Part I

Publisher's Preface

This book represents the second part of Paul O'Neill's history of St. John's, Newfoundland. As the book is arranged by subject matter, rather than chronologically, each part can be read on its own, or the two can be enjoyed as a complete work.

This volume contains an index to both parts, the complete bibliography from Part I expanded to include new sources used in Part II, and addenda relating to both volumes. The acknowledgements to Part I are repeated here as they apply equally to both parts.

The pictures included in this volume, many just recently discovered by the author and never before in print, vary greatly in quality. In large part this is due to the state of the originals. The nineteenth century photographs were often not as clear as might have been desired; however we believe they add greatly to the volume.

The complete work represents a thorough and entertaining study of Canada's oldest city—a study which should help to keep alive its past and give pleasure in the present.

Acknowledgements

This work is history in a particular pattern. Because it is the first history of St. John's ever to be compiled, I feel it would have been extremely difficult to have told the story in chronological order and include the mass of information and detail these volumes should contain.

For those wanting a complete picture of the life and history of the town at any specific period the work will be frustrating as they will have to refer to many chapters. However, for those interested in the numerous small details, events, dates, and human interest happenings that tell of the story of entertainment, education, sport, religion, and other facets of life, in the development of St. John's, I hope the book will prove a satisfaction.

The historical evolvement of each sphere covered by this book has been investigated exhaustively. Wherever possible, sources, dates, etc., have been carefully checked and counterchecked. Unfortunately, much valuable material has been lost in the numerous fires that have swept St. John's. What errors are to be found in the manuscript are due to the vagueness of sources, contradictory information, or the author's own inability to recognize an inaccuracy. Sources quoted in the chapters may be checked in the bibliography. It was the author's intention to compile rather than interpret the events recorded in this work. What is important is that they are now available in a single source. My concern has not been to startle, but to unify. A search on two continents for unpublished diaries, letters, reports, drawings, photographs, and other material, has proven to be generally unavailing.

The quest for confirmation of certain facts and stories was often exasperting and frequently time consuming. Some cherished myths had to be exploded for the sake of historic fact. The frustrations of my quest were relieved by the generous assistance of many people and especially the following.

I am most deeply indebted to Claire Pratt for such a thorough job of editing and an indefatigable determination not to let any of my inadvertent errors slip by. For introducing me to Press Porcepic and bringing to an end my publishing woes I offer my sincere gratitude to Clara Thomas.

In Ireland I should like to thank the staffs of the National Library in Dublin, the Waterford City Council and Chamber of Commerce, and the

Water Street in Chapter 8. I was also fortunate to have the co-operation of many people who supplied information on their families and businesses. They were too numerous to list here. For their generous help I acknowledge my debt.

My thanks to the Hutchinson Publishing Group Ltd., London for permission to quote from *My Air Armanda* by Air Marshal Balbo and to Charles Scribner's Sons, New York, for permission to quote from *The Spirit of St. Louis* by Charles A. Lindbergh.

Among those who kindly helped by their encouragement were Lewis and Phyllis Brookes who planted the seed for this book in my mind. Kay Breen, Jean Neary and Jim Long listened with patience and criticized most helpfully. My mother was often forced to dredge nearly forgotten facts from the depths of her memory to satisfy my impatience for accuracy and I am grateful.

Lastly, I am under a special obligation to mention my debt to the Most Reverend J. M. O'Neill, DD., and Dr. A. B. Perlin, who by their advocacy of my cause, enabled me to obtain Canada Council aid for research. The project was completed with the assistance of a Canada Council grant under its Canadian Horizons Program. A. B. Perlin has been most generous with his help, which was always as close as the nearest telephone.

I would also be remiss if I did not here record the memory of a beloved little dog Toby, who looked on with patient sympathy night after night, year after year, as the story slowly took shape. He listened in devoted silence as I read aloud the troublesome chapters, winced with me when my frustrations became too much to bear, and often licked encouragement when I felt near defeat. He died, age fifteen years, one month to the day before the work was completed. With him I buried at Briarcliff many of the memories of trying to compile this work.

Briarcliff, Bay Bulls.
St. John's, Newfoundland.
May 9th, 1973.

Contents

PUBLISHER'S PREFACE   ix

ACKNOWLEDGEMENTS   x

1.   THE ART OF GOVERNMENT (Politics—National to Civic) *433*

Agitation for self-government *455*   Secret ballot *456*   Mary Travers and the Assembly *456*   Erection of a Colonial Building *456*   Social activities *460*   1861 Hogsett-Furey riot *460* Bloodshed on Water Street *461*   1886 "railway riot" *462* More social events *463*   The carpet affair *464*   Disturbances of 1921 *465*   Julia Salter Earle *466*   1932 riot *467*   Commission of Government *472*   National Convention *472* Confederation *473*   Confederation Building *475*   St. John's Charter *476*   Windsor Lake named *476*   Mayors of St. John's *477*   City Halls *477*   Symbols of office *478*   Suffragettes *479*

2.   TO TRAVEL HOPEFULLY (Transportation and Accommodation) *483*

First public transportation *503*   First road out of St. John's *503*   Conception Bay packets *504*   Stage coaches *505*   First mention of a railway *506*   Steam communication and the Mullock affair *507*   Early coastal boats *508*   Coming of the railway *509*   Bell Island ferry tragedy *510*   The omnibus *511*   The cycle, jaunting car and automobile *512*   Construction of a gas works *513*   The new "electric fluid" *513*   First incandescent light *514*   Completion of a railway *515*   1898 contract *516*   Branch lines closed *517*   Paving Water Street and electric railway *518*   A gasoline powered bus system *518* Early inns *519*   Palliser's ball *520*   House on Prince William Place *521*   The Ugly Club *522*   19th Century hotels *522* Some catered fetes *524*   New Atlantic Hotel *528*   20th Century hotels *528*   A hotel at Fort William *529*   Atlantic Place *530*

3. CRIMES AND MISFORTUNES (Law, courts, trials and murders) *531*
Early trials and punishments *545* Whipping in the Navy *548* Bonfoy orders gallows *549* Public hangings *549* First laws in 1711 *550* Crow's command *550* Rule of naval surrogates *550* Vanburgh introduces Courts of Oyer and Terminer *551* Permission to execute in Newfoundland *552* The Keen murder *553* John Reeves, first Chief Justice *555* Other justices *555* Butler and Landergan affair *556* Abolition of Surrogate Courts *557* Charter of George IV *557* Cochrane and prisons *559* Signal Hill jail *561* Bank of England Robbers *562* H.M. Penitentiary at Quidi Vidi *563* Notable escapes from St. John's prisons *563* Pindikowski and ceiling frescos *568* Story of Valdmanis *569* Political trials of 1894 *570* Riots and a prison ship *570* The Market House *572* The new Court House *572* First lawyer *572* Law Society formed *573* Evolution of police force *573* Mitchell to O'Neill *575* IWA strike tragedy *576* Some courtroom dramas *577* Murder and its consequences *580*

4. A HANDFUL OF ASHES (Fires—great and small) *597*
Jones report of 1809 *620* Fire of 1816 *620* Great Fire of 1817 *621* Fire of 1819 *625* Some merchant families *625* Fire of 1833 *626* Great Fire of 1846 *627* Broomfield's report to Phoenix Fire Office *627* Rebuilding the town *631* Destruction of Tarahan's Town *631* Mullock and Bennett help save town in 1856 *632* Apple-Tree Well fire *633* Sundry other fires *633* Fire Brigades organized *635* Electric alarm boxes installed *636* Firemen's parades and celebrations *636* Great Fire of 1892 *637* Descriptions of Harvey and a Boston visitor *637* Rebuilding the city *643* Tragic fire on Southside *644* Hull Home fire of 1946 *645* K. of C., most tragic indoor fire in Canadian history *646*

5. OF BLOSSOMS, BIRDS AND BOWERS (Parks and recreation) *649*
The Garden *665* Lahey's Botanical Garden *667* Bannerman helps establish a park *668* Victoria Park *669* Bowring family donates a park *671* Signal Hill National Historic Park *673* Gibbet Hill *673* Chain Rock *674* The noon and Sunday guns *676* Cabot Tower *676* Governor Cochrane and Virginia Water(s) *678* Sir James Pearl *679* Develop-

ment of Glendale and Mount Pearl *680* Pippy Park *682*
Oxenham's story *683* Long Pond area *684* Edgell's Farm
and Confederation Building *684* Mumming *685* Soldier's
Meadow *686* Early St. John's graveyards *686* The Native
Society *687* Flag of Newfoundland *689* Catholics and Dis-
senters bury their own dead *690* Funeral customs *693*

6.   TRUE FAITH AND READY HANDS (Churches) *695*
First Church of England *711* Jackson-Lloyd affair *712* Rice
and his successors *712* Parson Langman *713* Constitution
of the See of Nova Scotia and Newfoundland *714* Appointment of Spencer as first Bishop of Newfoundland *714* Plans
for a cathedral *715* Bishop Feild *717* Completion of the
cathedral, the 1892 fire, and the rebuilding *718* St. Thomas'
Garrison Church *720* Christ Church, Quidi Vidi *721* St.
Mary's Anglican *722* Roman Catholics come to Newfoundland *723* Persecution under Penal Laws *724* Arrival of
Father O'Donel *725* Construction of Old Chapel *728*
O'Donel's successors to Fleming *731* Attempts to get land
for a cathedral *732* The grant of land *733* Three legends
735 Jones, the forgotton architect *737* The building of the
Basilica *738* Methodists establish in Newfoundland *742*
Pickavant, first minister *742* New Methodist Chapel de-
stroyed and rebuilt in 1816 *744* Fires and threats of fires
744 Building of Old Gower, George Street United, and
Cochrane Street Church *746* Destruction and rebuilding of
Gower Street Church *747* Building of the first Presbyterian
Kirk *747* Fraser's term *748* Split in Church of Scotland
749 Fire and destruction *749* St. Andrew's after 1892 *751*
The Congregational Church and John Jones *751* The first
meeting house *752* Queen's Road Congregational *753*
Unity with Presbyterians *754* Move to St. David's *755*

7.   IN THE MAZE OF SCHOOLS (Education and Schools) *757*
First schools *775* Newfoundland and British North America
School Society *777* Life in early schoolrooms *777* Bishop
Feild's establishments *778* B.I.S. and education *780* Bishop
Fleming's Franciscans *780* Irish Christian Brothers *781*
Bishop Mullock founds St. Bonaventure's College *782*
Methodist College *784* Diocesan Girls' School *784* Com-
ing of Presentation Sisters *787* Life in St. John's *789*

Arrival of Sisters of Mercy *792* First Orphanage *796*
Academy of Our Lady of Mercy *796* Salvation Army College
797 Charles and Emma Dawson *797* Memorial University
798 St. Bride's College *801* College of Fisheries *801*
Trades College *802*

8. ONE VERY NARROW STREET (Block by block—the firms
and people) *803*
The Lower Path *819* Early scenes of disorder *820* From
the ruins of 1817 *821* Staples in the stores *822* Temperance Street to Hill o' Chips *823* John Stripling's Estate
824 Hill o' Chips to Holloway Street *824* The Crow's Nest
825 The Newfoundland War Memorial *826* Holloway St.
to Court House Steps *828* Telegram Lane *830* Court
House Steps to Beck's Cove *832* Market House Hill *832*
Libraries and bookstores *833* Beck's Cove to Queen St. *838*
William's Lane *840* The General Post Office *841* Queen
Street to Hutchings St. *842* Paving of Water Street *844*
Newman's celebrated Port *846* Hutchings St. to Victoria
Park *848* Victoria Park *849* Victoria Park to the Cross-
roads *850* Sudbury Hall *851* The Crossroads to Mullins
River *852* Vail's Bakery *853* Kerry Lane *854* Mullins
River to Long (Job's) Bridge *854* The Marine Promenade
854 Long (Job's) Bridge to Steer's Cove *855* Peter and
Lewis Tessier *857* Steer's Cove to Bishop's Cove *859* The
Dowsley Tragedy *860* The Crosbie Empire *863* Bishop's
Cove to Beck's Cove *866* Meagher of Waterford *866* The
Bank Crash *867* Beck's Cove to Ayre's Cove *871* Daylight
Saving Time *871* Ayre's Cove to Clift's-Baird's Cove *872*
Charles Robert Ayre *873* The St. John's Library Society *874*
The first synagogue *877* James Baird *878* The City Club
878 Clift's-Baird's Cove to Hunter's Cove *879* Loss of S.S.
Lion *879* St. John's Board of Trade *882* The first Macpher-
son *883* Hunter's Cove to Harvey's Lane *884* Javelin
House *886* Harvey's Lane to Water St. East *887* Gill's
Cove Customs House *887* The Mall of 1969 *887*

9. THEIR NAME IS ON YOUR WATERS (Mercantile and
Harbour history) *889*
St. John's Waterfront *905* American Dock *906* Mercantile
firms *907* Furness Line *908* Galway Wharf and Allan Line
909 Queen's Wharf and Queen's Beach *910* O'Leary,

O'Brien and Stabb *912* Job's business *913* Baine, Johnston & Co. *915* Port in World War II *917* Ice Cutting Act *917* National Harbour of Canada *919* Bowring's *919* Lawrey Murder *922* Building of drydock *924* Long Bridge *925* St. Mary's Church and Shanadithit's grave *926* Dundee whalers *927* Royal Navy Hospital *927* Department of Transport *927* Canadian Overseas Telecommunications *928* World War II ammunition dumps *929*

10.   ITS LONG-LOST MULTITUDE OF SHIPS (Vessels great and small) *933*
Loss of the *Argo* and the *Connaught 953* The *Newfoundland* and the *Nova Scotia 955* The *Fort Amherst* and *Fort Townshend 956* Marvellous misadventure of Louisa Journeaux *957* Bowring's Shakespeare fleet *961* Wreck of the *Florizel* and sinking of the *Stephano 962* Shackleton buys the *Nimrod 964* The *Terra Nova* takes Scott to Antarctica *964* The *Bear* and the *Proteus 966* Mutiny on the *Diana 967* Tragedy of the *Viking 968* The seal hunt *969* Loss of many sealing vessels *970* The *Greenland* disaster *971* Great Sealers' Strike *973* Loss of the *Southern Cross* and tragedy of the *Newfoundland 974* Story of H.M.S. *Calypso 975* The Alphabet Fleet *976* Sinking of the *Caribou 977* Shelling of the *Erik 978* The *Kelmscott* story *978* Bob Bartlett and the *Effie M. Morrissey 979* Portuguese fleet and the *Gil Eanes 980* Harbour pilots *981* Practice of a "let-pass" *982* Wrecks in the Narrows *982* To Gibraltar and The Hebrides *985* *Lady St. John's 986* Two stowaway stories *986* Some shipboard visitors *987* Merlin Rock *990*

Table of Illustrations

Chapter I

Statue of Corte Real   435
Patrick Morris   436
King's Beach, 1780   437
Government House, Fort Townshend, 1831   438
The Honourable Philip Little   439
Sir Frederick Carter   439
The Interior of the Lower House, Colonial Building   440
The Ceiling of the Upper House, Colonial Building   441
Market House, Water Street, 1880   442
Water Street at McBride's Hill, 1880   443
Sir Robert Bond   444
Lord Morris   444
Union and Commercial Banks, 1894   445
Sir Ralph Williams on the steps of the Colonial Building, 1910   446
A picnic at Pearces, Forest Pond, Goulds   447
Photograph of the Great Riot, 1932   448
West side of Colonial Building after Great Riot, 1932   449
The Billies, Kirkcudbright, Scotland   450
Inauguration of Commission of Government, 1934   451
The Honourable Joseph Roberts Smallwood   452
The Honourable Major Peter Cashin   452
Her Worship Mayor Dorothy Wyatt   453

Chapter II

Bishop John T. Mullock   485
William Whiteway   486
Sir Robert Reid   486
St. John's railway station, 1881-1903   487
Riverhead Railway Station, 1903   488
Accident, Reid-Newfoundland Company's Locomotive   489
Gentleman at the Battery   490
Interior, Reid-Newfoundland Railway Coach, 1900   491
The S.S. *Bruce*, 1900   492

Powerhouse and Petty Harbour   493
Tracks on Water Street, 1899   494
Streetcars, Water and Adelaide Streets   495
Motorcyclists, 1910   496
First car in Newfoundland, Rolls Royce, 1903   497
Motoring, 1927   498
Atlantic Hotel   499
Masonic Parade, Crosbie Hotel, circa 1893   500
The Balsam   501
Cochrane Hotel, Hawker and Grieve   502

Chapter III
Captain Henry Osborne   533
Chief Justice John Reeves   533
Gibbet Hill, 1800   534
The Constabulary at Fort Townshend, circa 1900   535
Market House, 1849   536
Chief Justice Boulton, 1790   537
Inspector General John McGowen   537
Water Street premises, scene of Sillars' murder   538
Regal Cafe, scene of Eng Wing Kit murder   539
Judge David Woodley Prowse   540
Funeral Parlour, New Gower Street   541
King George IV, Queen Mary laying cornerstone, 1901   542
Court House, 1901-04   543

Chapter IV
Chart of Fires of 1817, 1846, 1892   599
Drawing of Fire of 1846   600
Sir John Harvey   601
Reverend Moses Harvey   601
Firemen and the *Terra Nova*, 1885   602
Firemen of the West End Brigade   603
St. John's and the Narrows, circa 1890   604
Great Fire, 1892   605
Ruins after Great Fire, 1892   606
View of Destruction from Devon Row, 1892   607
View of Destruction from Devon Row, 1892   608
View of Destruction from Bell Street, 1892   609
McBride's Hill and Water Street, 1892   610
Ruins of Church of England Cathedral, 1892   611
Athenaeum before 1893 Fire   612

Athenaeum after the 1893 Fire   613
McAuley's Cooperage and H.M.S. *Alert,* 1901   614
Ruins of the Prince's Rink, 1941   615
First Traffic Light, Rawlins Cross, circa 1940   616
Burning Ruins, Knights of Columbus Hotel, 1942   617

Chapter V
Sketch, Upper Long Pond, 1831   651
Military Road, 1851   652
Soldiers Meadow, 1875   653
General Protestant Cemetery, 1880s   654
Painting by Hayward of Mummers Parade, 1850s   655
Patrick Street arch   656
Hawker and Grieve take off in the "Atlantic," 1919   657
Sir Edgar Bowring   658
Rudolph Cochius   658
Casino Theatre Stage   659
Sir Cavendish Boyle   660
Professor David Bennett   660
Pleasantville Camp, some Blue Puttees, 1914   661
Newfoundland War Memorial and Entertainers, 1943   662
Camp Alexander, 1941   663

Chapter VI
Dr. Aubrey Spencer   697
St. Thomas Church, 1850   698
Military and King's Bridge Road, 1821   699
St. John's Cathedral, circa 1885   700
The Reverend James O'Donel   701
Captain Henry Prescott   701
Detail, Brenton's Drawing of St. John's, 1798   702
Roman Catholic Complex, Henry Street   703
Pageant "Triumph and Sacrifice," 1955   704
Bishop Thomas Scallan   705
The Reverend Michael Howley   705
The Basilica of St. John the Baptist   706
March of Portuguese Fishermen, 1955   707
The Reverend John Pickavant   708
The Reverend Charles Pedley   708
Gower Street Methodist Chapel   709

Chapter VII
The Reverend John Jones   759

Samuel Codner   759
Church of England Boys' School, Colonial Street   760
Church Lads Brigade, circa 1900   761
Kindergarten scholars at Bishop Feild   762
Bishop Edward Feild   763
Bishop Power   763
Lady Morris   764
Dr. Robert Holloway   765
Orphan Asylum   766
St. Bonaventure's College, 1900   767
Irish Christian Brothers' Schools' Students, 1906   768
St. Bonaventure's College Hockey Team, 1928   769
Mother Bernard Kirwan   770
Littledale   771
Salvation Army founders   772
Early campus, Memorial University   773

Chapter VIII
Customs House, 1846-1892   805
Water Street East, 1880s   806
Water Street from William's Lane, 1880s   807
Water Street West of Adelaide Street   808
Salt fish drying on Water Street, circa, 1880   809
Ayre & Sons, rebuilt after 1892   810
James H. Munroe   811
Sir John Crosbie   811
E.J. Horwoods, Water Street   812
Water Street Merchants, 1901   813
McCarthy's Grocery Store   814
Ayre's Department Store, 1907   815
Haymarket Square   816
Water Street circa 1950   817
Water Street, circa 1945   818

Chapter IX
The Narrows, by Oldfield, 1831   891
St. John's, by Oldfield, 1831   892
Women drying Codfish, 19th Century   893
Scene at Sir Ambrose Shea's Wharf   894
Samuel Bulley   895
Shanadithit, the Last of the Beothuck Indians   895
Culling salt fish   896

Water Street   897
Port of St. John's, circa 1900   898
Replacing Drydocks, 1925   899
The S.S. *Beothic* during a Seal Hunt   900
Skinning the Seals, circa 1900   901
Scene from *The Viking*   902
The Mercantile District of St. John's, 1970   903
Finger Piers along Water Street, 1949   904

Chapter x
Chain Rock Battery, The Narrows   935
The *Argo*   936
The Liner *Connaught*   937
The S.S. *Adriatic*   938
Cabot Tower   939
Sir Hugh Palliser   940
Louisa Journeaux   940
S.S. *Ethie*   941
S.S. *Terra Nova*   942
S.S. *Nimrod*   943
S.S. *Bear*   944
Mutineers near the S.S. *Diana*   945
S.S. *Eagle*   946
S.S. *Proteus*   947
Captain Bob Bartlett as portrayed in *The Viking*   948
New Harbour Boat, 1910   949
Royal Mail Ship *Newfoundland*   950
Crew and Officers, S.S. *Caribou*   951
The Narrows in World War II   952

1

The Art of Government

Gasper Corte-Real seems most likely to have discovered St. John's in 1500 and named it Rio de San Johem. He was lost the following year on a voyage to Newfoundland. This statue in St. John's, by the Portuguese sculptor Martins Correira, was a gift to the city from the Portuguese Fisheries Organization as an expression of gratitude on behalf of Portuguese Grand Banks fishermen for the friendly hospitality always extended to them by the people of Newfoundland. (Courtesy Newfoundland Department of Tourism.)

The great Patrick Morris was born in Ireland in 1789. At the age of eleven he arrived in St. John's where his father conducted a business. Morris was second only to Dr. William Carson in fighting for full Responsible Government and other reforms. He died 22 Aug. 1849 without living to see the realization of his dream. .

King's Beach, St. John's (circa 1780), site of Newfoundland War Memorial. On the left is The Ship, a popular tavern of the time. The flag flies over the Customs House. This painting is thought to have been done by one of Governor Edwards daughters who accompanied him to St. John's in 1779, causing His Excellency to rent a dwelling on shore which became the first Government House. The Highland soldiers in the sketch were not stationed in Newfoundland until 1779. (Courtesy Chief Justice Furlong.)

Government House, Fort Townshend, in 1831. The gable roof addition at the back stands on the site of the present Central Fire Hall. This was the residence in which Governor Pickmore died. It was also the home of Waldegrave, Gower, Duckworth, and Lady Hamilton, the first Governor's wife to reside in the colony. The old barracks building on the left was torn down in 1947. (Courtesy Newfoundland Constabulary Archives.)

The Honourable Philip Little was born in Prince Edward Island in 1824 and came to Newfoundland to practise law in 1844. In 1855 he became Newfoundland's first Prime Minister at the age of thirty-one. He served in that capacity until 1858 when he was appointed a judge. After retiring to Ireland in 1866 he died there 15 October 1897.

Sir Frederick Carter was born in St. John's 12 February 1819. His father was Chief Magistrate Peter Weston Carter. In 1864 he and Sir Ambrose Shea were Newfoundland delegates to the Quebec Conference and are now numbered among the Fathers of Confederation. Prime Minister from 1865 to 1869 and an opponent of sectarianism, he invited leading Catholics like Shea and John Kent to form a coalition-type government. His platform of "Confederation with Canada" saw him defeated. He was again Prime Minister from 1874 to 1878. Appointed a judge in 1879, Sir Frederick died 1 March 1900.

The interior of the Lower House in the Colonial Building. Here the Government of Newfoundland sat with one interruption from 1855 to 1959. The fireplace around which members of the government clustered is behind the lamppost on the right while the staircase down which Sir Richard Squires escaped is behind the lamppost on the left. (Courtesy Newfoundland Provincial Archives.)

This ceiling in the Upper House of the Colonial Building is one of those painted by the Polish prisoner Alexander Pindikowsky in 1880. In this chamber the Legislative Council met. It also served as a ballroom for fetes honouring the Prince of Wales, Cyrus Field, and others and was a mortuary room when the corpse of Sir Ambrose Shea was brought home to Newfoundland for burial. (Courtesy Newfoundland Provincial Archives.)

In front of the Market House on Water Street around 1880. Ladies with parasols cluster under the window of O'Brien the butcher. During the riot of 13 May 1861 Father O'Donnell is said to have been wounded by a shot fired from this window as he tried to disperse a mob in front of the Market House. (Courtesy Provincial Reference Library.)

442

Water Street at the foot of McBride's Hill (circa 1880). The store on the right, M. Fenelon & Co., was Kitchen's property during the Great Riot of 1861. Here three people named Clifford, Hunt and Fitzpatrick were shot to death when the military under Colonel Grant opened fire on a mob that was smashing its way into Kitchen's store and turned to attack the troops. In the Pope Building, later erected on this site, Newfoundland's first broadcasting station VOS went on the air in 1921, giving its first official broadcast 9 July 1922. (Courtesy St. John's City Hall.)

443

Sir Robert Bond is considered by most people to have been Newfoundland's greatest Prime Minister. He served with distinction from 1900 to 1908. At one time he pledged his personal fortune to secure a loan in New York which helped tide the colony over a difficult economic period. He retired to his estate at Whitbourne in 1913 and stayed aloof from political life.

Lord Morris, born in St. John's in 1859, served as Prime Minister from 1909 to 1917. During World War I he left Newfoundland to become a member of the Imperial War Cabinet in London. He was created Baron Morris in 1918. He died in self-imposed exile in England 24 October 1935.

444

The day of the bank crash, 10 December 1894, when the Union and Commercial Banks suspended payment and locked their doors. Depositors are shown congregating in front of the Union Bank building which still stands on Duckworth Street. It is the only building in the east end of downtown St. John's to have survived the Great Fire of 1892. (Note the ruins of the Athenaeum next door.) On the left of the photograph more people congregate in front of the Commercial Bank across the street to the east.

His Excellency the Governor, Sir Ralph Champneys Williams, officially announces the death of King Edward VII and proclaims the accession to the throne of King George V from the steps of the Colonial Building 9 May 1910. Twenty-two years later an unruly mob gathered here for the Great Riot of 1932. (Courtesy Provincial Archives.)

446

A picnic at Pearces, Forest Pond, Goulds, held to celebrate the gaining of the Jubilee Scholarship by Richard Anderson Squires who (hands folded in his lap) sits in the lower left corner of the group. Seated beside the future Prime Minister are Elsie Holloway (the famous photographer), Eva Macpherson, Mr. LeSueur, and Harold Tessier. Left to right in the middle row are George Peters, Professor Thérouin, Sally (March) Thérouin, Mrs. Stephen March (wife of the M.H.A.), Mrs. Holloway (mother of Elsie), Mrs. (Dr.) H.E. Kendall, Violette Macpherson, Florrie Ayre, Clare (Edgar) Shirran, John Steer, Jessie Ayre, Charlie Syme, Cyril Tessier, and Will Shirran. In the top row are Janie Snelgrove, Jean Ayre, Emma Ayre, and Louise Bartlett. (Courtesy Newfoundland Provincial Archives.)

447

The Great Riot of 1932 took place when this crowd marched from the Majestic Theatre to the Colonial Building demanding an audience with the Prime Minister, Sir Richard Squires. At the front of the mob surging towards the steps of the Legislature are the bandsmen. A lone mounted policeman on a white horse moves through the crowd at the back. (Courtesy Newfoundland Provincial Archives.)

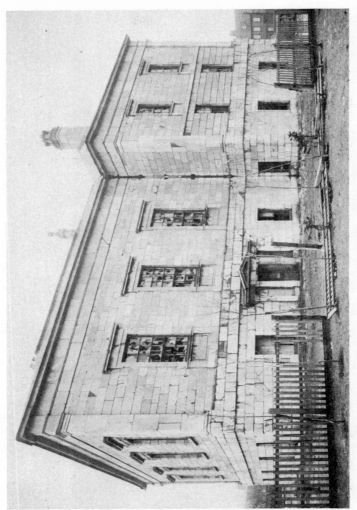

The west side of the Colonial Building after the Great Riot of 1932 in which all the windows were smashed and the building ransacked. Files, furniture, and a grand piano were dragged through this broken section of fence and burned in Bannerman Park. The entrance is shown here to the first bank in St. John's which was located in the basement of the building. (Courtesy Newfoundland Provincial Archives.)

The Billies, birthplace of the greatest man in Newfoundland history, Dr. William Carson. This farmhouse, three miles north of Kirkcudbright in Scotland, is where the fiery advocate of Newfoundlanders' rights was born in 1770. The house today is virtually unchanged. Carson's St. John's residence, also called The Billies, is at the top of Rostellan Street but its exterior has been drastically modernized. (Courtesy Galloway News Pictorials.)

A historic moment in Newfoundland history, as Commission of Government is inaugurated 17 February 1934 in the ballroom of the Newfoundland Hotel. Seated on the stage are the three English and three Newfoundland Commissioners. They are from left to right Noel Trentham (English), Sir John Puddester (Newfoundland), Sir John Hope Simpson (English), Sir William Horwood (Chief Justice), Sir David Anderson (Governor), Ex-Prime Minister Frederick Alderdice (Newfoundland), Thomas Lodge (English), William Howley (Newfoundland), and the Master of Ceremonies Arthur Mews.

The Honourable Joseph Roberts Smallwood on the campaign trail convincing
Newfoundlanders to vote their country into the Canadian Confederation in 1948. The
magnetism of his voice and hypnotic spell of his personality swept him into office
as Newfoundland's first provincial premier and kept him there for twenty-two dynamic and
turbulent years.

The Honourable Major Peter Cashin whose resignation from the post of Minister of Finance
in the government of Sir Richard Squires began the political unrest that led to the riot of
5 April 1932 which saw the Prime Minister fleeing with a mob at his heels. Here the Major is
seen, following World War II, leading the fight for the return of Responsible Government to
Newfoundland. His campaign ended in Confederation with Canada.

452

Her Worship Mayor Dorothy Wyatt was the first woman elected to a position of real prominence in Newfounldland on her own merits. A registered nurse and doctor's wife, it is said, "in a glare of watchful and frequently critical publicity she showed herself afraid of neither decision nor controversy." (Courtesy St. John's City Hall.)

The Art of Government

In general, the art of government consists in taking as much
money as possible from one class of citizens to give to the other.
                    VOLTAIRE *Dictionnaire Philosophique*

For the most part the story of the political life of St. John's is the story of
the political life of Newfoundland. It is far beyond the scope of the present
work to trace the rise and fall of systems and governments in the island
over the centuries. In this chapter we shall be content with tracing the history of the buildings that have housed national, provincial, and civic governments at St. John's.

Men like Thomas Oxford and John Downing began the agitation for
some form of government within the colony of Newfoundland in the
1770s. It was to take sixty years before the island's rulers in Britain paid
any real heed to the petitions of the settlers. The country was run for and
by the west country fish merchants of England and they had a strangle-
hold on emigration and development.

The Minutes of the Merchants Venturers Society of Bristol, 10
January 1764, reveal the power of these gentlemen. The Minutes read:
"The Committee agreeing with the opinions of Dartmouth and Poole that
the establishment of a purely civil government in Newfoundland would be
rather disadvantageous to the fishery, the master is desired to notify those
views to the Board of Trade." This minute resulted from a request by the
Right Honourable the Lords Commissioners for Trade and Plantations
who wanted to know the opinion of the merchants of the city trading in
Newfoundland.

The settlers were not consulted and they had no voice. The only
question to be answered was whether civil government "will or will not
be for the benefit and advantage of the fishery and navigation of this
kingdom." At the Bristol meeting letters were produced from the merchants of Dartmouth and Poole showing that civil government in Newfoundland would bring no advantage, rather a disadvantage.[1]

In 1832, years of agitation for self-rule by such men as Dr. William
Carson and Patrick Morris finally resulted in the granting of a peculiar
compromise called representative government. On polling day, 25 Sep-

455

tember 1832, fifteen members were elected from nine districts to the first House of Assembly. One of the defeated candidates was the man whose efforts made it all possible, William Carson. The system was rendered almost inoperative from the beginning by the creation of an appointed Upper House, a kind of local House of Lords, or Senate, which had virtual veto over the legislature.

Like the vote for women, the secret ballot was a long time in coming to Newfoundland. In early elections there was no problem in knowing whom the small numbers of eligible electors supported. Votes were counted by having those favouring one candidate assemble on one side of the person taking the count while those favouring the other candidate stood on the opposite side. Frequently votes were openly bought with liquor and other enticements, so that some voters moved from one side to the other until a final count was taken. The first local politician elected by secret ballot is said to have been Edward Morris, who was returned in 1885 by "the free and independent electors of St. John's West."

Before the use of indoor halls, public meetings in St. John's were held on street corners. The most popular location for these political harangues was a platform that was erected for the purpose on the corner of Barter's Hill and New Gower Street and that was reached by stepping through the second-storey window of the adjoining house. The platform was above the reach of the spectators so as to assure the orator that he would not be dragged down by an unsympathetic mob.

Election headquarters for the first Newfoundland elections, in 1832, was the inn of Mary Travers, at King's Place, opposite the present War Memorial. On 26 December 1832 this two-storey frame building, just west of King's Road, became the Parliament of Newfoundland when the first session of the local legislature met in the former tavern. The upper floor was used by the Council and the lower floor by the Assembly. Governor Thomas Cochrane officiated at the opening and there was a nineteen-gun salute from the forts. John Bingley Garland, member for Trinity, was elected Speaker.

One of the things overlooked by the first session was an appropriation due Mrs. Travers for rent on her property. On Friday, 26 July 1833, she reminded the House of the attention of herself and her servants toward the comforts of the House, and intimated the inconvenience and loss she had suffered by not yet receiving the sum awarded her for the use of her premises. Her creditors had instituted expensive lawsuits against her and she wanted her rent from the infant government. No reply was received by the anxious lady.

Immediately she took matters into her own hands, causing a restraint warrant to be issued. She seized the Speaker's chair, the cocked hat, dress suit, and sword of the sergeant-at-arms, and a desk full of books and papers belonging to the Assembly. Mrs. Travers advertised the Speaker's chair for sale in the Press as being "elegantly upholstered and finished in black moreen and ornamented with brass." The desk, its contents, and even the mace were up for sale by auction.

The mace, sword, and regalia were brought from London, England by the first sergeant-at-arms, Thomas Beck. At the auction most of the articles were purchased by a Mr. Leary and were eventually bought back by the embarrassed Assembly. Having been dispossessed of its King's Place headquarters by the angry Mrs. Travers, the second session moved to the old Court House, east of today's Court House Steps, where the Union Bank building still stands.

The business of the House was unable to proceed because of certain papers still in the possession of Mary Travers. The Clerk, Edward Archibald, called on her to return the articles but she absolutely refused until the five months' rent owing her was paid. The truth was they had already been sold to Mr. Leary.

On 3 February 1834, on a motion by Dr. Carson (who by then had gained election), the former landlady was ordered to attend the Bar of the House. Several questions were put to her by the Speaker and she was ordered to retire. A resolution was then passed requesting the Governor to take the necessary steps for the return of the papers and furniture. Arbitration was agreed upon, but Mrs. Travers refused to recognize the board. In 1836, after four years of wrangling, the lady was awarded £108.6.8. for rent and £83.13.5. for incidental expenses.[2]

The Court House proved to be a most inconvenient assembly chamber. It was much too small. On 20 February 1834, the Colonial Secretary was requested to add an extension to the west side of the Court House. When nothing came of this request it was proposed, 7 April 1836, that a site should be sought for the erection of a new building to house the Assembly. Vacant land west of the Court House, then an extension of Church Hill, was recommended to the Governor for the "accommodation of the Legislature, and for a public Market House for the town of St. John's and for other purposes."

On 2 May 1836 the Upper House passed the bill sent up for the Assembly, entitled "An Act to authorize the erection of a Colonial Building in the town of St. John's, and the raising by loan of a sum of money for that purpose." William Haddon, an Englishman who had superintended the construction of the new Government House for Sir Thomas Cochrane, wrote to Governor Prescott, saying he felt himself qualified to superintend the erection of the Colonial Building. Nothing more was heard of Haddon's offer.

On 2 March 1837 Prescott wrote to Lord Glenelg in London: "I have the honour to transmit an application addressed to your Lordship by the Commissioners for the erection of a Colonial Building in this town, Which at their request I beg to recommend to your Lordship's favourable consideration." There matters rested until 9 August 1838 when John Kent brought the proposal to the attention of His Excellency.

On 17 May 1839 the Governor told the Assembly that the commissioners for the erection of a Colonial House had determined upon a plan for a building. Little seems to have happened until 2 January 1841 when a proposal was made to take over one of the military buildings at Fort William for the Assembly. There was much discussion and numerous visits to the site. On April 20 His Excellency was requested to draw from the Treasury "the sum of £300, to be applied for the purpose of setting up and preparing the building at Fort William for reception of the Legislature."[3] With that the matter died and there was no further talk of passing over Fort William to the fledgling Government of Newfoundland.

On 19 March 1844 William B. Row proposed "An Act to authorize the raising by loan of a sum of money for the erection of a Colonial House." After various readings and amendments it was finally given assent by the governor. There was silence for another two years. On 11 March 1846 Patrick Morris asked leave to introduce a bill to authorize the raising of a loan of seven thousand pounds for the purpose of the completion of the Colonial Building and Market House which was not to cost more than fifteen thousand. James Purcell, the Irish architect and builder, had already been engaged to oversee the project. Purcell was against uniting a market house and a Colonial Building on the same site. He felt it was "too contracted" even if the whole of Church Hill (Court House Steps) were added. Patrick Kough, a politician who was also a builder, held that "the site at Church Hill is not calculated for a Colonial Building . . . being so much lower than Duckworth Street, the most conspicuous part of the building will not be seen." He felt a Colonial Building should go elsewhere and that the Duckworth Street site should be reserved for a market place. Following the 1846 fire a new Court House and Market House did get erected on the property.

Meanwhile, Major Robe of the Royal Engineers was sent to the Barrens to examine a site. On 18 May 1846 he wrote of the swampy land opposite Marsh Hill, between Government House and the Roman Catholic Cathedral: ". . . the ground selected is in the very centre and lowest part of a springy marsh or swamp. . . . The swamp never completely dries up . . . the springs which supply the south swamp afford the most abundant flow of water. . . ."[4] The major did not favour the location because a house erected in the midst of a marsh might be both unhealthy and unstable, even were the ground subject to the expensive process of drainage.

On 9 June 1846 the Great Fire drove the legislators from the old Court House. Members fled with books, papers, furniture, and other paraphernalia, but much was lost in the devouring flames. Temporary accommodation was found on the upper floor of the Orphan Asylum on Queen's Road, a school run by the Benevolent Irish Society. The first session in the Asylum took place on 16 June 1846. There was a guard of honour from the Royal Newfoundland Companies to greet the governor, judges, clergy, and other dignitaries, and a salute of artillery from Fort Townshend echoed over the blackened ruins of the city.

In spite of Major Robe's fears that a house in the marsh might prove unhealthy and unstable, James Purcell was granted the sum of £14,935 and told to have a building completed there by January 1848. The corner stone was laid on Queen Victoria's birthday, 24 May 1847. The event was accompanied by "many demonstrations of joy and loyalty usual on the happy occasion." At one o'clock Governor LeMarchant, watched by his Lady and "hundreds of the curious, roused to hearty cheers," laid the cornerstone which contained current coins of the realm, copies of local newspapers, some grains of locally grown wheat, and a parchment inscription.

After two years on Queen's Road the B.I.S. informed the Assembly that it needed the space in the Orphan Asylum for classrooms and the Government was once more homeless. The Hon. James Tobin came to the rescue by offering his new building on Water Street, opposite Holloway Street, and the Governor opened the new session of the Assembly there 19 December 1848.

Because of "disappointment in the arrival of some materials and a variety of other causes," Mr. Purcell was unable to complete the Colonial Building within the specified time. In fact, he eventually ended up more than two years behind schedule. The official opening took place Monday, 28 January 1850, at half-past two in the afternoon, when the booming of guns and the peal of church bells announced the arrival at the site of Sir Gaspard and Lady LeMarchant "in their well appointed sleigh," through ranks of soldiers from the garrison who lined both sides of Military Road. The band struck up the national anthem and shortly after three o'clock His Excellency took his place upon the throne. According to one newspaper he was

> clad in the rich uniform of Windsor, in deep mourning for the demise of the Queen Dowager, and according well with the sense and dignity which the occasion and place inspired. . . . Conspicuous in the great assemblage by his vigorous person and frank countenance we observed the veteran of Badajoz and Waterloo, Lieutenant Colonel Law . . . and directly below His Excellency's throne we saw the son of the gallant father (Lt. Robert Law) late from the bloody fields of the Punjab with wounds still unstaunched. . . . The ladies were accommodated on both sides of the Chamber, Lady LeMarchant . . . investing the important ceremony with a further interest by her presence. She was attended by a brilliant crowd of the fashion, elegance and beauty of the city but so numerous it would be impossible for us to enumerate them.[5]

No mention is made of James Purcell, the architect who designed and erected the structure.

White limestone was imported from Cork for use in the construction.

By the 1960s this stone was starting to crumble and had to be replaced. The cost of the building was around a hundred thousand dollars. It measured eighty-eight feet along the front and went back to a depth of a hundred and ten feet. The portico, supported by six Ionic columns about thirty feet in height, was surmounted by a pediment showing the Royal Arms. The Upper and Lower Chambers were at the back of the structure and each measured thirty by fifty feet. The Colonial Building was to become the scene of some of the most stormy, fatal, and tragic moments in Newfoundland history.

There was a savings bank in the basement, where Newfoundland's first bank robbery took place on the night of Saturday, 30 November 1850. The thieves forced a window and carried off the chest of the savings bank which contained four hundred and thirteen pounds. The offer of a reward of a hundred pounds and a free pardon to an accomplice brought no clues. In March 1851 James Kavanagh and Michael Whelan, one of whom had been a labourer at the Commercial Bank, were arrested on suspicion, confessed their guilt, and were committed to jail. The sum of two hundred and seventy pounds was recovered.

The Colonial Building became a social centre, and balls, concerts, and agricultural exhibitions were held there. The first public ball was held there on Tuesday evening, 25 July 1852, to honour Vice-Admiral Sir George Seymour and the officers of H.M. Ships *Cumberland, Bermuda,* and *Buzzard.* Dancing was in the Legislative Chamber and supper was served in the Assembly room. Edward Moore decorated the place with over two hundred wax lights and two side chandeliers of candles festooned with flowers. Monsieur Toussaint catered to over three hundred persons.

Of all the balls held in the Colonial Building the most memorable was the one which took place on the evening of Tuesday, 10 August 1858, to honour Mr. and Mrs. Cyrus Field, and to celebrate the laying of the Atlantic cable. It was a crowded and brilliant assemblage with the bells of the Roman Catholic cathedral ringing in the background. The midnight supper was set out by Lash's "in their best style."

Lash's firm catered again Wednesday, 25 June 1860, when a ball was held in honour of the visit of the Prince of Wales, later King Edward VII. His Royal Highness opened the event by dancing with Lady Brady, the wife of the Chief Justice. About seven hundred guests packed the building and the prince stayed until half-past two o'clock the following morning. He closed the finale with the "amiable and accomplished daughter of the Hon. James Tobin." The press accused one member of the executive of taking five persons to the ball without a ticket or payment. The scoundrel then presumed "to force his dancing acquaintance to the notice of His Royal Highness."

On Monday afternoon, 13 May 1861, Governor Bannerman arrived at the Council Chamber at two o'clock, after being hooted by a violent mob surrounding the Colonial Building. The excitement was occasioned chiefly by the known determination of the government to reject the claims of George Hogsett and Charles Furey to take their seats in the Assembly as members for Harbour Main. When the session began Mr. Hoyles objected to the presence of Messrs. Hogsett and Furey, claiming that their certificate from the returning officer was obtained by intimidation. They refused to withdraw and were removed by the police. The mob, hearing this, tried to force its way into the building.

The *Newfoundlander* says of the scenes which took place outside:

> The day was one of dread and horrors which assuredly can never be forgotten and never atoned for. . . . These feelings attained a fearful height at the time Messrs. Hogsett and Furey were obliged to withdraw from their seats, and it was with the utmost difficulty that the crowd who surrounded the Colonial Building could be restrained from violent demonstrations by the presence of the military and police forces, and even by that which always proves more powerful than either or both—the presence and exertion of the Catholic priests.

The mob gradually became more tranquil, thanks mainly to the Reverend Jeremiah O'Donnell, and began to disperse about six o'clock. Kenneth McLea received some blows as he left the building, but Father O'Donnell quickly rescued him and his injuries were slight.

From the grounds of the Colonial Building the crowd scattered about the town, later congregating in Water Street where they began smashing the glass in store windows. The premises of Nowlan, and that of Kitchen, both relatives of Patrick Nowlan, the member for Harbour Main, were broken into and their goods scattered about the street. Judge Little, at risk to life and limb, hurried into Water Street and managed to stop the smashing and looting. Father O'Donnell, in a hoarse voice, entreated and implored the people "for Christ's sake" to go home.

At that moment, the military, under Colonel Grant, marched onto the scene at the foot of McBride's Hill where Kitchen's store was located. Stones were thrown at the soldiers, and the Colonel was insulted and pulled from his horse. During these provocations the order was given to fire, and soldiers discharged their rifles into the frenzied mob. When the volley was over, three people were dead in the street and four others were injured. A lad named Clifford, the only support of an aged widow, was killed instantly. Two others, Hunt and Fitzpatrick, lingered a few minutes before dying. Fitzpatrick was an elderly invalid released from hospital the day before. With stones and musket balls flying about, Judge Little and Father O'Donnell did what they could to stop the massacre.

The priest, who was suffering from exhaustion, asked a man named Patrick Myrick if he could lean upon him. Myrick agreed.[6] While engaged in trying to disperse the mob in front of the Market House, Father O'Don-

461

nell was shot through the ankle, and Myrick was very seriously injured in the thigh by a musket ball. The two injured and bleeding peacemakers were carried into a neighbouring house. The shots were said to have been fired from an upstairs window in the house of O'Brien, the butcher, next to the Court House.

Magistrate Bennett refused Judge Little's request that he retire the troops. The Judge then went to Colonel Grant assuring him of peace if he would withdraw the soldiers. Colonel Grant consented and asked Judge Little to accompany him and his men to barracks. Between eight and nine o'clock the ringing of the Roman Catholic cathedral bells summoned the multitude to the church where Bishop Mullock rose into the pulpit in pontifical wrath and denounced the riot and rioters,[7] sending them all scurrying home to wash their wounds and bury their dead.

The Colonial Building witnessed its next riot twenty-five years after the events of 1861. On 30 March 1886 the Chamber was invaded by an excited crowd, consisting mostly of unemployed men and boys who had marched through the town with a banner bearing on it, in blue letters, the word "railway." They reached the House around three o'clock but were denied admission. Judge Prowse and Major Fawcett, of the constabulary, tried to get them to disperse, but their efforts failed and the mob smashed down the door and swept into the building, the flagpole shattering the gasolier in the main hall. Workers crowded the floor of the House, the galleries groaned under the weight of people, and shouts and banners filled the air.

The Speaker took the Chair and ordered the House be cleared but the police were powerless. Sir Ambrose Shea walked through the mob to lead them outdoors but they did not follow. He returned and condemned the action of the throng. Prime Minister Thorburn rose and said that he was powerless to act on their demands for railway employment. The House was adjourned and the crowd spilled out on the grounds where Sir Ambrose addressed them again from the steps, assuring them that the government would try to meet their demands for employment. He promised money would be spent on levelling Bannerman Park.

When the disturbance ended, two of the demonstrators, Patrick Dempsey of Casey's Lane and a young man named Earles, were taken into custody at an early hour in the morning. When word of their arrest spread, a mob gathered once more in the streets and a large body of men proceeded to the Court House where they demanded that they all be tried for the alleged offence, or that the arrested men be set free. Once again the city was on the verge of a bloody riot. The police were hastily summoned and the whole force, foot and mounted, with loaded revolvers, rifles, fixed bayonets and swords, hurried to the spot. Meanwhile, the alleged culprit, Dempsey, was arraigned before Judge Prowse who, finding no evidence of any violent deed by the prisoner, discharged him, and the mob dispersed peacefully.

On April 2, the flag bearer, a young man named Connell, was arrested about four o'clock and escorted by two policemen to the lock-up. The mob gathered again, in front of the Court House, and the police resumed their positions. As night wore on many in the assemblage went home for some sleep. In the morning charges of malicious mischief, the breaking of a gasolier, and an assault on Sergeant Coughlan[8] were preferred against Connell. Earles was charged only with malicious conduct. The case did not conclude until April 5 when Earles was discharged and Connell given thirty days, not for flag bearing, but for striking the police.

Between political fights and mob riots the building reverted to social events. At one o'clock on Tuesday afternoon, 10 October 1882, the first show of the St. John's Agricultural Society was held on the grounds with prizes going for horses, colts, bulls, cows, swine, sheep, poultry, butter, grain, potatoes, turnips, beets, and cabbage. The Society itself is said to have first met at the Factory, Garrison Hill, on Wednesday, 5 January 1842, at noon, with Governor Harvey presiding. Dr. William Carson was its mentor.

The *Evening Telegram* likened the political activity of the Legislature to a theatre when, on 15 February 1883 under the headline THEATRE, THEATRE, it announced

> The Royal "Terra Nova" Theatre will open for the season when the grand combination comedy company will have the honour to appear in the highly sensational and thrillingly interesting domestic Drama in an unlimited number of acts and scenes—entitled "The Bandit's Bride" or "The Fate of Poor Old Terra Nova"... [the cast to include] Willyam Whiteway as a plotting attorney and Ambrose Aye as Oily Gammon, afterwards the Hon. Happy-go-lucky Shillitoe. . . . The whole to conclude with the screaming farce, in one act, entitled "Beggar my Neighbour". Characters by the company. The performances will be at the expense of the colony.

Back in July 1859 the building had been used for a genuine performance when Agnes Heywood, a contralto of some repute in London and New York who was washed ashore from the wreck of the *Argo*, gave an operatic concert in the Colonial Building to raise some money with which to replenish her lost wardrobe, before continuing on her way.

The public ball, held 11 August 1887 to mark the Golden Jubilee of Queen Victoria, came in for strong criticism in anti-government sections of the press. The *Evening Telegram* called it "The Breakdown at the Colonial . . . a bacchanalian spree on money stolen from the Treasury of the Commonwealth . . . a mushroom and shoddy affair. . . . There was much heavy drinking during the night, and one or two fellows managed to make themselves as obnoxious as could be."[9]

The pro-government *Royal Gazette*, on the other hand, said: "The

463

Public Ball at the Colonial Building was a brilliant success. The music (by Bennett's Brass Band) and the catering (by Messrs Ayre) were both everything that could be desired. The floor was in excellent order and it was well on for three o'clock when the weary dancers could tear themselves from the fascinations of the Jubilee Ball."

To accommodate dancers at the Jubilee Ball, the carpet was removed from the floor of the Assembly and placed in one of the anterooms whence (unlike Johnson's famous cat which came back the very next day) it never returned. According to Devine, writing in the *Trade Review*, the cry of "Who stole the carpet?" rang throughout the country and did more to bring about the defeat of the Thorburn administration than did the history of all their other alleged misdeeds put together. Devine says he heard afterwards that one of the officials of the House locked the carpet up in a certain room in the basement and confided its whereabouts to only one other man. The latter was promised a good slice of the carpet but, on finding out that the first man intended to deceive him, boldly lifted the thing from the thief. A carman, who hauled birch junks to the Colonial Building, carried it away snugly tucked in his cart. Whatever the truth, it was never seen again.

On 22 August 1905, as mentioned in Volume I, the Colonial Building served as a mortuary for the first and only time, when the remains of Sir Ambrose Shea were brought back from England where he had died in self-imposed exile. Shea was the outstanding Roman Catholic politician of his day and he had the misfortune to be appointed Governor of Newfoundland following the bitter sectarian election of 1885 which saw returned a totally Protestant government full of Orangemen who would in no way accept Sir Ambrose. His pro-confederate views were used to whip up public sentiment against him by such fellow confederates as Carter, Whiteway, and Winter. Sir Robert Thorburn, the anti-confederate Prime Minister, felt a political animosity against Shea while some of the others felt a more personal one. Frederick Carter wanted the governorship for himself and was most annoyed when he was passed over by the Colonial Office. William Whiteway gave Carter his backing because he was after Carter's job as Chief Justice. So much bitterness was created that Shea was sent instead to govern the Bahamas, which he did with much approbation, while another English governor was sent to Newfoundland. Following his stint in the Bahamas Sir Ambrose moved to London where he died. For his funeral the pillars in front of the Colonial Building were draped in black crepe. An honour guard of police stood beside the corpse which was waked in the House of Assembly while thousands of the curious streamed past the coffin.

Britain went to war 4 August 1914. The government of Newfoundland did not get around to shaking its fist in the face of the Kaiser until September 2 when a special war session of the legislature was held in the Colonial Building. In the presence of Bishop Power, Chief Justice Horwood, Mayor Gosling, Inspector General Sullivan, Canon Bolt, and other important personages of church and state, Governor Davidson was escorted to the throne to declare Newfoundland at war with Germany. Outside a vast mob cheered the decision.

Sniffing the wind, the Prime Minister, Sir Edward Morris, scented honours and, abandoning his dreams of making the Southside Hills white with sheep, departed for London in September of 1917 to become a member of the Imperial War Cabinet. Created Baron Morris in 1918, he remained in England until his death, 24 October 1935. His one return visit to Newfoundland in 1921 was that of a lonely exile ignored by his old colleagues and others who felt he had deserted them when he left for England in 1917. His residence on Topsail Road, named "Beaconsfield" after Disraeli, became the home of the Roman Catholic Archbishop of St. John's.

The year 1921 brought more trouble to the aging House. In describing the events of 13 April 1921, the *Evening Telegram* exaggerated somewhat when it said: "Never in the history of Responsible Government has such a scene been staged as that which took place yesterday, April 13, in the House of Assembly. It took but a spark to set the whole crowd which thronged the ancient building aflame." Evidently the reporter was not familiar with the tragic riot of 1861.

The house met at three o'clock and Sir Michael Cashin, the Leader of the Opposition, arose to continue his speech of the Address in Reply, unfinished from the previous session. While he was talking a supporter cried out his approval from outside the Bar. When he would not be silenced the Speaker interrupted Sir Michael to order the Sergeant-at-Arms to eject the man from the House. As a policeman tried to hustle the fellow out, the crowd broke into an uproar of protest. The Speaker then ordered the public galleries cleared. However, Sir Michael, who still had the floor, admonished the crowd "Stay right where you are."

Cashin, who had been Prime Minister before the last election, saw his government defeated on sectarian lines by a united Protestant vote. However, he held most of the Catholic districts, including St. John's where he had strong support. The fiscal year 1920-21 was a disaster for the government with an unprecedented deficit of $4,271,474. The total revenue of $8,438,039 was down by over two million, attempts to regulate the fisheries had broken down, and an imminent financial crisis, coupled with a threatened collapse of the island's railway system, charged the atmosphere of St. John's with much political tension. Demonstrations by unemployed city workers were threatening to become violent. It was these partisans of the Opposition who greeted Cashin's admonition to stay where they were with vociferous and deafening cheers.

Sir Michael's behaviour was immediately questioned by the Government and the Speaker ordered him from the House while his case was being discussed. The Leader of His Majesty's Loyal Opposition defied anyone to throw him out. At that point Sir John Crosbie rose and put himself

465

in accord with the views of Cashin. The House was now in a state of utter turmoil and, although the Speaker declared the session adjourned for the afternoon, few seemed to pay much heed to the honourable gentleman.

The floor was thronged with a crowd of people, smoking and carrying on the argument in loudly vocal groups. It needed only the wrong word to be spoken for a scene of violence to ensue. Finally Sir Michael was able to shout above the din and get the attention of the Chamber. He defused the explosive situation by thanking the crowd for their support and telling them they had all acted like gentlemen. His short speech was greeted with tremendous applause and then in deference to his wishes the crowd began to disperse.[10]

The pot of political discontent simmered until April 21 when a crowd of unemployed gathered at the Casino Theatre on Henry Street and prepared to parade to the House of Assembly where resolutions were to be presented to the government. Ex-Private F. Jordan was called upon to bear the Union Jack and, marching behind the flag, the men paraded up New Gower Street to Hutchings Street, along Water Street, up Cochrane Street, and along Military Road to the Colonial Building. Some members of the Cadets Band played airs during the march. The procession was followed by a large number of teamsters with their horses.

At the Colonial Building the band played "God Save the King," after which a delegation entered the Assembly and proceeded to the Bar of the House, stating that they brought with them a flag that protected them all. The man that bore it had only one arm; the other was in France. Prime Minister Sir Richard Squires extended a hearty welcome. Sir Michael Cashin rose to say he was surprised to hear such a hearty welcome from the Premier, as in reality it was an occasion for shame and grief seeing the Union Jack brought to the Bar by a needy people. It was promised that an employment bureau would be opened in the Municipal Council office, and the members and workers' committee withdrew to the steps to be photographed. Among the group was the real founder of the Women's Liberation movement in Newfoundland, the colony's own Emmeline Pankhurst, Julia Salter Earle, President of the Women's Branch of the Newfoundland Industrial Workers Association, who lived nearly opposite in a house just east of Bannerman Street. Although male chauvanism and female jealousy prevented her ever being elected to office she did not hesitate to offer herself as a candidate. Her motto was "Vote for Julia—She won't fool ya." The St. John's women of today owe a great deal to the often-ridiculed Julia Salter Earle.

On April 25, just four days after the march of the unemployed, a disorderly scene was witnessed in the House when two government members were heckled by the gallery. On May 14 a committee of working men and women appeared unexpectedly in the Assembly. In a pathetic and moving speech, according to the *Evening Telegram*, "Julia Salter Earle brought tears to the eyes of many an auditor." She accompanied the delegation from the House and was widely cheered by the large body of men outside. Later, in a conversation with the Prime Minister, she asked him what he would do if his little boy was hungry. His reply was most enigmatic, "I'd shoot!" Who or what he would shoot he did not say. With that the demonstrations of 1921 petered out.

The political unrest of 1932 began February 1 when Peter Cashin, son of Sir Michael and Member for Ferryland, resigned as Minister of Finance, giving no reason and refusing to make a public statement. When the Legislature opened on February 4 and Cashin rose to speak, the cards he held in his hand were neatly stacked against the government of Sir Richard Squires. As it turned out he also held in his palm the destiny of Newfoundland. Most subsequent events from the collapse of Responsible Government to Confederation can be traced to that crucial moment. In an emotion-packed speech Cashin charged that Prime Minister Squires had been guilty of deliberately falsifying Minutes of Council so as to deceive the governor and his Cabinet colleagues regarding certain fees he had been paying himself out of public funds. Similar charges of corruption were hurled against other members of the Cabinet and Cashin claimed that one of them had even failed to file income tax returns. The political scandal resulting from these charges portended trouble among the ranks of the unemployed. Their street gatherings led on February 11 to a mob of several hundred marching on the Court House where the Prime Minister had his office. After standing about for some time in the cold snow they finally brushed aside the police and forced their way into Squires' chambers. Sir Richard was shoved roughly about and there were fears of worse violence until calm was restored by the immediate distribution of dole orders.

The affair at the Court House was merely the overture to a comic opera of ineptitude, corruption, and tumult that rang down the curtain on Newfoundland's political independence forever. Peter Cashin elaborated on his dramatic charges in the Legislature by naming Dr. Alex Campbell, a man paid to be Minister of Immigration in a country that had no immigration, as the income tax evader in the Cabinet. He accused the Unionist member for St. Barbe, Walter Skeans, of forgery, but his most damaging indictment was made against Squires who was either a wily schemer or naive blunderer. The man remains an enigma. Cashin claimed the Prime Minister had taken five thousand dollars per year from funds of the War Reparations Commission. As a distinguished war veteran himself Cashin was able to say with bitter sting:

> Those who fought for their country and the relations of those who died will no doubt feel aggrieved that no mean portion of their small recompense fell into the hands of slackers under the pitiful guise of payment for services rendered . . . one is forced to the

dreadful conclusion that what we won by honour and death is
fallen into dishonour and decay.

On February 18 it was moved by the Opposition that the charges be
investigated by a select committee of the House but Squires succeeded in
pushing through an amendment to the effect that the Governor, Sir John
Middleton, should conduct an inquiry only into the charges made against
himself. Since Squires knew that the funds he had taken from the War
Reparations Commission were not for personal use but to keep the badly
leaking ship of state afloat he felt this delay would give him time to plan
new strategy. It was the inaccuracy of the Minutes rather than personal
corruption that had led to the charges and Middleton chose this as a way
out in his reply of 22 March 1922 when he wrote: "I have the honour to
inform you that there has not been any falsification of the said Minutes and
that I have not been deceived or been induced to deception to sign the said
Minutes." There was much His Excellency kept to himself that might have
been said. Only by the narrowest technicality could his reply be considered
as a true statement of the facts.

Regardless of Sir John's pronouncement, the confidence of the public
in the Squires government was seriously impaired. Cashin's blow was to
prove fatal. When the House met on March 23 Dr. H.M. Mosdell, a minister without portfolio, and two members of the governing party used the
occasion to resign. The House adjourned until 5 April 1932. At 2:15 that
afternoon, what the *Daily News* termed a "mass of moiling humanity"
gathered at the Majestic Theatre on Duckworth Street waiting to start an
orderly parade to the Colonial Building to present some resolutions passed
at a public meeting the previous night calling on the Legislature to investigate certain charges made against Prime Minister Squires and his Secretary of State, Dr. Arthur Barnes. Before the parade got underway, H.A.
Winter K.C., called on the men and women not to breach the peace.

A crowd of two thousand marchers started from the theatre for the
Legislature picking up another fifteen hundred persons along the way. At
3:30 p.m. a committee representing the marchers, consisting of J.M.
Howell, Rev. W.E. Godfrey, J.H. Devine, and Mr. Winter, was admitted to
the Colonial Building and presented a petition. Instead of accepting the
document from the committee and having done with it the Prime Minister
perversely requested a legal opinion on the rights of the delegation. This
obstinate behaviour was inexplicable with a mob literally howling at the
door. The considerable delay caused while legal counsel was sought played
into the hands of the agitators in the crowd leading to an attempt to force
the door of the building.

Someone called Mr. Godfrey outside but he was unable to restore
calm. The committee, realizing that things were getting out of hand, tried
to re-form the dangerously unruly mob and march back to the Majestic
Theatre. When an effort was made to lead off with the flag someone tried

468

to grab the banner. The national anthem was played by the band and there was a momentary lull. As soon as it was over the flag was torn from the staff and carried into the building. Eventually the Guards Band and the committee led the parade back to the theatre. When they got there, they were surprised to find that a large part of the mob had stayed behind on the grounds, and the Colonial Building was under siege.

The area in front was in turmoil with youths pelting stones at the windows while their elders battled the police. Constable Lake was dragged from his horse and beaten. Also beaten was Constable Leaman and a civilian named Healey. All three were rushed to the General Hospital to have their wounds looked after. With batons flying, the police charged the mob, hitting right and left, and blood flowed freely. Fifteen of the injured, including a boy of ten years, were taken to O'Mara's Drug Store, at Rawlin's Cross, for treatment. Stones and pickets from the Bannerman Park fence were used against the police.

The mob eventually gained the rooms occupied by Miss Morris, Librarian of the Legislature. Her piano was dragged out to the park where it was smashed to pieces. Two attempts were made to set the building on fire but these were frustrated. After wrecking some of the rooms, the crowd was finally driven back outside where a group of rowdies lay in wait, supposedly to lynch the Prime Minister. Squires hid himself in the basement while various members departed unmolested. Peter Cashin mounted the steps late in the afternoon and announced that the Prime Minister would resign later in the day. The crowd demanded he do so immediately. Superintendent of Police, Patrick O'Neill, came to the front of the steps and appealed to the mob to go home. Many seemed to drift off but the hooligan element remained.

About seven-thirty in the evening some friends arrived in a car to take away the Prime Minister. Squires climbed into the automobile without incident, aided by the Reverend Mr. Godfrey, and the car moved slowly through the crowd. At first, most people were unaware of the identity of its passenger. As it started down Colonial Street, however, a cry went up "There he is," and the mob suddenly gave chase, blocking the path of the vehicle. Mr. Edward Emerson, who was watching nearby, quickly decided to try and divert the attention of the mob. This small-statured man, who later became Sir Edward, the Chief Justice, cried out for some men to put him on their shoulders so he might see better what was happening. During the few brief moments in which attention was turned to Mr. Emerson who was being hoisted aloft, Squires jumped out of the left side of the car and darted into the residence of a Mrs. Connolly, at 66 Colonial Street. The Reverend Mr. Godfrey and Father Joseph Pippy, of St. Joseph's Church, kept the angered mob at bay while Sir Richard dashed through the house, over some fences to Bannerman Street, along the alleyway on the side of Cochrane Street Methodist Church, to Cochrane Street, where he leaped into a passing taxi. He made his escape to the home of E.J. Godden,

136 Waterford Bridge Road. When the clergymen were pushed aside, a crowd of some eight or ten men searched the Connolly house. Angry that their bird had flown, they decided to turn to other objectives. Part of the mob marched to the East End Liquor store, opposite City Terrace on Duckworth Street, where they chopped down a telephone pole and used it as a battering ram to break into the store which was quickly looted. Others of the rioters marched to the West End Liquor store, at the foot of Springdale Street, and completely emptied the building of its liquid contents.

Back at the Colonial Building, almost every pane of glass had been smashed, doors and window frames were battered to matchwood, furniture, office equipment, and clothing had been taken out and destroyed, documents and files were strewn all over Bannerman Park.[11] The Inspector General made good his escape, about an hour after the Prime Minister had fled. Meanwhile, Monsignor McDermott, all the priests of the Palace, Father Gibbs, the Reverends Johnson and Pike, the Reverend Dr. Clark, and a number of other clergymen of all denominations tried to get the crowds to go home.

During the height of the riot one youth seized the mace and was making off with it when he was caught by a spectator who returned it to the House. Another youth got away with the sword of the sergeant-at-arms and dashed to the front of the building holding it high in his hand. The efforts of the clergy, Peter Cashin, and Superintendent O'Neill to restore order were in vain. The place was a shambles. Large stoves had been flung into the Assembly room and Council Chamber. Only the chandeliers had escaped damage.

Miss Morris and the Ryall family, who occupied quarters in the basement, lost almost all their possessions, which had been either destroyed or stolen. The cost of damage done to the Colonial Building was estimated at ten thousand dollars.[12] An election was soon called and Squires, game to the last, offered himself in Trinity South. He was subjected to a rough campaign by people who had previously given him a massive majority and soundly defeated by Harold Mitchell who, on his return to St. John's, was given a torchlight procession through the streets. Drays were lighted with Greek Fire, and Mitchell, installed in a Victoria cab, was pulled along by a dozen of his supporters. Squires sold his house, at 44 Rennie's Mill Road, and left Newfoundland for good. He died in self-imposed exile, 26 March 1940, at the age of sixty years.

In 1932 the Amulree Royal Commission, on which no Newfoundlander sat, was formed to examine into the future of Newfoundland. Its report was presented to the Legislature of Prime Minister Alderdice in November 1933. It stated that during the last two years it had become increasingly apparent that the Dominion was unable, from its own resources, to meet the interest charges on the public debt. Urgent action was required, therefore, if the island was to be saved from default, a fate which was averted in December 1932 and June 1933, only by the generous assistance of the United Kingdom and Canada.

The Amulree Commission recommended that an immediate appeal should be made to His Majesty's government in the United Kingdom for their sympathetic co-operation in a joint plan of reconstruction. A telegram, received from the Secretary of State for Dominion Affairs, indicated that such an appeal, if made, would be assured of a prompt, favourable, and indeed gracious response.

Lord Amulree's report claimed that Newfoundland's political problems were due to "extravagant expenditures and political abuses of the past." This was an oversimplification and even a distortion of the truth since most of the country's politicians were no more corrupt than many of their neighbours on both sides of the Atlantic. Responsible Government seems to have been doomed from the beginning by two factors. First of all, the decline of the salt codfishery and dwindling markets stripped the government of the only real economic basis it had for providing public and social services. Secondly, the security of Canada and its prestige in United States' eyes made it imperative for that nation to swallow up Newfoundland. It is ironic that Canada today is fighting an almost identical battle against American intrusions on her sovereignty. While other places in financial difficulties similar to those of Newfoundland, with no mother country to fall back on, accepted a lower standard of living and fewer public and social services, Newfoundlanders appear to have been unwilling to make the sacrifice. Attitudes had changed since the days of William Carson and Patrick Morris, and the people of the island were unprepared to fight the arduous battle required for the survival of an independent Newfoundland.

On Tuesday, 28 November 1933, the House resolved itself into a committee of the whole to consider the matter, and an address was sent to "The King's Most Excellent Majesty" in which his "most Dutiful and Loyal Subjects, the Legislative Council and Assembly of Newfoundland" humbly approached His Majesty praying that ". . . until such time as Newfoundland may become self-supporting again, there should be substituted for this existing Government a form of Government under which full legislative and executive power would be vested in the Governor acting on the advice of a specially created Commission of Government over which His Excellency would preside. The existing Legislature and Executive Council would for the time being be suspended." In the meantime His Majesty's Government in the United Kingdom should assume general responsibility for the finances of Newfoundland and make arrangements for a reduction of the burden of the public debt. Many felt the country should have defaulted but this was as unthinkable then to Britain as it was to the United States government to let New York City default in 1975.

The last meeting of the Parliament of an independent Newfoundland took place on Saturday, 21 December 1933, when the Governor addressed

both Houses of the Legislature. His Excellency, Admiral Sir David Anderson, said: "Should the Parliament of the United Kingdom take the desired
action it will provide a means of relief from our financial anxiety, and I
hope enable us to enter upon an era of prosperity."

The President of the Legislative Council, by command of the Governor, then said: "It is His Excellency's will and pleasure that the General
Assembly be prorogued until Wednesday, the seventeenth of January,
1934."[13] There was never to be another session. The sun had set on the
dream of William Carson and Patrick Morris. It would never rise again on
a totally politically independent Newfoundland.

Commission of Government, in many ways a fair and progressive system, if an uninspired one, was inaugurated in the ballroom of the Newfoundland Hotel, on the north side of the lobby, Saturday, 17 February
1934, at a few minutes past three in the afternoon. Prime Minister
Alderdice was there as one of the newly appointed members of the Commission. He was to die three years later, 28 February 1936, and be buried
with a state funeral, from his residence, 3 Park Place, Rennie's Mill Road,
almost opposite the home of Sir Richard Squires.

The Commission of Government never met in the Colonial Building
during its term of office, from 1934 to 1948. The place was taken over for
offices by the Department of Natural Resources, under Sir John Hope
Simpson. The old Chamber was not to witness history again until the
opening of the National Convention on Wednesday, 11 September 1946.
That body came about as the result of years of agitation by Peter Cashin for
a return to Dominion status. When Major Cashin started his campaign he
was a small and lonely voice crying in the political wilderness over radio
station VOCM every Saturday night. Gradually he became bolder and a
growing audience began to listen to his fiery speeches, which were filled
with patriotic rhetoric and a lively sprinkling of accusations and revelations.

Others took up Cashin's cry for independence and the movement
could no longer be ignored. The result was the election of delegates to a
National Convention to choose the form of government best suited to the
needs of Newfoundland, commission or responsible. In the background
unseen forces were at work to make sure there would be a third alternative,
confederation with Canada. On opening day Major Cashin moved an
address of loyalty to the King, and the convention got underway. It made
history by being broadcast on wax recordings every evening over station
VONF and VOWN (Corner Brook).

As the sessions began, a David appeared on the horizon of the
Goliath, Major Cashin. He was a pig farmer from Gander, elected to
convention membership by the fluke of being in Gander instead of his
usual home, St. John's, at the time the convention was called. His name
was Joseph Roberts Smallwood and the stone in his slingshot was Confederation.

On the afternoon of 30 January 1948 the National Convention held its final session. After much acrimonious debate it recommended to the United Kingdom that Responsible Government, as it existed prior to 1934 (an unfortunate wording), and Commission of Government be placed before the people at the proposed referendum. The resolution that Confederation with Canada be added to the ballot paper was defeated by a vote of twenty-nine to sixteen. However, the delegates reckoned without the interference of Governor MacDonald, who was dedicated to the task of ridding England of its troublesome colony, once and for all, by seeing that it became part of Canada. The Smallwood faction, urged on by its messianic leader, petitioned for a third choice on the ballot paper, and His Majesty's government graciously consented.

In the referendum which followed, Responsible Government won the day. The vote was: Responsible Government, 69,400; Confederation with Canada, 64,066; Commission of Government, 22,311. However, instead of granting the people their choice, as had been promised, the Government of the United Kingdom decided to hold a second referendum, leaving out Commission of Government. This time a misguided editorial on the front page of the Roman Catholic newspaper, the *Monitor*, in which Archbishop Roche, unwisely guided by patriotic fervour, urged his faithful to vote for Responsible Government, was ruthlessly exploited in the Protestant outports, where support for Confederation was strongest. A secret letter went out to members of the Orange Society urging resistance to the wiles of the Catholic Archbishop. The result was that Confederation squeaked by with a majority of 6,989 votes, and the half-healed wounds of political religious animosity were again running sores that would infect the country for nearly twenty more years. The vote in the referendum was Confederation, 78,323; Responsible Government, 71,334.

Mackenzie King welcomed the new province into the great Dominion of Canada. Many of those opposed to Confederation were not so much against the idea of Newfoundland becoming the tenth province, as they were against the idea of her entering without any bargaining position of her own. Had political independence come first, there can be no doubt that the terms of union could have been immeasurably improved, as was seen when it came time to renew Term 29. Instead of entering the union of her own free will, while making the most of her meagre dowry, Newfoundland was hastily handed over by her mother country, anxious to be rid of a troublesome daughter, who had been shamefully raped by the undisguised corruption of some of her politicians and the inability of her electorate to see beyond their own self-interest and religious differences.

Confederation was a benefit and a boon to Newfoundland, and most people feel it was bound to have come eventually. The first session of the first Provincial Parliament of the Province of Newfoundland, opened in the Colonial Building's old Assembly Room, at three o'clock, on the afternoon of 13 July 1949. Confederation itself had taken place one minute before midnight, March 31 of that year—one minute to April Fool's Day. The new Liberal premier was the David from Gander, Joseph R. Smallwood. Having broken with his fellows, Major Peter Cashin sat as an independent. The Anti-Confederates were all thinly disguised as Progressive Conservatives.

Following the speech from the throne, 28 July 1959, and the departure of the Lieutenant-Governor, Premier Smallwood moved the House of Assembly into adjournment. It was the last active session of government to be held in the old building. A special session, a sentimental journey back to the old quarters, took place 29 June 1960. No business was enacted. Premier Smallwood rose from his old seat to recall Sir William Coaker as the greatest orator of his day, Lord Morris as a brilliant master of sarcasm, Sir Robert Bond as the last Edwardian, gracious and learned, and Sir Michael Cashin as a man who took advantage of the ancient privilege of protecting his head from flying missiles, thrown by the spectators, by always wearing his hat in the House.[14] Opposition Leader, James Greene, making his first and last speech in a House where his great uncle had been Prime Minister, recollected the events of "1932, the year of the riot."

Restoration of the ceiling frescos, painted in both Chambers of the House by the Polish prisoner, Pindikowsky, in 1880, was undertaken by a local painter, Clem Murphy, in 1940. He carried out the task with great fidelity, in regard to both colour and design. The smoke of nearly a century was removed, crumbling cornices and other mouldings were repaired, and in some sections, where the ceiling was destroyed, the frescos had to be restencilled. The initials W.J.P., the date 1878, and the name J. Graham (probably Pindikowsky's local assistant) were found cut on one of the brackets in the legislative room. It was estimated by Murphy that the original job took about two hundred books of gold leaf. Each book contains twenty-five leaves.

Repair work was begun on the outside east wall in 1955, and the job was completed a year later. A new cornerstone was laid in 1956. Stone for the west wall was imported from Ontario in 1958 and the work, begun in 1959, was completed in 1960. The restoration of the front section was finished in 1965. The portico and steps were replaced and the new columns of Ontario stone were installed.

On 22 June 1960 the Newfoundland Archives, held by Memorial University since their establishment in 1956, were turned over to the Newfoundland government and moved into the Colonial Building. Allan M. Fraser, a former Memorial University professor and ex-federal Liberal M.P., was appointed first Provincial Archivist. He was followed by F. Burnham Gill, a former newspaperman and a direct descendant of the famous Gill family of Bonavista and St. John's.

George Whitney Limited of Kitchener, Ontario, was given a contract, early in 1957, to survey the accommodation occupied by various government offices in St. John's, and present a proposal to the Newfoundland government for a large building to accommodate all branches under one roof. The result was the eight-million-dollar Confederation Building. While no thing of beauty, it had the advantage of being financed to owner-ship on a lease-buy-back basis that did not add to the provincial capital debt.

It is the custom throughout the world for the Parliamentary Government of a country, or province, to sit on the right-hand side of the Speaker and the Opposition on the left. In Newfoundland the custom is reversed. This local tradition came about because in the Assembly room in the Colonial Building, the stove was on the Speaker's left and the Government of the day always availed itself of the opportunity of sitting near the fire-place, while the Opposition suffered the cold drafts on the Speaker's right. The tradition was maintained in the new legislative chamber on the tenth floor of the Confederation Building.

The Coat of Arms of Newfoundland was granted by Charles I in 1637, some twelve years before he lost his head in the altercation with Cromwell. Its existence appears to have been forgotten until 1927 when the New-foundland government was made aware by Sir Edgar Bowring, who was in London, that there were certain records in the College of Arms relating to the grant of a Coat of Arms to Newfoundland by King Charles. After a thorough investigation the Coat of Arms, showing two Beothuck Indians holding up a red shield containing a white cross, two lions rampant and two unicorns rampant, surmounted by a moose (frequently mistaken for a caribou) was officially adopted by the Newfoundland government, 1 January 1928.

In March 1834, with the sympathy and encouragement of Governor Cochrane, Dr. William Carson introduced into the House of Assembly a bill "to establish a Town Council and Police in the town of St. John's." It was defeated by the merchants, led by George Hutchings who had a patho-logical fear of municipal taxes that is still virulent in many parts of New-foundland today. Hutchings and others petitioned the Assembly against creating St. John's a Corporation, 2 April 1834, "fearing taxation by irre-sponsible persons." By defeating the doctor's proposal they succeeded in retarding the growth and planning of the city by a civic authority until 1887 when St. John's was finally granted its Charter. Even then there were those who shook their heads, predicting that the population would be beg-gared, and some foresaw revolution as the final outcome.

The first municipal election took place in 1888, and the Council returned to office consisted of Moses Monroe, W.D. Morison, John Car-nell, Frances St. John, and Mogue Power. There were two government appointees, James Fox and James Goodfellow. Each householder had one vote and this system of election remained in effect until 1973 when universal suffrage was extended to all adult city residents.[15]

Until the year 1902 there was government representation on the council by two of the seven members who composed the board. That year saw the first election of an official mayor (George Shea) and six councillors with no appointed members. For the first time in its long history the city was in charge of its own affairs without any outside intervention or control. It was to prove itself incompetent for the task.

The main asset the City of St. John's acquired in 1887 was the Water Company. In February 1845 a bill was brought before the General Assembly by John Valentine Nugent, "To make provision for supplying the town of St. John's with fresh water." Even though the Water Company was incorporated by the legislature in 1846 it took another fourteen years before the hope was realized and wells, such as Bray's, east of City Terrace, remained in use. In 1851 four public tanks and reservoirs were erected in the town. One on Garrison Hill had a pipe running to the nearby Orphan Asylum School. A second reservoir on Cuddihy Street, which became known as Tank Lane, held thirty thousand gallons of water. There was another on the upper side of Beck's Cove with wooden pipes laid across Water Street. The fourth was located at the top of Long's Hill. In 1859 a new reservoir was opened near Long's Hill and two hundred feet of pipe were laid out to carry the overflow of the old cistern to save water.

The St. John's Water Company was finally formed in 1859 to bring water to the town from one of four suggested sources: Petty Harbour Long Pond, Windsor Lake, Monday's (Mundy) Pond, and Virginia Lake. On 5 April 1860 a ship arrived from Galway carrying "seventy-four Irish youngsters" (young men) to work on building the water works.

Windsor Lake was eventually chosen and the water supply from there to St. John's was turned on for the first time on 16 June 1862. Windsor Lake, originally called Twenty Mile Pond, was renamed on 28 January 1812. The newspaper, *Royal Gazette*, tells the story.

> On Tuesday, the 28th instant, a large party of gentlemen appeared at the Merchant's Hall by appointment, and at ten o'clock set off for the head of Twenty Mile Pond, where they assembled agreeable to invitation at the house of Thomas Kearsey, and partook of a plentiful refreshment, the pleasure of which was much increased by the satisfaction of using excellent bread made from the wheat grown in the vicinity of St. John's. After regaling themselves and enjoying "the comforts of a clean room and a good fire" they took some excellent Old Madeira Wine, provided for the occasion, and pouring generous libations, called the village Windsor, with many good wishes for its prosperity and increase. They also named that noble and delightful piece of water adjoining (before called Twenty Mile Pond) WINDSOR LAKE; and immediately proceeded over the immense sheet of ice which covered its romantic surface to the commencement of the New Road on the North Side of it, and continued their journey to Mr. George Goff's at Portugal Cove, highly pleased with the New Road, and the varied and picturesque scenery which skirted its borders. They

dined at Mr. Goff's with the greatest hilarity imaginable, and leaving his house at three o'clock returned over Windsor Lake, renewing their refreshments at Windsor, succeeded by the loyal song "Heart of Oak" reached St. John's at 5, much gratified with the amusements and occupations of the day.

Before Governor Cochrane's time there was no road around the lake. One led from St. John's to the edge of the lake, then the traveller crossed the water, or the ice, to the far shore from where another road, little better than a trail, led down to the Cove. Windsor Lake was the scene of a tragedy on 14 February 1891 when a man named Squires and a girl named Noseworthy were caught in a storm and perished on the ice.

The chore of watering vessels in the port is first mentioned in the estimates of the General Water Company in 1867 when the contract was awarded to Edward Flynn. Born in Tipperary, Ireland, in 1805 Flynn was the brother-in-law of the company secretary, Pierce Barron, former M.H.A. for Placentia St. Mary's. He supplied water to the ships by horse and cart for sixty-four pounds ten shillings and received extra payment for repairing tanks and extra services. In 1870, for example, this amounted to over three hundred and fifty-four pounds. When the genial old Irishman died on 29 September 1890 he had already been succeeded in the position of Superintendent of Watering Vessels by his son John, a grandfather of the author, and the position was held by father and son for more than sixty years.

In 1898 the Council found itself in financial troubles as a result of trying to extend water and sewer services without sufficient finances. It collapsed, and a commission of three persons was appointed by the government to replace it. In 1902 an Act restored civic government to the citizens of the city but in 1914 it again became necessary to put municipal affairs in charge of an appointed commission. In 1916 the Council was restored for the third time. A new Charter giving the City Council new powers and consolidating all previous laws was granted in 1921. Following a Royal Commission in 1966 another City Charter was granted.

George Shea was followed as mayor by Michael Gibbs (1906-10), William J. Ellis (1910-14), William G. Gosling (1914-21), Sir Tasker Cook (1921-29), Charles J. Howlett (1930-32), Andrew G. Carnell (1933-49), Henry (Harry) Mews (1949-65), and William G. Adams (1965-73). Mayor Howlett died from physical infirmities after fifteen months in office.[16] In that short time, he gave an energetic lead to modern city planning and was responsible for paving Duckworth Street. Mayor Carnell continued the paving policy and had many of the side streets treated with macadam.

Mayor Mews's major contribution was to formally approve construction of a new City Hall in 1960, from the proceeds of a secret fund which he had established for the purpose. The first Council offices were in a building on Duckworth Street, the Keough Estate, opposite the Commercial Bank.

Today the *Evening Telegram* publishes on the site. The Great Fire of 1892 not only robbed Council of a meeting place but also destroyed most of the books, papers, and records of the city. Some invaluable historic documents were lost in the flames.

After the fire meetings were held at the home of the secretary on Maxse Street. Eventually arrangements were made to use a fish market in Clift's Cove. In 1893 Council secured the upper floor of the Renouf Building, at the west end of Church Hill and Duckworth Street. An effort was made to purchase the Union Bank Building, east of the Court House Steps, when the bank went into liquidation after the 1895 bank crash, but it was not successful so Council remained in the Renouf Building until 1903 when it removed to the Kennedy structure next door to the west. There it remained for eight years.[17]

Lady Glover, wife of Sir John Glover, the only governor of Newfoundland to serve two separate terms, mentioned in her journal, 13 July 1877, that a sailor's Home was under construction in St. John's. Her hope seems to have been premature. In 1880 J.J. Rogerson and James Murray headed a provisional committee to organize a campaign for the erection of a Fishermen's and Seamen's Home in the city. It was figured that ten thousand foreign seamen and twice that number of outport fishermen visited St. John's each year. The foreigners, and local lads with no place to go, stayed on board their vessels and got drunk in local taverns, causing many a disturbance.

The committee estimated the cost of the building to be seven thousand pounds. It was hoped to raise five thousand locally, and the remainder from foreign friends. The campaign was boosted by a bequest of a thousand pounds from the estate of the late Robert Alexander. The money was raised and the cornerstone laid on 6 June 1885, as the last public act of Governor Glover. The silver trowel was presented to her Ladyship while the band from H.M.S. *Tenedos* rendered suitable airs. The site for the brick-faced building was to be Duckworth Street at Blockmaker's Hill. Mahon, a blockmaker, had a shop on the east side of the hill below where George Street is today. Blockmaker's Hill is now known as Mahon's Lane.

At a meeting of the Fishermen's and Seamen's Home Joint Stock Company, 11 August 1886, the shareholders were told that another fifteen hundred pounds were needed to complete the furnishings. There was only a small attendance at the meeting "owing to the arrival of the mail steamer that morning." More delays were experienced and the building was finally opened on 11 December 1886. The dormitories were able to accommodate up to a hundred lodgers. A bed was thirty cents; a meal, twenty-five cents; a cup of tea or coffee, three cents; and a bath, ten or twenty cents. The building's glass door was locally made by the Newfoundland Glass Embossing Company at its factory in Casey's Field, at the head of Flower Hill.

When Sir Wilfred Grenfell opened his Seamen's Institute on Water Street in 1911 it was decided to close the Duckworth Street Home. The place was offered for sale and the City Council, then engaged in a search for permanent quarters, jumped at the chance. Considerable changes were made in the building, both inside and outside, in order to meet the requirements of the city's business.

On 9 August 1911 Sir William Horwood formally unlocked the doors of the former Seamen's Home on Duckworth Street at the east corner of Mahon's Lane, his Lady unfurled the flag, and Mayor Ellis led the way into the recently purchased building which was to remain the Council's home for nearly sixty years. For the first time the City Fathers occupied quarters that were not rented.

On 5 August 1969 a cornerstone of Bristol pennant was laid on the north side of New Gower Street, and work was begun in earnest on the erection of a modern City Hall. Constructed of cast-in-place concrete, it was designed to dramatize the rugged terrain on which it was built. The place was officially opened on 10 October 1970.

The old Fishermen's and Seamen's Home was pulled down with indecent haste in 1971, with little or no attempt being made by Council to sell the structure to private enterprise so as to ensure its preservation. Protests in the newspapers and over the media proved ineffectual. The historic building disappeared leaving a gaping foundation on Duckworth Street, which was filled for a time with some haphazard playground equipment.

The Emmeline Pankhurst or Susan Anthony of the Newfoundland suffragette movement was Mrs. J.B. Mitchell, mother of Harold Mitchell. Immediately after World War I she gathered a group of ladies about her and they held meetings at Mrs. Mitchell's house at 1 Devon Row to pioneer voting rights for women. The demand was circulated in a petition which gathered seventeen hundred signatures. It was arranged by Mrs. Mitchell, a niece of the illustrious Richard Barnes, to have two former soldiers who were members of the House of Assembly, named H.H. Small and F.P. LeGrow, present the bill. The Legislature threw it out. One member advised the suffragette leader: "Go home, madame, and learn to bake bread." She replied, "I bake excellent bread."

Another important torchbearer was Mrs. Hector McNeil who arranged meetings for the cause in the Pitts Memorial Hall, Casino Theatre, and Mechanics' Hall, to which she brought women to speak on the suffragette movement from as far away as the United States. When Mrs. McNeil died, the mantle of leadership passed to Mrs. T.B. Goodridge.

The battle was won first on the municipal level when the St. John's City Council enfranchised women who were property owners in 1921. Three ladies offered themselves for election that year. Two of them were soundly beaten but Julia Salter Earle came within a dozen votes of becoming a councillor.

Walter Monroe's first official act as Prime Minister, when his government took office in June 1924, was to present the suffrage bill to the

Legislature and ensure that it was passed.[18] Four years later the first crack in the all-male façade of Newfoundland political life occurred when Lady Helena Squires was elected to the Newfoundland House of Assembly as the member for Twillingate. The irony of the situation was that both Lady Helena and her husband, Prime Minister Squires, had strenuously opposed giving women the vote. When Sir Richard fell out of popular favour after the riot of 1932, and his government was wiped out at the polls, Lady Squires suffered personal defeat at the hands of Norman Gray and departed from political life with her husband.

Credit for first suggesting to the Legislature that the vote be extended to women goes to Cyril Fox, who was afterwards elected Speaker of the House, and ended his career as a judge in the Supreme Court. Judge Fox, who was Chairman of the National Convention, dropped dead on November 16 in the Colonial Building during that noisy and acrimonious affair in 1946.

Civic history was made in 1969 when Dorothy Wyatt, a nurse and wife of a medical practitioner, Donald Wyatt, was elected to the St. John's Municipal Council. She had campaigned under the slogan "Vote for Wyatt — She won't be quiet," and she wasn't. As the fearless Councillor took her place beside her male colleagues in the Council Chamber for the first time, one could imagine the ghost of Julia Salter Earle smiling approval from the gallery. Smiling beside her was probably the ghost of the very first woman in recorded history to have set foot on Newfoundland soil. She was the ill-starred Marguerite de la Roque, who landed in St. John's, 8 June 1542, on board the ship of her uncle, Jean-François de la Roque, Sieur de Roberval, sent by King Francis I to establish permanent French colonies in New France.

Marguerite paid the price for being revealed a passionate woman in the male-dominated society of her time. She was accompanied on the voyage by her old nurse, a Norman peasant named Damienne, who turned a blind eye on her mistress' dalliance with one of the gentlemen on board ship. The affair probably got a bit out-of-hand while Roberval was in St. John's with Jacques Cartier, but it is doubtful it ever went beyond the slap and tickle stage on the crowded vessel. However, even that was enough to outrage the Calvinist ethics of Uncle Jean-François when he heard of the couple's carryings-on as he headed into the mouth of the St. Lawrence River. To teach Marguerite and Damienne a lesson, old Roberval marooned his niece and her nurse on one of the windswept Harrington Islands off Quebec, Labrador, and left them to their fate armed only with a couple of arquebuses.

The lover was to be put in chains, but in the confusion of landing the ladies he leaped overboard and swam ashore with more guns and ammunition. It is said by the pious that Roberval had the couple married by an abbé before landing the ladies so as to safeguard the family name. In the ninth

month of her exile a child was born to Marguerite but it died almost immediately.

During the long winter, the lover went mad under the strain and fell
or leaped off a cliff and was killed. The gentlewoman developed into quite
a good shot and killed three bears, one of which was "as white as an egg."
The following winter, old Damienne died. Surrounded by three graves,
Marguerite de la Roque began to hear demonic voices shrieking about her
shelter in the bitter white night. They were stilled by her reading aloud
passages from the New Testament.

We know these incredible facts because, strange to say, the lady
survived the ordeal. In the spring of 1544 some passing French fishermen
saw the smoke from her fire and rescued Marguerite who was emaciated
and in tatters. She returned to her home in Picardy and is thought to have
ended her days as a schoolmistress in a convent.[19]

On 13 November 1973, four hundred and thirty-one years after
Marguerite de la Roque walked the beaches of St. John's harbour, Dorothy
Wyatt was elected mayor of the rapidly expanding city of one hundred
thousand people. As she donned her robes and chain of office and took her
place with her male colleagues in the Council Chamber it soon became
obvious that Mrs. Wyatt still had no intention of becoming quiet.

2

To Travel Hopefully

Bishop John T. Mullock was a dominent figure in the St. John's of his day. Born in Ireland in 1807 he was consecrated Bishop and came to Newfoundland in 1847. In his fearless letter to the press he denounced governments, flayed opponents, promoted the island's first coastal boat service, and was the first to propose an Atlantic cable. He consecrated the Basilica and established St. Bonaventure's College. The fearless prelate died 29 March 1869. (Courtesy Roman Catholic Episcopal Corporation.)

485

Sir William Whiteway, born in Devonshire in 1828, came to Newfoundland in 1843. He served as Prime Minister three times: 1878-1885, 1889-1894, 1895-1897. Soon after he had assumed office in 1878, the government decided to go ahead with the building of the controversial cross-country railroad but fearing French objections, the British government terminated it at Hall's Bay. Whiteway, knighted in 1880, died 24 June 1908.

Sir Robert Reid, born in Scotland in 1842, came to Newfoundland in 1890 to finish the Hall's Bay Line. When he arrived he had a personal fotrune of about six million dollars. When he left, most of it was dissipated in spite of the fact that he had owned the railways, the coastal boats, the telegraph system, the electric light company, and the St. John's street railway.

St. John's first railway station opened in 1881 inside this last building left standing at Fort William. The old stone barracks served the travelling public until 1903. It was in front of this station that an angry crowd gathered to bid farewell to Signor Marconi when the inventor was forced by a court order to move his wireless experiments from Newfoundland to Cape Breton. (Courtesy Newfoundland Reference Library.)

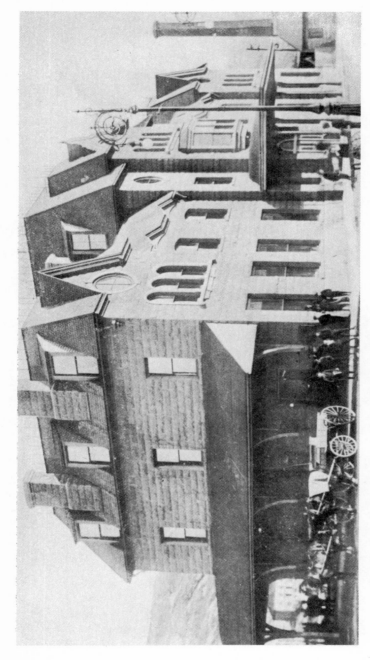

This classic Victorian railway station opened at Riverhead in 1903 on what had been the banks of the Marine Promenade. The architect was W. H. Massey, chief engineer with the Reid-Newfoundland Railway Co. Although some of the windows have been changed and the wrought-iron decoration has vanished from the roof, the building remains virtually unchanged. (Courtesy Newfoundland Provincial Archives.)

This photograph by Sir Leonard Outerbridge shows an accident to the Reid-Newfoundland Company's locomotive No. 60 on the old railway track near the present intersection of Empire Avenue and King's Bridge Road. Quidi Vidi Lake can be seen at the left. The mishap was caused by a cow on the tracks, a regular occurrence in the early days of the railway. (Courtesy Newfoundland Provincial Archives.)

489

A gentleman in a bowler hat sits on the shore at the Battery and contemplates the railway tracks which were the eastern terminus for the Newfoundland Railway before the station moved to Riverhead. This area became the American Dock during World War II. Fort Waldegrave is on the height of land above the Narrows. (Courtesy Newfoundland Provincial Archives.)

This view of the interior of one of the Reid-Newfoundland Railway coaches around 1900 shows a sleeper on the Foreign Express of the Overland Limited. At night the seats became the lower berths and the sections overhead were pulled down to become the upper berths. The narrow-gauge railway swayed considerably as it rattled down the track but still there was an elegance to it all that modern transportation lacks.

The S. S. *Bruce* was placed on the Port aux Basques to North Sydney run when the railway to the west coast of Newfoundland was completed in 1898. In this photograph taken around 1900 she is shown loading passengers from the Foreign Express at dockside in Port aux Basques. The return excursion fare from St. John's to North Sydney by train and ship was fourteen dollars.

The barren valley of Petty Harbour provides a backdrop for the powerhouse built by Sir Robert Reid in the late 1890s to supply electricity to St. John's. Water was fed to the plant by a sluice which can be seen running along the hillside and down to the powerhouse. By 1900 this plant was generating enough electricity not only to light the city but also to supply a street railway.

493

In 1899 Sir Robert Reid's company began work on laying streetcar tracks along Water Street in order to operate a train service. At the same time it agreed to pave Water Street from the foot of Cochrane Street to the Crossroads with granite cobblestones. The small crowd in front of Knowling's West End Stores, opposite Buchanan Street, is unexplained. (Courtesy CBC Newfoundland Region.)

The streetcar at the left is turning up Adelaide Street from Water Street while a westbound car sits on the double tracks at the intersection. Bishop Sons & Co. hardware store is on the right of the photograph. This site was later occupied by Gerald S. Doyle, and after Mr. Doyle's death by the Big 6 of J. M. Devine. The Broadway House of Fashion (with awnings) was destroyed by fire. (Courtesy Provincial Reference Library.)

495

This 1910 group of motorcyclists near St. John's consists of (left to right) Alex Dryden, G. H. M. Bursell, Dr. T. P. Smith, R. Baxter, Dr. Cluny Macpherson, F. Brehm, and Dr. N. S. Fraser. The pioneer cyclist in Newfoundland was Dr. Fraser who first thought of this method of conveyance as a help in his extensive practice. (Couresty Newfoundland Centre, MUN.)

In 1975 there were 191,765 motor vehicles registered in Newfoundland. The first of them was this elegant Rolls Royce open touring car which Robert Reid Jr. (seated behind the wheel) imported from England in March 1903. On Sundays Mr. Reid obligingly displayed the car to the curious townspeople at the railway station, Fort William.

497

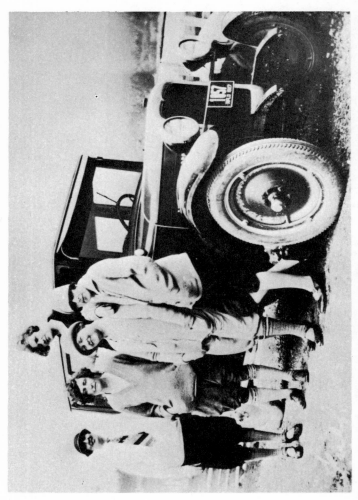

Motoring was a popular ladies' sport in the roaring twenties, and knickers were the height of fashion. These belles are on a day jaunt from St. John's to Fulford's, Placentia, in 1927. The Chevrolet belonged to the photographer Maude Ryann of Theatre Hill. The motorists are (left to right) Gertrude Phelan, May Ross, Nan Phelan, and Josephine Flynn (mother of the author). Standing on the running board is Mary Hogan.

The ultimate in luxurious hotel accommodation in nineteenth-century St. John's was the Atlantic Hotel which John Foran opened in May 1885 on the site of what is now the Sir Humphrey Gilbert Building on Water Street. Gutted in 1892 the Duckworth Street portion at the back was rebuilt and became the Customs House. Walsh's Grocery building (on the left) now houses the famous Crow's Nest on the top floor. (Courtesy Provincial Reference Library.)

A Masonic parade passes the Crosbie Hotel on Duckworth Street during the reconstruction period which followed the Great Fire of 1892. George Crosbie, the hotel's owner, was the father of Sir John Crosbie. In recent years the hostelry has been known as the Welcome Hotel. The churchlike structure on the left of the hotel is the Longshoremen's Protective Union Hall, built on the site of John Jones's Meeting House. (Courtesy Newfoundland Provincial Archives.)

One of the most elegant Edwardian hotels in St. John's was The Balsam on the west side of Barnes Road. Sir Robert Bond stayed here when in town for sessions of the Legislature. It also played host to the London Theatre Company in the early 1950s before being torn down. (Courtesy Newfoundland Reference Library.)

The Cochrane Hotel on the northwest corner of Cochrane and Gower streets played host to many famous guests in the early years of the century from Guglielmo Marconi to Alcock and Brown. Standing on the steps of the hotel, Harry G. Hawker shakes the hand of Commander Morgan as F. P. Raynham and Lieutenant-Commander McKenzie-Grieve (extreme left) look on. Hawker and Grieve were the first to attempt to fly the Atlantic non-stop. (Courtesy Agnes Simms.)

To Travel Hopefully

To travel hopefully is a better thing than to arrive.
ROBERT LOUIS STEVENSON *An Apology for Idlers*

The first public transportation available in St. John's was not for travel within the town but to the outports of the island.

It began in the 1830s. In those days journeys to and from the settlements of the Southern Shore, or Conception Bay, were both time-consuming and hazardous on whatever vessel happened to be sailing. With regard to the Bay, Governor Cochrane felt matters could be improved by making Portugal Cove a packet-boat terminal for such places as Brigus, Bay Roberts, Harbour Grace, and Carbonear. Under his direction work was begun on a road to link St. John's with Portugal Cove.

There was already a well-constructed track leading from the town towards the Cove. This first highroad on the island was the work of W.J. Epps. Late in October 1792, according to the Colonial Records, Epps asked for approval of the Governor for the intention of a committee of the inhabitants of St. John's to make a road to Portugal Cove for which a subscription was entered into on the twenty-second of the month. His Excellency gave his approval and asked for the names of committee members. A start was made but the project was never completed.

Aaron Thomas, in his journal, tells of a journey he made to the Cove in June 1794. He reports the road was perfectly good for a distance of three miles, because of its having been recently made, but at the Tilt House it dwindled to a rough path. This small travellers' rest he describes as a miserable hut put together at the expense of Colonel Skinner, Chief Engineer of Newfoundland.[1] It stood close to where the airport road and Major's Path join Portugal Cove Road.

The hut was fitted out with a fireplace and was used as a rendezvous for the partaking of provisions and liquor brought there by the "Gentlemen and Ladys who go a Tilting in the winter on the ice on a Pond about three miles further in the woods call'd Twenty Mile Pond."[2] Beyond the Tilt House trees were felled as far as the pond, but the way was over bogs and stumps of trees.

Able Seaman Thomas tells us that the citizens of St. John's were

503

drawn in sledges to Twenty Mile Pond as soon as the ice was formed. Lapped in furs they skimmed over the glittering surface while "totally laying aside all apprehensions of danger." This sport was what they called "tilting."[3]

From the pond an Indian path led to Portugal Cove. This path was single file with large stepping stones in the bog sections. Similar paths led from Torbay, Topsail, and Bay Bulls. In fact, the Bay Bulls path presented such obstacles that the purser of the frigate *Rose*, who walked it in 1790, "rendered his Breeches in such a manner as decently forbid him entering St. John's until after night had sett in."

In his journal, Aaron Thomas describes Portugal Cove as a village of about twenty fishermen's huts, a fish room, a fish flake, and a public house run by Madam Hartry. He drew a sketch of the place showing a single stage and one large fish flake. Judge Prowse gives the number of families resident in the cove during the winter of that same year, 1794, as being thirty-four, consisting of some two hundred people. The charges for Mrs. Hartry's salt pork and dry biscuits, according to Thomas, were commensurate with those of Saunders in the Strand or the Garrick's Head in Bow Street.[4]

Within thirty years of this visit Portugal Cove, supposedly named by the great Portuguese navigator, Corte-Real who is said to have discovered Conception Bay in 1500, was linked to St. John's by a crude road, and Bay packet boats were already using the port in growing numbers. According to the historian, H.F. Shortis, the first of these was operated by a man named Michael Dooly who placed the following ad in the *Royal Gazette*, 14 April 1808.

> PACKET BOAT—For Harbour Grace, Carbonear or any of the Out-Harbours. The subscriber respectfully informs the public that he has provided a New Skiff that rows six oars for the purpose of conveying passengers etc. to any of the Out-Harbours. Persons desirous of obtaining quick passages either may be accommodated at short notice by applying to Michael Dooly, a Resident of Portu-
> / gal Cove.

The phrase Out-Harbours refers to such places as Brigus, Bay Roberts, and other communities in Conception Bay. Dooly had a daughter who was afterwards manager of William Toussaint's Hotel in Harbour Grace.

If these skiffs were not the most comfortable means of transport, they were the only way of reaching communities around the Bay from St. John's, except by waiting for a coastal schooner. As with all pioneers in any venture, some packet travellers paid the price with their lives. For example, on 11 November 1822, Murphy's boat was lost with all her passengers and crew on the way to the north shore.

The week of the Murphy tragedy, James Neary, of Portugal Cove, was advertising his packet boat *Lively* to sail twice a week from the Cove to

Harbour Grace. Hire of the boat was thirty shillings, tradesmen and labourers fare was four shillings, while Ladies and Gentlemen paid five shillings. Letters were ninepence each.

To enable passengers to reach the numerous packets plying the Bay the first highroad in Newfoundland was opened between St. John's and Portugal Cove in 1831. The following year a stagecoach service was introduced to transport people to and from the sailing terminal. These stages were the island's first public transport. They were owned by a man named William Coughlan and consisted of half a dozen coaches. Each was pulled by four horses and driven by men with names like Bennett, Cruett, Bulger, Murphy, and the most colourful of all, Bill Somers, a stout, red-faced man and skilled driver, who wore a leather covering over the stump of a missing hand.[5] Coughlan, a nonagenarian, died 15 January 1906 and was buried from his residence, Allandale Farm, at Belvedere.

Each coach had its own name, *Victoria, Velocity, Ketch,* and so on. The coachmen were attired in long greatcoats with several capes and a top hat. They looked for all the world like an etching from *David Copperfield,* or *Pickwick Papers,* as they sounded their posthorns and started along Duckworth Street for Portugal Cove. Archbishop Howley has left us a romantic account of Coughlan's Coaches. In an article written after their passing he recalls:

> How we loved the rumbling, clumsy old vehicle, full as our youthful minds were at the time of the daring deeds of Dick Turpin. . . . How often and with what admiration and awe have we watched it roll along with its heavy yellow wheels, all dashed with mud, and its great, comfortable looking body, all painted in red and gold, its leather aprons tacked with large, round brass nails, its "boot" and "well" and inside and outside seats all filled with passengers, their trunks and wallets packed on top . . . and then we looked up and saw the driver perched on his lofty seat,—oh, how we envied him that glorious position, and how we admired the dexterity with which he twirled and cracked his long whip over the backs of his well-managed four-in-hand.
>
> And finally we heard the horn winded in the crisp morning air, it was a scene to be remembered. It seems incredible that . . . a picture so romantic could have been witnessed in St. John's, yet, so it is![6]

The coaches departed the Commercial Hotel, opposite the present War Memorial, for Portugal Cove, at nine o'clock every morning, and for St. John's immediately after the arrival of the packets. The one-way fare was five shillings for each passenger, and luggage over twenty pounds could not be carried without a "reasonable charge." Travellers wishing to obtain seats could secure them at the hotel. John Flood, who held up the stagecoach on Portugal Cove Road in 1834, was publicly hanged on 12 January 1835.

In 1833 John Crute took over the premises two doors east of the old London Tavern and offered a second passenger service to the Cove. Two years later he introduced wagons, which Archbishop Howley described as "Unpoetic and rigid with stiff, straight, meeting-house looking seats." It was also in 1835 that Patrick Mullowney brought into use, what his newspaper ad described as,

> A neat, light Jaunting Car to carry four between this and Portugal Cove during the fall. The car will start from the subscriber's house, calling at Mr. Stephenson's Hotel for passengers and luggage at half past nine o'clock every morning and return to town on arrival of the Conception Bay packet at the Cove.

Sometimes passengers had to share accommodation with such unusual companions as the corpse of Patrick Downing, who had been publicly hanged in St. John's on 5 January 1834, now on its way to Portugal Cove for transport to Harbour Grace where it was to hang in chains.

By 1838 the packet business was booming. Samuel Cozens's "fast-sailing, coppered cutter *Ariel*" was offering after-cabin passage to Brigus for seven shillings sixpence and fore-cabin at five shillings. Letters were down to sixpence and were to be left in the letterbox at the shop of Mr. Alexander M'Ivor, Stationer, Water Street. The *Ariel*, a thirty-ton vessel belonging to the Brigus Packet Company, had commenced service in July 1836. She had a separate cabin amidship for the ladies, and class distinctions were rigidly maintained.[7] In 1827 Skipper John Stevenson of the *Express* had been dismissed for, amongst other charges, "permitting steerage passengers to go into the Cabin to the annoyance of Cabin passengers." The *Express* was owned by Andrew Drysdale and sailed for Harbour Grace three times a week. Perchard & Boag were her St. John's agents and no accounts could be kept. The rates were "ordinary fares 7s 6d, servants and children 5s." On the other hand, another Harbour Grace packet, Maurice Doyle's *Nora Creina*, preferred to advertise its fares as "Ladies and Gentlemen 7s 6d, other persons 5s." Mr. Doyle would hold himself accountable for all letters and packages given him.[8]

The queen of this large fleet would appear to be the Carbonear ship, *Native Lass*. The owner, James Doyle, gave notice to the traveller that

> Her character for speed and safety is already known. She is divided into separate compartments. Her cabins are superior to anything in the Island. Select books and newspapers are kept on board for the accommodation of the passengers. . . . She leaves Carbonear Monday, Wednesday and Friday. Leaves the Cove for Carbonear Tuesday, Thursday and Saturday.[9]

On 22 May 1847 we find the first public demand being made for a railway in Newfoundland. The St. John's *Morning Post*, on that day, proposed the laying of a rail line to Portugal Cove to link with a steamship service on Conception Bay. A rail line and a steamship service to the Bay were both established in later years, but not as the newspaper envisioned them.

In January 1852 it was moved in the House of Assembly that a grant be made available for steam communication in Conception Bay and five hundred pounds was granted for three years to a company consisting of Thomas Ridley, John Munn, James Rorke, William Donnelly, and Joseph Devereux. They purchased the S.S. *Lady LeMarchant* in Scotland. On 4 October 1852 she reached St. John's after a voyage of twelve days from Greenock and sailed from Harbour Grace on her maiden voyage in the Conception Bay service on October 11.

The Roman Catholic prelate, Dr. Mullock, achieved some notoriety in 1860 by broadening his fields of endeavour to include steamship chartering for the Newfoundland government. That year a bill was passed providing three thousand pounds a year for five years to provide steam communication between St. John's and the outports. Without official authorization the Bishop and Judge Joseph Little, who were in New York, thought they saw just the ship, the S.S. *Victoria*, and entered into a virtual contract to charter the vessel. The government refused to honour the agreement. In one of his famous letters to the press the chagrined Dr. Mullock scathingly denounced the Kent administration:

> The great and paramount want of Newfoundland is a facility of communication between the capital and the outports; as long as the outports are left isolated, so long will education, religion and civilization be left in the background. Newfoundland must remain in that state of darkness to which ages of bad government have reduced it. I solemnly declare that without steam communication the people must remain poor, degraded and ignorant.... A beautiful steamer, in every way adapted for the purpose, engaged to do service north and south twice a month, was offered in New York; I visited the ship myself, and if she was not all that was specified the contract could be terminated at three months notice. She had every accommodation for passengers and would have done more to develop the interests of the out-harbours than all the Houses of Assembly that ever met on the island. The government when they saw the matter brought to a point refused to engage her. ... Will strangers believe that in a British Colony the shire town of Fortune Bay is in reality further away from us than Constantinople? But then we have the satisfaction of seeing thousands upon thousands of pounds distributed among our locust-like officials ... the collection of revenue under the present system is nothing but *legalized robbery*. . . ."[10]

In 1862 His Lordship had the pleasure of seeing the government engage the S.S. *Victoria*, the ship he and Judge Little had contracted for two years earlier. She began on the Bay run 2 November 1862 and was succeeded by the S.S. *Ariel* the following year. The *Ariel* was lost at Red Bay in 1875.

The year that the *Ariel* began her passenger service to Conception Bay, Stewarts were operating the screw steamer *Walrus* regularly, between St. John's and the western outports, as far as Sydney. Her first stop on the western voyage was at Ferryland. Fares seem to have been reasonable at three pounds ten cabin and two pounds steerage to the Cape Breton port. The price included meals, but no wine or liquor, and passengers had to look after their own luggage. The S.S. *Tiger* later supplemented this service.

The Rt. Rev. Dr. Mullock who, as we have seen in the *Victoria* affair was no shrinking violet where public utterances were concerned, again turned from episcopal tasks, in 1860, to push for a railway that would connect "the Conception Bay and St. John's trading communities, and be most highly advantageous to both." The Bishop's plea was ignored.

Five years later the noted physician, Dr. Henry Stabb, went a step further, and made the first public proposal for a railway to the west coast to link St. John's with Canada. That same year, Sir Sandford Fleming, a Scotsman who was building the Canadian Pacific Railway, proposed to Sir John A. MacDonald to link St. John's by locomotion to the cities of America.[11] The city was intended to be the Atlantic terminus of the Great American and European Short Line Railway. Passengers from as far away as Vancouver and San Francisco would be able to journey to St. John's by train, take a fast ship across the Atlantic to Valentia, in Ireland, and then go by train across Europe, and into Asia. The route would cut four days off the sailing time between London and New York. Had the dream been realized much of the North American traffic for nearly half a century would have passed through St. John's. It foundered on the rocks of politics.

The island population of one hundred thousand could not hope to finance such a venture, and the price Sir John A. MacDonald demanded, to find the cost for a steam ferry and railway, was that Newfoundland confederate with Canada. This the government and people of the island were not prepared to do. Fleming tried to negotiate a personal deal with the Newfoundland government in 1874, offering to pay for the whole thing himself.

The offer was taken up, and in the summer of 1875 a survey was begun to find a suitable route from St. John's to St. George's Bay. The final cost worked out for a standard-gauge single track was between six and seven million dollars, not a very large sum. Urged on by Bishop Mullock and others, the scheme seemed near fruition when political considerations once more blocked the plan.

In the Treaty of Utrecht, Britain had recognized French treaty rights to fish from what was known as the French Shore, on the west coast of Newfoundland. A treaty clause prohibited any foreign installation within one mile of the shore and the French interpreted a railway to be a foreign installation. The British government was unwilling to push the point, on behalf of the island, and Sir Sandford Fleming finally abandoned his plans for the Great American and European Short Line Railway. The famous engineer turned his attention to inventing standard time, and laying the Pacific cable to Australia.[12] Instead of becoming a crowded metropolis, catering to nearly one hundred thousand travellers yearly, St. John's settled back to slumber in obscurity.

The great leap forward in Newfoundland transportation was to be a legacy of Robert Reid, another Scotsman who worked on building the C.P.R. The Newfoundland railway was not originally Reid's concern. In 1880 an American company undertook to build a narrow-gauge rail line to link the capital with Notre Dame Bay and there was to be a branch line to Harbour Grace, then the second largest town on the island. Bonds were floated in England.

Plans were laid to turn the first sod on August 9, but the ceremony did not take place until 16 August 1881. Ground was broken near John Dwyer's residence, Oak Farm, at the northwest corner of Empire Avenue and Carpasian Road. Dwyer, M.H.A. for St. John's West at the time of his death in 1917, and known as "Honest John," was a governor of the Newfoundland Savings Bank. The track ran along what later became Empire Avenue, to the station at Fort William, site of Hotel Newfoundland. That first day a party of fifty men began digging up the road bed along a route known as Freshwater Valley.

On October 8 the S.S. *Standard* arrived from Cardiff, Wales, with a cargo of railway iron and the work of laying track proceeded immediately. The first steam engine was lost overboard in a shipping mishap. Its replacement arrived on board S.S. *Merlin*, December 5, by which date twelve hundred men were employed in construction at a dollar per day. The engine had been purchased, second hand, from the narrow-gauge Prince Edward Island Railway. It was put to steam and ran for the first time on 13 December 1881, carrying ballast along the track. Before the termination of the season it was hoped to see a continuous line as far as Topsail.

A fatal accident soon marred the venture. It happened on 18 November 1882 when a number of labourers were riding back to St. John's from Holyrood for the weekend. Contrary to regulations some were seated on the front of flatcars with their legs dangling. At Indian Pond, six miles from Holyrood, a startled cow leaped onto the tracks and was run over. A group of men riding on the front of one of the cars were thrown off as the car bounced over the carcass of the animal. Three fell beneath the wheels and were killed instantly, and three others were seriously injured. This was the first of several fatal railway accidents in Newfoundland, the worst of which took place near Glenwood, 25 March 1906, when eight men were burned to death in a derailment.

By 1883, extravagance and waste had dissipated the money raised in England and the construction company defaulted. Sixty miles of track had been laid. The English bondholders took over the project and completed the eighty-four miles to Harbour Grace the following year.

The first passenger trip on the line was a grand excursion to Topsail, 29 June 1882. The train left Fort William station at nine o'clock sharp, accompanied by Professor Bennett's Band. Tickets were eight shillings double and five shillings single. Besides the music of the Professor's boys, the Star of the Sea Band and one other were in attendance during the day. The whole thing concluded with a Grand Bonnet Hop in the Star of the Sea Hall. The tired, but happy, revellers returned to the city at seven o'clock thrilled at having made history by being the first passengers on the new-fangled contraption.

A spike-driving ceremony took place during the visit to St. John's of H.M.S. *Canada* in 1884. The president of the Newfoundland Railway Company, who had just arrived from New York, invited the officers of the ship to go on a picnic to Mile 50, which had just been laid. At the site, a midshipman from the ship, the Duke of Cornwall and York (afterwards King Geoge V), drove in a ceremonial spike.

On November 24 the line was opened for traffic to Harbour Grace and three trains a week linked the north shore communities of Conception Bay to the capital. There were so many stops at wayside stations that the journey took most of the day to complete. In March 1905 it was to take five weeks to get from Harbour Grace to St. John's when snowdrifts blocked the tracks. The longevity record for trans-island train travel had been established two years earlier, in February 1903, when the express was blocked for seventeen days in fifteen-foot drifts at Kitty's Brook. Supplies of food and fuel ran out and a relief train was derailed and the parties frostbitten.

The hammers of the railroad gangs sounded the death knell for the packets sailing out of Portugal Cove. By 1885, less than a year after the commencement of train service, all had vanished completely from the seas, and the stagecoaches and wagons that transported passengers and freight to and from the packet boats creaked to a halt.

Portugal Cove is still used as a ferry terminal. It links the City of St. John's to the once great iron-ore community, Wabana, on Bell Island. Now used by daily commuters, the service has, for over half a century, been the subject of endless complaint. It has also been marred by tragedy.

On the evening of Sunday, 10 November 1940, during the wartime blackout, the eighteen-ton, fifty-five-foot-long passenger ship *Garland* left the Cove at 5:30 p.m. with thirty-one passengers on board. As she headed out from the dock the night was clear with a full moon. However, when the vessel was about two-thirds of the way across the Tickle she ran into a brief snow squall. As the squall cleared the fifteen-ton ship *Golden Dawn* was seen crossing the bow of the ferry.

No evasive action was taken on board the *Garland*, nor were the engines cut. She struck the smaller craft amidships on the starboard side and foundered within minutes. Many of the passengers were still below decks in the saloon as she slid beneath the black waters. Even if there had been time for them to scramble out on deck there was little they could have done. The ferry carried no life belts, no lifeboats, or any other kind of life-saving appliances. Twenty-seven of the thirty-one persons she carried were drowned, including three women.

The *Golden Dawn* continued without stopping to Bell Island where she was beached. The people on shore heard the screams of those drowning in the waters of the Tickle. Another ferry, *Maneco*, searched in vain for survivors until two o'clock in the morning. The wreck of the *Garland*, which had begun on ferry service that year, was found two-thirds of a mile offshore in 168 feet of water.

On 7 August 1860 there appeared on the streets of St. John's a new wonder in public transportation. The strange vehicle, drawn by two horses, was called the "omnibus." Imported from the Old Country, it had two large wheels at the rear and two smaller wheels at the front. The driver, who wore a coat of tails and a stovepipe hat, sat up front in a bracketed seat called a "dickey." The conductor stood on a running board at the rear and clung to handles like those of a police wagon.[13]

The proprietor of the omnibus, S.G. Archibald, a man accused by his political opponents of having "Yankee notions," also operated the Prince's Baths on the south side of Water Street. The omnibus service ran from the Baths in Maggoty Cove to Riverhead, and a report of the times says it "rolled along in stately grandeur induced by Bucephalus and Rosinante...."

There were windows along both sides of the omnibus and there was a window in the door at the back. Fourteen passengers sat facing each other, seven to a side. Generally the floor space was also occupied. The omnibus left the Prince's Baths at half-past eight in the morning and began the return trip from the Cross Roads, Riverhead, at nine o'clock. It then ran every half-hour alternately up and down until 6:00 p.m.[14]

On September 14 Archibald added a station-wagon service for out-of-town transportation. This contraption left Maggoty Cove at eight o'clock for Waterford Bridge in Kilbride, and the return trip was commenced at 8:45 a.m. No description of it exists but it was probably some sort of goods wagon.

Omnibus fares along Water Street were in two parts. From the Baths in Maggoty Cove to Mrs. Warrington's Union Hotel at Steers' Cove the fare was sixpence, and from the Union Hotel to the Cross Roads it was another sixpence. After passing the halfway mark the fare doubled. Tickets could be had from the conductor or at the Prince's Baths,

The omnibus lasted two years. In 1862 we find Mr. Archibald employed by the government as a commissioner inquiring into the damage caused to householders in Harbour Grace and Carbonear by the political riots of the early 1860s.

The cab or cabriolet was not known until 1820. These carriages, with two or four wheels, and drawn by one horse, seated two or four persons. By 1827 the word cab had come into the language and by the end of the decade most major cities in the world had a public cab service. When they first appeared on St. John's streets is unknown, but by 1862 they were popular enough to bring about the demise of the short-lived omnibus. There were three well-known cab stands where cabmen waited for fares. At the east end of Water Street there was one at Haymarket Square; in the centre of the business district there was another stand at Market House Square; and the west end had a third one at Post Office Square. The first rules for regulating traffic on the streets were issued by Judge Prowse in 1874. By 8 August 1891 cabs had become so numerous that the council ordered cabmen and vehicles to be licensed in an effort to enforce some kind of control. A cabmen's shelter was opened at the Post Office Square stand 24 March 1898, and in its warmth cabbies could gossip among themselves while awaiting fares.

Transportation history of another kind was made on 26 May 1869 when the first cycle was ridden in public. That day R.H. Earle peddled his velocipede beyond Topsail and returned to receive the acclaim of his fellows.[15] The bicycle, as we know it, did not reach North America until one was sent from England for the Philadelphia Exhibition of 1876. The velocipede, an early version of the bicycle, had a large wheel at the front and one or two small wheels at the back. It did not have air-filled tires and, as a result, was aptly known as the "boneshaker."

The first jaunting car to take to the streets of St. John's was imported from Ireland by John Boggan, Sr., in 1878. This odd-looking two-wheeled cart sat four persons facing each other, and there was a seat up front for the driver. It made its local debut on the tenth of June. Twelve years later, in the summer of 1890, an even more peculiar looking vehicle was seen when the first steamroller appeared on city streets.

The gasoline-driven automobile began its invasion of Newfoundland in March 1903. The hundreds of thousands of motor-driven vehicles that have since choked Newfoundland highways and byways can take pride in the fact that their first ancestor to reach these shores was no frivolous Model T from the United States, but an elegant Rolls Royce open touring car, imported from England by Robert Reid, Jr. The second car arrived soon afterwards for Sir Edgar Bowring. There was an immediate outcry against these monsters hurtling through the streets at ten miles per hour. On Sundays Mr. Reid's Rolls was displayed to admiring crowds gathered at the railway station. By 1906 there were enough cars in St. John's to bring about the first Motor Car Act and registration. The first traffic light was erected at Rawlins Cross, its signals installed on a post set in the ground in the middle of the intersection. They were operated by a policeman who stood in a little box on the southwest corner. Traffic switched from driving on the left to the right side of the road in Newfoundland on New Year's Day 1942.

The next important advance in public transportation was the coming of the street railway. Before this could happen, however, tallow candles had to give way to oil lamps, oil lamps to gaslight, and gaslight to electricity. The April session of the House, in 1844, passed an act incorporating the St. John's Gas Light Company and, on May 13, a meeting of the shareholders was held under the chairmanship of Robert Job. The shares list was opened that month and a grant of land was given for the construction of a gasworks. This portion of ground, formerly known as the "parsley bed," was a semi-circular beach on the south side of Water Street between Alexander and Patrick Streets (then known as Foote's Lane and Gas Works Fire Break).

By October all the apparatus had been received and it was hoped to start laying the pipes in November. The "fairest promise" was given of being able to introduce light into the lower street by the end of the year. The work took longer than expected and it was not until 4 September 1845 that the principal shops were lit by gas for the first time. Bowring's is said to be the first gas-lighted store in St. John's. Water Street was thronged with spectators 'till a late hour that September evening. The hope was expressed that soon the public thoroughfare itself would be illuminated.

J. J. Broomfield, an agent visiting St. John's from the Phoenix Fire Office, London, wrote home in October 1845:

> Gas pipes are being laid down in Water Street and supplied from a Gasometer erected at the western extremity of the town by River Side—the works are already in operation—several of the street lamps are in use and it is intended to be introduced into the shops and retail stores generally thro'out the town.[16]

The year 1860 saw the gas company advertising in the newspapers for "a man to take charge of and light the street lamps of St. John's." By 1885 there were twenty-four hundred gaslights in operation about the city. That was also the year when the community was first illuminated by arc lamps. A.M. MacKay promoted the use of the new "electric fluid," considered by many a kind of miracle. A share list for the Electric Light Works was opened in June and a warehouse on the east side of Flavin Street, that had been the Terra Nova Bakery, was leased. During the first half of the twentieth century the Imperial Tobacco Company manufactured cigarettes and tobacco on the site.

The apparatus for the Flavin Street plant, then known as Flavin's Lane and later as Electric Street, was shipped to St. John's on the S.S. *Miranda* in the fall of 1885. That same week another ship, the *Hanovian*, on her regular Halifax-Liverpool run, struck the rocks at Portugal Cove South on September 2, in a dense fog, and was a total loss. All her passengers and much of the cargo was saved and brought to St. John's three days later on board the *Miranda*. Among the rescued was the inventor of the telephone, Professor Alexander Graham Bell, his wife, two children, a nurse, and a Mr. A.M. Bell. They were put up at the Atlantic Hotel until two o'clock on the afternoon of the eighth when they departed for England on board the *Polynesian* which called in from Quebec to pick up survivors of the wreck. Alexander Graham Bell's father had served as a chemist with McMurdo's in St. John's before the great inventor's birth.

With the arrival of the equipment poles were erected from the plant down Prescott Street to Water Street. By Saturday, October 17, all was in readiness, and many turned out to see the lamps that evening in the eleven stores connected to the plant. They were disappointed. The contact of a wire with a pole of the Telegraph and Telephone Company caused a short circuit, and telegraph operators for miles around were given quite a shock. The jolt hurled one of them six feet from his apparatus. On Monday evening the arc lamps were lit again and this time they stayed lit. There were twenty-eight lights in stores and twelve on the streets.[17]

The *Evening Standard,* reporting the event, noted: ". . . hundreds of thousands saw the electric light for the first time and crowds in front of the business places where it shone stopped to gaze and admire the new wonder." In the globes, which were as large as those of the gas lamps, a solenoid was energized bringing together the carbon pencils to establish an arc. The carbons were replaced each day.

In 1888 a new machine was purchased from the Edison Swan Company in England. It enabled the electric company to offer an indoor system of incandescent lights and these were immediately requested for Government House and other public buildings. Switches were placed in every room of the governor's mansion to enable the lights to be turned on and off at will. About 165 lamps were installed in Government House and the huge cut-glass chandeliers were converted from gas to electricity. By January 4, the company announced it would soon be in a position to supply private houses and public buildings within a radius of two thousand feet of the station.

According to Brian Wadden, in a paper entitled "St. John's Electric Light Company, 1885-1892," the first incandescent light was lit, not from the station, but from batteries installed in Government House, 1 January 1889.[18] By April the dynamo was in operation and the *Evening Telegram* was able to report, "important orders for the lights have now been carried out." Incandescent street lights were now burning without fanfare throughout the city. As an economy measure there were planned interruptions when street lighting was considered unnecessary as, when noted in the press, "The lights were out for the past five days, it being moonlight."

The first incandescent lights on Water Street, after the '92 fire, were installed in hastily erected sheds owned by William Frew, W.S. Clouston, and James Gleeson. They were turned on on October 5 and met with great approval.

On 29 August 1889 John Starr of Halifax advised a meeting of the

City Council that he was applying to the next session of the Legislature for a charter of incorporation for an electric tramway company. The bill did not reach the House until April 1891. Possibly as a result of the Great Fire, which took place the following summer, no action was ever taken on Starr's application and it was Sir Robert Reid who eventually received authorization to build and operate an electric street railway in St. John's. To learn how this gentleman became involved in the tram system we must return to the story of train transportation.

By 1883 extravagance and waste had dissipated all railway funds and the American company defaulted. The Harbour Grace railway line was placed in receivership and operated by the receiver on behalf of the English bondholders. This was done until 1896. In 1885 the Newfoundland government raised a loan which enabled it to complete a second branch line to Placentia. This line was a two-year project that cost the exorbitant sum of $20,500 per mile. The experience taught the government not to meddle in railroad building.

The Placentia train ran on the English bondholders' track as far as Whitbourne and this resulted in a costly legal battle that was settled in 1896 when the Privy Council awarded the bondholders $1,500,000 and the Newfoundland government the railway track. The Whiteway Government, in 1889, passed an act to raise four and a half million dollars to finish the construction of a railway to Hall's Bay on the northeast coast. Tenders were called and one of those who tendered was Robert Gillespie Reid, an experienced railroad builder born in the village of Coupar-Angus, near Perth, Scotland, in 1842. Besides working on the C.P.R., of which he was a director, he had built railways and bridges in Australia, the United States, Ottawa, and Montreal. In June 1890 he contracted with the Newfoundland government to finish the railway to Hall's Bay and arrived in St. John's November 20 to begin his engrossing involvement with the country.

When he came to Newfoundland, Reid was worth about six million dollars. Why he found the proposition inviting is hard to imagine. His tender was accepted, not only because of his vast experience, but because his bid of $15,600 per mile of track was the lowest, most straight-forward, and unqualified. He was to receive five thousand acres of land for every mile of railway completed. When construction was begun he soon came to the conclusion that a terminus at Hall's Bay was a luxury the colony could not afford, so he used his influence to urge the government to reroute the road to Port-aux Basques, three miles beyond the disputed French Shore territory that ended at Cape Ray.

A further agreement was worked out with Mr. Reid whereby he would also operate the trans-island railway. At this point the story becomes one of long, involved political hassling, governments falling, and of new deals being made. The famous 1898 Contract is a story in itself. It is sufficient to note here that eventually the terms under which Reid assumed the completion and operation of the railway for fifty years were:

an additional grant of twenty-five hundred acres of land to be given him for each mile of railway; payment of $1,000,000 to the government, and in fifty years the railway to revert to him; payment of $325,000 for the dry-dock which the government built for $560,000 and was operating at a loss; payment of $125,000 for a thousand miles of telegraph lines through Newfoundland which he would operate at reduced rates; the building and operation, at his own expense, of eight modern coastal steamers to carry passengers, mail, and freight. For this latter service the government would pay him a subsidy of $92,000 per year.[19]

When Robert Reid tried to develop his eight thousand square miles of Newfoundland he ran into trouble. English investors would lend money to a legally established corporation but not to the huge empire of a private individual. He returned to Newfoundland to have his firm registered as a limited liability company, but the new government of Sir Robert Bond insisted the contract first be re-negotiated. Ownership of the railway reverted to the government and Reid's $1,000,000 was returned. The telegraph lines reverted to government control and Reid received back the $100,000 he had paid for them. He also gave up ownership to all lands acquired under the '98 contract. Ultimately he received another $2,500,000 for compensation of claims resulting from that contract.

After eighteen years of waiting, the first overland passenger train left St. John's Wednesday, 29 June 1898, with an excursion party and some fifty men and women on their way to a conference in Halifax. The return excursion fare from St. John's to North Sydney was fourteen dollars. A large crowd turned out that evening at the Fort William station, to witness the six-o'clock departure. The train, as it pulled out, consisted of one baggage car, one day coach, a dining car, and two sleepers, under the watchful eye of Conductor Stephen Howlett. The 541-mile journey to Port-aux-Basques took twenty-seven and a half hours. The S.S. *Bruce* carried the pioneer travellers to North Sydney.[20] When she docked on Friday night a big demonstration of welcome was staged at the Nova Scotia port.

The regular train run was begun at six o'clock, June 24, when the mail and a large number of passengers departed the city. The contract specified the minimum speed of the trains was to be eighteen miles per hour. Many who journeyed on the overland express thought it to be the maximum. This was especially true in the days of World War II when servicemen began to refer to the overtaxed train as the Newfie Bullet. The name caught on.

The American movie star, Joan Blondell, came to St. John's on 9 October 1942 to entertain American troops. On her return to Hollywood, Miss Blondell appeared on the famous radio show "Command Performance" and sang a song she found in Newfoundland called "Newfoundland Express." A witty and tuneful ditty, it contained such lines as:

A pretty lady passenger was sitting there close by,
She spied an American soldier with a twinkle in his eye,
He walked up beside her and asked her for a kiss,
Up with her hand and knocked him cold on the Newfoundland
    Express.

Another verse advised would-be suicides not to try going to heaven by tying themselves to the tracks or they would freeze to death waiting for the train. Following her singing of the song on the radio show, Miss Blondell was deluged with hate mail from overly-sensitive Newfoundlanders who took her performance to be an insult to their country. The star wrote to the *Evening Telegram* protesting her innocence.

Eventually all Newfoundlanders came to poke good-natured fun at the archaic, narrow-gauge replica of imperialist days that chugged and swayed along the island's tracks. The last passenger train ran on 2 July 1969. On 2 December 1968 the first passenger run was completed by C.N. bus.

Nearly thirty years earlier, on 1 July 1931, two branch lines were closed and the track taken up. One was from St. John's to Trepassey. It had opened on 1 January 1914. The other was from Carbonear to Grates Cove - Bay de Verde, a line which opened 11 October 1915.

Late in the 1890s Mr. Reid (later Sir Robert) acquired a franchise to light the city of St. John's. A dam was erected in an area of the Goulds, and water was fed by a flume from this dam to a powerhouse in Petty Harbour to replace the Flavin Street plant. From there the electric power was sent by transmission line to the city. By 1900 the Petty Harbour plant was generating plenty of juice to light much of the community, and there was enough spare electricity to supply a street railway. The Reid interests were engaged, not only to install and operate a streetcar service, but also to pave Water Street, with granite blocks, from Cochrane Street to the Crossroads. The paving was to cost $135,000.

On 30 April 1900 the Reid Company unloaded a streetcar at the railway station, Fort William. Two horses and a group of men hauled the car from there to the car barn which had been constructed on Water Street West, opposite the foot of Hutchings Street. The entrance faced the railway station. A trial streetcar run took place on May 1, starting at noon, from the foot of Holloway Street. While a big crowd gathered to watch, a lady cyclist almost turned the triumph to tragedy when, in her excitement on seeing the tram she ran down a small boy in front of the General Post Office. No serious injury resulted though the lad claimed to have seen "every star in the firmament" when his head hit the pavement.

The first regular car run began on 2 May 1900 on a set of double tracks, from the foot of Holloway Street, where the cobblestones began, to the foot of Hutchings Street, where they ended. Passengers could travel the distance for five cents and they were picked up or dropped off anywhere along a route which eventually extended up Holloway Street, east on Duckworth Street to Cavendish Square, where it turned into Military Road. At Rawlins Cross it twisted around to Queen's Road, down Theatre Hill, and south on Adelaide Street, to Water Street. At one time a branch line ran along Harvey and LeMarchant Roads to Patrick Street. In the west the track extended to the Crossroads. At Adelaide Street and at the Crossroads terminal the rod at the rear of the car, connecting it to the overhead transmission wires, was lowered and the one at the front raised, so that the back of the car became the front. The conductor would carry his operating handle and coin box to the other end for the return journey as small boys ran through the car reversing the backs of the wooden seats. At first there was a ticket man and motorman. These were soon combined in the single occupation of conductor who wore a grey suit with a peaked, pillbox cap and often ran personal errands for housewives living along the route or picked up letters to mail at the General Post Office.

The cobblestone paving was laid on Water Street only, and for approximately a quarter of a century mud and clay disrupted and plagued the service on the other unpaved streets. It was not unusual to see a group of citizens helping push the streetcar back on the tracks. In fact, on the very first day of service the car became stuck several times on Water Street because of mud on the rails. Within a few months, the first of many accidents took place, when a streetcar collided with a horse and cart at the foot of Alexander Street.

The *Evening Telegram* hailed the advent of the tram system by exalting, ". . . we shall be abreast of the age in spite of our isolation." The work of laying the rails was accomplished with no more serious mishap than a crushed finger and a broken plate-glass window. The finger was treated at Connor's Drugstore and the owner immediately resumed work. Minor cuts, scratches, and a few broken cart wheels, were added to the toll of sore muscles and aching backs, as the excavating, rail-laying, and paving went on. In connection with this work a curious entry in an issue of the *Evening Telegram* reads: "At 4:45 last evening, 40 or 50 men, with a large slab of portable platform on their shoulders passed up Water Street."

In 1924 the Reid Newfoundland Company sold out the City Lighting Company of 1898 to the Royal Securities Corporation of Montreal, who organized the present Newfoundland Light and Power Company, Ltd. In 1926 the new owners took up the old rails of the street railway and put down, on the newly paved streets of the town, single track of a heavier type, and imported eight new steel streetcars to replace the old ones worn out in service. At various places along the route double tracks were laid to permit the cars to pass. These double tracks were located in front of the railway station, at the foot of Holloway Street, the top of Cochrane Street, in front of the B.I.S. Clubrooms on Queen's Road, and at the Adelaide Street intersection.

By 1940 the area of the city had spread so much that it was necessary to supplement the street railway by a privately owned, gasoline-powered bus system. The streetcars ran for the last time in St. John's on 15 September 1948, when tram Number 17 completed its run. The demands of modern traffic had made them obsolete. Not one of these vehicles was preserved anywhere for the pleasure of future generations interested in this historic mode of public transportation. Their rusting shells could be seen along country roads for a few years, fitted out by purchasers as summer shacks or fish-and-chips shops.

The demand for service compelled the Golden Arrow Bus Company to expand its routes. It was refinanced as Capital Coach Lines. In April 1958 the City Council was forced to take over the financially unsuccessful operation and the deteriorating rolling stock, at a cost of $500,000. For a time the St. John's Transportation System showed a small profit, but by 1960 there had been a succession of deficits amounting to about a thousand dollars per day. In 1972 the system changed its name to Metrobus and painted the vehicles lime green, blue, and silver. This did not prevent the precarious financial position from future deterioration.

Wherever there is transportation, travellers moving about from place to place, there is also the need for accommodation and a bite to eat. In the old days, any wayfaring stranger, anxious to abandon himself to the luxury of gracious living, was due for disappointment when he reached St. John's. While the coachhouses of New England and the inns of the Old Country were unknown in colonial and nineteenth-century Newfoundland, many of the taverns offered comfortable beds and a hearty meal. Aaron Thomas, who visited the Mrs. Tree's London Inn, Ferryland, in 1794, reports he dined on "a Boiled Leg of Pork, Fowls, Lamb, Ducks, Pudings, Green Pease and other vegitables, served up with Sauces and Gravys. Had an Epicure been one of the Guests he could not a found fault with a single Dish."[21]

The earliest St. John's hostelry, of which we have any record, is the Ship, which stood on the north side of Water Street, east of the present War Memorial. The entrance was on the side, where the steps are now located. A painting, thought to have been by one of Governor Richard Edwards's two daughters who accompanied him to Newfoundland, and now in the possession of Chief Justice Furlong, shows the Ship Tavern around 1770, but the date is more probably 1780 if painted by Miss Edwards. In front of the tavern, townspeople and soldiers congregate and gossip. Opposite the door a crude foot bridge spans a stream. In all likelihood this is the brook that once ran down into Gill's Cove, that was rediscovered, some years ago, during the reconstruction of Water Street. A large Union Jack is seen flying from the Ordnance shed on King's Wharf. Next to it is the large Customs Building. The presence of soldiers in Highland dress also indicates 1780 as there were no Scots soldiers in St. John's much before that date. Admiral Lord Nelson was a customer at the Ship in 1781, when he visited St. John's on board H.M.S. *Albermarle*. Captain William Bligh is thought to have been another customer.

The Ship disappears from history before the turn of the century having been replaced in importance by the London Tavern which is first mentioned by Capt. George Cartwright in 1786.[22] The most famous inn of them all, Cornelius Quirk's London Tavern, was noted for the quality of its liquors and the excellence of its meals. Since it was primarily a place of feasting and drinking, it is dealt with in Volume 1, Chapter 5.

In the last years of the eighteenth century the East India Coffee House is thought to have been a centre of information in the town of St. John's. This establishment lasted well into the following century and was much frequented by shipowners and their captains. The services of harbour pilots were engaged at the Coffee House.

Persons of sensibility were invited to sample the gastronomic delights of John Wilson's Beef-Steak and Chop House, which was doing so well by 1812 that Mr. Wilson removed from his house to the more commodious quarters of Ryan the printer, near King's Beach. There, from July 23 onwards, he was able to offer "Dinners dressed in the best manner and furnished to families and others on short notice." Following Mr. Wilson's sudden and unexpected departure from this world, his sorrowing widow announced her determination to carry on the business herself.

By 1815 Widow Wilson faced competition from Samuel Thomas. His City of London Beef-Steak House, King's Place (on the east side of the War Memorial), made a point of the fact that his "...beds shall be unrivalled in goodness . . . rich soups every Sunday from 11 until 3 o'clock." The Gamecock Inn, on the west side of the foot of Long's Hill, attempted to lure customers in 1820 by offering patrons the sport of cock-fighting in a room at the rear.

Many of the old taverns and eating places were swept away in the Great Fire of 1817. Their place was taken in the rebuilt town by the Army, Navy and Commercial Hotel, on the north side of Duckworth Street facing today's War Memorial. Its first glittering event seems to have been the United Service Ball for 1821, held to mark the first anniversary of the accession of a king who was to merit almost universal hatred—the profligate George IV. This "truly splendid affair" was patronized by the Governor and Lady Hamilton.

The following year, the Officers' Ball, at the same establishment, was an even more sparkling occasion. On January 24 guests dined by candlelight to the music of rotating military bands, and "... the dancing kept up with much spirit from 9 o'clock to 5 o'clock in the morning when the company retired highly gratified."

The town had come a long way in the fifty odd years since 1766, when Sir Joseph Banks complained of the social standing of his fellow guests, at a ball given in St. John's, October 26, by Governor Palliser, to celebrate the Coronation of George III. Sir Joseph confided to his diary:

> . . . the want of Ladies was so great that My Washerwoman & her
> sister were there by formal Invitation but what surprized me the
> most was that after Dancing we were conducted to a realy Elegant
> Supper set out with all Kinds of Wines & Italian liquers To the
> Great Emolument of the Ladies who Eat & Drank to some Pur-
> pose Dancing it seems agreed with them By its getting them such
> Excellent stomachs.[23]

During the late eighteenth and early nineteenth centuries, military soirees took place in what is thought by some to be the oldest historic house still standing in St. John's. It is located at 9 Prince William Place. The front (now the back) faces Bonaventure Avenue at Newtown Road. This building may be the one marked on a map of St. John's made in 1741, even though the location is not exact. Some maintain that there was originally a small barracks on the property and that the present structure was erected around 1770. It was set in formal gardens somewhat like the knot gardens popular in New England. The place, which was used as a sort of country club for the recreation of the officers of the garrison and upper-class colonists, escaped destruction by fire and land developers because of having been so far outside the town.

The thick stone foundations may still be seen in the basement. Until recently movable oak panels separated the downstairs rooms and these were rolled back to make a ballroom. The two enormous fireplaces had pothooks showing until a few years ago. In a lamentable renovation, during World War II, the sloping roof was removed, the chimneys lowered, and the casement-style windowboxes replaced. Most of the wide verandah, to the south, was also taken away, and traces of the stables and flower gardens were wiped out in 1940, when Prince William Place was pushed through the property. Of the many trees that were planted around the house in the shape of the letter "H," more than two hundred years ago, only two still survive, for like the house they are protected by no provincial law or civil ordinance.[24] This building may well have been where Sir Joseph Banks danced with his washerwoman ten years before the American Revolution.

Another whose toes tapped the floorboards of the ballroom of the house was H.R.H. Prince William, later King William IV of England, who died without issue and passed the throne to his niece, Victoria. The Prince served in Newfoundland, with the Royal Navy, during the summer of 1786, and while he was in St. John's a ball was held in his honour at the house on Prince William Place. The street name commemorates this event.

Around 1820, if you were unattractive in appearance, there was always an invitation to dine with your fellows of the Ugly Club. They met for dinner, ". . . served at 4 o'clock precisely," every five or six weeks. They appear to have been a group of gourmets who took their business to various establishments about the town.

521

In May 1819 the Ugly Club had a few vacancies and these could be filled by applying to Mr. Uglymug, the secretary. A long poem in one newspaper ad began;

> Ye ugly men possessed of faces,
> entitled in our club to places,
> all whom their features qualify,
> with hideous gorgon's self to vie . . .

One reader, whose features failed to qualify him, lamented in a letter to the editor that there was no organization for handsome men, such as himself.

The Ugly Club was the forerunner of such dining fraternities as the Lions, Kiwanis, and Rotary. Whether or not it provided similar social services is unknown. None of this unusual club's records have survived.

Some spinster sisters, a few doors away from the Army, Navy and Commercial Hotel, vied with that establishment for the transient trade in the 1820s. They called their place the Misses Ward's Hotel. It was not nearly so staid as the name might suggest. A reporter wrote in 1829 that the St. Patrick's Day festivities there were "celebrated with great enthusiasm" and it would take him some days to recover from the all-night affair.

On 29 May 1832 Mr. and Mrs. Andrew Stewart opened the Scotch Hotel on Water Street, at the foot of Prescott Street, opposite Hunter & Co's. premises. Mrs. Stewart, who had served as housekeeper in distinguished families in Scotland, had been employed by Sir Thomas Cochrane. The same newspapers that announced the opening of the hotel also advertised for a housekeeper at Government House to replace Mrs. Stewart.

By 1838 the Commercial Hotel, which had dropped the Army and Navy from its name, was burned out. It was in the hands of Patrick Kielty who moved a few doors along Duckworth Street, into "houses formerly occupied by Misses Ward at King's Beach." The riotous old ladies appear to have either retired or taken their eternal rest. Mr. Kielty refitted the place and announced with pride that there was "an excellent billiard table kept on the premises." He also took pleasure in the fact that his new hostelry commanded an outstanding view of the Narrows, facing across the empty square, as it did. Kielty's ownership was to last into the 1850s.

In the 1840s, before the town was destroyed in the Great Fire of '46, a Mr. Parkins had a hotel on Water Street, west of Hunter's Cove, called Parkins's Hotel, where the Turf Club used to meet, under Dr. William Carson's leadership.

A little earlier the great man could be found at Sally Dooley's Colonial Inn, a notorious hangout for political agitators such as the doctor, Patrick Morris, R.J. Parsons, and John Kent. In 1833 Mrs. Dooley was burned out, but ". . . with the prompt exertions of friends saved most of her furniture from the ravages of the late fire," and she reopened the New Colonial Inn, Maddock's Lane (Ayre's Cove), in late July. On November 26 Winton noted in the *Public Ledger* that the agitators had returned to their old haunt. He wrote: "The celebrated Dr. Carson of much political and other notoriety, has been holding nightly meetings for some time past at the house of Mrs. Dooley from which he and his adherents have been accustomed to harangue the people very much in the style of ordinary mob-orators." The *Ledger* termed these sessions "Sally Dooley's Parliament."

There were a number of popular hotels in the expanding community between the '46 and '92 fires. In addition to Kielty's rebuilt Commercial Hotel, there was Cabot House at 159 Gower Street; Cochrane House at 45 Cochrane Street; British House on New Gower, near Theatre Hill; and Alexander Candow's Victoria House, 1 Waldegrave Street, on the west corner at Water Street. Other hotels, on the main thoroughfare, included the Metropolitan, Henry Earle's Prince of Wales Hotel at No. 171, and a hostelry on the east corner of Holloway and Water Streets, which Richard Matthews gave the resounding name of Conception Bay & Prince Edward Island Temperance Hotel.

On Waterford Bridge Road, the Torrington Hotel, opposite Syme's Bridge, opened in Tor Cottage. Before Candow's Victoria House there was an earlier place of the same name run by Mary Ann Mullowney "at Cathedral Place, near Mr. Barnes home." J.J. Broomfield, of the Phoenix Fire office, wrote to his London headquarters, a few months before the 1846 fire, that the Victoria House was "highly respectable." So much so that Judge Norton was among the boarders. This popular and highly cultured Irishman was the first Roman Catholic to serve as Chief Justice of Newfoundland. A kind of local John Fitzgerald Kennedy, he helped open the doors of the codfish aristocracy to many of his countrymen. In the 1840s auctions were held in the Victoria.

At one period Mrs. Mullowney moved her establishment to Duckworth Street, next door to the Commercial Buildings, west of Telegram Lane. She soon repented and returned to Cathedral Place, a small street behind Richard Barnes's house on Military Road. It is possible that Mrs. Mullowney's Victoria House was the site of the home of Sheriff Carter, which later became the Balsam Hotel.

Following his retirement in 1917, Sheriff James Carter turned his spacious house, Balsam Place, into a hotel. It soon became a fashionable wintering spa for outport merchants and their wives, as well as a retreat for many of the out-of-town members of the House of Assembly. Around the turn of the century, Sheriff Carter gave a long lease to E.R. Burgess, formerly of the Waverley Hotel. Mrs. Elizabeth Burgess eventually passed it to Mr. and Mrs. Leo McCrudden. After Leo McCrudden's death, his wife Alice carried on alone for many years until her own unexpected death in 1947. Mr. and Mrs. John Facey then ran it until the early 1960s, when it was vacated and torn down.

This family-style hotel played host to both the Alexandra and London Theatre companies during their years in St. John's. Among famous names of the theatre who found shelter at the Balsam, are Charles Jarrott, the director of the films *Anne of the Thousand Days, Mary Queen of Scots, Lost Horizon,* and other epics; Alec McCowan, the distinguished English actor who won a Tony Award on Broadway in *Hadrian VII;* and Ronald Fraser, a comedy star in many British movies.

Toussaint, a great name among St. John's hotel owners, operated from several locations during his career. He probably began in a house on the corner of Duckworth and Cochrane Streets that was taken over by Mrs. Goff in 1839 and operated as a boarding house. It was not until after the '46 fire that John C. Toussaint came into his own, with the opening of the splendid Hotel de Paris, "situated in the most central part of the commercial thoroughfare." It was opposite the foot of Holloway Street where part of the King George V Institute now stands. The Hotel de Paris closed its doors, 20 April 1865, after nearly twenty years. It reopened under new management as the Atlantic Hotel (not to be confused with the Atlantic Hotel of 1885). Another Toussaint, William, operated the International Hotel at Harbour Grace in the 1860s.

Born in Paris, France, 1 March 1808, Toussaint came to St. John's in 1832 with his twenty-year-old Irish bride. Besides operating his hotel, he served as Spanish Consul and also ran a catering business. The firm catered for many an affair of state, including the public ball, held in the Colonial Building in 1852 to honour Vice-Admiral Seymour, who had called at St. John's to convey Governor LeMarchant to his new post in Nova Scotia. That evening there was dancing in the Legislative Chamber, and at midnight an "elegant repast" was served to over three hundred people in the Assembly Chamber. According to one newspaper, the garrison band and that of H.M.S. *Cumberland* "produced their immediate and irresistible effect on the impatient votaries of Terpsichore."

In 1865, the year the hotel closed, a daughter of the Toussaints married a gentleman with the impressive name of Don Hipolito De Uriarte, who had taken over from her father as Spanish Consul. J.C. and his wife moved to Victoria Cottage, on Signal Hill, where he acted as French Consul.

One time Don Hipolito purchased a piano from Tom Mullock, 2 Queen's Road, a brother of the Bishop. Both brothers were noted for their Irish wit. Tom delivered the Don's piano on a hearse. A large crowd collected in front of the house on the west side of Prescott Street and the irritated Spaniard asked "What for, Signor Mullock, you send down my piano on a funeral cart?" Tom replied it was to convince the Consul that he had a dead bargain.

Mrs. Toussaint was a handsome, dignified, and stately lady, with whom no one would dream of taking the slightest familiarity. However, in a foolish mood, a Captain Conn, a dapper, daring, and egotistical little lady killer, who had just returned from the ice with a fair trip of seals in a vessel belonging to Captain John Barron, and who thought no female in the land could withstand his charms, undertook to steal a kiss from the lady before the assembled company or, in the event of failure, stand treat all round. He stole a somewhat unsatisfactory kiss from the back of the lady's neck when she wasn't watching for which he not only got his face smacked by Mrs. Toussaint, but had to pay a fine of ten pounds in the Court House next day. It is thought that Captain Conn never put up the treat for the boys, at least not at Toussaints, for he was never seen there again. The old lady was ninety-five at the time of her death. Her husband, who is buried near the Chapel in the C. of E. Cemetery, Forest Road, died 18 January 1887.

Toussaint's competition in the catering business came from J. and G. Lash. These gentlemen operated from one door east of Tim Phelan's Corner, at Adelaide and Water Streets. Following the '46 fire they relocated on the south side of the street, at No. 303, where they opened the Railway Hotel. This building is still remarkably well preserved. The bakeshop is now occupied by the east store of Thompson's Jewellery and the hotel portion, upstairs, has been taken over by a loan company. The outside is almost unchanged since 1847.

Lash's excellent Bakery put the firm very much in demand at parties and the brothers catered for many an illustrious event, including the ball given for Cyrus Field, in the Colonial Building, to mark the successful landing of the Atlantic cable.

Of the fete for Mr. Field and his wife, one enthusiastic newspaper reported: "The supper table groaned under the profusion of excellent cheer set off in Lash's best style."

The firm was also invited to handle the ball, given in the same building, to honour the visit to Newfoundland of the Prince of Wales, who was to become King Edward VII. It was reported in the press that the feast encompassed ". . . all procurable delicacies from New York and such wines including best claret and twelve dozen of champagne." The cost for a ticket to the prince's dance and supper was fifteen shillings for gentlemen, seven shillings for ladies. Lash's continued in the catering business in St. John's until after the turn of the century.[25] On state occasions they were known to decorate their tables with pink, white and green carnations, the colours of the colony.

Knight's Home opened on the south side of Water Street, at No. 173, in 1852. It was about a hundred yards east of Clifts'-Baird's Cove. Samuel Knight, a former hardware merchant, eventually sold out to George Crosbie, who changed the name to the Central Hotel and reopened on 1 May 1886. Upstairs hotels were universal in Victorian St. John's and the Central was no exception. A photograph of it appears in Volume I, page 160. With the destruction of the premises in the fire of 1892, Mr. Crosbie obtained a former newspaper property, on the east corner of Duckworth and Victoria Streets. Here he blasted away the cliff face to make room for an imposing four-storey, wooden structure of forty-one rooms. The Crosbie Hotel opened on 10 December 1894. It was the leading hotel of its day and boasted of having electric light and a bathroom on every floor.

When the Duckworth Street building first opened it was still known as the Central Hotel, but the name was soon changed to the Crosbie. The place narrowly escaped destruction, 12 January 1903, when the furnace room was discovered in flames. Quick thinking, and a handy fire extinguisher, averted a catastrophe. However, the hotel was the scene of a tragedy, 30 April 1920, when Captain Wilfred Pippy, a thirty-eight-year-old soldier with four years service in the Newfoundland Regiment, shot himself dead with his revolver, in a room on the second floor. He had returned from England three weeks earlier and, the night before his tragic end, played cards with friends until 1:00 a.m. He had shown no signs of despondency so that his violent action was unexplained.

Following the death of George Crosbie, his son, the future Sir John, helped his mother manage the business. Eventually it passed into the hands of Mr. and Mrs. Bell, Sir John's sister, and from 1937 to 1965 it was managed by William Spurrell. The hotel closed for a short period, was renovated, and reopened, under the ownership of John Murphy of the Arcade Stores, as the Welcome Hotel.

Before the '46 fire, the Metropolitan House on the north side of Water Street, a few doors east of McBride's Hill, was a very popular lodging with outport visitors. After it was swept away, another Metropolitan Hotel opened at 359 Water Street, in Goobies block opposite the Post Office, and lasted into the twentieth century.

Mr. and Mrs. George Greening's Albert Hotel was also much in demand. It stood on the northwest corner of what is now George Street and Beck's Cove. An oyster bar was opened there by the new owners, Mr. and Mrs. John Tobin, in 1860. The Albert was the last building in the west end of town to be destroyed by the Great Fire of 1892. The flames were stopped in Beck's Cove and all buildings west of the Albert were spared. George Street was afterwards pushed through part of the hotel site, as a firebreak.

Two days before Christmas 1875, the Albert Hotel became the focus of a mystery. A man named John Nowlan, of Catalina, paid Mrs. Tobin and checked out of his room about 9 p.m., to go on board a boat at Tessier's Wharf and sail for home. He called at Hogan's saloon on Water Street, bought a pipe, and continued on his way. He was never seen or heard of again, and the offer of a large reward failed to turn up information on his whereabouts. It was rumoured that he was killed in a house on Water Street, near the foot of Springdale Street, as he was known to have a large sum of money on his person at the time. He was a sober man, in the prime of life, and his fate remains a puzzle.[26]

The White House, a hotel on Carter's Hill, was run by Will Bursey of Old Perlican. The Newman House, at the west corner of Water and

Springdale Streets, was once the Whitten Hotel. The Brownsdale, on New Gower Street, between Springdale and Casey Streets, was opened three-quarters of a century ago by Mrs. Brown of Brownsdale, Trinity Bay. It was torn down in early 1975.

Queen's Hotel, above the popular Queen Restaurant, at the corner of Water and Holloway Streets, was operated in the mid-1880s by Alvin Tupper. In this vicinity, near the Market House, there was another hotel called the Langley.

Oysters seem to have been much in demand in 1860. Besides the Albert's oyster bar, that year it was announced by D. Adams "to the inhabitants of St. John's and the public generally," that he had opened the American Coffee House and Oyster Saloon, "immediately under his Ambrotype Rooms, opposite the premises of Messrs. Baine Johnston & Co., where he trusts by close attention to give those who may favour him with their patronage every satisfaction." Gentlemen from the outports were told they would find it a very convenient place to call and a bill of refreshments was always on the table.

In the 1850s and 1860s the Union Hotel on the west side of Water Street and Steers Cove was high in popularity. It was sold by auction in 1863, and eventually became the Warrington. Many considered it the most fashionable hostelry of its day. It was celebrated for its elegant saloon bar, attended by Miss Guzwell, whose father owned Jersey (Renouf's) Cottage, near the river, on Waterford Bridge Road. While Mrs. Warrington ran the hotel, her husband manufactured cod liver oil at Torbay. By the middle seventies its fortunes were on the decline and the Warrington finally closed. Its valuable English furniture was sold by auction.

Devine and O'Mara tell us that the Headquarters Hotel, a few doors west of Telegram Lane, was the "most popular saloon and restaurant in town." It opened in May 1860 and was destroyed by fire on December 31 the following year. The blaze broke out at 3:00 a.m., and the family of George De Forest, the proprietor, barely escaped with their lives. Sarah Holt's crockery shop and dwelling, next door, were also burnt.

In the late 1870s, Mrs. William Higgins chose a traditional hotel area on Duckworth Street, King's Beach, for her Mansion House, facing the site of the present War Memorial, and next to the shop of Chaplin the tailor, who afterwards moved to Water Street.

On 12 January 1883 the *Newfoundlander* complained, "one of the greatest wants known to St. John's is the want of a hotel suited to the status and character of the town." That year, John Foran took the matter in hand and proposed the formation of a company, for the building of a hotel on the site of the vacant ground, on the north side of Water Street, just below the Beach and west of Messrs. Rendell's office. He estimated its cost at about seven thousand pounds. Foran also built and owned a market on Water Street and a rink on Prescott Street.

The Atlantic Hotel was truly the most awesome building in the town. A splendid edifice, it soared an unprecedented four storeys into the sky.

Opening in May 1885, it catered to the whims of the quality for the next seven years, and its guest list included such illustrious personages as the inventor of the telephone, Alexander Graham Bell. The entrance to the lobby was on Duckworth Street, opposite King's Road. The Water Street level was rented to small shopkeepers such as barbers, watchmakers, and milliners.

The Atlantic Hotel was the scene of an unfortunate tragedy on 27 November 1887. A young clerk, William Shea, coming off duty in the office, opened the elevator gates to ascend to his room. Mr. Foran heard a cry and, with his wife, hurried to the basement where they found Shea dying at the bottom of the shaft. A doctor and Father Scott were fetched but the young married man soon died.

The '92 fire gutted the famous lodging house. The structure was rebuilt inside the shell, but it is doubtful if it was ever reopened. The building was sold by auction in December 1893 and purchased by J. Whitty. At the time, its fifty rooms were valued between twenty-two and twenty-five thousand dollars, a considerable drop in market value from the thirty-five thousand dollars it originally cost to build. The Atlantic assumed a new role in the life of the town on 25 October 1895 when it was purchased, through negotiation, by the Government of Newfoundland for sixty-five hundred dollars, a genuine bargain. Six weeks later it opened its doors as H.M. Customs House and continued in that service until 1956 when it was torn down and replaced by the characterless monolith of the Sir Humphrey Gilbert Building.

Following the total destruction of the east end of the city in 1892, there was a sudden boom in the hotel trade in the west end, especially in the unburnt section of Water Street west of Beck's Cove. Probably the most fashionable of these upstairs hotels was the Tremont, at No. 295, in rooms where the murderer Parnell had lived with his family. The building still stands next to the main branch of the Bank of Nova Scotia. Mrs. McGrath, mother of Dr. James McGrath, a minister in the Smallwood administration, opened Tremont House on 21 June 1886. The name was later transferred to the Waverley Hotel on Duckworth Street. Sir Michael Cashin often stayed at the Tremont before purchasing a house in St. John's.

It was also in 1886 that John Jinkenson advised "pleasure seekers" that he had fitted up in Morton Lodge "his residence at Freshwater," a suite of apartments consisting of a ballroom, refreshment room, and supper room where he was prepared "to entertain in first class style Dinner and Supper Parties, and Picnic and other parties." Morton Lodge was "twenty minutes drive from town over a splendid road."

There were several popular hostelries in Goobie's and Stewart's stone buildings, opposite the General Post Office, besides the already mentioned Metropolitan Hotel. The area is now entirely covered by Woolworth's store. The Balmoral Hotel was located over Garland's bookstore in Goobie's (then Tessier's) block. The nearby Osborne House was run by Mrs.

McGrath of Tremont fame, and a third name associated with English royalty, the King Edward Hotel, was also in the same block. On Christmas Eve 1907 the King Edward offered "Special cuisine, which is the best of any hotel in the city."

No doubt the pinnacle of Edwardian elegance was the turn-of-the-century opening of Yvette Cottage: Restaurant Française. Its twenty rooms offered "Modations fin de siecle." The place is pictured in sylvan loveliness, on the cover of a 1902 issue of the *Newfoundland Quarterly*. It is spoken of in the magazine as "One of the most frequented resorts in St. John's, two miles from the city ... deep set in that lovely and much admired vale of Kilbride. Madame Therouin is the obliging matron, vivacious and courtly in manner."

One of the hotels that rose from the ashes of Duckworth Street, in 1893, was the City Hotel, operated by E.R. Burgess. It was on the north side of the street, three doors east of Prescott Street in a building much changed but still standing. Burgess sold out to John Dooley, Chief Steward of the S.S. *Grand Lake*. When Mr. and Mrs. George Walsh took it over from Dooley they changed the name to the Waverley Hotel, and gave it a dedicated clientele. The place went through a third name change when Mark Delaney became its manager and called it the New Tremont Hotel. Delaney, a brother-in-law of the author's grandmother, was followed by John T. Meaney.

The hotel was a five-storey structure with a balcony along the length of the building, on the fourth floor, giving an unobstructed view of the harbour. The East End Post Office was located there for some years. In September 1930, Robert J. Coleman purchased the property and renovated it for his commission business. The top floor and balcony were removed, and Coleman's occupied the premises until going out of business in the late 1960s.

A favorite winter headquarters of outport society, in town to do "the season," was the Cochrane Hotel on the northwest side of Gower and Cochrane Streets. It opened sometime in the 1870s as Cochrane House, and suffered the fate of most of its colleagues in 1892. The rebuilt Cochrane Hotel was operated, early in the present century, by Mrs. Maher and later taken over by an American businessman named Drayton who made it a leading hotel in the city. Among the distinguished patrons of the Cochrane's thirty-two rooms have been most of the noted aviation pioneers, Hawker and Grieve, Raynham and Morgan, Alcock and Brown, as well as Charles and Anne Morrow Lindbergh. Guglielmo Marconi and his assistants stayed there while conducting the famous wireless experiment in 1901.

It was in 1901 that Governor Williams laid the cornerstone for the Avalon Hotel at Fort William. Most of the fort's building had been razed to make way for the nearby railway station and shunting yards. The Avalon Hotel was part of Sir Robert Reid's railway deal with the Newfoundland government. Work was begun on the hotel and the concrete foundations were poured. Structural materials were in preparation when a fire, in the nearby station buildings, resulted in difficulties that caused Reid to temporarily abandon the project. It was never resumed.

Around 1910 the movement for a hotel at Fort William regained vigour and new support. Eventually, the 137-room Newfoundland Hotel was completed by the government on the site of the ill-fated Avalon Hotel. The Newfoundland accepted its first guests on 30 June 1926. After fifty years it is still the leading hotel in the city.

With the coming of Confederation, its operation was assumed by Canadian National Railways and, as a nod to the French presence in Canada, the name was changed, in the 1960s, to the more Gallic-sounding Hotel Newfoundland. Its registers bear the names of many celebrated persons, from the world's greatest living operatic bass, George London, and novelists such as John Masters and John LeCarre, to Hollywood's beef-cake hero, Victor Mature, who carried on a telephone romance from its rooms with Hollywood pin-up queen Rita Hayworth, during World War II, when Mature was a sailor stationed for a time in Newfoundland with the U.S. navy.

In 1972 Ayre's premises on Water Street, including the former Knowling stores and several adjoining shops, were acquired from the property owners, the Newman Estate, for a twenty-million-dollar complex to be known as Atlantic Place. The twenty-storey building was to include a new C.N. hotel comprising twelve floors, a health spa, an indoor swimming pool, a three-storey shopping mall, roof-top cabaret, and other facilities. The hotel was to have three hundred rooms and convention facilities for a thousand people. Work on clearing the site was begun in 1972 and the project was slated to open in 1975. It proceeded with unbelievable slowness and by 1975 work on the erection of the concrete block exterior walls was only half-completed. The media was flooded with rumours that the hotel tower had been abandoned due to escalating costs. There are at present no plans to complete the hotel.

In 1973 Trizec, a Montreal development organization, applied to Council for permission to erect an office and hotel complex on vacant land west of City Hall on New Gower Street. The thirty-storey structure was to contain three towers but by the spring of 1975 rising costs had also placed that entire project in jeopardy.

3

Crimes and Misfortunes

Captain Henry Osborne was appointed Newfoundland's first governor in 1729 when Lord Vere Beauclerk was forced to turn down the honour. Osborne, lacking in experience and inspiration, nevertheless brought some semblance of law and order to the colony. He established seventeen justices of the peace and thirteen constables, erected stocks, a court house, and a prison at St. John's. He was Vice-Admiral of England before his death in 1771.

In 1791 the British House of Commons created the Court of Civil Jurisdiction of our Lord the the King at St. John's presided over by Chief Justice John Reeves, whom Prowse calls "an admirable official—industrious, painstaking, firm and resolutely impartial."
In 1793 Reeves published the real history of the island, *History of the Government of the Island of Newfoundland.*

533

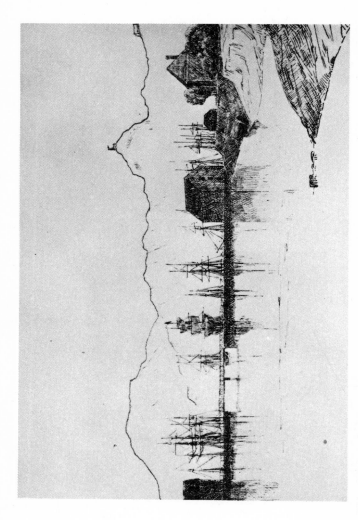

Gibbet Hill from the Southside Road as it looked around 1800. Between Mudge's premises to the right of Long Bridge and the rectory of old St. Mary's Church rises the top of Gibbet Hill and the infamous scaffold. When this sketch was drawn by the Reverend William Grey in 1851 the gibbet had long fallen into disuse and probably disappeared from the site. (Courtesy Public Archives of Canada.)

The Newfoundland Constabulary, with mounted police and band, assemble in front of one of the old barracks at Fort Townshend around the turn of the century looking as if "constabulary duty's to be done. . . ." The building, torn down in 1946, dated from 1779 and was occupied by married police. It appears in the 1831 sketch of Government House in Chapter 1. (Courtesy Newfoundland Constabulary Archives.)

This sketch of the Market House erected on the site of the present Court House in 1849 shows the three levels of the building. The ground floor was a produce market with cells for prisoners at the back. The post office occupied the second floor with an entrance from Market House Hill. The court occupied the top floor and was entered from Duckworth Street. The new Anglican Cathedral is at the top of the steps. (Courtesy Public Archives of Canada.)

Chief Justice Boulton, born in England in 1790, came to Canada at age seven. He was dismissed as Attorney General of Upper Canada in 1833 for having attacked the Colonial Office in connection with the reception accorded William Lyon Mackenzie at Westminster in 1832. Appointed to Newfoundland he became known as "the hanging judge." Prowse says he was "hated as no one else was ever hated in this colony." Removed from office in 1838 and cast adrift penniless he returned to Toronto where he died in 1870.

Inspector General John McCowen was the son of a British Army officer. Born in County Clare, Ireland, in 1844 he was appointed Governor of the Penitentiary in St. John's in 1879 and became Inspector and General Superintendent of Police in 1895. McCowen organized the St. John's Fire Department, the police band, the widows and orphans fund, and the Pension and Gratuities Scheme, and had all police appointed Tidewaiters.

The codfish behind the electric light pole on the right hangs over the entrance to Sillars and Cairns on Water Street. The discovery of the murdered body of Mr. Sillars in the basement of the store 1 December 1888 led to a pathetic court case in which the accused was seen as a defeated and browbeaten Bob Cratchit working for an unregenerate Mr. Scrooge. The building still stands, as does Lash's Bakery and Railway Hotel on the right. (Courtesy CBC, Newfoundland Region.)

The building on the right of Kent's Grocery at the Crossroads, seen here around the turn of the century, became the Regal Cafe where the bizarre murder of the Chinese proprietor, Eng Wing Kit, caused a sensation in 1938. A milkman from Kilbride discovered the crime, often referred to in St. John's as the tong murder.

Judge David Woodley Prowse, LL.D., Q.C., the greatest historian whose *History of Newfoundland* has not been equalled since its publication in 1895. Born at Port de Grave in 1834 and appointed a judge of the Central District Court in 1869, he was openly disappointed at not receiving the honours he rightly felt should have been his. Prowse died 17 January 1914.

The most celebrated aspect of the Murray Street laundry murders was probably the exhibition of the three corpses in the window of this funeral parlour on New Gower Street. There was a long line-up of the curious who waited to glimpse the corpses placed in tilted coffins. Note the horse-drawn hearse in the lane beside the undertaking establishment. (Courtesy Provincial Reference Library.)

Rain did not deter the future King George V and Queen Mary from laying the cornerstone for the present Court House, 24 October 1901 when they visited St. John's as Duke and Duchess of Cornwall and York. Here they are shown alighting from their carriage at the site watched by spectators beneath a sea of umbrellas. The building opened in 1904. (Courtesy Newfoundland Provincial Archives.)

The present imposing neo-Romanesque Court House shown at the time of its construction (1901-04). It also served as an office for the Prime Minister and cabinet. It was here that a threatening mob descended on Sir Richard Squires. The police lock-up is entered by a side door at the foot of the steps. Magistrates court is entered by the black door above. The Supreme Court occupies the Duckworth Street level.

Crimes and Misfortunes

History is little else than a picture of human crimes and misfortunes.
VOLTAIRE *L'Ingénu*

A legate from Florence was so appalled at English trial methods in 1615 that he wrote back home: "This seems a strange kind of justice, that the accused is not permitted to have a lawyer to defend him, not even to be able to produce documents or testimonies in his favor, but has to depend on himself to speak for himself against the charges of the more expert advocates of the court, who ARE able to use against him testimonies and writings."

A seventeenth-century English law court was a place where preliminary examination determined guilt. There was no point in placing somebody on trial who was not guilty. It was the duty of juries to acquiesce in conclusions already reached. Prisoners had no defence counsel, and no way of knowing what the indictment was until it was read in court, too late to prepare a reply. Hearsay evidence was in popular use.

Once the accused was tried and found guilty, the punishment was often swift and brutal. There was no nonsense about appeals, mainly because there were almost no rights and therefore few violations on which to base an appeal. The lone effectual appeal was to the king, and this was reserved for traitors and murderers only among the aristocracy.

The lowly sailor or fisherman in Newfoundland stood little or no chance of either justice or mercy when accused of a crime. In 1755, at a time when the Penal Laws against Catholics were strictly enforced, Michael Keating of Harbour Main was fined fifty pounds for allowing mass to be celebrated in his fish store. His property was ordered demolished, his goods seized, and he was banished from the colony. As late as 1859 John Ryan was sentenced to banishment by Judge Little for the larceny of two watches, a writing desk, and four geese. In the middle of the eighteenth century a drunken soldier, who stole a lamb he found grazing on the barrens (now the Military Road area), had all his goods and chattels confiscated and, the next day at the Court House, he was branded with the letter

545

"R" on his right hand. This was a rare case of mercy being shown because the usual punishment for sheep and cattle stealing was hanging, as two of Colonel Haly's servants found out when they stole and killed a cow.

In November 1794, John Coady was condemned to death at St. John's for forging the name of Martin Walsh to a bill of exchange for £2.9.7. (about $12), and for "personating the same Martin Walsh." Thirty-three-year-old Mary Ryan was found guilty of doing some shoplifting, 18 December 1839, and "Sentenced to be banished from this Island and its dependencies for 14 years and to be imprisoned with hard labour until her passage be procured to some port or place beyond the Government of Newfoundland. . . ." On March 31 the following year she was put on the schooner *Venus* for Halifax.

Extreme youth or advanced age saved nobody from the harsh sentence of banishment. In 1854 George Tough, an unfortunately named lad of fifteen years, was convicted of larceny and transported to Boston on board the schooner *Marcia*. In 1852 Joseph Rose, age seventy years, was given a like sentence for the same crime. "Throwing corrosive fluid in the face of R. Blundon," got thirty-two-year-old William Hayden banished for life, 15 May 1856.

Sixteen-year-old Elizabeth Ward gave the authorities some trouble in carrying out the punishment passed on her in April 1855. The young lady was sentenced by Judge Carter to banishment from the colony for seven years for the theft of a velvet bonnet and scarf. Elizabeth is probably the first female juvenile delinquent whose deeds are recorded in St. John's for, in addition to having a hankering for finery, she was also in a delicate condition without a husband. The wayward lass was placed in the old jail on Signal Hill to await transportation. On April 30 she was put on board a vessel bound for Prince Edward Island but escaped before the ship sailed. She was recaptured a few days later and returned to jail. On June 9 another attempt was made to transport the girl, but once more the wily teenager escaped ship. Apprehended, she was returned to jail where "She exhibited symptoms of insanity and was sent to the asylum, from which she effected her escape but was again brought back to the Gaol on January 12th, 1856." The Government gave up trying to deport her and on May 1 the Governor issued her a pardon.[1] She must have given birth either in the jail or the asylum but there is no record of the fate of the child.

An unusual punishment appears in the Colonial Records for 1757 as being meted out to the first of the town's numerous ladies of the night known to us by name, Elenor Moody. The winsome tart lived near Fort William. One autumn evening, in late September 1757, Elenor met up with John Moye, a seaman belonging to Governor Richard Edwards's ship, and induced him to follow her home where she robbed him "of his money and buckles (first making him excessive drunk) and then with the assistance of a soldier, dragg'd him out of the house, upon the Down and there left him. . . ."

On October 1 Governor Edwards required and directed His Majesty's Justices of the Peace "to cause the Constables to apprehend the said Elenor Moody, and to put her in prison 'till 4 o'clock in the afternoon, at which time to cause her to be put in the Whirligig, where she is to remain One Hour, & to be properly punished, and to be sent out of this island the first opportunity, being a Nuisance to the Publick."

In 1777 being found innocent could land you in prison just as easily as being found guilty. About nine o'clock on the evening of November 24 the previous year, a St. John's merchant named John Cahill was having a drunken spree in his house on the Upper Path. Some boys peeped in the window and Cahill and his guests rushed out to strike the unwanted spectators. In the melee Cahill himself was struck with a stone, languished a day or so, and died. Richard Power, an Irish "youngster" (labourer), who happened to be passing, was arrested. There was no evidence to show that he was in any way involved in the violence. In fact, the unfortunate Power had himself been struck several blows which were treated next day by Doctor Delaney. Found not guilty, the prisoner was discharged, on condition he pay the fees of the court. Richard Power faced jail if he could not pay the court costs for a trial which proved his innocence.[2]

The same year Lawrence Hallohan was found guilty of forging a bill of eight pounds (less than forty dollars) and was sentenced: "That you be carried back to the place from whence you came and thence led to the place of execution and there be hanged by the neck until you are Dead, Dead, Dead, and the Lord have mercy on your soul." He was hanged on 10 May 1777. That same year Lawrence Dalton, who forged orders for only twenty shillings and seventeen shillings (less than two pounds), suffered the same sentence.

Patrick Knowlan, who stole a counterpane valued at tenpence (less than twenty cents) from Peter Prim, was given the following sentence:

> That you P. Knowlan be whipped by the common whipper with a halter around your neck. That is to say you are to receive on your bare back twenty lashes at the common whipping post, then to be led by the halter to the Publick Path just opposite Mr. Peter Prim's door [on Water Street between Holloway and Prescott Streets] and there receive twenty lashes as before, and then led as before to the Vice-Admiral's Beach and there to receive twenty lashes as before; to forfeit your goods and chattels; to pay the charges of the court, and to depart this Island by the first vessel bound for Ireland, never to return on pain of having the same punishment repeated every Monday morning; to be kept in prison till you go abroad.

The magistrates responsible for most of these harsh sentences were Michael Gill, John Stripling, Edward White, Dr. Thomas Dodd, Robert Bulley, and the Church of England clergyman, Edward Langman.

547

At the time, whipping was almost a way of life, especially in the Navy. The Log Book of the H.M.S. *Pegasus*, written on a visit to Newfoundland in 1786, has somebody whipped for something almost every day the ship was in port at St. John's. For example, the entry for September 16 reads: "Alexander McMullem, Fras Brown, Richd Burke, Chas Tebey, William Melcomb and James Butter seamen with twelve lashes for Drunkenness and Moses Williams with twenty lashes for Drunkenness and scandalous behaviour on shore. loosed sails. washed between decks."

As late as 21 August 1804 James Brown and Richard Nickells were found guilty of forgery in the court of Justice Tremblett and sentenced to hang. The same session also sent Catherine Brown to the gallows for the murder of her husband. She was publicly hanged 1 September 1804. If or how the two cases were related is not clear. James Brown was also executed but a hue and cry arose over the conviction of Nickells. The merchants of the town signed a petition for his reprieve and Tommy Tremblett himself wrote the governor, "I consider him a proper object of mercy." Erasmus Gower was hesitant that the granting of a pardon might result in a rash of forgeries but His Excellency finally succumbed to pressure and Nickells was allowed to go free.

Public whipping posts were located about the town. Historians are not in agreement as to the exact sites of these posts. We know there was one somewhere in the vicinty of the foot of Garrison Hill. It is generally agreed to have been on the site of the present Sergeants War Memorial. Petty thieves (this must have been the theft of farthings) and disturbers of the peace (brawlers, drunks, etc), were secured to the whipping post where a husky arm delivered anywhere up to one hundred lashes with the cat-o'-nine-tails. In one case, at Placentia, His Royal Highness, Prince William (King William IV), presided as surrogate in the Court House. Here is how it is described in the records:

> A riot happening on shore at 4 o'clock, the Magistrate attending to suppress it was insulted. The Prince came on shore with a guard of marines, arrested the ringleader, called a court, and sentenced him to receive 100 lashes—he was only able to receive 80. Next day inquired into the facts of the case; (and report has it that they had whipped the wrong man).

Such crimes as a servant sticking a tongue out at an employer could get him placed in the stocks which were set up on the more public paths. The prisoner was then pelted with filth by the townspeople of St. John's as they passed by the culprit.

Law and order, as we know the process, was slow in evolving. It did not reach the American west, for example, before the present century and, until recent years, the Negro of the deep south often had little hope of either trial or justice. Therefore, in many ways, Newfoundland was not isolated in its search for a workable legal system. A commission was given, in 1615, to Captain Whitbourne, out of the Court of Admiralty, for impanelling juries. This seems to have resulted from an agitation by commissioners of the customs to appoint an officer to prevent illicit trade in Newfoundland. Other than trade cases were brought to the attention of these juries.

To put some backbone into the sentences of the courts, in 1705 Governor Bonfoy ordered justices of the peace in Newfoundland to erect gallows on the public wharves in their districts, for the execution of persons found guilty of robbery or felony. St. John's had a number of such scaffolds to which crowds were drawn for hanging spectacles. The most famous was Gibbet Hill just below Cabot Tower. This site was used more for military offenders than common felons, so that their service comrades might look up and take heed. In the late seventeenth and early eighteenth centuries a gallows stood on Church Hill but this had to be moved elsewhere when the expansion of the Church of England required the ground. West of Bates Hill was known as Gallows Hill in 1822 when the New Amateur Theatre was built on the old hanging property. There was a gallows erected at the top of Belvedere Street where five culprits were hanged in 1800. Four were strung up in 1750 on a gallows that stood on Keen's Wharf, on the west side of Hunter's Cove, the site of today's Royal Trust Building.

In 1811 some daring soul chopped down the public gallows as a prank. Governor Duckworth did not see the humour of the situation and issued the following proclamation: "Whereas certain indisposed and wanton persons lawlessly deemed to cut down the gallows on or about the night of the 12th this is to give notice that whoever will detect and secure the offenders so that they may be brought to immediate punishment shall receive a reward of £30."[3] There is no record of anyone claiming the reward.

In spite of the large public turnout for the various hanging events in the old days, the hangman who supplied these diversions was generally scorned by the populace, as this notice from the *Newfoundlander*, 16 January 1834, seems to show:

> A report having been maliciously set afloat through the town that some of the crew of the Colonial yacht FORTE performed the office of hangman at the execution of Downing and also at that of Mandeville and Spring, we the undersigned, being crew of the yacht FORTE take this public method of pronouncing such a report to be false and an unjust aspersion on our characters.

It was signed by seven men.

Eventually, malefactors were hanged from a window on the west side of the old Court House, east of the present Court House Steps. Besides theft and murder, a rape could get you the rope, as Private William Fielding discovered when he was found guilty of raping seventeen-year-old Elizabeth Melville, in the Strawberry Patch on the barrens in July 1750. John Stackebald, of the Kingdom of Ireland, was convicted of performing a rape on the body of Esther Merrifield of Torbay, 26 July 1762, between three and four o'clock in the afternoon, on the kitchen table, while her besotted husband who was Stackebald's drinking companion, watched from the settle by the stove. He was convicted and sent back to jail to await hanging. In an attempt to escape the scaffold, the prisoner set the prison on fire.[4] Young Stackebald was obviously determined not to be led as a lamb to the slaughter.

Chief Justice Reeves says he found that in 1711 there was

> what is called, a record of several laws and orders made at St. John's for the better discipline and good order of the people, and for correcting irregularities committed contrary to good laws, and acts of parliament, all which were debated at several courts held, wherein were present the commanders of merchants' ships, merchants, and chief inhabitants; and witnesses being examined, it brought to conclusion between the 23rd day of August and the 23rd day of October 1711.[5]

Captain Crowe, the commander, presided at this voluntary assembly in 1711, and his successor seems to have followed his example by holding subsequent meetings. Reeves adds, "These assemblies were somewhat anomalous, a kind of legislative, judicial and executive, all blended together; and yet perhaps not more mixed than the proceedings of parliaments in Europe, in very early times."

The earliest system of justice known to the settlers was that of the fishing admirals, which was no justice at all. This meant that the first skipper to arrive in a port, at the start of the fishing season, was absolute ruler of that port for the rest of the year. Often these were totally ignorant men with no qualifications except command of a ship. Their ways were oppressive and their punishments harsh and partisan.

Documents from the correspondence of naval commodores and commanders, on the Newfoundland station to the Board of Trade in England, in 1729, show that in spite of the law of the fishing admirals disorders were on the increase. One wrote, "It is certain the admirals are seldom or never at leisure to hear any complaints whatsoever, except one of their favourites is the plaintiff." Another writes,

> I flatter myself that as there was no garrison here (namely at St. John's) to terrify or interfere, I should find a stricter obedience to the laws and regulations that had been made for the government of the place, and that a proper regard was shown to the authority vested by law in the fishing admirals, but on the contrary I find...
> that unless the captains of the men of war are present and assist

and countenance them at their courts, their meetings would be nothing but confusion, and their orders of no use. . . .

In a letter written by Captain Kempthorn, in October 1715, he says there is always great disorder in winter because of the neglect of deputizing somebody to maintain order:

> At that time, theft, murder, rapes or disorders of any kind whatsoever, may be committed, and most of them are committed without control, and time enough given for the offender to make off.... St. John's is the metropolis of the island [the captain was the first to make this claim], and the discipline which is kept up there, whether bad or good, will have a great influence upon all the rest of the harbours. If good order might be established here, it might easily be effected in all other places. . . .[6]

In 1729 Lord Vere Beauclerk, the commodore of the Newfoundland station, was appointed first governor and commander-in-chief in and over the island of Newfoundland, "with authority to appoint Justices of the Peace and to erect Court Houses and prisons...." It was also decreed that a person skilled in the laws was to be sent annually to the island with His Majesty's Commission of Oyer and Terminer (to hear and determine). Instead of this skilled person, Judge Prowse tells us, copies of the Acts of Parliament and eleven sets of *Shaw's Practical Justice of the Peace*, impressed in covers with letters of gold, were sent to the colony.

As mentioned in Volume I of this work, Lord Vere was unable to accept the office of governor because of his seat in Parliament.[7] Instead of this capable man, his subordinate, Captain Henry Osborne, was given the task of acting as Newfoundland's first governor, while Beauclerk remained commodore of the station. Osborne was an equitable and honest young officer, if uninspired. He had neither the years, nor the experience, to cope with the task successfully.

With the arrival of Governor Osborne in 1729, the rule of the fishing admirals came to an end. It was replaced by that of naval officers who were commissioned as deputies, or surrogates, to hold court in summer. When the naval convoy returned to England in the autumn local justices of the peace were appointed to try all cases in Courts of Session during the winter months. However, many of these justices were as incompetent and corrupt as the fishing admirals they replaced. One St. John's judge, John Stripling, was an illiterate tavern owner. There is a record of three magistrates of the town having levelled a $750 fine on one man for being drunk and using improper language. This fine money was divided among the gentlemen on the Bench. Since magistrates received no fixed salary, they were paid so much for each trial and kept a portion of the fines they imposed. The same three lawmen are said to have issued licences for 108 taverns at $23.50 each. Half of the more than $2,500 they collected went into their own pockets. Justice was usually denied the poor because, unlike the rich, they were unable to buy off such magistrates.

In 1729 Governor Osborne created six districts between Bonavista and Placentia and within them he established seventeen justices of the peace and thirteen constables. Stocks were erected in several places and a tax was imposed for the building of a prison at St. John's. By September 1730 a court house and prison were completed, but the magistrates were threatening to resign because of the indignities and obstructions of the fishing admirals, who were reluctant to admit to the authority of the governor and his legal aides.

The fishing admirals contended that the magistrates were only winter justices. On their return to Newfoundland in the spring they claimed their old rights and went on licensing public houses, seizing, fining, and whipping. The merchants joined them in opposing the new authority because they and the ships' masters had been summoned to pay wages, then an unknown thing in the colony.

Criminal cases were still required to be sent home to England for trial. This was done at local expense and often involving long delay. Two murder cases, one in Torbay where a man named Gosse was accused of killing a fellow called Blackmore, and the other a murder by a person named Steele, led to a recommendation by Governor Lee (1735-37) to permit the trial of capital crimes and felonies in Newfoundland and the establishment of a court of vice-admiralty to cope with illegal trade. In the Gosse and Steele cases the accused and witnesses were transported to England where they were put up at great expense for some considerable time. When Governor Vanburgh received his commission in 1737 there was a clause inserted giving him the authority to hold Court of Oyer and Terminer while he resided in the colony. However, the Privy Council struck out the clause on the ground that such an action might involve the Crown in a controversy with Parliament. It was not granted for another thirteen years.

In 1750, Governor Drake was finally given the power to establish courts superior to those of the magistrates and to try all offenses except treason. He was also granted the right to pardon offenders and to remit offences, fines, and forfeitures, except in cases of wilful murder. In the latter case he could grant a reprieve according to the circumstances. Transcripts of all the capital cases had to be transmitted in full to enable the Crown to allow or disallow them.

The Court of Oyers and Terminer could not hold more than one assize a year and that had to be during the residence of the governor. His Excellency found the limitation on his power to execute, for capital offences, detrimental to the judicial system. Condemned men had to wait nearly a year to know their fate and during the winter it was almost impossible to prevent their being set free by friends. Governor Drake asked that he be allowed to execute capital offenders immediately, and permission was granted in 1751, in all cases except treason. That year the first gallows was set up in St. John's, but the power was used sparingly, for Drake sentenced only two men to death during his term. He reprieved others of doubtful guilt and they were all eventually pardoned.[8]

The most notable murder of the period was that of William Keen, a justice of the peace at St. John's. The motive for the crime appears to have been a mixture of money and revenge, for Keen had frequently put soldiers in jail without notifying their commandant, a practice which led to a dispute between the military and the local magistrates.

In 1723 William Keen had been the leader of a group of citizens of St. John's who tried to establish a local government to cope with disorder and crime. In this he was assisted by John Jago, the Church of England chaplain, and fifty others. The association held its own courts almost every week during the winter of 1723-24. As a result of these activities, Keen was one of the first magistrates created by Governor Osborne in 1729-30. In 1741 he was appointed Naval Officer for the port, and Judge of the Vice-Admiralty Court, which was another attempt at creating a court of justice.

Ten persons were implicated in his murder in 1754. Only nine of them were brought to trial, for one of them, Nicholas Power, turned King's Evidence. It was conclusively proven at the trial that the group, organized by a soldier named Edmund McGuire, had conspired to rob the judge's house several times. The instigator of the plot seems to have been a woman, Eleanor Power, possibly somebody once in Keen's employ, for she professed to know where the old man had hidden enough money to gain each of them one thousand pounds.

The conspirators, McGuire and three other soldiers all belonging to Captain Aldridge's company, John Munhall, Dennis Hawkins, John Moody, as well as Eleanor Power and her husband Robert, Paul McDonald, Lawrence Lamley, and Matthew Halluran, all of Freshwater Bay, swore on a prayer book to be true to each other. On the appointed day they rowed from Freshwater Bay to St. John's and landed at the King's Wharf where they were joined by the soldiers. They met again at midnight at Magistrate Keen's summer house, believed to be at Quidi Vidi. However, as there were still people in the nearby stages splitting fish, they were forced to await a more favourable opportunity.

The next time they tried to carry out their plan they were again frustrated by finding young Keen's sloop and that of another tied up at his father's wharf. On 29 September 1754 they met again near the summer house and once more went through a form of swearing. They proceeded to break down the door in the darkness. Some of the conspirators kept watch with muskets while others entered the house, stole some silver spoons, and followed Eleanor Power, who, dressed as a man, led them to a chest she said contained the fortune they all hoped to share.

Once outside they broke open the case only to find it contained liquor. Some of the men wanted to abandon the project and go home but McGuire threatened death to any who left. They went back to the house a second time and McGuire and Matthew Halluran went upstairs to the magistrate's room. Keen woke up and McGuire put a quilt over his head. The old man rose in the bed and put out a candle the soldier was holding. When he cried out "Murder!" Halluran struck him twice with a piece of old scythe with a sharp point he had carried on each of the robbery attempts. The magistrate was also given a blow on the head from the butt end of McGuire's musket. Dr. Thomas Allan and Dr. John Burton testified at the trial which followed the arrest of the murderers that Keen died from the wounds.

Michael Gill presided over the trial which took place on October 8. Within half an hour of his charge to the jury they returned a verdict of guilty of the felony and murder charge. Gill ordered that all nine be hanged by the neck until dead and that Edmund McGuire and Matthew Halluran "be hanged in chains on some Publick Place, when and where the Governor shall be pleased to appoint." Governor Bonfoy was pleased to appoint that they be hanged at noon on the morning of October 10 "on the Gibbet Erected on the Wharf of Mr. Wm. Keen, until they are dead, and their Bodys to be taken down and Hung in Chains, on the place appointed for that purpose." The following day Robert and Eleanor Power were hanged by their necks on the same gallows (now Hunter's Cove, site of the Royal Trust Building) and "their Bodys to be taken down and Buried near the said gallows." Eleanor Power is believed to have the distinction of being the first woman to be hanged for murder in Canada. Bonfoy thought fit to respite the execution of the others, and they were subsequently pardoned by the King.[9] As a result of this murder by a lawless few Irish Roman Catholics, the entire Irish Catholic community of the island was to suffer incredible persecution in the months that followed. There was an outburst of anti-Catholic fanaticism and Governor Bonfoy issued such strict orders that many fled to the other colonies of North America, or home to Ireland.

The next notable event in the development of law and order in St. John's took place in 1792 with the establishment of the first Supreme Court. Three years earlier Aaron Graham, who was secretary to Governor Mark Milbanke, recommended that His Excellency create a court of common pleas, with regular judges, instead of justices of the peace. Prowse tells us this fortunate mistake (of recommending that the governor create something he had no power to create) led to the investigation and inspection of our judicial system by the House of Commons, and Graham, who was the virtual governor of the Colony, is credited, along with Milbanke, with having instituted Newfoundland courts of justice.[10]

The merchants, whose interests were again no longer served by the courts, were firmly opposed to Admiral Milbanke's new tribunal, the first one being established by the House of Commons in 1791 as "The Court of Civil Jurisdiction of our Lord the King at St. John's, in the island of

Newfoundland." John Reeves, law adviser to the Board of Trade, a diligent, persevering, steadfast, and dispassionately fair official, was appointed Newfoundland's first Chief Justice for one year. The next year the court was designated "The Supreme Court of Judicature of the Island of Newfoundland," and Reeves was again chief justice. This matter of a yearly appointment was continued until 1809. Under Reeves, Aaron Graham, who afterwards became a police magistrate in London, and D'Ewes Coke were made assessors in the court. During the third year Reeves returned to England, where he wrote a history of Newfoundland, and Coke, who had been a magistrate, and before that a surgeon and notary at Trinity, succeeded as Chief Justice. Reeves had been paid five hundred pounds per year, Graham and Coke two hundred pounds each. When Coke rose to the top position he was given a salary of three hundred pounds. The clerks received forty pounds each. It was thought that one clerk would be sufficient to conduct the business.

D'Ewes Coke presided as Chief Justice until 1797, when Richard Routh, Collector of Customs and an exemplary official, received the post. Routh asked permission to go to England on leave in 1800. This was granted and on the journey he was shipwrecked and lost at sea. There was no appointment in 1801, but in 1802 another surgeon, Jonathan Ogden, became Acting Chief Justice. He was also lost at sea while on a cruise for his health. The next appointment was that of Thomas Tremblett, a crusty old merchant with a terrible temper. His decisions were scrupulously fair and he gave as much offence to his fellow merchants as he did to "the lower orders." The merchants drew up a long list of complaints against him which they presented to the Governor, Sir J.T. Duckworth, who sent them to the irascible Chief Justice. Tremblett wrote back: "To the first charge your Excellency I reply that it is a lie, to the second charge I say that it is a d---d lie, and to the third charge that it is a d---d infernal lie, and Your Excellency I have no more to say."[11]

The charges against Tommy Tremblett, as well as an accusation that Reeves had participated in the salary of the Chief Justice after he had ceased to fill that situation, were dismissed by the Governor and the authorities in England, as prefabrications. No act of wilful injustice, partiality, or accountable delay could be proven against old Tremblett, and Reeves was obviously innocent. However, it was apparent that Tremblett knew little about the law and it was deemed advisable to switch him with an Irish gentleman, Caesar Colclough, who was in similar difficulties, as Chief Justice of Prince Edward Island. From that time on, the head of the Supreme Court in Newfoundland was required to be a barrister of not less than seven years' experience. Colclough arrived in St. John's in September 1813. His reaction to his appointment may be summed up in the following letter to a friend, written September 29: "Fate has removed me for my sins to this cursed spot as Chief Justice. . . . I wrote this in the counting house of a fish merchant, whose ship is bound to Lisbon. I have been here but a few days. . . ."[12] His penance lasted three years. A humorous man of letters, he succeeded in having his salary raised from five hundred to one thousand pounds per annum. Prowse characterizes him as a sorry administrator, "little better than an old woman."

Francis Forbes was born at Smith's Island, Bermuda, in 1787. He was called to the English Bar in 1812 and the following year was appointed Attorney General of Bermuda. In 1816 Earl Bathurst offered him the post of Chief Justice in Newfoundland. During his term Sir Francis was greatly loved. Henry Shea, the father of Sir Ambrose and Sir Edward, said he was "one whose inflexible adherence to impartial administration of justice, had nobly gained him love, esteem, gratitude and applause, of all descriptions of people in this island."

In May 1822, Chief Justice Forbes left Newfoundland. Lady Forbes wrote later: "After six happy years at St. John's, the severity of the climate made it necessary for my husband to return to England." In 1824 Sir Francis took his seat on the Bench at Sydney as Chief Justice of New South Wales, Australia. Newfoundland, however, remembers him less for his outstanding judicial qualities than for his musical abilities as the composer of "Up the Pond," the St. John's Regatta anthem that has become immortalized as "The Banks of Newfoundland." The composition was published by Oliver Ditson, Boston, and it brought Justice Forbes undying fame. The Newfoundland statesman, Lord Morris, has written:

> How surprised would have been Sir Francis Forbes, could he have looked into the future, to find his composition (attempted no doubt to relieve the strain of official duties) being played before royalty, and at the parade of the Lord Mayor of London. In France and in Scotland, the home of the old Forbes family, was heard the music of "The Banks of Newfoundland."

Forbes was a learned man whose court at St. John's was a place above criticism where, for the first time, the full benefit of the law was extended to all. The same situation was not true of the outports. There, surrogate courts were still being conducted by naval officers. Two incidents in 1820 brought about an end to this form of injustice.

The 1818 fishing season was an extremely poor one in the island and a fisherman of Harbour Grace, James Landergan (or Lundrigan) fell in debt for supplies to the amount of twelve pounds (then about sixty dollars). This sum due to his suppliers was immediately put in suit in the surrogate court at Harbour Grace, and judgement passed against the man by default. Shortly afterwards his fishing room was sold and the clerk of his suppliers purchased it for the amount of the debt. Landergan had personal property at the time fully equal to satisfy the judgement, and his fishing room was estimated to be worth about one hundred and fifty pounds. When the sheriff's officer went to deliver possession of the room Landergan was away and some strong language passed between the officer and the fisherman's wife. This was interpreted as resistance to authority and a complaint was made to the court.

When Capt. David Buchan of H.M.S. *Grasshopper*, and Rev. John Leigh, Anglican parson at Harbour Grace, held a surrogate Court at Port de Grave, Landergan was summoned to appear before them. As he was hauling some fish for his family at the time he apologized for not being able to attend court then but promised to go the following morning. That night the military returned and seized Landergan in his bed. He was confined on board H.M.S. *Grasshopper* until next morning when he was brought before the court. Adjudged guilty of high contempt he was sentenced to receive thirty-six lashes on his bare back. His property was to be confiscated and he, his wife, and four children turned destitute upon the world. The fisherman was taken and held by the wrists and legs to a stake where he received fourteen lashes from a bo'sun's mate with a cat-o'-nine-tails before fainting. Richard Shea, a surgeon of Port de Grave, asked that the punishment be stopped. The unfortunate man "was then taken down and carried into the house where he was much convulsed." A similar fate was handed out to a man named Philip Butler for another trifling matter.

When news of the Landergan affair and the Butler punishment reached St. John's the people of the town were incensed. Protest meetings were organized by Dr. William Carson, assisted by Patrick Morris and others, and a fund was raised so that Landergan and Butler were able to bring an action in the Supreme Court against the surrogates. Chief Justice Forbes found there was no cause against the defendants but he soundly condemned the system which could place ignorant and incompetent men in a position to deal with the difficulties of law.

Dr. Carson called a meeting on the old Parade Ground at Fort William and resolutions were formulated which he immediately sent to England, denouncing the summary power of the surrogates and calling for a better system of judicature. What the reformers were really after was a local legislature and these two cases played directly into their hands so that they were able to find immediate sympathy for their cause in England. As a result of agitation over the Landergan-Butler affair, the Imperial Parliament, in 1824, passed "An Act for the Better Administration of Justice in Newfoundland." A Royal Charter was issued by King George IV in 1825. It was promulgated, 22 January 1826, and on that date the Supreme Court, as we know it, was duly constituted. The Act has been revised in some respects but it still forms the basis of the procedure and jurisprudence in force today in civil matters.

In 1968, while investigating an old building in St. John's, David Webber, Curator of the Newfoundland Naval and Military Museum, found a dilapidated roll of parchment behind a radiator. The roll had been scorched by fire and the pages had been bound so closely together, and were so brittle and fragile, that Mr. Webber decided specialist help would be required to unroll it. The roll was sent to Dr. W.I. Smith, Dominion Archivist, in Ottawa. It took Dr. Smith and his staff two and a half years to restore the parchment to something close to its original position. There are six pages, two feet by three feet, and it contains the 1825 Charter issued by George IV. It names Richard Tucker as Chief Justice, along with Wallet Des Barres and John Molloy as assistant judges.[13] Tucker served from 1823 to 1833. Judge Prowse says in a letter to Judge Alley of Prince Edward Island, 23 April 1894, that when Des Barres was earlier made Attorney General of Cape Breton he was so young looking he put on a pair of false whiskers when he went to the Colonial Office to receive his commission.

When Des Barres was pensioned in 1858 his position was filled, on November 2, by Bryan Robinson who, as a rising young lawyer, had defended Dr. Kielley in the celebrated case of Kielley *vs.* the House of Assembly, heard by Judge Lilly. Elected M.H.A. for Fortune Bay in 1843, Robinson was an enthusiastic road-building supporter of the Hon. Lawrence O'Brien, who was known as the "Colossus of Roads." In 1877 age and infirmities forced Sir Bryan Robinson's retirement, after a very distinguished career, and he left Newfoundland. His residence, "Pringlesdale" on Pringle Place, which he disposed of in March 1870, became the home of Prime Minister Winter and later of Lieutenant-Governor Sir Leonard Outerbridge. Robinson's Hill, nearby, was called after him.

In the days when British knighthood was in flower in Newfoundland, that is until Confederation with Canada put an end to it in 1949, many of those on the Supreme Court were handed knighthoods. One judge who appears to have coveted the honour and been denied has long since triumphed over his detractors and won for himself a greater immortality. Daniel W. Prowse went so far, in 1897, as to write Governor Sir Herbert Murray asking some recognition for his services to the Crown and sending along a handwritten document which he called "Record of D.W. Prowse's Public Services." However, it is not by his public services in the law courts that Judge Prowse had gained undying fame but by his fantastic *History of Newfoundland,* one of the greatest colonial histories written in North America.

Prowse was born at Port de Grave in 1834. His family, which originally came from Devon, was long in Newfoundland trade. After being called to the bar in 1859 he was involved in politics and succeeded his brother, R.H. Prowse, in the Hoyles administration of 1861 as member for Burgeo - La Poile. He left political life in 1869 when he accepted an appointment as magistrate and judge of the Circuit Court. While staunchly loyal to Newfoundland and an international booster of the colony his sympathies were pro-confederate until the late 1890s when he began to favour an economic union with the United States.

Sir James Winter, the Attorney General, commenting on Prowse's services to the law in a private communication to Governor Murray, said:

... I think he has somewhat overstated the value of his work and in [other matters] he went a little outside of his proper sphere ... I can bear testimony ... to the fearlessness of consequences which he had always shown in what he believed to be the discharge of his duty, tho' on the other hand his judicial conduct has frequently been characterized by eccentricities and idiosyncrasies not compatible with strict justice.

With people like Winter working against him behind the scenes it is no wonder Murray sent the judge a curt refusal of recognition.

Whatever his judicial conduct there can be no question that the denial of a knighthood for his scholarly and monumental history was a great injustice, especially at a time when almost every petty politician who ranked as a cabinet minister was romping off to Government House to be knighted. As a historian, D.W. Prowse was a man of outstanding ability. His *History of Newfoundland*, published in 1895, remains the only complete history of the colony ever written. It became fashionable to sneer at the work for inaccuracies and questionable interpretations of certain events as well as the flavouring of them with the author's own tastes and prejudices but it is these so-called flaws woven into prodigious research that have distinguished the work for nearly a century.

As early as 6 February 1890 the judge was maintaining that owing to his stand on the French Shore question he lost the opportunity of a knighthood. Whatever the reason, his old age was sadly devoid of the honours that should have been his, and his deafness seemed to confirm him in his "eccentricities and idiosyncrasies." He had a number of problems with government and education authorities that resulted in the collapse of several publishing ventures including an updated third edition of his famous history. Prowse died on 27 January 1914 at his home on Portugal Cove Road, site of the present Mary Queen of Peace church-school.

The growth of local courts meant an expanding need for prisons and jails. The first prison and court house at St. John's was a combined building erected on the order of Governor Osborne and was ready for business by 1730. A wooden structure, it stood on Duckworth Street, opposite Cathedral Street.

As we have seen, about the year 1729 Courts of Sessions of Justices of the Peace were erected at St. John's with very limited powers for repressing petty crimes and breaches of the peace. In 1812 Governor Duckworth wrote to Earl Bathurst asking for fifteen hundred pounds for a debtors' prison which might also serve as a dwelling for the High Sheriff. No action seems to have been taken on the request, and debtors continued to be housed with common criminals. By 1825 that enlightened Governor, Sir Thomas Cochrane, wrote to the Secretary of State:

It is difficult to paint in proper colours the lawless and disgraceful

state of the town of St. John's, and considering the age of the Colony, the population of the capital, and wealth that has from time
to time circulated through it, it is really discreditable to the Colony that any part of it should be so circumscribed. . . .

In Newfoundland the higher class of society is composed sole-
ly of those whose commercial transactions bring them daily in
collision with the lower; in Harbour Grace there are but ten or
twelve of the former; in other places two, three or four, from
whom the magistracy must be selected, and who in consequence
are frequently placed in the situation of presiding over and deter-
mining their own cases. . . .[14]

Along with this letter, Cochrane transmitted to the Secretary of State
a letter from Chief Justice Tucker, who was in agreement with him
respecting the Court House and jail at St. John's. Alterations and improvements to the ancient building were contemplated for some time. The old
structure had been erected of wood, and on a confined site that was not
capable of the improvements necessary to make the jail efficient. Cochrane
felt that the cells were little better than cellars, neither wholesome nor
secure. As many as ten men would be confined together in a single cell at an
expense to themselves of ninepence per day each. In consequence of the escape of a prisoner, an expense of more than one hundred and fifty pounds
was incurred in order to ensure the confinement of the other prisoners.

Under the circumstances, His Excellency felt there was an obvious
necessity for a separate prison, built of stone, which would combine a jail
with a house of correction. He trusted that the obvious need would induce
its immediate erection. Strange to say, his appeal did not fall on the usual
deaf ears, and a new court house and prison arose at St. John's. A painting
of the city, done for Governor Cochrane by William Eager in June 1831,
shows the new institution as an imposing structure.

Both court house and prison were, however, still combined in a single
building and on the same confined site as the previous one. In spite of good
intentions, prisoners were still confined to the basement, and their cells
appear to have been but little improvement on the previous cellars. They
consisted of a range of small rooms. Light and air was admitted through a
hole, ten by twelve inches, in the three inch thick door which opened from
each room into the passage. The yard attached to the place was so small
that none of the prisoners could take exercise in it.

A newspaper article styled "A Voice from Prison" had this to say of
the place:

> The ventilation is dreadful and the air stale and feotid. Here too
> the MONOMANIAC resides—and hence is sent forth his noxious
> ravings. We do not throw censure on the assiduous or humane
> officer who had the chief control of the gaol. Not the least blame
> can be attached to him. Nor do we attach any censure to the
> keeper. He is the personification of good nature.

Richard Perchard, who had been in charge of the Duckworth Street quarters, died on 19 January 1846. The Great Fire of June 9 of that year destroyed the Court House and jail and an abandoned barracks, located where the Signal Hill National Park Visitors Interpretation Centre now stands, became the first separate prison in St. John's. Prisoners were transferred to the middle of three ramshackle stone buildings on the hill. The roofs had blown off the two end structures rendering them useless. The remaining one was so insecure that whenever there was a windstorm the jailer kept himself ready to release those in his custody at a moment's notice for fear the walls might start to tumble down on top of them. There was no exercise yard and the women's cell had to double as a bath house. When a male prisoner was admitted he was stripped naked and washed in the ladies' quarters while the dispossessed females were herded into an adjoining closet, without ventilation, and the keyhole plugged. According to written testimony, new female prisoners had their faces, necks, bosoms, and feet "washed by males."

In spite of its many disadvantages, some attempt at rehabilitation was made in the Signal Hill jail. One officer brought books at his own expense and tried to teach the young men in his charge to read and write. The statements of Richard Brace, who became superintendent of the institution in 1855, show him as a progressive man dedicated to the principals of such reformers as the Quaker, Elizabeth Fry. He went to England, and on his return advocated a prison like Pentonville for St. John's, so that prisoners could be re-educated to enter society. Brace felt the rules and regulations at the Halifax prison, which he also visited, were too severe.

The *Royal Gazette*, 16 September 1852, had carried an advertisement asking tenders for the supply of "dimension stuff, lumber, etc., required in the Colonial Penitentiary." Plans called for the erection of an elaborate building on Forest Road, on the south bank of Quidi Vidi Lake, opposite Quidi Vidi Road. The design, based on Pentonville, was drawn up by R.D. Hill, an architect of Birmingham, England. In payment for his services he received the sum of £194.3.0. The spacious, modern structure was to accommodate forty-four males, six females, and six debtors.[16] The basement was completed to ground level late in the year of 1852, but the building Mr. Hill envisioned never materialized.

With the coming of Responsible Government in 1850 there had been a great hue and cry for economy, and one of the major works on which the new administration ordered a cutback was the prison. In 1858 a start was made on a building of much smaller size. It was occupied for the first time on 24 August 1859, with Richard Brace in charge, but was still incomplete.

In 1855, when Brace took charge of the St. John's prison, after having served as jailer at Harbour Grace for several years, the situation on Signal Hill was so bad that the Governor wrote to Colonel Law to ask if the barrack on the road ascending the lower part of the hill, then occupied by married soldiers, could be assigned as a prison without inconveniently restricting accommodation for the troops. He also wanted to know if there was sufficient ground to make a good airing for the prisoners. The answer would appear to have been in the negative for the convicts remained in the old prison atop the hill until their transfer to H.M. Penitentiary, on Forest Road, in 1859.

The old prison had held an average of twenty inmates at a time. In 1860, the first year the new institution was in full operation, it admitted 175 inmates at a weekly cost of four shillings per head. By 1962, just over a hundred years later, their number had grown to 1,211. Uniforms were worn by the Penitentiary staff for the first time in 1877, after officials complained about the embarrassment they suffered in being mistaken for prisoners.[17]

Richard Brace reported that his assistants could not be persuaded to inflict corporal punishment. Even some of the inmates, who had been offered a remission of part of their sentences if they would punish their fellow prisoners with the whip, refused. In time the Criminal Code was amended to abolish corporal punishment.

On 20 February 1874 the old building on Signal Hill, by then in a bad state of decay, again served as a prison for a brief period. Because of an outbreak of fever, all the inmates at the "Pen," as it came to be known, had to be transferred back to the hill while their quarters were being fumigated.

There have been a number of notable escapes from St. John's penal institutions over the years. As far back as 12 August 1828, there is a record of a man named Power, who had murdered his wife, breaking jail. It was said that a fishing skiff was stolen from Maggoty Cove that night and the murderer was thought to have made good his escape to some outport.

In 1848 the Manchester Branch of the Bank of England was robbed of the sum of nineteen thousand pounds (about a hundred thousand dollars), a fortune for those days. While Scotland Yard worked overtime to find the culprits, they were walking the decks of the world's leading luxury liner, *Britannia*, enjoying the company of Mr. and Mrs. Charles Dickens. Their names were Brady and Naughton. Not long after they had landed in New York the duo realized their means of escape had been discovered.

They hurried to the Cunard dock and found a ship there sailing for Fogo, Newfoundland. Two seamen had deserted and the fugitives signed on in their places. After helping unload the cargo at Fogo they came on to St. John's by schooner. Being debonair and well educated, the two gentlemen were soon the toasts of the town and much in demand at many a fashionable home, where their recollections of their friend, Mr. Charles Dickens, enlivened the dinner table, for the plight of Little Nell was everyone's concern.

When their small change ran out, they took from their bundle a one-hundred-pound note which they asked Mr. Bernard Duffy, of the Dublin Bookstore, to change. Amazed at the size of the note, he said he was short of ready cash and invited them to return for the money after dinner. As soon as the two were gone, Duffy hurried to his friend Bishop Fleming who advised him to take it to the manager of the Bank of British North America. The manager took note of the number but refused to handle the bank note. Meanwhile, the Bishop recalled reading in a newspaper he had been sent about a bank robbery in England. More amused by the thought than anything else, His Lordship hunted around and found the paper. It contained the numbers of the stolen notes. He sent for Duffy and the note and, sure enough, its number, 38455, was one of those listed in the paper. The Chief of Police was alerted and Brady and Naughton were arrested at Mrs. Johnson's semi-private hotel where they were registered as Bradshaw and O'Kelly. When word of their arrest spread through the town the quality, who had befriended them, rushed to the jail on Signal Hill to protest the ghastly blunder.

One friend is said to have brought them a cake containing files and, incredibly, the age-old trick worked. Patiently the two men sawed the bars of their cell and, on a foggy night, made their escape. Naughton tripped in the bars as he was fleeing and the guard struck him in the leg with a shot. He was soon overpowered and his wound treated by the military surgeon, so that he was returned to England for trial, in the charge of the High Constable.

His partner Brady seems to have been more fortunate. He fled down the hill to Maggoty Cove and being an excellent swimmer threw himself into the waters of the harbour. He swam across the Narrows and landed just inside Fort Amherst, from where he made his way on foot to a community of squatters living on the top of the Southside Hills. After searching the White Hills, Quidi Vidi, and Torbay for two weeks, the hunt for the escapee was given up. It is thought that Brady settled down to the life of a fisherman, married the daughter of one of the men who had given him shelter, and left many descendents who are living in St. John's today.[15]

In 1862 Mr. Brace reported that two culprits, sixteen-year-old John Lennox, and twenty-eight-year-old John Farrell, slipped out of H.M. Penitentiary about 5:30 a.m., on May 12. They waited until two guards entered their cells and crept out behind the men slamming the door and locking in the guards. In those days prisoners' clothes were taken from them at night so the two had to make off in their long underwear and barefooted.

Lennox had been given nine months the previous Friday for the theft of a ham. It was his seventh commitment. Farrell, who had served thirteen previous terms, was in jail for improper assault on a female on Rennie's Bridge. The two vanished as soon as they were out of the prison. It was reported in the press that they had been furnished with the means of getting out of the country and the police gave up the search. The duo were recaptured on August 6, and young Lennox was released twenty-three days later.

Twenty-year-old Joseph Richardson was at the lakeside prison awaiting trial for the larceny of a dog when he made his escape, about 4:00 p.m., 2 August 1879. He had been working in a field, under guard, when he removed some pickets from a fence and escaped. Three times that afternoon the police ran him to the water's edge. Three times he plunged into the ocean and got away. The third time it was reported that a boat had picked him up and he was taken off somewhere. That was Richardson's second escape. The previous year he had scaled the Pen fence and was gone two days. This time he was recaptured and released on September 29. He was back in jail November 1, accused of assaulting the police and of larceny of clothes. For that he got six months.

Michael Whelan, a model prisoner twenty-three years of age, serving a life sentence for voluntary manslaughter near Horse Cove (now St. Phillips), was sent out with a gang of six or seven prisoners, between 7:00 and 8:00 a.m., 25 November 1887, to work on a drain that ran from the General Hospital to Quidi Vidi. He asked leave to retire for a natural purpose and disappeared into the White Hills. Next day, and every day until January 13, the newspapers offered a reward of two hundred dollars for information leading to his capture. The last mention of this reward in the press is 8 February 1888. Whelan is thought to have made good his escape to the United States. In those days visas and passports were unknown and it was possible to travel anywhere in North America with few, if any, papers.

A twenty-nine-year-old sailor, James Rigby, serving five years for the manslaughter of a shipmate named Hookey, escaped from the Pen around 10:30 p.m. on 20 July 1890, by using a broom knife to unscrew the catch which held the bolt of his cell. Once out of the room he had to get past two wardens on duty at the end of the corridor. This presented no challenge when he discovered both of them soundly asleep at their posts. Rigby tiptoed out into the night, scaled the wall, sailor-fashion, and was off. Next day, from his hideout near Horse Cove, he watched the police scour the countryside in search of him. When he thought they had gone he went to beg food from Frederick Squires, who recognized him from the description given by the police. Squires fed the fugitive and, when he was gone, took off over a back-fence trail to intercept the detectives. Rigby was apprehended on the road near Horse Cove, still wearing his prison pants with one leg white and the other blue. The sailor was released at 10:00 a.m., 13 October 1891 by order of His Excellency the Governor.

Phil Brady's escape was the stuff of which legends are made. He became the hero of the hour and his feat was celebrated in verse as well as on the local stage. Like that damned elusive Pimpernel, they sought him here, there, and everywhere without success. It all began at 5:45 p.m., 6 October 1906, when the five-foot, four-inch, blond, blue-eyed, eighteen-year-old Englishman climbed the Penitentiary fence and headed for Mt. Carmel Cemetery where he hid until midnight along the old railway track (now Empire Avenue).

As the days went by, the fugitive was reportedly seen in all directions. The police began to resemble the Keystone Cops as they commandeered carts, wagons, and carriages in their pursuit of the elusive felon. Poets blossomed to celebrate the great escape in the local press. One wrote of the Inspector General:

> The public smile at each endeavour
> "Away, Away," cries Sullivan,
> Nor e'er give up the chase.

A man named Paddy Coughlan, who had a farm on the Old Placentia Road (now Brookfield Road), was robbed of a pair of trousers on the night of Brady's flight and prison garb was found on the floor in their place. Paddy complained a few days later that a can containing a hundred dollars was also missing. The gentlemen of the law proved this a falsehood and the song "Who Stole Paddy Coughlan's Can?" attained instant popularity. Today it is among the lost masterpieces of local literature.

Young Brady's noticeable English accent inspired another bard to versify:

> All the jailers are nearly wild,
> Their grief is awful sad,
> Because they've lost their darling boy,
> Their little English lad.

On November 8 an embarrassed police force offered a reward of fifty dollars for the capture of the notorious youth. There were no takers until the night of the 13th, when a man from Petty Harbour picked up a bottle in a local saloon and cried out, with great indiscretion, "Brady will have a drink out of this before midnight." An informer rushed to the law with the news and the police tailed the man to Murphy's cellar, on Petty Harbour Road, where they cornered Brady. He put up a fight with a hay rake before he was subdued and brought to George Knowling's cottage, "Silverton," near Kilbride Bridge, where he was kept overnight. Next morning, around 10:30, the officers of the law bore their captive in triumph through gaping crowds to the Penitentiary. Johnny Burke wasted no time in writing a short play about the escapade and it met with delighted audiences.

Unfortunately, the story ended in tragedy. Nearly two years later, 5 March 1908, Brady was released from jail suffering from some disease. It was most probably tuberculosis contracted in the barn where he slept during the cold, damp nights of his escape. Just over three months after his release he died at 3:20 a.m. in the old hospital, on Signal Hill, the place where Marconi was to receive his first wireless message. The youth had yet to celebrate his twenty-first birthday.

Gertrude Bursey has the distinction of being the only female to escape custody in St. John's history. The twenty-one-year-old woman, in jail for disorderly conduct, her third prison sentence, and thirty-five-year-old Thomas Evans, who had four convictions for vagrancy and disorderly conduct, escaped over the wall in the late autumn of 1911 and were seen making off toward Logy Bay. H.M. Mosdell reports that one of them was captured the same day but that the other one got off scot free, went to the United States, and became a respectable citizen. Prison records show that this was not the case. Both convicts were apprehended. Gertrude Bursey was released from prison on 26 March 1912 and Thomas Evans got his discharge two days later.

Kitchener Edwards was obviously named by patriotic parents swept away in the euphoria which followed Lord Kitchener's relief of Khartoum and his conquest of the Sudan. The slender, five-foot, two-inch native of Change Islands made his own kind of history on 5 June 1922 by escaping from His Majesty's custody. The twenty-two-year-old was completing one month of a twelve months' sentence for larceny when he made a rope of twines used in the manufacture of brooms and, attaching it to an iron bar, flung it over the wall of the Pen and climbed to freedom. Like Bursey and Evans he was last seen making his getaway along the Logy Bay Road.

A massive manhunt failed to reveal his hiding place, but he was finally undone by a girl in Whitbourne. At an early hour on the morning of June 21, Miss Foley noticed a mysterious light in the shop of her neighbour, G.N. Sparkes. She alerted her brother, a brakeman on the railway, who got Mr. Sparkes out of bed. The two overcame the trespasser as he was leaving the store and were amazed to find their captive to be the elusive Kitchener Edwards. The young man was returned to the prison at St. John's by train.

On 17 November 1939 there escaped a quartet of prisoners: James Wynott, twenty-three; Maxwell Lush, twenty-one; Hector Tuff, twenty-two; and Frederick Noftall, twenty-three. Wynott, Lush, and Tuff were in jail for theft of a motor car from R.J. Murphy who lived in Mayfield, Waterford Bridge Road, opposite Road de Luxe. Noftall was in for an offence committed on Bell Island. Around 6:30 p.m., on the 17th, Wynott asked to go to the toilet. On the way back to his cell he suddenly turned on the warden, overpowered him, and released Lush. They made their way to the floor below where they throttled another unsuspecting warden and released Tuff and his cellmate, Noftall.

As a result of a telephone tip, three of the escapees, Wynott, Tuff, and Noftall, were captured the next day in a shack hidden in the woods at Mount Pearl. Even though they had three fully loaded revolvers on them at the time, the men were taken without a struggle. Lush was not captured until November 25 when the police received another telephone tip saying that he was in a house on Hunt's Lane. At ten o'clock that evening the law officers went to the house and caught Lush, who was hiding behind a bedroom door.

On 9 March 1955 James Robbins was sentenced to serve two and a half years at St. John's for robbery with violence. He had already served seven years of a ten-to-twenty-year term for manslaughter in Albany, New York, in 1948, and been deported to Newfoundland. There were also charges against him in Toronto, Kingston, and Montreal. After several aborted attempts at escape from the local Pen, one of which earned him a bullet in the leg, Robbins finally made it on 10 January 1956. Shortly before five o'clock that afternoon he found a door in the prison yard, propped it against the wall and went over the top. The wardens saw him escape but he disappeared before they could reach him.

In spite of the fact that the 175-pound, twenty-nine-year-old seaman was wearing khaki pants and a dark brown windbreaker, he got completely away. Even his upper front gold tooth did not betray him. About eight o'clock that evening it was noticed that another prisoner was also missing. He was twenty-two-year-old Gerald Hanlon who had a long police record and was serving two and a half years for break and entry. Around ten o'clock next morning Hanlon was recaptured in a house on Murphy's Lane, Mundy Pond.

In spite of a most intensive manhunt, nothing was seen or heard of Robbins until December 10 that year, when he was picked up in a rooming house in Toronto where he was living under the name of James Parker. It was believed the Ontario police acted on a tip from someone who saw his picture among those of Canada's ten most wanted criminals in a *Weekend Magazine* article.

The eleven-month search by baffled police officers provided the same kind of merriment in St. John's that the escape of Brady had provided half a century earlier. In the London Theatre Company's spring revue, two of the actors had appeared on stage dressed as prison wardens and delighted audiences by singing, "Robbins, Robbins, hear our plea, will ye no' come back again."

Following his eventual release from prison, nothing more was heard of James Robbins until 29 July 1963 when he was arrested in Montreal and charged with the fatal beating of a woman in a downtown rooming house. The Court of Queen's Bench jury took six hours to find him guilty of murder, for which he was given a life sentence.

One of the shortest-lived escapes to freedom took place early on the morning of 13 January 1960, when Alfred Howell, forty-two, serving a five-year term; Cyril Lush, twenty-one; and John Colbert, thirty-two, both serving lesser terms broke out of the Pen about 1:30 a.m. and made a quick getaway. Shortly after their flight, Lush and Howell broke into Gaden's factory on Duckworth Street. At 3:00 a.m. they were seen by the police on Hamilton Avenue and taken into custody. Colbert was recaptured at 4:30 a.m. when he broke into Marshall Motors, then on Water Street.

The most recent jail break in the long history of H.M. Penitentiary took place in 1973 when Maurice Skiffington, a nineteen-year-old youth from Bonavista Bay, got away on October 7 by climbing a fire escape to the roof of the prison and jumping twenty feet to the ground. He stole a car belonging to a Lake Avenue man and used it to make his getaway. Skiffington was picked up October 9, at 6:15 a.m. by the police who removed him from a westbound train at St. Ann's siding on Topsail Road. For his pains he had an extra six months added to his two-year sentence for break, entry, and theft.

In the middle years of the nineteenth century, St. John's newspapers published a weekly list of the names of prisoners at H.M. Penitentiary, as well as a notation of their offences, and the length of each sentence. For example, on 24 November 1860, one read in the press that the Pen contained twenty-two males and one female.

One of the most interesting felons to occupy a cell at Her Majesty's Penitentiary was probably Alexander Pindikowsky, whose name appears several times in both volumes of this work. He was arrested 10 March 1880 and charged with uttering forged cheques upon the Commercial Bank, in the name of E. Weedon, Esq., of Heart's Content, Trinity Bay.

Pindikowsky arrived in Newfoundland in 1879 as a professional artist and fresco painter with a rather unusual assignment. The Anglo-American Telegraph Company had hired him to give art instructions to interested employees and their wifes at the Heart's Content Cable Office. His course was an extensive one and seems to have found favour among its participants.

The painter was also given another task. When the new cable office was constructed in 1873, the old office, which had been built in 1867, was converted into a theatre for the use of the employees. It was called the Victoria. Variety concerts were staged there and Pindikowsky was commissioned to paint half a dozen twenty-five-foot-long backdrops for use on the stage. These are all believed to have disappeared.

The year 1880 found the man in St. John's with financial problems, which he attempted to solve by forging two cheques in the name of the company superintendent at Heart's Content, Ezra Weedon. The first of these, for £232, he tried to pass at the Commercial Bank. The teller refused to hand over such a large sum of money to a stranger until he had contacted Weedon. A telegram was sent to the gentleman. After leaving the bank, Pindikowsky tried to cash a second cheque for £65 at a drugstore, also in the name of Weedon, but the firm did not have such a sum on hand.

Meanwhile, the cable superintendent advised the bank that he had not issued any cheques to the artist. On the evening of 10 March 1880, as Pindikowsky was refreshing himself in the Temperance Coffee House on Water Street, the police entered and placed him under arrest. He came to trial on June 8 and was convicted.

The *Public Ledger*, 11 June 1880, commented: "Alexander Pindikowsky for forgery was sentenced to fifteen months from his commitment, and is ordered to leave the country." The *Royal Gazette* added the information that "Pindikowsky was ordered within five days of his release to quit the country for life, in default of which, on his return to the country at any time, he is to receive further imprisonment." The further imprisonment was to be an additional two years.

The Polish artist's talents as a fresco painter were brought to the attention of the authorities and they were soon put to official use, in return for a remission of five weeks on his sentence. He was set to work designing and painting ceiling frescos, to relieve the drabness of the state rooms at Government House. There were rooms in which no hint of the delicate charm of Adam's Neo-Classical designs had ever penetrated. Governor Glover was so delighted with the frescos that he suggested to Prime Minister Whiteway that the prisoner also decorate the ceilings of the two legislative chambers in the Colonial Building.

Each day Pindikowsky and his assistants were brought from the penitentiary to his place of work until the fresco painting was completed. A sum equal to the amount of the forgery was subscribed by his admirers and the prisoner was released. His banishment from the country was also withdrawn.[18] In 1882 he was advertising his services in a local newspaper, as a fresco painter. The Athenaeum hired him and he painted some very fine murals on the interior walls of the building. Unfortunately, they were destroyed in the Great Fire of 1892. He also worked on the Presentation Convent chapel, Cathedral Square. After that he left the country and disappeared from sight. His name lives in the much-admired frescos he painted in Government House, the Colonial Building, and the Presentation Convent.

Of the many persons who have been confined to the Pen in its long history, perhaps the most prominent guest to stay any length of time was Dr. Alfred Valdmanis.

In March 1950 Premier Smallwood hired this Latvian economist, of impeccable credentials, for the job of provincial economic expert, to spearhead the industrialization of Newfoundland. On May 24, he was appointed Director of Economic Development. By 1953 this old-world genius had become Chairman of the Board of the Newfoundland and Labrador Corporation (NALCO). He brought many industries to the province, most of which have been long forgotten. His resignation was tendered 15 February 1954. His departure from Newfoundland was greatly lamented by the Premier who, like blind Anna on the steps of the Temple, foretold great things for this man, including the belief that one day Newfoundlanders would erect a monument to his memory. According to reporters, there were even tears in Mr. Smallwood's eyes as he hugged his departing friend on the tarmac at Torbay Airport.

On April 24 Dr. Valdmanis was arrested in Montreal and charged with extortion. Two days later, Premier Smallwood assumed responsibility for the arrest. In May the Premier laid additional charges against the former economic tzar, who was granted a bail of a hundred thousand dollars and released on May 15, but it was a short-lived freedom. On May 17, Valdmanis was again arrested, when the provincial government laid a civil charge against him to recover two hundred and seventy thousand dollars. The actual sum involved was said to be close to four hundred thousands.

On 9 August 1954 the doctor asked for trial by magistrate. The following day he was committed to the Supreme Court. He pleaded guilty to a fraud charge of two hundred thousands, was convicted on September 16, and remanded for sentence. Two days later he was given four years on the fraud charge. Paroled on 2 January 1955, he flew to Montreal. Alfred Valdmanis died tragically on 11 August 1970 in a highway automobile accident fifteen miles west of Edmonton, Alberta, at the age of sixty-one.

Nothing like the Valdmanis affair had been known before in the storm-tossed political seas of Newfoundland. On 22 April 1924 Prime Minister Warren had authorized the immediate arrest of his predecessor in office, Sir Richard Squires, who was charged with the larceny of twenty thousand dollars. While Squires supporters claimed that he was the victim of a conspiracy, the London *Times* commented: "That it should have been possible to level such accusations against the Prime Minister of a great Dominion of the Crown seems incredible; that it should have been possible to prove them is nothing short of a tragedy."

The perennial farce of Newfoundland politics has consistently contributed absurdities to relieve the grim humour of the St. John's courts. Back in 1894, Prime Minister Whiteway, Robert Bond, and other Whiteway supporters found themselves arrested and hauled into court to answer charges under the Bribery and Corruption Act. In the subsequent trials Sir William, Bond, and a number of others were unseated. While there was no personal dishonesty, the judges felt that technically there had been patronage given. Mr. Justice Little remarked, ". . . although under the law there is nothing left for me to do but unseat and disqualify Sir William Whiteway, Mr. Bond and Mr. Watson, I deem it only due to them to say that they leave this court without a stain on their honour, integrity and morality."

Not all prisoners in St. John's were sent to languish in the Penitentiary beside the lake. An old rhyme goes,

> The Judge said "Stand up, boy, I'll pin your ears.
> You're sentenced to the *Meigle* for twenty-one years."

The *Meigle* was a former coastal steamer. By 1932 she was out of service and gathering rats and barnacles in St. John's Harbour when the Penitentiary became seriously overcrowded.

The dole riots in Carbonear, 6 October 1932, resulted in the arrest and trial of sixteen people at St. John's. Businessmen in the Conception Bay town were assaulted and injured by a group of hungry men, dissatisfied with their six cents a day dole. Windows in the community were smashed and the rail line was blocked. Six others were arrested in Spaniard's Bay. This sudden influx of prisoners, added to the thirty-odd arrested in the House of Assembly riot earlier that year, taxed the Penitentiary beyond its limits and resulted in the S.S. *Meigle* becoming a prison ship. The vessel was rented from the Newfoundland Railway and her passenger cabins became jail cells for the more trustworthy of His Majesty's miscreants. She was able to cater to between twenty and thirty prisoners, and a number of convicts were transferred from the Pen to the ship.[19]

With the release of the rioters the prison population returned to normal and the prison ship was dispensed with in June 1933. She was later returned to active service and during World War II carried freight between Canada and Newfoundland. The career of the S.S. *Meigle* came to an end in 1947 when she was lost off St. Shotts.

The stone Court House, built in Cochrane's time, was destroyed in the Great Fire of 1846. It was from a second-storey window, on the west side of this building, that public hangings had been staged. After the fire, a rugged, unsightly structure, known as the Market House, was built to the west of the former Court House, on a site occupied today by yet another Court House. The Market House was not only depressing on the outside, but we are told that on the inside it was incredibly dingy, full of dark rooms and cold drafts.

On the Water Street level, the Market House contained a fish, meat, poultry, dairy, and vegetable market where housewives and house maids came every day to purchase fresh supplies from stall owners. At the back of the market were the windowless cells of prisoners awaiting trial. The second floor, with an entrance on the side, from Market House Hill, was used as a post office and later a telegraph office. The top storey, entered from Duckworth Street, contained the courtrooms.

The Market House opened on 6 July 1849 with John Boone of Flower Hill as keeper. In addition to the holding of trials, the Court House portion was often given over for use by theatrical performers, especially visiting concert artists. How accompaniment was provided is unknown, unless there was a piano hidden behind the bench.

The sorry state of the building almost caused one lawyer to suffer a broken ankle in November 1887, when a large chunk of plaster fell from the ceiling, narrowly missing his foot. On the night of 15 February 1890 officials reported seeing a ghost on the premises. There were many who felt it was that of Catherine Snow who had been hanged from a window of the old Court House next door, for the murder of her husband. Others wondered if the spirit which was troubling the officials did not originate from among bottled spirits.

In May 1889 the Grand Jury found the Penitentiary "in its usual cleanly and efficient condition as regards the management and treatment of prisoners." It was sorry no reformatory or industrial institution had yet been provided for the juvenile class of offenders. However, when it came to examining the Court House, the Grand Jury condemned "the delapodated [sic] and unhealthy state of the Supreme Court room" and urged the necessity of erecting a new Court House in the suburbs.[20] Within three years of this report the Great Fire of 1892 made this necessity absolute when it left the Market House a gutted ruin.

Tom Power, a brother of the famous blacksmith, Rhodie Power, won immortality of sorts by climbing the wall of the Market House, on the Water Street side, with his bare hands and feet. It was reported that Tom's achievement, which took him almost to the clock, was performed by getting a hold with his hands and toes in the mortar crevices between the stones.

Following the 1846 fire, until 1849, when the new court in the Market House was ready, Supreme Court sessions were held at the old Factory, off Garrison Hill, behind the present Synod Hall. After the 1892 fire the wait for a new building proved even longer. From 1892 to 1894, court sessions were held in the Colonial Building, between sessions of the Legislature. This was unsatisfactory so temporary quarters had to be found. From 1894 to 1904 the Supreme Court met in the Star Hall on Henry Street.

The cornerstone for the present Court House building was laid on the morning of 24 October 1901. The previous day, the Duke and Duchess of York arrived in St. John's after a tour of Canada. At eleven o'clock, on the twenty-fourth, they landed and went to Government House. By noon they were at the site of the new Court House and the stone, with its Latin inscription, was well and truly laid by the Duke, afterwards King George V, while May of Teck, the future Queen Mary, looked on with impassive dignity.

Stone for the building, mined at Petites Quarries, was furnished by W.G. Ellis from the Ellis stone yard which was on the site of the Sir Humphrey Gilbert building. The woodwork for the Court House, which opened 11 May 1904, was executed by the Horwood Lumber Company and this included some fancy wood panelling in the courtrooms. Construction of the Court House was not accomplished without tragedy. On 9 December 1901 James McNeill fell from a scaffold and was killed.

The first lawyer to reside in St. John's was probably George Larkin, "a gentleman bred to the civil law," whose name appears in the records of the British House of Commons as being sent out in 1701, for the purpose of making a report "on the fate of the plantations and the execution of the laws of Trade and Navigation." The appointment of an Attorney General for Newfoundland was recommended that same year but the position was not granted until 1821, with the appointment of a lawyer named Westcott, who appears to have been quite hopeless and was quickly retired on a pension.

The first local lawyers were a class known as "special pleaders." By

1820 they had become so numerous as to be the subject of a complaint by Governor Hamilton to the Secretary of State. His Excellency wrote:

> I beg to inform your Lordship that a practice has crept into the Courts of Justice, within these few years . . . by the encouragement of petty attorneys who are employed in almost every case which comes before the Chief Justice. . . . This is an evil the growth of which is rapidly increasing, and the earlier it is checked the better.[21]

Two of these pleaders are known to us. The resolution passed at the public meeting, held in connection with the floggings of Landergan and Butler in 1820, mentions that "thanks be passed to the lawyers Dawe and George Lilly for their disinterested conduct in conducting the case in the supreme court." William Dawe and George Lilly are, therefore, the first local lawyers we know of to fight a case in the Supreme Court.

The barristers' Roll, commenced in 1826, contains the following names as having been enrolled that first year: James Simms, George Lilly, William B. Row, John Broom, William Hayward, Charles Simms, William Dawe, and William Dickson. The Law Society of Newfoundland was incorporated 1 July 1834 under the leadership of E.M. Archibald who had come from Nova Scotia in 1832, at the age of twenty-one years, to be Chief Clerk and Registrar of the Supreme Court.

Linked to the development of the courts of justice is the development of that arm of the law known as the police. St. John's can claim to have the first police force in English Canada. In writing the Duke of Newcastle on 14 October 1729 regarding particulars of his arrival in Newfoundland as first governor, Captain Henry Osborne said that he had appointed over the districts into which he divided the island "Justice of the Peace and Constables according to the bigness of the fishery they presided over." These constables were inhabitants of good character who served as part-time police officers. A century would pass before there was any thought of the formation of a regular police force.

There is no indication that these gentlemen wore a uniform but they did carry one item of police equipment as shown by the following edict of Governor Richard Edwards on 3 October 1757;

> Whereas the Peace in the Execution of Justice is lyable to be disturbed, by the Constables not appearing properly with their Staffs in the Execution of their Office, It is hereby strictly required & directed, that for the future no Constable ever fails in carrying same, & demeans himself according to Law in the Execution of his Office.

Around 1807 a plan was devised thereby anyone wanting to be licensed as a tavern keeper in St. John's had to agree to perform police duties. Robert

Parsons, proprietor of the West India Coffee House, was put in charge of the thirty-four persons, including two women, who were tavern owners, and therefore, constables.

In 1812, the year of the war between Canada and the United States, Governor Duckworth exempted publicans from constabulary duty, and hired twelve efficient stipendiary constables, who were required to perform the duty or night patrols. Their salaries were twenty-five pounds per year, to be paid out of the fund the tavern licences created, and the licence fee was increased to twelve pounds (sixty dollars) from eight pounds. How long this arrangement lasted is not clear.

On 28 November 1825 Governor Cochrane directed the Chief Magistrate, John Broom, that all persons applying for licences to operate taverns should once again pay eight pounds for each licence and that the money should go toward paying the salaries of special constables. There would be no regular police for nearly half a century. William Phipard was given the post of High Constable, at a salary of eighty pounds per year. He was assisted by eight constables who wore blue coats, red waistcoats, buttons with a crown and the letters "G.R.," and a cockade in the hat. These eight men were divided into four tours of duty and they were to live in houses distributed throughout the town.

By 1834 Duckworth's night patrols were evidently a thing of the past. That year Chief Magistrate Broom and High Constable Phipard petitioned the House of Assembly to be able to retire from public life while on July 15 Patrick Kough, M.H.A. for the district of St. John's (his name is often misspelled Keough), petitioned the House for an efficient night watch for the town. The retirements were granted and Kough's Bill passed, July 27, but no action was ever taken. There was another heated debate in February 1845, but it was not until 10 January 1848 that a regular night watch was established. It consisted of sixteen specials and four constables under the management of High Constable Finlay. This force appears to have been a sometime thing. Like Alice's Cheshire Cat it kept appearing and vanishing over the years. On 31 March 1865 Bishop Mullock sent a petition to the House of Assembly asking for a permanent night watch, but his plea failed.[23]

Back in 1834, at Governor Cochrane's urging, a Bill to establish a Town Council and Police in the town of St. John's had been brought before the House, but George Hutchings and his fellow merchants prayed "that it may not pass," and their prayers were answered. They were in deathly fear that a town council would require them to pay taxes for the upkeep of the community, a fear which still strikes terror in the hearts of Newfoundlanders.

Starting in 1836, with six police, a permanent force of sorts began to emerge in the capital. In 1841, the newly arrived Governor, Sir John Harvey, ex-inspector General of Constabulary in Ireland, appointed Timothy Mitchell, a Roman Catholic who had served under him in the Irish police, as Superintendent of the existing force. Mitchell, a native of Ballinasloe, Galway, was thirty-one years old. He filled the position for the next thirty years. He died on 18 September 1871 at the age of sixty-two and is highly spoken of by Governor Hill and all who knew him. His grave in Belvedere Cemetery is directly opposite Calver Avenue.

In addition to this force, which grew with the years, the soldiers of the garrison were also charged with maintaining order. One wonders about their effectiveness when reading the order of the day, of the Major General Commanding, 23 July 1856, "almost daily in the early hour of 11 o'clock in the morning he sees grog shops and other disreputable places filled with soldiers of the garrison, which fact mainly explains the great increase in crime that he has lately noticed to have taken place."

In the late 1860s the British government decided on a general reduction in its colonial military establishments. One of the places affected by this decision was Newfoundland but there appear to have been no immediate plans to carry out the intention. However, following the decisive refusal of Newfoundlanders to confederate with Canada in 1869, an angered Britain decided on an immediate withdrawal of the garrison. Even though this would have come about within a few years in any case the confederates and anti-confederates made political capital out of an apparently punitive action which left the colony virtually defenceless. Even Governor Hill, who must have known of the decision to reduce the Imperial Garrison, was appalled at the haste of the withdrawal and wrote to England complaining of how easily the place might be taken by an enemy attack in the absence of the garrison.[24]

Deprived of military protection, the local government was forced into the formation of a constabulary. Head Constable Thomas Foley of the Royal Irish Constabulary was picked to head up the new police force. Foley, "a sound Protestant," was given an address and testimonial by the leading citizens of Belfast before departing for Newfoundland. The head of the new police force was appointed in February 1871, seven months before the death of Mitchell. He arrived from Ireland, April 17, and immediately set about organizing his force. The Constabulary Act was introduced in the House of Assembly, February 1872, and given royal assent, April 24 of that year. The Newfoundland Constabulary, however, dates its formation from the appointment of Foley in February 1871. Foley died suddenly in the police court on 18 April 1873. He was succeeded in office by Paul Carty, another member of the Royal Irish Constabulary, on 21 August 1873. Carty was pensioned in 1885.

Major Morris J. Fawcett, a retired army officer, was personally chosen by Governor Glover to fill the job. He remained at the post ten years, until 1895, when he resigned to become Inspector of Police at Jamaica. John R. McCowen was born in Ireland in 1841 and came to live in St. John's thirty years later. He attained the rank of Head Constable, but resigned in 1885 to become Governor of the Penitentiary. On 26 March 1895 he was appointed to be the first Inspector General of Police and Chief of the Fire Department.

McCowen reorganized the Police Department and saw that an electric fire-alarm system was installed in the town. He stationed unmarried police, from Fort Townshend, in the East, Central, and West Fire Halls. In 1909 McCowen was followed by John Sullivan, a native of Trinity. Charles Hutchings became the last Inspector General and Chief of the Fire Department in 1917. When he retired the office was abolished.

Patrick J. O'Neill became the first Chief of Police in 1934. The force under him consisted of three hundred men and was at its peak of efficiency.[25] O'Neill died in office, 6 December 1944.

Just after World War II, in a barbarous destruction of an historic site, the old barracks at Fort Townshend, dating from 1773 and extensively repaired in the 1880s, was torn down to make room for a place where the police could deposit wrecked automobiles. The buildings were in very good condition at the time of their destruction and were being lived in by married police officers and their families.

With the end of the war, the Constabulary began to grow smaller as the Newfoundland Ranger Force took over from it in the outports. Confederation with Canada brought the Royal Canadian Mounted Police to Newfoundland, and the Constabulary was finally restricted to the City of St. John's and some highway patrol work.

In 1959 there was a serious loggers' strike in central Newfoundland involving recognition of the International Woodworkers of America. When violence was threatened in the town of Badger, near Grand Falls, two detachments of the Newfoundland Constabulary were sent to the aid of the R.C.M.P. In the ensuing riots, Constable William Moss, of the Constabulary, was allegedly struck on the head by someone wielding a piece of pulpwood. He was unconscious from March 10 until his death on March 12, on which day the body was returned to St. John's, from Grand Falls, amidst a great display of public emotion. The Legislature paid the deceased officer the tribute of two minutes of silence.

His funeral took place on Saturday, March 14, from his residence, 136 University Avenue, to the Railway Station where a train stood waiting to convey the young man's remains to his birthplace, Port Blandford, for interment. The Premier seized the opportunity to solicit public sympathy by turning the funeral into a state occasion watched by angry crowds.[26]

On March 19 a murder charge was laid against thirty-nine-year-old Ronald Laing of Lomond in connection with the death of Moss. In a four-day trial the following June he was acquitted in fifty-two minutes. In the melee between the police and loggers in the pitch dark there was no way anybody could identify the murderer. Smallwood told the Legislature that the real criminals were the I.W.A. organizers. He said: "All Newfoundlanders know who they are: Ladd, McCool, and Hall. They are the criminals. Up to now they have succeeded in evading arrest."

The Premier continued to emphasize the martyrdom of the constable by instituting a six-hundred-dollar "William Moss Memorial Scholarship" to be given each year to the son or daughter of a Newfoundland policeman. This gesture was followed by the placing of a small monument in the middle of the square in front of Police Headquarters at Fort Townshend. The inscription on the bronze plaque reads: "In memory of Constable William J. Moss, who died March 12th, 1959, from injuries received in the line of duty during the I.W.A. loggers' strike at Badger, Nfld."

The trial of Ronald Laing was just one of the many compelling cases scattered throughout Newfoundland legal history. Some of them, such as the Lawrey press-gang murder, the Lieutenant Rudkin duel trial, the Dr. Kielley affair, and the Stick-a-Pin-Here case are to be found in the first volume of this work. There are others worth recalling such as the celebrated case, in 1853, when a daring attempt was made on the life of Peter Weston Carter, senior stipendiary magistrate, an otherwise fine man who suffered the disease of religious bigotry. He once tried to supplant Superintendent Timothy Mitchell with his own man, because he disliked Mitchell's religion. The Governor intervened and dismissed Carter's crony.

The attempted murder, which was unrelated to the Mitchell affair, took place Wednesday afternoon, 25 May 1853, when a cooper named Long called at the residence of Judge Carter, Hawthorn Cottage, Carter's Hill, and asked for a proof-relief (a dole note). He carried a double-barrelled gun which Carter laid hold of when the man told him not to touch it. In the scuffle Long dragged the Magistrate down half a dozen steps to the street, and three paces away from him took aim and pulled the trigger. The gun misfired. The man immediately fired the other barrel sending two balls through the victim's arm. Carter's son, who was in the garden, rushed to his father's aid and secured the fellow.

The *Public Ledger* commented: "It is worthy of notice that although a large crowd had collected not one person had assisted in the capture but rather encouraged the fellow to make his escape." It has been suggested that the watchers were mostly Roman Catholics who, knowing of the Magistrate's religious bigotry, were delighted at his distress. At the trial Long said his reason for attempting to kill the Judge was the fact that Carter was a bad friend to the poor. Judge Prowse claims the reverse was notoriously the fact.

Around 1862 a woman named Mary James left a child with a Mrs. Walsh and went to Canada. The mother of the infant was Church of England, but Mrs. Walsh reared the little one as a Roman Catholic. When the girl was eleven years old, the Reverend Mr. Johnson, acting on behalf of the Church of England, claimed the child. The foster mother refused to give her up. The case was brought to court at St. John's.

When officials sought the girl she could not be located. Mrs. Walsh refused to say what she had done with the child, and was found guilty of contempt of court for refusing to reveal her whereabouts. On 15 June 1873 she was sent to prison to loosen her tongue. On July 17 a petition was vainly circulated asking her release. Mrs. Walsh was finally let out of prison on December 10, but nobody ever found out what became of the James girl.

On 12 October 1881 Mr. Winter (later Sir Marmaduke) found himself in court charged with having assaulted, on October 7, W. Crichton, editor of a satirical paper, *Mosquito*. The case was heard with due reverence and the verdict was in favour of Crichton, for one cent, the smallest award ever made in a Newfoundland case.

Anyone attending court on 20 November 1903 might have thought himself in Transylvania, listening to a charge against old Count Dracula. The *Daily News* reported the case under the heading "A Fiend in Human Form." It seems that Elizabeth Fewer of Chapel Cove, Conception Bay, a twenty-five-year-old woman, married less than one year, passed to her heavenly reward on 22 September 1903. On the Tuesday following the burial, some of her family visited the grave and discovered the ground disturbed. It was decided to dig up the coffin. Elizabeth was found lying face down, without the protection of the lid. The corpse was nude from the waist up, and there were stab wounds on the body. The remains had been sexually molested.

A jilted suitor, Joseph Murray, was arrested and charged with malicious injury to private property. The trial produced its own cast of Dracula-like characters when one of the witnesses turned out to be a dumb girl, and another her brother, a cripple who "crawled to the witness box on his hands with such agility as made all wonder." Of the "human fiend" the papers said: "All through the trial Murphy stood and watched vacantly." His speech was incoherent. In spite of these signs of insanity he was sentenced, December 14, to sixteen years hard labour.

The wartime blackout and presence of thousands of servicemen in St. John's during World War II gave the local police an additional responsibility in trying to prevent theft, rape, and street brawls. One of their most trying nights was that of Christmas, 1941, when the Chinese owners of the Imperial Cafe on Water Street, a couple of doors west of Prescott Street, closed it to the public for a private party so they might celebrate the arrival of some Chinese friends by ship the previous day. About 9:30 in the evening three Canadian sailors were passing and saw lights in the place. When denied entry they beat down the door. A fist fight followed which spilled into the street and involved about a dozen sailors, the Chinese, and the local constabulary. One of the boys in blue rushed away for aid. A short time later a hundred and fifty ratings of a ship's company marched on the place and within minutes the sailors had gutted the Imperial Cafe leaving the building in shambles. The Chinese escaped out the back, climbed to the top floor, and locked themselves in for protection.

For some months Canadian-Newfoundland relations were on a wobbly foundation in St. John's. That summer, fisticuffs again erupted in

578

Bannerman Park with the United States Army and Newfoundland Home Defence fighting the combined Canadian services. The Canadians were rescued by the constabulary and a riot was averted.

No doubt the most fascinating aspect of law and order, court, trial and prison, is murder. There have been many interesting murder cases in St. John's over the centuries. Most of these crimes were deeds of passion, sudden actions in which some overwrought person killed. It is impossible in a work such as this to mention, even briefly, all the trials and executions that have taken place in the city, but there are some important cases that cannot be ignored. Murder will always remain a puzzle, socially, psychologically, and morally, as the tragic histories which follow illustrate.

Michael Darrigan (1780)

Some time in the month of December 1779, a few days before Christmas Eve, Michael Darrigan, a labourer and native of Ireland, broke off the irons from his hands and feet and escaped from His Majesty's sloop of war *Cygnet*, in St. John's harbour, where he was being held prisoner for murdering Cornelius Gallery, on October 24, with a cutlass. Gallery was probably the last person to die by the sword in Newfoundland.

On or about Christmas Eve, John Hall of the Royal Artillery was on duty at Bay Bulls when a skiff came into the harbour and the men on her attempted to board a little brig that was moored there. The Captain repulsed them and they went ashore. Hall and a comrade went in pursuit of the boat's crew and surprised four of them in a thicket of woods where they had a fire going. They were armed with forelock, pistol, and sword but seemed to have surrendered without a struggle. One of the quartet was Michael Darrigan.

While Hall was gone to get help, Darrigan escaped into the woods but was soon taken prisoner again and returned to St. John's with his companions. On 29 September 1780 Darrigan was brought to the bar and arraigned on a murder charge along with Thomas Burke, John Mahoney, John Crow, and Daniel Crow, all natives of Ireland.

The trial was delayed to await the Governor's arrival from England in the summer. It produced the following evidence. On Sunday 24 October 1779, shortly after eight o'clock in the evening, John Kennelly and a young comrade, James Mahoney, had gone to the house of John Mahoney, somewhere in the vicinity of the present Newfoundland War Memorial, where Kennelly paid Mahoney's wife a debt of three shillings and sixpence. There were seven or eight men in the house, which may have been a tavern, possibly even the famous Ship. The men invited the newcomers to come in and sit down. Kennelly did so, but Mahoney said his messmates would be going to cabin and that "it is a most time to be going home." A simple fellow who appears to have been easily led he was finally persuaded to sit down, whereupon Thomas Burke taunted him, "You have not behaved like a man or boy since you came in" and said that he was more

579

like a blackguard. Instead of being riled, Mahoney arose, took off his hat, and begged pardon if he had offended. Kennelly said it was a shame for young fellows to fall out when they came together. Darrigan then asked Kennelly if he would take young Mahoney's part in a fight. He replied that he would not be willing "to see him hurt or ill used."

Darrigan went to a bed in the room and returned with a slightly bent cutlass in his hand. He gave Kennelly a blow on the head with his fist. Mahoney got up and went outside where he was followed by Kennelly as neither of them wanted a fight. Mahoney was pinned against a fence while a group of men attacked his companion who probably showed more of a willingness to fight back than Mahoney.

Kennelly eventually escaped down a lane near a brook of water (probably Gill's Cove). When he looked up he saw Darrigan in his shirt-sleeves coming from the direction of Gaden's flake (near Holloway Street) brandishing the cutlass. He begged him to spare his life. Darrigan swore by the Lord Jesus he would not let him pass without putting his mark upon him. He gave Kennelly a violent cut on the head and on the arm he had raised to defend himself. After this the wounded man was dragged back into the house.

Young James Mahoney got home to find his messmates in bed. He told them he thought Kennelly was dead and wanted help to fetch him. Cornelius Gallery walked back with him to John Mahoney's door which was shut. When they asked if their friend was inside Kennelly himself answered that he was. Suddenly the door opened and seven or eight men rushed out with spades, shovels, sticks, and the cutlass. In the melee that followed, Darrigan cut Gallery in the head with the sword.

Dr. Thomas Dodd was sent for as Gallery was placed on a bed in the house of John Mahoney. The doctor found a large wound on the left side of the head five inches long and two inches deep. A large portion of the skull was driven into the brain. Next day Major Pringle visited the victim who was "perfectly in his senses" and told the major all that happened. Nicholas Gill, a justice of the peace, was sent for and in the presence of James Haye and Nicholas Mudge, Gallery, shortly before he died, made a signed declaration in which he named Michael Darrigan as his murderer, and stated that Thomas Burke had broken his arm.

Darrigan was charged with the murder and brought to trial. "The evidence being summed up the jury withdrew and in about a quarter of an hour returned, and gave their verdict of guilty of Murder." Darrigan was also found guilty of a felony in making his escape from H.M. Sloop *Cygnet*. Burke, Mahoney, and Daniel Crow were found guilty of unlawful flight but John Crow was declared innocent of both the murder and flight.

Michael Darrigan was ordered taken to his place of execution and hanged by the neck. His three companions were to be transported to the Kingdom of Ireland and never to return to Newfoundland on pain of death. For some reason, the innocent John Crow was separately given the

580

same sentence. This was probably for having taken part in the fight. Darrigan begged for a day or two to make his peace with God and this request was submitted to His Excellency.[27] Having squared things with his Maker the penitent was launched from the scaffold into eternity.

John Hearn (1815)

In 1815 a harbour pilot named John Hearn was a respected member of the community, but his wife Mary was an alcoholic. There had obviously been many quarrels before the one in which he killed her in their St. John's home. He testified at the trial that the unfortunate victim of his anger had, "yielded herself up to the daily practice of drunkenness, and to a total neglect of her maternal duties."

On June 2, John Hearn ". . . in a fit of passion and gust of indignation excited by the repeated and degrading exposure of his wife's person, and irritated by her approbuous [sic] language and abuse, unpremeditatedly struck her in a vital part and caused her death." Hearn claimed he had harboured no intention of committing any serious harm by the blows he inflicted. The witnesses who appeared on behalf of the prosecution gave ample evidence of his general good conduct toward his deceased wife.

The trial took place on Monday, September 11, and Hearn was found guilty. He was sentenced to be hanged on the Barrens and then gibbeted (hanged in chains). He sent an appeal for mercy to Governor Keats who advised him that he was pleased to remit the latter part of the sentence. Public sentiment was in favour of commutation and the troops were called out on the day of the hanging to put down any disturbances.

Friday morning, 22 September 1815, the populace and soldiers assembled at the gallows on the Barrens, somewhere in the present vicinity of the Colonial Building. At ten o'clock the prisoner, having spent some time in prayer with the Reverend Mr. Fitzgerald, was hanged by the neck until dead. There is no record of disturbances having taken place, or of Hearn's appreciation of His Excellency's remission of the latter part of the sentence.

Patrick Downing (1833)

Patrick Downing and Patrick Malone were accused of the murder of Robert Crocker Bray at Harbour Grace in 1833. The trial in the Court House at St. John's was presided over by Chief Justice Bolton.

The events were claimed to have begun, according to Downing, three or four days after a big fire which destroyed much of the town. Downing and Malone were working on the Bray farm, engaged in starting stumps with crowbars. Downing claimed Malone told him he had carried into the house a bag of money belonging to Bray containing forty or fifty pounds, which had been buried in a field during the fire. He said he slept in an adjoining room and theft of the bag would be a simple matter. Downing told Malone two men could not pull it off, that four would be needed, and

581

the matter was dropped. When Malone returned from the ice the following spring they plotted again and an elaborate plan was worked out which was to involve the housemaid, Ellen Coombs. They were to kill the family of Bray, his wife and son, wound themselves, and run out crying that they had been attacked.

On the night of the murder, Bray was killed downstairs by two blows of a tomahawk; Ellen Coombs, and the child, Samuel, were killed in a like manner in the bedroom. The maid had probably refused to take part in the scheme. Mrs. Bray happened to be out of town at the time. The house was set on fire in the bedroom and at the foot of the stairs, after the two had searched the place and took what cash and valuables they could find. There was no bag of money. Their loot was hidden on the beach, at Bear's Cove, one and a quarter miles away. On their way back they were greeted with news that Bray's house was on fire and ran about crying "Fire!" As the building had not burned, the bodies of the murdered occupants were quickly found.

Suspicion centred on Malone from the first and the confession which was taken from him, under illegal circumstances, led to the discovery of the stolen goods and the arrest of Downing. The cash take was between thirty and forty shillings. At their trial in St. John's Malone claimed he was sitting rocking the baby when Downing called and murdered the family. He admitted to helping him hide the loot.

The perverse Judge Boulton told the jury to disregard any part of Downing's confession against Malone, and that the evidence against Malone was very slight. Both men showed no emotion during the proceedings and greeted the joint verdict of "Guilty," with indifference. Court adjourned at 7:30 p.m. on 3 January 1834, after a nine-hour trial.

Downing was executed two days later. Bishop Fleming was with the prisoner the whole of Sunday night and on Monday morning offered mass in his cell. Fathers Troy and Ward walked with him to his execution. The scaffold was set up on Market House Hill outside the sessions room at the northwest corner of the Court House. The sashes of the northwest window were taken out and, as the prisoner stepped through, he showed "the most astonishing composure and fortitude." Before the drop fell he thanked Mr. and Mrs. Perchard for their kindness to him in prison. According to a reporter, "The execution was witnessed by an immense concourse of people, who behaved in the most decorous and orderly manner." It was the first execution in nearly nineteen years, since that of Hearn in 1815. Orders were given for Downing's body to be cut down and conveyed to Harbour Grace, where it was to hang in chains, near the spot where the murders were committed.[28]

Canon Wood, who was Church of England vicar in Portugal Cove at the time, records in his diary that when the body arrived at Portugal Cove, for conveyance across Conception Bay to Harbour Grace, it was taken from the coffin and hanged in chains on the wharf while awaiting the arrival of the packet boat.

Once it reached Harbour Grace the corpse was gibbeted at The Reef until Tuesday, April 29, when it was taken down by friends and placed on the doorstep of Dr. W. Stirling who had examined the bodies of the murder victims. On 30 April 1834 the Chief Magistrate at Harbour Grace, Thomas Danson, wrote the Colonial Secretary that during the night just passed

> the Gibbet on which the Malefactor Downing was suspended was cut down and his body removed from the irons and then brought and placed at the Front Door of Mr. Stirling's House, where it was first discovered at five o'clock this morning; from the decomposed state in which the body now is, it has been found necessary to place it in a shell and bury it in the Northern extremity of the Court House Ground.

A note poked under Dr. Stirling's door read:

> Dr. S. This is your man you were the cause of bringing him here take and bury him or Lookout should you be the cause of allowing him to be put up again we will mark you for it so Do your duty and put him out of sight. truly A friend from Carbonear.

Owing to the illegal inducements of the investigating police, who promised him a pardon among other things, Malone was reprieved and given a life sentence. The newspapers of the day were not happy with the police or Judge Boulton. They felt that Downing was a victim of circumstances who had gone to his death for a crime instigated by the conniving Malone.

Mandeville, Spring, and Snow (1833)

What is probably the most interesting case of murder, trial, and execution to be witnessed in St. John's, began in the spring of 1833, when twenty-five-year-old Tobias Mandeville had "criminal intercourse" with Catherine Snow in the woods near Harbour Grace. An illicit relationship of a permanent nature grew out of this tryst.

Catherine was the wife of John Snow of Port de Grave and the mother of seven children, the two eldest of whom were daughters about sixteen or seventeen years of age. There was also a maid in the house, Kit White. Mandeville, who claimed to be a cousin of Mrs. Snow, lived at Bareneed. There was a twenty-eight-year-old hired hand, Arthur Spring, working for the Snows.

Spring was not happy with his wages and felt he was being cheated by Snow out of what was justly his. Mandeville was said to be madly in love with Mrs. Snow and wanted to marry her. Both men had a reason for wanting to do in the husband, both claimed the other first suggested the murder, and both claimed the other fired the fatal shot.

On August 31 Mrs. Snow sent her two eldest daughters, accompanied by Kit White, to a wake where they were to stay all night. The young ones were asleep in bed. She was said to have given her husband's shotgun to Spring and sent him off to the fishing stage to meet Snow, who was returning by boat with Mandeville from Bareneed, according to plan. Mandeville was ashore first. As Snow was coming in from the stage-head, Mandeville claimed he stepped aside, and Spring fired the fatal shot. Spring claimed that he was unable to bring himself to do the deed and when he dropped the gun Mandeville picked it up and shot Snow in the breast, from a distance of three or four yards, as the man was advancing from the stage-head. They then tied the body with a rope, lowered it into the water, and towed it out into the bay where they fastened it to a grapnel and dropped it to the bottom. It was claimed that Mandeville planned to marry Mrs. Snow as soon as rumour died away, and that the two had promised Spring full wages for his part in the deed.

Snow was missing from August 31. No one suspected murder. A partial search was begun on September 5, and on the 10th fifty men in eight boats dragged the harbour, but it was felt that if the man had fallen overboard the dogfish, which were plentiful, would have devoured the body.

On the fifth of the month, murder was considered a possibility and Spring was arrested on suspicion. Mandeville was taken later in the day. Finally, Spring confessed to Mandeville's having done the deed. Mandeville quickly confessed that Spring had done it. Both claimed the deed was perpetrated at the urging, and with the help of Catherine Snow. In admitting their illicit relationship, Mandeville said the last time he "connected with her" was the night following the murder, and his trousers had been found by Kit White in her mistress's room. Mrs. Snow, who had fled the community, was not taken into custody until about a week later.

On Friday, 10 January 1834, the trio stood in the dock, accused of the murder. The jury retired around 10:30 p.m. Within half an hour it returned with a verdict that found all three guilty as charged. Mrs. Snow's lawyer then announced that she was pregnant. As it was 11:30 p.m. Chief Justice Boulton sentenced the three to death and adjourned court. Next morning a jury of matrons was empanelled and the ladies reported back that Mrs. Snow was "quick with child and in an advanced stage." She was respited until the next session.

The crowds were treated to a double hanging on Monday, 13 January 1834, their second and third executions in just over a week. Bishop Fleming spent the two nights before the fatal day with the prisoners, and said mass in their cells on the morning of the hangings.

The gallows was again erected at the western end of the old Court House, where Downing had been hanged eight days previously. The reporter for the *Newfoundlander* noted that the prisoners were composed and met death without flinching. He added that "They were fine young men . . . and wore blue jackets, white trousers and gloves of the same colour." These were the executions disclaimed by the crew of the yacht *Forte*, and mentioned at the beginning of this chapter.

After the delivery of what was probably a love child, Mrs. Snow was most unwell. It was, therefore, decided to try and improve her health before hanging her. During the trial she claimed total innocence and said she had given the gun to Spring thinking he was taking it to shoot dogs. The Attorney General admitted there was no direct or positive evidence of her guilt, but she was caught in a circumstantial web. The Chief Justice had remarked to the jury, "You will observe that nothing said by any of the prisoners can be admitted to implicate her in the act." However, her affair of passion with her very much younger cousin was enough to condemn her.

On 22 July 1834, having recovered her health, Catherine Snow was sent to the scaffold. She was informed of the date a week previously. On the appointed day she was awakened at five o'clock in the morning and was dressed in the usual costume worn by a corpse. When she looked in a mirror, and saw herself in the garb of the grave, she uttered a piercing cry and her reason left her for a while. By nine o'clock, when she stepped through the window of the sessions room to the gallows, again erected on Market House Hill, she was calm and walked with a firm step. Having heard mass celebrated in her cell by Bishop Fleming, she prayed a few minutes with the priests, declared herself a sinful but innocent woman, and was hanged by the neck in front of thousands. She struggled briefly before she died. That night her remains were interred in the Catholic burial ground because her guilt was not considered to have been proven. A petition for a reprieve, handed around earlier by the Catholic clergy, had failed.[29]

Catherine Snow was the last woman hanged in Newfoundland and hers was to be the second last public hanging. The following year a highway robber was hanged.

Richard Roleston (1833)

Richard Roleston and Samuel Gower went out for a friendly walk in the woods near St. John's one fine day in 1833. They had with them a quantity of liquor and Gower urged Roleston to drink freely. After a while Gower became intoxicated and began to doze. Roleston, probably freed of inhibitions by the liquor, is said to have attempted to commit an unnatural crime upon his drowsy companion who awoke and not only resented the interference with his person, but struck his friend a blow with a deadly weapon. Gower attempted to take Roleston into custody by marching him to the barracks where he would be charged.

During the trek back to town Roleston tried to break away. In the scuffle he stabbed Gower with a knife. The victim lingered a short time, possibly long enough to tell the story, and died of the wound.

At the trial in January 1834 Chief Justice Bolton pointed out, "Death ensued in the prosecution of an attempt to commit another felony in which he was resisted as he might lawfully be, by the deceased." Roleston went to the scaffold. It was a busy year for the hangman and the executions of Downing, Mandeville, Spring, Snow, and Roleston, after a nineteen-year lapse, earned Bolton the title of "The Hanging Judge."

John Flood (1835)

The last person to be publicly hanged in Newfoundland would appear to have been John Flood whose crime was merely "Highway Robbery." Few details are available in the Colonial Records or newspapers except that he was tried 9 December 1834 and found guilty of robbery and assault. Court records of the trial are missing. He is believed to have held up the St. John's - Portugal Cover stagecoach somewhere in the vicinity of Kent's Pond on Portugal Cove Road. Flood was given a sentence of death and his hanging was set for "the second Monday of January next." This was 12 January 1835. There is no record of commutation of his sentence so we assume he is the man we are told was hanged the year after Catherine Snow's death, the last person to be given a public hanging in Newfoundland. It was to be forty years before there would be another hanging and by that time execution had become a private affair conducted behind prison walls.

Issac O'Neil (1848)

On the morning of 27 December 1848 a soldier, who was chasing a wild horse, found the body of a man lying in a pool of blood on the barrens, off Military Road. He ran to the nearby barracks with the news, and an officer and three men conveyed the corpse, by stretcher, to their quarters. It was recognized as being that of Mr. Wilson, a citizen of the town. He had been dead seven or eight hours as the result of a blow on the head with a heavy implement. A diligent search was conducted for clues but no arrests were made.

During the last week of August, the following year, one of the crew of the brigantine *Star* was taken ill as the ship was being made ready to leave port. A crew member reported to the captain that there was a fellow on the wharf looking for a job and he was hired to replace the sick sailor. The man gave his name as Issac Neil (O'Neil). During the voyage he appeared to grow morose and kept completely to himself. He slept little and shared his friendship with nobody.

The captain was finally forced into asking O'Neil what was his trouble, as the man was obviously seriously bothered by something and unable to do his work. He broke down and wept to the captain that he had killed Wilson with a club, on the barrens, St. Stephen's night. The officer comforted him and he was dismissed. About seven o'clock the next evening O'Neil was on watch when he overheard the captain and mate discussing his fate. He immediately jumped overboard. A boat was launched and rowed in pursuit of the swimmer. As he was about to be overtaken, O'Neil turned in the water, waved his right hand, and plunged into the depths of the ocean, never to be seen again.

A Person Unknown (1855)

On Tuesday, 2 October 1855, a murder on Water Street created a hue and cry in the press for police protection which did not seem to exist. Between eleven o'clock and midnight, a scuffle broke out on the pitch-black roadway, near Baine Johnston & Company premises, opposite Mc-Murdo's Lane. Dennis Summers, a lad of twenty years, was stabbed with a knife in the heart, and left dead in the gutter. Though suspicion centred around several individuals, no proof of anything could be found. The coroner and jury returned a verdict of "Wilful murder against a person or persons unknown."

Alarmed citizens clamoured for protection against crime on the streets of St. John's. The newspapers demanded the establishment of a night watch. The *Newfoundlander*, in an editorial, said such a force "composed of sober and in every respect, efficient men, would be at this moment a most useful, and to the whole public, a most acceptable provision."

Michael Carey (1863)

Michael Carey was accused of killing his wife, Jane, at Broad Cove, Bonavista Bay, 13 May 1863. Jane was his second wife, and they had been married two years. Between six and seven o'clock, on the night in question, the couple sat in the chimney corner quarrelling. Carey lost his temper and took up the fire tongs with which he struck the woman two blows. She fell to the floor and he continued to hit her until she died.

The trial opened in St. John's on December 5 and closed on the sixth when a verdict of guilty was received with a great deal of surprise, as the nature of the testimony had indicated insanity. His lawyer successfully contended that he should have been acquitted because he was obviously insane, and Carey got off on grounds that the constitution of the jury had been irregular or illegal.

On Tuesday, December 15, Chief Justice Brady set aside the conviction and issued a pardon, on condition of Carey's being imprisoned, according to Her Majesty's pleasure, in the Lunatic Asylum at St. John's. The newspaper *Newfoundlander* used this case as a strong argument for abolition of the death penalty. It pointed out that a less severe alternative would enable jurors to find many guilty who go free because the jurors are reluctant to deprive a felon of his life for a crime with mitigating circumstances. The argument is still very much in use by abolitionists over a hundred years later.

Patrick Geehan (1871)

Though the crime of Patrick Geehan took place in Harbour Grace, he and Joanna Hamilton, an illiterate maid in his employ, were tried in St. John's before Justice Bryan Robinson. The trial was unusual because of the fact that it had to be started twice. After it began, and the first witness was examined, it was discovered that one of the jurors was from Carbonear and not entitled to sit in the district of St. John's. The proceedings were annulled, a new juror found, and the trial begun again.

On 20 November 1871 neighbours heard a gun fired between noon and one o'clock at the farm of Patrick Geehan at the southern end of Harbour Grace, near Riverhead. Three days later the body of Geehan's wife was found on the Spaniard's Bay Road about two miles from her house. There were marks on her head and throat. Then, a hand was seen sticking out of the earth on the farm and the body of Mrs. Geehan's brother, Garrett Sears, was dug from a pit of clay and fish offal. He had been shot to death. Patrick Geehan had told neighbours that Sears had gone with his sister to St. John's to get his toes fixed.

Following the discovery of the bodies, Geehan was arrested along with the maid, Joanna Hamilton, who had returned with her master from the Labrador fishery just one week before. It was alleged that a criminal intimacy between the two was the motive for the crime. At the trial, a fisherman from the north testified that Geehan and Joanna slept on two beds in one room on the Labrador, and that Sears had a bed in a shanty at the back of Geehan's place. Joanna was also quoted as having said of Mrs. Geehan, "It was a pity a smart young man like the skipper should be tied up with such a bloody old hag." It was the first court case for one of the defence lawyers, Richard Raftus, who was admitted to the Bar the day the trial commenced.

It took the jury two hours and forty-five minutes to find both defendants guilty as charged. When Judge Robinson asked him if he had anything to say, Geehan, declaring that he was perfectly innocent, asked that his statement be read again to the court: ". . . as I done the deed. I want to have it read as I said. . . ." Dick Raftus complied. Joanna had nothing to say, but "burst into a flood of tears and cried aloud piteously, 'Oh, must I die with a rope 'round my neck . . .', and a good deal more in this strain of terror and lamentation." When it was brought to the attention of the court that she was pregnant she was reprieved.

Like most nineteenth-century Newfoundland murderers Geehan was Roman Catholic, and Bishop Michael Howley and a bevy of nuns daily entreated him to repent and seek absolution. Shortly before his date with the hangman the town rejoiced to hear news of the Bishop's victory. His soul saved, Geehan was granted an interview with his mistress, in the presence of Dr. Howley, and they forgave each other everything. When Joanna found the farewell was becoming unbearable, Geehan "prayed her not to give way to grief, but to be calm, not for her own sake alone, but for that of the unconscious and innocent being whose chances of life, he said, would be jeopardized by any yielding on her part to violent distress." He then willed all his property to her and to their child.

Shortly before eight o'clock on the morning of July 1, he was led to a gallows on the western side of the Penitentiary. The execution was the first to take place inside the prison walls. A recently enacted British law stated that hangings would, in future, be held in private. The man fell six feet but his neck did not break. His legs kicked up and down until he finally strangled. He was buried in the northwest corner of the prison yard.

William Parnell (1888)

The first building west of the present main branch of the Bank of Nova Scotia, on Water Street at Beck's Cove, was the premises of Sillars and Cairns. When Cairns passed away the business was sold to William Parnell who had been an employee of Bowrings for twenty years. However, Parnell was not able to make a success of the venture and it reverted to Mr. Sillars who managed it on behalf of himself and the other creditors, and Parnell became a clerk in the store.

Parnell lived over the shop, with his wife and children, as did several of the unmarried clerks. It was the fashion in those days for clerks to live above the stores where they worked. On the night of 30 November 1888 Sillars announced an early closing because it was winter and trade had fallen off. At 9:15 p.m. the doors were locked. At ten o'clock one of the clerks, who was going out, saw Sillars and Parnell in an office and ware-room in the basement. Later Parnell was seen going upstairs. At eleven o'clock Mrs. Parnell alarmed the maid and others in the household by calling for a doctor, as her husband had apparently been taken seriously ill. The doctor arrived and discovered the man had swallowed a quantity of strychnine.

Next morning around seven o'clock the body of Sillars was discovered at the foot of the stairs. He had three bullets in him and the five-shot chamber of a revolver was on the floor nearby, from which four shots had been fired. The police surmised that the merchant had been shot in his office, but not killed there. Rasputin-like, he had crawled to the stairs where a violent blow on the skull finished him off. Parnell was charged with the crime.

The trial opened on 4 June 1889 before the Chief Justice. Parnell pleaded not guilty and his tale was that of a defeated and browbeaten sufferer, a Bob Crachit working for an unregenerate Scrooge. Sillars, a man of violent temper, had often abused and taunted him. He had called Parnell's wife a slouch and said the unfortunate man had no business having a family he couldn't support. For three nights before the murder, a child of Parnell's had been suffering from an illness, and he had been forced to sit up with it all night. After supper, on November 30, he had fallen asleep from exhaustion. When he awoke and came downstairs to work, at nine o'clock, Sillars berated him for sleeping on the job. When the clerks were gone the two began to argue over a creditor's compromise which Sillars adamantly refused to grant. Parnell called him a damned, heartless old reprobate, a swindler, and a hypocrite. The smouldering temper of his boss exploded and he went after the harassed clerk with a coal shovel. Parnell, who carried a pistol for protection of the firm against thieves, pulled the gun from his pocket. It was a self-cocking pistol and the four shots were instantaneous.

On June 8 the jury returned a verdict of "Guilty." By then the prisoner appeared to be truly demented. One newspaper said he had a wild look in his eyes and had to be led into court clinging to the arm of a warden whom he refused to let go. He appeared not to know where he was or comprehend his sentence. According to one reporter, "he certainly gave the impression he was insane."

The day before his execution the newspapers rejoiced in news from the Penitentiary that the man appeared to be truly penitent. That night, from six to ten o'clock, he was permitted a visit from his wife. The Reverend A.C.F. Wood then stayed with him until midnight.

The morning of 8 July 1889 was dismal and gloomy. Rain fell in torrents. Parnell arose at seven o'clock in a new cell. The night before he had been brought from his old cell, on the upper floor, to one on the ground floor, as a kindness, to shorten the time it would take him to reach the scaffold. The press noted the distance was sixty feet.

A few minutes before 8:00 a.m. Parnell climbed the six easy steps to the gallows, erected close to the eastern wall out of sight of the curious public gathered in front of the prison. With his face to the north and crying out "Lord Jesus receive my soul," the anguished creature was dispatched without a sign of a struggle or a quiver of the rope.

Francis Canning (1899)

A hanging on 29 July 1899 roused strong abolitionist sentiments in many Newfoundlanders. The tragedy began on the afternoon of May 12 in an upstairs room of the saloon of Francis Canning at 190 New Gower Street, just east of Casey Street. At three o'clock that afternoon, a Miss Tracey was entering by the back door when she heard three shots ring out. She met the proprietor hanging over the bannister. He yelled at her and she hastily retreated.

When others arrived to investigate, Canning was gone and Mary Nugent, a barmaid who worked in the tavern, was found wounded and unconscious. Four days later she regained consciousness in the hospital and made a deposition regarding the apparently motiveless attack. She had been removing her coat when she was shot from behind. On May 23 she passed away and the tavernkeeper faced a charge of murder.

Canning, who was said to have been born in St. Helen's forty-eight years previously, was twenty-two years in Newfoundland. He was actually a native of St. Helier on the island of Jersey. Described as the kindest and most genial of men, he had lately taken to drink and when under the influence was disposed toward violence. His trial, which commenced June 26, ended on July 5, with a verdict of "Guilty."

The execution is memorable for the violent storm which occurred the night before the hanging. It was reported that the thunder was the loudest heard in St. John's in nearly a quarter of a century. Nuns and clergy of the city spent twenty-four hours in continual prayer, on the eve of the execution, and Msgr. Scott asked that the rosary be recited for the unfortunate man in every Roman Catholic home that night. For years afterwards people told how they cowered in terror and prayed fervently as the dreadful storm raged overhead.

A gallows was erected on the north side of the prison grounds. Fifteen minutes before the time set for the execution the Penitentiary bell began to toll. The prisoner climbed the three-foot scaffold. According to the *Daily News* reporter, he "looked the picture of misery and died firmly believing in the salvation of his immortal soul." At 8:00 a.m. the black flag was hoisted over the jail as a sign that the ordeal was ended. The remains were interred in the prison cemetery thirty feet from the gallows. Local newspapers expressed the sentimental wish that never again would they have to report an execution in Newfoundland. It was to prove an empty hope.

Wo Fen Game (1922)

The sensation of 1922, in the courts at St. John's, was the trial for murder of Wo Fen Game. The thirty-one-year-old Chinese purchased a revolver from the Martin Royal Stores on the afternoon of May 3 and, at eight o'clock that evening, shot to death three other Chinese in the Jim Lee Laundry where he worked on Murray Street, just off the top of Long's Hill. Then he seriously wounded his brother-in-law, Hong Wing, in a Casey Street laundry before turning the gun on himself on Barron Street. After the suicide attempt, he staggered to the nearby door of Wing Ling's New Gower Street laundry, where he fell to the sidewalk in a pool of blood. A revolver and bullets were removed from his pocket.

Meanwhile, in the Jim Lee Laundry, halfway up the west side of Murray Street, the police, alerted by a next-door neighbour who had heard the shots, found Hong Lee, Hong King Hig and So Ho King, all dead. One of them was in the street about thirty feet above the laundry, another was found in a laundry basket, and the third in the washroom. Wo Fen Game recovered from his self-inflicted wounds and was held on a charge of "wounding with intent to kill."

The trial, which was held in the Supreme Court before Chief Justice

Horwood, lasted six days. It emerged in the testimony that the man had come from China with the understanding that he would be paid twelve dollars per week, which was four dollars more than he had been earning in China. Instead, he got twelve dollars per month, according to his claim. Another laundry worker said the pay was seven dollars per week plus board. Dissatisfaction with his wages played on the emotions of Wo Fen Game. He decided in his mind that the other workers at the laundry were going to kill him and on the afternoon of the murders purchased from the Martin Royal Stores on Water Steet the revolver with which he shot to death three co-workers. The wounding of his brother-in-law, on Casey Street, he claimed was accidental. Gossip had it that the slayings resulted from a family blood-fued in China but this was never mentioned during the trial. It is probably popular myth.

While he was giving his testimony through an interpreter, Wo fainted away and the trial had to be adjourned. Next day he was carried in bodily, in a state of hysteria and collapse. He lay on the bench and moaned so loudly that the judge ordered him put in the corridor outside the door. At 4:30 p.m. on the sixth day the jury went out. In thirty minutes it was back. Wo Fen Game was placed in a heap in the dock to hear the verdict "Guilty! Guilty on all counts." He was asked three times if he had anything to say but, as he was insensible, he said nothing and Justice Horwood pronounced the sentence of hanging.

The prisoner appears to have gone mad for he made several attacks on the warden and sheriff in his cell. A deputation of clergy from the Methodist community arrived to comfort him but he declared himself a Confucian. However, the day before his hanging he resigned himself to the Methodist faith, and was visited by the Reverend Mr. Joyce who helped compose him for the final ordeal.

At 7:35 a.m. on the morning of his death the bell began to toll in the Penitentiary. The prisoner was led from his cell to the gallows, in the northeast corner of the grounds with his hands bound to his sides by half a dozen turns of a rope. When he saw the masked hangman a look of terror came over his face and he trembled uncontrollably until he disappeared in the pit of the scaffold at 8:09 that morning. By nine o'clock the body was taken down and buried in the prison yard, as the black flag was run up.

Que John Shang (1938)

What appeared to have been a Chinese ritual murder in the tradition of the tongs was discovered on 3 July 1938 by a milkman from Kilbride, delivering milk to a Chinese restaurant, the Regal Cafe, located at the Crossroads, junction of Water Street and Topsail Road, in an area now occupied by a drugstore parking lot.

Eng Wing Kit, the proprietor and lone occupant of the building, was found dead in the kitchen, suspended from a manila rope. The body was hanging parallel to the floor by the neck from a piece of metal pipe placed from the stove to the table. The face was about one foot from the floor. Three different kinds of cord were wound around the neck four times and a flour sack was draped from the neck to the floor. The whole throat had been cut from ear to ear. An examination showed bruises on the face and there was blood over an area of the floor. A portion of skin about the size of a quarter had been sliced from the left breast. The man had obviously died the previous day, Sunday, as the body was quite stiff.

Five Chinese lived in a laundry next door, but they professed to have heard nothing. Finally they admitted to hearing parts of a conversation and two of them placed a fellow countryman, Que John Shang, in the vicinity of the cafe at the time of the crime. A knife which was found wiped clean, in a cleat at the end of the table, was thought to have been the murder weapon.

Shang was charged with the crime and his trial commenced 31 October 1938. Nothing conclusive was proven against the man and what evidence there was to link him to the murder was circumstantial. He had been a part owner of the Holland Cafe at 23 New Gower Street, but had sold his share. It was believed there were financial problems between himself and Eng Wing Kit. On November 3 the jury retired at 4:40 p.m. to consider the evidence and returned at 8:50 p.m. with a verdict of "Not Guilty." The accused was released into the arms of friends and left the Court House in a taxi. The murderer of Eng Wing Kit was never made to pay for his crime. Citizens of St. John's spoke of the killing as a tong murder because it had some of the elements of a ritual Chinese killing about it.

Herbert Spratt (1942)

Another tragic episode was acted out on 17 March 1942 in a house at 33 Plymouth Road, in the east end of the city. Herbert Spratt, a twenty-two-year-old recently discharged from the Navy as being medically unfit, went, in the afternoon, to the Plymouth Road home of his brother, with a girl he hoped to marry in June, twenty-year-old Josephine O'Brien. It was St. Patrick's Day, a holiday in St. John's. Around 5:30 p.m. the brother and his wife left the house. When they came home about 11:30 that evening they found the girl dead on a couch in the kitchen. She had been struck on the head with an electric flat iron and died of skull fractures, a haemorrhage, and shock. She was also discovered to be pregnant.

Meanwhile, a distraught Herbert Spratt was going about the town confessing to people that he had killed Josephine. To one he said "I killed my girl. She was going to have a baby. I never had anything to do with a girl in my life." Arrested at 144 Water Street, the young man signed a confession. It seems that the girl's news that she was pregnant by another filled the ex-sailor with an insane rage. He groped blindly for the iron and struck her a blow on the skull.

The jury found him guilty but recommended mercy in view of his "youth and indifferent health and good service record." The condemned man showed no emotion as he was sentenced to hang by the neck until dead. Nobody dreamed that he would. His record of questionable mental health went back to his school days. However, the recommendation for mercy failed to set aside the sentence of the court.

To the revulsion of many in the community Herbert Spratt was hanged at eight o'clock on the morning of 8 May 1943 on a scaffold erected in the northeast corner of the courtyard at the Penitentiary. The press tells us, "The condemned man faced his ordeal without flinching. The execution was carried out in a most expeditious manner by an unmasked official from Canada." The hangman appears to have known his business for the whole of the execution ceremony took only two minutes, yet the effect on some of the witnesses was to last a lifetime. Two hours later the body was passed over to the distressed father, James Spratt, a highly respected member of the St. John's City Council, who had the sympathy of the whole community. The execution of this pitiable young man may well make history as the last instance of capital punishment being carried out in Newfoundland.

Melvin Young (1964)

A chain of errors led to the escape of four prisoners from the Penitentiary on 17 December 1964. They were James Thorne, seventeen, of Fortune; Melvin Young, nineteen, of St. George's; John Snow, nineteen, of St. John's; and Winston Noseworthy, twenty-one, of Bell Island. The escapees' offences included breaking, entering and theft, car stealing, failure to remain at the scene of an accident, breaches of the Alcoholic Liquors Act, and destruction of property. After escaping at different times from Salmonier Prison Camp, all four ended up locked in the same four-inmate cell at the Penitentiary. Regular inspections of the cell were not made and as a result they were able, using a knife and razor blades, to cut a hole through the floor of their cell, thereby securing entrance to the basement. From the basement they got through a hatch in the doctor's office, which should also have been bolted, and were able to get outside the building where they climbed over the wall, with the aid of two blankets tied together and hooked to a barbed wire on the wall. The prison towers were not manned after midnight.

The four petty crooks stole a car from near the Penitentiary and abandoned it on Topsail Road where they stole another, and headed west on the Trans-Canada Highway. Three miles east of Whitbourne, two R.C.M.P. constables, Robert Amey and D.C. Keith, had set up a roadblock. The fleeing convicts smashed through it. About 8:30 a.m. the two constables came upon the quartet in the stolen car on a side street in Whitbourne, about five hundred feet from Barrett's store. The police drew their revolvers and ordered the unarmed convicts out of the car. The criminals made a break for it but were backed up against the front of the store. Keith covered them while Amey ran down the road to call for help on the police car radio. The four jumped the lone Mountie, grabbed him by the hair and banged his head again and again on the ground. Young took his gun as shouts, curses, threats, and obscene language filled the cold, morning air. Amey ran back to see what was happening and found himself face to face with Young. Both demanded that the other drop his gun. Then a shot rang out and Amey fell into the snow with blood coming from a hole in his chest and from his mouth.

Young ran into Barrett's store while the other three took off over the fences. Fred Barrett, who was just opening his shop for the day, was made a hostage. After much talking, Constable Keith got Young to take the bullets from the revolver and give himself up, and as he emerged from the store he was taken by two R.C.M.P. officers who had just arrived on the scene. Amey was found dead in a snowbank.

On the morning of 23 March 1965 Young, a short, brown-haired, boyishly good-looking teenager, stood in the dock to hear Chief Justice Furlong say: "The sentence of the court is that you be sentenced to death, to be hanged by the neck until you are dead." Young's face flushed as he bowed his head. There was silence in the courtroom. The jury's foreman stood up and said, "We recommend clemency."

Few wanted to see capital punishment brought back to St. John's after nearly twenty-five years. There was a hue and cry in the press against adding Young's death to the tragic loss of Amey's life, a loss that would not have occurred had the policeman been unarmed. Except for vengeance, it appeared that little else would be gained. The execution, set for July 15, three days before the murderer's nineteenth birthday, was rescheduled for October 15, while new appeals were heard in the courts. The Melvin Young case eventually concluded with a commutation of his death sentence to life in prison.

4

Handful of Ashes

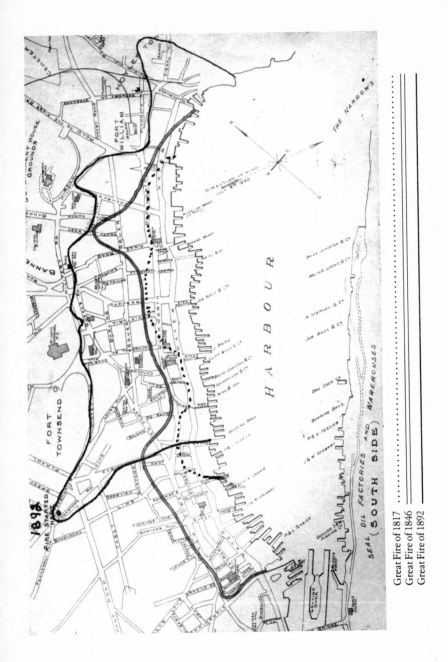

Great Fire of 1817 ·············
Great Fire of 1846 ═══════
Great Fire of 1892 ═══════

599

This recently discovered rough drawing, the earliest of a fire in St. John's, is unique in that it is the only known pictorial record of the Great Fire of 1846. The scene is one of the coves along Water Street looking east towards the Market House seen outlined against the white patch of flame in the sky. It is not known if the drawing was done by an eye-witness or from a description after the event. (Courtesy Provincial Library.)

Sir John Harvey was born in 1778 and entered the British army in 1794. He served in Canada in the War of 1812. He was Lieutenant-Governor of New Brunswick (1834-41), Governor of Newfoundland (1841-46), and Lieutenant-Governor of Nova Scotia (1846-52) where he died 22 March 1852. His bungling attempt to halt the Great Fire of 1846 helped spread the flames and destroy much of the city.

The Reverend Moses Harvey, like Lewis Anspach, Charles Pedley, Philip Tocque, and Archbishop Howley, was a clergyman as well as historian. His description of the Great Fire of 1892 is the most graphic account available. Born at Armagh, Ireland, in 1820 he was Presbyterian pastor in St. John's until 1874. Harvey died 3 September 1901 in his eighty-first year.

601

A group of proud firemen show off the first steam fire engine in Newfoundland, the Terra Nova, in front of the Colonial Building in 1885. This vehicle, manned by eight firemen and drawn by a pair of horses, was the ultimate in modern firefighting equipment. (Courtesy Newfoundland Provincial Archives.)

This supposed view of St. John's from the Basilica towers during the Great Fire in 1892 is a hoax. An artist has superimposed flames on the preceding photograph by S. H. Parsons. The flames are shown sweeping towards the west. The fire actually spread from the west to the east. Strange to say there are no known actual photographs showing the 1892 fire in progress.

The Great Fire of 1892 had its beginning a short distance northwest of this vantage point on Harvey Road. In the foreground are the ruins of the Methodist College (now Holloway School). The gutted remains of Gower Street Methodist Church are in the centre on the right side of the photograph, with the ruined walls and tower of the Church of England Cathedral above them to the left. (Courtesy St. John's City Hall.)

606

Due to the efforts of the tenants and an army of housemaids, Devon Row at the east end of Duckworth Street was saved from destruction. This photograph, taken from the roof of Devon Row, shows the destruction of the city. The trees in Cavendish Square on the right seem to have been spared.

607

This 1892 view also was taken from the roof of Devon Row. It shows Hill o'Chips twisting down to Water Street stretching west along a waterfront lined by rubble, the shells of burned-out buildings and the pilings of burned wharves. Duckworth Street meanders through the ruins on the right side of the photograph (Courtesy St. John's City Hall.)

Duckworth Street looking east from Bell Street in the summer of 1892. Beyond the chimneys of Scotland Row, on the left, are the gutted remains of the Anglican Cathedral of St. John The Baptist. The gaunt shell on the right is the Presbyterian Church where the Reverend Moses Harvey attended a prize-giving the afternoon of the Great Fire. (Courtesy St. John's City Hall.)

A coachman with whip in hand drives his mistress, shaded from the sun by a parasol, up McBride's Hill from rubble-littered Water Street. The gutted structure on the left was Goodfellow & Company. Between the chimney walls of the building in the centre of the photograph, part of the Bowring property seems to have been spared. This was the western limit of the 1892 fire. (Courtesy St. John's City Hall.)

610

This old magazine photograph shows the ruins of the Church of England Cathedral in the summer of 1892. The gutted shells in the foreground were the homes of the Lord Bishop of Newfoundland and the cathedral clergy. The Union Bank Building on Duckworth Street at the left of the cathedral ruins.

612

The Athenaeum, seen here before and after the 1892 fire, was the cultural heart of St. John's. The cornerstone of the building was laid by Sir Hugh Hoyles 4 November 1875, fourteen years after the organization was founded. With it were lost many priceless manuscripts and historic documents. The site opposite Cathedral Street was afterwards occupied by the Museum building which served for a time as the Gosling Memorial Library. (Courtesy Provincial Reference Library.)

The tragic fire at McAuley's cooperage on the south side, 11 September 1901, did $200,000 damage. Moored in front of the blazing building is H.M.S. *Alert*. The ship's doctor went immediately to the relief of the severely injured. (Courtesy Newfoundland Provincial Archives.)

On 28 November 1941 the Prince's Rink, then called the Arena, was totally destroyed in a spectacular $100,000 fire. It left St. John's without an artificial ice surface throughout the war years and almost dealt local hockey a mortal blow. This photo shows the ruins behind Hotel Newfoundland the day after the fire. (Courtesy Leslie Simms.)

615

This was St. John's first traffic light at Rawlins' Cross (circa 1940). It was manually operated by a policeman in the box in front of Dr. Cluny Macpherson's surgery. Constable Steve Reynolds was on traffic-light duty here 12 December 1942 when he noticed a glow in the wartime blackout and rang in the first alarm for the tragic Knights of Columbus fire. (Courtesy Arthur Fox.)

On 12 December 1942 hundreds of servicemen and their girlfriends were attending a broadcast of the "Barn Dance" at the Knights of Columbus Hostel on Harvey Road when the building was discovered in flames. One hundred persons died in what has been called the most tragic indoor fire in Canadian history. In this photograph a policeman is outlined against the burning ruins. (Courtesy Newfoundland Reference Library.)

Handful of Ashes

Theirs be the music, the colour, the glory, the gold;
Mine be a handful of ashes . . .
                                    JOHN MASEFIELD *A Consecration*

While the cities of North America boomed with increasing prosperity and their silhouettes grew higher and wider, St. John's was becoming the most burned-over capital on the continent. Through several centuries it was gutted in whole or in part. Three of these calamities were consuming enough to be called Great Fires.

Ordeal by fire is a test of survival that goes far back in mythology. St. John's has not been found wanting. After each conflagration this urchin of the west Atlantic has sifted through its handful of ashes and built again on its charred remains with a folly and shortsightedness that led to ever greater disasters. San Francisco, Boston, Chicago, Quebec, Saint John, N.B., and other cities have all been tried on the anvil of flaming destruction but none of them have been so consistently and needlessly tried as St. John's.

The first indication we have of a serious conflagration in St. John's is found in a note in the files of the Phoenix Fire Office, London. In 1805 the Phoenix company insured the St. John's firm of Messrs. Marmaduke Hart & Co. (afterwards Hart, Robinson & Brooking) for three years. On 24 February 1807 Mr. Hart wrote to the insurance company:

> The town of St. John's, Newfoundland is about a mile in extent running NW to SE. The principal stores are situated in the center of the lower street. Many of them are contiguous to and some of them are built over *Coves* of Water which run up into the Town and are intended to preserve Fishing Boats during the winter. It appears that St. John's is very much within the Hazard of one fire, altho no Accident of Fire has happened since 1780. There are 4 or 5 engines in the Town and regular fire companies under good regulation.

Hart's statement about fire engines and fire companies is a bit puzzling in view of the subsequent history of these machines and organizations in St. John's. For some reason they must both have fallen into disuse.

619

Two years after the fire of 1780 the Phoenix people wrote the first fire insurance policy ever issued on property in Newfoundland. On 28 November 1782 they insured the St. John's premises of Newman & Roope for three thousand pounds. This was only the second policy written by the Phoenix office on an overseas risk. The first was written a month earlier on a sugar house in Russia.

In the year 1809 Jenkin Jones, a representative of the Phoenix Fire Office who was visiting St. John's wrote to his headquarters in London:

> The body of the town is comprised of the Lower Street, which is from one extreme of the harbour to the other, not much less than one mile and ¾ long. This street, as you will see, is formed on one side by the stores and buildings on the wharfs, on the other by rows of buildings used for retail shops. Altho' called a street, it is in fact only a crooked and narrow alley, in some places contracted to 6 feet wide, in others expanding to as much as 12 or 18 feet. This street runs nearly in the direction of the prevailing winds, and is a tunnel through which they blow occasionally with great violence. The buildings are uniformly, thro'out the town, of wood and have the roofs covered with shingles. There is not a private building of a different description in the whole town.
>
> St. John's has of late years rapidly increased in population and buildings, and the properties on the water-side have become of great value. In proportion with these causes, the buildings upon them have become more numerous, and indeed a more crowded range of wharfage and stores I have yet seen in no places. Even the narrow coves reserved by government for boats have been encroached upon, and every year adds to the list.[1]

As can be seen from this description the place was one enormous fire hazard. This was borne out on 12 February 1816 when fire broke out in the newly erected house of a person named Walsh at King's Beach, near the site of the present war memorial. This fire, which began in the upper part of the house, was discovered about eight o'clock in the evening when it suddenly broke through the roof. It burned with such fury that it spread to adjoining buildings on all sides before anything could be done to stop its progress. In no time at all it was rampaging through the flimsy dwellings on the Upper and Lower Paths and leaping over the cross streets until it had destroyed everything from today's Prescott Street to Fort William and as far north as the present Gower Street.

The fish flakes that covered what open ground there was helped spread the flames as they were tinder dry and many were covered with "blasty" (dried out) boughs. This fire left nearly a thousand people homeless out of a population of ten thousand and cost half a million dollars, a considerable sum for those days. A hundred and twenty family houses were totally destroyed as well as two printing establishments and a newly erected Methodist chapel on McCarthy's Lane (Prescott Street). The customs house was also on fire but the blaze was extinguished without much damage to the building.

It was reported that there were "many acts of plunder during the awful confusion of the scene." The looting of their rescued belongings added considerably to the sufferings of the victims. Some looters were arrested, convicted, and publicly punished for the offense. The buildings on the harbour side of Water Street were spared, but these were mostly warehouses and fish-storage sheds. In those days all the shops were on the north side of the street.

The following year, 1817, the town was visited by the first of the Great Fires. It happened in two parts. At ten o'clock on the night of November 7, in a small house adjoining Water Street and very near the scene of the fire the previous year, a blaze was discovered soon after it started. However, it burned with such rapidity that in a very short time the neighbouring houses were also on fire. A wind carried flaming embers to the south side of Water Street and soon all the buildings between King's Beach and Governor's Wharf (opposite the present Court House) were doomed by the ravaging flames. Every measure that was practicable was resorted to in order to stop the progress of the blaze. On Water Street a large building near the east corner of Governor's Wharf and the street (Clift's-Baird's Cove) was torn down with extreme difficulty and the great exertions of the army and navy. This kept the fire from spreading west along the main thoroughfare.

The progress of the flames along the north side of the street was halted by tearing down a group of houses on the east side of the church hill (now Court House Steps). This effort also succeeded in keeping the fire from spreading to the upper town. To the eastward the flames continued to rage with much fury until the whole of the area from the present Court House to Hill o' Chips was entirely consumed. The work of destruction was completed in six hours. East of Hill o' Chips there was hardly anything like a street left—only detached houses, sheds, and wharves.

The loss of the leading provision shops with their supplies for winter consumption, in a year of near famine, was a terrible blow. In ruins lay the great merchant houses along Water Street, Duckworth Street, Holloway Street, and (old) Gambier Street. Most downtown retail stores did not move west of Clift's-Baird's Cove until after the Great Fire of 1846. King's Wharf, then just west of Hill o' Chips, was saved by hauling down two storehouses adjoining the Fort William Ordnance and Commissariat on the wharf. The fire took with it a hundred and thirty dwellings, the Court House, and numerous business premises, storehouses, sheds and wharves. No lives were lost but property losses were in the nature of $2,500,000. Only a few more private dwellings were consumed than had been in 1816 but the destruction of many more business firms and stores of provisions increased the cost of the loss five times.

Governor Pickmore, who was spending his first winter in the country as the first governor to take up permanent residence, was alarmed that so many of the supplies, intended for winter consumption by the inhabitants of the town and the island generally, were lost at a season when no adequate relief could be obtained. He placed a temporary embargo on shipping until the extent of the loss could be ascertained and he was saddened to find that the stock left appeared to be inconsiderable. If he had been gifted with enough clairvoyance to see fourteen days ahead he would have been plunged into despair.

The curtain rose on the second act of the Great Fire of 1817 on the morning of November 21 around half-past three of the clock in the premises of Messrs. Huie & Reed, situated on the lower side of Water Street near Adelaide Street. It was first discovered from one of His Majesty's ships in the harbour and, although every possible effort to contain it was made with great promptness by the army, navy, and inhabitants of the town, the blaze was soon out of control. In spite of the fact that there was no wind blowing, the flames spread with great speed among buildings composed almost entirely of wood and stored with dried provisions and other inflammable articles. Every attempt to stop their destructive progress eastward was baffled until all the dwellings and stores on both sides of Water Street almost to the present Court House were totally destroyed.

All that remained of the town, between Adelaide Street and Hill o' Chips, were some detached buildings on the north side of Water Street between present day McBride Hill and the Court House Steps. These were saved by pulling down a house and range of fish flakes adjoining a large shop near the foot of McBride Hill. The westward progress of the fire was halted about a hundred and fifty yards from the end of Water Street only with extreme difficulty and the most powerful exertions. West of Huie & Reid's, two houses, one on each side of the street, were demolished at the first practical opening. The narrow space between buildings presented a great problem.

Some 260 dwellings were destroyed for a value estimate of $1,500,000. Upwards of two thousand people, nearly one quarter of the inhabitants, were homeless. The combined total for both calamities, known jointly as the Great Fire of 1817, was four hundred buildings destroyed at a cost of $4,000,000, and one out of three people left homeless. In the second fire an area, 650 yards long by 50 to 150 yards wide, was laid waste.[2] People were deprived of habitation, food, and clothing at the start of what was one of the most bitterly cold winters ever known in Newfoundland.

This period of extreme distress is termed in local history "the winter of the rals." The word rals was used locally for rowdies. Lawlessness prevailed as gangs of these rals roamed the streets and lanes assaulting and robbing with impunity. They were seen daily rooting through the charred embers of the town for half-burned fish to feed their starving families. Two men were found dead in the snow-covered ruins, having perished from cold and hunger. Even those with money could find little food to buy. Funerals were commonplace as people froze to death in makeshift shelters or succumbed to starvation.

Governor Pickmore cautioned people, on December 1, not to put up any other than temporary erections, and then only by special authority. He was a farsighted man, and it was his hope to rebuild the growing town on a proper plan, so that it would be not only safe from future fires but also a pleasant place in which to live.

It seems that a firebug might have been the cause of the disasters of 1817. At the end of December an attempt was made to set fire to the house of William Hogan in Maggoty Cove, an area of the town that had so far been spared. On January 1 a proclamation was issued offering a reward of three hundred pounds (a whopping fifteen hundred dollars) for information leading to the capture of the culprit.[3] The proclamation said that the new attempt was probably connected with the unexplained fires of November 7 and 21 and left little doubt that somebody was setting them.

Captain Sir William Eliot, who was in St. John's in the year 1819, gives another explanation in his biographical *Naval Sketch Book*. According to Sir William:

> It is whispered amongst the better-informed of this island that some of the mercantile community have most opportunely escaped bankruptcy, by what might almost be termed a providential conflagration. [He adds that the annual fire was looked for with the coming of the frost.] If the governor suggested any precautionary expedient for the prevention of fire, or, in the event of its occurring, issued orders calculated, as he thought, to avert the inevitable destruction of property that must in such cases be expected to ensue, he was sure to be attacked through the medium of the radical press and anonymous pamphlets; if not opposed by the "grand jury", or even a grand deputation from the commercial community, on the subject of this presumed encroachment on civil rights.[4]

Following the second fire, in November of 1817, Governor Pickmore entertained grave doubts that his request for provisions from Halifax, after the first fire, would be adequate, and he asked that further supplies be sent out from England before the season was too far advanced and ice had closed the port, which it did with a vengeance. Within three months His Excellency was himself a corpse and it took three hundred and fifty men chopping at the ice for three weeks to open a channel out of the port so that his remains might be conveyed home to England.

The year 1818 saw only one fire disaster of any consequence in the town. It broke out in September "through gross negligence" and consumed twelve dwelling houses near Fort William and part of the Ordnance property at the foot of today's Ordnance Street where the East End fire hall stands. Meanwhile the almost totally unrestricted building that went on along the waterfront guaranteed the success of the conflagration of 1819.

It began between 1:00 and 2:00 a.m. on July 19 in an empty house somewhere in the area of Beck's Cove recently occupied by George Garland and separated by a space of only ten or twelve feet from the residence of Thomas Williams, a leading merchant and one of the founders of the Amateur Theatre. Sir William Eliot was an eyewitness. Again in his *Naval Sketch Book* he tells us:

> . . . a flame was first discovered by the vigilance of the look-out from the flag-ship. The alarm-gun was instantly fired, the report of which echoing among the surrounding hills at so silent an hour of the night, was truly appalling, more particularly as its cause could not be misunderstood. The affrighted inhabitants, suddenly roused from deep sleep, issued forth in dismay from their dwellings at the well-known clang of the fire-bell. Women with children in their arms, and many with helpless infants at the breast, were seen flying in every direction, *en chemise,* for refuge to their more fortunate friends, situated at a distance from the fire— which rapidly spread amongst the streets consisting almost entirely of wooden houses—or to the church, the constant asylum on each of those calamitous occasions. . . . Parties were dispatched provided with buckets, hatchets, hawsers and every auxiliary implement that the experienced could devise for subduing the fire, with the exception of engines, as, from the proximity of the men-of-war . . . the ships were in readiness to slip from their moorings, and haul out of reach of the fast-falling flakes, which showered constantly around them.
>
> Being amongst the first of those officers who proceeded on shore, with a view to tranquillize the tumult of the people, we were surprised to witness, amid this scene of horror and destruction, such a manifestation of opposite feeling. Those who were insured, were philosophically passive, and submitted to their fate without a murmur; whilst, on the contrary, those uninsured, were either too irresolute or too furious in their conduct to be practically useful. The rich, awaiting the inevitable destruction of their property, were almost frantic with despair; whilst the poor, (particularly the *Paddies*) were delighted beyond measure at the prospect of plunder which presented itself . . .[5]

Sir William goes on to say that the military and navy behaved with much coolness and courage but that their exertions to extinguish the flames were severely hindered by those whose property they were attempting to save. One or two demagogues vociferously disputed with the soldiers and sailors and "literally exhausted the Billingsgate vocabulary of abuse, in exciting the lower orders to riot with the troops."

According to Sir William's narrative, wet blankets and carpets were placed along the tops and sides of the houses to make them less liable to catch fire. A captain of the navy was subjected to "showers of abuse, which rained thick and threefold" for suggesting the levelling of one or two houses to make a firebreak. A military officer proposed blowing up the houses with a few barrels of gunpowder but the axe and the saw were finally chosen.

> The principal upright beams which supported these buildings were sawn through at the base . . . a seaman taking the end of a hawser in his hand, ascended by a ladder the top of the dwelling . . . and succeeded in securing it sufficiently firm round the house. An hundred hands now hastily grappled the rope . . . but the "miracle" of making a breach in this modern Jerico was reserved, as of old, for the clergy; for just then the well-known shrill voice of the priest was heard vociferating from the crowd, "Follow me, boys—follow Father Fitzgerald!" when a phalanx of fishermen flocked round their pastor . . . and with a hearty hurrah hurled the building to the ground.[6]

Sir William ends his eyewitness account by telling us no lives were lost but that much valuable property, insured and uninsured, perished in the flames, "or was plundered by the *Paddies*." He says that on other occasions it was notorious that a considerable part of the property plundered was secreted and carried away in boats, called "jack-asses," to the outports.

The 1819 fire managed to make considerable headway very quickly because of the continued dryness of the weather and the inflammable condition of the building materials. The only hope of controlling it, to the east, lay in preventing its crossing a narrow street on the corner of which stood Mrs. Eliott's house and shop. Dinah Eliott appears to have lived on the west corner of present-day McBride's Hill. It was hoped to contain the blaze in the west before it reached Codner & Tracey's, on the west side of what is now Bishop's Cove. Within two and a half hours the entire lot of houses, shops, warehouses, and wharves in this area was completely destroyed. The wind blew moderately from the southwest throughout the conflagration.

A small garden (now Bishop's Cove) separated the firm of Thomas Meagher, Sons & Co., from Codner & Tracey. It was here that Charles Fox Bennett, who also had considerable property in the area, made a stand with his engine. After an arduous struggle, the fire in the west was finally subdued, but not until Meaghers was destroyed and the dwelling house of the Codner & Tracey firm had caught fire several times.

Meanwhile, at the eastern end of the conflagration, there was a space of some sixty feet between Mrs. Eliott's and some buildings remaining from the three previous fires of 1816 and 1817. At this point the cliff face jutted out into the Lower Path. These factors enabled the fire fighters to prevent the flames spreading further east and, as Captain Eliot tells us, the

625

fire "was subdued by degrees, or spent itself . . . for want of fuel."

The *Mercantile Journal* said it was instantly to be desired in rebuilding that the example of Baine Johnston & Co. and Hunter & Co. would be copied in erecting stone buildings. There were congratulations for the job done by Colonel Manners and the troops. The military gave to the engine from the ordnance department "all the effect that could be deserved while Mr. Job, with a small patent engine belonging to his house, watered the shingled roofs of the buildings on the north side of the street." Upwards of eleven hundred persons were driven from their habitations and, as the paper observed, "Even though it was summer, much misery was found among the lower orders." It observed with pleasure "H.E. the Governor [Sir Charles Hamilton] affording such aid by his presence at different points of fire, as would naturally be expected from his character and station, and we are happy in recording that we hear of none of these complaints of plunder which upon similar occasions disgraced the lower orders of the community."[7]

Eliot was obviously better informed than the newspaper on the behaviour of the lower orders, for the following day the governor issued a proclamation placing an embargo on all vessels leaving port without inspection because of improper attempts to convey rescued property out of the harbour. A day or so later the *Journal* itself noted that discoveries were made on the south side of goods stolen from sufferers in the fire and much property was recovered. Mr. Justice Blaikie evinced his usual alacrity on this occasion and half a dozen culprits, including one woman, were sent to trial.

Of the 1,061 people officially left homeless, one publican was burned out for the fourth time. Andrew McCoubrey, the hairdresser, was left homeless for the third time. Among the dispossessed was Dr. Kielley's family of six, Benjamin Bowring's household of eleven, fourteen in the family of Thomas Williams, and twelve in the family of Thomas Meagher. Having lost all in the fire, the Meaghers returned to Ireland where the old man's famous grandson, General T.F. Meagher, was born soon afterwards. Jenkin Jones had written of the Meagher property, "We are better without these risks." In all, one hundred and seventy buildings had been destroyed. The agent for the Phoenix Fire Office observed of the reconstruction that, "Since the city could not afford to build of stone only; firebreaks should be compulsory."

The next conflagration of note took place on 17 July 1833, which was a Sunday. This most extensive fire broke out between 2:00 and 3:00 a.m. in the house of J.B. Thompson, three doors away from Bowring's on Water Street. Within minutes of breaking through the roof, the adjacent buildings were aflame. Though the town and garrison engines responded immediately and the alarm was raised, the body of the fire was so immense and the heat so intense that it could not be prevented from crossing the street. It was finally stopped at the house of J. Renouf, east of Ayre's Cove.

To the westward it was brought under control at the premises of McGregor & Co and Mr. Kielty's near Queen Street. Before six o'clock that morning all the houses in one of the finest stone ranges in the town were entirely consumed. Over fifty families were homeless and there was a tragic loss of life. Having saved his wife and infant from the fire, J.B. Thompson discovered that his seven-year-old daughter was still inside the house. As he went to rescue her the floor caved in and both father and daughter perished in the flames.

Among business firms wiped out was the extensive mercantile establishment of McBride & Kerr, opposite McBride's Hill, Stewart's, and Bowring's. Writing back from retirement in Liverpool the following year, old Benjamin Bowring admonished his staff not to "go to bed yourselves without seeing every fire and candle safe."[8] The holocaust of 1833 had been caused by a Thompson servant who did not properly extinguish a candle on going to bed.

At three o'clock on the morning of Friday, 23 August 1838, flames were seen to suddenly burst through the roof of the premises of Thomas Hayes, a publican. Crowds jumped from their beds and rushed to the scene of promised excitement, but the fire was extinguished before many buildings were burned. The *Royal Gazette* said, however, that except for the assistance of those in the street a large portion of the town would again have fallen prey to its old enemy. No doubt could be reasonably entertained, the paper continued, that the fire was the work of an incendiary, and two women were committed to jail on strong suspicion.

Pyromaniacs were treated to another feast of rare delight in 1846. The previous year an agent for the Phoenix Fire Office, J.J. Broomfield, arrived in St. John's and wrote home to England on 25 October 1845:

> . . . I may remark *generally* that St. John's, Nfld. is the worst built town that I have seen since I left England [he had been in Canada]—the streets are all of a very irregular width, especially Water Street, which is in one part 60 feet, in another 40 feet wide. This is owing to the operation of the recent Act of the Legislature, which provides that in every case, upon the expiration of a lease, the building shall be pulled down and not allowed to be re-erected at a nearer approach to its opposite neighbours by 60 feet, so that in process of time, when the leases of all the wooden buildings shall have fallen in, a clear open space of 60 feet wide will be secured thro'out the whole line of Water Street, and as the same Act requires that all the buildings facing the street shall be of brick or stone construction and slated, a very great improvement will be thereby created.
>
> Gas pipes are being laid down in Water Street and supplied from a Gasometer erected at the Western extremity of the town by the River Side—the works are already in operation—several of the street lights are in use and it is intended to be introduced into the shops and retail stores generally thro'out the town. A meeting

of the merchants was held on Wednesday last (21st inst.) prepara-
tory to the formation of a Coy. for the purpose of supplying the
town with water, which can be obtained from 2 sources, viz., St.
George's Pond on Signal Hill or the main river at the other end of
the town, both of a sufficient elevation to secure an abundant
supply to Water Street, Duckworth Street and Gower Street. The
expense is estimated at six thousand pounds.[9]

Before any of these contemplated improvements could be effected,
the Great Fire of 1846 broke out on the very windy morning of June 9.
Shortly after 8:30 a.m. a pot of glue that had been set on the stove in the
shop of Hamlin, a cabinet maker on George Street (at the back of the present General Post Office), boiled over and caught fire.

In describing the events of that memorable day, the *Newfoundlander*,
which did not resume publishing until July 18, says:

> ... in a short time the whole collection of stone and wooden houses
> in the locality were on fire. It was hoped that a stand might be
> made at the corner of Queen Street and Water Street, but the fire
> spread on consuming Messrs. Rogerson's, Stewart's, and C.F. Ben-
> nett's premises; it was stopped by an heroic effort at Newman's
> premises, at River Head.

Bennett's and Stewart's oil vats exploding in sheets of uncontrolled
flame, and a change in the wind to an easterly direction, made the
destruction of much of the town inevitable. The governor, Sir John
Harvey, rushed to the scene and was everywhere offering counsel and sympathy. He might have been more helpful had he done nothing. Sir John,
determined on trying to control the flames by a firebreak at Beck's Cove,
ordered Stabb's house, on Water Street at the southwest corner of the cove,
to be blown up. The action was not successful, and because of the velocity
of the wind the explosion sent a shower of burning timber into oil vats
across the cove igniting Bowring's block. An artilleryman was killed by the
reckless blast and another seriously wounded.

At McBride & Kerr's the flames had no difficulty jumping Ayre's
Cove and continuing to race along both sides of the street destroying shops
and dwellings. A man, either ignored or forgotten in the confusion, died in
the destruction of the Court House and jail where he had been left in his
cell. Another man, struggling to save his possessions, collapsed and died in
the street. A few days later, John King and Joseph Row, labourers employed in clearing away some ruins, were killed when a wall tumbled in on
them. This brought the immediate death toll to five persons.

Besides the Court House and jail, other important buildings which
fell before the onrush of fire included the Church of England Cathedral (a
wooden building), the Commercial Buildings, Merchant's Hall, the Amateur Theatre, the Customs House, the Bank of British North America, the

628

Savings Bank, and the Colonial Treasurer's. The money that was in the banks was saved and taken to Government House. An unusual loss was the new Presentation Convent, south of Murray Street, on Long's Hill. Far removed from the scene of devastation, it was ignited by embers brought into the building in a refugee's clothing bundle. So rapid was its destruction that the nuns had no time to save anything, including some priceless works of art brought back from Europe and presented to the sisters by Bishop Fleming.

A number of ships in the harbour were burned to the waterline by "flankers" (flaming embers) carried on board by the high wind. Most of them caught fire first in the masts and rigging. In all, some £70,000 ($280,000) worth of docks were burnt. Several times the stores on the south side of the harbour caught, but these outbreaks were extinguished by men stationed on the roofs. The fire passed over a one-hundred-ton brigantine in Wood's slip, Maggoty Cove, but burned the houses on the hill beyond.

The homeless and destitute were accommodated in tents which were promptly erected by the military on the barrens between Government House and Rawlin's Cross. Within a fortnight they had moved to temporary wooden sheds built on the Parade Grounds, west of Fort Townshend, and these dwellings eventually became a shelter for the poor of the city. Some people were housed and fed in the Old Factory and Orphan Asylum School, both on Queen's Road. More found refuge in the Roman Catholic chapel and school on Henry Street. Two of those quartered in the Native Hall, in Bannerman Park, were killed when the building blew down in a September gale. It could be said that the final death toll as a direct result of the fire was seven persons. Fortunately the weather was warm and most sufferers were able to rebuild or find permanent shelter before winter.

J. J. Broomfield wrote from St. John's, July 23:

> I am told that in less than an hour of the breaking out of the fire, the houses on both sides of Duckworth St. and Water St., together with all the buildings in the intermediate space were wrapped in one vast sheet of flame, which the fury of the wind (blowing with a gale at the time) drove before it with such frightful rapidity that the engines that were brought to the fire could not appear near enough to throw a single drop of water on the burning mass—and as the fire proceeded, the men who should have assisted to extinguish it, hastened to their own homes to endeavour to save the little property they possessed.[10]

In another letter, written August 3, he reported:

> . . . the general opinion of the commencement of the fire was that the flames would not cross the Fire Breaks, so fully persuaded

were the merchants of this, that very few persons living on the eastward of Warren's [Bishop's] Cove attempted to remove any of their property, until the fire had passed that boundary—then and not till then the occupants of the block bounded on the E. by Beck's Cove began to remove—but still the merchants in the next block eastwards were not apprehensive of the fire communicating with their range of stone built stores, and I am assured by those who have resided for many years in St. John's and been present at the former large fires, that the fire of 9th June might have been stopped (on the Water side at least) at Beck's Cove but for the injudicious step taken by the Governor of blowing up Stabb's wooden house with gunpowder, the result of which was that the shattered fragments of timber were ignited by the explosion and the burning brands scattered in all directions, several alighting on the oil vats of Messrs. Bowring Brothers in the rear of their stone buildings and immediately caused a terrific blaze, which involved the destruction of the whole of the block. Even then it was supposed that Messrs. Baine Johnston & Co's solid stone buildings on both sides of the street in the next division would offer resistance to the further spread of the fire, and many that lived to the eastwards of the latter premises delayed moving until it was too late—and so on till the whole town was consumed.[11]

He added that:

The work of destruction comprises almost the whole of the town . . . not a vestige of any timber building [remains]. The once substantial stone buildings having iron doors and shutters present the appearance only of crumbling, shattered ruins rent from top to bottom, warped and twisted in all directions.

The last steamer brought £15,000 in gold, a donation from the Home Government with a promise of £15,000 more, for the relief of sufferers.

August 24 he wrote again to the London office from New York claiming that: "The frequency of calamitous fires in timber towns on this continent during the last few weeks has been truly alarming." Besides St. John's he alluded to outbreaks at La Prairie, Quebec, Nantucket and Lynn in Massachusetts, and Dartmouth (presumably Nova Scotia).

Nearly three quarters of what was then St. John's was in ruins that stretched from Springdale Street to Hill o' Chips, and on the harbour side of Water Street to Maggoty Cove. Of the six leading mercantile firms, only Newman's in the west end escaped destruction. The value of property lost was over £800,000 or almost $4,000,000. The population of the town was 16,000.

On June 23 a bill was passed authorizing the raising of a loan in England, or elsewhere, to the amount of £250,000 to be applied to the rebuilding and improvement of the town. The governor followed this with a proclamation warning all persons against the reconstruction of wooden buildings upon the burnt district before the intentions of the local Legislature on the subject were declared.

His Excellency gave assent, on August 3, to a bill for re-erecting the town on an improved plan. Water and Duckworth Streets were to be of a parallel width of sixty feet each, for the whole length of the town, and all buildings on both sides of the streets were to be of brick or stone, with slated roofs. No timber building was to be permitted and eleven firebreaks were to be opened sixty to eighty feet wide.[12] Another bill, incorporating a company for supplying water to the town, was also passed. However, in spite of restrictions, half of both sides of Water Street had already been rebuilt with wooden houses and stores. Many of these were ordered removed, but not the ones along Duckworth and New Gower Streets. Little saddle-roof houses sprang up around old chimneys that were left standing, many cracked and unfit for use. The stage was being set for an even more spectacular holocaust.

Things were relatively quiet along the fire front for nearly ten years after the Great Fire of Forty-six. Then the sleeping giant awoke again, on 31 July 1855, about six o'clock in the evening, in a house on Pokeham Path. The newspapers commented that the fire took place in the western suburbs of the city.

A widow went out and left some children at home alone. They amused themselves by burning shavings that eventually caught fire to the house. The Phoenix and military engines responded with alacrity but they were ineffectual because of the dryness of the wood and the scarcity of water. In a very short time sixteen houses were consumed. The *Newfoundland Express* commented that "the Phoenix Company took the commonly viewed honourable position of supplying the military engine with water."

It was only necessary to wait six weeks for the next chapter in the city's flaming history. About seven o'clock on the evening of Tuesday, October 19, a fire broke out in the residence of a cooper named Summers, in an area of the city called Tarahan's Town. This was roughly that section between Gower Street and Queen's Road bounded by Prescott and Cathedral Streets. The name came from a local merchant who owned the property.

The Tarahan's Town fire began in the second or third house back, in a lane leading from Gower Street to Queen's Road. It spread quickly through the densely populated locality and the scarcity of water again doomed the efforts of volunteers and the military. In three to five hours the flames laid waste an area from the Congregational stone church on Queen's Road down Meetinghouse Hill (Chapel Street) to Gower Street, west to Cathedral Street and north to Garrison Hill. Both sides of Gower Street were in smouldering ruins and the backs of the houses on the eastern section of Queen's Road were singed. The Congregational Church was saved for another day. In all, five acres were levelled. One newspaper claimed that

3,600 were "turned out of their fetid dwellings" of which 240 were destroyed. Another paper said 400 families of 2,000 persons were left homeless. As in 1846, victims who were of the poorest classes were housed and fed in the nearby Orphan Asylum and Old Factory.

No sad songs were sung for the loss of what was termed this "disease retaining locality." All the newspapers claimed the fire to be a real blessing. The *Public Ledger*, after maligning the whole of Tarahan's Town, went so far as to say that "The stench emitted from the blazing mass offered full evidence of the filthy condition of the place." It was no secret that the calamity was especially appreciated by the nearby Church of England Cathedral congregation.

The city went to blazes twice in 1856. About 9:30 p.m. on July 21 flames came through the roof from the attic of a house owned by Mr. Kellond, a boot and shoe maker, who lived on the east side of Garrison Hill near Bond Street in a row of houses that had been spared in the Tarahan's Town fire. As the burning tongues licked up the range, the Phoenix and volunteer companies, aided by a detachment of Royal Newfoundland companies under Colonel Law, took part in a well-directed effort that saved the Church of England rectory and the Old Factory. The fire spread to the rear and to the eastwards of Kellond's destroying about twenty houses. This completed the work of the Tarahan's Town fire of the previous fall, so that almost nothing remained standing between Duckworth Street and Queen's Road.

Citizens had only to wait three months for the second 1856 spectacular. Between three and four o'clock on the morning of October 24 a bakery on New Gower Street, near William's Lane, was discovered on fire. The flames spread southwest to Adelaide Street while others jumped across and started up Theatre Hill. Thanks to the exertions of Bishop Mullock, who was routed from his bed, a house was pulled down on Theatre Hill, and that was credited with saving the town to the north and east. Charles Fox Bennett, with his engine, also rendered excellent service in another direction.

Though the various fire companies and the military, still under Colonel Law, did their best, they appear to have been seriously hampered for want of water. The *Times* claimed that there was also want of apparatus and organization, and that superabundant confusion was the order of the morning. J.J. Rogerson and Hugh Hoyles, whose life was at one time in imminent danger, were also said to have done yeoman service. The whole event seems to have been a sort of triumph, for the *Times* exulted that "the storming of Sebastopol scarcely eclipses the determined, unflinching and successful stand that was made. . . ."

The four to five-hour blaze had taken ninety houses and plunged numbers of people into great distress. Only about eight thousand pounds was carried in insurance on the lost property, less than half its value. The disaster had begun at Flaherty's property, which was to figure in another outbreak later. The collapse of a chimney in the ruins, November 17, claimed the lives of two young lads, Barron and Quigley.

The tragic conflagration which broke out on 16 September 1858 is known as the Apple Tree Well Fire. This well was on New Gower Street, between Pleasant and Casey Streets. On 13 May 1859 a child, Anastasia Raftus, drowned in the well and it was never used again. About seven o'clock on the September evening in question flames were seen issuing from Jonas Barter's stable, just above the well, on Pleasant Street. Within minutes the adjoining houses were on fire. The Phoenix and Royal Newfoundland companies responded immediately, with the Garrison engine, but the flames spread rapidly east and west, due to the shingles being dried out by a prolonged drought. Only by strenuous efforts were they prevented from crossing to the south side of New Gower Street.

In less than two hours, between forty and fifty houses, valued at five thousand pounds and insured at a little over one fifth of their value, were lost. Jonas Barter, owner of the hayloft where the outbreak began, had remained in his house rummaging for some important papers he wanted to save and was last seen trying to make his escape by a window. He fell backwards into the flames and his body was recovered next day from the ruins. Nothing was left standing between Lazy Bank and Flower Hill. The *Newfoundland Express* said in an editorial, "Within the past two years £15,000 have been lost by fire within a few hundred yards of the wooden district. . . ."

December, 1858, brought two more outbreaks. The first originated about 4:30 a.m. on December 4, in some soot which was thrown against a house in Georgestown (Hayward Avenue - Fleming Street area) after sweeping a chimney. A large group of people was rendered homeless in the seven or eight overcrowded tenements destroyed.

About 4:00 a.m. on the fourteenth an accident with a night light resulted in a house fire, in a range of shops and dwellings just west of Robert Alsop's premises at Steer's Cove. With winter beginning, the range was destroyed and twenty-five families left homeless.

A servant in the house of George Gear, on Monkstown Road, attempted to trim a camphene lamp after it had been lighted on the evening of 11 August 1859. The lamp blazed up suddenly and in minutes the house was in flames. The fire spread to the north and the intense heat ignited houses across the street. Besides the fire companies, men of British and French ships of war, then in port, fought the blaze. It was stopped by pulling down the house of Captain Haleran, the noted sealer, who has an impressive tombstone at Belvedere. Sixteen houses valued at five thousand pounds were destroyed.

A candle left burning on a bedroom table, when the family of a cooper on Henry Street, opposite Bell Street, retired for the night, caused an early morning blaze on 8 December 1859. The flames spread with terrible rapidity consuming much property before being brought under control. It was feared the old Roman Catholic chapel and Bishop's residence, on Star Hill, would go but the complex was saved by the efforts of the Phoenix and volunteer companies.

The newspaper *Patriot* felt there would have been a major disaster but for the fact that these companies were so quickly on the spot and there was plenty of water. On the other hand, the *Newfoundland Express* and the *Royal Gazette*, while stating that twenty houses were destroyed and fifty families homeless, commented on the usual scarcity of water. On 26 October 1860 in the very same area a fire which began in a cooperage destroyed five dwellings.

Garret Dooley had a house on the west side of Prescott Street, just above Bond Street. On 8 June 1862, at two o'clock in the morning, it burst into flame as the result of an accident. Nine houses were gutted in two hours and it was only with a great deal of exertion by the Phoenix and Cathedral brigades that the fire was prevented from crossing the street and also from extending to the houses on Queen's Road, at the back of the burnt-out area.

About 1:30 on the frosty morning of 17 January 1865 a house in the street west of the Parade Ground and leading to Freshwater Road was found to be on fire. The Phoenix and Cathedral brigades responded immediately to the fire bell, but because of the chronic scarcity of water on the higher levels they were unsuccessful in controlling the blaze until between fourteen and sixteen houses were consumed. One report had only twelve families homeless. Some insurance was carried on the lost property in what became known as the Cookstown fire.

Rags and such junk, stored in a rag depot between Hutching's Lane (now Street) and Bambrick Street off Water Street west, caused the major fire of 1866. It broke out about 1:00 a.m. on July 17 on Steven Street and leaped freely along to Hutching's Lane, due to a want of water from the six-inch pipe in the street. Eighteen or twenty dwellings housing fifty or sixty families were levelled and a number of blooming potato and cabbage gardens were destroyed. The whole of the area from Hutching's Lane to Bambrick Street was left in ruins. The *Morning Chronicle* raised a hue and cry to have such places as the rag depot banished from built-up sections of the community.

On August 25 that year a fire bell is said to have been erected on Duckworth Street near Cochrane Street. It was rung for the first time September 20 when a fire broke out on Pokeham Path east of the gasworks near Riverhead Convent. The *Newfoundland Express* reported that a major conflagration was averted by the Phoenix company and Cathedral brigade which were quickly on the scene and only ten tenements were consumed.

The Southside Hills were swept by fire from Blackhead Road almost to Fort Townshend on 25 August 1870. Powder was stored in a magazine cut into the base of the hills and it was feared that if this exploded the

whole of the growing city might be decimated. At great personal risk the
soldiers succeeded in removing the powder minutes before the flames
reached the magazine. Because of the thin soil on the hill the roots of the
trees were destroyed and the stands of spruce, fir, and birch never grew
back. This was a pity because they might have relieved the gruesome scars
of pipelines and oil tanks that a succession of City Councils allowed to per-
manently disfigure these impressive heights in the middle years of this
century without any compulsion on the oil companies involved to landscape or beautify.

A much burned-over area of New Gower Street was again visited by
its old enemy on 31 August 1875. The fire began in a stable at the rear of
Mr. Flaherty's property on New Gower Street, east of Adelaide Street.
Flaherty's, as we have seen, was where the major fire occurred in 1856.
This time the volunteer company and Mr. Carty, with a company of police,
got the blaze under control in two hours, but not until Flaherty's property—three cooperages, ten dwellings, and a number of stables and out-
buildings—were reduced to ashes. Only partial insurance was carried.
With this fire the preliminaries ended. All was now in readiness for the
main event.

Before examining the Great Fire of 1892 it is important to trace the
story of fire fighting in St. John's. The first brigade, The Society for the
Prevention of Fire, was organized in 1811, with Major James McBraire, a
local merchant, in command. The volunteers faced unbelievable hazards
and their work was often at the risk of their own lives. In 1822 Newman
Hoyles placed an advertisement in the newspapers asking for volunteers
for a brigade of which he became the captain. By 1824 there were two fire
engines in the town. One of these man-pulled wagons was at Fort Townshend. The Phoenix insurance people kept another at the wharf of Brown,
Hoyles & Morris. The town was divided into three wards: east, central, and
west. The volunteer force for the central ward was organized in 1826.

In 1835 the Chamber of Commerce wrote Governor Prescott, expressing regrets over the proposed removal of the military from Fort Townshend to Signal Hill. It was felt that their position at the Fort commanded
the town so that the military were generally the first to raise the alarm, and
their services in putting out fires were badly needed.

The most important of the volunteer forces was the brigade organized by the Phoenix Fire Office in 1846. Two new engines, promised in
January of that year by Mr. Broomfield, sat on a wharf in England awaiting
shipment, from April until mid-June, when they were finally sent out to
Newfoundland as freight on the *John & Mary*. Unfortunately, they had
arrived six weeks after the town had been reduced to cinders in the Great
Fire of 1846. The brigade was finally formed, on January 6 of the following
year, and it continued to fight fires in St. John's until it was disbanded in
1876. Another famous group, the Cathedral Fire Brigade, operated from
Power's Corner on Waldegrave and George Streets. It, too, was disbanded

in 1876. In December of that year, four months after the break-up of the volunteers, the Phoenix Fire Hall, at the foot of Long's Hill, burned to the ground. The fire bell for this hall, and for the town itself, was on a vacant lot on Henry Street, opposite the top of Bell's Shute, and it is thought to have given the Bell Street of our day its name.

The work of the Phoenix and Cathedral companies was taken over by the St. John's Volunteer Fire Brigade which came into being on 4 July 1877, with Frank Boggan as captain. It lasted until after the Great Fire of 1892 when a professional fire department was organized. In March 1895 John McCowen was appointed to head the constabulary and one of his first duties was to organize a fire department for the city. It was established by law on July 8 under the control of the head of constabulary. McCowen's force had 125 men consisting of one Chief Officer, three District Officers, nineteen regular firemen, and 102 reserve men.[13]

On 25 June 1895 the East End Fire Hall, on the former site of the Ordnance stables at the foot of Ordnance Street, was opened. The Central Fire Hall, opposite the driveway leading to St. Bonaventure's College, got its fire bell on September 1 of that year. The West End Fire Hall was opened at the eastern corner of New Gower and Bambrick Streets. In addition to these three stations the steamer *Favourite* was fitted up, at a cost of two hundred dollars, for use as a fire boat.

There were plans to test the men and equipment in a mock fire but this proved unnecessary when the furniture store of Callahan, Glass & Co., on the corner of Theatre Hill and Duckworth Street, caught fire at 5:30 on the afternoon of 17 July 1895. The four-storey building was saved "by the heroic manner in which [the firemen] worked in extinguishing the blaze." The *Evening Telegram* called it "the baptismal fire under the new regulations." Callahan, Glass & Co. was eventually completely gutted in a spectacular fire on Sunday morning, 10 June 1917.

Thirty-five Gamewell electric fire-alarm boxes were installed and the three halls were connected by telephone. The first steam engine arrived on July 18 but the horses had some years to go before being displaced by the gasoline engine. By the end of 1895 all three stations had a steam engine each, with thirteen horses to pull them. By 1896 the number of alarm boxes increased to forty-five and an extension ladder was acquired.

The first annual parade of the Constabulary and Fire Department was held on Thursday, 18 June 1896, arriving at Government House at 11:30 a.m., where Governor Murray and his daughter inspected the force. The flag adopted by Inspector General McGowen, as the official banner of the force, was handed over to the governor for safe keeping. It was a huge five-by-twelve-foot silk Newfoundland tri-colour of pink, white and green, edged all around with gold fringe. Until recent years this flag was on display at the Central Fire Hall but it has since disappeared.[14]

The Victoria-Cabot celebrations of 24 June 1897 were the occasion of spectacular displays by the firemen. During the day there was a parade and

636

on the following evening a torchlight procession of the constabulary and firemen which left the Central Fire Hall around 9:15 p.m., accompanied by three bands. The illuminations at the Central Station, which began at 8:30 p.m., attracted many thousands. About seven hundred candles and a blaze of gas lights formed a diamond and a crown with the letters "V.R." above the legend VICTORIA JUBILEE 1837-1897. Some six hundred candles were used in a similar display at the East End Fire Hall.

The building of the three fire stations in St. John's did not pass without critical comment. As recently as 1895 there were people writing to the press who felt that these halls were a monument to the incapacity and wanton waste of the Whiteway government. It seems incredible now that there could be any opposition to building fire stations in a city that had so frequently been devastated in whole or in part by fires.

During the Jubilee celebrations a decoration for courage was conferred on several fire constables as the result of a fire which broke out on board the steamer *Aurora* on 15 November 1895. The ship, which was moored at Bowring's southside premises, was tied up close to five hundred pounds of gunpowder and ten thousand rounds of ammunition. By their skill and courage the men brought the fire under control before it reached the explosives. Subsequently there were to be many tales told of the brave deeds of the firemen of St. John's.

The early summer of 1892 was extremely hot. The lack of rain had withered the grass and dried out the vegetables in gardens around the city. There was a plague of suburban brush fires and a few forest fires raged in Conception Bay. Their smoke hung over the city so that the air smelled of burning wood. By July 8 one of these fires, in the western suburbs, was causing some uneasiness because of rising winds. At two o'clock that Friday afternoon the temperature in the city was 87 degrees, in spite of a strong breeze that blinded the eyes with dust and covered the harbour with white caps.

About 4:30 in the afternoon the Reverend Moses Harvey was attending a distribution of prizes to the pupils of the General Protestant Academy, in the basement of St. Andrew's Church at the corner of Cathedral and Duckworth Streets. Henry O'Meara, a young Boston poet who was visiting the city of his birth, was preparing to take tea at the home of friends in the west end of the city. In the barn of Timothy O'Brien, at the junction of Freshwater and Pennywell Roads, one of his drivers, Tommy Fitzpatrick, stumbled as he went about his chores and the pipe on which he had been puffing fell from his mouth. Burning ash ignited some hay that was stored in the barn. There would normally have been no cause for alarm as a bucket of water could easily have extinguished the smouldering embers; however, they soon discovered there was no water to be had. The water supply to the city had been turned off that morning to permit the laying of new mains at Rawlins' Cross and, though it was turned back on at three o'clock that afternoon, it had not yet reached the higher levels.

There was a reservoir tank nearby but this had been emptied by the fire brigade in a practice drill a month previously and through someone's negligence had not been refilled.

The hay in the barn burned unchecked and soon the whole building was enveloped in flame. At five o'clock the fire bells rang in the fire hall near the foot of Long's Hill. By the time the horses and engines reached the scene the wind had carried the flames southward to the adjoining houses. Without water there was little the brigade could do but stand by helplessly and watch the wind carry the flames from house to house.

It was at five o'clock that the Reverend Mr. Harvey, who had left the meeting and was walking with his friend near the Parade Ground, noticed the glare of fire some distance beyond. Hastening to the spot he found three houses on fire. He remarked to his friend that it was a bad day for a fire as a high wind was blowing from the northwest hurling sparks on the roofs of the clustered wooden houses. The Long's Hill station firemen passed the cleric on their way to the fire.[15] The Bostonian also heard the fire bells as he took tea and had some misgivings because the wind was blowing fiercely.[16]

At the scene of the fire a call went out for volunteers, and though many townspeople responded they were just as helpless as the firemen. Soon half a dozen houses were in flames, then twenty. At the intersection of Harvey Road and Long's Hill the fire divided. One tongue licked westwards down Carter's Hill while the other started to the southeast down Long's Hill. The wind kept the fire from crossing Lime and Wickford Streets in the west so that it burned back over itself sparing the west end. In the east Long's Hill was becoming an inferno. The firemen were overpowered and their hoses burned.

The Reverend Moses Harvey saw the roof of the Methodist College on the north slope of the hill begin to smoke. In half an hour the college and the whole mass of buildings surrounding it were engulfed in a fiery torrent. Gower Street Methodist Church, the Orange Hall, Synod Hall, the schools of the Church of England, and the residence of Bishop Jones collapsed in flames. A ring of fire surrounded the Cathedral. The Bishop saved only what he was wearing and was seen to borrow a topcoat to protect him from the wind.

Lawyers rushed to their threatened offices, around the Court House, and managed to save most of their legal documents. Throngs of people living in the path of the blaze carried or wheeled their belongings to the open grounds in front of the Benevolent Irish Society on Queen's Road or the Anglican Cathedral churchyard. Confusion mounted almost to panic. Many who lived in parts of the town not threatened by the fire were hiring out their horses and carts to the less fortunate at exorbitant rates.

The O'Mearas from Boston saw, from the window of their host which overlooked the city, that it would be advisable to hasten to their hotel and rescue their luggage if it was to be saved. Their party of four, including a lady, hurried toward Water Street, remembering that their trunks were unpacked and on the third floor. When they arrived within a few hundred yards of the hotel (probably Knight's, halfway between Baird's and Job's Coves) the Court House, which was nearly opposite, was a sheet of flames, the woodwork flying in great flankers across the street. Looters were grabbing whatever they could get their hands on. Women were seen rolling barrels of pork along the crowded street as young girls ran past with bolts of yard goods tucked under their arms. Some merchants threw open their doors and let the crowds have whatever they could save.

The party from Boston found the door of their hotel blocked with the luggage of boarders who happened to be near enough to reach the place, and it was only with the utmost difficulty that they reached their rooms, now literally walled in by fire, a large store below them having burst out into roaring flames. Hastily thrusting their things into trunks and bags, they started over the stairs dragging what they could.[17] On reaching the street they were surprised to find it comparatively clear, the heat and the danger having driven away most of those whom they had encountered on their way up to their rooms.

Bishop Jones, to be on the safe side, was storing papers and documents in the crypt of the Church of England Cathedral, at the door of which policemen stood guard to make sure no ember got into the massive building. Almost unnoticed, however, the intense heat melted the lead around the panes of glass. Shortly after seven o'clock the huge oak rafters ignited under the slate roof and the Gothic masterpiece, erected at a cost of five hundred thousand dollars and just nearing completion, was soon a magnificent ruin. The beautifully moulded arches and massive pillars crumbled, and with a mighty crash the lofty roof fell in, the flames leaping hundreds of feet into the air.

Gower, Duckworth, and Water Streets blazed as the evening turned to darkness. Moses Harvey watched as St. Andrew's Church caught fire. In an incredibly short space of time nothing remained but the tower and blackened walls where, only a few hours before, he had witnessed the graduation exercises. Across the street desperate efforts were underway to save the Athenaeum. The handsome structure contained a lecture and concert hall, a library of seven thousand volumes, the Savings Bank, and the Surveyor General's office. It had been erected at a cost of sixty thousand dollars and was an institution in which the city took great pride.

Next door to the west, the Union Bank made a stout resistance. Protected by iron shutters, it escaped destruction. The Commercial Bank, opposite to the east, three doors west of Victoria Street, was gutted. The Market House fell before the common enemy at about the same time as the B.I.S. building on Queen's Road. The most strenuous efforts, by the Christian Brothers and a group of volunteers, could not keep it from joining the general conflagration. Those with goods piled on the B.I.S. and Anglican Cathedral grounds saw them turn into huge bonfires.

In Water Street the Boston visitors searched vainly for a man or boy whom they might impress into service. They could find none, as money was being too freely offered everywhere for aid. Finally, by dint of dragging and carrying, they got what they had with them along about a quarter of a mile or so and rested. Their host for the tea party, seeing one of his men in the crowd, hailed him, and a handcart and willing hands soon put them under their friend's roof with the greater part of their luggage saved. Those of the host's family who were familiar with the city were out all night helping to save property while the visitors stood at the window and gazed on the awful scene of destruction.

The Congregational Church on Queen's Road burned through neglect, while two houses just to the east, on the other side of the street, escaped untouched. A massive effort was made to save the fire hall at the top of King's Road. This met with success and resulted, as well, in saving the houses on the south side of Military Road.

By eight o'clock Water Street was an inferno. Bowring's premises, shops, stores, warehouse, and wharves were enveloped in sheets of flame. Goodfellow's, Ayre & Sons', Baird's, Baine Johnston's, Thorburn & Tessier's, Marshall & Roger's, and Job Brothers' disappeared one by one as Water Street was swept on both sides. The Reverend Moses Harvey watched as these tumbling buildings sent out flakes of fire and tornadoes of fiery particles. He began to think of his own house in Devon Row and through a suffocating atmosphere, laden with burning sparks and blinding smoke, wended his way homeward where he found the inhabitants of the Row packing their goods and preparing to remove them, as it was believed to be impossible to save the range of houses.

It was late in the evening by the time the fire started to eat its way through the handsome houses on the upper part of Cochrane Street. The west side above Bond Street did not catch but the east side was ablaze. Bishop Howley encouraged the crowd to tear down the house of Mrs. Kelligrews which stood next to the mansion of George Rendell at the top of the street. It was feared that if Rendell's went, the flames would cross the road to Government House and St. Thomas's Church. The Bishop himself hauled with the rest and the Kelligrews's home, which was already on fire, tumbled into the street. A few lengths of hose were found and attached to a hydrant but the water that came from them was little more than a dribble. Still the action of making the firebreak saved, not only the Rendell house, but all the buildings to the east on Military Road, Government House, and the church property on the north side of the street.

Meanwhile, back at Devon Row, Moses Harvey and the residents were doing all in their power to save their property. A strong force was assembled at No. 5, the house next to the fire. The roof was kept damp by wet blankets, and brooms in active service swept off the sparks as they fell in myriads onto the balconies. The house next to the Row blazed up and the red tongues of fire licked the gable end and mounted toward the roof.

The Reverend gentleman held his breath waiting for the final catastrophe. The roof of the burning house next door fell in and the flames began to collapse. With a sigh of relief the clergyman realized Devon Row was saved. It was half-past two o'clock in the morning.[18]

The railway station at Fort William was also saved, but buildings in Hoylestown were not so fortunate. The Mercy Convent, Bavarian Brewery, and the United States Consul's residence on Signal Hill were among the last buildings to burn. By the time the fire reached Walsh's Square the old St. George's Barracks, then being used as a fever hospital, were already a charred ruin as flying embers had caused them to burn much earlier. With nothing left to consume, the Great Fire of 1892 began to die down. It was nearly 5:30 o'clock in the morning.

A thick canopy of smoke hovered over what had been a city. Flames still tumbled about in the rosy expanse of ruins. The waters of the harbour were like a reflective pool of blood. Charred hulls of the *Sharpshooter, Dover, Huntress,* and a number of lesser vessels floated aimlessly. The *Nelly, Ethel, Prince Le Boo,* and other schooners that had caught fire were saved by moving them out into the stream. The stifling night air was alive with the sound of foundering walls and exploding charges of forgotten gunpowder. Brush fires, started by flying sparks, burned on the Southside Hills.

Few slept that night. The homeless were too heartsick, their helpers too weary, and the scavengers too excited. People wandered aimlessly until dawn. Moses Harvey heard the crying of weeping women as they hurried along with their children. It made his heart ache to see the groups of men, women and children, with weary blood-shot eyes, standing over their scraps of furniture and clothing. As he walked about he saw many asleep on the ground from utter exhaustion, their faces filled with despondency.

Never did such a pyrotechnic display meet the eyes of any of the Boston visitors. When daylight came they walked as far as they could to see the ruins and came within sight of their hotel. The end walls of stone and the chimneys were still standing and the coal was burning in the basement. All else had vanished. Overhead thick clouds of smoke hid the sun and it was some hours before it cleared.

Almost nothing remained standing from Signal Hill to Beck's Cove and north to LeMarchant, Harvey, and Military Roads. Few fires have so totally destroyed a North American city. The only comparable Canadian fire, excepting the Halifax explosion, is the one which destroyed Saint John, New Brunswick, 20 June 1877. While not so extensive, the Saint John disaster was far more tragic, costing a hundred lives.

The Bostonians planned to go to Harbour Grace by the ten-o'clock train. On their way to the Fort William depot the sights they saw were pitiful. The poor, with the commonest things in their hands, and those who were better off, with the choicest, were on the ruined streets, some having a definite object in view, some not knowing where to turn in the rubble. They heard acquaintances ask each other "Did you save anything?" and the answers were "Yes, my books," "What I have on," "Nothing."

At the railway station the visitors boarded the train, along with one hundred passengers bound for Harbour Grace, including a baby, six weeks old, in the care of a nurse and maid. They engaged the maid in conversation and she told them they had saved the wedding silver of two years ago, and little else. Before the train reached Topsail the passengers could see the country was all ablaze with forest fires. They spent the day dashing through gaps in the flames and then being forced to back up and wait hours until the track was clear. They were due in Harbour Grace at 3:30 in the afternoon but did not arrive until 1:30 the following morning. Even at that odd hour about a thousand people turned out to greet the soot and smoke-covered refugees.[19]

In St. John's the homeless filled the parks and open spaces. The military erected tent towns in Bannerman Park and on the north bank of Quidi Vidi Lake. Many hundreds had escaped with nothing but what they were wearing, and the problem of providing food and shelter was enormous. At least twelve thousand people had been burned out. As the citizens of the devastated city tried to pick up the broken threads of their lives that morning nobody paid much attention to the small vessel that arrived in port from England with a young doctor on board making his first visit to the island. His name was Wilfred Grenfell.

More than two thirds of the city, and by far the better portion and most important mercantile area, lay in ruins. This included nearly every law office and doctor's surgery. The newspapers *Herald, Times, Gazette, Advocate, Telegram,* and *Colonist* all lost their plants, and for most of them it was a fatal blow. All the principal churches were gone with the exception of the Roman Catholic Cathedral and the Methodist churches on George and Cochrane Streets. St. Thomas's Garrison Church, too, had been spared. The Atlantic, Central, Waverley, Knight's and Gordon Hotels as well as the Star, Temperance, British, Masonic, Victoria, Total Abstinence, and Mechanics' halls were charred rubble. Numerous factories, stores, warehouses, shops, wharves, and other business premises had been razed to the ground. Of the $20,000,000 worth of property that was lost, only $4,800,000 was covered by insurance. Nearly two thousand dwellings were consumed.[20]

The middle class were the greatest sufferers. Hundreds of families, from comfort and independence, were brought to penury, and had to begin life anew. The blow to St. John's affected the whole of the country, its trade and its industries. From all quarters liberal, generous, and sympathetic aid poured in. Most of the great cities of the United States and Canada sent help and many countries in Europe responded to the plea. Germany sent pianos which were to be sold for the benefit of the sufferers. In England the governor, Sir Terence O'Brien, who was on holiday with his wife at the time, cancelled all private engagements, and the two devoted themselves to raising relief money and supplies. Bishop Jones, who took ship to England immediately, aided in this appeal.

In spite of the enormity of the calamity only two lives were lost. These have been variously reported as a Miss Stevens and her maid, a daughter and the housemaid, or a mother and daughter. P.K. Devine, writing of the fire twenty years after the event, says the victims were Mrs. Stephenson and her niece who had stayed too long in their house on Victoria Street at the back of the Crosbie Hotel. Their attempt to save some possessions had cost them their lives. Devine also gives the final total for destruction at 1,572 private homes, 150 stores and shops, and 1,900 families burned out.

Timothy O'Brien, who owned the barn where the fire started, fired Tommy Fitzpatrick whose carelessness had wiped out his employer's property and most of the city with it. However, the crusty old Irish drayman was unrepentent. The *Royal Gazette* reported on July 29: "A discharged man-servant of Mr. T. Brien named Fitzpatrick was arrested this morning on suspicion of having cut out the horses tongues." It seems the rascally villain took revenge on his former master by an act of great brutality to O'Brien's horses.

In late August Judge Daniel Prowse laid the preliminary report of an investigation by him into the cause of the fire upon the table of the House of Assembly. The chief points were:

(1) That the tank near the place where the fire began had been emptied sometime before by Superintendent Dunn, and never completely refilled, (2) that the water was turned off on the 8th of July under the orders of Chairman Mitchell for the purpose of repairing pipes, and turned on again before the fire, but not long enough before to have filled the higher pipes by the time the fire began, (3) that the fire department was numerically insufficient to cope with the flames.

The report said its materials were old and rotten, and the whole fire service was half starved for supplies of implements of all kinds.

When rebuilding commenced, Water Street was widened even more and, with Duckworth Street, was straightened as much as possible. The old twisted roadways of the upper and lower paths disappeared forever. In their place stood modern streets of brick and stone. Some few new streets appeared and some old ones vanished. Duke of York Street, site of the first Government House, was gone. The place where it had been was intersected by a new street called York, connecting Cochrane and Wood Streets. With the removal of the ruins of the British Hall, in the middle of Prescott Street, it was possible to extend Darling Street to Cathedral Street. The entire length became known as Bond Street, named for Sir Robert Bond.

The brick and stone edict was enforced on Water Street but not, as it should have been, on Duckworth Street. Much of the city was quickly resurrected in rows of attached, wooden houses. People were anxious to get settled before the autumn cold set in. This hasty and often unsupervised reconstruction has been a headache to the City Council and fire department ever since. Nearly a hundred years after the fire many of these houses have now become firetrap slums and each year finds inhabitants burned to death as the old dwellings go up in flames. Some of the more elegant of the rebuilt houses, such as those on Church Hill, erected on the ruins of Scotland Row, a range of buildings similar to Devon Row, have given the city a pleasing and distinctive character.

St. John's has witnessed a number of less spectacular, though far more tragic fires, since 1892. On Wednesday, 11 September 1901, there was a $200,000 blaze at McAuley's cooperage on the Southside. Just after eight o'clock in the morning the water glass in the boiler burst. Benjamin Clarke, a man in his early fifties, was working on replacing it at 8:30 when the boiler exploded killing Clarke instantly. His eighteen-year-old son, Walter, who was working nearby, was the worst among several men who were severely injured by the blast. A ship's doctor from H.M.S. *Alert,* moored nearby, was immediately on the scene rendering assistance to the sufferers.

The fire spread from the cooperage to Job's seal oil store and for a time it was feared that the newly rebuilt city might be in danger. Eight hundred casks of oil were thrown into the harbour and this relieved the threat. By ten o'clock sparks, driven by the high wind, spread the fire to Prowse & Sons, Baine Johnston & Co., and to the store of Newfoundland Fish Industries. On the far side of the road eight dwellings, whose inhabitants had barely time to save themselves, were destroyed. Men from the H.M.S. *Alert* were put ashore with fixed bayonets to protect property from the eternal scourge of looters.

Parts of the cooperage boiler were discovered a hundred yards away. The steamers *Greenland, Iceland, Panther,* and *Vanguard* narrowly escaped destruction. They were towed away from the docks, where they had been moored, by a ship that was to face a tragic doom of her own, the S.S. *Southern Cross.* The decks of the threatened vessels were too hot to stand on. At 1:45 that afternoon the death toll from the fire reached two, when young Clarke passed away in terrible agony and still fully conscious.

At seven o'clock on the morning of 10 February 1948 a building on the southwest corner of Springdale and New Gower Streets was on fire. By the time the firemen got there the place was a mass of flames. What made this the second most tragic fire in St. John's history was the fact that the premises was being used as an infirmary and housed forty-three patients at the time. There were twenty-seven more in two adjoining structures.

In 1946 an inspector had recommended a fire escape be built at the back of the three-storey building. When the Council requested that this be done by the government, the Department of Public Health and Welfare replied: "As this Department neither owns, occupies or manages Hull Home we do not agree that any obligation is imposed upon us to make the alteration suggested."

Unfortunately for the inmates, the Department was right. The place was a private nursing home operated by a Mrs. Hull who gave her name to the institution. The City Council claimed it did not know the rented building was being occupied as a hospital and infirmary for the aged and infirm.

Nothing was done about installing the fire escape, so that when the Home was swept by fire few of the forty-three persons in the building at the time escaped. When flames blocked the narrow staircase the only way out was through the windows. One man was killed when he jumped from the third floor into New Gower Street and two women died in jumping at the rear, where the building was actually four storeys high. In all, thirty-three persons between the ages of twenty-two and ninety-one years lost their lives. Most of the victims were on the top flat where there were nine bedrooms containing two to five beds each. Though many of the bodies were burned, firemen said they believed the majority had suffocated before the flames reached them.

The morning was one of the coldest that winter. The water from the hoses froze almost as soon as it hit the building. The intense frost formed it into giant icicles. Great difficulty was found in moving the hoses about because they kept freezing to the street. Several fire fighters were treated for frostbite.

During World War II there were a number of fires in St. John's military installations. These were believed to have been the work of enemy agents. A barracks on Signal Hill was destroyed in a spectacular blaze, and on the night of 10 December 1942 a barracks was discovered on fire at Shamrock Field, the headquarters for the Newfoundland Home Defence force, at the east corner of Newton and Merrymeeting Roads. The quick thinking of one of the soldiers resulted in the blaze being immediately brought under control.

Two nights later, on Saturday, December 12, the temperature was a cold 14 degrees above zero. No light showed anywhere in the city because of the wartime blackout. The daily papers and radio stations advised property owners of the hours of blackout, which changed according to sunrise and sunset. That evening, anyone passing the Knights of Columbus Hostel on Harvey Road, at the west corner of the dirt road leading to Memorial University College and Fort Townshend, would have noticed an endless stream of servicemen and their girlfriends climbing the steps of the large two-storey building to attend the regular Saturday night broadcast of Barry Hope's "The Barn Dance," about to take place on the stage in the auditorium.

It had been a rather eventful week in some ways. Besides the apparent sabotage at Shamrock Field, Ellen Carroll of North River, Conception Bay, had passed away at the age of 115, being the oldest person in the British Empire. On Tuesday, everyone was shocked to hear that shortly after midnight on Monday a prominent businessman was knocked unconscious with a bottle by two naval ratings on Monkstown Road. A rape was attempted on his wife. By Saturday the excitement was over and the hapless lady was recovering. In homes throughout the city, families settled back to listen to "The Barn Dance" from the K. of C. Hostel, on radio station VOCM.

The audience in the crowded auditorium was fully enjoying the show. About ten minutes past eleven, Edward Adams, a Canadian soldier, was standing at the microphone singing "Moonlight Trail." He was halfway through the song when listeners to VOCM heard a woman's shrill cries of "Fire! Fire! Fire!" This was followed by a commotion and shouts of "Keep quiet!" At that moment the broadcast went dead. A musical fill was substituted. At the radio station on Parade Street, just west of the hostel, the horrified staff continued to listen to the screams and shouts coming over the line.

The nearly five hundred people who were in the hostel saw flames suddenly breaking out everywhere. Panic seized many in the auditorium as they rushed for the exits. The lights flickered and went out, as tongues of fire swept overhead catching alight the paper streamers that fell on the heads of those underneath igniting the hair of many. To the horror of those being pushed against some of the exits it was found that they opened inwards.

There was a manually operated traffic light at Rawlin's Cross. Located in the middle of the intersection, with KEEP LEFT painted on it, this was the only traffic light in the city. The policeman who was on duty operating the light noticed a glow in the sky and 'phoned the fire department from his little sentry box on the southwest corner. He did not know where the fire was located. According to his watch it was five minutes past eleven o'clock.

The first alarm was rung in at 11:17 and it took the firemen one minute to respond from two hundred yards away. When they reached the scene the building was already doomed and the intense heat prevented all hope of rescuing the trapped. All the firemen could do was try and save the Church Lad's Brigade Armoury to the west and Catholic Cadet Corps Armoury to the east. Both buildings were on fire but the flames were extinguished before much damage resulted.

Forms could be seen to appear at window openings in the awful inferno only to drop from sight. Many who managed to escape were burning torches. Some of the locked doors were smashed down and a handful of people were pulled to safety before the heat drove the rescuers away. There were a number of fine acts of heroism. A Chinese was dragged out by two servicemen, at great personal risk, only to find that he was already dead. When the policemen got back to barracks their greatcoats were frozen so stiff with water that they stood by themselves on the floor.

In little more than forty-five minutes the disaster was almost over. By midnight the first bodies were brought out and laid on the floor of the C.C.C. armoury, on the east side of the dirt road by the K. of C. Hostel. The old building had been used by the Catholic Cadet Corps as a drill hall before the corps became defunct. The terrible task of carrying out the dead went on until four o'clock in the morning. All day Sunday a parade of friends and relatives viewed the corpses in an effort to identify the remains of charred victims. The smoking ruins had claimed ninety-nine lives and a hundred and seven were injured by flame and glass. Only nine remained unidentified. On December 15 the final toll was given as one hundred dead. Next day the hostel would have celebrated its first birthday.

Pipers and military brass bands played mournful music as thirty-five members of the armed forces were buried in a mass grave at the General Protestant Cemetery on Waterford Bridge Road and another nine were interred at Mount Carmel Cemetery on the Boulevard. The flag-draped coffins of sixteen airmen were paraded from Torbay Airport to the railway station and taken by train to Gander for burial.

In the report of the inquiry conducted into the tragedy by Sir Brian Dunfield a number of building and operational blunders were found to have led to the awful loss of life. Dunfield guardedly concluded that the fire was of "incendiary origin," possibly "a case of sabotage." The phrase "enemy agent" was also used.[21] It was thought that about 10:30 p.m. someone had set a match to a trail of toilet paper in a storage cupboard on the second floor leading to the lofts. This could have caused the open attic of the building to become a ball of flame so that when the fire was discovered it seemed to be breaking out everywhere within minutes. According to the evidence the blaze was first noticed at 11:10 p.m. by a soldier who went to the cupboard to get some bed linen. The watch of the policemen on Rawlin's Cross might have been slow.

The theory of sabotage was given substance later when the lofts of the Red Triangle, a Y.M.C.A. Hostel on Water Street, opposite Alexander Street, and similar in structure to the Knights of Columbus Hostel, were said to have been found strewn with oil-soaked toilet paper during an inspection before a Saturday night dance. The Y.M.C.A. stood only yards away from the large storage tanks used by the gas works.

To this day the Knights of Columbus Hostel fire at St. John's, in the early days of World War II, still ranks as the greatest indoor fire disaster in Canadian history.

5

Of Blossoms, Birds and Bowers

This sketch of Upper Long Pond (now Long Pond) was drawn from Mt. Scio Road in 1831 by Oldfield. Behind the house on the far shore what is now Allandale Road leads towards the town. Government House can be seen in the distance standing in the Narrows. Behind the scene of this sketch were the Queen Victoria Hills. (Courtesy St. John's City Hall.)

651

This detail from a drawing by W. R. Best shows Military Road looking west from Government House around 1850. In the centre is the hothouse of the Botanical Garden in what is now Bannerman Park. Notice also the tower of the old Mercy Convent in front of the Basilica. (Courtesy Public Archives of Canada.)

652

This photograph taken around 1875 shows Soldiers Meadow at the junction of Ordnance Street, Gower Street, and King's Bridge Road. The trees were planted in 1864. Today it is known as Cavendish Square. Fort William barracks, to the left, on the site of Hotel Newfoundland, was sold by auction 22 August 1883 and torn down within ten days. Devon Row, in the background, constructed by the Southcott Brothers for James and Hannah Martin in the early 1870s, still stands.

653

The General Protestant Cemetery was promised by Governor LeMarchant in 1849. It opened May 25 of that year in a field opposite Syme's Bridge. This photograph taken in the 1880s shows the cemetery on the right with the road to Syme's bridge below it. The Waterford River meanders along the bottom of the picture. The cemetery later spread west along Waterford Bridge Road taking in the meadow in the centre of the photograph. (Courtesy Newfoundland Provincial Archives.)

654

This painting by J. W. Hayward re-creates the mummers parades of the early 1850s. While fools cavort in fancy costumes along Duckworth Street, sealers block the foot of Victoria Street with a woodpile. It was woodhauls such as this that led to the creation of Newfoundland's traditional pink, white, and green flag. On the right is the newspaper office of the *Courier*. The Scotch Free Kirk stands west of the Commercial Bank on the left. (Courtesy Newfoundland Provincial Archives.)

655

This arch of spruce boughs (note the men on top) was erected at the foot of Patrick Street to welcome Archbishop Hughes of New York when he went to Riverhead to lay the cornerstone for St. Patrick's Church in 1855. The Marine Parade is on the right. The line of trees in the centre was planted in 1847. Many of them still stand along the sides of the railway tracks which obliterated the shallows and beautiful promenade. (Courtesy Roman Catholic Episcopal Corporation.)

656

A historic moment in world aviation. This is thought to be the only photograph in existence of the take-off of Hawker and Grieve's Sopwith aeroplane "Atlantic" from Glendenning's Farm, Mount Pearl, 18 May 1919. They were forced down at sea 1050 miles out from Newfoundland. Glendenning's Farm was originally the home of Sir James Pearl. (Courtesy Agnes Simms.)

Sir Edgar Bowring was born on Mt. Scio farm, St. John's, 17 August 1858. Married to Flora Munn Clift, he serves as a member of the Newfoundland Legislature as well as a director of Bowring's and as Newfoundland's Trade Commissioner in London. He donated Bowring Park to the City of St. John's.

Rudolph Cochius, born in Arnhem, Holland, 2 January 1880, joined a firm of landscape architects in Montreal in 1911. From 1912 to 1917 he was engaged in laying out Bowring Park, St. John's. From 1922 to 1925 he worked on the Newfoundland War Memorial Parks in France at Beaumont Hamel, Monchy-le-Preux, Gueudecourt, Masniéries, and Courtrai. He settled in Newfoundland in 1925.

On this stage in the Casino Theatre (circa 1900) the "Ode to Newfoundland" was performed for the first time by a visiting actress, Frances (Daisy) Foster, 20 January 1902. The song was performed again, in the author's presence. May 2 when Miss Carroll, robed in pink, white, and green stood on a pedestal on stage to represent Terra Nova. (Courtesy Newfoundland Provincial Archives.)

659

Sir Cavendish Boyle was a whimsical and poetic Governor of Newfoundland from 1901 to 1904. He gave local hockey the Boyle Trophy and the colony its national anthem, "Ode to Newfoundland," set to music by his friend Sir Hubert Parry.

Professor David Bennett was the Sousa of Newfoundland. His various bands played for every important event for half a century including the Roman Catholic Cathedral fencing, laying the Atlantic cable, and the first train excursion. He was Professor of Music at St. Bonaventure's College. (Courtesy Centre for Newfoundland Studies, MUD.)

Pleasantville on the shores of Quidi Vidi Lake was a quiet place for picnics and sports activities. With the outbreak of World War I in 1914 it became a military camp. This is tent No. 1 at Pleasantville and the first men to enlist in the famed Blue Puttees. Standing (left to right) Walter Janes, John Thompson, Neil Patrick, Michael Sears, John Long. Seated (left to right) James Irvine, Ralph Andrews, George Langmead (killed 1917), James Carter, Roland Williams.

The Newfoundland War Memorial stands on Haymarket Square at King's Beach. On 16 July 1943 Edgar Bergen and Charlie McCarthy paused on the steps of the monument to purchase a tag from a servicewoman. Beside the dynamic duo above, such stars as Frank Sinatra, Joan Blondell, and Phil Silvers found their way to St. John's to entertain U.S. servicemen during World War II. M. J. O'Brien's grocery in the background burned down in 1975. It was formerly Billy Bearn's.

An area between Pine Bud Avenue and Long Pond Road, known as Carpasian Park, became Camp Alexander in 1941 when the United States Army constructed a temporary military camp on the site while awaiting completion of Fort Pepperrell. The boardwalk-lined path stretching south towards Pine Bud Avenue and the Basilica is now Sycamore Street. Piled in the path are birch junks for burning in camp stoves. (Courtesy Leslie Simms.)

Of Blossoms, Birds and Bowers

I sing of brooks, of blossoms, birds, and bowers
Of April, May, of June, of July flowers.
　　　　　　　ROBERT HERRICK *Hesperides (1648)*

The first bower to be sung of in St. John's is that described by Edward Hayes, the captain of the *Golden Hind*, the only one of the five ships in Sir Humphrey Gilbert's ill-fated 1583 expedition to North America to complete the whole voyage safely. In his narrative of the adventure Hayes speaks of the hospitality extended to Sir Humphrey by the merchants of St. John's who presented them with "Wines, marmalades, most fine rusk or biscuits, sweet oils and sundry delicacies; also we wanted not of fresh salmons, trouts, lobsters and other fresh fish brought daily unto us."[1] Later in the discourse he adds:

> The next morning being Sunday and the 4 of August, the Generall and his company were brought on land by the English merchants, who shewed us their accustomed walks unto a place they called the Garden. But nothing appeared more than Nature it selfe without art: who confusedly hath brought foorth roses abundantly, wilde, but odoriferous, and to sense very comfortable. Also the like plentie of raspis berries, which doe grow in every place.[2]

Most likely we shall never know the location of "the garden." Judge Prowse says it was probably somewhere around Cherry Garden, a glade between Waterford Bridge Road and the river, just west of Syme's Bridge. Sunday, 13 June 1886, about three-thirty in the morning, a fire broke out in the cottage of the late Captain Richard Rhodes which the newspapers reported was on the former site of the Cherry Garden on Waterford Bridge Road at the foot of Cherry Garden Hill. It is unlikely there was even a footpath to this area in Gilbert's time, let alone a cultivated garden.

Stephen Parmenius of Buda, a Hungarian poet drowned on the Gilbert voyage, seems to confirm this in a letter to Richard Hakluyt, Master of Arts and Philosophy, Christ Church College, Oxford.

The whole terrain is hilly and forested: The trees are for the most

665

part pine. Some of these are growing old and others are just coming to maturity, but the majority have fallen with age, thus obstructing a good view of the land and the passage of travellers, so that no advance can be made anywhere.[3]

If it were possible to walk a mile or more along the Waterford River, Parmenius is unlikely to have said *no* advance could be made *anywhere.* In a harbour devoid of houses, where only the beach was occupied, "the garden" was probably a place of relaxation not very far from the ships. Flower Hill, near City Hall, the traditional site of an ancient flower garden, seems a much more likely spot than Waterford Bridge Road.

Parmenius adds: "We made representations to the admiral to burn the forests down, to clear an open space for surveying the area; nor was he averse to the idea, if it had not seemed likely to bring considerable disadvantage." The poet also said, of the area around St. John's harbour: "All the grass is tall, but scarcely any different from ours. Nature seems even to want to struggle towards producing corn. . . . There are blackberries in the woods, or rather very sweet strawberries growing on bushes."[4]

The Colonial Records for 1751 tell of a strawberry field on the marsh near where the Colonial Building now stands. On the afternoon of July 8 three soldiers from Fort William, Philip Coffee, Michael Ryann, and William Fielding, were strolling over the terrain when they chanced upon Ann Moore, a widow; Katherine Wheyland, "of full age"; and Moore's servant Elizabeth Melville, who had been berrypicking. The soldiers asked the ladies if the berries were thick, then, "not having God before their eyes but being moved and seduced by the instigation of the devil on the 8th day of July in the woods near St. John's," they committed a rape upon the body of "Elizabeth Melville of the age of 17 years then and there being in the peace of God." It appears that Ann Moore, described by Fielding as an "old bitch," and her friend Katherine dropped their baskets of strawberries and fled towards the town, leaving poor Elizabeth to struggle alone, for her virtue, in the clutches of the trio. At their trial Coffee was released for want of evidence, Ryann was found not guilty, but Fielding was pronounced guilty and sentenced to hang.[5]

Could the scene of the strawberry rape have been the merchants' bower of nearly two hundred years earlier? The words strawberry and raspberry were often interchangeable and it is not impossible that a small footpath led up along the banks of the river that became King's Road to the strawberry field near Military Road.

A bower of loveliness was created in St. John's around 1811 when an officer of the garrison erected a small grotto on Signal Hill. Anspach tells us it was "fitted up and ornamented with considerable ingenuity and taste, provided with a table in the center and seats around. Above the entrance, low and narrow, was the following inscription 'Pro Amico', and in another place, 'Ne Vile Fano'." A brother officer, inspired by the grotto, rhapsodized in a poem to the *Newfoundland Gazette*, January 1812:

> But in that happy spot we ever find
> The soulful joys that elevate the mind.

In 1813 Governor Keats wrote that St. John's had grown into a large commercial town of ten thousand inhabitants. His Excellency remarked: "The environs of the town, the natural beauties of which are very striking, present to view several neat, well cultivated and productive farms."[6] A military officer who published a book in 1867 found it far less agreeable. He complained there was "not a sign of a monument or ornamental fountain, or anything else to denote a love of country existed. No athenaeum, rink or library; no greenhouses, conservatories or parks, only the bare, cold, unappealing necessities of life." Back in 1817 there had been a movement to erect a Martello Tower on Signal Hill but construction was stopped by orders of the Ordnance Board that no new works be carried on.

The claim of the military officer that the town contained no greenhouses, conservatories, or parks seems to indicate that the Botanical Garden had become a thing of the past by 1867. Back in 1847 William Thomas and John Stuart surrendered title to a parcel of land on the north side of Military Road which was granted for an ornamental garden under the direction of a committee not exceeding five persons. The plot was not quite big enough for the proposed Botanical garden. The adjoining property, which was owned by Governor Bannerman, was therefore added to the original parcel by "Yielding and paying therefore . . . the yearly rent of sum of one shilling lawful money of our United Kingdom on the second day of September in each year." The grant was made to William Lahey, 23 July 1847.

As proprietor of the Botanical Garden, Mr. Lahey offered subscriptions to private families at twenty shillings. The single rate was ten shillings and nonsubscribers paid one shilling and threepence per visit. The garden opened on 1 October 1847 and the newspaper *Patriot* observed: "Floral beauty and music combine to invite a visit and they compose a voluptuous treat nowhere else to be found in the city or suburbs." The garden was open from 6:00 a.m. to 7:30 p.m., and Colonel Law permitted the garrison band to attend on Tuesday afternoons at three o'clock. Lahey supplied bouquets to subscribers for one shilling threepence. Others paid two shillings sixpence. He also took in plants to board in the hothouses during the winter months and promised replacement if they died before spring. Nonsubscribers were unable to enjoy the "voluptuous treat" from the roadway, for the whole was enclosed by a board fence about seven and a half feet high.

The Botanical Garden seems to have lasted nearly twenty years. A more public place of recreation which came into being that same year was the Marine Parade or the Promenade. When it was announced that it was intended to turn the parcel of land skirting the harbour above Job's (Long) Bridge into a promenade, petitions were drawn up by the fishermen of the area not to divert this public beach from its original purpose. They complained of having nowhere to haul up their boats should the beach be converted to a parade. The petition was lost and a grassy bank was built along the shore of the river mouth from Hutchings Street to the Parsley Garden, opposite Alexander Street. Trees were eventually planted along the Promenade. The area has long since been swallowed by railway tracks and sheds, and the wide expanse of water from the edge of Water Street to the foot of the Southside Hills has dwindled to a small, polluted brook.

In summer the quality of the town sailed their boats along the steep embankment on the north side of the Marine Parade while their social inferiors looked on with mute envy from the shore. In winter the area became a gigantic open-air skating rink, and on frosty nights thousands would gather there by moonlight to try their skill on skates. All that remains today to mark the shores of the Marine Parade are the giant trees which line the south side of Water Street between Long Bridge and Patrick Street.

The beauty bug seems to have been quite virulent in 1847. That was also the year in which the town got its first public fountain. Erected of stone, it was "on New Gower near the streamlet which divides the properties of Holdsworth and Cuddihy." This would be somewhere between our present Holdsworth and Adelaide Streets. There is no record of the fate of this ornamental fountain.

The property next to the hothouse was in the possession of the Native Society. On 24 May 1845 Governor Harvey laid the cornerstone for the society's hall near the present bandstand in Bannerman Park. The hall blew down in a wind storm on September 19 the following year, killing a boy, aged five, and his sister, aged twenty, victims of the Great Fire who were sheltering there. Three others were injured.

The *Times* noted on 9 April 1864:

> Land heretofore occupied by the Native Society and lately surrendered by that body to the government, as also the adjoining grounds used as a Botanical Garden, not being sufficient for the contemplated Public Park, His Excellency, Sir Alexander Bannerman, has consented to add thereto a portion of land (and private property of the governor for the time being) situate on the South side of the Circular Road, which will give "Ample field and scope enough" for the much desired park—for the establishment of which an act had passed the Legislature. A finer or more commanding site could not well be chosen and we doubt not it will tend to promote the health and comfort of the inhabitants as expressed in the Act before us.

Four days later, on April 13, Governor Bannerman gave assent to the Act to establish a public park in St. John's. However, on the sixth, the Attorney General had already announced that the park must be deferred for want of money. The *Newfoundlander* moaned: "They have yet to wait awhile all those who were excited by the thought of the salubrious air and green trees and ramblings over pleasant walks. . . ." Then it complained of a "perverse misdirection of activity which aims first at establishing a place of recreation and amusement, while the health and comfort of the inhabitants were ignored in the poisonously filthy state of the whole town."

The "salubrious air and green trees" were a long time in coming. As the years went slowly by with no park in sight, the Victoria Rink was built on the Military Road site in the late 1860s. It proved so popular that the Avalon Rink was built next to it a few years later, and opened in 1870. In 1872 the Victoria Rink became known as the Exhibition Hall when Archdeacon Edward Botwood promoted a great exhibition and sale to pay off a debt on St. Mary's (Southside) of which he was incumbent. Shops were closed for the day to celebrate the event. Bishop Feild was heard to admonish the Archdeacon, "Edward, be sure and give change." These skaters' palaces were burned to the ground on the same night in 1878.

On Saturday, 25 August 1883, a lumberyard on the north side of Military Road, "being the South West corner of Bannerman Park," was leased by public auction. It is the first notice that the name Bannerman Park had come into use, even if there was no park. In 1888 the first Municipal Council of St. John's assumed liability of ten thousand dollars for developing Bannerman Park and another park on the site of the old St. John's Hospital, on Water Street West, to be known as Victoria Park.

The date given for the official opening of Bannerman Park is 1 September 1891. However, the following item in the *Evening Herald,* for August 19, seems to indicate this particular sylvan refuge was already in business.

> Professor Bennett's Band attracted an immense crowd to Bannerman Park last night. The night was gloriously fine and bright, but a great disappointment fell upon every person present when, about half-past eight, the band left the park. . . . If the Municipal Council could not afford to pay them until 10 o'clock, it would have been better had its members left the matter alone . . . it was a shabby trick . . . in no other part of the world are parks conducted on such miserly warm water principles.

The yearly rent of "one shilling lawful money" which William Lahey of the Botanical Gardens yielded to the governor became eighty dollars after His Excellency added his private property on the south side of Circular Road to the growing park site. This added another ten acres to the original lots.

At first, when the parkland was in the hands of the Surveyor General, it was his duty to see that the governor received his yearly rental fee. What the early landlords did with their eighty dollars nobody knows. It was theirs to dispose of as they wished. In 1917 Sir W.E. Davidson informed the civic authorities, who had assumed the Surveyor General's responsibility for seeing that the rent was paid after the City Council was established, "I intend to utilize this in preparing land in the government house grounds for potato allotments."

His Excellency later abandoned the lowly spud and informed Council he wished to devote the eighty dollars to ". . . the possession of such permanent improvements to Bannerman Park which might suggest themselves to you." The City Fathers came back with the suggestion that "a bubble fountain for drinking purposes" would be an ideal improvement, and so it is there to this day, just east of the bandstand. With no further suggestion from the Council, Governor Davidson diverted the money toward the landscaping of the Government House grounds establishing a traditional way of spending the rental fee which has continued to this day. A greenhouse was built at Government House in 1849.

The City of St. John's owns Bannerman Park. There is no reason other than tradition for the Council to continue paying rent to the governor on property it owns. When the park finally opened in 1891 it was named for Governor Bannerman in gratitude for his generous gift of land and "vested in Her Majesty [Queen Victoria], her heirs, and successors . . . set apart, dedicated and appropriated for the sole use and purpose of a public park for the use and accommodation of the inhabitants of St. John's and all others resorting to the same." The following year hundreds of tents and other temporary dwellings were erected in the park to shelter refugees from the Great Fire of 1892.

In time Bannerman Park acquired a monument to Father Morris, a Roman Catholic priest who founded Newfoundland's first orphanage, St. Thomas Court, located at Villa Nova in Manuels. He was also the founder and editor of a magazine called *The Orphan's Friend* which had a circulation of twelve thousand. The orphanage was begun in 1880 when Father Morris was twenty-eight years old. He was a brother of Sir Edward Morris, the Newfoundland Prime Minister. In April 1889 a typhoid epidemic broke out and spread to St. Thomas Court. While nursing the stricken boys, the priest contracted the disease and died on the first of August.

His monument consists of a dado of rough, native granite, with a shaft about ten feet high surmounted by a bust of Father Morris. The inscription states that the monument was erected to his memory by the people of Newfoundland. Nearby, in front of Government House, opposite the top of Cochrane Street, there is a monument to another self-sacrificing citizen. It commemorates the death by drowning on Boxing

Day, 26 December 1869, of twenty-three-year-old Weston Carter, a son of Judge Carter. Young Carter drowned in Deadman's Pond on Signal Hill while vainly trying to save the lives of two girls, named Brewin and Martin, who had fallen through the ice. His funeral on December 29 was attended by thousands.

As indicated, Victoria Park on Water Street West was developed and opened about the same time as Bannerman Park. In 1888 the St. John's Hospital, which stood on the site, was abandoned and the following year was burned to the ground as a possible health hazard. Victoria Park also sported a bandstand and a monument. A fifteen-foot high stone goblet, mounted on a pedestal ornamented by two metal lion heads, was erected to honour Moses Monroe, a local philanthropist. It was originally a fountain, with water from the lion heads pouring into a shallow dish. The inscription reads: "1897. In Memoriam Moses Monroe. Erected by voluntary subscriptions of all classes and denominations in the island, in token of the respect and esteem with which they cherish his memory."

Beyond Victoria Park, in the western suburbs, a beauty spot named Bowring Park was laid out in 1911, rather like an English public garden. The property was donated to the city by Sir Edgar Bowring to mark the centenary of the firm of Bowring Brothers in Newfoundland and was officially opened on 14 July 1914 by H.R.H., Prince Arthur, Duke of Connaught, while on a visit to St. John's. The Duke was a very much younger brother of King Edward VII and uncle of the then monarch, King George V. The Royal Duke's opening of the park is commemorated by a plaque under a tree which he planted not far from the main entrance. The Connaught Stone, which holds the plaque, was originally the cornerstone for a sanitarium which was to be built on the nearby Squires property. Sir Richard Squires later used it as a headstone for his dog. All that can be read of the dog's inscription today is "Humber _____ 192_, — 1936."

The original fifty acres were laid out by a Dutch landscape expert named Rudolph H.K. Cochius. He planned a botanists' haven containing many hundreds of species of trees, shrubs, and flowers. Sir Edgar Bowring added to the trees in 1921 by planting an oak to officially mark the deeding of the place to the St. John's City Council. In 1952 the Council erected a sundial to the memory of the great benefactor.[7]

Two rivers run through the park. The one on the north side, originally called the North River and which flowed all the way to the harbour, is now the Big Castor River, while the original South River is known as the Little Castor. When these two waterways leave the park, they become the Waterford River, a name which came into use around 1834. The area of Brookfield, located between the two rivers, is quite large and was once called the Island. On the death of James Brian, the original owner of Brookfield, the estate was sold in July 1858. Being a very desirable location, the area was occupied by many prominent citizens down through the years. Land on both banks of the Waterford River, below the bridge at

Kilbride Church, was once the property of Captain David Buchan, and it was he who opened the road along the south shore.

On entering Bowring Park there is a Y intersection. From this Y, traffic turns right along the banks of the Big Castor River. On the left is the tree planted by the Duke of Connaught. Beyond the Connaught Stone, on the right side of the road, is the Caribou monument, partly hidden in a copse of trees. This bronze animal was designed by Basil Gotta for the Newfoundland park at Beaumont Hammel in France. It was near that little French village that all but sixty-eight members of the Royal Newfoundland Regiment were wiped out or wounded in a foolhardy charge against the German lines, 1 July 1916. A decision to cancel the attack had already been made, but it did not reach the trenches in time. The copy of the caribou in Bowring Park was presented by Major William Howe Green, O.B.E., a cousin of Sir Edgar Bowring, as a tribute to the Regiment. The caribou was the national animal of Newfoundland. The monument was unveiled Memorial Day, 1 July 1928, by Mayor Tasker Cook. A cross at the base lists the names of battles in which Newfoundlanders fought and died, such as Suvla, Gueudecourt, Armentiers, and Passchendaele.

Beyond the green, in front of the bungalow, there is a famous statue known as the Fighting Newfoundlander. This sculpture, showing a soldier of the Newfoundland Regiment about to throw a hand grenade, was a gift to the city from Sir Edgar Bowring and presented to the undying memory of the Regiment. The fifteen-foot memorial was unveiled on 13 September 1922 by Sir William Horwood. The work, also executed by Basil Gotta and posed for by a member of the Regiment, Corporal Thomas Pittman, was featured on a stamp of the Dominion of Newfoundland.

Peter Pan, that whimsical creation of Sir James Barrie, who has become the symbol of eternal youth, is the figure atop a monument near the lake, inside the main gate. A fairy on the monument is seen gazing at an engraved name, Betty Munn. Elsewhere on the statue an inscription reads: "In memory of a little girl who loved the park." Betty Munn was the daughter of a well-known St. John's and Harbour Grace commercial family and godchild of Sir Edgar Bowring. On 23 February 1918 the girl and her father left St. John's for a visit to Betty's mother, who was receiving medical treatment in New York. They had booked passage and sailed on board the S.S. *Florizel*, a ship of Bowring's Shakespear fleet. Early next morning the vessel went ashore on the reefs off Cappahaydn. Nearly one hundred people lost their lives in the tragedy, including Betty Munn.[8]

The death of his beloved godchild greatly upset Sir Edgar and he determined to erect a monument to her memory in the park. An approach was made to Sir George Frampton who agreed to make available a copy of his famous "Peter Pan." The statue was unveiled by the sculptor, 29 August 1925.

Sir George Frampton, R.A., a world-famous sculptor, had created the original Peter Pan statue for Kensington Gardens, London, and copies were made by him for Brussels, Melbourne, Toronto, and Bowring Park. The erection of the St. John's statue was personally supervised by Sir George on a site which he selected, at the same time expressing the feeling that the Bowring Park setting was more appealing than the one in Kensington Gardens.[9] It is interesting to note that in Barrie's immortal play, *Peter Pan*, Wendy and Peter had a big Newfoundland dog named Nana.

In recent years the park has been expanded by acquiring the adjoining property to the west known as "Midstream," once the estate of Sir Richard Squires, the controversial Prime Minister of Newfoundland from 1919 to 1923 and from 1928 to 1932. All that is left of "Midstream" are the fire-gutted ruins of the former summer residence of the Prime Minister. The charming two-storey house was already a victim of neglect and public apathy when vandals set it ablaze on 23 October 1971. Four different fires appear to have been deliberately set in the bungalow at the same time, destroying stairways, walls and kitchen.[10] The major damage was done by one at the rear which started in the bathroom in the basement.

Signal Hill, a natural lookout which commands the approaches to St. John's Harbour, is the site of Signal Hill National Historic Park, covering 243 acres. The second largest National Historic Park in Canada, it was created by the federal government in May 1958. A complete restoration of its many fortifications will take years to complete.

The park begins at Deadman's Pond. Above this pond there is a high tor visible from anywhere in the harbour or along the waterfront. Known for years as the Crow's Nest, it later became notorious as Gibbet Hill. A gun battery built atop the knoll in 1696 was replaced by a gibbet in 1750, and the device seems to have been kept in fairly constant use for the next half-century. Any miscreant hanging in chains from one of the projecting arms of the gallows would be clearly visible to sailors and fishermen on ships below in the harbour. It was hoped this example would deter them from other felonies.

In his journal the young English sailor, Aaron Thomas, wrote in 1794 of a walk to Quidi Vidi on a day when: "The sun was transcendently bright and the air serene." He sat down by the lake and saw "a gibbet on which was suspended an unhappy object as a monitor to the living to refrain from the dreadful act of spilling blood. . . ."[11] However it was not necessary to spill blood to earn a place on the gallows. Rape assured the guilty of a hanging, but petty theft could and did lead to execution under eighteenth-century laws.

A poorly planned and ill-fated shipboard mutiny in the harbour almost got some sailors hanged on the hill. In 1797 the mutiny of the Nore broke out in England over pay among ships of the Royal Navy at Spithead. The Nore was an anchorage for the British fleet in the Thames estuary. The mutiny was led by a seaman named Parker, and spread to Newfoundland, 3 August 1797, when the foretopmen, serving on board H.M.S. *Latona* moored in St. John's harbour, refused orders to go aloft. Others joined them and this was intended as a signal for crews in all the ships in port to follow suit. None did, however, and the group of mutineers was subdued after some sword-play in which blood was drawn by their officers. Their threatened fate may be seen in the words used by Governor Waldegrave to address the crew of the H.M.S. *Latona* the following Sunday: ". . . your great delegate Parker is hanged, with many others of his atrocious companions. You looked up to him as an example when he was in his glory, I recommend you look to his end as an example also. . . ."[12] The Governor regretted that his commission did not allow him to conduct courtmartials in Newfoundland, as they were in Nova Scotia. If it had, the foretopmen of the H.M.S. *Latona* would have been displayed on Gibbet Hill.

Those hanged there were always left suspended for days, until they began to get a bit "ripe" and offended more by their odour than by their deeds. When finally cut down it is said they were packed in wooden barrels along with a generous helping of heavy stones. These barrels, with holes punched in the sides, were supposedly rolled down the hill to the bottomless pond at the base, where they promptly sank from sight, thus saving mightily on funeral expenses. It is said by some that this is how Deadman's Pond got its name. Once considered bottomless, much gravel fill has been pushed into it over the years, so that now it is little more than a medium-sized pool.

George's Pond, originally St. George's Pond, is to the left up the hill from the entrance gate. It, too, has a reputation for being bottomless. It is actually nearly eighty feet deep at the centre. Once used as a reservoir by the city, today it is an alternate supply in case of serious fire or drought. Opposite this pond there is a visitors' information centre and museum. This area was formerly the site of a barracks that became Signal Hill Jail.

Queen's Battery stands on the heights four hundred feet above the waters of the Narrows. Begun in 1763, it was completed in 1796 and enlarged and made stronger in 1809. The last remaining building on the site, built around 1705 as a powder magazine and barracks, was destroyed by an arsonist, 10 February 1961. It had been lived in by a family up to two years before that. Rumour had it that the place was burned in revenge by a labourer denied work at Signal Hill Park. The present gun mountings probably date from the 1860s. The guns at the site are not original, but were placed there when restoration was begun in 1929. The fort has been filled with about three feet of gravel so that in the days when its guns blazed in defence of the town the parapet was shoulder high and the mountings for the guns, which are now level with the ground, were waist high and soldiers could push and pull the cannon into position. A stone floor has been discovered beneath the clay fill.

From Signal Hill to Fort Amherst, on the far side, the distance is about fourteen hundred feet. Between Chain Rock (beneath Queen's Battery and occupied by a light) and Pancake Rock, directly opposite, the distance is six hundred feet. In 1762 a large chain was attached from Chain Rock to Pancake Rock. Every evening, during the years the town was under threat of enemy attack, this chain and log boom was raised by two capstans so as to obstruct enemy vessels attempting to enter port through the Narrows.

Signal Hill was first fortified by private individuals early in the 1600s to protect their homes and fishing gear from the French and marauding pirates. The most notorious of these brigands were a group of Englishmen who, disguised as Turks, plundered Newfoundland waters. They flew the Star and Crescent and called themselves the Sallee Rovers, after a seaport in Morocco. They were driven from Newfoundland waters by Henry Mainwaring who was knighted for his actions by King James. Sir Harry then turned to piracy himself and operated out of Newfoundland harbours. He died in Europe, a hunted exile, after having dissipated a fortune.

A gun battery was placed on shore, above Chain Rock, in 1673 when Dutch pirates, under Captain Jacobs (Jakob Everson), attacked the town in October. They were driven off by Christopher Martin and thirty men who manned the Narrows.[13] Jacobs sailed off to Jamaica to invade the stronghold of the notorious Captain Morgan.

Twice in this century Chain Rock has been put to use in order to keep enemy ships from entering St. John's, or attacking shipping lying at anchor. During World War I a log boom was again employed to protect the harbour, and during World War II some anti-submarine nets were secured to Chain and Pancake Rocks, to keep vessels in the port safe from underwater attack by U-boat packs patrolling the North Atlantic.

The claim has been made that British Admiralty records of the early 1800s indicate the daily firing of a noon gun from Signal Hill. Sister Magdalene O'Shaughnessy, one of the founding sisters of the Presentation Order in Newfoundland, wrote home to Ireland in November 1833:

> You will be surprised to hear they have no town clock; the reason given is, that it could not be kept regular in consequence of the extreme cold, so that the only way they have of regulating the time is by the discharge of guns which are fired at stated times during the day.[14]

The *Royal Gazette* for 25 January 1842 says: "It will also be satisfactory to know that a gun will in future be fired from Fort Frederick (on the Southside) exactly at noon every day which to a certain extent will supply the want of a public clock so much needed in this town." This would seem to indicate that the "discharge of guns" mentioned by Sister Magdalene was discontinued and replaced by the regular firing of a noonday gun from Fort Frederick in 1842.

The Southside cannon was later replaced by an old screw gun from the Boer War installed near Cabot Tower on Signal Hill and still in position there. It was, in turn, replaced by a saluting gun said to have been taken from H.M.S. *Calypso,* the former Royal Naval Reserve ship, which was then fast becoming a derelict hulk in the harbour.

There have been two interruptions to the firing of the noon gun. The first occurred in 1906 when it was claimed by some long-winded preachers that people attending Sunday morning services habitually checked pocket watches when the gun was fired to the consternation of the orator in the pulpit. The gun was stopped on complaint of the clergy and it gave rise to a verse called "Who Stopped the Sunday Gun?" by M.A. Devine, which began:

> "Now hasten forth, reporter man," the editor did say,
> "For some important news is out about the town today."
> "Go down to Skipper Eli Dawe and question him, my son;
> He knows, I s'pose, who told Tom Rose
>   To stop the Sunday gun."

The cannon was silenced again 15 March 1949 by a shortage of percussion caps used in the gun, and the practice was not revived until 1 January 1959 when a piece of iron pipe jutting from the ground near the steps to Cabot Tower became the famous noonday gun. In 1974 a proper cannon was placed on Signal Hill and it took over the midday chore from the piece of pipe in the ground.

Besides announcing midday, the noon gun was also used to signal various events such as the arrival of the new year, or the fact that the day's weather would be fine and fair enough for the Regatta to take place on Quidi Vidi Lake.

Cabot Tower, 510 feet above sea level, was built on a site formerly occupied by the Blockhouse. During much of the nineteenth century this building was used to signal the arrival of ships. Each mercantile firm had its own house flag. When the man on duty atop the hill lifted his spyglass and identified the banner flying from the mast of an incoming vessel, the flag of that firm was hoisted on the Blockhouse. Spotters in the offices of business firms along the waterfront would lift a glass to see whose ship was approaching, and those concerned would then hurry to the dock to greet the arrival. If there was illness on board, other flags warned the firm to have a doctor on hand to render assistance.

When those in the town saw a red flag with a white dot in the centre, flying from the Blockhouse, they knew the incoming vessel belonged to W. & G. Rendell; if it had a white diamond on a red field the ship was owned by C.F. Bennett and Co.; a white cross on a blue field denoted it was Duder's; a red star on white, Tessier's; a red and white checkerboard, McBride and Kerr, and so on. The practice of flying house flags from the top of Signal Hill was not discontinued until 1958.

On 29 March 1880 Frank Scott, who was on duty in the Blockhouse, was startled to see a steamer travelling at immense speed through the ice, twenty miles off port.[15] Scott, who swore to having witnessed the mirage ship was generally a sober man.

On the afternoon of Saturday, 28 April 1894, at four o'clock smoke and then flames were seen coming from the old building. Gunpowder stored in the Blockhouse for the noonday gun exploded. Fortunately, those in the place at the time were able to escape and there were no injuries. The blaze, which had been started by a defective stove, was watched by crowds on wharves along the waterfront. A successful effort was made to save the nearby powder magazine, but the historic signal house was no more.

Cabot Tower was erected on the ruins to commemorate the four hundredth anniversary of the discovery of Newfoundland by John Cabot and also Queen Victoria's Diamond Jubilee. The leading proponent of the idea for building a tower on the hill was Bishop Howley, and the plan he finally convinced the authorities to adopt was a square, castle-like structure, with four turrets. Probably due to a lack of funds, the present tower is one-quarter of the original design. The Bishop laid the cornerstone on 22 June 1897, construction was begun the following year, and the edifice formally opened on 20 June 1900.

The architect was William Howe Green, and the contractor was Henry J. Thomas. The stonemason in charge of construction was Samuel Garrett, who lived at 2 Duckworth Street, the only slate-covered house in St. John's. Garrett was the son of John Garrett, a stonemason with the garrison. While working on the construction of Cabot Tower he used some of the left-over stone which came from the old barracks and prison opposite George's Pond to erect the range of stone dwellings on the west side of Temperance Street for each of his four daughters.

In December 1901 Guglielmo Marconi gave Signal Hill a place in world history when he used the area as headquarters for his transatlantic wireless experiment. The historic message from England was received in a hospital close to the old powder house. The building was later destroyed in a fire but part of the foundations may still be seen, beyond the wall of the parking lot, on the ocean side. Below the parking area, in Ross's Valley, a few tumbled stones still mark the site of the seldom used smallpox hospital known as Prowse's folly. The Judge's only involvement seems to have been in trying to convince the government to build a road from the top of the hill down to the hospital.

Signal Hill was flown over by Alcock and Brown, as they headed out over the ocean to complete the first transatlantic nonstop flight in 1919, and also by Charles Lindbergh on his historic solo flight to Paris in 1927. He called it, ". . . the last point of land on the last island of America."[16] The famous Hill also saw the end of French dreams in the New World. The last battle of the Seven Years' War in North America took place here in 1762, which was also the last engagement between the English and French in Canada. The story of that fight is told in the first volume of this work.

The steep slopes from the tower to the sea have claimed surprisingly few victims considering the numbers of persons who frequent Signal Hill each year. On 8 October 1894 Richard Peters of 3 Parade Street, a tanner who was doing carpentry work for eight dollars a week, fell over the face of the hill and was killed. What makes Mr. Peters unique among the several who have met their deaths in the area is that he was observed falling by most of the crew of H.M.S. *Cleopatra,* at 10:30 a.m., yet the incident was not reported by the sailors until his body was discovered the following day. The most recent victim to fall to his death was Joseph Groke, a former Newfoundlander who was visiting from Ontario on 8 May 1975 when he fell two hundred feet while sightseeing.

To the east of the main road, at the crest of Signal Hill, is the highest point of land in St. John's called Ladies Lookout. Known by that name since 1702, it was probably a place where soldiers took their young ladies for a stroll when they were, what was called, "walking out." Near Ladies Lookout are some excavated ruins of a canteen, storage hut, latrine, and some fortifications used by the British garrison a couple of centuries ago.

Early in the 1800s a road was built from Fort Townshend in the direction of Long Pond. It more or less followed Newtown Road and Mayor and Bonaventure Avenues. Known as Arundel Cottage Road it took its name from a fashionable country estate, once called Coote's Farm and later Hope Cottage, owned by John Steer, which stood on the site of the Arts and Culture Centre. Before demolition, the house was a Church of England orphanage. The road was constructed to link the fort with a line of outposts built in what was to become known as the Queen Victoria Hills, a ridge stretching from Oxen Pond to Windsor Lake. Another road was built from Fort William to Portugal Cove, and a third from Fort William to Torbay. The Portugal Cove and Torbay roads were joined by Major's Path, named for Major Brady, a landholder in the area who was a soldier in command of engineering and related construction and whose company left St. John's in 1789. There was an alternate road to Torbay, by way of Logy Bay and Outer Cove. This road followed the original footpath between St. John's and Torbay, and it was over this footpath that the British Forces, under Colonel Amherst, had marched to recapture the town from the French in 1767.

About two and a half miles from Fort William, along the Logy Bay Road, is the entrance to Virginia Water. This fashionable estate was, for many years, the closest thing to a park in the environs of the town. In 1815 the six hundred and fifty acres of meadows, lake, and trees, known as Gaden's Marsh Farm, became the property of Burrell Rutledge. When Governor Sir Thomas Cochrane was looking for a farm in the country he purchased the Rutledge property through Payne and Simms and changed the name to Virginia Water. The grounds, with the exception of the cottage, were open two days a week for the public to enter and ramble at will.

His Excellency lived there in summer with his two sons and two daughters. The Anglican parson of Portugal Cove, Reverend Mr. Wood, has described the boys, Frederick (18), and Charles (16), saying he had little liking for "such feminine creatures."

The Governor is thought to have named the estate after Virginia Water, an artificial lake in Windsor Great Park, twenty-two miles from London, in the English county of Surrey. Local use of the plural, waters, is an interpolation of a later age. Cochrane called the residence Virginia Cottage. Some have maintained the name was given it by George H. Emerson, a later owner whose United Empire Loyalist family moved to Nova Scotia from Virginia, following the War of Independence. However, the property had already been named by Cochrane when Emerson acquired it.

Sir Thomas spent £382.12.0 out of public money to fix up the estate. When an inquiry was later conducted into the phenomenal cost of the government house which he had built in the town, a supply of paving stones was found to be missing. The Governor confessed to having borrowed them for Virginia Water but said he intended replacing them with a shipment from Halifax. When His Excellency was recalled in 1834, his country estate was sold. The cottage burned between six and seven o'clock on 18 November 1887 after catching on fire in one of the upper rooms. George Emerson, who was living there at the time, sent a servant galloping to the city on horseback, requesting assistance. It never came.

At the opposite end of the town Governor Cochrane's friend and later enemy, Captain James Pearl, acquired five hundred acres of land which he turned into a residence of considerable prominence. Born in Nova Scotia in 1790, Pearl became a naval hero of some standing. In the Basque Roads engagement he was severely wounded, and he also distinguished himself in the East Indies where he received the thanks of the government of Bengal for his services during the Burmese War. There can be no doubt that he displayed meritorious heroism. The King of the Netherlands awarded him a gold medal, and a piece of plate was given him by the British Merchants of Canton for a gallant rescue he performed in the China Seas. He was retired in 1827 as Commander but Cochrane and others refer to him as Captain.

In October 1829 he arrived in St. John's with his wife, Anne, and went immediately to Government House where he personally delivered to Sir Thomas Cochrane an order from the Colonial Secretary of State for His Excellency to grant him a thousand acres of land belonging to the Crown. He had probably visited Newfoundland during some part of his naval service and was not a complete stranger. In December, a grant was made of a thousand acres of Crown land adjoining Brookfield, then the estate of William Dunscomb, west of St. John's. By the time George Holbrook, the Surveyor General, got around to surveying and laying out a plan of the land, Sir Thomas had reduced the grant to five hundred acres because of numerous petitions for property in the area. Pearl was not pleased and, while he tried to put as brave a face as possible on the deal, he inwardly began to build a long smouldering resentment. Still anxious to cultivate the friendship of the Governor, he called the mansion he had built Mount Cochrane, in honour of His Excellency. At great personal expense he constructed a road from Dunscomb's property to his own place which, in time, became the Old Placentia Road. Pearl was irritated at having to build what he considered a public road for the convenience of others. By June 1830 he had spent over five hundred pounds on the property. Later that year he became involved in another controversy with the Governor when the other five hundred acres, for which he had applied, was granted to two Scots immigrants named Hood and Gibson. Controlling his anger, Pearl allowed the newcomers temporary use of his road and helped them clear their land by the free employment of his labourers, ploughs, and farming implements.

Of this neighbourly gesture the Captain wrote: "My liberal conduct towards them met with a most ungrateful return. They allowed their cattle to destroy my crops, left open my fences, by which cattle got into my cultivated land, and did great injury."[17] Highly incensed, Pearl forbade Hood and Gibson passage through his estate; however, against his will, he let the Governor persuade him to withdraw the ban. In any case, he now had a new interest.

On 11 November 1830 Captain Pearl was off to England where he placed a petition for representative government before William IV, who had just come to the throne and was familiar with Newfoundland where he had served in his youth. There can be no doubt that Pearl's audience with William, and his talks with Mr. Robinson of the Colonial Office and Lord Norsland, were an important factor in the eventual granting of representative government, a credit he seems seldom to have been given.

On his return in May 1831, Hood and Gibson caused Pearl additional trouble when they tried to clear more of their land by burning the woods. The fire destroyed a hundred acres of the Captain's property and did great injury to his crop of oats and potatoes. It came close to destroying his house and barn. A complaint in writing to the Governor brought no result and, in mid-June, a fire started by James Halliday destroyed two hundred acres of young and thriving timber belonging to Pearl as well as fencing, posts, and other timber he had collected during the winter to build a new house at Riverhead. On June 20 he wrote to the authorities to complain that the fire started by ". . . the disgraceful and criminal conduct of James Halliday and his workmen, continues to rage with great fury through the country to the southwest." His Excellency's only reply was to ask for rent due on the piece of land he had granted at Riverhead.

Perhaps the Governor's laconic reaction was due in part to his knowledge that the Captain was actively trying to have him removed from office. Earlier that spring Pearl wrote from England to the private secre-

OF BLOSSOMS, BIRDS, AND BOWERS

tary, Captain Campbell, "The Governor's doom is sealed." This information caused a sensation when it reached St. John's, but sensation was
nothing new to the Captain. When he first arrived in England in 1830,
before he got around to asking for representative government for the
colony, he rocked the authorities by demanding a knighthood for himself.
His failure, on both counts, was not due to any lack of determination on his
part.

Late in 1831 Hood and Gibson appear to have sold out. With their
departure from the area, the ex-naval officer's fortunes as a landowner
seem to have improved. An attempt by Governor Cochrane to patch up the
quarrel, by having the Pearls to dinner at Government House, was re-
buffed by the Captain who informed His Excellency in a letter that he and
his lady could not contemplate dining with the likes of the Governor's
cronies. The breach did mend before the departure of Cochrane from
Newfoundland and the Captain eventually got the knighthood he so
diligently sought. In 1836 he was made a Knight of the Royal Guelphic
Order of Hanover. Two years later, at the hands of the young Victoria, he
received the accolade of Knight Bachelor. In 1837 he renamed his residence, substituting his name for that of Cochrane. On 13 January 1840, at
the age of fifty years, Sir James Pearl died suddenly. His remains were
interred in the Church of England burial ground and the tombstone which
marked his grave can still be seen on the Church Hill side of the cemetery
where it lies flat, almost hidden in the grasp of weeds.

Mount Pearl, like Jane Eyre's Thornfield, was soon left a blackened
ruin. The mansion burned on August 1 in the year of its owner's death.
Lady Anne was granted another three hundred and fifty acres at about this
time, and her sister-in-law, Eunice Blamey, was given a long strip of land
on the east side of the Western Cross Road. Following Pearl's unexpected
passing, the farm was managed for the widow by John Lester, a Dorset
man brought to Newfoundland in 1836 to work for Sir James. Whatever
the reason, Lady Pearl decided to move to England in 1844, and the
property was rented to Lester. She died at 57 Brompton Row, London, in
1860 and, as there were no living relatives, Mount Pearl was bequeathed to
John Lester, Mrs. Eliza Bulley, and Mrs. Wix Saunders. The two ladies
appear to have disposed of their holdings by selling them to Alexander
Smith and Judge Little. Sandy Smith later sold his acres to an Englishman
named Studdy who, in turn, sold out to Andrew Glendenning. Judge Little
did nothing with his property and it eventually passed to his son. The site
of the Pearl farm was converted by Glendenning into a race track, and it
was here that Hawker and Grieve took off on their ill-fated pioneer transatlantic flight. The government bought the race track property in 1935 and
turned it into an experimental farm. Administrative offices now stand
near the site of the old mansion house occupied by Sir James and Lady
Anne Pearl.

Soon after World War I a Marconi radio station was established just west of the corner of Old Placentia Road and the Western Cross Road (which became known as Marconi Road and later Commonwealth Avenue). The Old Placentia Road was renamed Brookfield Road. The Canadian Broadcasting Corporation now has its radio transmitters for CBN and CKZN on the Marconi site.

In 1923 Roland Morris became interested in the area and acquired Lady Pearl's grant from Judge Little's son. He called it Glendale, after a community which had impressed him near Burbank, California, and set about clearing the land and building roads. In 1928 Morris interested a group of businessmen in forming the Mount Pearl Park Company Limited and they acquired additional acres from Glendenning's land for the development of a garden city. The plans for this suburban haven were prepared by Rudolph Cochius, the designer of Bowring Park. Unfortunately, the Great Depression of 1929 ended the dream. The shareholders disposed of much of the land and Morris left for Toronto.

The garden city was never realized but development did continue. The area became popular for summer homes and these were later converted to year-round dwellings as the limits of the city spread west. By the beginning of World War II between a hundred and a hundred and fifty families had become permanent residents. Roland Morris returned to Newfoundland in 1940 and began to develop Glendale. The town of Mount Pearl - Glendale was incorporated in February 1955, with Hayward Burrage as first mayor. It was a hundred and twenty-five years since Sir James Pearl was given his grant of land. Except for his name, no monument anywhere in Newfoundland honours the founder of the town and one of the fathers of self-government in the colony. In 1959 an historic plaque honouring Pearl was attached to the County Court House at Yarmouth, Nova Scotia.

The newest park in the city of St. John's is Pippy Park which came into being in 1966 when C.A. Pippy, a local millionaire, donated a million dollars, over a twenty-year period, to the provincial government. Premier Smallwood directed that the money should be used to purchase land between Elizabeth Avenue and Nagle's Hill. A grandiose scheme was envisioned which would place the Trades College, Confederation Building, and Memorial University in the huge urban parkland. The dream was later adjusted to the reality of the fortune it would have cost to expropriate such areas as the Churchill Park housing development. The government was forced to settle for the creation of a green belt by placing a freeze on all building in the area of Nagle's Hill and acquiring all unused land in the immediate vicinity.

The northern boundary of Pippy Park is the old Queen Victoria Hills stretching from Thorburn Road to Portugal Cove Road. Early in the last century a trail known as Burnt Pinch Path ran along this line of hills and connected Logy Bay Road with Mount Ken, now Kenmont Road. Parts of this path still exist as Mount Scio Road, Nagle's Hill Road, and Ridge

Road. These streets were formerly known by such colourful names as Hangman's Path, Governor's Path, and Peat Marsh Trail. West of Mount Scio a rough road was begun to link St. John's to St. Phillips, then called Broad Cove, but it never progressed much beyond Casey's Farm. This road had the distinguished name of the Water to Water Overland Trail.

There is a legend in the Nagle's Hill area of a lost treasure in Oxen Pond, formerly called Oxenham Pond. The legend has to do with a Lieutenant Oxenham, an army paymaster. According to the tale he was on the trail with an armed guard distributing pay to soldiers manning sentry posts in what became the Queen Victoria Hills when he was set upon by a French scouting platoon from Placentia. Rather than surrender the payroll, Lieutenant Oxenham attempted to escape by dashing into the bush. Unfortunately he found his path of retreat cut off by the shores of the pond. With the enemy hot in pursuit he threw the strong box, containing the coin of the realm, into a deep muddy section of the pond. Some storytellers have him executed on capture for this deed, while others say he was taken prisoner to Placentia. In any case his brave action in keeping the money from falling into the hands of the French was rewarded by his having the pond named for him.

The tale is contradicted by a second legend which states that Lieutenant Oxenham arrived at the sentry post bordering the pond to find the soldiers gambling away the pay they had recently been given. He took the money from them, placed it in a small sack of some sort, and threw it into the waters from which it was never recovered. This seems unconvincing. The University Vivarium, including a botanical garden, animal and bird farm, is now located on the shores of the pond.

Another legend of the area has it that there is a grave site beyond the northwest ridge of Big Pond. The graves are said to be those of three British soldiers who were shot, either by French or their own officers, but no British military sources have any historical record of soldiers having been buried in the area. It is possible some British troops were surprised at an outlying sentry post by the French during one of their raids on St. John's. If shot in a skirmish, they would probably have been buried where they fell.

There is a bog in the vicinity of Rocky Pond which, according to tradition, contains a cannon or large field piece. This ordnance property was supposedly lost during the days of the British garrison and lies submerged in a marsh near the pond.

Five distinct excavations, made by an old prospector named McGrath, lie within the boundary of Pippy Park. Early in the present century this man believed that the Wabana iron ore on Bell Island began in the vicinity of Nagle's Hill. He made two small excavations near Oxen Pond. Further north he made three deeper ones, the deepest being approximately thirty feet. McGrath never found the vein of ore. His diggings may be seen to this day, though they are partly overgrown.

These excavations should not be confused with a large gravel pit known as Split Rock. This exposed surface, near Big Pond, became a picnic spot when a grass cover grew over much of the rock. Besides Big Pond and Oxen Pond, Pippy Park and the nearby area contain three bodies of water once called Long Pond. Upper Long Pond has now become Long Pond and is part of Memorial University campus. A residence for the president was erected on the north slope. Nearby, south of the junction of Mt. Scio and Nagle's Hill Roads, the beer baron Lindbergh, whose large brewery on the site of St. Joseph's School on Signal Hill Road was destroyed in the '92 fire, had a home with the impressive name of Lindbergh Castle. Oddly enough, the only other castle in St. John's, Castle Rennie, was located directly behind Lindbergh's Brewery on Signal Hill. Gutted in the Great Fire, Castle Rennie was rebuilt and used as a Convent by the Mercy Sisters teaching at St. Joseph's School.

A short distance north of where Long Pond empties into Rennie's River, there stood a well-known country residence, North Bank, built by Colonel Rendell and set in a grove of trees on the shoreline. In the early days of World War II, before the opening of Fort Pepperrell, the United States Army turned the building into a military hospital to serve the needs of servicemen on board the troopship, *Edmund B. Alexander,* and later at Camp Alexander, on the corner of Long Pond and Carpasian Roads.

In the last century Middle Long Pond became Kent's Pond when John Kent, Newfoundland's second prime minister, occupied a country residence on its shores. Lower Long Pond, behind the Holiday Inn, skirted by Brady's Path, is now called Kenny's Pond and is just outside the boundaries of Pippy Park.

At the top of Gooseberry Lane, below Confederation Parkway, there was a country estate known as Captain Edgell's farm. Edgell came to Newfoundland in 1801 in command of the sloop *Pluto.* This ship was in Newfoundland waters for twenty years, off and on. Captain Edgell is spoken of in the *Royal Gazette,* 27 August 1807, as "a gentleman whose name will long be remembered . . . with pleasure." The Confederation Building, the home of the Legislature for the province, sits in the Captain's pasture. West of his farm there was a wedge-shaped property that ran along the north bank of Rennie's River as far as Long Pond. This was "The Billies," an estate granted to the great William Carson in 1831. It is described in Chapter 6, Volume I.

The word "pond" is used almost exclusively throughout eastern Newfoundland for any inland body of water, regardless of size. The reason for this is that the area was first settled by people from the English west country where there are ponds but no lakes. The word "lake" was unknown to these early settlers so they called every body of water a pond. If it was of immense size the name still applied, as in Bay Bulls Big Pond and Twenty Mile Pond.

St. John's parks provided the citizens of the town with somewhere to walk abroad and re-create themselves in summer, but a favourite winter gathering place was the kitchen or parlour of thousands of homes where young and old joined in the popular pastime of Christmas mumming. This folk tradition of informal house visits by roving groups disguised of face and body (often with sex-reversal) was celebrated throughout Newfoundland with uninhibited revelry during the twelve days of Christmas from Christmas Eve to Twelfth Night. The "strangers" or "fools" also disguised their voices as they sang, played, or danced, while their hosts attempted to penetrate the disguise by playing a guessing game, sometimes with much roughness. When a mummer was identified the person was unmasked.[18] Before the visitors moved on to the next house food and drink were offered and consumed with high spirits.

There was some tradition of house visiting in disguise in Britain and Ireland at certain times of the year but nowhere does the custom of Christmas mumming seem to have acquired the popularity it did in Newfoundland. Dressed in strange costumes, their faces often blackened with soot or burnt cork, the mummers went their rounds causing apprehension and even terror among people they met on the way. Women and children who ventured along the unlighted streets and roads could expect to be pounced on by the "fools."[19] St. John's streets were especially hazardous after dark during the holiday season because of the numerous lanes leading off them which provided the mummers with hiding places.

Early in the nineteenth century mummer plays and mummer parades were an important facet of the town's Christmas celebrations. As they marched along the streets on their way to perform their play, dressed in elaborate costumes of the traditional characters they were to portray, the ribald merrymakers slapped at watching bystanders with whips and inflated bladders.[20] The pranks and colour enlivened the drabness of winter for the lower orders who could afford few diversions. As the years passed, the outlandish behaviour of the "fools" sometimes ended in violence, and a fear of uncontrollable riot in St. John's led to the banning of the parades by law.[21]

The edict on marching probably contributed to the demise of the mummers' plays as well. These performances were not conventional plays but folk dramas with set speeches performed by actors playing such characters as Cromwell, Father Christmas, and St. George. They were quite stylized hero-combat epics in which good triumphed over evil. For some reason not fully understood, the acting of these plays died out all over Newfoundland just prior to World War I.[22] An attempt at revival has been made in the 1970s by a professional group of local wayfaring actors called the Mummers. For several years now they have been going from house to house in St. John's during the holiday season performing the traditional play in fancy costumes.

Although mumming (or jannying) still survives in some of the outports of the province, the celebration was seriously curtailed almost everywhere in the island by a murder which took place in the Conception Bay town of Bay Roberts in 1860. After dark on the evening of Friday, December 28, Thomas Mercer (sometimes wrongly identified as Isaac), a young man who had been married two weeks before, was on his way back from working in the woods with his two brothers-in-law when they called at his mother-in-law's house for a cup of tea. The trio then left for Mercer's home. At a turning in the road they were pounced upon by six mummers who jumped from a hiding place and beat the three with sticks before fleeing into the darkness.

The injured Mercer was carried home by his companions. To his mother he said, "Oh, mother, I am killed!" and fell unconscious. He died next day from a skull fracture.[23] It was said in Bay Roberts that the three men, who were Protestant, were set upon by Roman Catholics, and this led to serious religious disturbances all along the shore of Conception Bay. Bishop Feild became embroiled in the controversy when he tried to sort things out and was accused of fomenting religious animosity by some who saw the chance to make political hay. Six names were freely mentioned in Bay Roberts. The six were examined but dismissed for want of evidence.

The coroner's verdict was "wilful murder." A reward of a hundred pounds was offered, but to no effect. After the Attorney General returned to St. John's without discovering the identity of the murderers, a magistrate was sent to the community to follow up but he found no new evidence. Because of the religious unrest which followed the murder of Mercer the Legislative Assembly passed an Act, 25 June 1861, making it illegal for any person in Newfoundland to go about wearing a mask or otherwise disguised unless licensed by a magistrate. The Act, which was frequently ignored but never repealed, gradually diminished the century-old tradition of Christmas mumming in the colony, especially in St. John's where there were constables to enforce the restriction.[24] As late as 1975 it was resurrected by the Chief of Police to control Hallowe'en hooliganism when teenagers, who sometimes robbed the small mummers of their trick-or-treat collections, were advised that they were subject to arrest if found on the streets in disguise.

Soldiers' Meadow is probably the oldest parklike setting in St. John's. From the 1600s this green slope outside Fort William was a popular place where children romped in the summer sun and winter snow. In this century it has been renamed Cavendish Square. Trees were first planted there in a special ceremony 1 May 1864. In the early days Soldiers' Meadow was bounded in the west by a river which still runs under Ordnance Street.

Another popular place for "walking out," in the days before the town had a public park, was the graveyard, and we can be sure that many a slap and tickle disturbed the quiet of trees and tombstones in years gone by. There were a number of early burial grounds in the community but their location has been lost. The oldest cemetery we know of is in front of the churchyard of the Anglican Cathedral on Duckworth Street. When the first chapel was opened there, a few years after the turn of the eighteenth century, burials followed almost immediately. For over a hundred years it was the only place of interment permitted in the town. Church of England, Roman Catholic, and dissenter were buried there side by side.

The earliest headstones still to be seen in this cemetery date back to the 1830s. Among them is that of Rev. Frederic Carrington, "Rector of St. John's, October 7, 1839." This clergyman was succeeded by the Reverend Mr. Bridge (later Archdeacon), who came out to Newfoundland in 1825 as tutor to the two sons of Governor Cochrane. A few months before Carrington's death, Dr. Aubrey Spencer was ordained Newfoundland's first Church of England bishop, but he did not arrive in the island until after the passing of the rector and the Reverend Bridge was in charge.

The only stones which mark actual grave sites are those of William Carson and Richard Barnes. Dr. Carson's is near the Duckworth Street wall, opposite Court House Steps.

In the southwest corner, near the foot of Church Hill, the monument to Richard Barnes fights an almost losing battle against vandals, the elements, and wildwood. This island of neglect in a sea of weeds marks the final resting place of a man who, by his education Act, ended centuries of illiteracy in the colony and forced Newfoundlanders to learn to read and write. The fading inscription states:

> Erected by the Newfoundland Native's Society to the memory of Richard Barnes, late of St. John's, Merchant, MHA, and founder of the society who died September 3rd. This tribute is a testimony of his great talents, many private virtues and untiring efforts for the welfare and advancement of his native country.

About the only legacy of Mr. Barnes's Native Society still around is a flag. Its beginnings are obscure but we can be sure no Canadian province has a banner so rich in origin, or as dear to the hearts of the people, as the pink, whites, and green tri-colour of Newfoundland, one of the oldest flags in North America.

Shortly after the granting of Representative Government in 1832, resentments between the established settlers and recent immigrants, mostly Irish, grew into open conflict. The result was the formation of the Native Society by Richard Barnes, and on 15 June 1840 Dr. Edward Kielley, an Irishman from Ulster, became its first president. Its purpose was to protect the imagined rights and privileges of landed planters from the flood of newcomers. The natives felt they were not getting a square deal in their own land. On 24 May 1845 Governor Harvey laid the corner-stone for the society's hall, in Bannerman Park. As we have seen, this building blew down in a gale, 19 September 1846, killing two people sheltering there. The society never quite recovered from that disaster.

Besides having its own quarters, the organization had its own flag. It consisted of a green spruce tree, on a pink background, with two clasped hands beneath. The motto, "Philanthropy," was later added. Although the society was formed to protect natives of all faiths and origins, it seems to have increased religious animosities, so that in the end it turned the Protestant English and Catholic Irish against each other. This ill feeling was accentuated annually by the woodhauls.

In the era of the 1840s there would be as many as ten thousand sealers in St. John's each spring waiting for ships to take them to the icefields. In order to keep such a vast congregation busy and out of mischief, arrangements were made to divert their energies by voluntary woodcutting to supply churches, schools, and charity institutions. The wood was cut outside the town and pulled on sledges to various places where it was stacked on end. There is an excellent painting by J.W. Hayward of one such woodpile on Duckworth Street, at the foot of Victoria Street, in 1854. The stacks were decorated with flags and bunting, and there were bloody fist-fights over whose was the largest. The Protestant English sealers used the pink flag of the Native Society, while the Catholic Irish flew a green banner.

On 16 January 1839 Bishop Fleming tried to encourage brotherhood by writing a letter of thanks, for hauling wood, to the Citizens of the District of St. John's. He said: ". . . to the numerous highly respectable Protestants who assisted, both by their personal exertions and contributions of timber, to render the returns valuable, I owe a debt of gratitude." This attempt at conciliation failed.

Early in the 1840s the rows and disorders created by the woodhauls became a matter of grave concern. A tragic riot could erupt at any time. Something had to be done to make peace among the various factions, and it seems Dr. William Carson suggested that Dr. Fleming, a man who had the respect of all, be asked to use his considerable influence.

The Bishop was familiar with the flag of the Native Society, and had been presented with one as early as 1837. This is the first authentic knowledge we have of its existence. The *Carbonear Sentinel,* 15 November 1838, carried a long item regarding his recent visit to Harbour Grace. The report said: ". . . among the banners were seen that beautiful flag which was presented by the Roman Catholic NATIVES OF ST. JOHNS to his Lordship on his departure from the island last year." The Union Jack did not assume its present form until 1848, about a dozen years after the birth of the first Native's flag which for over a hundred and twenty-five years has been steeped in the traditions of the people of Newfoundland.

The delegation which called on Bishop Fleming asked if he would use his pulpit to denounce the sealers' quarrels. The cleric is said to have believed the solution lay in uniting the warring troops rather than in thunderous harangues. He hit upon the idea of uniting their two flags into a single banner that would be meaningful to all Newfoundlanders. Protestants and Catholics approved the idea. His Lordship designed a tri-colour by taking the pink from the banner of the English Native's, the green from the banner of the Irish fishermen's flag, and separating them by white, taken from the banner of Scotland, as a symbol of peace between the foes and respect for his great Scottish friend, William Carson.

The compromise worked. Following the death of Richard Barnes the society adopted the new form of the flag as its own and the banner immediately attained great prominence in the social and commercial life of the colony. There are reports of its having been flown at Government House, as well as from the staffs of private homes, commercial concerns, public buildings, and from the mastheads and sterns of Newfoundland vessels at sea. As late as 1907 an official mail steamer entered the port of St. John's, flying the pink, white, and green. It was ordered hauled down because by then a device, known as the Red Ensign, had become popular throughout the colonial Empire. This flag, designed by England for its possessions, appeared around the turn of the century. Although it had a kind of official recognition in some places it was never distinctive and engendered little real affection in many of the countries in which it flew. Canada was the exception. The ensign consisted of a red, white, or blue field with a Union Jack in the upper, inside quarter and a symbol of the colony or dominion in the lower, outer corner. The symbol for the Newfoundland Red Ensign was actually the design of Adelaide Lane, a niece of Governor Boyle, who was his hostess at Government House until 1903. She represented Newfoundland as a kneeling fisherman with the harvest of the sea beside him being presented to Britannia by Mercury, god of commerce and merchandise. With one minor alteration the lady's design was approved on 18 May 1904. Miss Lane's symbol was later replaced as the coat of arms of Newfoundland by that awarded Sir David Kirke on 13 November 1637, consisting of a shield with lions and unicorns in the quarterings, two Indians as supportings, and a caribou as crest.

There was a song written about the native flag and the chorus went:

Fling out the flag of Newfoundland
Pink, white and green so fair so grand . . .

The tune became a kind of national anthem for the country and was sung at many gatherings until Governor Boyle wrote his famous ode. During the visit of the Prince of Wales (Edward VII) in 1860 the chambers of the Colonial Building were decorated with pink, white, and green bunting for a public ball in his honour. The *Evening Telegram* of 22 June 1892 reported on a triumphal arch made of boughs standing at the foot of Cochrane Street: "[It] attracted great admiration . . . at its apex . . . the tricolor of Newfoundland. . . ." Inspector General McCowen chose the banner as the official flag of his newly formed police and fire department. This pink, white, and green flag, edged in gold braid, was paraded through the town and presented by the Inspector to Governor Murray for safekeeping at Government House in June 1896.

In April 1909 the Newfoundland flag gained world prominence by being brought to the North Pole on Admiral Peary's historic trek of discovery. Newfoundland's famed Captain Bob Bartlett reached within six miles of the Pole in advance of Peary and a pink, white, and green banner, which was presented to Bartlett at New York on 4 July 1908 by a Miss Phelan, was planted there by the Captain. An officer of the S.S. *Invermore,* on being questioned as to the veracity of the report, said there was no doubt about the feat being performed. The *Daily News* headlined the story "Crew of the Invermore say Capt. Bob Bartlett was within six miles of North Pole and planted the Pink, White and Green there."

Newfoundland has always been depicted in the eyes of her country-men as a woman who bears a striking resemblance to Miss Liberty without a torch. She wore a flowing gown of vertical stripes of pink, white, and green. It was in this raiment that she appeared on stage at the Casino Theatre in 1901, when in the presence of its author, Governor Boyle, the first authorized public performance of his "Ode to Newfoundland" was given. Next day the colours appeared on the cover of the sheet music published by His Excellency. They were also seen at the masthead of Colonial Commerce, an important local periodical for over a quarter of a century.

After much agitation by Newfoundland citizens for a distinctive flag of their own, the Honourable Ank Murphy, then Minister of Provincial Affairs, announced in 1971 that his government was at last going to give the province its own distinctive flag. He later stated in a press interview that the vast majority of people who contacted him favoured adopting the traditional Pink, White, and Green. However, nothing happened and Mr. Murphy was moved to another portfolio. On 23 January 1974 the Honour-able Tom Doyle, Minister of Tourism, unveiled a proposed new flag. It proved to be a pathetic design, in no way distinctive of the province.

In January 1975, Dr. Whitney Smith, Executive Director of the Flag Research Center in the U.S.A. chose the Pink, White, and Green to be in-cluded in a set of silver ingots of flags being produced by the Franklin Mint. He felt its inclusion would "help to give it the publicity it deserves." Dr. Smith, one of the world's leading flag experts and consultants, was also including the story of the Newfoundland tri-colour in a book he was preparing on the history of Canadian flags as he felt its history made it one of the most interesting flags anywhere in Canada.

His Lordship, Patrick Lambert, the second Roman Catholic Bishop of Newfoundland, began the first agitation to get his flock the right to bury their own dead in their own cemetery. His efforts were rewarded in 1811 when Lord Liverpool wrote to Governor Duckworth: "It is desirable that you will immediately comply with the request of the Roman Catholic Bishop that the Roman Catholic Church may be allowed the same rights which that of Nova Scotia possesses, of burying its own dead.[25]

Bishop Lambert was away at the time so the Governor sent the glad tidings to Father Ewer, the Vicar General, and added: "Until a burying ground has been set apart distinctly for the Roman Catholics, they must, of course, continue to be interred in that of the Protestant Church, and the Roman Catholic Ministers will officiate on these occasions."

Governor Duckworth had written Bishop Lambert in October 1810 to say:

> I am sorry to acquaint you that an instance of the irregularity of which I spoke before to you has again occurred. On Friday evening last a corpse was to have been interred at 4 o'clock. Mr. Rowland (C. of E. clergyman) waited a considerable time, in vain, and the corpse was brought after he had gone away and interred without a minister. It is with much reluctance that I am compelled to interfere: but it is my particular request that until some arrangement can be made upon this subject, you will endeavour to prevent a practice which cannot surely be admissable.

Roman Catholics were evidently skulking around the back streets with their corpses waiting for the Church of England clergyman to go home so they might bury their dead without the person being prayed over by an Anglican.

Finally in 1811 the Governor received the sanction of the Prince Regent for the authorities to "set apart distinctly" a burial ground for the Roman Catholics. Thomas Coote, the Chief Magistrate, reported a vacant plot of ground on Long's Hill, a street thought to have been named for Richard Long who owned land on the west side of the hill above Livingstone Street. Old Judge Coote described the site as: "Situate near Fort Townshend on the road leading by the Charity School towards the Western Barrens." It covered much of the area now occupied by the Kirk and Holloway schools, running ninety-two yards along Queen's Road and Long's Hill.

The first body interred in the new graveyard was that of an English woman, the wife of John Butt, who died in 1784 at the age of ninety-four years and was the oldest inhabitant of St. John's at the time of her death. Her body was removed from the general cemetery and buried in the new Roman Catholic one.[26]

The earliest tombstone found on Long's Hill in later years was that of a Mrs. Aylward, dated 1813. This cemetery was also the final resting place of two priests. Father Whitty, a curate in the old chapel on Henry Street, was interred there in 1823. Near him were buried the remains of Father Edward Murphy, a young priest from Wexford, Ireland, who passed away in St. John's just six months after his ordination.

The deed granted on 30 June 1838 for the ground on which the Basilica now stands mentions, among other things, that it is to be used as "a cemetery for the benefit of the loyal and faithful Roman Catholic sub-jects. . . ." There is no evidence of this property having been put to such a use by that denomination. However, there is an old military map, dating from the late 1700s, in the Provincial Archives, showing a small cemetery at the junction of Bonaventure Avenue and Military Road. This might have been a place to inter fever victims, used briefly during an epidemic, and then forgotten. There were a number of such burial grounds scattered around the outskirts of the town. Two corpses were unearthed during excavations for the Basilica foundation. They were said to have been the bodies of the two Irishmen, Farrell and Power, hanged in 1794, for the murder of Lieutenant Lawrey of H.M.S. *Boston* (see Chapter 9). Whatever the basis was for this belief, it has not come down to us.

In his speech, at the opening of the Legislature in 1849, Governor LeMarchant said:

> As a very obvious method of improving the sanitary conditions of this town, I recommend having an Act passed, prohibiting after a certain early period, any interments within the limits of this town, and in anticipation of some measure of this description, I have provided a suitable piece of ground for the purpose of a General Cemetery at a short distance from the town.

All graveyards within St. John's were supposedly closed by law on July 1 that year.

On May 25 the General Protestant Cemetery referred to by LeMar-chant opened on Waterford Bridge Road, just west of the former home of Judge Des Barres and opposite Syme's Bridge. Mr. Syme, who gave his name to the bridge, lived west of the river crossing. Offlay Farm stretched towards the Crossroads, to the east of the bridge.

Relatives attempted to have some of the remains of dissenters, lying in the old Anglican churchyard, disinterred for transfer to the General Protestant Cemetery at Riverhead. It was thought that opening the old graves might give rise to the outbreak of some plague, so the transplants were quickly forbidden. Many of the dear departed had perished from typhus, cholera, and other afflictions which were a hazard of life in those days, and it was believed their bones might still harbour the pestilence.

On June 25, one month after the opening of the General Protestant Cemetery, Bishop Feild consecrated the new Anglican necropolis on Forest Road. The Governor's secretary, Mr. Rushworth, handed the Bishop the deed of trust, "granting the land for the purpose of a cemetery for members of the Church of England, but also reserving the rights and privi-leges of such of Her Majesty's subjects who were not of that church, which they had in the old St. John's burying ground." The deed of consecration was read by the Reverend Blackman and signed by the Lord Bishop.

The former cemetery, in the Cathedral churchyard, was the scene of some excitement a few years previously when, on 10 July 1846, a tailor named George Raynes was found dead among the headstones with his throat cut. His murderer, if there was one, was never found and the mystery faded from memory, unsolved.

Anticipating Governor LeMarchant's recommendation to the Legislature, the Roman Catholic prelate, Dr. Fleming, in 1848 acquired McKee's Grove adjoining the estate of Belvedere, which he had purchased from H.E. Emerson. It was his intention to open a cemetery on the site. That same year, the Benevolent Irish Society took possession of John Dowsley's property on the road to Bally Haly Farm, at the top of Kenna's Hill, next to Sir William Archibald's Retreat Cottage. In July 1849 the Bishop purchased ten acres of land adjoining Dowsley's, facing on Quidi Vidi Road, for the purpose of a cemetery. He joined the two lots and made one large burial ground known as Mount Carmel Cemetery.

The partisan newspaper *Patriot,* in reporting the Roman Catholic purchase of the Quidi Vidi Road property by the bishop, took the occasion to trample some sour grapes in printer's ink. On 21 July 1849 it spoke of the beautiful piece of land, in a delightful situation, and added:

> This munificent act of Dr. Fleming is in accordance with his whole ecclesiastical career—never hesitating to devote his private purse to the well-being of his flock; but we do think that it was despicably mean and niggardly of the government to permit his Lordship to make this sacrifice—particularly when it is recollected that the Church of England possesses in this district of the colony alone, some thousands of acres of land as Glebe—and besides, by its influence plundered the fire sufferers of £13,000! While the Catholic church does not possess a rood, nor receive a farthing of the fire funds.

The plundering referred to was the collection of funds for fire sufferers and building a cathedral made by Bishop Feild in England which he split on a fifty-fifty basis. Some felt, without justification, that all the money should have gone to fire sufferers.

Bishop Fleming was soon dead and his successor, Dr. Mullock, opened the two new cemeteries. The old graveyard on Long's Hill continued to receive guests for five or six years after the government ordered it closed. Mount Carmel was consecrated on 26 June 1855, and Belvedere Cemetery a few days later on July 1. An extension to Belvedere was consecrated on 8 July 1881.

In the old days, the deceased's clergyman and doctor generally preceded the cortege on the way to the churchyard. The last such funeral seen in St. John's took place on 17 November 1870 when Patrick Kelly, youngest son of Captain William Kelly of Cochrane Street, died at the age of forty-two and was buried.[27] It was also the practice to send gloves and black crepe for the hat to invited mourners. The first funeral at which

693

these were not sent was that of forty-six-year-old John McMillan who was buried from his Water Street residence, at 2:30 p.m., Sunday, 1 October 1876.[28]

Most of Newfoundland's great men and women of the past, as well as the humble, lie in weed-covered ground, beneath tilting headstones. It is strange that a people who have such a high regard for religion as Newfoundlanders have such a low regard for the final resting place of their dead. The poet would be required to conjure all his powers of imagination in order to sing "of blossoms, birds and bowers" in most St. John's cemeteries.

6

True Faith and Ready Hands

The Church of England diocese of Newfoundland was separated from that of Nova Scotia in 1828 and the following year Dr. Aubrey Spencer was consecrated as the first Lord Bishop of the colony. Born in Mayfair 12 February 1785 he was a grandson of the second Duke of Marlborough. Consecrated to the see of Newfoundland at Lambeth Palace 4 August 1839, he later served as Bishop of Jamaica for ten years. Retired to Devon he died there 24 February 1872 and is buried in Collaton. (Courtesy Queen's College.)

697

St. Thomas's, the oldest church still standing in St. John's, and the Narrows beyond, as seen from Government House (circa 1850). In this painting by W. R. Best the church-like structure in the centre is the Anglican theological college which eventually became Queen's College. (Courtesy St. John's City Hall.)

This sketch by Oldfield shows the junction of Military and King's Bridge Road in 1821. Fort William can be seen behind the horse and cart. The high board fence on the right enclose the house which became the residence of Bishop Spencer when he was consecrated Bishop of Newfoundland in 1839. The ghostly figures on horseback in front of the fence are pencil drawings not completed in ink. (Courtesy St. John's City Hall.)

Comparing this photograph of the nearly completed cathedral (circa 1885) with the previous drawing, very few changes are seen Bishop Feild's residence peeps out from behind the cathedral on the right while Old Gower Street Methodist Church is at the left. In front of Old Gower is the Methodist Chapel which was dragged across the street to the corner of Church Hill. (Courtesy Newfoundland Provincial Archives.)

The Reverend James O'Donel arrived in St. John's in 1784 to find the place a "howling moral wilderness" with an indifference to all religious observances. Twelve years later he was consecrated first English bishop in Canada. He left Newfoundland in 1807 and died in his native Ireland, 15 April 1811. (Courtesy Roman Catholic Episcopal Corporation.)

Captain Henry Prescott from a painting by W. Gosse. The Captain, who was Governor of Newfoundland from 1834 to 1841, engaged in a battle of wits with Bishop Fleming over the site for the proposed Roman Catholic Cathedral which the Bishop eventually won. Prescott became an admiral in 1860 and died 18 November 1874. (Courtesy Newfoundland Provincial Archives.)

This detail from Brenton's drawing of St. John's in 1798 shows the Anglican church in the upper right on the site of the present cathedral. The building with the T-shaped roof in the centre left is the Roman Catholic chapel erected by Bishop O'Donel in penal times when a Catholic church had to look like a private dwelling. (Courtesy Public Archives of Canada.

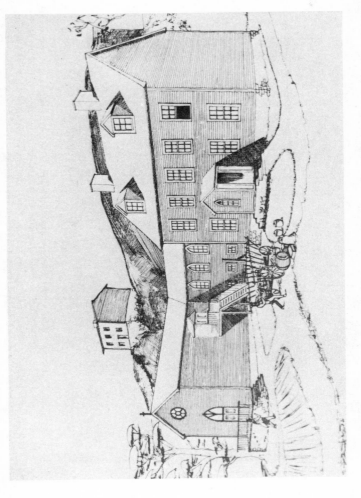

This is how the Roman Catholic complex on Henry Street looked during Bishop Fleming's time. On the right is the episcopal residence with the building known as the Old Chapel on the left. Connecting the two structures is the Catholic Academy. The steps lead from the gallery of the Old Chapel. The Star of the Sea Hall stands on the site today. (Courtesy Roman Catholic Episcopal Corporation.)

703

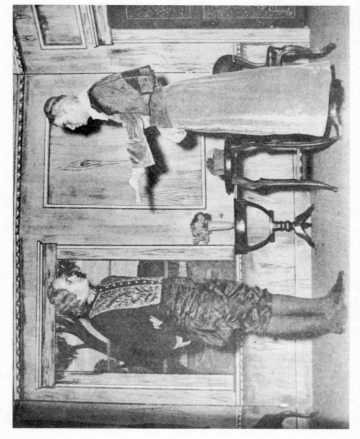

In 1955 the stage pageant "Triumph and Sacrifice" was presented to honour the one hundredth anniversary of the consecration of the Basilica of St. John the Baptist. This scene from the production shows a determined Bishop Fleming (Michael Cashin) demanding that an obstinate Governor Prescott (Paul O'Neill) give him the grant of land he wants on which to build a cathedral. (Courtesy Roman Catholic Episcopal Corporation.)

Bishop Thomas Scallan was a literate, sophisticated, and urbane man devoted to culture. He was consecrated Roman Catholic Bishop of St. John's in May 1816. His ecumenical greeting to Bishop Inglis of Nova Scotia got him in serious difficulties. Scallan requested that Father Michael Fleming be his successor. (Courtesy Roman Catholic Episcopal Corporation.)

The Reverend Michael Howley was born at St. John's 25 September 1843. A scholar, poet, and historian of note he succeeded Dr. Power as Roman Catholic Bishop of St. John's in 1894. He was elevated to the archepiscopate in 1904 and became Newfoundland's first archbishop. His fame as a historian rests on his *Ecclesiastical History* and numerous pamphlets. Archbishop Howley died 15 October 1914.

The Roman Catholic Cathedral of St. John the Baptist was a legacy of Bishop Fleming who made a number of trips across the Atlantic to obtain the land. It was completed and consecrated in 1955, five years after the death of Dr. Fleming. In this 1900 view the pink, white, and green Newfoundland flag flies from the left tower while the green Irish harp flag flies on the right. The cathedral was raised to the rank of Basilica in 1955.

706

Thousands of Portuguese fishermen with flambeaus in hand gather on the RCN dock in St. John's 17 May 1955 to march to the Roman Catholic Basilica to present statues of the Fatima apparition brought from Fatima, Portugal. Flag-decorated ships of the Portuguese White Fleet are seen in the background. (Courtesy Roman Catholic Episcopal Corporation.)

707

The Reverend John Pickavant was born in Lancashire in 1792. Ordained in 1814 he was a Methodist missionary in Newfoundland for thirty years. In 1816, when he was twenty-three years old, he arrived in St. John's as the first Methodist minister in the capital. Pickavant died in England in 1848. (Courtesy Gower Street United Church.)

A recently discovered photograph of the Reverend Charles Pedley, Congregational parson and a learned historian whose *History of Newfoundland*, published in June 1863, probably ranks second only to Prowse's. Pedley served the Congregationalists in St. John's from 1857 to 1864. He died at Cobourg, Ontario, in 1872. (Courtesy Rev. James Armour.)

708

Gower Street Methodist Chapel at the foot of Long's Hill opened on Boxing Day 1816. It survived many disasters including the Great Fires of 1817 and 1846. On 1 July 1847, after numerous renovations, the old building was moved to the other side of the street to make room for a new brick Wesleyan church on Gower Street. (Courtesy Gower Street United Church.)

True Faith and Ready Hands

A time like this demands
Strong minds, great hearts, true faith
And ready hands.
JOSIAH GILBERT HOLLAND *The Day's Demand*

Surveys indicate that St. John's has the largest per capita church-going population of any city in Canada. Religion has always played an integral role in the lives of most of its citizens. The story of the town might almost be traced through the history of its churches.

The Roman Catholic clergy have played a very active role in the island's affairs from the time of their first bishop, Dr. O'Donel who helped to put down a rebellion by Irish troops of the garrison in 1799, to Archbishop Roche whose bold front-page editorial in the diocesan newspaper, the *Monitor,* opposing confederation with Canada in 1948, united the Orange Societies of the island in a determination to defeat Responsible Government at the polls.

In a less obvious way the bishops and clergy of the Church of England have also taken a role in political, economic, and cultural matters. In more recent times the voices of Methodists and Presbyterians have been added to the chorus. In tracing the story of the St. John's mother church of these four important denominations we find a fascinating and contradictory tale of bigotry and co-operation that was the way of religion in Newfoundland before the twentieth century.

THE ANGLICAN CHURCH

In a petition to the Bishop of London in 1699, asking for the services of a clergyman, the Church of England people of St. John's not only promised to support a pastor but "upon his arrival to rebuild the church that was here destroyed by the French." This is the first recorded mention we have of a church in St. John's. The chapel was probably little more than a room set aside in Fort William, for no such building has ever been found in plans of the town. It would appear from the petition that it was destroyed in 1696 when the fort fell to invading French forces.

In 1699 Rev. John Jackson, who seems to have served as a naval chaplain on the Newfoundland station, arrived in St. John's with his wife and eight children, as pastor of the flock. Several years later, in 1702, he built "a small but handsome church in the precincts of Fort William." The following year he was described as being in want and deplorable circumstances. This did not prevent the garrulous divine from engaging in a bitter personal feud with the garrison commander, Captain Lloyd. A loose-living martinet, Lloyd was accused of having ordered soldiers whipped for the pleasure of his mistress and profaned the Lord's day with fiddling and naked dancing. He was also said to have hired out soldiers and kept most of the payment for himself.[1] The story is told in some detail in Chapters 2 and 5 of Volume I.

The three-year-old church was destroyed in 1705 when the town fell to five hundred French troops who burned the fort and houses. In that same year the bitterness between the parson and commander ended with Lloyd's recall to England to defend himself against charges. He was convicted but seems to have bought back his commission and returned to the town the following year promoted to the rank of Major. The Reverend Mr. Jackson was also recalled to London but he, with his small army of children, was shipwrecked off the Isle of Wight on the way home and, though they all escaped with their lives, he lost what little possessions he had. For some years afterwards he went about London in want and poverty until appointed to a living by Queen Anne.[2]

His successor, Rev. Jacob Rice who was also given the promise of a decent living by the congregation, rebuilt the church at St. John's in 1706 but it was again laid in ruins by the French when the place was captured and destroyed by their forces under St. Ovide de Brouillon in 1708. There is no record of its having been repaired so the congregation was, for a time, without a chapel.

Twelve years later Jacob Rice erected a larger wooden church of fir and spruce close to the site of the present cathedral. By 1730 he was also said to be "much distressed through want of means." The Rev. Mr. Fordyce, who succeeded Rice, had to return to England six years after his appointment, also because of his inability to procure subsistence for himself and family from the congregation.

With the departure of Fordyce in 1736, the mission at St. John's was abandoned for nine years. In spite of their repeated assurances to the Bishop of London, the Church of England congregation of soldiers, immigrants, and planters had consistently failed to live up to their promises once a parson was installed. During the nine years in which the mission was closed, the spiritual welfare of the people was cared for in summer by chaplains of the naval station. One of these, Rev. Thomas Walbank, chaplain on board H.M.S. *Sutherland,* ministered to the flock of five hundred during the four months of summer in 1742. He reported the church at St. John's to be large and well furnished.

The year 1744 saw the Reverend Mr. Peasley transfer from Bonavista on the assurance that a house had been procured for his use and the usual promised payment of a stipend for his maintenance. He stayed in St. John's seven years until the failure of the flock to give him either a house or a living forced his removal to North Carolina.

Next to come was Rev. Edward Langman, M.A., a scholarly gentleman of Balliol College, Oxford. On assuming his duties in 1752, he reported the population of St. John's, exclusive of the garrison, to consist of a hundred families of which fifty-two were Roman Catholic, forty Church of England, and eight Dissenters. Rev. Langman decided to put up a new church in 1758, and the following year construction was begun on the present cathedral site near the east corner of Duckworth Street and Church Hill. The area was used for public hangings and the gallows had to be moved elsewhere.

The building of this house of worship was still not accomplished without coercion on the part of the authorities. Governor Richard Edwards made prisoners of thirty persons who failed to contribute toward the erection of the church and gave them a choice of making a donation, working on the construction, or going to jail.

In spite of the fact that Parson Langman was forced to go and "beg for alms as a poor man would," in order to eke out an existence, he was able to raise four hundred pounds for his new church. The Governor's tactics undoubtedly helped but even so the promises made by the faithful to support their pastor were again unfulfilled. Reverend Mr. Langman had a small house on Henry Street, probably little more than a shack. He ate out of his garden, which was near today's Dicks Square. John Jones, the founder of Congregationalism in Newfoundland, says that Parson Langman was dismissed in 1783 without a pension and with "the contemptuous speeches of the public." Rev. Samuel Greatheed, a strict Puritan, characterized him as "notoriously immoral" and a "lover of the bottle."

In 1762 the French landed at Bay Bulls, marched to St. John's, and captured the town. The garrison were made prisoners and all who were not Roman Catholics were forced to leave and their property was seized. The Reverend Langman was too ill to be moved so he stayed behind where he was roughly treated, his house plundered, and his property confiscated. His losses were a hundred and thirty pounds. When the town was recaptured by Colonel Amherst, Langman resumed his missionary work until his faculties failed him in 1784.[3] He was the first permanent clergyman of the Anglican faith in St. John's, and he also served as a very strict magistrate.

A new church was opened just above the old one on 19 October 1800. It measured sixty-seven and a half by sixty-four and a half feet and was twenty-one feet high. It had a cottage-style roof that was later raised so that it consisted of four triangles. To the building of this church King George contributed two hundred guineas and Governor Waldegrave an unspecified amount. In all, some fifteen hundred pounds was collected.

The year 1787 saw the See of Nova Scotia constituted. Newfound-

713

land, which had been under the nominal care of the Bishop of London, was included in the new see. However, the Bishop, Charles Inglis, was never able to visit the island, and the same was true of his successor, Dr. Robert Stanser. It was not until the time of Bishop John Inglis, a son of Charles Inglis, that Newfoundland was visited for the first time by its Church of England ecclesiastic in 1827. During the six weeks of the bishop's stay in and around St. John's, the twenty-seven-year-old church was finally consecrated. Dr. Inglis found it to be commodious and in good repair but spoke of the lack of a belltower or steeple. Two drawings of the town in 1831 show the tower completed.

In 1825 Governor Cochrane wrote to the Colonial Office pointing out that St. John's, with a population of twelve thousand, had

> . . . one Episcopal Church, one Wesleyan, and one small Presbyterian chapel. The Episcopal Church contains 70 pews and 60 free seats. . . . It is unnecessary to point out the total inadequacy of such an establishment to the wants of so large a population . . . there is no part of the world where an efficient Church Establishment would be productive of better effects than among the lower orders of this colony, or where the expense attending it would be more likely to be repaid by an increasing industry and economy, and consequently by fewer calls upon government for support.[4]

A Protestant bishopric was established in the colony in 1839 under the title Bishop of Newfoundland. The words of the instrument and establishment are:

> Whereas by letters-patent under the Great Seal of the United Kingdom of Great Britain and Ireland, bearing date at Westminster, the 17th day of July, 1839, in the 3rd year of our reign, we did erect, found, and ordain, make and constitute the Island of Newfoundland to be the Bishop's see, and to be called henceforth the Bishopric of Newfoundland.

The first incumbent was a man who had served the island as a missionary, Dr. Aubrey Spencer. At the time of his elevation he was Archdeacon of Bermuda. A grandson of the second Duke of Marlborough,[5] Bishop Spencer was a highly accomplished man and born aristocrat. His daughter married the son of the Governor of Newfoundland, Sir John Harvey.

Dr. Spencer, who took the title Aubrey Newfoundland, tells us:

> At my consecration to the see of Newfoundland, I found only eight clergymen of the Church of England in the whole colony; the church itself is a most disorganized and dispirited condition; the schools languishing, many of them broken up, and all destitute of

that spirit of unity and order so essential to their real efficiency. I am very thankful that I have been permitted, within the short space of two years, to remedy some of these evils, and to supply the most craving of their deficiencies. . . .

The clergy in Newfoundland are maintained mainly by the noble Society for the Propagation of the Gospel in Foreign Parts, but the people are called on by the Bishop to provide a house and a small stipend, according to their respective means, for their several missionaries. . . .

With the liberal aid of the Society for Promoting Christian Knowledge, and that of the Society of Dr. Bray's Associates, I hope also to enrich the clerical and parochial lending libraries, to erect several new school-houses, and to establish a printing press at the Theological Institute at St. John's. In many of these works I look for assistance from the Diocesan Church Society, in which I hope to see enrolled almost every member of our communion throughout the land.

In 1849, soon after his consecration as Bishop, Dr. Spencer found that "the condition of the church was indeed so deplorable as to divest the service of religion of much of the veneration and dignity which rightly belong to it." The rundown building, raised to the rank of Cathedral, impressed him "with a mournful sense of the small proportion of our worldly substance which has been bestowed on the sanctuary of God."[6]

An attempt was begun to raise funds for a proper cathedral. Bishop Spencer dispatched Archdeacon Bridge to England with an appeal to the "liberal and wealthy supporters of the Still Established Church in England."

This appeal was probably the same as one which appears in the second edition of Archdeacon Wix's journal and is remarkable today as a footnote to the bigotry prevalent in England at the time. Termed "An Appeal on Behalf Of The Protestant Episcopalians Of The Town Of St. John's, Newfoundland," the document reveals some excellent insights:

The town of St. John's contains above 13,000 souls; about 8,000 are Roman Catholics, and the remaining 5,000 are principally attached to the Protestant Church; and it is for the poor emigrant Protestant settlers in Newfoundland that this appeal is made . . . the present church in St. John's does not accommodate more than 800 persons. . . . Whilst a second Popish chapel is soon to be erected in our capital—and this in a colony where the state of society equals, if it does not exceed, in ignorance, superstition, and insubordination, the worst parts of Ireland. This want of Church-room exists in a town . . . where a resident Roman Catholic Bishop and three or four priests are not only the most zealous and indefatigable in the spiritual duties and endeavours to make many converts, but where they also use every means in their power to encourage the natural superstition of the people; and by forbidding the children of Roman Catholic parents attending Protestant schools, they effectually keep them in that state of ignorance which best suits their false and idolatrous doctrines.

A Nunnery has been established, where a variety of fancy work is taught, to induce the Protestant children to attend the school attached to the establishment; and no scheme of allurement or intimidation is omitted to ensnare the poor and ignorant into the trap laid for them. . . .

The statement continues with a warning to the Parish Sunday School to watch and pray for its pupils, "Who may be scattered through the wilds of America, or settled amongst idolaters, infidels and scoffers." It ends by calling on the faithful to recall the blessings of "a seed sown by English Missionaries, watered by English bounty" and adds the hope that "this appeal will not be made in vain for funds to build a new Protestant Episcopal Church in St. John's."[7]

Unknown to those in England who were moved by the appeal, the nunnery referred to was a house which the Presentation Sisters were renting, on an eight-year lease, from the Church of England pastor of St. Thomas Church—none other than Archdeacon Edward Wix.

Either the heady emotion of the appeal, or the eloquence of the handsome Archdeacon Bridge, resulted in a substantial sum of money being raised for the new cathedral. Liberal donations were received from the Queen Dowager as well as the Archbishops and Bishops of England. The Governor, Sir John Harvey, gave a hundred pounds and the Bishop added a hundred of his own.

Construction was delayed by dissentions which soon surfaced, over the site where the new church was to be built. In a pastoral letter Bishop Spencer called on his flock "to lay aside all animosities, to abandon or reconcile all trifling differences of opinion, unite as men confessing One Lord, One Faith, One Baptism, in building up the Lord's House." The Bishop's own view was that the best place for the cathedral was in the existing churchyard, provided the foundations were laid "with due care to the rights of those who have an interest in the graves."

Within a few months Dr. Spencer was able to announce that the differences had finally been settled regarding the site and construction would proceed on the spot he had chosen at an estimate of seven thousand pounds. Plans were drawn up locally by a Mr. Purcell at a cost of twenty pounds. James Purcell had been brought to Newfoundland from Cork, Ireland, to superintend the building of the Roman Catholic cathedral, by Dr. Michael Fleming. According to the Cork Constitution, 18 May 1843, eighteen hundred tons of cut limestone were shipped to St. John's for the Church of England cathedral which was to be 120 feet lone, 56 feet broad, and with a spire 130 feet high. The Constitution said the church would cost ten thousand pounds. The plans for the entire project were the work of Mr. Purcell himself. A drawing of the proposed cathedral appears in the front of Philip Tocque's book, *Wandering Thoughts*, as the "Church of England Cathedral, St. John's."

The limestone ordered from Ireland was delivered in crates at the site, and on 21 August 1843 the foundation stone was laid by Bishop Spencer just four days before his leaving the see to take up new duties in Jamaica.[8] Beneath the plate on the stone were deposited the seal of the Bishop of London, a glass bottle containing coins of the reign, a parchment copy of the inscription on the stone, and numbers of the *Royal Gazette* and *Times* newspapers which carried in their pages the order of the proceedings. The location of this stone is unknown.

The Governor, Sir John Harvey, spoke at the ceremony and Bishop Spencer delivered an address in the old church nearby. With the establishment of a see in Newfoundland that ramshackle building had been automatically designated a cathedral. It was, in all respects, unworthy of the title. In spite of the laying of the foundation stone for the new house of worship, construction on the design by Purcell was never begun.

Less than three years after the arrival of Rt. Rev. Edward Feild, successor to Dr. Spencer, St. John's was devastated by the Great Fire of 1846, which left in ruins most of the business section, many of the churches, and a number of private dwellings. One of the churches lost in the flames was the old Church of England on Church Hill.[9]

In the autumn of that year Bishop Feild took ship to England to send relief back to fire sufferers and try and raise money with which to rush to completion the unstarted cathedral. It was decided to scrap Bishop Spencer's design, and while in London Dr. Feild met Sir George Gilbert Scott, a noted architect prominent in the Gothic revival, and engaged his even more famous son Sir Giles Gilbert Scott, to draw up a new and more elaborate design. Scott's reputation is built on his work in the neo-Gothic tradition. Among London churches of his design are St. Agnes, Kennington, and All Hallows, Southwark.

Bishop Feild arrived back in St. John's on 25 May 1847 on board the little church ship, *Hawk*. While in England he had been approached by Jacob Mountain, a twenty-nine-year-old clergyman who had heard of the need in Newfoundland. They sailed together on what turned out to be a stormy passage. As the weeks went by, the voyagers were all but given up for lost by the waiting congregation, and it was decided to go ahead with the opening of the new foundations without the Bishop. To the relief of all, the ship appeared off St. John's on the very day of the ceremony.

The prayer book used by the Reverend Mountain on the voyage is inscribed:

> A thank offering from those who sailed in the Hawk, Church Ship, from Torquay on Sunday, April 18th, 1847, on their mission to Newfoundland, and by the mercy of God arrived at St. John's after

a tempestuous passage on Whittuesday, May 25th. On which day
the ground for the foundations of the new cathedral of St. John
The Baptist at St. John's were opened.

Mountain, who became principal of Queen's College, died of typhoid
fever at the age of thirty-seven. His prayer book was used in the cathedral
until the 1880s when it was sent to the church at St. Pierre. With the
dismantling of that church in 1940, it went to the rector of Lamaline, for
use at Point Crewe. When the people of Point Crewe moved to Fortune, in
the late 1950s, it was taken to High Beach. Following the last service
conducted there in 1966 it was given over to the Venerable W.G. Legge,
who passed it over to the rector of the cathedral in November of that year,
and it is now on display in the church museum.

With the opening of the ground for foundations by Bishop Feild,
construction was at last begun. The original limestone had been ruined by
heat in the Great Fire and a new supply, of twelve thousand tons of cut
stone, was ordered from England and Ireland. The new building was to be
188 feet long, 99 feet wide, and 80 feet high to the ridge of the roof which
was to be vaulted with a tower and spire. Flagstone for the floor was
brought from France. The Bishop was able to open the completed nave to
worship on 21 September 1850. After that, construction bogged down and
did not get moving again until 1880 when Bishop Llewellyn Jones urged its
completion as a memorial to Bishop Feild.

In March of that year men and boys of the city, as well as the crews of
sealing steamers waiting to leave port for the ice fields turned out in the
hundreds, every day for a week, to volunteer their labour to haul the stone
from the quarries to the site. Those who helped were not only members
of the Church of England, but Roman Catholics and dissenting Protestants as well.

The choir and transepts were completed from plans reworked by Sir
Giles Gilbert Scott, son of the original architect. When excavations for this
part of the project were being dug on 18 June 1880, the skeleton of a military man was unearthed. Buttons found with the bones indicated the
corpse was that of a naval lieutenant, who some thought may have been
that of Lt. Philpott, a young naval officer killed in the last fatal duel fought
in St. John's in 1826. Others have suggested they might have been those of
Mr. Lawrey, a lieutenant on H.M.S. *Boston,* killed in a press gang murder
in 1794.

By 1885 work on the cathedral was finished and the choir and
transepts were finally consecrated. Seven years later the whole edifice was
left a blackened shell when the Great Fire of 1892 swept through St. John's
leaving much of the city a smouldering ruin.

Of the cathedral, only the walls remained. This crushing blow was
made all the more severe by the loss of the Cathedral Rectory, Clergy
House, Synod Hall, and other property. A decision was taken to restore the

718

TRUE FAITH AND READY HANDS

cathedral immediately. With the help of members of the Anglican communion throughout the world, funds were raised and at a cost of sixty-five thousand dollars the present choir and transepts were completed. The repaired structure was dedicated anew on 28 June 1895. After that, all activity once more ceased.

In an address to the Synod of 1902 Bishop Jones urged the completion of the cathedral. There was still an immense mass of debris left by the fire. The work of clearing this away was done by free labour, which commenced on June 24 after a brief service held by the Bishop who stood amidst the ruins. By July 18 the work was completed. Day after day, when their regular working hours were over, men and boys laboured into the night to get the job done. Again, Roman Catholics, as well as dissenting Protestants, loaned a helping hand and the Star of the Sea Society organized a football match that raised four hundred dollars toward expenses.[10]

The restored nave was blessed on 21 September 1905. The sermon for the Benediction was preached by the Right Reverend Frederick Courtney, Rector of St. James's Church in New York and a former Bishop of Nova Scotia. The completion of the tower was proposed that same year but the project was considered too expensive at the time. Later it was felt that the native stone used in the construction might not take the weight of the spire, the crowning glory of any Gothic cathedral. In recent years there have been suggestions that the work be carried out in aluminum. It is to be hoped that this will be done to bring out the full beauty of the finest Gothic church in North America and the masterpiece of George Gilbert Scott.

In 1955 reconstruction and replacement of much of the stone was considered a necessity and the work was commenced. It has continued ever since. During the renovations, which were carried out by the Rambuch Decorating Company of New York as a result of the firm's work in redecorating the Basilica, the plaster which covered the inside walls was removed, revealing the true beauty of the stone. It is obvious from the unevenness of the wall stones that they were not originally intended to be exposed.

Much of the early history of the Church of England in St. John's is not told in the story of the cathedral but in that of the church called St. Thomas's. This oldest church building in Newfoundland is still in continuous use. Known as the Old Garrison Church, it is located on Military Road, just east of the Mall, in front of Government House.

The first garrison church in St. John's goes back to 1699 when the town consisted of eight hundred people living in small cottages clustered around Fort William. As mentioned, that church seems to have been destroyed by the French when they took St. John's in 1708. The next garrison church does not make its appearance until 1827 when the Venerable George Coster and Governor Sir Thomas Cochrane recommended its erection.

In 1833 Archdeacon Edward Wix went to England to plead the cause.

719

He returned with some financial help and offers of aid to erect "a Church sixty-two feet by thirty-six, with galleries, capable of holding seven hundred persons. . . ." Governor Cochrane secured from the Imperial Government a gift of the land on which the church stands, on the stipulation that seating be provided for the church members of the garrison.[11]

No account can be found of the consecration and opening in official records or newspapers of the day. We do know from an advertisement placed in *The Times,* for the sale of the opening sermon at one shilling ninepence per copy, that the discourse was delivered on 28 September 1836 by Rev. Charles Blackman, Rector of St. Luke's, Port-de-Grave. It appears that the sermon was delivered on the day of the official opening, but in a letter dated 24 August 1843 Bishop Spencer writes:

> On my arrival in St. John's the Church of St. Thomas became one of the earliest objects of my care, and I am happy in having been enabled *to complete and embellish the building, to consecrate it to the worship of the Almighty,* and to establish it as a district church in this large and increasing city.

To judge by this letter the building was not completed and consecrated until after the arrival of Dr. Spencer in June 1840.

The site is described in the contract for the church as "A plot of land on the barrens bounded on the North and West by the Public Mall and on the South and East by land in the occupancy of the Royal Engineers and the Commissariat Department."[12] The workshop of the Royal Engineers, on Military Road first west of King's Bridge Road, was later renovated for use as an orphanage and then as a hostel for students of Bishop Feild College. In time it was replaced by a Tudor-style building for theological students. Canon Wood Hall, which afterwards occupied the site, was seriously damaged by fire in May 1966 and torn down.

The Queen's Bakehouse, on the corner of Military and King's Bridge Roads, jutted so far out into the intersection that you could stand on the doorstep and look along Gower Street. Behind the bakery, where a school now stands, was the Commissariat Coal Shed. A short distance down King's Bridge Road were the offices and dwelling of the Assistant Commissary General, built in 1818. This building is still standing and has been restored by the federal government as a national historic site. It served as rectory for the incumbent of St. Thomas's Church from 1870 until 1969. A curate's house, located at 6 Forest Road, was sold in 1971.

The Old Garrison Church has much in common with Uncle Tom's Topsy—it just growed. Many changes have been made to the original structure erected by Patrick Kough, a builder who came from Ireland in 1824, and worked on the construction of Government House before going into business for himself. From 1832-37 he was a member of the Legislature for St. John's. Kough died on 9 November 1863. His stone house on Kenna's Hill is still standing.

There are many items of historic fascination in St. Thomas's Church. In front of the rear gallery there is a cast-iron Hanoverian coat of arms—the Royal Arms of 1815. With the accession of Queen Victoria and the separation of Hanover from the throne of England the Hanoverian symbols were removed from the Arms adopted by the young Queen.

There was once a large square pew at the front of the lower gallery for the use of the governor. Fitted out with crimson rep curtains and up-holstered in the same material, it was furnished with a table and several wooden armchairs. Here Governors Prescott, Harvey, and LeMarchant sang praises to the Lord. A sour note was struck by Governor Hamilton when, in the winter of 1852-3, he complained of the cold draft and was moved to what was known as the bishop's pew, immediately in front of the reading desk on the ground floor. The governor's pew was removed when the gallery front was renovated by the addition of the war memorial wood-work.

Not quite so old as St. Thomas's, but an interesting relic of the ecclesiastical past of the Church of England in St. John's, is Christ Church, Quidi Vidi, once a chapel of ease to St. Thomas's. The first house of worship on the site was a sort of ecumenical chapel. How it came into being is not clear. Methodist annals for 1822 mention materials having been obtained in that year for a chapel at Quidi Vidi. The next information we have is that a church opened in the village on 30 July 1834, to be shared by Methodists, Church of England, and Congregationalists. In John Jones's Journal, belonging to the Congregationalists, it states that the chapel was "built by the sole exertions of the Congregational Church in St. John's." Even the opening date mentioned above is a matter of controversy for a newspaper of August 31 says "the neat little chapel which has lately been erected at Quidi Vidi" opened for worship on Wednesday last. That would be in late August. According to John Jones the land was given by a man named Brace.

The ecumenical project was apparently premature, for dissensions began to surface and in nine years the venture ended. Somehow the Church of England got hold of the property and decided to erect a new chapel on the site. Bishop Spencer wrote of it in his journal: "We are founding a new church, the old one being in a decayed state."

It is not clear whether the old church was completely demolished or built into the new one. Again there is controversy on this point. Since nothing has been proven, one way or the other, we must accept the Bishop's statement as indicating that the old building was razed. In any case the new church opened on 9 November 1842.

The Times, describing the event under the heading NEW CHURCH AT QUIDI VIDI, had this to say: "The church, recently erected at Quidi Vidi, under the direction of the Lord Bishop of the Diocese ... opened yesterday. The desk was occupied by Rev. O. Howard, the clergyman in charge of the settlement ... the sermon was preached by Rev. Mr. Bridge...."[13] The item went on to say that the congregation was very numerous, with between thirty and forty communicants. A collection resulted in about eight pounds being taken up.

The chapel was designed by James Purcell, and he gave his plans to Mr. Brett whose active exertions led to the erection of the Quidi Vidi church. On opening day it was lamented that Brett had moved away from St. John's. Rev. Oswald Howell lived in the little village at King's Bridge until April 19 when his house, barns, carriage, and other worldly goods were sold by auction. *The Times* concluded its article on the opening by adding "Tho' it is not yet completed this church promises to be quite a model for a village church."

In 1888 Christ Church was closed for six months while the building underwent extensive repairs and a paling fence was erected around the outside. With the coming of the automobile the congregation began to dwindle, as the faithful drove to services in the city. By the 1960s it was decided to close out the church and tear down the dilapidated structure. An organization called the Newfoundland Historic Trust was formed for the purpose of preserving the old church. On 10 July 1966 the chapel was deconsecrated and secularized in a special service. The following July it was taken over by the Trust and funds were raised for its restoration. These ran out and money problems and vandalism plagued the project so that it was not completed until 1973. Besides age, Christ Church has another historic claim. It was used by a New York film producer, Varick Frizel, for the climactic scene in the first sound feature film made in Canada, *The Viking,* with Charles Starrett.

To conclude the story of the Anglican church in St. John's, mention must be made of the Church of St. Mary the Virgin, which was on the Southside Road a little to the east of Long Bridge. A monument now marks the site. St. Mary's grew out of a suggestion in a Lenten pastoral letter of Bishop Feild in 1857. The cost was estimated at around three thousand pounds (twelve thousand dollars). Plans and specifications were prepared by Rev. Wm. Grey, M.A., incumbent at Portugal Cove and a noted artist who has left us many valuable sketches of St. John's in his day. The Reverend Grey was a direct descendant of the family of England's nine-day Queen, Lady Jane Grey, who was dispatched heavenward in the Tower of London by Mary Tudor. Grey's son succeeded to the title and Earldom of Stanford as the ninth earl.

The contractor was Richard Harvey who completed the construction for a total cost of £3478.2.11. The new church was consecrated on Friday, 24 June 1859, in the name of St. Mary the Virgin, by Dr. Edward Feild, then Lord Bishop of Newfoundland, Labrador, and Bermuda. The wife of Rev. Jacob Mountain gave a pair of brass candlesticks for the altar. Later that day baptism was administered and the first child to receive the sacrament was the three-month-old son of the builder, Richard Harvey, who was named John Richard. Rev. John Pearson was the parson in charge.[14]

Built on twelve acres of Admiralty property, which included the old Admiralty store, the new church stood "with no nakedness or shabbiness within." On the outside it was "not only simple but severe in style," suited to the rugged Southside Hills. In 1911 the church was enlarged to nearly twice its original size, but by 1959 it was felt that still more space was needed. Since the federal government was anxious to acquire the land, some parishioners saw this as an opportunity to erect a modern church in a more fashionable part of the west end. On June 21 that year Bishop John Meaden, whos parents had been married in old St. Mary's in 1876, broke ground for a new St. Mary's on Craigmillar Avenue. A cry went up to save the old building but a remote Ottawa was impervious to the distant voices. Old St. Mary's was recklessly and needlessly pulled down in 1963.

The Anglican Church in Newfoundland got its first Archbishop on 15 October 1975 when the Lord Bishop of the diocese, Rt. Rev. R.L. Seaborn, was elected Archbishop and Metropolitan of the Ecclesiastic Province of Canada. There are four in the country: Canada, Ontario, British Columbia, and Rupert's Land.

A native of Toronto, Bishop Seaborn, at the age of sixty-four, was the first Bishop of Newfoundland to become a Metropolitan, a position in the Anglican Church in Canada second only to Primate. Archbishop Seaborn, a World War II chaplain who was awarded the Croix de Guerre, served as Assistant Bishop in Newfoundland for seven years before becoming Bishop in 1969. His formal installation and enthronement as Archbishop was at the Cathedral in St. John's, 16 November 1975, at the closing of the last synod of the Anglican Church of Newfoundland, following which three diocese were created for three bishops instead of the former single diocese with a bishop and an assistant bishop.

THE ROMAN CATHOLIC CHURCH

The Roman Catholic religion was planted in Newfoundland by Sir George Calvert, who became Lord Baltimore, at Ferryland in 1628. That year he made the first grant of freedom of religion in an English colony of America and brought three Jesuit priests to Ferryland from England. They were Fathers Smith, Longville, and Hackett. When the crusty Rev. Erasmus Stourton of John Guy's Cupids Colony, the first Church of England clergyman in Newfoundland, got wind of Popish practices on English territory, he travelled at once from Cupids to Ferryland. His investigation led to a clash with Calvert, and Sir George had the parson expelled from the island for his pains in uprooting Popery. It is reported that one of the priests from Baltimore's colony was travelling about the south of England the following year in want of means. It had been Calvert's dream in his province of Avalon to renew the Catholic glories of ancient Verulam and Glastonbury, but the seed withered with his departure in 1629.

It was not replanted until 1662, this time by the French at Placentia.

723

An unnamed French abbé came out with the settlers that year and was murdered by them when they later mutinied. He was probably followed by other unidentified clerics until 21 June 1689 when two priests of the Recollect Order established a monastery. One of them, Father Joseph Denys, remained at Placentia for at least half a dozen years. In 1692 a decree of the Sun King, Louis XIV, established the first Roman Catholic parish in Newfoundland, Our Lady of the Angels.

The lily of France was no more durable than the Catholic rose of England and it perished with the departure of the last French governor in 1714. The church that was left behind was transferred to the Church of England. The root that finally took was that of the shamrock planted by unlettered Irish labourers.

These hardworking people, mostly fishermen and servants, came out to the colony for what was known as a "Newfoundland season," a summer, a winter, and a summer, following which they were returned to their homes in Ireland. They were so numerous that, at home, the island was known as "transatlantic Ireland." Early in the nineteenth century Robert Kent, a Waterford merchant, settled in Newfoundland and established a prosperous import and export trade, which included the transportation of permanent settlers to the island in large numbers. The wages were high, and while harsh penal laws prohibited the Roman Catholic faith, they had been relaxed to such an extent by the 1780s that persecution was far less than in Ireland.

It had not always been so. For example, in 1755, we find Governor Dorrell, writing to the magistrates of Harbour Grace:

> Whereas I am informed that a Roman Catholic priest is at this time at Harbour Grace, and that he publicly read mass, which is contrary to the law, and against the peace of our soverign lord the king. You are hereby required and directed on the receipt of this, to cause the said priest to be taken into custody and sent round to this place. In this you are not to fail.[15]

It was actually Caplin Cove where the offending service had been held and the culprit cleric escaped to Harbour Main, where Michael Katem allowed him to use one of his fish rooms to celebrate a public mass at which Katem was present. The Justice of the Peace for Harbour Main, Charles Garland, was ordered to fine Katem "the sum of fifty pounds, and to demolish the said fish-room or store-room where said mass was said, and I do likewise order the said Michael Katem to sell all the possessions he has or holds in this harbour. . . ." The same day Michael Landircan of the same place stood accused of a similar crime. Garland was instructed "to fine him the sum of twenty pounds, to burn his house and stage down to the ground, and he to quit the said harbour. . . ." At the same time, Darby Costley,

Robert Finn, Michael Mooring, and Ronald McDonald confessed to being Roman Catholics. Costley and Finn were fined ten pounds, Mooring eight pounds, and McDonald two pounds ten shillings, and all were banished from the island.[16]

That was not the end of the affair. According to Prowse, sixteen others in Harbour Main, and as many at Harbour Grace and Carbonear, were convicted, and in every case the building in which the offensive service had been held was ordered destroyed. The name of the cleric who brought about these burnings, fines, and banishments is unknown. Several Irish priests did mission work in Newfoundland, prior to 1755, before the English penal code was so rigorously enforced by Governor Dorrell. Some believe these men to have been unfrocked in their homeland. With the coming of Dorrell no Papist clergyman was tolerated in the colony, partly due to the brutal murder of Magistrate William Keen by Catholic Irishmen. In order to be married, or have their children baptised, in their own church, it was necessary for Irish Catholics to return to their own country. The old parish registers in the southern ports of Ireland contain many marriage and baptismal entries relating to "Terra Nova."

A search of the registers of old St. Patrick's, in Waterford, shows Newfoundland entries from 30 January 1734 to 23 June 1780, by which time a more benevolent attitude appears to have emerged. Many of these registrations reveal that priests in Ireland solemnized marriages performed in Newfoundland by common consent, or by ship's captains. Some entries have couples being married and their children being baptised at the same time. For example, old St. Patrick's registry shows "John Roache and Joan Dunphy of Terra Nova" had their marriage vows solemnized and their four children baptised, 4 January 1762.[17] The business of transporting whole families to Ireland for the administration of the sacraments must have entailed not only much expense and hardship, but a great deal of personal hazard.

Most of the disabilities of the penal laws against Roman Catholics in Great Britain were removed in 1791 for those who took the oath of loyalty, but Ireland did not experience Catholic emancipation until 1926. Newfoundland's Irish Catholics were more fortunate. On 24 October 1784 a proclamation was published by Governor John Campbell, granting liberty of conscience to all persons in Newfoundland and the free exercise of such modes of religious worship as were not prohibited by law.

One immediate advantage of this relaxation of religious prohibitions against Roman Catholics was the arrival, that same year, of Rev. Dr. James O'Donel, who reached St. John's as the first regular authorized missioner of the church of Rome in Newfoundland. Tradition has him born at Biothrin Glas, in Garryntemple Townland, on the road leading from Marfield to Knocklofty, four miles south of Clomnel, County Tipperary. The year was 1737. After receiving his early education from a private tutor he went with his brother, Michael, to a classical school in Limerick where he decided to enter the Franciscan Order. He went from there to Prague, in Bohemia, as chaplain to various aristocratic families. In 1775 O'Donel returned to Ireland and was appointed Guardian at Waterford, where he was elected Provincial of the Order in Ireland from 1779 to 1781. Three years later he became Prefect Apostolic of the Roman Catholic church in Newfoundland.[18]

There was no chapel in St. John's at the time. There was not even a priest's house. Dr. O'Donel went to live in Tom William's house at the foot of Lime Kiln Hill, now a parking garage, east of City Hall. The clergyman soon found a desirable property, and the lease was signed, 20 October 1784, for ninety-nine years between John Rogers and Rev. James O'Donel, for a dwelling house, outhouses, and "two small gardens, the Cheery Garden and Court Yard before the door commonly called or known by the name of Parson Langman's, which was lately occupied by the said James Rogers." The property was on Henry Street above City Terrace. Its length along the Upper Path was sixty yards in front, fifty-three yards at the rear. Its depth was twenty-seven yards in the east and thirty-seven yards in the west. Bishop Howley has described the dwelling as a small cottage. A painting of St. John's in 1798, by R.P. Brenton, shows it as a substantial house with three dormer windows on the upper floor. Part of the dwelling was converted into a chapel and the remaining rooms were reserved by the priest for his own use.

In 1786 a chapel was built west of the cottage above the Upper Path. This T-shaped building is also visible in Brenton's painting. In 1787 an old man of unknown name was found lying dead behind this chapel. He was buried, October 10, in a pauper's grave. Exactly one month later we find Dr. O'Donel writing to Dublin asking for two clergymen who will be able to enforce obedience to lawful authority. His suggestion of "a Father Yore, who . . . offered himself" was acted upon and the man was sent out from the Archdiocese of Dublin.[19] Yore was to serve the church in Newfoundland with distinction for the next fifty years.

Shortly after the arrival of this assistant, O'Donel found himself in court answering accusations aimed at his expulsion. A letter was read out in the Court House in which the surrogate, Pellu, a man of French extraction, who had caught the eye of Governor Milbanke, publicly denounced Pope, Popery, priests, and priestcraft, and "in an extacy blessed his happy constitution that was cleanly purged from such knavery."

The small chapel which the priest built seems to have excited Pellu's ire. O'Donel, a superb Anglophile, suggests the man was jealous of the esteem in which he had been held by Governor Campbell. The surrogate closed his appeal to Milbanke with the request that priests should be turned out of the country; that circular letters should be sent to all magistrates; if any more priests arrive, to ship them off immediately; and that no priests should be left but where there was a garrison to keep them in awe. Writing to Ireland, 16 November 1788, Dr. O'Donel says,

When I heard this, I waited on the secretary, who told me that the admiral had made up his mind, and adopted the measures of his favourite Captain Pellu . . . with what depression of mind and spirits I returned from the garrison; however, I drew up my defence in writing, waited on the governor, who most politely received me, entirely changed his opinion, and assured me that he came to this country with a great regard and esteem for me. As his friend, Captain Campbell, so often spoke respectfully of my name to him, and that from what he could personally observe from my conduct, that he quitted the island with the same good opinion of me. I am truly a son of persecution and a child of affliction since I came to this country.[20]

The cordial meeting at Fort Townshend does not appear to have eased matters for long. Just before his consecration as bishop, Dr. O'Donel made application for leave to build a chapel in Ferryland. In his reply, from on board the *Salisbury*, 2 November 1790, the secretary states:

The Governor acquaints Mr. O'Donnell [sic] that, so far from being disposed to allow of an increase of places of religious worship for Roman Catholics of the island, he very seriously intends, next year, to lay those established already under particular restrictions. Mr. O'Donnell must be aware that it is not the interest of Great Britain to encourage people to winter in Newfoundland, and he cannot be ignorant that many of the lower order who would now stay, would, if it were not for the convenience with which they obtain absolution here, go home for it at least once in two or three years; and the Governor has been misinformed if O'Donnell instead of advising their return to Ireland, does not rather encourage them to winter in the country.[21]

An hour later His Excellency sailed out of St. John's for the winter, so that the priest had no opportunity of reasoning with the Royal representative. Milbanke was greatly influenced by Pellu who, by changes and quick promotions, was unexpectedly appointed the Admiral's captain for the year. Though he seems to have become hostile to O'Donel, the governor feared public opinion enough not to take any direct action against the man.

The year 1791 saw John Reeves appointed Judge Advocate, and this enlightened man not only brought law and order to the island, but true religious liberty, as well. O'Donel wrote of him:

Providence guided the steps of a Mr. Reeves to this country. . . . This truly good and benevolent man would not suffer me even to expostulate with the governor on his foul misrepresentation, as he assured me that the state of the Catholic church should remain unmolested here, and so it happened . . . it is to be supposed we shall never more be molested by governors, from this favourable prospect, I wish to have another missionary . . . it is absolutely necessary he should speak Irish.[22]

Accounts of the savage barbarity and inhuman cruelty of the Jacobin Club in Paris, in 1792, horrified the cultured O'Donel and left him intolerant of mutiny and revolution, as we shall see. Through the diplomatic cultivation of officials he began to find acceptance even in government circles. He wrote to the Archbishop of Dublin that

> Our present Governor and the judge advocate have made very solemn professions of friendship to me; the former returned me public thanks at his own table for the unremitting pains I have taken those eight years in keeping the people amenable to the law; and on being told he overrated my slender endeavours, he said he was too well informed to think so. You may judge he had not this information from his predecessor.

This friendship with William Waldegrave blossomed and a year later the Prefect was writing of the Governor: "I was the only landsman who dined with him on the eve of his departure aboard his elegant ship, where I had the pleasure to hear him declare in the presence of five captains of frigates, that the Catholics were the best subjects his majesty had."

In November 1795 Dr. O'Donel was appointed Vicar Apostolic of Newfoundland, St. Pierre, and Miquelon. A year earlier an appeal had been sent to Pope Pius VI, requesting that "Jacobum Ludovicum O'Donnell" be appointed as bishop. Besides the names of some of the leading Catholic laymen of the territory, the list also contained the signatures of one Dominican and two Franciscans, which shows there were four Catholic clergy in the island at the time. In a bull dated 5 January 1796 O'Donel was given the title of Bishop of Thyatira in partibus, the third Roman Catholic prelate in British and French North America. He wanted to go to Baltimore for his consecration, but the possibility of war with America made the venture impracticable, so he went reluctantly to the French Bishop of Quebec. He returned from his consecration by a stormy and perilous voyage to Placentia and was the first episcopal gentleman to set foot in Newfoundland since the visit of the Bishop of Quebec to the French colony, in 1689.

Two years later, in 1797, construction was begun on the Old Chapel, an imposing, if plain, wooden structure at the back of the first small church, on the north side of what is now Henry Street hill, where the Star of the Sea Hall stands today. The building was, in fact, a cathedral because of having a bishop, and its presence changed St. John's from a fishing port into a cathedral town. For the next fifty years this edifice served the Catholics of the community. When it was destroyed, a stone was discovered in the foundations, bearing the date 1754. It seems unlikely that this could have been the foundation stone from an earlier chapel, for we have seen that Catholics, at the time, had their property burned and were banished for allowing mass to be celebrated on their premises. The origin of the stone remains a mystery.

There is also a story of some sort of church having been built on the spot around 1774. We have a description of it from a man named Harry Black who claims to have "brought the first stick of wood that was ever placed in it. It was laid under the altar in the north-west corner." It would appear from this hand-me-down narrative that there might have been a structure there that was renovated for use as a sort of chapel. The date could be 1784 and Black might have been referring to the chapel of Dr. O'Donel.

The Bishop's dislike of the French was not only extended to Jacobins. In 1793 he wrote to his superior in Ireland:

> We have had 300 French prisoners here during the summer. Their officers were at liberty, and I must own, I did not like to see them coming every Sunday to my chapel with large emblems of infidel-ity and rebellion plastered on their hats. It was much more pleasing to see three companies of our volunteers, headed by their Protestant officers, with fifes and drums, coming to the chapel to be instructed in the duties of religion and loyalty.[23]

By 1794 Dr. O'Donel was intimating a desire to be put out to pasture in Ireland. However, his eloquent hints were ignored by his superiors. While delighting in his episcopal dignities, he wrote:

> I went to Ferryland, only fourteen leagues from this place, last June, was blown off to sea for three days and three nights; during the nights we could not distinguish the froth of the sea, which ran mountains high, from the broken ice with which we were entirely surrounded. I am now in the fifty-sixth year of my age, and con-sequently will not be long able to bear the great hardships and fatigues of this mission. It would suit me better to spend the short remainder of my life in retirement. . . .

As regards Pellu's charge that O'Donel encouraged people to winter in the colony, Bishop Mullock writes: "We believe he was guilty of the charge made against him by Governor Milbanke, of encouraging the Irish to winter in the country. . . ." Guilty or not, he soon recovered in the esteem of the authorities, and on 6 October 1797 applied for some property, stating that Governors John Campbell and Sir Richard King had offered to allow him a grant of a piece of ground. He sought eight or nine acres 560 yards long (unoccupied) on the north side of Riverhead. The nearest house was William Fortune's, 393 yards to the northeast. In time this piece of land became known as the Bishop's Farm. Rent for the land, on Patrick Street between Water Street and Hamilton Avenue, nine or ten pounds per year, was paid to Dr. O'Donel's sister in Ireland. In 1816 Simon

729

Solomon, the postmaster, was collecting the rent for her. St. Patrick's Church and convent were later built on part of the farm site.

The Bishop's zeal for exorcising the rebellious spirit manifested itself in 1799. He received information that some Irish soldiers of the greatly depleted St. John's garrison, who were followers of Wolf Tone's United Irishmen, planned an insurrection against the British Crown. The story is told on a petition to get the Bishop a pension, sent to Governor Erasmus Gower by the magistrates, merchants, and principal inhabitants of the town. They wrote:

> In the spring of 1799, when, next to General Skerritt, [Bishop O'Donel] was the person who saved this valuable island from becoming a scene of anarchy and confusion by making the most unwearied exertions and using the extensive influence he had acquired over the lower classes, by which means they were prevented from joining the mutineers of the Newfoundland Regiment at a time when General Skerritt had not sufficient force to oppose such a dangerous combination. This the General with candour often acknowledged, and regretted that he had not sufficient interest at home to procure Dr. O'Donel a pension from Government for the many essential services he had rendered the country. . . .[24]

As a result of the information which the Bishop passed along to the General, arrests were made among the soldiery, but without signifying a specific charge. The garrison was kept under keen vigilance and this prudence paid off the following April. An historic marker, which was on a building at the east corner of Belvedere Street and Hayward Avenue, reveals the plot already detailed in Chapter 2. It reads:

> A army powder shed which occupied this site was chosen as a place of rendezvous by fifty United Irish mutineers of the Royal Newfoundland Regiment on the night of the 25th of April, 1800. Nineteen men stationed on Signal Hill deserted their posts and met as planned. But others at Fort William and Fort Townshend were prevented from joining. In June, 1800, five of the mutineers were hanged on the gallows erected on this site after being found guilty of mutiny at a general Court Martial.

The petition for a pension fell on receptive ears and Governor Gower informed O'Donel that it had been granted. The Bishop wrote to the Governor, 24 July 1806:

> I had the honour of receiving your esteemed letter this morning and have to thank you for your condescending attention to my welfare in securing me fifty pounds per year [a purchasing power of more than two thousand dollars today], together with the rest of your benevolent acts of friendship . . . I must confess myself at a

loss for words to express my feelings upon the occasion. . . . I would
do myself the honour of waiting on you this morning had not I
thought you'd come on shore, however should I've been even the
last I would not be the least in respectful regard and real affection.[25]

Bishop Mullock, writing in a later age, was at no such loss for words to
express his feelings about the pension. The irascible prelate thundered:
"While the profligate favourites of royalty and the cadets of a beggarly
aristocracy were drawing their thousands annually from the pension list,
FIFTY POUNDS was considered a sufficient reward for the acknowledged
and invaluable services of a Catholic Bishop."[26]

The first Bishop of Newfoundland returned to Ireland in 1809. He
died at Waterford in 1811 and is buried at St.Mary's, Clonmel, outside the
walls of the old church. When the building was enlarged, his grave stone
was imbedded in the floor of the new church to the right of the nave. Today
he lies under a window dedicated to an Australian bishop, and the plaque
to his memory is elsewhere in the church. The almost defaced gravestone
lies beneath the churchyard wall, to the left of the main entrance.

Bishop Patrick Lambert was appointed coadjutor, 2 August 1805, and
succeeded as Bishop in 1807. Failing health compelled him to return to
Wexford in 1816, where he died. His ten years left little or no real impact
on the social, cultural, or political life of St. John's. He seems to have been a
pious man, in poor health, who devoted himself exclusively to the spiritual
welfare of his flock. Lambert's main achievement seems to have been
obtaining the right for Roman Catholic clergy to perform the marriages of
Catholics and to bury their own dead.

Rt. Rev. Thomas Scallan, O.S.F., was also a Wexford man. Literate,
urbane, and ecumenical far beyond his age, he guided the church in
Newfoundland from 1817 to 1830. He was no stranger at the dinner table
in Government House, and gave the arts a boost by frequenting the
Amateur Theatre. He avoided politics, but an ecumenical gesture in 1827
toward his church of England brother, Bishop John Inglis of Nova Scotia
and Newfoundland, got him in very hot water indeed. During the first visit
to St. John's of an Anglican bishop, Dr. Scallan walked up the lane from his
residence on Star Hill to pay a friendly call on Bishop Inglis, some say with
mitre and crosier. A group of bigoted Irish Catholics were scandalized
when they saw Dr. Scallan accompany his opposite number in the Protestant church in broad daylight. Archbishop Howley felt the most charitable explanation for this peculiar behaviour on the part of his predecessor
was that Scallan was already ailing and suffered a temporary lapse of
sanity. The affair reached Rome and the Bishop was sent a reprimand,
which arrived when he was on his death bed. Many Roman Catholics in St.
John's were convinced that Dr. Scallan passed away excommunicate. His
memorial plaque, in the Basilica, was designed in such a way as to assure
the faithful that he died in the arms of Mother Church.

On 7 October 1823, according to a letter in the Franciscan Friary at Kilinny, Rev. Martin Fleming, a high ranking member of the order, wrote to Dr. Scallan to inform him he was sending his nephew to join the Bishop in Newfoundland: "I hope your Lordship will not be displeased with him. . . . Your Lordship will soon know him to be a most useful, indifatigable missioner." The nephew, Michael Anthony Fleming, was to become one of the outstanding men of Newfoundland history. His uncle asked him to write the Bishop that he was coming, but the letter was found still in his room after he sailed. The young priest had received his habit in Wexford from Dr. Scallan, then Superior of the House, in 1808. Ordained on 15 October 1815, he was stationed at Carrick-on-Suir, where he had been born in 1792. Father Fleming was recalled from Newfoundland by the provincial, but was sent back again to the colony a year or two later. He was consecrated coadjutor Bishop to the ailing Scallan, at the latter's request, 28 October 1829, in the Old Chapel on Star Hill. His title was Vicar Apostolic and Bishop of Carpasia in Partibus. This was an extinct see in Asia Minor. The coadjutor was in Conception Bay, on church matters, when he was summoned to the death bed of Dr. Scallan in May 1830. The ailing Prelate begged forgiveness for his sins, hoped that his protégé would guard the faith well, and passed on to his reward.

The episcopacy of Dr. Fleming appears to have been a quiet one until 1834, when storm clouds began to gather. Governor Cochrane's reading of the Riot Act, Christmas Night 1833, when an Irish rabble tried to lynch Winton, editor of the *Public Ledger,* estranged the Governor and the Bishop. The clouds broke in 1834, when Dr. Fleming determined to erect "a temple at once beautiful and spacious, suitable to the worship of the Most High God." Unable to find a satisfactory site, penniless, and almost friendless, probably because of his great arrogance, his prospects appeared quite gloomy. He tried to circumvent the new governor by sending his appeal for a piece of land near Fort Townshend directly to England. A fair, but unbending bureaucrat, Governor Prescott was unwilling to ignore the slight and meet the demands of the Bishop. The clash of wills reverberated through the next century and a half.

Dr. Fleming writes of his plans:

> I began literally without a penny my arduous struggle, in 1834, by memorializing the government for a piece of ground; it is certainly a valuable spot, beautifully situated, almost in the centre of the town and containing eight acres . . . before I succeeded in obtaining the object of my prayer to the Crown, it cost me nearly five years of vexation and annoyance. . . . How much of tribulation did I not endure. . . . Every effort that malice the most ingenious could devise has been resorted to thwart my views; calumny, insult and opprobrium were heaped upon me . . . after having travelled 20,000 miles of the Atlantic Ocean solely upon this business, amid storms, tempests, danger, and death, and undergoing all the hard-

ships and privations human nature could endure. . . . I was put
in possession of the present valuable piece of ground that forms
the site of our cathedral.[27]

' It would be difficult to chronicle the enormous correspondence, as
well as moves and countermoves, involved in Fleming's struggle to obtain
the site of land. A brief outline will have to suffice. In the autumn of 1834
he forwarded his first request directly to the Secretary of State for the
Colonies. In August 1835 he was informed by Governor Prescott that the
application was "unavoidably deferred." The application was renewed in
June 1836 and followed up by a trip to London in the autumn. Lord
Glenelg, the new Secretary for the Colonies, informed the cleric that
without further information from the Governor and Officers in Newfoundland no decision could be made on the application.

On his return to St. John's, Fleming was informed that a jail and
penitentiary were contemplated on the land he was seeking. He was
offered instead the "Commandant's Field" at the top of Long's Hill,
opposite the present C.L.B. Armoury, or the "Soldier's Garden," site of
Mount St. Francis Monastery, on Merrymeeting Road. The first of these
contained slightly more than two acres and the second about four and one-
half acres.

The Bishop, recognizing the desire to temporize, sailed immediately
for London where he addressed more letters to Lord Glenelg. He was in
Rome, in the spring of 1837, when he received word that "The Governor . . . will be instructed to grant you so much of the land in question as
may be necessary for the ecclesiastical buildings which it is your intention
to erect." News of this success preceded him, and when Dr. Fleming
reached St. John's he was greeted by cheering crowds. The Assembly
adjourned and Members of Parliament came to the wharf to compliment
him.

When the Prelate waited on the Governor it was immediately apparent that the celebrations had been premature. Prescott again offered
him the Commandant's Field or the Soldier's Garden. Fleming stated his
objections and His Excellency finally agreed to give the original request his
backing. However, when he called the Bishop to a meeting with him the
following day, Governor Prescott told Fleming he had changed his mind
and offered one of the two previously mentioned sites.

Dr. Fleming wanted neither. The land he was after, known as Williams Plantation, was east of the road to Fort Townshend, and used as a
garrison woodyard. He knew there were no plans for the restoration of the
fort, as new barracks were to be constructed on Signal Hill and the garrison
transferred there. In spite of the dangers of winter travel, the Bishop
decided on another trip to London. Fearful that the land might be sold by
auction during his absence he arranged with some front men to bid for him
if such a sale took place.

He landed at Falmouth on January 19 and hastened to London where he joined Dr. William Carson, Patrick Morris, and John Valentine Nugent, who were in England trying to get Judge Bolton dismissed from his post in Newfoundland. Representations to the Colonial Office, and a lengthy letter to Lord Glenelg, finally brought results. On 7 April 1838 His Lordship advised the Newfoundland authorities to put the Bishop in possession of the land he sought once and for all. Dr. Carson is thought to have brought the triumphant news home.

Winton, editor of the *Public Ledger,* was less than enthusiastic. He sniffed:

> As for Dr. Fleming having obtained a "scrap" of ground upon which to build a chapel, or a cathedral, or whatever else of that nature it might be—we, for our part, see no objection to it. By all means let it be obtained. The grant, however, would be for the use of the Roman Catholics generally, not as a personal favour to Dr. Fleming, of whom it is impossible to believe that he stands in such odour at the colonial office, after what has taken place. The grant, therefore, if any such there is, stands apart from all personal considerations for Dr. Fleming, who has rendered himself so obnoxious in this country both to Protestant, and to the thinking order of Roman Catholics, as to make it not only highly desirable, but absolutely necessary for the peace and comfort of society, that he should as speedily as possible be succeeded by some gentleman possessing very different views and feelings. . . .[28]

In commenting on Carson's return, the *Public Ledger* added that he was "leaving the other two persons associated with him in this mission kicking about somewhere on the other side of the Atlantic." This refers to Morris and Nugent who, along with Dr. Carson and Bishop Fleming, had shared London lodgings at 63 Paternoster Row, next to St. Paul's, an address of the infamous Mrs. Turner who was hanged in 1615 for her part in the Sir Thomas Overbury murder and scandal.

On instructions from Dr. Fleming, Father E. Troy went to Governor Prescott in May, to receive the grant of land. Registered 30 June 1838, it consisted of nine acres, three roods, and thirteen perches given for no consideration of money

> to Rt. Rev. M.A. Fleming and his successor and successors as Roman Catholic Vicar and Vicars Apostolic of Newfoundland [as a] free grant for the purpose of erecting a Roman Catholic Cathedral, schools, residence for clergy and a cemetery for the benefit of the loyal and faithful Roman Catholic subjects and for no other use or purposes whatsoever.[29]

John Valentine Nugent says Father Troy informed the Governor that

734

he would finish the enclosure of the property in half an hour. He adds: "The idea of fully enclosing with a strong and lasting complete wooden fence nine or ten acres of ground in the short space of half an hour, by those who did not know the people of St. John's was laughed at; all else thought it barely possible." Nugent says that Father Troy told the congregation of his boast to the Governor, and

> On the morning appointed, the whole Catholic population attended and very many worthy Protestants with them. Every man, woman and child brought something useful; either longures, or posts or nails, or saws, or hammers. Everyone was at his post when the signal to commence was given. The last stroke of a hammer was made and the work complete within 15 minutes!! Thus was the first installment of labour given by the people for the new cathedral, and the necessary material for the work supplied perfectly gratuitously, nor was a single glass of spirits tasted on the occasion.[30]

Professor David Bennett's Band played for the fencing as it did for so many other historic events.

Strange to say, this outburst of fencing activity gave rise to a legend that has persisted to this day. According to popular myth, the Bishop was informed that he could have as much ground as could be fenced within a given period of time. Some say the period was sunup to noon, others say noon to three o'clock, and still others claim one hour of the clock. It is clear from the beginning that Dr. Fleming was after the piece of land he was granted. In a letter written to Sir George Grey, in 1836, he says: "The piece of ground I pray for is that part of 'The Barrens' on which the garrison wood yard stood, containing about ten acres. . . ." In October of that year Captain Walker, head of the Engineer's Office in St. John's, sent Grey "A plan of the ground applied for by Dr. Fleming."

The Bishop in his final letter to Lord Glenelg wrote:

> Surely your Lordship may then estimate the propriety of granting or withholding, not grounds I have never asked for, but the lands I have been five years soliciting. I trust, therefore, your Lordship ... will bestow upon the Catholics of that country the piece of ground I have prayed for, or allow them to purchase it at its full value, which, under the circumstances, will be considered as great a favour as a gift.

Dr. Raymond Clark of Memorial University, in an offprint published in 1970, suggests that the fencing myth is a typical foundation legend found in many parts of the world and going back to the founding of Carthage, as described by Virgil in the *Aeneid*. There is another fascinating story handed down in connection with securing the site, that Dr. Clark says

735

is also common in foundation folklore. It has to do with the burial of a body to ensure the possession of land.

According to a local tale, Catholics were not merely content to enclose the property. They had learned from bitter experience that a fence around a plot of land was no guarantee of anything. Fearful that Governor Prescott would find some way to withdraw the grant, they were determined to obtain undoubted possession. It is said that somebody suggested that if a corpse were buried on the grounds, in keeping with the permission to use them as a cemetery, then not even the Bishop's worst enemies would try to wrest the land from him. Unfortunately, nobody chose to die at that particular time. Suddenly it was announced that a notorious character of the town, named Mullins, had gone to his reward. Mullins was buried with great mourning in the area which later became the handball alleys at the back of St. Bonaventure College. Within a few days a spectre, in the image and likeness of the late Mullins, was seen to haunt his favourite tavern. On closer inspection, it was found to be no ghost at all, but a resurrected Mullins. Instead of being dead, the old sot had merely been dead drunk. Just before the lid of his coffin was hammered into place, the "corpse" was surreptitiously removed and the funeral honours were for a box of stones.

During excavations, two genuine *corpus delicti* were uncovered. They are believed to have been the mortal remains of the two Irishmen, Power and Farrell, who had been hanged, drawn, and quartered in 1794 on the barrens, for the murder of Edward Lawrey. Old maps of Fort Townshend, in the latter part of the eighteenth century, indicate a cemetery on the site of the cathedral yard. This could have been the Potter's Field of which mention is made in several journals, or one of many plague burial grounds. It is possible that by Bishop Fleming's time its existence was forgotten.

There is also a legend of the Queen's involvement in the project. The story is so elaborate that it almost has the ring of truth. On the whole, the tale would appear to be a myth, but it cannot be completely dismissed. The Queen Victoria legend is based on an unconfirmed story handed down by the Dempsey family of St. John's, who were close friends of Bishop Fleming. This family has it as a tradition that it was their personal financial assistance that enabled the Bishop to go to England. Mrs. Dempsey is supposed to have suggested that Dr. Fleming approach Queen Victoria directly. She had information that the eighteen-year-old Queen rode her carriage through Rotten Row, in Hyde Park, each morning. If he were to stand there in clerical purple and offer her a salutation, she would likely stop.

According to the story this is just what he did. Her Majesty called for the carriage to stop and asked the identity of the reverend gentleman. When advised he was the Roman Catholic Bishop of her Colony of Newfoundland she invited him into her carriage. In the course of an interview at Buckingham Palace, Dr. Fleming acquainted the Queen with the numerous problems he faced in acquiring land for his cathedral. The young Victoria promised to take measures to overcome the difficulties. Shortly after this interview, the Bishop is supposed to have received word that the grant of land had been finally made.[31] Though it is not mentioned in the Prelate's very incomplete papers, there seems to be some far-fetched corroboration for the story in his statement that the new cathedral would be a lasting memorial to the benevolence of Queen Victoria. In a sermon preached by Bishop Howley, on her death in 1901, he spoke of the procuring of the land as "due to the gracious gift of Queen Victoria," and stated that the signing of the deed of grant was one of the first acts of the young Queen, who had only come to the throne the previous year.

This peculiar story does not end there. Her Majesty is supposed to have opened a coffer containing gold and offered some to Dr. Fleming who, somewhat embarrassed, took but a few sovereigns. More were pressed upon him. As he was about to depart, Victoria is said to have requested a return favour from the Bishop. She asked that the new cathedral in St. John's be named for St. John the Baptist. The Bishop willingly agreed and, as he was leaving the palace, the Queen, seeing the day was damp and cold, took off her stole, folded it lengthwise and wrapped it around the neck of the inadequately protected clergyman. This supposed shawl of the Queen is still in the possession of descendants of the Dempsey family in St. John's. It is purple, with an elaborate ornamental silk design of the Thistle, Rose, and Shamrock.[32]

An architect known as Herr Schmidt has always been credited with the design of the Cathedral which Bishop Fleming built. However, there is a letter in the National Library in Dublin (a draft copy in the Bishop's hand) which seems to prove that the architect was not Schmidt, but John Jones. On the outside the communication is marked to Thomas Jones, Esq., Architect, Clonmel, "Requesting his speedy execution of plans for cathedral." Dated 11 July 1838 on the inside, it reads:

> To John Jones. As I have now arranged all my affairs in this country and am solicitous as soon as possible to sail for Newfoundland, I should feel extremely obliged if you could let me hear as soon as you conveniently could that you have finished the design for the intended erection at St. John's, when I shall feel great pleasure in remitting you the amount of your expenses. I should also feel thankful if you accompanied your account with a statement of the quantity of tons of block stone, etc. which you judge would be necessary for the ornamental work of the cathedral and the probable expense of their conveyance from Cashel to Waterford in order that I may now lose no time in their preparation and also your instructions regarding the laying of the foundation which I should be desirous of accomplishing as soon as may be practicable, after my arrival. I cannot close this without once more expressing my sense of the favours I have already received at your hands and

> my expectation that under the auspices of a gentleman of your eminence, in your interesting profession, the church which I contemplate will rise in beauty alike creditable to the designer and an embellishment to the country. . . .

There is another draft letter, in the Dublin archives, dated "November 38?" The address on the outside appears to be "Smidth [sic] Esq. Architect, Hamburg." Inside it reads

> To Schmidt — I take the earliest opportunity that offers on my arrival here [Newfoundland] after an exceedingly protracted voyage to transmit to Mr. Graham of the Belvedere Hotel three thousand marks being the full amount I have engaged to pay you for the construction of a model of the church of which you furnished me with plans. . . . Permit me here to acknowledge your polite attention in the *preparation of the plans I have already had* and my entire and unqualified satisfaction at the style of their execution and to reiterate my hope and expectation that the model you are building will realize all my wishes to have an erection raised in this country worthy as well of the great object for which it is destined as also of the high character of the distinguished artist to whose superior talent the design is due.

There is ambiguity in the last sentence. Does the distinguished artist refer to Jones or Schmidt? It appears conclusive from the two letters that John Philpot Jones did the original designs in consultation with the Bishop, who then took them to Herr Schmidt, at Altona on the Elbe, a consulting engineer in the pay of the Danish government, who was recommended as an expert on problems of building in stone in a northern climate. In 1859 John Jones was practising in London where he won an international competition for the Genoese Prison in Sardinia. That same year he entered the competition for the Church of SS Peter and Paul in Cork, but lost out, "as I am a Protestant." However, Canon Murphy thought his design superior to the others, went against the prejudice of the committee, and bought Jones's plans from him for his price.

An Irish architect, Michael McGrath, was hired to oversee the project in St. John's. In a letter addressed to Michael McGrath, Waterford, in the National Library, Dublin, from Dr. Fleming in St. John's, November 1838, the Prelate refers to the cut stone:

> . . . give me a statement . . . also for what charge you would make me for coming out to this country with them and superintending the erection until its completion, a work that will be rendered particularly easy of accomplishment as I shall be prepared with a model of the building erected in the proportion of half an inch to a foot. . . .

In another undated letter to McGrath, he speaks of stone from Kelly's Island, in Conception Bay: "A considerable quantity has been already landed in St. John's without expense by the ship owners of Conception Bay, Protestant and Catholic. . . ."

McGrath soon arrived on the scene, but did not long remain on the job. When the Bishop insisted on a number of innovations that were not architecturally wise, there was a strong clash of opinions and McGrath resigned. The project was finally handled by the Dublin firm of Murphy. McGrath stayed on in St. John's and advertised his architectural services as being available at John Dillon's, in Queen Street.

The return of Dr. Fleming and Nugent, 18 October 1838, after an arduous fifty-two-day passage from Hamburg, on the *Kingaloch,* seems to have been a time of great rejoicing. Winton's *Public Ledger* chose to ignore the event, but the *Patriot* crowed that

> the arrival of the beloved and venerated Dignitary of the Catholic Church . . . filled the bosoms of the entire community (with the exception of course, of Tory malcontents) with the sublimest feelings of gratification and pleasure. . . . From an early hour in the morning, the entire population was astir, hurrying to the wharf where, it was expected, his Lordship would disembark, and by eleven o'clock a body of people "which no man could number", surrounded O'Brien's wharf and blocked up Water Street. By-and-by a shout of welcome that rent the air "and made the welkin ring" announced that the beloved gentleman had left the ship, and was proceeding to the shore, and on looking in the direction of the Narrows, the yacht freighted with its esteemed charge was seen, the Native Flag flying, cleaving the waves shoreward surrounded by a fleet of others loaded with friends lay and clerical and having every variety of banners waving to the freshest breeze. Anon she reached the quay and a long shout re-echoed from the expectant and anxious populace, and numerous happy greetings and affectionate embraces were exchanged between His Lordship and his more immediate friends. (But who is not the friend of Doctor Fleming?). As his Lordship moved up the street, awaiting him, already formed, was a procession of the female scholars of the Convent Schools (established by his Lordship) dressed in pure white, followed by the Benevolent Irish Society and the Mechanics Society. . . . The entire body then proceeded up Water Street to the Episcopal Palace and as they proceeded discharges of fire arms greeted them at intervals.

By 1838, with the fencing finished, the work of building the cathedral was ready to begin. The excavation of 8,800 cubic yards of earth was completed in two days, with the women carrying away the clay in their aprons. There was a quantity of red granite lying about on Signal Hill which had been removed from its bed when a roadway was opened to the barracks. Glad to be rid of it, the Colonel of Engineers granted the Bishop permission to take the stone away. One Sunday Dr. Fleming announced the project for the following Wednesday. At nine o'clock that morning six thousand persons were waiting on the hill. Before evening twelve hundred tons of stone were slide-hauled over the snow to the cathedral site for the foundations.

Bishop Fleming himself supervised the cutting of the stone at Kelly's Island, off Chamberlains, in Conception Bay. He lived there in a hut, working daily with pick and crowbar. There was no road out of St. John's at the time so the cleric was often seen up to his waist in water helping load the schooners which were volunteered to transport the stone to St. John's where farmers, with horses and carts, brought it from the wharves to the site. The main walls were faced with cut limestone imported from Galway. The quoins, mouldings, and window frames were made of Dublin granite. The cut stone was cast under the direction of James Purcell of Cork. Hundreds of thousands of tons of stone were landed at the Ordnance Wharf and carted by all religions and all classes of society to the cathedral grounds without a shilling's expense for labour or cart hire. Even more so than in Europe in the Middle Ages, the construction of the Roman Catholic Cathedral at St. John's was a labour of love by people of faith. The Bishop boasted to the Governor that he would build the church for twenty thousand pounds (a purchasing value of about half a million dollars today).

On 20 May 1841 the foundation stone was solemnly blessed and laid by Dr. Fleming. At noon a procession formed at the Old Chapel and proceeded along Water Street, up Cochrane Street, along Military Road to the cathedral site where a model by a Mr. Butler of Dublin was displayed beside the stone. The number assembled on the grounds was estimated at ten to twelve thousand, half of the population of St. John's. In a collection, taken on the spot, the amazing sum of $10,400 was raised. The Cathedral was said to be the largest church structure in any of the North American colonies. By 1843 the outside walls were finished and the inside walls had been raised to about thirty feet. Then the supply of stone ran out. The Bishop took ship to Ireland for the last time. By 31 January 1848 Dr. Fleming was able to write: "I have now completed the structure of this beautiful edifice as to externals. The walls, the roof and the towers are all finished, and I have only the interior now to struggle through."

Sister Mary Xaverius Lynch, one of the first four Presentation Sisters to come out from Ireland, gives us the following portrait of Fleming, in a letter she wrote home in 1834:

> He is a very strict Superior and knows the Religious Life very well and expects the greatest perfection from a religious. He is the greatest stickler for rule and discipline and is most observant. . . . As for himself, he appears not to care for anything in this world. His only breathing seems to be for the good of Religion and the

salvation of souls. He stayed up all night with two men who were to be executed [Mandeville and Spring]. It was the first execution here these sixteen years. He is now getting two beautiful school-rooms built to contain 200 children. It will be a very handsome building when finished. Night and day he is continually over the workmen who are giving their work for nothing and since he began it he has often had two or three hundred men in the day and by his own exertion he is getting all this done. We sometimes think he will be famished with the cold for in the most severe weather and the snow coming down in flakes, he will be with the workmen in the open air and perhaps will not eat a bit until 5 o'clock and sometimes not then itself. We wonder how he lives for he takes no care of himself, his whole heart being on the good of Religion.[33]

In another letter that same year, the foundress of the Presentation Convent, Mother Bernard Kirwan, adds this information. "The Bishop's house is a handsome comfortable one. Furniture, plate, retinue correspond with the appearance he made in Galway. His sister, a very nice amiable little girl, lives with him."[34] This sister, Johanna, afterwards married John Kent, Newfoundland's second prime minister. The story is told that the Bishop, who could not tolerate noise while he preached, once turned on his sister who was coughing her way through his sermon and cried, "Johanna, go home out of it!"

On 6 January 1850 Dr. Fleming made his last public appearance, at the scene of his labours and triumphs, when he offered the first mass in the new cathedral. He was so weak he had to have a chair placed on the altar where he rested from time to time during the ceremony.[35] On July 14 he passed away at Belvedere. His remains were interred under the high altar.

In 1854, just before the consecration of the church, Bishop Fleming's successor, Dr. Mullock, moved into the new palace. On 9 September 1855 Bishop Mullock consecrated the completed cathedral. It had taken twenty-one years to finish the work. According to Mullock the basilica, residence, and convents cost a hundred and twenty thousand pounds (about six hundred thousand dollars). On hand for the consecration was Archbishop Hughes of New York, and the Bishops of Toronto, New Brunswick, and Arichat (now Antigonish), Nova Scotia. The occasion is said to have inspired Archbishop Hughes to construct St. Patrick's Cathedral on his return to New York.

During repairs, 2 November 1870, when the congregation was coming from evening prayers at the Cathedral at ten o'clock, a large plank fell from the belltower instantly killing two cousins, Miss Martin and Mrs. Sullivan, who were standing chatting underneath.

Unfortunately, conflicts with McGrath had forced Dr. Fleming to do without sound architectural advice so that exterior repairs were imperative by the time Bishop Howley began his episcopate. Internal repairs were a project of Archbishop Roche. In 1953 Archbishop Skinner ordered a complete restoration of the interior. On 30 May 1955 His Holiness Pope Pius XII, on the occasion of the centenary celebration of its consecration, elevated the Cathedral to the rank and title of Minor Basilica. It was the ninth church in Canada to be so honoured.

The four Major Basilicas are all in Rome. In 1972 work was finally begun on the beautification of the grounds, after a hundred and seventeen years.

THE METHODISTS AND UNITED CHURCH

The story of the United Church of Canada in Newfoundland begins in Harbour Grace between 1765 and 1772 when an ordained Church of England clergyman, Laurence Coughlan, abandoned that faith and converted some two hundred people to the teachings of his friend John Wesley. In 1809 Rev. John Remmington, an itinerant preacher working in Conception and Trinity bays, called at St. John's to take ship to England, and while in the town organized a small group into the first Methodist Society.

It was not until 1813 that the Methodist faith in St. John's grew to a point where the need for a clergyman was deemed a necessity. Investigations were carried out and, in 1814, these resulted in the British Methodist Conference instructing its missionaries in Newfoundland to pay particular attention to St. John's. It listed the town as one of its missions, sought the establishment of a Methodist Society there, and began negotiations with the government in England for a grant of land on which to build a chapel. When these negotiations failed, as well as some conducted in St. John's with Governor Keats, it was decided to go ahead with the building of a chapel on a plot of land leased from a member of the fledgeling congregation.

In the spring of 1815 work was begun on the erection of this chapel. Early historians tell us it was on Gower Street, near the foot of Long's Hill. However, this belief is quite conclusively contradicted by Dr. David Pitt in *Windows of Agates,* a short history of the founding and early years of Gower Street Church, which he compiled in 1966 from carefully considered sources. Dr. Pitt is of the opinion that the chapel of 1815 was probably erected on Prescott Street, then called McCarthy's Lane.[36] There is also contradictory evidence as to whether this building was actually completed before it was destroyed in the fire that swept part of the town on 12 February 1816. It is generally agreed that it opened for public worship on December 26, and vanished in smoke and flames six weeks later. The first minister, twenty-three-year-old John Pickavant, had reached St. John's in October. Rev. Thomas Hickson was actually appointed to the living, but his arrival from England was so long delayed that Mr. Pickavant was transferred from Port de Grave to the capital.

A Lancashire man born in 1782, John Pickavant was converted to Methodism in 1808, the year the St. John's congregation was organized. He is said to have been a person of rare evangelical gifts, "an orator both charming and subduing." The fire of 1816 not only destroyed the new chapel but left many of the congregation homeless in a severe winter of near famine conditions. Prospects were dim for rebuilding the small house of worship. For this reason it was decided to seek help by an appeal in England, whereupon Pickavant sailed off to solicit funds with which to rebuild the chapel.

Official church history tells us he sought the means, not only to rebuild the chapel at St. John's, but one at Carbonear which had also been destroyed by fire. Again Dr. David Pitt has corrected a longstanding error. His research shows us that the Carbonear fire did not occur until the following year. He suggests the confusion may have come from the fact that the chapel at Carbonear was still quite new at the time, and also somewhat in debt. Pickavant may have included an appeal for it in his solicitation of funds for St. John's.[37]

Meanwhile the Church of England minister, in a gesture of brother-hood, obtained the use of the Charity School for public worship by the Methodists of the town.[38] Since the new site was beyond the settled area, special permission had to be obtained from the Governor in order to build on it, and this had to await the return of Governor Keats in the spring. His Excellency was so long delayed that the congregation decided to go ahead with construction on a plot of land for which a grant already existed. An eligible spot of ground was purchased "in a part of town every way convenient, and secure from any future accident by fire."

The cornerstone for the new chapel was laid at four o'clock on 17 September 1816, at the foot of Long's Hill on a rise of land at the western end of a street Governor Gower had pushed through twelve years earlier as the northern limits of the town and which had been named for him. The stone was set in place by Rev. William Ellis who delivered an address based on the text "And all the people shouted with a great shout, when they praised the Lord, because the foundation of the house of the Lord was laid." Mr. Pickavant had, meanwhile, been sent to Western Bay and his replacement was a twenty-five-year-old missioner just arrived from England, George Cubit. He brought out two assistants who were permitted to remain with him at St. John's for the winter. We have the Reverend Cubit's word that the new Governor, Admiral Francis Pickmore who had arrived in St. John's just four days previously, and his secretary came to the ground on which the foundation stone ceremony was being held and remained till the conclusion of the service.[39]

The new Methodist chapel on Gower Street was opened 26 December 1816, with a sermon preached by the Reverend Cubit at eleven o'clock in the forenoon. The building stood opposite the foot of Long's Hill. This street, as we know it, was not completed until October 1888, so the entrance was from Gower Street. Another entrance, at the back, led to a basement Sunday School. In the spireless chapel there was said to be room for six hundred under a high, peaked roof. Because the building was only fifty by forty feet, it was necessary to surround the auditorium with a gallery containing two rows of pews, in order to accommodate the congregation. The pulpit was at the north end facing the Gower Street entrance. Light was supplied by five windows in each side wall and between these windows candles were placed in hanging brass sconces. A small chandelier was added later.

Dr. Pitt tells us that the choir of this early chapel was especially noteworthy. Besides singers of both sexes, it included several violinists and a substantial bass viol, played by a gentleman who occupied a centre front seat, above the large clock that surmounted the lintel of the main entrance. These instruments were later joined by a seraphine.[40]

Even though the chapel saw its first service on Boxing Day 1816, it seems that construction was not completed until late in 1818. By October 1817 the plastering of the walls was done and they had been given one coat of paint. A newspaper notice for 1818 advised readers that Rev. George Cubit would be preaching at the new Methodist Chapel on December 26 and that a collection would be taken up to help offset erection expenses as a large debt was still outstanding. The words "New Methodist Chapel" would indicate fairly recent completion. Rev. James Sabine was noted as the attraction at the Protestant Dissenting Meeting House that same week.

Meanwhile the Great Fire of 1817 devastated much of St. John's, in two November outbreaks that occurred less than two weeks apart, destroying some $2,500,000 worth of property. Two thousand were left homeless in conditions of unbelievable want. While the chapel was spared, the congregation once more suffered crippling losses. Most were scattered by the need to find alternative accommodation before winter set in. Gangs of starving rowdies, called "rals," roamed the streets terrorizing the citizens by assault and robbery. Some idea of the situation can be realized from the fact that the Reverend Mr. Cubit, who had lost an infant son in April, was without bread, flour, and potatoes for some time during the bitterly cold winter, and thought himself fortunate in being able to obtain a half-barrel of potatoes "frozen and not as large as walnuts, by sending eight miles for them, fourteen shillings."[41]

Mr. Cubit's health failed and, in the autumn of 1818, he took leave in London. He found himself facing censure for having left St. John's without permission, although it had been requested as early as May, and his leave was on the advice of a medical doctor. For some reason his case was resolved without the censure. His place was taken by Rev. John Bell, a very neat and precise person whose "preaching abilities were not of a high order."

Another fire, in 1819, again laid to ruins a large part of downtown St.

John's and brought the church supporters, who had already suffered much in the three previous fires in as many years, to the verge of utter ruin. In February 1820 disaster threatened the church building as well when, at midnight on the twentieth, a man living opposite noticed the place was on fire. Some cinders which had been raked out of the stove and left in a pan on the floor after the Sunday service had ignited the wood. The chapel was found to be full of smoke, the stove had fallen down, and the pulpit railings were just catching fire. The response to the alarm was sufficient to douse the flames and the building was saved.[42]

During summer, from 1820, open-air services were conducted at Riverhead and Maggoty Cove. The St. John's clergy also travelled on foot over trails of rock and bog to preach at Torbay, Portugal Cove, and Petty Harbour. They were treated with the proverbial Newfoundland hospitality everywhere except at Petty Harbour where, because the people were either Church of England or Roman Catholic, none would invite them to their table. Sometimes in winter the Methodist preachers would have to spend two or three nights in open lofts, on a bed of shavings, with only a couple of horse blankets for warmth.[43]

If any ill will existed between Roman Catholics, Anglicans, and Methodists, it was soon dissipated by a boyish-looking blond, of twenty-three years, who was known as Father Croscombe, an unusual title for a Methodist. Called the "eloquent whiteheaded boy," he reached St. John's from England in 1824, and a crowded house greeted him on his arrival. He made friends with Bishop Scallan and the leaders of all denominations. We are told by Dr. Pitt that his friendship with Governor Cochrane "gave him a social standing in the community that his predecessors had not enjoyed, but which from this time on seems to have been generally accorded to his successors." In after years, "even Roman Catholics, who met him in other places" were said to greet him with a "bright face and cheery remembrance."[44] On his departure in 1828, John Pickavant returned to the town.

On 30 January 1833 Bishop Michael Anthony Fleming presented a petition to the House of Assembly asking that Wesleyan clergymen be permitted to perform the marriage ceremony and that marriages celebrated by them to date be confirmed and legalized. Judge James Higgins claims this action led to a picture of Dr. Fleming being placed in the cornerstone of Wesley United Church, Patrick Street. Other petitions followed, and on March 19 William Thomas, a member of the House, proposed a bill which was adopted by the Assembly.

In 1839 there were over a thousand members in the congregation and it was necessary to build an addition to the aging Methodist chapel. Even the extension proved inadequate and in 1846 plans were made to erect a new church. While the Great Fire of that year destroyed much of St. John's the old building was again spared. As usual, many in the congregation lost everything in the blaze of July 9, and it was necessary to shelve construction plans. Years of poverty and distress followed, including a cholera epidemic which carried off large numbers of parishioners. By 1852 no seats could be obtained in the chapel. Most of the calamities were overcome by 1 July 1857 when the old structure was "launched" from its site so that construction could begin on a new church. The launching consisted of moving the wooden chapel to a platform that had been erected over a sloping vacant lot on the opposite side of the street, a site donated by Walter Grieve. The feat was accomplished by the captain and crew of a ship that was in port. The spot has been occupied during much of the present century by the Orange Hall.

On Thursday, August 21, the foundation stone for the new Wesleyan Church was laid in a teeming rain and dense fog which kept many from attending. The newspaper accounts of the event tell us that "the ministers of the Church of Scotland, the Free Church, and the Congregational Church evince by their presence their brotherly kindness towards the Wesleyan ministers." The Honourable J.J. Rogerson proceeded to lay the stone, which contained inscriptions, coins, and newspapers. The collection resulted in a hundred and three pounds.

The new church was built of brick with a slate roof. Unlike the old chapel it was erected side-on to Gower Street with an entrance at the eastern end off Church Hill. There was room to seat one thousand persons. The basement was at street level on Gower Street. A stone wall topped by wrought iron railings was added in 1883 to enclose a small garden with two ornamental shade trees. The church was opened for worship, in an unfinished state, 29 November 1857 by Rev. Matthew Richey, President of the Eastern British America Conference. It had the first hot-air furnace in Newfoundland and the editor of the *Courier* congratulated the trustees for having shown "the spirit of progress without which no progress could take place." The new church, which in time came to be known as Old Gower, lasted until its total destruction in the Great Fire of 1892.

Meanwhile the population of the city was expanding rapidly. A large financial contribution from Charles Ayre made it possible to build another Methodist church on George Street, at a cost of thirty thousand dollars. This was opened on 14 December 1873. There was a chapel on Alexander Street and another on the south side. A graceful wooden church was opened at the head of Cochrane Street in 1882. In 1892 Cochrane Street Church barely escaped the flames of the Great Fire which levelled the opposite side of the street. However, one hour after the evening service on Sunday, 18 January 1914, it was totally destroyed by a blaze of unknown origin. It was rebuilt the following July.

Old Gower was not so fortunate. The 1892 fire left the mother church in St. John's, as well as the former chapel across the way, in smouldering ruins. Once again most of the congregation lost everything to the insatiable flames. Sunday services were held at Fleming Street School Chapel, near Monkstown Road, but by October the congregation was able to move into a large temporary structure known as the Tabernacle, on the east corner of Parade Street and Harvey Road. The site was later occupied by a school, radio station VOCM, and finally a supermarket. The Tabernacle remained in use four years.

In 1893 discussions over plans for a new church resulted in substantial disagreements of so serious a nature that there was a move by the Quarterly Board to buy land and build a separate church, on the west corner of LeMarchant Road at Carter's Hill. The Trustee Board ignored the dissenting group and pushed forward its own plans for a new building on the Gower Street site. Rev. Dr. Carmen, General Superintendent of the Church of Canada, laid the foundation stone, 5 July 1894.[45] The financial problems involved were enormous and could only be overcome by heavy borrowing. The Quarterly Board finally abandoned its plans for a rival church and the congregation was reunited.

The splendid red brick edifice we know today was formally opened by Rev. Dr. Potts, 4 October 1896. A number of turrets and towers, as well as a tall and impressive spire, gave it a massive appearance. Because of defective construction the spire was unfortunately removed. It has never been replaced and the result has been to dwarf and stunt the beautiful lines of the church. Gower Street United, which seats sixteen hundred, cost seventy-five thousand dollars. The debt was not liquidated until 1916. As with most St. John's churches there have been large outlays for repairs.

On 10 June 1925 the Methodist Church was joined in union at Toronto with the Congregational and some Presbyterian churches. The new church was named the United Church of Canada. In Newfoundland it meant only the changing of the name of the denomination from Methodist to United Church, as the general work of the church was in no way affected. Congregationalists joined the Presbyterians and stayed out of the Union in Newfoundland. Gower Street Methodist Church became the Gower Street United Church we know today. The event was celebrated by a great mass meeting at Gower Street.

THE PRESBYTERIAN CHURCH

Presbyterianism grew strong in sixteenth-century Scotland under the leadership of John Knox. At the Westminster Confession (1645-47) the name Kirk of Scotland took the place of Church of Scotland. Subsequently the word "kirk" came into common English usage when describing a church of the Presbyterian creed.

In January 1838 a group of six Presbyterians, living in St. John's, gathered together in Joe Bacon's schoolhouse to discuss the question of building a church and calling a minister. The six were James Douglas, John MacDonald, Thomas McMurdo, David Sclater, Kenneth McLea, and Dominie Rogers.[46] A general meeting of Presbyterians was held on 1 June 1838. The Governor was petitioned for a piece of ground on which to build a kirk. The land sought was on the west side of King's Bridge Road, just north of the entrance to Government House, now occupied by the United States Consulate.

Governor Prescott was no more disposed to grant dissenters the property they wanted than he had been to allow Bishop Fleming the land he was after for his cathedral. He advised the Presbyterians he would be willing to grant them permission to build a church on property already held, and available on a rental basis, on condition that a church be erected and completed within two years. Four years of discussion and dissention within the congregation followed, and the permit was withdrawn.

In 1840 it was recorded in Scotland that "Mr. Stevenson, belonging to Edinburgh, has been appointed to St. John's and will go out for three years." There is no further record of the man. In 1842 the private quarrels were overcome and it was finally agreed to erect a kirk at St. John's. A building fund was set up and Governor Harvey contributed twenty pounds and promised to find a suitable site. Rev. Donald Fraser from Nova Scotia spent July and August of 1842 in St. John's, organizing the congregation. He was invited to remain and, after returning to Nova Scotia to arrange for his transfer, he arrived as minister of the new congregation on Christmas Eve 1842. Services were generally held in the old Factory, although sometimes evening services were held in the Wesleyan Chapel.[47]

Governor Harvey granted a "beautiful and commanding site," on the road which bears his name, and the cornerstone was laid in May 1843 by Kenneth McLea, who was President of the Scottish Society. The superintending architect was Mr. Norris and the church was completed at a cost of twenty-eight hundred pounds. It opened 3 December 1843 and was described as a "singularly neat, well-constructed and substantial edifice . . . elegant and spacious" with a beautiful and conspicuous spire which could be seen from all approaches to the city.[48]

The kirk was badly damaged by vandals on the night of 25 February 1846 when all the windows were smashed in an orgy which also broke a few panes of glass in Gower Street Church. The offer of a hundred guineas reward brought no result. Prints in the snow showed the culprits to be two men, one in good boots, the other in moccasins.

Bishop Fleming leased to the kirk the land in front, on Long's Hill, which had been a Roman Catholic burial ground, for a nominal rent, on condition the graves not be disturbed. When pounds, shillings, and pence were replaced by dollars and cents in Newfoundland, 1 January 1888, this rent is said to have become one dollar per year. At one time, when it was thought to build a gradually sloping driveway to the kirk from Long's Hill to replace the present incredibly steep roadway, some of the presbyters pointed out that the agreement with Dr. Fleming was that the graves not be disturbed and the project was shelved.

Rev. Donald Fraser, a son of the manse, was born on the island of Mull, Scotland, in November 1793, and ordained at Tobermory. He came to Newfoundland from Lunenburg, Nova Scotia, where he had gone in

1817 to serve Pictou County. On 7 February 1845, less than two years after the opening of the kirk, he was dead of cancer at fifty-one years of age. On the day of his funeral the shops of town were closed and the vessels in the harbour lowered their colours. Fraser was "buried in the very spot he frequently admired, near the steeple of his own church."[49] In 1884 his own and his wife's remains were removed to the General Protestant Cemetery at Riverhead.

In his short ministry Mr. Fraser became engaged in controversy when he fought for "one educational institution totally free from all religious and sectarian domination or preference." In this he was strongly opposed by the Church of England Bishop, Edward Feild, and the denominational schools bill became known as the Church of England Measure. To a lesser extent the Roman Catholic Bishop was also involved. Fraser's crusade failed and denominational education became a reality. It was to be nearly a century and a quarter before the system showed signs of disintegration.

In 1843 a matter of conscience split the church in Scotland. Nearly five hundred ministers gave up their parishes over the question of patronage and formed the Free Church of Scotland. This split spread to Newfoundland at the time a new clergyman was being sought to succeed the late Donald Fraser. Some wanted a member of the Established Church while the majority favoured a parson of the Free Church. These differences could not be resolved and the local congregation was divided in two with the courts deciding that the property belonged to the Established Church.[50]

Adherents to the Free Kirk decided to build their own church on Duckworth Street, a few doors east of Cathedral Street. This church can be seen in a drawing by W.R. Best (*circa* 1858), and also in J.W. Hayward's painting of old-time fools cavorting at the foot of Victoria Street in 1855. When this second Presbyterian house of worship opened in St. John's in 1850, it was known as Free St. Andrew's. In 1852 Rev. Moses Harvey, who was to make a name for himself as a Newfoundland historian, became its pastor.

Early on the morning of 30 January 1876 a police patrol noticed flames coming from inside the old church of St. Andrew's-on-the-Hill. The fire bell was rung, but by 3:00 a.m. the building was an inferno. The fire lit up the town for miles around and a wind carried flankers as far east as Cochrane Street. Had it not been for the fact that the shingled roofs were covered by a snowfall, earlier in the evening, the whole of St. John's might have gone up in smoke twenty years sooner than it did. The cause of the outbreak was the overheating of the furnace by an inexperienced hand, hired to warm up the church for Sunday during the absence of the regular attendant. The loss was valued at over four thousand pounds.

The homeless congregation of the Old Kirk met in the "Temple," a small billiard room just to the west of Free St. Andrew's on Duckworth Street. They might have gone on meeting there for a long time were it not for the fact that within eight months the Free Kirk was dealt the same fate as the Established Kirk.

On the afternoon of Friday, 15 October 1876, a fire broke out around 4:00 p.m. in Bennett's iron foundry at Riverhead, just east of Sudbury Street, when some woodwork had been ignited by coming in contact with molten metal. The fire was supposedly put out. However, after closing hours it burst out again, and by 6:00 p.m. the foundry was in flames and soon demolished.

Around 9:30 that evening a second alarm was sounded when the former newspaper office of the *Chronicle* on Duckworth Street, just east of the foot of Cathedral Street, caught fire. It was being rented by Mr. Davy, a carpenter, and the place was littered with wood chips, shavings, and bits of lumber. A westerly breeze drove flankers to the adjoining building, the Temple, already mentioned as the refuge for the Established Kirk. This place, lately occupied by the Catholic Institute, had lawyer's offices below on the ground floor.

No water was ever poured on Davy's carpenter shop, though some water did partly save the Temple. Then it was noticed that the Free Kirk, which was immediately to the east, had taken fire in one of the ornamental pinnacles of the tower. It was claimed the place burned for about fifteen minutes without any effort being made by firemen to extinguish the flames. Some said afterwards that a bucket or two of water would have done the job, but when at last an attempt was made to fight the fire the roof was already alight. Forty sailors and marines of H.M.S. *Bullfinch* assisted the men of the Phoenix Company in a losing battle. Nothing could be done to save the church. It collapsed in a heap of burning embers.

Before these had cooled, at one o'clock the next morning, a third alarm was raised. A house belonging to Mr. Bennett, and standing just west of his gutted foundry, had burst into flames. When the smell of an unusual quantity of kerosene was detected, the tenant, Mary Shea, was arrested on suspicion of arson.

The eventful weekend was not over for the firemen. On Sunday it was boldly insinuated that after the first fire they had indulged too freely in liquor, at Bennett's Brewery, and were incapable of doing their work at the second fire. One of them was quoted as shouting in a drunken stupor, "Let the bloody Protestant church burn down!" For a few weeks the indignant firemen, many of them Irish Catholics, found themselves the centre of controversy, even though it was an almost total lack of organization, rather than religious bigotry, that caused the loss of the kirk. One newspaper cried that unless the methods of fire-fighting were overhauled a greater calamity might soon engulf the whole of St. John's. Cassandra, in her heyday at Troy, was not more gifted with prophecy.

Within months of the fire which destroyed the second Presbyterian church, the two groups agreed to reunite and build a single kirk. Meanwhile, the congregation of Free St. Andrew's met for services in the Court House.

The cornerstone for the new church was laid on 18 June 1878 by the Reverend Dr. Muir on the east corner of Cathedral and Duckworth Streets.[51] It opened on 20 November 1879, with a service conducted by L.G. MacNeil. In little more than a dozen years this beautiful new kirk was a smouldering ruin when the Great Fire of 1892 swept along the street. The large Bell clanged ominously as it tumbled from the falling steeple into the cinders.

Reconstruction was agreed upon almost immediately but, again, not without dissention. A vote favoured building the new St. Andrew's on the hilltop where the first St. Andrew's had been built. An influential minority wisely opposed the site as being too inaccessible. Meanwhile the congregation held services in the West End Presbyterian Hall, on lower Hamilton Street, and later in the Church Hall, Queen's Road.

Plans for the new Kirk were drawn up by Wills & Sons and the cornerstone was laid, 24 August 1894, by the Governor, Sir Terence O'Brien. Built in Gothic style, of Accrington brick and trimmed with Scotch freestone, the church, manse, and hall were completed at a cost of eighty-five thousand dollars. However, like its counterparts in the city, repairs have since been out of all proportion to the cost.

The main porch is composed of the same stones as were used in the Duckworth Street Church. Over the front door of the former kirk there was cut in the stonework, in bold relief, THE BURNING BUSH—the emblem of the Church of Scotland. This emblem survived the flames and can now be seen in the tower portion of St. Andrew's Kirk.

Following debate on union with the Methodists and Congregationalists, a motion was unanimously carried in St. John's that "the interests of Christian Unity would be better served by this congregation remaining as it is, Presbyterian."[52]

THE CONGREGATIONAL CHURCH

The story of the Congregational Church in Newfoundland begins just twenty-five years after the Pilgrims brought the faith to America in 1620. The movement arose in the sixteenth and seventeenth centuries in England as a revolt against ritualist worship and the Established Church. It was formalized in 1582 when Robert Browne, an English clergyman, first expounded the principles of Congregationalism. In 1645 the Independent Church of Christ, as it was then known, was established in Newfoundland by members exiled for their beliefs by Queen Elizabeth I. Eventually it withered away.

In 1756 a soldier named John Jones came to Newfoundland with his artillery company. His life in St. John's was, at first, one of drinking, swearing, and carousing with profligate companions. Born thirty years earlier in Wales, Jones wasted his time in idleness until, at the age of twenty-two, he joined the Royal Artillery as a private soldier. It was not until five years after his arrival in St. John's that he was "awakened to

751

spiritual concern by the plight of a fellow soldier who died blasphem-
ing."[53] In that year, 1770, Jones turned preacher and re-established Congregationalism in Newfoundland.

In 1773 Jones's military unit was returned to England. For two years
he was stationed in Chatham where he joined the Independent Church.
"To his surprise and regret" he was told to return to St. John's with
another artillery company in 1775. His duties at the garrison were those of
sergeant-major, quartermaster, paymaster, and clerk. In his room Jones
held public worship on Sundays when a jailer, a sergeant and his wife, and
three soldiers met for prayer. He was later allowed the use of the Court
House by the Magistrate, but Governor John Montague soon forbade this
on his arrival from England in the spring.

Open-air services were held that summer on the barrens. However,
when the weather became cold Jones was forced to turn his thoughts to
erecting a small shelter for indoor worship and somehow obtained a lease
on some land. It is believed that this was on Forest Road outside the town
limits. Trees were cut down in the winter of 1777 and in the spring the
congregation set about erecting a small Meeting House before the return
of the governor. It could not have been very ostentatious for the building
was completed in twenty-eight days.

When Montague returned a few weeks later and heard of the Meeting
House, he went into "a great rage" and swore to tear it down "stick and
stone." However, Jones says "the lease held." The Governor tried to
banish him to Placentia but that failed and the soldier went on preaching
every Sunday as the first minister of the Dissenting Church of Christ in St.
John's until the military obliged him to return once more to England the
following year.

The congregation of seventy or eighty people that Jones left behind in
St. John's begged him to leave the army and "come out next year to reside
with them as their minister." By July 1779 the former soldier was ordained
and back in St. John's preaching at his suburban Meeting House.

At first his only problem seems to have come from "the so-called
Gentlemen of the Navy" who attempted to amuse themselves by pouring
gunpowder down the funnel of the stove during services. Jones requested
of the magistrates "a licence to preach according to law." Nicholas Gill was
willing to grant one but Magistrate Edward Langman, the Anglican
parson, swore he would send the constables if Jones dared to preach.
Sunday, 1 August 1779, Jones had just begun his sermon when the constable entered the church and ordered him "to desist from preaching and
holding unauthorized Meetings and Assemblies in this harbour."

Governor Richard Edwards, who mistrusted Dissenters, forbade
them the use of the building for meetings, whereupon services were
restricted to the private lodgings of Mr. Jones. He was tempted to give up
and return to England but his flock prevailed on him to stay.

The preacher petitioned Governor Edwards without effect. He and his elders finally saw His Excellency on board his ship in September just before he sailed home and the Admiral treated them to "much abusive language." Once Edwards reached England he had a stormy interview with a Dr. Stafford who pointed out to the governor that he "had access to Mr. Pitt and even to the throne." Blame for the clash in Newfoundland was put on Parson Langman. When the Admiral returned to St. John's in July 1780, Jones presented him with another petition, supported by Colonel Pringle, and the Meeting House was reopened for services. In 1784 Governor John Campbell rescinded all restrictions on religious liberty and the little building was dedicated to the serious business of saving souls without further interference.

When the lease expired on the Meeting House property, Jones decided to build a more commodious place of worship at a more convenient location within the town. The chosen site was one hundred feet above the Upper Path (Duckworth Street) "centrical to the Town, a desirable circumstance where the inhabitants have to make their way through Snow more than knee-high several months of the year." Two lots on what became Meetinghouse Hill (now Victoria Street) were purchased for one hundred pounds from Andrew Barnes, and Governor John Elliot granted permission to erect "a Meeting House, School and Minister's Dwelling."

The building committee consisted of John Jones, Nathan Parker, Henry Phillips, Wallis Lang, Joseph Lowman, Edward Freeman, James Barnes, and George Brace. The foundation stone was laid "with the accompaniment of a quarter cask of rum ordered by the committee. . . ," and construction was completed, except for the galleries, by 1789. The total cost was just over seven hundred and eighty-two pounds. The Meeting House measured forty-two feet by thirty-two feet, and attached to it was a "tenement" containing the School, Vestry, and Mr. Jones's apartments. When Rev. Daniel S. Ward arrived in 1842 he found the building in "a state of decay" and raised money to erect a stone church on Queen's Road at the west corner of Chapel Street. However, the death of Ward the following year and other problems delayed completion of the new chapel until 1851. The Meeting House above Duckworth Street became Temperance Hall. Both the old and new structures were destroyed in the Great Fire of 1892. During much of this century, the Longshoremen's Protective Union Hall stood on the Meeting House site. After 1892 a plan was devised to erect a new church of brick on the Queen's Road site but financial considerations dictated that the attractive new structure be of wood. In 1834 Methodists, Anglicans, and Congregationalists had rebuilt Christ Church at Quidi Vidi. That ecumenical venture lasted about nine years.

Dissenters seem to have been blamed more for religious unrest in Colonial St. John's than Roman Catholics. Captain Sir William Eliot writes of these two sects, in 1819:

> The power of the priests here is fully as great over the lower
> orders of the people, who are principally papists, as it is in other
> countries; but there is a more pacific disposition, and less persecu-
> ting feeling, on their part, towards those who entertain a different
> creed. Indeed, the persons most prone in this colony to religious
> differences are of that sect so appropriately denominated "Dissen-
> ters". En passant, it would be unpardonable here to pass unnoticed
> the singular difference in the state of society in this island and that
> of Ireland, to which it bears, in a religious point of view, a strong
> resemblance. Though the vast majority of its population are
> Roman Catholics, no rivalry nor discontent prevails, although the
> government and all official situations are filled by Protestants.
> The Roman Catholic Bishop entertains and is entertained by the
> governor and official persons, not excepting the officers of both
> army and navy; and, unlike the policy pursued at public dinners in
> Ireland, no controverted topics of religion are ever discussed, nor
> political toasts introduced, which could be construed into the
> slightest attempt to foment disunion or embroil religious profes-
> sors.[54]

However, Jones was on excellent terms with Langman's successor, Rev.
John Harries, even loaning him the use of the Meeting House in 1799-
1800 while the new Church of England was being built. He also carried on
a very cordial correspondence with Bishop O'Donel in which the two men
found agreement on several matters including religious tolerance.

Even though John Jones, like his Church of England contemporary,
Rev. Edward Langman, was forced to go about begging his livelihood, he
earned the respect of the town. In 1799 he suffered a paralytic stroke and
passed away on 1 March 1800. Nearly two thousand persons, including the
whole company of artillery, turned out for his funeral, conducted by the
Reverend Mr. Harries in a severe snowstorm. It was a simple happening
in keeping with his wish that "my funeral be conducted in the most frugal
and least expensive manner that decency will permit of."[55]

A committee was appointed in the spring of 1936 by the Queen's
Road Congregational Church to meet with a committee from St. Andrew's
Kirk "to investigate the avenues of approach, and the possibility of the
Congregational Church being received in its entirety into the Presbyterian
Church in Canada."[56] They were also to investigate the possibility of unity
with the United Church. In a vote taken 8 March 1937 a majority of New-
foundland Congregationalists favoured union with the Presbyterians. The
application was granted in 1938.

In December 1956 the Presbytery gave the congregation permission
to sell "the freehold property on the south side of Queen's Road vested in
the St. John's Congregational Church together with the building there-
on."[57] It had been decided to re-establish the church on the north side of
Elizabeth Avenue, just west of Portugal Cove Road. The old property went
to the Seventh Day Adventist Church for thirty-two thousand dollars. In

the summer of 1958 work was begun on the new church with a sod-turning ceremony. The cornerstone was laid on October 13 and the new edifice was officially opened and dedicated 26 April 1959 the day the final service was held in the Queen's Road Church.

The name of the Congregation was officially changed to St. David's Presbyterian Church in 1957.[58] The new name was significant in view of the fact that the first minister of the congregation in Newfoundland, John Jones, was a native of Wales whose patron saint is St. David. It is in that church that the John Jones Journal is lovingly preserved.

7

In the Maze of School

The Reverend John Jones never took no for an answer. He started the Congregational church in St. John's in 1770 in the face of strong opposition. In 1798 he constructed the first proper school in the town as part of a Meeting House which he opened on what is now Victoria Street. (Courtesy Rev. James Armour.)

Samuel Codner, who founded the Newfoundland and British North America School Society as a thank offering, was an English merchant. When he left Newfoundland John Bond, father of Sir Robert, acted as his agent until Wilson and Maynell bought out the firm. Codner's Central School was a stone building that could take four hundred pupils.

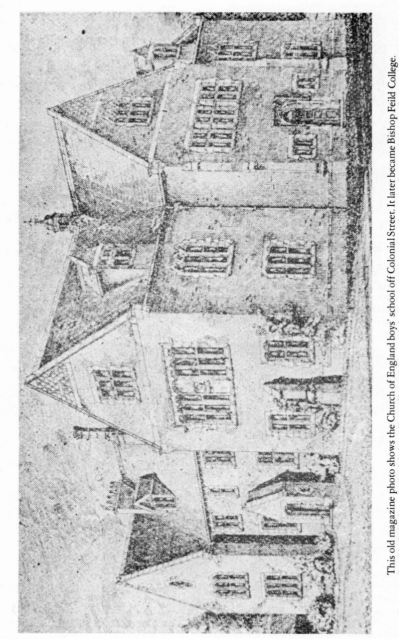

This old magazine photo shows the Church of England boys' school off Colonial Street. It later became Bishop Feild College. Dr. Blackall, the principal, led a valiant effort which saved the impressive structure from the flames of 1892, only to see it torn down a few years later and replaced by the present building. (Courtesy Newfoundland Provincial Archives.)

760

Members of the quasi-military caders known as the Church Lad's Brigade pose in front of old Bishop Feild College around the turn of the century. Roman Catholics and Methodists also had their own cadet movements but the CLB outlasted them all. (Courtesy Newfoundland Provincial Archives.)

761

Under the eagle eyes of two school mistresses and the headmaster, the kindergarten scholars at Bishop Feild join their hands in morning prayer in this very old photograph. All St. John's schools are still privately operated by religious denominations. (Courtesy Newfoundland Centre, MUN.)

Bishop Edward Feild, the second Bishop of the Church of England in Newfoundland, is credited with fostering the denominational system of education which continues to this day. Consecrated 28 April 1844 he was Bishop of Newfoundland and Bermuda. He died 8 June 1876 while on a visit to Bermuda.

In 1875 Bishop Power requested that the Irish Christian Brothers come to St. John's and teach. They arrived 2 September 1875 and rented a house at 173 Duckworth Street. The first superior was Brother Holland who reached St. John's 3 October 1875.

763

Lady Morris was Isabelle Langrishe LeGallais, the daughter of Wm. Le Gallais, a Church of England clergyman from the Channel Island of Jersey who drowned on a pastoral call between Channel and Isle aux Morts in a fearful gale 27 October 1869. A schoolteacher, she was one of the sisters who founded Jersey Lodge which grew into Bishop Spencer College. In 1887 Isabelle married the Honourable James Fox. He died two years later and she married the future Baron Edward Morris.

Dr. Robert E. Holloway was an outstanding Methodist teacher and scholar. Born in England in 1850 he was for thirty-two years principal of the Methodist College, St. John's. At the time of his death in 1904 he was preparing the publication of his book *Through Newfoundland With A Camera* which was completed by his daughter Elsie, the noted photographer.

The Orphan Asylum Schools on the corner of Garrison Hill and Queen's Road never sheltered an orphan. The building housed a non-denominational school run by the Benevolent Irish Society. During its colourful history the Orphan Asylum served as a legislature for the Newfoundland government following the Great Fire of 1846. (Courtesy Benevolent Irish Society.)

No school in Newfoundland seemed able to compete with St. Bonaventure's College, seen here around 1900, for all-round excellence. It was outstanding in academics, athletics, debating, theatricals, and music. The original college was the four-storey building on the right, erected by Bishop Mullock with stone left over from the construction of H. M. Penitentiary. (Courtesy Newfoundland Provincial Archives.)

The scholars of the Irish Christian Brothers' schools in St. John's Holy Cross, and St. Patricks Hall, show their numbers by assembling in sailor suits and Buster Brown outfits in front of the B.I.S. Hall on Military Road in 1906. (Courtesy Benevolent Irish Society.)

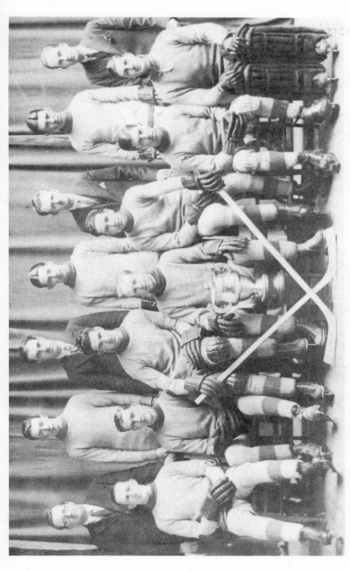

St. Bonaventure's College won the first of a fantastic twenty-six Boyle trophies for hockey in 1928. The 1928 team included many prominent men. Top row (left to right): Senator John Higgins, William Cotter, Patrick Keegan, John Wood, Eric Robertson (Mgr.), Frank Graham, Chief Justice Robert Furlong (Sect.). Front Row: H. M. Opposition Leader Gordon Higgins, Q. C., Michael Monahan, Gordon Halley (Vice Captain), Edward Phelan, Q. C. (Capt.), Thomas Sutton, Ashley Graham, William Kendall.

Mother Bernard Kirwan was superior of the Presentation Sisters who came to Newfoundland from Ireland in 1833. It was her task to organize the first group of English-speaking nuns in Canada. She died at Fermuse 27 February 1857. (Courtesy Presentation Sisters Archives.)

Littledale, opposite Waterford Bridge in Kilbride, was the home of Newfoundland's first prime minister, the Honourable Philip Little. Bishop Power purchased the residence from Judge Joseph Little and opened it as a Roman Catholic girls' boarding school in 1884 under the direction of Mother Bernard Clune. The original house was later torn down. (Courtesy Newfoundland Provincial Archives.)

When Emma Churchill of Portugal Cove married Charles Dawson in Ontario and returned to Newfoundland on her honeymoon the couple held a meeting in Temperance Hall, St. John's, that led to the organization of the Salvation Army in Newfoundland. Shown above are (front row) Charles Dawson, Beulah, Helen, Mina, Emma Churchill; (back row) Fred, Bernard, his wife, Archie, William. (Courtesy the Salvation Army.)

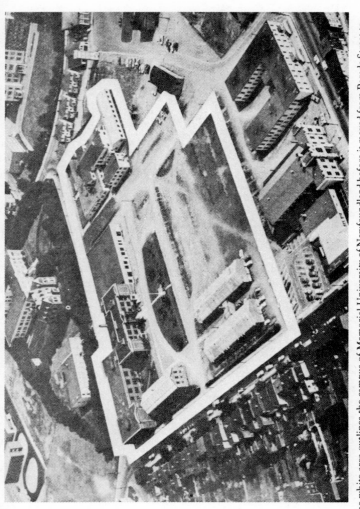

The white area outlines the campus of Memorial University of Newfoundland before it moved from Parade Street to Elizabeth Avenue. The original building is behind the stretch of lawn in the centre. On the right is the former U.S.O. where American servicemen were entertained during World War II. The building in the lower right corner is the second Knights of Columbus Hostel built on the site of the first Hostel which was destroyed 12 December 1942 in the most tragic indoor fire in Canadian history. (Courtesy Newfoundland Historical Society.)

In the Maze of Schools

Some are bewildered in the maze of schools
And some made coxcombs nature meant but fools
                    ALEXANDER POPE *Essay on Criticism*

Newfoundland's first school was not founded in St. John's, but at Bonavista where in 1723 Rev. Henry Jones, a Church of England clergyman, started one with the help of the Society for the Propagation of the Gospel (S.P.G.).

The first school at St. John's of which we have any knowledge was opened in 1744 by another Anglican clergyman from Bonavista, Rev. Mr. Peaseley, also with help from the S.P.G. His object was to provide a school "for want of which a large number of children attended a Papist one."[1] This reference is a mystery since Roman Catholics of the time had no freedoms of any sort under the Penal Laws which were being vigorously enforced. For some reason the Peaseley school did not survive.

In 1788 another attempt to start a school in St. John's was made by the S.P.G. when Mr. Price, a missionary of the society, opened a free school in his residence where he taught with the aid of an assistant. The 1794 census of the town lists one Mich Hearn as a Roman Catholic schoolteacher. He was probably in the employ of Bishop O'Donel.

John Jones, the founder of Congregationalism in Newfoundland, started a day school in St. John's around 1785 and it was attended by children of all faiths, including Roman Catholics. A Charity School was opened by Jones in 1790, connected with his new Meeting House, and taught by George Brace. When the parson suffered a stroke in 1799 the assistant schoolmaster, Lionel Chancey, continued to teach at the Meeting House until 1802 when the school was transferred to his home.

The next attempt at establishing a regular school was a venture undertaken by twenty-five St. John's merchants. On 10 December 1798 Rev. John Harries; Richard Routh, Chief Justice and Collector of Customs; and others wrote to Governor William Waldegrave pointing out that: "The want of a good school for the education of the children of both sexes, and the number is very great, has been frequently and is long lamented by the inhabitants of this place."[2] The group informed the governor they were willing to subscribe £273.3.0 for three years to overcome the want.

They asked His Excellency to advertise in the papers, while he was in England, for a man of classical education and a mistress to teach the rudiments of English, ornamental needlework, and French.

To the task came another Anglican Divine with the unlikely name of Louis Amadeus Anspach. This scholar was to leave behind a most valuable contribution by writing and publishing the first comprehensive history of Newfoundland. However, his school venture was premature and, when expenses proved greater than expected, the attempt ended in much bitterness, hostility, and a lawsuit.

The St. John's Society, organized by Governor Gambier in 1802, opened two schools, one Protestant and one Roman Catholic. By 1809 they had combined and enrolled 378 girls and 247 boys. Denominational differences disappeared and were not to reappear with any real effect for half a century.

On 22 June 1815 John Sullivan was advertising in the *Royal Gazette* a list of subjects, mostly to do with mathematics, that he would be teaching "a select number of youth" at the "School now established in the town of St. John's." He advised that he had added his own school "to that in which Mr. Coyle kept his." Coyle would appear to have been a private tutor.

Also in 1815 James Warner, who was teaching in St. John's from 1805 at a salary of forty pounds per annum, was appointed Principal of the School of Industry which was still operating in 1826. Jemima Rearnell, a teacher at the school, was paid twenty pounds, probably for teaching dressmaking or allied arts. The abstract of Net Revenue and Indenture for 1822 in the Provincial Archives reveals that Joseph Bacon was appointed a schoolmaster in 1819 by the Governor and Commission at a salary of sixty pounds per annum. He was appointed catechist by the Society for the Propagation of the Gospel in Foreign Parts and given apartments in the schoolhouse.

In 1804 Lord Liverpool wrote the Governor of Newfoundland, Lord Gambier:

> Newfoundland has for a long time been gradually increasing in population, and in that respect is become a sort of colony, and in the end it will become so entirely. It is proper, however, to counteract this tendency as long as possible: at the same time, concessions must occasionally be made so as to prevent tumult and disorder among the people of this island, who are in general of a very low and a very bad description. . . ."

His Lordship became Prime Minister of England in June 1812 and his unusually long ministry lasted until April 1827. In 1822 a Newfoundland merchant, Samuel Codner, born in 1776 at Weston-Super-Mare, Devonshire, was saved from shipwreck in a terrible storm while sailing from St. John's to England. As a thank offering for his deliverance Codner established the Newfoundland and British North America School Society with the inspiration of Lord Liverpool who had obviously undergone a change of heart regarding the very low orders in Newfoundland after becoming Prime Minister. Liverpool appointed himself Vice-President. The inaugural meeting of the society took place in London 30 June 1823 and in the following year the British government made a grant of five hundred pounds to the venture plus a schoolmaster's salary of one hundred pounds per annum. Codner pointed out that in consequence children would be "early trained to subordination and their moral habits . . . generally improved."

Patrick Morris took strong exception to the picture presented by Liverpool, and others, of Newfoundlanders living in "a savage and besotted state." He wrote in 1827, "Possibly their object is to represent us as great sinners that they may have the merit of converting us into very great saints."

There can be no doubt that conversion was in the minds of the evangelical members of the School Society even though their first advertisement in the *Mercantile Journal* on 16 September 1824 announced that "education would be non-denominational, the Authorized Version of the Bible would be read without comment, and instruction in the Catechism and formularies of the Established Church would be given after school hours only." The school was opened on September 20 and was taught by Mr. and Mrs. William Jeynes, Mr. William Fleet and a female monitor. Temporary quarters were found in an old stone structure next to a bakery. Within two years the scholars moved to a newly erected stone schoolhouse on Duckworth Street between what is now Holloway Street and St. John's Lane. It could accommodate four hundred and fifty children but only half that number were enrolled and they were about equally divided between boys and girls. Dr. Bell's system was in use. In 1825 the school offered a course in teacher training and thus became Newfoundland's first normal school.

The low enrolment figures at these early schools resulted from the fact that only the most ambitious or dedicated parents bothered to have their children educated. Almost all the women were illiterate, even some of the ladies of quality. There was not much to attract pupils to colonial schoolrooms. Equipment consisted of little except ink powder, a bell in the master's hand, and a clock on the wall. Slates arrived on the scene about 1815 and were common until the present century. Quill pens were in use until after 1850. There was no blackboard and little paper. For a copy book, sheets of wrapping paper were folded over and sewn together, with wallpaper used for a cover. Learning was done by rote, a dreary and noisy method, since textbooks were an innovation of the late eighteenth century. The job of the master seems to have been to hear reading, set sums, teach parsing, mend pens, and thrash the disorderly.

A well-behaved class was a silent body, seated on long benches, in a cramped and badly ventilated room. Scholars were read and spelt twice a day and the rest of the time were busy keeping still. Every ten or fifteen minutes the master would pound his cane on the desk and its sound sent shivers through the hearts of those whose restless feet were threatening the silence of the room.

Benches and desks were slabs of wood overlaid with jack-knife literature. Yet any scholar who pinched a splinter from these deeply carved planks was apt to feel the cane of an eagle-eyed teacher on the offending fingers. The girls were required to keep the place swept and dusted, while the boys were charged with looking after the wood supply, lighting the fire, and disposing of the ashes. When the stove got overheated snow was brought in to quench the fire. In winter pupils nearest to the stove sweltered, while children in the far corners of the room suffered chillblains.

Despite the primitive conditions and the fact that those in the most need of financial support were often employed as teachers and were very poorly paid, there was some who were born to the calling and loved their work so greatly that they were able to instill a love for learning in their pupils.

In the 1835 session of the newly created House of Assembly notice was given "that at the commencement of the next session of this House leave would be asked to bring in a Bill to found and establish an Academy in this island." Nothing much seems to have come of the proposal and in 1843 another Act was passed. That year the first School Inspector, John Valentine Nugent, was appointed. He had been M.H.A. for Placentia in 1837 and for Conception Bay District in 1842. The Colonial Secretary advised the Roman Catholic Irishman: "His Excellency wishes you to confine yourself to inspection of Roman Catholic Schools except that where Protestant Boards may desire you should visit schools in their district."[5]

The Act of 1843 did not bring about the harmony and contentment hoped for in educational matters. It met with spirited opposition from Protestants and Roman Catholics alike. The government opened a non-denominational academy in St. John's in 1845 with John Valentine Nugent as Principal. The General Academy, as it was called, opened in Castle Rennie on Signal Hill Road, a site occupied by a Sisters of Mercy convent for most of this century. Castle Rennie had been the home of the Honourable John Dunscomb whose business near the foot of Cochrane Street, begun in 1809, was burned out in 1844 in a forty-thousand-dollar fire. In August of the following year Dunscomb left Newfoundland, and Castle Rennie became the General Academy a few months later. It was not a popular institution, with an enrolment of never more than sixteen students.[6] In 1850 the government ended the experiment and Nugent opened a private school, the St. John's Academy, on Monkstown Road.

Bishop Fleming had opposed the General Academy because the regulations would not allow him any control of the school. Bishop Feild was an even more determined opponent. In 1844 he established the

Collegiate (Boys) School for Secondary Education and the following year founded the Diocesan Girls School in a building on Military Road, in front of St. Thomas Church. By these moves he hoped to pressure the government into separating the Church of England school grant from that of the Methodists. There was already resentment among Anglicans over the inroads Methodism had made upon the Church of England, and in places this proselytism had led to violence. The Bishop was determined to establish separate Anglican schools and to force the government to divide the Protestant grant according to population, with the Methodists getting the lesser share. By these actions it was Dr. Feild who was mainly responsible for the denominational system of education which Newfoundland has to this day.

The Education Act was changed in 1851, 1852, and 1853 before it was finally rendered acceptable. Separate schools were established for Roman Catholics, Anglicans, and Methodists in St. John's but there was still friction. The new Roman Catholic Bishop, Dr. Mullock, objected to the condition that the daily scripture readings be given from the Authorized Version of the Bible. Dr. Feild put forward the claim that "Education cannot be carried on without religion." In 1874 the government gave in and agreed to the establishment of a straight denominational system of education under church control.

The Church of England Academy eventually absorbed Bishop Feild's Collegiate School, occupying "Avalon," a large house on Forest Road at the west corner of Factory Lane. Here it stayed until 1861 when it moved to new quarters on Bond Street, where a Tudor-style brick building had been erected along with a headmaster's residence and boarding dormitories. The title "college" seems to have come into use around 1892, when the various academies in St. John's adopted the name applied to schools in the British Isles, organized by clerics for grade-school instruction.

In the seventeenth century the word "college" was slang for a prison and it is quite certain that many a reluctant scholar "creeping like snail unwillingly to school" felt the St. John's institutions deserved the soubriquet. One of them, as we shall see, was built of stones intended for a penitentiary.

A new building was added on the Colonial Street side of the old Church of England College and in September 1894 the place was named Bishop Feild College, in honour of its founder. By 1926 these school buildings, which survived the 1892 fire through the efforts of the headmaster, Dr. W.W. Blackall, had fallen into disrepair. Work on a new and much more elaborate institution for all grades was begun and completed in 1928. By 1959 it had outlived its usefulness and, with the October opening of Bishop's College, in the north end of the city, Bishop Feild College was forced to wrap its traditions in memory and become an elementary school.

The story of Roman Catholic education in St. John's goes back to 26 June 1826, when the Benevolent Irish Society obtained a grant of land on

779

the northeast corner of Queen's Road and Garrison Hill. There the society erected a building called the Orphan Asylum, although it was never used as an orphanage.

In the spring of 1827, when construction was finished, pupils were moved from Gill House into the Orphan Asylum. Gill House, the former home of the famous Gill family, was leased in 1826 for use as a temporary school, while the Orphan Asylum was being completed, and in it were enrolled a hundred and thirty-six boys and seventy girls, with Henry Simms and Mrs. Edens as teachers. Unable to meet Mrs. Edens's salary of twenty-five pounds per year, the society was soon forced to dispense with her services. At the turn of the century, ten pounds was the average yearly salary of a teacher, and even in 1827 Mrs. Edens's demands were away out of line.

The Benevolent Irish Society was a non-denominational, fraternal organization and the school which it opened in the Gill House, in 1826, was also rigidly non-denominational though, for some unknown reason, almost the entire student body was soon Roman Catholic. In 1827 the Orphan Asylum Schools opened their doors. In those days each classroom was called a school. With the coming of the nuns in 1833, the Asylum began to take boys only, and in 1836 a course in navigation was introduced. Following the 1846 fire the school building, which was outside the area of destruction, housed sessions of the Amalgamated Legislature.

In spite of the good work being done by teachers in the Orphan Asylum Schools, Dr. Fleming was not happy. The B.I.S. refused to allow him to enter the school to teach religion. In the 1830s he wrote to a friend:

> The boys at a very tender age are employed in some way or other about the fishery, in order to earn as much as will support themselves and render them altogether independent of their parents. The consequence is that, free from every domestic restraint, they are much exposed to the temptation to drink rum, which, according to custom, is served out to them regularly three times a day.[7]

The Bishop felt an urgent need for a religious order to teach and care for these rum-soaked lads. It was not until 1847, however, when he was worn out by his labours on behalf of his cathedral, that he succeeded in procuring a branch of the Franciscan Brothers in Galway, Ireland. At one time Dr. Fleming, himself a Franciscan, had dreams of establishing a house of that order in Newfoundland and he set to work to construct a monastery, Belvedere, off Bonaventure Avenue. The building still stands. It was to Belvedere that the Franciscan Brothers came in 1847.[8] Known about the town as "the Monks," they were not religious but Third Order laymen who were entitled to wear the brown robe.

The Franciscans took charge of the Orphan Asylum Schools with great success under Brother Angelus. The experiment, however, ended in failure, mainly because of the loss of Brothers, who seem to have had a falling out among themselves. Several of those who came out chose to return to Ireland and there were no new recruits. In 1853, three years after the death of Bishop Fleming, the Benevolent Irish Society agreed to the remainder returning home. In an atmosphere of some bitterness the school reverted to secular teachers, although some monks may still have been around in 1863. A newspaper ad in the *Newfoundlander,* June 12, announced that members of the Third Order of St. Francis had established a Religious Literary Library, attached to the Episcopal Library, March 14, and that it was open from two to three on Sunday afternoons.

In 1875, at the request of the B.I.S., Bishop Power invited the Irish Christian Brothers to come to St. John's and teach.[9] That order was founded by a Kilkenny man, Edmund Rice, in Ireland in 1817. Brother Rice was a widower and a well-to-do businessman in Waterford. He had a brother, Thomas, who died leaving four, or possibly five, children. His widow passed away soon afterwards and two of the children, a boy and a girl, went to the United States where they are thought to have perished in a train accident. Two others, Patrick and Michael, were sent out to Newfoundland to become wards of Morgan Doyle, a friend of the family in Grates Cove. Patrick married Doyle's daughter, Mary, and settled in nearby Red Head Cove. Michael moved to St. John's where he became a man of considerable means before he died in 1883.

When the B.I.S. was looking for another order to take over the Orphan Asylum Schools in 1875, it appears that Michael Rice suggested that an 1863 invitation given to his uncle's order, and refused on the grounds that demands for brothers in Ireland were too great, be renewed. The society's president made the motion, which was seconded by Rice.

On 2 September 1875 Brothers McDonald and Hoope arrived from Ireland to prepare the way for the coming of their order to the New World. On the date of their arrival, another member of the flock, Brother Holland, sailed from Ireland. He arrived in St. John's on October 3 and was to become Superior of the first North American house of the Irish Christian Brothers. Today the order has branches across Canada and the United States, as well as in the West Indies and Australia.

Brothers McDonald and Hoope had rented a house for use as a temporary dwelling at 173 Duckworth Street. It belonged to a Mr. St. John and was on the south side of the street about midway between Prescott Street and St. John's Lane. As soon as everything was in readiness McDonald and Hoope departed for home leaving Brother Holland behind. He was joined when the *Moravian* docked at St. John's on 20 January 1876, by Brothers Mitchell, Prenderville, and Tully. Prenderville was later to teach Ireland's future President, Eamon DeValera. Tully was a thirty-one-year-old lay Brother who soon returned to Ireland and resigned from the order.

Eleven days after their arrival in the western world, 31 January 1876, the Irish Christian Brothers opened three classrooms on the second floor of the Orphan Asylum.[10] Over three hundred pupils sought admission that first day but, because of a lack of space, a hundred were turned away.

The following year it was decided by the Benevolent Irish Society that the fifty-year-old wooden building was no longer adequate. On 22 July 1877 the cornerstone was laid for a stone structure. The new school on Queen's Road, known as St. Patrick's Hall, was officially opened on 15 August 1880. On May 19 of that year the Orphan Asylum School, which stood on the southwest corner of the lot, was sold by auction for thirty-five pounds and torn down. Twelve years later St. Patrick's Hall was completely gutted in the Great Fire of 1892. Classes were held in a temporary structure, erected by the government for the St. Vincent de Paul Society on Harvey Road, at the east corner of the path to Fort Townshend Parade, while reconstruction took place inside the burned-out shell of St. Patrick's Hall.

The new hall opened in the rebuilt Benevolent Irish Society building in the fall of 1894. Here the Brothers taught until 1945, when classes were moved to the newly erected St. Patrick's Hall School on Bonaventure Avenue. In 1947 the Presentation Sisters reopened the old classrooms in the B.I.S. building for use as an elementary school.

Construction of a monastery for the Brothers was begun in 1878. On September 9 Bishop Power laid the cornerstone on a plot of land, off Merrymeeting Road, known as the Soldier's Garden. While Mount St. Francis was under construction, the Brothers moved from Duckworth Street to St. Bonaventure's College where the priests gave them the use of five bedrooms and a parlour, although they were required to maintain a separate kitchen. They moved into the Mount on 21 August 1880.

St. Bonaventure's College had an entirely different beginning from its compatriots. It was founded by Dr. Mullock, 1 December 1856, in the Old Palace on Henry Street, as a diocesan seminary for the development of vocations to the priesthood. Dr. Mullock did not share Bishop Fleming's opinion that local persons (male or female) should not be accepted for the religious life and he saw to it that the first native-born priest to serve in Newfoundland, Father Brown of Carbonear, was ordained in Ireland in 1856. The first person born in Newfoundland to be raised in Holy Orders, according to Archbishop Howley, was Patrick Meagher, a son of the Water Street merchant, Thomas Meagher. St. Bonaventure's was a college in the true sense of the word and taught courses at university level. Over the years there was a long wrangle about having it accredited. For this reason the headmaster at St. Bon's was always called the President, instead of the Principal.

On 27 April 1857 Dr. Mullock laid the cornerstone for St. Bonaventure's first building, on the grounds of Halley's Cottage on what became Bonaventure Avenue. In 1852 the governing council decided to build a new penitentiary on the south shore of Quidi Vidi Lake, with building materials imported from the United Kingdom. Before it could be completed, Responsible Government took over the affairs of the country and funds for the prison were withdrawn, so that the original plans were only partly completed. At noon on 5 August 1856, thirty thousand Irish bricks were sold by auction on the penitentiary grounds and the highest bidder was Bishop Mullock. These Irish bricks (actually heavy granite stones) were used in the construction of St. Bonaventure's College.

The school was ready to receive its first day-student seminarians in March 1858. Boarding accommodations, not at that time ready, were completed in 1859, and on October 4 the place was finally opened to boarders. The President was an Italian priest, Father Carfagnini, who was later to become Bishop of Harbour Grace. Soon after his appointment to that see, a bitter dispute broke out between the Italian Bishop and the Harbour Grace members of the Benevolent Irish Society. It was settled by a decision from Rome in December 1875, stating that the Irishmen were right in claiming that the B.I.S. was "not a religious but a civil society." The action of the Bishop in trying to impose his control on the B.I.S. was pronounced by Rome to be irregular. Dr. Fleming had earlier been frustrated in an attempt to impose his will on the society and teach religion in the B.I.S. Orphan Asylum Schools at St. John's. The Harbour Grace episode created great enmity between prelate and people until, finally, the Bishop had to be withdrawn. According to local legend he is reputed to have cursed the community as he left saying, "The grass will grow on Water Street." To this day residents blame the supposed curse for a long series of destructive fires and commercial disasters that have hit the town. Carfagnini, the first President of St. Bonaventure's, ended his days as an Archbishop in Italy.

In 1865 Bishop Mullock put the deserted Belvedere to use as a boarding hostel for students attending the Catholic Academy, a school he had established in the vacated Old Palace on Henry Street. Before his death in 1869 the Bishop changed the character of St. Bonaventure's from seminary to secular school. In the fourteen years of its existence as a diocesan seminary it had sent forth about thirty students who were elevated to the priesthood, but only one of these completed all his studies at the institution.

At 11:00 a.m., 3 October 1870, St. Bonaventure's opened its doors to its first non-clerical students. The President was the new bishop, Dr. Power, with Rev. John Lovejoy as Vice-President. The teachers were Rev. Dan Lynch and Messrs. Thomas Talbot, Fitzpatrick, and O'Regan. Professor Bennett, the famous bandmaster, taught music. On 9 October 1889, at the request of Bishop Power, the school was taken over by the Irish Christian Brothers, and the first president under this new regime was Brother J.L. Slattery. Sod for a new wing was turned by Archbishop Howley in May 1907, and the cornerstone laid by him on July 4. The building was opened in 1909.

The name St. Bonaventure's was chosen by Dr. Mullock for two reasons. First of all, he was a member of the Order of St. Francis, and St.

Bonaventure is called the second founder of the Franciscans. After St. Francis, the learned Bonaventure is the greatest saint of the order. Secondly, the name commemorates the death of Bishop Fleming who passed away on July 14, the feast day of St. Bonaventure.

In the years that followed, the fame of this college, as an institution of learning and sports prowess, spread around the world and boarding students came from as far away as the United States and England. A list of its graduates is a Who's Who in Newfoundland. They include a baron, various knights, a governor, archbishops, bishops, prime ministers, chief justices, ambassadors, and just about anything else you can name.

The story of this great hall of learning, with its fantastic achievements in sport, came to an end in September 1962, when senior students were transferred to the more modern Brother Rice and Gonzaga High Schools, and the old buildings were given an unfortunate face lift and called St. Bonaventure's Grammar School.

The third denominational body to emerge from the collapse of the General Academy, when the education grant was split three ways, was the Wesleyan Academy. It got its name in 1859.[11] In 1886 Governor Des-Voeux laid the cornerstone for the Methodist College on Long's Hill. Unfortunately, this building was totally destroyed in the Great Fire of 1892, and all records of its early days were lost and details of its history are unavailable. The school was rebuilt in brick with an adjoining residence for the sons and daughters of Methodist clergymen serving throughout the island. Fire again gutted the Wesleyan College in 1925. The present building, now known as Holloway School, arose from the ashes.

Land for a senior school was acquired on LeMarchant Road east of Golf Avenue. Although the foundation stone was laid in 1919 by the Prince of Wales (later King Edward VIII), the school was not occupied until 1928. It was called Prince of Wales College in honour of the heir apparent. The old Wesleyan name had become obsolete in 1925, when the United Church was formed by a union of Methodists, Wesleyans, some Congregationalists, and some Presbyterians.

With the opening of Prince of Wales Collegiate in 1960, the old building on LeMarchant Road sent its elementary students next door to Harrington School and became United Junior High School. Prince of Wales College was the only coeducational institution run by the three major denominations in St. John's. Its successor, Prince of Wales Collegiate, had the same distinction.

Meanwhile, during the nineteenth century, the education of Church of England and Roman Catholic young ladies was not neglected. The Diocesan Girls' School, which Bishop Feild founded in 1845, was in a building that had been Dr. Spencer's residence, on Cochrane Place (Military Road), at the corner of Gower Street. Bishop Feild had moved to a brick dwelling on the northwest corner of Gower and Cathedral Streets. Under the direction of a Miss Cooksley the school expanded rapidly and twelve years later it moved to 22 King's Bridge Road where it became known as Jersey Lodge and for the next eighteen years was under the direction of the Misses Le Gallais whose father, Rev. Wm. Smith, was from the Channel Island of Jersey. He drowned near Isle aux Morts in 1869. One of his daughters, Isabelle, became the wife of Lord Morris.

By 1857 the institution had become known as the Church of England Girls' School and the principal, Clara Butler from Quebec, was in charge from that year until 1882 when she was replaced by Armine Nutting, sister of the celebrated nurse, Adelaide Nutting. At her boarding house in St. John's Miss Nutting met a pale young man named Gilbert Gosling. She resigned as headmistress in 1887 and married Gosling in Halifax the following year. He later became mayor of St. John's and her donation of his books to the city after his death became the Gosling Memorial Library.

The Church of England Girls' School became the Synod Girls' School following the departure of Miss Nutting and a move from King's Bridge Road to Synod Hall on Queen's Road. In 1895 the deserted Jersey Lodge became Bishop's Court, official residence of the Church of England Bishop of Newfoundland. It was demolished in 1956 and replaced by an unfortunate venture into modern architecture, occupied by Bishop Meaden, the following year. This new residence, which cost over a hundred thousand dollars, was sold in 1972 for sixty thousand, and Bishop Seaborn moved to a more modest residence on the west side of Portugal Cove Road, three doors north of Roche Street.

In 1892 the Synod Girls' School, then in charge of a Miss Cowling, and its two neighbours, the Central School and the General Protestant Academy, both dissenter institutions, were razed in the Great Fire. The General Protestant Academy, known as the Academy School, stood near the site of the present kirk on the corner of Queen's Road and Long's Hill.

When the Church of England school reopened in 1894, it got a new Principal, Edith de la Mare, and a new name, Bishop Spencer College. Four years later Emilie Stirling took charge and she remained headmistress from 1898 until 1920 when an Englishwoman, Miss A.M. Richards, took over for two years. In 1922 another Englishwoman, the highly competent if somewhat formidable, Violet Cherrington, became principal and she held the post for the next thirty years. In 1918 the Church of England purchased the British Hall on the southwest corner of Bond and Flavin Streets and this became the last home of the college. The British Society had been founded in 1837 by a group of staunch male Protestants devoted to church, king, and country. The first British Hall opened 1 November 1852 and was burned in '92. The cornerstone for the Spencer structure was laid by Governor O'Brien in 1893. In time, as the British Society membership dwindled, the Hall was sold. In 1972 the society became non-denominational but its days were numbered. The decision to dissolve it was made in 1976 and its papers were turned over to the Newfoundland Provincial Archives.

The first residence for boarding students at Spencer College was a double house at 25-27 Forest Road. A small legacy from the estate of Bishop Jones made it possible to search for more convenient quarters closer to the school.

In 1927 Bishop Jones Hostel, a house on Rennies Mill Road opposite Bannerman Park, was acquired and opened as a lodge where resident girls could, in the words of Headmistress Violet Cherrington, get "plenty of nourishing food under careful supervision." Bishop Spencer College fulfilled Miss Cherrington's aim of "preparing girls for life" until the senior students were sent to the newly erected Bishop's College in 1959, where they shared facilities, and some classes, with the boys. Spencer was operated as an elementary school until 1972, when its doors were finally closed and the building offered for sale. The last principal was Jean Murray, daughter of David Murray, and editor of *The Journal of Aaron Thomas.*

Young ladies of the Roman Catholic faith got their education from the Presentation Convent School, or at the College of our Lady of Mercy, the fifth school in St. John's to be called a college.

In 1833 Bishop Fleming determined to cross the Atlantic and obtain the services of a community of Presentation nuns to come out and try to educate what he called "the poor little girls" of St. John's. The semi-cloistered order was founded to teach the poor by a well-to-do Irish lady named Nano Nagle. To raise money for the venture the Bishop auctioned off his fashionable carriage, which had large gilded mitres emblazoned on the panels. The vehicle was purchased by his good friend, Dr. William Carson, and for years Dr. Carson amused himself by driving about the town on his calls with the episcopal emblem gleaming from his carriage doors.

Dr. Fleming felt "the necessity of withdrawing female children from under the tutelage of men, from the dangerous associations which ordinary school intercourse with the other sex naturally exhibited."[12] On the morning of 29 June 1833 these sentiments brought the reverend gentleman to the door of a convent just outside the town of Galway in Ireland. He carried his belongings in a carpet bag and introduced himself as an American bishop.

The convent, which still stands on Presentation Road, welcomed the "American" bishop and allowed him to say mass. Following breakfast he was shown about the building by a young nun, Sister Magdalene O'Shaughnessy. During their tour of the school Sister Magdalene asked endless questions while the Bishop spoke to her in the most fervent tones of the desolation of his diocese. Suddenly he cried out, "You must come out with me to Newfoundland. There is the only way you can save your soul." He had no need for the impassioned plea. Sister Magdalene had already made up her mind.

After breakfast Mother John Power called all the Sisters in the thirty-three-member community together and the Bishop explained his mission.

He wanted four volunteers to teach in Newfoundland.[13] The response was immediate and Sisters Magdalene, Xaverius Lynch, Xavier Molone, and Bernard Kirwan, who was to be Superior, agreed to accompany the Bishop. "If you do not like the place," he promised, "I will land you safe back in this parlour again without a penny of expense to the house." Before giving her final consent Mother John insisted that Dr. Fleming stipulate in writing that the ladies would be sent back to Galway should such a course become necessary.

The volunteers were astir at four o'clock on the morning of 12 August 1833. At the request of the Bishop the mail coach was sent from Kilroy's Hotel to the convent and soon after dawn the passengers were aboard. Dr. Fleming sat on the box with the driver. There was "great weeping and lamentation" as the community said goodbye to the four Sisters they knew they would never see again in this world. Horses were changed at Athlone and by evening the coach reached Dublin, where they were quartered in the house of a Mrs. Hughes on Ormand Quay.

During their stay in the Irish capital, a young priest was sent over one morning to say mass for the Sisters. A venerable deacon was already on the spot and sent the youthful father away saying, "Well, my boy, what do you know about nuns?" The young priest's name was John Mullock, who was to become Bishop of Newfoundland and spiritual Superior to the little community from which he had been turned away.

Leaving Dublin, the Sisters travelled, again by coach, to Waterford, a favourite starting point for emigrants to the "Wild Plantation," as Newfoundland was known. On August 28, accompanied by Dr. Fleming and "his boy Phil," the Sisters boarded the *Ariel* at Passage East on what they considered a long and dangerous passage.[14]

The letter from Sister Magdalene, containing news of their arrival, went astray in a Liverpool post office, and when four months went by without hearing from them, the convent in Galway gave the travellers up for lost. Solemn requiem masses were celebrated, copies of the four Sisters' vows were burned, and the community went into general mourning.

The passage had indeed been hazardous, as the missing letter from Sister Magdalene to Mother John, written the day after her arrival, shows.

> We were only a few hours on board when we all got sick. . . . We were almost insensible. . . . On the third day after we left Ireland we had a storm. One of the masts was broken and some others damaged. It lasted for three days but we were not much frightened because we were almost regardless of what was going on we were so deadly sick, but we soon had another storm to encounter which was most awful. . . . It lasted 36 hours. The sails were torn to pieces, it came on so suddenly, the waves were monstrous high and used to wash over the deck in so terrible a manner that you would suppose every moment was your last. . . . The vessel heaved so

much we could not stand even for a minute. You may be sure there is not a saint in the calendar who was not invoked during this violent storm.[15]

The ship became unmanageable so that the crew had to leave her to the mercy of wind and wave. Eventually, when the storm ceased and the vessel came in sight of land, heavy fogs and contrary winds prevented their entering the Narrows, so they tossed about for another three days, in sight of the town. They finally entered the harbour on the twenty-first of September.

Sister Xaverius Lynch wrote:

> We arrived in the harbour of St. Johns 6 o'clock Friday morning . . . as soon as there was intimation of the bishop having arrived, there were crowds of people coming on board to see him at that early hour . . . they had the greatest preparations for him. Before we left the vessel, there was an address presented to him by the members of Parliament. . . . It was a most grand sight. We crossed the harbour in a small boat and when we came near the shore there were crowds of small boats, full of people, the banks, and hill were crowded and as soon as the boat that the bishop and we were in arrived there was nothing to be heard but shouts of joy and acclamations. Our ears were stunned with the noise and cries . . . all hats were off and several gentlemen were dressed in scarves [shoulder sashes]. Protestants, Orangemen and all kinds of people came to welcome us . . . as soon as we were handed into the carriage. We drove off to the bishop's house followed by crowds. . . . There were Protestant merchants who put up their colours. . . . The bishop told us that our entry made the greatest impression on the people. . . . Everyone is most anxious to see us; several of the most respectable called and left their visiting cards. Protestants among the rest, but we appeared to no one until we opened school. . . ."[16]

Sister Bernard Kirwan, the leader of the little band of pioneers, said in her first letter home.

> I almost despaired of ever writing to you again. I was so ill for ten days I was almost insensible to everything. The Sisters thought I would never reach St. John's. . . . Nothing can equal the kind attention of the bishop. . . . We are still in his house but he is looking out for us. We have two bedrooms and a parlour entirely for our own use. . . . This day six weeks we left Galway. I can scarcely think it possible, dear Rev. Mother, that I am never again to see you and all my dear sisters. . . . The bishop expects a great deal from us, he never lets us forget that we are nuns and he our Superior. . . . The Bishop's house is a handsome, comfortable one. Furniture, plate, retinue, correspond with the appearance he made in Galway. His

sister, a very nice amiable little girl, lives with him. . . . I trust as the Lord has always made use of his weakest instruments to promote His Glory it will be so with us. . . .[17]

A month later they moved into their own quarters, a former tavern, adjoining a slaughterhouse, just east of the corner of Duckworth Street and Pilot's Hill. Over the door hung a sign: "The Rising Sun," which the Sisters took to be a propitious omen. They opened their first school in the slaughterhouse on Monday morning, 21 October 1833. In the former tavern a very small parlour and two bedrooms only were reserved for their own use. Into the two buildings they managed to cram 450 "poor little girls" before the end of the first week.

There was a stable in the garden at the rear of the slaughterhouse. The only way in which a horse could be got in or out of this stable was by leading him through the hallway of the building. One day Dr. Fleming, who was visiting the nuns, was obliged to step into one of the school rooms to let an animal pass. Aghast to find the community suffering such an inconvenience he decided to remove them at once, in spite of the year's lease he had taken. Within a month they moved to the comfortable and commodious dwelling recently vacated by the Venerable Archdeacon Wix, the noted historian and first incumbent of St. Thomas's Anglican Church. Rev. Wix leased the property to the Bishop for eight years. The Archdeacon's house was in the present locality of Holloway Street, and here the Presentation Sisters stayed for nearly nine years, until the lease ran out.

The winter of 1834 seems to have been one of intense cold. In the Archdeacon's house, off Nunnery Lane (the site of the convent is now called Nunnery Hill), the ladies struggled against the severity of the weather. Sister Xaverius, in one of her voluminous epistles wrote:

> We would require all the fervour of our devotion to keep us warm. You may imagine what the cold is when in our bedrooms we cannot leave a drop of water in the basins or jugs. We must wait ever so long before we can get it to melt. As for our towels . . . they are frozen quite hard and stiff. . . . Water freezes in a room even with a fire and the water which is left on the altar for the priest is in ice before he uses it, though only left a little before he comes. As for the milk for breakfast, it is like lump sugar and we are obliged to cut it with a knife. . . . When we are out walking our breath freezes on our cloaks. Everything we leave out of our hands, jugs and mugs, are frozen to the table. . . . As for the clothes, when they are put in to steep they become a complete mass of ice; and the meat is obliged to be sawn. I suppose, dear Ann, you think all this incredible for we thought so ourselves until we began to experience it. . . . Since I began this letter so intense had been the frost that while Biddy was mopping the stairs the water was frozen on the boards so that it was like glass though she used boiling water. . . . The water in our mugs at dinner became ice before we

> drank though there was a fire in the room and at night the breath
> on our sheets is frozen. While Biddy was pumping water her hand
> was frozen to the handle. . . . Let not all this frighten you for we
> can bear it very well and we were never better in health but I think
> we would be obliged to put on warmer clothing than in Ireland. . . .[18]

A school was erected near the nun's residence at a cost of six hundred pounds, and twelve hundred pupils were enrolled. Sister Xaverius wrote of this school: "They are two beautiful rooms more lofty than our schools in Galway but not quite so long. There are five windows each side of the room made in Gothic Style."[19] Of their pupils, Sister Magdalene had this to say:

> I have scarce anything particular to mention regarding them except that
> they improve on acquaintance, are very docile and most anxious to come to
> school. . . . They are very fond of dress-wear, necklaces, rings, etc. so that
> from their appearance you would scarcely think you were teaching in a
> poor school. No such thing as a barefoot child to be seen here, how great
> the contrast between them and the poor Irish! How often do I think of the
> poor children of Galway. . . .[20]

Many of these letters were interrupted, in the course of being written, by the ink freezing in the inkwells.

By 1843 the old residence of the Archdeacon was showing signs of decay. When the lease expired, the nuns were uprooted and moved to "a house which had been a ball-alley, situated a little outside the town." Construction was begun on a new and permanent convent at the top of Long's Hill, near what is now Young Street. This beautiful building, with its handsomely finished front flanked at the angles by hexagonal castellated towers and a spacious portico, was ready for occupancy on 14 December 1844. Less than two years after opening, it was destroyed during the Great Fire of 1846.

This blaze, which consumed much of the town, was confined to the lower streets, and the Presentation Convent, on the upper level and far from the scenes of flame and panic, became a refuge for many of the dispossessed who streamed up Long's Hill seeking asylum. One of the refugees is thought to have brought the fire into the convent in some smouldering blankets, unnoticed by anyone until the fire in the town was nearly out and the convent suddenly began to burn. So rapid was the spread of flames that all the historical archives belonging to the order were lost. The Sisters had barely time to save themselves and the throng they were sheltering before their convent was in ruins.

Bishop Fleming was visiting Europe at the time so the homeless nuns were forced to manage for themselves. They finally decided to take refuge in a barn at Carpasia, a small suburban farm and cottage belonging to His Excellency. At the time of Dr. Fleming's consecration as Assistant Bishop, the ailing Dr. Scallan was still Bishop of Newfoundland, so the new assistant was given the title of an ancient and extinct see in Asia Minor, called Carpasia. Fleming later gave the name to his country residence, just north of Patrick's Pinch, and the road which passed the property became Carpasian Road.

Walter Grieve, a Protestant gentleman who was an admirer of the Bishop, is said to have donated all the ropes and scaffolding used in erecting the Roman Catholic cathedral walls. As a mark of his gratitude Dr. Fleming either made a gift of Carpasia, or sold it for a nominal sum, to Mr. Grieve. The estate afterwards passed to the Duder family and eventually came into the possession of Gerald S. Doyle, who erected an imposing country residence on the land. Following Mr. Doyle's death the Presentation Order purchased Carpasia for a fairly considerable sum and used it in the 1960s as a training house for novices. A lack of candidates caused it to become a "House of Prayer," a place for religious retreats, in 1972.

For five months in 1846 the nuns slept on the floor of the barn at Carpasia and taught in the nearby fields on fine days. In wet weather the stable and out-buildings became classrooms. When Bishop Fleming returned to find the Sisters living in these most desperate circumstances, and most of the town lying in ruins, he arranged for the Mercy Convent on Military Road to be partitioned, and the Presentation nuns moved in to share the building. But the already ill prelate had received a shock which undermined his health completely and eventually brought on his death.

On 23 August 1850 Bishop Fleming's successor, Dr. Mullock, the young priest who had been turned away from the community years before in Dublin, laid the cornerstone for a new Presentation Convent and school adjacent to the cathedral. As soon as the walls of the school were up the Sisters moved into the uncompleted building, with a roof made of sails loaned to them by Walter Grieve. Here they lived until their convent, adjoining the school to the west, was ready. They took possession of it from Bishop Mullock on 2 July 1853, and the building at Cathedral Square is still the Mother House of the first order of English-speaking nuns in Canada. It was the eighth house that Nano Nagle's daughters had occupied in the twenty years since they had arrived in St. John's from Galway.

Bishop Mullock seems to have brought his family with him from Ireland. His brother Thomas taught music at 2 Queen's Road, and his sister, Mother di Pazzi, who lived with him in St. John's before entering the convent there, was Superior of the Presentation Order in Newfoundland. As a result of this connection the order was gifted with a number of art works such as the famous *Veiled Virgin* of Giovanni Steazzo, and an exquisite marble altar in the convent chapel, carved with local scenes.

Sir Richard Bonnycastle made the following observation, while visiting St. John's early in the spring of 1842:

There is a small convent of nuns, of the presentation order, con-

791

sisting of four ladies, who devote their lives to the education of
children, and to purposes of similar utility; but they are never
seen, as in Canada, abroad in their conventual habit; nor do the
Roman-Catholic clergymen wear a distinctive dress, as in that
country; these also superintend their schools, which, in St. John's,
particularly, are very extensive and well conducted.[21]

If Sir Richard's observation is factual, and there is no reason to believe it is
not, nuns and priests in St. John's appear not to have worn distinctive
dress in public in 1842.

For some years after he brought the Presentation Sisters from Galway to teach the poor, Dr. Fleming contemplated introducing another
order of nuns to teach the daughters of those who could afford to pay for an
education. The beginnings of the Mercy Order in Newfoundland are not
nearly so well documented as those of the Presentation Sisters. No early
letters or reports appear to have survived either in Ireland or in St. John's.
Through neglect or indifference they were lost or destroyed.

On one of his visits to Ireland Dr. Fleming met Catherine McAuley.
This woman had used her immense fortune of thirty thousand pounds and
her yearly income of six hundred, inherited from her foster parents, to
purchase land and erect a school for poor children, as well as a hostel for
girls who were homeless and a hospital on Lower Baggot Street in Dublin.
The date the complex opened was 24 December 1827. The following year
it was named the Institute of Our Blessed Lady of Mercy. Catherine, and
her increasing band of followers, began to wear a uniform. She decided
that they should become nuns and requested permission of the church for a
small group of them to enter the Presentation Order for training, but not
to become members of that sisterhood. This little band of women was professed on 12 December 1831 and the foundation of the Order of the Sisters
of Mercy dates from that event.

Nine years later, on 12 July 1840, Bishop Fleming said mass in the
chapel of the convent on Lower Baggot Street. After mass the Bishop and
the Foundress discussed a Newfoundland branch. Mother McAuley said
she would open the proposed convent immediately except for the fact that
one was already being planned for Birmingham, England. However, she
promised Dr. Fleming to come herself and establish a Newfoundland congregation as soon as the one in Birmingham was launched. It was hoped
to open this first overseas house in May or June 1841. That evening she
announced that whoever could take tea without milk should go to Newfoundland as Superior. Sister di Pazzi followed up the humorous suggestion by taking tea without milk next morning. As it turned out, however,
neither of them was to lead the tiny flock over the ocean.

The Bishop had arranged for an Irish girl who lived in St. John's for a
time, and was acquainted with the circumstances of the country, to enter
the order and prepare for the Newfoundland mission. She was Mary Ann

Creedon, a native of Culowen, Cork, whose sister was married to John Valentine Nugent. It is assumed that Miss Creedon came to Newfoundland to visit her sister. How long she stayed we do not know. While in the colony she met Dr. Fleming and undoubtedly told him of her wish to join a religious order on her return to Ireland. It seems likely that he convinced her to enter Mother McAuley's convent in Dublin, with the intention of having her return to Newfoundland. In August 1841 she was professed as Sister Francis and became the fiftieth member of the Mercy Order.[22]

Catherine McAuley's illness that year caused the Newfoundland venture to be postponed. By the end of 1841 she was in her grave at Baggot Street and Sister di Pazzi was the new Superior of the congregation. It was not until 11 May 1842 that the overseas group was ready to sail. Besides Sister Francis it consisted of Clara Frayne, a Dublin-born girl who, as Sister Ursula, was the twenty-second member of the Mercy Order, and Sister Rose Lynch. Some histories speak of a postulant named Miss Supple, but she is not mentioned in the *Annals,* and she vanishes from the story once the Sisters reach St. John's. It is known that the foundress always endeavoured to send a novice on a foundation so that a ceremony of profession could soon occur for the edification of the people whom the Sisters would serve. If Miss Supple was such a novice she soon changed her mind. That she did arrive is proven by the following item in the *Newfoundlander* (9 June 1842): "The ship SIR WALTER SCOTT arrived from Dublin on Friday last, having on board four ladies of the religious order of Mercy, and two for the Presentation Convent of this town."

There is also confusion as to who was in charge of the venturesome trio (or quartet). The Register at Baggot Street styles Sister Mary Ursula, "First Superior of St. John's, Newfoundland," yet the *Annals* state that Sister Mary Rose was Superior.

When the little band of travellers reached Newfoundland, on 3 June 1842, Bishop Fleming went out in the pilot boat and met them four miles off port. So anxious was he to get the nuns ashore that he had them lowered into the small craft and taken back with him, when it was feared an off-shore wind would keep the *Sir Walter Scott* from docking until the following morning.

Rousing cheers greeted the ladies as they landed at the wharf of the Honourable James Tobin, whence they were taken to a nearby house and received by Mrs. Tobin. There a carriage was sent to fetch them and, as they drove through the narrow, unpaved streets to tea at the Presentation Convent, off Nunnery Lane, crowds waved them welcome. Since their own house was still under construction they spent the next six months as guests of the Bishop at Carpasia. By spring the convent was finished and the Sisters moved into a modest wooden structure, on the site of the present chapel on Military Road, just east of the entrance to the Basilica grounds. The building was oblong and terminated, for some unexplained reason, in a turret. Bishop Fleming writes that the Sisters "Opened their schools May

1st, 1843, and in a brief space had a considerable number of pupils whose progress . . . gives much satisfaction." On opening day forty-two students were enrolled.

If the harvest was great the labourers were soon to be very few indeed. The venture faced collapse in November 1843 when Sisters Ursula and Rose suddenly returned to Ireland. As the prospects for carrying on alone were dismal, Sister Francis was also urged to return home, but she asked for, and was given, permission to stay in St. John's. There is a tradition that the Sister was the undisguised favourite of Bishop Fleming, who told her the dreams, plans, and confidences he should have communicated to the Superior. This attitude is said to have caused problems among the ladies that could only be solved by the return of the other two Sisters to Ireland.

In 1857 Sister Ursula went to Australia and, at Perth, established the Mercy Order on that continent. Sister Rose remained at Baggot Street until September 1859, when she was sent on foundation to Geelong, Australia. The Register records the fact that she died in a mental hospital, in France, in 1890.

Sister Francis was not entirely alone. Early in 1843, the group was joined by a novice, Maria Nugent, who was a sister of John Valentine Nugent. Born in Waterford in 1799, Maria was highly educated and a scholar in Greek and Latin, as well as in Italian and French. She joined the Ursulines but severe sciatica forced her to leave the order. In 1833 she accompanied her mother to Newfoundland, where her brother and his family had recently settled. Within two weeks of their arrival the mother died and Maria entered the Presentation Convent at St. John's. Though admitted to the habit, ill health again prevented her from making her vows. In 1836 she returned to her brother's house. Here she lived the life of a recluse for six years, writing, translating, and overcoming her infirmities.

When the Sisters of Mercy arrived in 1842, Maria Nugent felt that at last her true calling had come. Because of her novitiate in the Presentation Convent she was professed and accepted by Mother Creedon, and on 25 March 1843 she became Sister Mary Joseph, the first Mercy nun to be professed outside the British Isles.

On 3 July 1847 Sister Joseph was at St. John's Hospital, Riverhead, nursing thirty-six patients suffering from typhus, the "famine fever," brought to Newfoundland by starving immigrants from Ireland. One eighteen-year-old victim lay cursing the captain who carried the fever to port. He was determined to die without forgiving the man he called his murderer. Sister Joseph spent two hours with the youth easing his pain and beseeching his forgiveness for the captain. In the face of such determination he finally turned to the pleading nun and said, "Well, madame, for your sake I'll forgive him." The priest he had earlier rejected returned to his bedside and the lad died at peace. That night Sister Joseph felt the fires of fever in her own veins and a few weeks later, on July 17, she died in agony.

Mother Francis Creedon was now entirely alone. The Mother House in Dublin once more begged her to write off the Newfoundland mission as a failure and return to Ireland, but she refused. Forced to close the school, she devoted her time to the sick and the poor. Within a few months her perseverance was rewarded, when Agnes Nugent, daughter of John Valentine Nugent and a niece of both the late Sister Joseph and Mother Creedon, came knocking on the door. Born in Waterford in 1830, Agnes came to Newfoundland with her parents in 1833. On 8 December 1848 she received the white veil from her aunt, and was professed by Bishop Mullock on 28 May 1850,[23] on which day a twenty-three-year-old novice, Theresa Bernard, arrived from Limerick, Ireland.

The profession of these two girls was the turning of the tide. Others soon followed. With the death of Mother Creedon, 15 July 1855, Theresa Bernard, now Sister Xavier, became Superior. During the fifteen years of her administration seven convent schools were established in Newfoundland and forty sisters were professed. Fifteen of these were natives of the island.

The first native-born girl to enter a convent was Sister Veronica Collins of St. John's, who joined the Presentation Order in the 1840s but was not professed until 1856. The first Newfoundlander to become a professed nun was Sister Francis Mullaly of Bonavista, who entered the Presentation Convent after Sister Veronica but was professed in 1851, a year after Dr. Fleming's death. The first Newfoundland-born nun of the Mercy Order was Anastasia Tarahan, who was denied admission to that order by Bishop Fleming because of being "native born." She finally joined the Sisters of Mercy in December 1854 and was professed on 15 August 1857 as Sister Mary Baptist.

The name of Mother Francis Creedon is not only to be found among those of the most distinguished members of the Mercy Order, it is to be found among the outstanding women of Newfoundland history. Deserted by her colleagues, alone in a land that was not her own, she struggled against almost impossible odds to keep her fledgeling convent alive. After the death of Sister Joseph, the temptation to heed the call from Dublin and return home must have been almost unbearable, yet she was determined to make a success of the first overseas venture of her order.

Today, as a result of the undaunted will of Mother Francis Creedon, the Mercy Sisters of Newfoundland are scattered in some twenty-five communities. Their junior college, St. Bride's at Littledale, was one of the most modern in Canada. Mercy nuns operate the magnificent structure that is St. Clare's Hospital, and they care for senior citizens in St. Patrick's Home. In 1961 they opened a house in Peru, where two of the Newfoundland sisters were killed on mission duty. From the first overseas convent, in St. John's, the order has grown to the point where thirty thousand

Mercy nuns now teach and tend the sick on six continents of the world. They were even with Florence Nightingale, at Balaclava, in the Crimean War.

During the great cholera epidemic that swept St. John's in 1856, Sister Xavier and her followers worked among the stricken from daylight to dark and often through the night. They entered plague-ridden houses in the filthiest slums to light fires and feed the abandoned wretches. They scrubbed floors and cleaned the tenements. They dressed and washed the sick and finally carried their dead bodies to the coffins which were placed outside the door by fearful officials who refused to enter the plague houses.

It was on 8 December 1854 that the Sisters of Mercy opened St. Clare's, the first orphanage in Newfoundland. This home for girls was in an annex attached to their convent on Military Road and built by Bishop Mullock in 1852. By 1856 the convent and annex were inadequate and overcrowded, and Dr. Mullock decided they should be torn down and a proper building erected. The Sisters moved into the orphanage and lived there for fifteen months while their wooden home was demolished and the present stone convent was constructed. By 1857 the building was ready for occupancy. The oratory, or convent chapel, was erected on the site of the old building. In 1916, when a commercial course was added to the academic one, the school became known as the Mercy Convent Academy.

At the time of his death in 1850 Bishop Fleming left his Belvedere property to the Mercy Order for use as an orphanage,[24] and bequeathed some funds for its maintenance. However, because it was occupied by ecclesiastical students and later by boarders attending the Catholic Academy, it was not possible to occupy the building until 4 July 1858 when it was decided to allow lay boarders residence at St. Bonaventure's College. The Sisters moved their thirty orphans from Military Road to Belvedere and opened the orphanage there on 16 November 1859. It closed a hundred and ten years later when the government decided to place the female orphans in foster homes.

Following World War I, the Knights of Columbus informed Archbishop Roche of their intention to erect some sort of memorial to their brother knights who died in the Great War. Knowing there was a crying need for more teaching space in the city, for Catholic girls, the Archbishop suggested the knights consider erecting a school. His suggestion was accepted and construction was begun at Cathedral Square, just above Mercy Convent Chapel. The new building, called the Knights of Columbus Memorial School, was opened by the Mercy Order on Columbus Day 1921. Later, the school became known as the Academy of Our Lady of Mercy and, in the mid-1940s, it was named the College of Our Lady of Mercy. With the opening of Holy Heart of Mary Regional High School on 15 September 1958, the college was given over to the teaching of elementary students under the name of Our Lady of Mercy School.

There is a large red stone in the wall, south of the entrance to the

Knights of Columbus Memorial building, behind the convent chapel. This polished granite stone, which bears the monogram "M," was obtained by Bishop Mullock from the Carmelite Convent of St. Theresa in Avila, Spain. He himself had been a student of the famous Carmelite University of Salamanca and as such was anxious to link his new convent building to that of the great Teresa of Avila.

At three o'clock on the afternoon of 14 September 1908 the Salvation Army College and Training School was officially opened, on the north side of Springdale and George Streets, by the Governor Sir William MacGregor, turning a key in the door. As its name implies, the building was more than just an all-grade school. It also housed a Training College for officers of the Salvation Army and there were living quarters upstairs. The first principal was a woman, Ensign E.N. Mercer.

In 1944 the Newfoundland Department of Education agreed to the appointment of a Salvation Army officer, Major W.C. Brown, as an executive officer in the Department. This gave the Army the same recognition as was previously extended to the other three major religious denominations in Newfoundland.

By the end of World War II, the Springdale Street building was beginning to show its age. School needs, and the efficiency of the Training School, made the erection of more modern quarters imperative. The necessary finances were found and, in September 1950, the school moved to a modern building on Adams Avenue, which was known as the Salvation Army College. The Training School for officers moved to several buildings on the west corner of LeMarchant Road at Barter's Hill.

The principal of the Salvation Army College at the time of its move to Adams Avenue was W.C. Woodland, who remained in charge of the new school for most of its life. In 1960, with the opening of the nearby Booth Memorial High, the Salvation Army College took on a new role as Dawson Elementary School.

In the 1880s two Christian Mission preachers in an Ontario town held open-air services and won a number of converts. They persuaded General Booth to link their work to that of the Christian Mission in Great Britain, which had recently become the Salvation Army. Two of the Christian Mission converts in Ontario were Charles Dawson and Emma Churchill. Miss Churchill was a native of Newfoundland, and when she and Dawson married they spent their honeymoon with her parents in Portugal Cove. During their stay in Newfoundland Emma and her husband conducted Salvation meetings in Temperance Hall on Victoria Street.

The group of Mission converts the Dawsons left behind when they returned to Canada became the nucleus of the Salvation Army which was organized in Newfoundland by visiting officers at an open-air meeting on the Parade Grounds, Parade Street, in 1886.[25] The name of Dawson Elementary School commemorates Emma Dawson of Portugal Cove, the first

797

Salvationist and a woman whose efforts led to the establishment of the faith in the island.

An enduring award for student achievement was announced in the *Royal Gazette,* 12 May 1891, when it was proclaimed that:

> the Governor in Council shall appropriate, annually, the sum of four hundred and eighty dollars for the institution of a Scholarship in the London University to be given and awarded to the student who shall take the highest place amongst competitors in this Colony at the Matriculation Examination holden in June of any year. . . .

The Jubilee Scholarship is still awarded but not for London University.

Memorial University of Newfoundland began with the joint dream of three men: Vincent Burke, William Blackall, and Levi Curtis. Dr. Burke, born in St. John's on 3 August 1878, graduated from St. Bonaventure's and Columbia University. He was appointed Superintendent of Roman Catholic Schools in 1899. Dr. Blackall, born in Middlesborough, Yorkshire, 16 January 1864, graduated from the University of London and came to Newfoundland as Headmaster at Bishop Feild in 1891. He became Superintendent of Anglican education in 1908. Dr. Curtis, born at Blackhead, Bay de Verde, 22 February 1858, attended Methodist College and Mount Allison University before becoming a Methodist minister in 1889 and was made Superintendent of Methodist education in 1899.

As School Superintendents for their denominations throughout Newfoundland, the three men often met and came to the conclusion that, if there were to be any appreciable progress in Newfoundland education, the country must have its own university. They made their dream public in 1913 but World War I put an end to all plans. In 1917 Burke, Blackall, and Curtis approached the Carnegie Foundation and in 1919 that body gave them the promise of one hundred and fifty thousand dollars in grants spread over nine years. On 22 January 1919 the Patriotic Association passed a resolution stating:

> This Patriotic Association agree to take into consideration the advisability of erecting in St. John's a memorial to the 1609 young men; soldiers and sailors, who had died in the great World War; in the form of an educational building which should raise to a higher level the whole status of education in Newfoundland and materially assist our young people to achieve greater success in life.

Sir Giles Gilbert Scott who was the architect for the Anglican Cathedral designed the proposed building. In 1920 Sir Richard Squires' government voted the sum of one hundred thousand dollars for the establishment of a Normal School. The cost of Scott's proposal was estimated at two hundred and fifty thousand dollars but economic problems and political unrest delayed a start on the hoped-for institution until 1922 when it was built for three hundred thousand dollars on a greatly modified scale. Meanwhile, a Normal School for teachers' training was begun in 1921 in the Synod Hall on Queen's Road. The dream of Burke, Blackall, and Curtis was realized on 15 September 1925 when the new Prime Minister, Walter S. Monroe, officially opened the new Normal School and junior college on Parade Street which was known as Memorial University College, an institution giving the first two years of the B.A. and B.SC. courses.[26]

The first president of Memorial was John Lewis Paton, retired High Master of Manchester Grammar School, England. Student enrolment was fifty-seven students. By 1973 the University had a full-time enrolment of 10,990 students. In 1949 the first session of the Newfoundland House of Assembly under Confederation heard in the speech from the throne: "It is considered that Newfoundland should have its own degree conferring university and you will be invited to consider legislation which would confer upon Newfoundland Memorial University College the status of University." The following month, August 1949, the Act was passed. In 1950 Memorial granted its first five degrees when regulations for Bachelor of Arts were approved, and in 1951 the degree of Bachelor of Science was granted. A graduate degree program was added a few years later with the approval of regulations for the degree of Master of Arts and Master of Science. In 1955 the degree of Bachelor of Commerce was introduced and in 1960 that of Bachelor of Education. In 1961 a degree program in Physical Education was added. The first doctorates were granted in May 1970. On 16 June 1973 the Faculty of Medicine awarded twenty-three new doctors the first medical degrees.

By the early 1950s, with the post-war interest in higher education, the old Memorial University College on Parade Street was badly overcrowded. On 9 October 1952 the Right Honourable the Viscount Rothermere of Hempsted, first chancellor of the University, laid the cornerstone for a new campus on Halliday's Farm, Elizabeth Avenue. The Rothermere family had for many years controlled the destiny of the paper mill and town of Grand Falls. Lord Rothermere was followed into the chancellor's role by another newspaper magnate, Lord Thompson of Fleet, who held the post from 1961 to 1968 when the first Newfoundland chancellor took over.[27] He was St. Pierre-born Dr. G. Alain Frecker whose wife, Helena McGrath, was the first graduate of Memorial University College.

An attractive feature of the new campus, which opened officially in October 1961 when Mrs. Eleanor Roosevelt presented the keys to Lord Thompson, was the beautiful complex of Georgian residences. Located on the north side of the campus, on the shores of Long Pond, were three theological colleges: St. John's (Roman Catholic), Coughlan (United Church), and Queen's (Anglican). They doubled as residences and theological institutions for the training of clergy.

In 1967 the University opened the Marine Sciences Research Laboratory at Logy Bay and received federal government approval for the establishment of Canada's sixteenth medical school. That same year saw the start of the Educational Television Centre. There was already a school of nursing established under Joyce Nevitt, an English nurse, in 1966-67. Work on a forty-six-million-dollar medical complex, including a four-hundred-bed hospital, was due for completion in 1977.

The first president of Memorial University was a Newfoundlander, Dr. Raymond Gushue. He was followed in the post by an English Labour Party Peer and medical doctor, Lord Stephen Taylor of Harlow, whose wife Charity had been matron of Holloway Prison in England. A residence was built for the president on the north shore of Long Pond. When Taylor returned to Britain in 1973, Moses Morgan, another Newfoundlander, became University President.

Ireland has many saints. Three are ranked as Great: Patrick, Columba, and Bridget. The last of these was a holy woman who lived around the year 500. Little is known of her but that she founded a monastery at Kildare and is buried, with Patrick and Columba, at Downpatrick. We do know that she was also called Bride and it is by this diminutive that she is remembered in the name of Newfoundland's only junior college.

In 1850 Philip Little, a Roman Catholic from Prince Edward Island, became Newfoundland's first Prime Minister. By the time he retired to live in Ireland in 1866, he was the owner of a country estate in the suburbs of St. John's called Littledale. On 3 November 1883 this estate, which consisted of a handsome three-storey white house as well as a great deal of valuable land, was purchased from the former Prime Minister's family by the Sisters of Mercy for use as a young ladies' boarding school. A classroom was added to the eastern side of the house and a dormitory at the rear. Called St. Bride's Academy, and with Mother Xaverius Dowsley as first Superior, the small institution, of four boarders, was blessed by Bishop Power in 1884. On August 20 of that year it was formally opened by the Right Reverend Monsignor Scott, in the absence from the country of Bishop Power. By the end of the year enrollment had risen to thirteen.

By the close of the nineteenth century the original buildings had become totally inadequate and Archbishop Howley ordered the construction of a new wing. Mother Joseph Kelly procured the funds and saw the building completed, in 1901, to the east of the Little home, and the old house was pulled down. Thirty thousand dollars had been spent on the new structure which the Archbishop designated Talbot Wing, to perpetuate the memory of Thomas Talbot, a generous benefactor to the cause of Catholic education in Newfoundland.

By 1908 still more accommodation was required and the west wing was begun according to plans in the original design. Commenced in 1909, the building was ready for occupancy in 1912, at a cost of sixty thousand dollars. The centre building, on the site of the old residence, was still on the drawing board at the time of Archbishop Howley's death, but his successor, Archbishop Roche decided to continue the work of building at Littledale. However, the greatly increased cost of labour, and the difficulty of obtaining workers and materials in wartime, meant that the Howley plan for a six-storey central tower had to be abandoned and a vulgar three-storey tower structure, linking the east and west wings, arose on the site of the original Little house.

With the acquisition of a college grant from the government in 1917, the institution was raised to the status of a college and was styled St. Bride's Roman Catholic College for Women. It became a normal school in 1938, when a course in teacher training was introduced. In 1942 serious consideration was given to plans for the completion of the originally contemplated six-storey central building. But, again, it was wartime and the unstable economic conditions resulted in a more modest wooden structure. The building, known as St. Augustine's Hall, was erected to the west of the driveway. Commenced in 1943, it was opened by Archbishop Roche on 1 February 1944.

A year before his episcopate ended in 1949, Roche negotiated an affiliation between St. Bride's College and Memorial University College.[28] St. Bride's was fully accredited by Memorial University, 1 July 1952, as a two-year junior college. At the same time it was given a seat on the University senate.

The beautiful, modern St. Bride's College complex, to the west of the old buildings, was opened 12 April 1967 by Archbishop Skinner, in the presence of Lieutenant-Governor O'Dea, Premier Smallwood, Bishop O'Neill, and others. The college's new residence could accommodate a hundred and fifty boarders. Appointed president was Sister Mary Nolasco Maloney.

In 1964, in accordance with the Memorial University Act, the affiliation was renewed, with a second year added. Students at St. Bride's could receive their degrees through Memorial. Under terms of the affiliation, instruction could be given at the college, in history and philosophy, for all four years. In 1974 the institution was suddenly closed and the future use of the structure became a subject for debate.

The College of Fisheries, Navigation, Marine Engineering, and Electronics was officially opened on 15 January 1964, on Parade Street, in buildings erected in 1923 for Memorial University College. It was the only educational institution in eastern Canada exclusively teaching subjects related to fisheries. Plans for its establishment were worked out by the government of the province in 1963. Dr. William Hampton was appointed first President of the College, professors were recruited from all over the world, and many competent instructors joined the staff.

A residence for boarding students was opened at Pleasantville, the former U.S. military base of Fort Pepperrell. Students come from all over the world, even from as far away as the island of Mauritius, in the Indian Ocean. Various loans, aids, and scholarships enable Commonwealth coun-

801

tries in Africa and Asia to send their young people to Newfoundland to study fisheries and related subjects. When the college opened in 1964, 146 students were enrolled. It operated two training ships from a branch building on the south side of St. John's Harbour; the longliners *Zilk* and *Beinir*. On board these vessels students could learn the practical application of what they were taught in the classrooms.[29]

On the southeast slope of Kent's Pond, where Confederation Parkway begins, John Kent, Newfoundland's second Prime Minister, erected a fine residence which he modestly termed a cottage. It consisted of six bedrooms on the upper floor. Set in its four acres of meadowland were a stable for two horses and a coach house. Following the decease of Kent, the property was sold by auction on 24 November 1858. The only reminder of the Irish landowner in the area today is his name, which was given to the the former Middle Long Pond.

The "cottage" was removed when the provincial government decided to open Confederation Parkway through the property, and erect the College of Trade and Technology at the back of the Kent family meadow.

In 1960 the government determined to provide a province-wide Vocational Education System which would include a College of Trades and Technology in St. John's, for which 75 per cent would be paid by the federal government. The cornerstone of the building was laid in May 1961. The facilities were designed to provide training for a thousand students, but by 1975 enrolment had risen to eighteen hundred and fifty.

The building opened on 12 September 1963 and provided training in over forty technical, trade, and occupational courses. It was operated by the Department of Education until 1970, when in September of that year it came under the administration of a Board of Governors.[30] At that time the school's first principal, Ken Duggan, became its first president.

8

One Very Narrow Street

Following the Great Fire of 1846 this Customs House was erected at King's Beach on the west side of Haymarket Square. It burned to the ground in the Great Fire of 1892 and was replaced by the Newfoundland War Memorial and Mechanics' Hall. This structure on the roof is a leading light to guide ships entering port.

This was Water Street East in the 1880s. The black and white buildings in the centre on the corner of Hunter's Cove, belong to Job Brothers and are the site of the Royal Trust Building. The two-storey structure in the upper left is Lindberg's brewery. The barracks in the trees to the right of the brewery were the first buildings on Signal Hill consumed by the 1892 fire. (Courtesy Provincial Reference Library.)

Water Street looking east from William's Lane in the late 1880s. The two stores on the right are those of the Honourable Moses Monroe while the large boot on the left hangs outside David Smallwood's. The boot manufacturer was the grandfather of Newfoundland's first premier under Confederation, the irrepressible Joey Smallwood. Many of these buildings are still standing. (Courtesy CBS Newfoundland Region.)

Water Street west of Adelaide Street in the halcyon days of the Edwardian era when ladies kept the sun off with parasols, and carriages lined up at the cab rank in front of the General Post Office awaiting fares. Woods West End Candy Store (below the Post Office tower) afterwards became the Sterling Restaurant. Note the double streetcar tracks and the sign of the gun on the left. (Courtesy St. John's City Hall.)

808

Every inch of space on this old Water Street premises, believed to be P & L Tessier's (circa 1880), is covered with salt fish spread out to dry. Cod was known as "the currency of Newfoundland" and was so designated on one of the country's postage stamps. (Courtesy Newfoundland Provincial Archives.)

Water Street from Beck's Cove to Temperance Street was levelled by the Great Fire of 1892. Within days of the disaster Ayre & Sons built this temporary shop on the ruins. It is said to be the first firm to reopen after the fire. Atlantic Place now stands on this site. Mr. Ayre's motto reads: "Fire can destroy; labor can restore."

810

James H. Monroe might be called the father of Newfoundland's manufacturing industries. In 1882, with his brother the Honourable Moses Monroe, he founded the Colonial Cordage Company with a capital stock of $160,000, of which $124,000 was paid up. Prowse termed its Rope Walk "The most important social industry in St. John's." It gave employment to five hundred persons. Burned out three years later the plant was replaced within six months.

Sir John Crosbie was born in Brigus in September 1876. He entered the hotel business with his father George Crosbie moving from that to the general fishery business where he headed Crosbie & Company. Within eighteen months he became sole owner of a firm that now controls Eastern Provincial Airways, Chimo Shipping Line, Atlantic Place, and various other enterprises. His wife was Mitchie Manuel of Exploits.

811

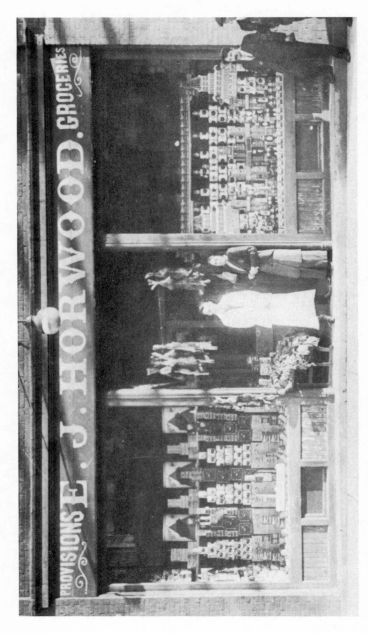

No modern supermarket could possibly replace the leisured pace of shopping at such stores as E.J. Horwood's on Water Street East. Besides the fresh cabbage and braces of rabbits hanging in the doorway the store was stocked with English canned goods and other supplies of superior quality. The lady is probably a shop assistant (Courtesy Provincial Reference Library.)

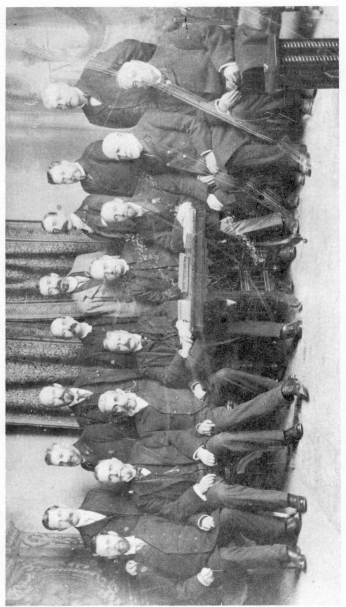

The committee organized to handle the children's demonstration for the visit to St John's of the Duke and Duchess of Cornwall and York in 1901 brought together some of the great merchants of the day. Front row: Sidney Woods, James Stott, Sir. J. S. Winter, Walter Baine Grieve, Rev. Alex. Robertson, Charles Steer, Hon. J. J. Rogerson, Hon. James McLoughlan. Back row: William Martin, W. A. B. Sclater, Henry Youmans Mott, Rev. J. Thackery, John Barron, John Harvey, Hon. R. K. Bishop, E. H. Davey.

Mr. T. McCarthy's grocery store at the corner of 437 Water Street and Hutchings Lane. It was the fashion to display casks of fat-back pork, spare ribs, and corned beef on the sidewalk. Urchins, corner boys, and others were always in plentiful supply. McCarthy's brother supplied piano music for the silent films at the Nickel Theatre. (Courtesy Provincial Reference Library.)

After the fire of 1892 Ayre's opened their big new department store 23 September 1907. In the china department a salesgirl looks on as a young gentleman examines a teacup while other clerks and customers hover over china which today costs a fortune in antique shops. (Courtesy Newfoundland Provincial Archives.)

Haymarket Square (now the Newfoundland War Memorial), between Duckworth and Water Streets, was a popular place in the days before the automobile when labouring men, businessmen, and the wealthy had to keep their barns plentifully supplied with hay for the numerous horses in the city. (Courtesy St. John's City Hall.)

This unburned section of Water Street, looking east from Waldegrave Street retained its post-1846 look until recent individual fires gutted most of the building in the range. In this photo (circa 1950) the York Movie Theatre, formerly the Queen, is on the right. (Courtesy Public Archives of Canada.)

A winter's day on Water Street in the period just after World War II. Bon Marche on the
left faces Ayre's in the Pitts Building on the right. At the foot of McBride's Hill (behind the
couple crossing the street) James Vey, the photographer, had his studio in the Bank
of Montreal Building. (Courtesy Public Archives of Canada.)

818

One Very Narrow Street

*The Capital of Newfoundland consists of one very narrow street
extending entirely along one side of the port.*
  LT. EDWARD CHAPPELL *Voyage of H.M.S. Rosamond*

Anyone standing at the foot of Temperance Street and looking west will
see a street that is probably the oldest commercial thoroughfare used
exclusively by the white man in North America. From the beginning of the
sixteenth century Water Street has been a place of buying and selling, trade
and barter, commerce and gossip.

Originally the line of beach cliffs ran close to what is now the north
side of the street, and there was a narrow foot path along this shore
interspersed by many rivers and several marshes. The coves of today were
the mouths of these rivers and marshes.

When St. John's was visited by contemporaries of John Cabot and
Corte-Real, the harbour was almost twice its present size. The hills on
both sides of the Narrows were thickly wooded with spruce and fir trees
that ran down to the water's edge. A high cliff skirted the north shore from
Temperance Street to Hill o' Chips, on top of which Devon Row now
stands. A beach stretched almost from Chain Rock to St. John's Lane.
Prescott Street was a substantial river running from the Barrens and
emptying into a marsh that extended from St. John's Lane almost to
Telegram Lane. West of Telegram Lane a high wall of rock followed the
shoreline jutting out to the water's edge at the foot of McBride's Hill. At
that point the beach was so narrow that it was almost impossible to get
past the cliff at high tide without getting wet feet. Beyond Beck's Cove the
outcrop levelled off to an area of flat bogland intersected by small streams,
the largest of which ran down Adelaide Street. Here the first settlers are
believed to have erected their wooden tilts possibly because the flat ground
could be more easily cultivated for kitchen gardens. The Oxford family, the
first planters in St. John's known to us by name, are thought to have
erected a permanent house in this area soon after 1600. In succeeding years
humble fishermen's dwellings were built along the north side of the
harbour foot path. Opposite them the shoreline was dotted with storage
sheds, fish flakes, and fishing stages which ran out into the water.

In time these early settlers were ordered away from the shore as large

819

areas were set aside for ships' rooms, plots of land reserved almost exclusively for the preparation of fish for market. Any encroachment on a ships' room was forbidden by law and the fishermen were forced to move their homes to higher land along what became known as the Upper Path, now Duckworth Street.

Because of the high wall of rock to the north, the only way for the Lower Path to expand was to move out into the harbour. Over the centuries fire rubble, rock, and other fill pushed the shore out from the original beach by as much as two or three hundred feet in places.

In the seventeenth century St. John's was little more than a small fishing village. It was not until the early years of the eighteenth century that its character began to change to that of a town. The most natural place for this growth to occur was along the waterfront, although building on the Lower Path was impeded by the presence of the ships' rooms. No person could fence off these grounds or erect any building on them without permission of the authorities, and this was seldom given. For this reason the Lower Path was almost totally devoid of business premises until midway through the eighteenth century when merchants and others began to defy the law and build on those rooms that had fallen into disuse. The area gradually turned from the curing of fish to trade and commerce.

With the formal abolition of the ships' rooms early in the nineteenth century and the granting of land to settlers, the Lower Path changed from a dank lane running under fish flakes into a busy thoroughfare. In summer it was thronged with fishermen and sailors from all parts of the world. They crowded such taverns as the Globe, Royal Oak, Jolly Fisherman, Shoulder of Mutton, and Rose and Crown to lower a pint while shoppers picked their way through mud, boulders, and piles of offal to small shops with multi-paned windows and half-doors. Outside were piled boxes and barrels containing goods of every description. Red-coated soldiers from the garrison helped housemaids carry their market baskets as tightly corsetted ladies in fancy bonnets nodded to dandies in close-fitting trousers and high collars who tipped silk hats when they passed.

At night the scene changed to one of sinister perspective. Footpads lurked in the shadows to rob the unaccompanied. There was little law and almost no order. Liquor was cheap and plentiful and men were ready to fight at the drop of a hat. Their raucous shouts cut through the stillness as they staggered from the taverns and grog shops. Along the whole length of the Lower Path lanterns and torches bobbed about in the darkness. Press gangs lay in hiding waiting to impress some able-bodied unfortunate into the King's Navy.

Lieutenant Edward Chappell in his journal of a visit to St. John's in 1813 wrote of the town:

> It consists of long, irregular, and in some places very narrow
> streets, the principal one being Water Street, which has been

much improved of late years, by the addition of stone houses, and some superior shops; but still requires a good deal to raise it above the usual appearance of a sea-port water-side. . . . The houses are principally built of wood; and there are very few handsome or even good-looking edifices in the place. The street stands upon very irregular ground, and is not paved; therefore, in wet weather, it is rendered almost impassible, by mud and filth.[1]

After commending the London Tavern as the only tolerable inn, Chappel says:

Shops of all descriptions are very numerous; but their commodities are extravagantly dear, particularly meat, poultry, and vegetables, as the town receives all its supplies of these articles from Nova Scotia. The number of wharfs for lading ships is remarkable; almost every petty merchant, indeed, possesses his own; and there is besides a very broad quay, called the Government Wharf, which is open for the accommodation of the public.[2]

While the lieutenant makes no mention of it, Water Street was a place where riots and other "shameful scenes" were commonplace and sometimes the military had to be called out to quell these disturbances. Of one such affray in 1815 Chief Justice Caesar Colclough wrote to Governor Keats:

I have ordered those who were only convicted of being in the crowd to be confined for one week each and to find ample security to keep the peace for three years; and one handsome, fine young man as I ever saw, who was convicted of two riots, I have ordered to be publicly whipped tomorrow morning from Sawyer's Corner to the Court House for the first, and confined six months for the last, part of which time I shall pardon as the support of his mother and sisters depend on his exertions.

Colclough blamed the rioting on the big wages most of the men earned at the fishery and the cheapness of strong liquor.

The first of the three Great Fires to sweep St. John's wiped out most of Water Street in 1817 destroying the last of the fish flakes and the old waterside sheds and warehouses that had been spared in a serious fire of the previous year.

The street that grew from the ruins was a twisted line of stone instead of wooden dwellings generally two stories high with slate-covered gable roofs. It continued to follow the meandering shoreline with no architectural pretence. These simple shops opened at seven or eight o'clock in the morning and stayed open six days a week until nine or ten o'clock at night. It was not until 15 June 1863 that St. John's stores closed at 6:00 p.m. for the first time. Nineteenth-century shopowners had to cope with a system of credit and barter that frequently led to financial ruin. St. John's news-

821

papers of the period are filled with the insolvency notices of firms great and small. Those who survived and prospered were those who were best able to adjust to the changing times as the prices of fish and cod-liver oil rose and fell on the world markets. It took a special talent for a merchant to balance the people's need with their ability to pay.

The Great Fire of 1846 once more left Water Street in ruins and the reconstructed town took on the appearance of an Irish city of the period. There was still no pavement but many shopowners put wooden or flag-stone sidewalks in front of their stores for the convenience of shoppers. The merchants generally lived upstairs over their businesses. There was still no regular police force or any street lighting so all was in blackness after nightfall. Candles glowed in store windows until the discovery of kerosene. Inside these shops the side walls were unbroken to allow maximum shelf space. Long counters ran down each side. Drygoods, hardwares, and the like were on one side with groceries on the other. At the rear was kept the molasses, with a bevy of flies buzzing about the spigot. Also kept at the rear was the forty-cent-a-gallon rum, barrels of pickled goods, and casks of kerosene oil.

The staples carried by mid-nineteenth century St. John's stores included groceries, drygoods, crockeryware, glassware, hardware, fishing supplies, and medicines. The patent cures such as Extract of Mustard, sarsaparilla, Balsam of Life, Genuine Eye Water, and antibilious pills were practically the only things prepackaged and sold with the name of the maker. Everything else was cut, measured, poured, weighed, wrapped, or tied. Salt beef and flour came in barrels, tea in chests, pickles in kegs, butter and lard in firkins, molasses in puncheons, and liquor in casks. Most purchases were seldom free of *insecta animalia*.

What follows in this chapter is not an attempt to describe the street with any sense of time or place in a historical narrative but to provide in as concise a form as possible biographies of shopowners and occupiers, mostly from the middle years of the last century to the present, who made Water Street the economic heart of Newfoundland. Since this chapter is more a story of people than of the street itself the only coherent way to treat such diverse material is to deal with each block biographically.

TEMPERANCE ST. TO HILL O' CHIPS

The street which Lieutenant Chappell found so lacking in architectural inspiration begins its mile-long amble to the Crossroads at the foot of Temperance Street, once a fairly large river. West of here, on the north side of the street, Alexander Harvey had a bakery in the second half of the nineteenth century. Next to Harvey's bakery there was a school conducted by the Sisters of Mercy. After the Great Fire of 1892 these ladies moved up Signal Hill to the site formerly occupied by Castle Rennie. Adjoining the convent was Archibald's tobacco factory. The Standard Manufacturing Company, which now covers the whole of the area, was incorporated in

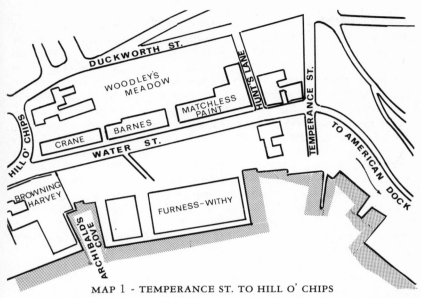

MAP 1 - TEMPERANCE ST. TO HILL O' CHIPS

1903 under the presidency of Sir Marmaduke Winter for the manufacture of soaps, blues, candles, and so on. In 1907 it began the manufacture of Matchless Paints, now sold in many parts of Canada.

At the beginning of the last century Woodley's Meadow was an open field between Water Street and Devon Row when William Woodley built his cottage there. In the 1830s the property passed into the hands of his widow, Mary. After her death there was little or no building on the property until E.F. Barnes occupied the open space. This firm, which was begun in 1932 on Waldegrave Street, moved to Woodley's Meadow in 1945, was incorporated in 1958, and opened a shipyard opposite Temperance Street in 1962.

The Newfoundland Woodworking Company had a factory next to the Hill o' Chips retaining wall. It is said that this factory gave the hill its name; however, this is in error. The name Hill o' Chips is probably the oldest in St. John's. It may originally have been Biskin Hill, a name which appears in ancient documents, but in the late 1700s it was already known as Hill o' Chips, while Water Street was still called Lower Path. It is the only street mentioned by its present name in a survey for altering the roads in St. John's conducted in 1780.

West of the hill William McGrath had his house and forge. It was here that Thomas McGrath was inspired to found the Total Abstinence & Benefit Society. The founders' meeting was held at the back of the blacksmith forge, using a rock that jutted out of the hill as a table. Temperance Street had just been built when the organization held its first parade on 6 January 1859. It was named to commemorate the event. On 14

823

April 1831 the property west of Hill o' Chips was granted to Thomas Brooking, William Thomas, and John Bland for the erection of a billiards and reading room for the use of the members.

The huge estate of John Stripling whom Prowse describes as a staunch Protestant and a publican from Weston-Super-Mare, England, began at McGrath's forge and went to Lady Eliza Tonkin's estate near King's Beach. To the north the publican owned land almost as far as Winter Avenue, on the shores of Quidi Vidi. Stripling came to St. John's some time before the middle of the eighteenth century. Though utterly ignorant and totally illiterate, he used his influence with the governor and garrison to obtain vast tracts of land. In 1757 he was captain of a company of militia. His house probably became the first Government House in 1779 when Admiral Richard arrived as governor with two of his daughters on board and sought a land residence. Stripling's unmarried daughter, Mary, who lived at Ashburton, Devon, inherited the property. To this day some of the people living between King's Road and King's Bridge Road pay ground rent to the heirs of the Stripling Estate in England.

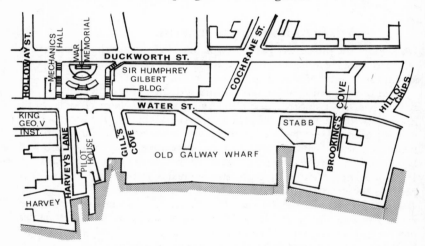

MAP 2 - HILL O' CHIPS TO HOLLOWAY ST.

In the nineteenth century a range of private dwellings stretched west from the foot of Cochrane Street. These were destroyed in 1892 and replaced by others. The first home of the Canadian Broadcasting Corporation in Newfoundland, following the eviction of VONF from the Newfoundland Hotel at the time of Confederation, was the end building in this range. The rat-infested quarters were known as the O'Driscoll King of Pain Building because of a large Minard's Linament ad painted on the west side next to the stonecutters' yard. Sir Ambrose Shea's office was here, opposite his wharf. It employed Henry Stabb, the first St. John's author of

824

a published novel, *Florimel Jones*. In 1780 there lived nearby a merchant named Livingstone, whose son served with distinction as a lieutenant in McBraire's volunteers during the war of 1812, by filling the harbour of St. John's with American prizes. Livingstone also helped Carson and Morris fight for Responsible Government. A Dr. Rowe had his house in the area in the late 1700s.

The stonecutters' yard, which was in the middle of the block between Cochrane Street and the War Memorial, belonged to the firm of William Ellis who started business in 1890. This was also where W & G Rendell had offices and where the Rendell family lived. Next to the stone yard was the Atlantic Hotel, opened by John Foran in May 1885. Before that he had taken over Toussaint's Hotel, opposite Holloway Street, and ran it as the Atlantic. His new hostelry fronted Duckworth Street. The Water Street level consisted of small stores rented to watchmakers, milliners, and others. Gutted in 1892, the hotel was partly rebuilt and eventually became the Customs House. In 1956 the entire area west of Cochrane Street was torn down to make way for the Sir Humphrey Gilbert Building, which houses many federal government departments, including customs. There is a post office on Water Street where the CBC once had its studios.

In the 1760s and '70s the inn known as The Ship stood on the east corner of Haymarket Square, now the site of the Newfoundland War Memorial. There is a sketch of this inn in existence.[3] Today there is still a tavern of sorts on the site but it is not apparent from the outside. The fourth floor of the second building east of the corner steps was converted during World War II into a service club for seagoing naval officers. Organized by Vice-Admiral Edmund Mainguy, who was then a Captain in the R.C.N., the location was suggested by Lady Outerbridge, who died in 1973, the one honorary female member: Her husband, then Colonel Leonard Outerbridge (later Sir) offered vacant space on the fourth floor of his warehouse building, rent free, for the duration of the war. A Canadian Army Officer, who puffed his way up the fifty-nine steps that lead from a small alley at the side of the War Memorial to the door of the club, remarked that the place was a crow's nest and it has become famous all over the world by this name.

The club opened on 27 January 1942 and soon built up a store of legends. After the opening formalities an officer of the Canadian Mine-sweeper *Georgian* took a sharp spike and carved the name of his ship in the floor where it can still be seen. A contest followed to see who could drive spikes into the flooring with the least number of blows. It was won by Lt. H. Shadforth, Captain of the Canadian corvette *Spikenard*. A few days later this ship was torpedoed in the North Atlantic and the crew lost. At the Crow's Nest a brass ring was cast with the words SPIKENARD—HIS SPIKE and put around Shadforth's nail. It has since been sawed out of the floor and is displayed behind the bar.[4]

Captain Mainguy conceived the idea of placing ships' badges on the wall.

He ruled that each navy ship visiting port would be allotted two square feet of wall space. The resulting artwork was considerable, a favourite being a lush drawing of fan dancer Sally Rand, to represent H.M.C.S *St. Laurent* or "Sally" as she was called. Officers of H.M.S. *Greenwich* donated a ship's bell which is rung twice a day to denote closing of the bar. Sir Percy Noble, who commanded the Western Approaches during the war, called the Crow's Nest "a repository of the legends and folklore of the men who sailed the little Canadian ships which saved the day for Britain, perhaps for human freedom itself, back when the British Commonwealth stood alone and long after the invasion of Russia and the iniquity of Pearl Harbour." Stephen Leacock, another famous visitor, called it, "One of the strangest clubs in the United Nations."[5]

The Seagoing Officer's Club, as "the Nest" was officially known, closed its doors 13 June 1945. It was then decided in May 1946 to form a Newfoundland Officer's Club. Colonel Outerbridge offered the vacant Crow's Nest at a rental of one dollar per year until revenue exceeded expenses. Architect Graham Rennie used his talents to try to make the place resemble an English Pub and, on 8 July 1946, the place reopened. Over the years since then it has played host to a long list of distinguished persons, including Prince Philip, Earl Alexander of Tunis, and Lord Montgomery of Alemain.

On an evening in June 1963 someone bet Commodore E.N. Clarke of the Royal Canadian Naval Dockyard, Halifax, that he could not produce a periscope for the club. The challenge was accepted and soon two naval men arrived to mount the periscope, with the aid of a giant crane in Water Street. It came from the U-190 which surrendered off Newfoundland at the end of the war. The top of this periscope can be seen today rising from the roof of the building.

In 1965 the club purchased the premises for fifteen thousand dollars. The ship's plaques, which had gone to McGregor House in Montreal at war's end, were recovered and remounted in the club. In 1950 Sir Leonard Outerbridge was elected Honorary President in perpetuity.

The Newfoundland War Memorial stands on what used to be Haymarket Square. The steep slope that had been here was cut down to a gentle hill on orders of Governor Edwards in 1780. In the early years of the present century, when a horse was as necessary as a car is today, people came to this square to sell or purchase loads of hay. It was earlier known as Customs House Square. The Newfoundland War Memorial was designed and executed by two English sculptors, F.V. Bludstone and Gilbert Boyes, at a cost of something over twenty thousand dollars. It was unveiled Tuesday, 1 July 1924, by Field-Marshal Earl Haig on a visit he made to Newfoundland. It was known as the National War Memorial until the time of Confederation with Canada, when it became the Provincial War Memorial. The figures in bronze represent liberty, the Forestry Corps, the

Merchant Marine, the Army, and the Navy. Markers on the grounds indicate trees planted by visiting British Royalties.

A plaque on the front of the memorial, at the Water Street level, bears the following inscription composed by Rudyard Kipling:

> Close to this commanding and historic spot Sir Humphrey Gilbert landed on the 5th day of August, 1583, and in taking possession of the new found land in the name of his sovereign Queen Elizabeth thereby founded Britain's overseas empire.

The Customs House was a brick building erected after the 1846 fire just west of the centre steps of the War Memorial. It was set forty feet back from Water Street and angled slightly toward the square. Hannibal Murch opened an Auction House next to the square in 1841. Darling Street, which connected Water and Duckworth Streets and ran behind the Customs House, disappeared after 1892 when the Mechanics' Hall was built over the area. The cornerstone for the hall was laid by Governor Sir Terence O'Brien, 26 December 1892. The Mechanics' Fraternal Society had been organized on 2 March 1827. Its first club was on Duckworth Street at the west corner of Darling Street. Trade unionism eventually made the society obsolete.

The Water Street portion of the merchants' building was occupied by the Commercial Bank. This branch achieved a certain notoriety on 26 April 1904, when R.L. Mare, a prominent broker and commission agent committed suicide by shooting himself in the office of the bank. The Anglo-American Telegraph Company was also here at one time.

During World War I the upstairs meeting hall became a movie theatre. In the Roaring Twenties it was a fashionable dance hall syncopating to the beat of the flappers and returned military officers who gyrated through the Charleston or wiggled through the shimmy. In the Mechanics' Hall flaming youth danced the hours away with young men who had known the hell of No Man's Land. The Knights of Columbus had clubrooms in the building after that. Following World War II it became a series of seedy nightspots.

S.O. Steele, who had begun business in drygoods in 1886, took over Mrs. J.H. Martin's crockeryware business next door to the Mechanics' Institute, in May 1899. This shop is one of the few on Water Street to retain its pre-twentieth-century atmosphere and charm. Mrs. Matthew's Golden Lion Inn, on the corner of Holloway Street in the 1800s, was the site of the East End Liquor Control Store until the building was torn down in the 1960s.

HOLLOWAY ST. TO COURT HOUSE STEPS

The east corner building in the next block, formerly Patrick Gleeson's property, was occupied during the first half of the present century by Ellen Stewart who ran a tearoom and bakery. Her husband was one of twenty

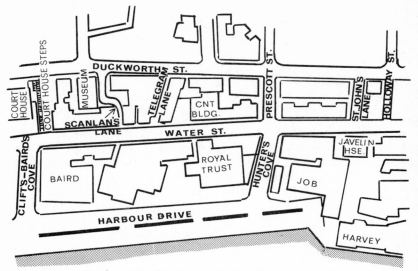

MAP 3 - HOLLOWAY ST. TO COURT HOUSE STEPS

men lost in the wreck of the S.S. *Regulus*, at Petty Harbour motion, 23 October 1910. Mrs. Stewart made headlines when she clamed in a lawsuit that the thirteen year-old ship wasn't seaworthy. Her daughter, Margaret, married Patrick Linegar, an officer on the Red Cross boats and a later well-known harbour pilot. The block to Prescott Street was taken up with rooming houses, small shops and restaurants. In 1860s Mark Chaplin, the tailor, was located here. A leading restaurant in the area before the 1892 fire was H. Tapper's Queens.

With the closing of Haymarket Square some of these houses were torn down in an effort to widen the narrow path, then called McLarty's Lane, west of Dennis Dooley's butcher shop. Up this path, Edward St. John, who lived on the corner, had a bakery and supplied bread to the military until he died in 1868. The new street was called St. John's Lane, after him, and not after the city as many people think. John Studdy, a farmer from England who became an M.H.A. for Fortune, had a dairy in the lane.

In the section from here to Prescott Street, known as Frog Marsh in the 1600s the ground was occupied in the eighteenth century by William Peagrum, Widow Lester (Mary), and Gaden's premises. Olive Gaden owned land on both sides of the Lower Path,[6] which appears to have been originally granted to her husband. George Gaden, probably an offspring, was another who supported Carson and Morris in the fight for self government. Much of this property was later Patrick Tarahan's.

On the west corner of St. John's Lane Rothwell & Bowring sold provisions on the site of the old Devonshire Inn where, before the

1892 fire, Professor Danielle had his Royal Restaurant. Two famous names in the history of the town were also located here. One was Charles Kickum, now remembered in Kickum Place, who, as President of the Benevolent Irish Society, brought the Christian Brothers to Newfoundland. The other was the controversial merchant, James McBraire, organizer of the B.I.S. and of the Newfoundland Volunteers in the War of 1812.

Before the 1892 fire the east side of Prescott Street was known as Reardon's Corner, for the father of Monsignor Reardon of Placentia. A tragic accident took place here in September 1871. Michael Lawlor, of the famous meat market family, an apprentice at Frank Boggan's cooperage, was coming down Prescott Street with a cartload of fish drums. He lost control of the horse, and the cart crashed into Reardon's porch, crushing him to death. After the '92 fire a Mr. Keating built a double house on the site, which became known as Keating's Corner until his death, when Woodstock Sales & Service took over for many years.

Prescott Street to Duckworth Street used to be known as Keen's Hill and was originally a river and marsh. North of Duckworth, along the banks of the river, there was a slide path to the Barrens. A bridge crossed the stream on the Lower Path, or Water Street level. In 1780 Gaden's flake, between the Upper and Lower Paths, was removed to lower the upper side of what is now Prescott Street.[7] The reason for this activity was the determination of Governor Edwards to open Water Street to a width of twelve feet. Fences were moved back, verandahs torn off houses, and flakes demolished. This was the first attempt to make the Upper and Lower Paths into proper streets with several new connecting streets being built. It marked the period of transition when St. John's changed from a village to a town.

The Academia, organized by Lord Morris, was located at the western foot of Prescott Street until the 1892 fire. After that the photographer Simeon H. Parsons, had his studio upstairs in the new building, with an entrance to the photographic rooms from Prescott Street. The outline of his skylight, removed in recent years, is still visible in the side of the building.

Close to this corner a man named Parker operated the Royal Oak Tavern in 1809. He either bought or rented the building from Richard Perchard who had been the proprietor in 1807. Occupants of this corner have been many. Crossman's Forge and Shambler's Sail loft were at the rear of the Royal Oak. Later the Atlantic Bookstore was here. During World War II a Chinese restaurant called the Imperial Cafe, the second building from the corner, was the centre of a riot by R.C.N. ratings who totally wrecked the establishment. It is of interest to note here that Chinese involvement in the community life of St. John's dates from 24 August 1895, when Tong Toi and Wang Chang opened a Chinese laundry.

The fiery Henry Winton, editor of the outspoken newspaper *The Public Ledger*, had his house and early printing establishment at, or near, the foot of Prescott Street. It was here that a mob came to lynch him on Christmas night 1833. This story is told in Volume I, page 186.

Gregory's Lane (actually Gregory Lane), which used to run from Duckworth Street, now ends above the street in a retaining wall. The lower portion was removed to widen the *Evening Telegram* parking lot. Here stood the auction market of James Hynes, a detached old building whose gable roof faced Water Street. John Foran later built his ill-fated Market House on the same site. The property was once part of the Clapp Estate of which we will hear more later.

John Williams McCoubrey came from Waterford, Ireland, with his wife 26 August 1823, and published the first issue of *The Times*, from the area between Gregory's Lane and Telegram Lane, a site now occupied by the *Evening Telegram* printing plant. *The Times'* offices were taken over by the *Telegram* after the death of Andrew Wright, a grandson of the founder, in 1920. Andrew Wright's daughter, Elizabeth, married John T. Carnell, a carriage builder on the corner of Duckworth and Cochrane Streets and she became the mother of Mayor Andrew Carnell. Following the '92 fire the top floor of the *Evening Telegram* building was occupied by J. W. Nichols's St. John's School of Art. A certified art teacher under the the art department, South Kensington, London, Nichols arrived in St. John's in 1894 and began giving classes in 1895.

Originally the *Evening Telegram* was printed in a small building behind *The Times'* office on Gregory's Lane. The next alleyway, called Johnny Power's Lane until the middle of the last century, is now Telegram Lane. Mr. Power's residence was on the east corner with a forge at the rear. Rhodie Power, as he was better known, was the most famous blacksmith of his day. There were four daughters who were highly accomplished musicians and the Power family used to give concerts at Fishermen's Hall. Around the turn of the eighteenth century much of this property was held by the famous Meagher family of Waterford, who lived further west, near the corner of Bishop's Cove.

Michael Connors' Butcher Shop was located in the block between Telegram Lane, a series of steps built after the '92 fire, and Parsons' Lane (now just a tiny opening between two buildings). His son, Frank, later opened a saddle shop on the site of the meat stall. Frank succeeded John McKenzie in the saddlery business in May 1891, and was in turn succeeded by Thomas Ring. This store was remarkable for the lifelike image of a horse displayed in the window. The animal was later purchased by Premier Smallwood and mounted on a peak above his farm on Roche's Line where it is still displayed.

W.J. Parsons, who gave his name to Parsons Lane, was a watchmaker and jeweller who specialized in nautical instruments. He emigrated to Canada in the year that country was founded, 1867. His daughter, Mrs. Dicks, was the mother of Mrs. John Leamon, whose son took over Dicks & Co., when the male line died out. The son also took over the home of

William Leamon Solomon, the postmaster, at 29 Monkstown Road. Parson's sign over the front door of his store at the corner of the lane was a life-size figure of a ship's officer holding a quadrant in the act of taking the sun.[8] In the old days, when most of the citizens were illiterate, a name over a store meant little. As in other parts of the world each firm had a recognizable sign. The following are some of the Water Street firms and their signs in the late 1800s; Woods, electric lamp; James Baird, lion; Robert Rutherford, golden fleece; W.R. Firth, Newfoundland Dog; Sillars & Cairns, fish; David Smallwood, boot; John Steer, polar bear; Martin's Hardware, circular saw; and almost every jeweller had a large pocket watch over the store front.

William Fling, an eccentric old bachelor, kept a junk store west of Parsons Lane. Moving along the street from this peculiar establishment there was another passageway which connected Water Street to Duckworth Street coming out opposite Cathedral Street. This twisting path was known as Funny Lane and is now called Scanlan's Lane. Between Parsons Lane and Funny Lane Simon Solomon had his watchmaker's shop which became the first post office in St. John's. Solomon began shortly after the turn of the nineteenth century, and in 1809 was proclaimed Post Master by Governor Holloway.

Michael Scanlan operated a wine merchant's shop on the east corner of Scanlan's Lane and had a house behind it up the lane. This pathway marked the eastern boundary of John Flood's old estate. Scanlan died in 1859 but his name survives.

At the top of Scanlan's Lane was the Athenaeum and on the east corner the publishing office of the *Newfoundlander*. Sir Edward Dalton Shea, editor and proprietor, lived on the premises with his family.

Dr. Dearin's Medical Hall was located west of the lane on Water Street. This flamboyant chemist's wife was a sister of Laurence O'Brien Furlong. Cash's Tobacco Store was in the middle of the block. This store was remarkable for its wooden cigar store Indian which stood outside the shop until the middle of the present century. Earlier, the site was occupied by a Mr. Mainwaring. There was a popular rumour, in the middle of the last century, that the gentleman had dug up a pot of gold while excavating to lay the foundation for his shop after the '46 fire. For some reason, possibly nothing more romantic than a legacy from abroad, Mainwaring did suddenly come into some money and his contemporaries believed the pot of gold story.

It was also in the middle of this block that P. Jordon & Sons had a downtown provisions store. On 24 February 1895 plasterers, who had been redecorating the upstairs room, left salamanders burning to dry out the plaster. The smoke from these iron pots suffocated the brothers William and Andrew Jordan during the night. Professor Danielle took over the Jordan building and ran it as a restaurant for a time. J.P. Wood opened a photography studio a few doors west of Jordans in 1870.

The site on the corner of Market House Hill, now Court House Steps, was taken by the tinsmiths, McCoubrey & Clouston. In the late 1840s McCoubrey left the partnership and William J. Clouston carried on the business under his own name. He was also a maker of cast-iron stoves. A nephew apprentice, John, later began his own firm on Duckworth Street, in 1904, at the age of thirty-three years. It is still there.

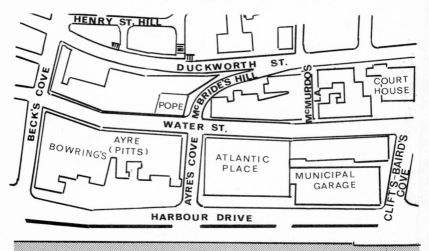

MAP 4 - COURT HOUSE STEPS TO BECK'S COVE

Market House Hill was an open space, originally an extension of Church Hill. The first Court House and jail were behind Clouston's tinsmith shop on the east side of the hill. After the '46 fire it moved to the top floor of the Market House erected on the opposite side of the hill. Sketches show the Market House building as being quite graceful. In actual fact it was rather ugly. The generally uncritical Hatton and Harvey said of it in their 1883 history: "The Court-House, Police-Office, and Post-Office are under the same roof, and little can be said in commendation of this building."[9]

A grim edifice of local granite, there was a stone gallery along the front with steps at the eastern end. This gallery was only used on ceremonial occasions. Normally one entered the Market House through an archway underneath the gallery while the Post Office on the second floor was entered from a door in the side of the building facing the hill. The Market House, opened by Governor Sir John Harvey, 6 July 1850, was under the management of Thomas Farrell.

Farmers, butchers, dairymen, and fishermen came there to sell their wares. At the back of the stalls were cells where the prisoners were kept with no light and very little air. The second-storey Post Office was equally dank and dreary. The damp, chilly quarters were credited with making the Postmaster as forbidding as his surroundings. He seemed to take revenge by having the public wait outside for hours on cold winter days before the mail was sorted and called. The telegraph office was later located in an adjoining room, one in which Shanadithit, her mother and her sister, were quartered on straw when first brought to St. John's.

In the 1860s and 1870s Market House Square was a place of pandimonium. On a summer's day, through the open windows of the courtroom came the voices of lawyers orating before judges "who would never ever budge." Outside the post office, milling throngs of men, women and children, accompanied by a large assortment of mongrel dogs, yelled and heaved as they waited for the mail bags to be opened and their names called. In front of the Market House unsold animals bleated, neighed, oinked and mooed, and left things underfoot, while orators held forth from the tops of kegs, and wits regaled their hearers, provoking unbridled mirth. Drunks and petty thieves swore unprintable oaths as they were hauled off to the cells or up to the dock. The Market House tumbled in ruins when swept by the Great Fire of 1892. It was replaced by the present Court House which opened 11 May 1904.

In the space now used to park police cars and vans, just west of the Court House, stood the butcher shop and dwelling of Thomas O'Brien. The butcher was suspected of the wounding of a priest, Father Jeremiah O'Donnell, during the 1861 election riots. The man of God was trying to quell the rioters in Market House Square when he was said to have been shot by a gun fired from an open window in the O'Brien house. However, no arrests were made. Ten days later on 23 May 1861, Thomas O'Brien placed his house and stall on the auction block. Because he was leaving the island he sold the place without any reserve. It is not known if the riot and sale were related incidents.

From O'Brien's to the corner of McMurdo's Lane several historically interesting persons were located. In the middle of the block, where R. and J.J. Rutherford operated Rutherford & Company, Dowsley the druggist had a dispensary for a time. The story of the tragedy that befell his son, Felix, is told elsewhere in this chapter. Next to Dowsley in the 1860s and '70s the Misses Duggan had the Maid of Erin shop. Upstairs were the photographic rooms of McKenny and Adams, later in the possession of the the famous portrait photographer, E.W. Lyons. With the passing of D. Adams, who began alone on the site around 1858, McKenny entered a new partnership, McKenny & Dicks, which eventually became Dicks & Company. After the 1892 disaster Dicks opened a few doors east of his former location and operated the Central Post Office in his store. The firm later moved to the opposite side of the street. Next to Dicks' John Bulley Ayre had his bakery and pastry shop.

The Maid of Erin property became Grey and Goodland's after 1892. The firm operated a book store and printing press there for three quarters of a century before the building was briefly occupied by the *Daily News*. It was here in 1817 that the first theatre in St. John's is thought to have opened in William B. Row's store. Next door, in the building on the corner of McMurdo's Lane, Dr. Samuel Carson had a house and surgery before the 1846 fire. His father, the great William Carson, died there in 1843.

In the early years of the nineteenth century McMurdo's Lane was known as McCallum's Lane, a corruption of the name McCalman who had a grocery business on the corner. When Valentine Merchant acquired the block it became Merchant's Lane until his death in 1867 when it was changed to McMurdo's Lane as we know it today.

Upstairs over Mr. Merchant's shop, a group of businessmen organized a billiards room and literary institute known as Merchant's Club. Artifacts connected with the history of Newfoundland were donated to the club and it became the city's first museum. The club was disbanded in 1851 and the collection stored. When the Newfoundland Museum was organized in the old Gerneral Post Office in 1885, the collection from Merchant's became the foundation for that museum.

With the closing of the club the upstairs rooms at Merchant's became a kind of public library, known as the St. John's Library and Reading Room. Several bookstores of the period also ran rental libraries and most of the clubs and fraternal societies had reading rooms. Some of them were located in taverns.

On 16 January 1859 Merchant's corner building caught fire at an early hour and was almost completely destroyed. Mr. Adams's Ambrotype Rooms and Restaurant next door to Merchant's shop were partially gutted. The rooms of the St. John's Library were seriously damaged and the greater part of the contents destroyed.

On the west corner of McMurdo's Lane was T. McMurdo & Co., one of the first drugstores to open in St. John's. The founder, Thomas McMurdo, came to Newfoundland from Aberdeen, Scotland, in 1823. The firm was on the site for well over a century and did not move elsewhere until 17 March 1973. In 1898 control of the business passed to Thomas McNeil who married Miss McMurdo in 1870.

In the 1860s McConnan's Book Store was next to McMurdo's. Thomas McConnan's wife, when Miss Fanny Moore, raised eyebrows in the town and set tongues wagging by becoming the first female to defy custom and skate with the boys at the rink.[10] Before Fanny no female was ever seen to skate with a male. Her husband died in British Columbia in 1892.

West of McConnan's the Catholic Literary Institute was upstairs over Chancey & Heath's bakery shop, run by Lionel Chancey and John Heath. Then came Mrs. Allen's crockeryware shop. Next to her Fred Smallwood, an uncle of the Newfoundland Premier, had a boot and shoe store. Beyond him was the provisions shop of T.J. Murphy where J.M. Byrnes, the author of *Paths to Yesterday*, was an apprentice clerk and book-keeper, before moving to the United States in 1887.

Charles Hutton, a professor of music, established a business on Water Street in 1883. Around 1907 he moved to the Murphy site and the firm has been there ever since. In 1932 it became Charles Hutton & Sons when Hubert and Basil entered the business. The Hutton family has always lived upstairs over the music store.

The Metropolitan House, a popular lodging place for outport travellers, run by Mrs. Gosse, was west of Hutton's. The corner property, once occupied by the *Gazette* Building, and now by the Bank of Montreal, was at one time owned by Robert Newman, whose brother William held the opposite corner on McBride's Hill.

The *Gazette* newspaper office was an imposing red brick structure erected on the east corner of the hill after the '92 fire. It was one of less than half a dozen architecturally interesting buildings on Water Street. James Vey, the photographer, had his studio in the tower. A characterless modern building, of little artistic pretention, stands on the site today, put up by the Bank of Montreal. Just east of it, the Royal Bank of Canada stands where Patrick Jordan had his uptown drygoods business. Also on the Royal Bank site was the watchmaking establishment of Barney Whiteford of Dunlace, Ireland. He was an uncle of the well-known law family of McNeilly. The old gentleman built Dunlace Cottage, at 139 Portugal Cove Road, in recent years the residence of G. Rex Renouf.

Many early plantations and estates overlap so that it is sometimes difficult to distinguish one from another. Robert Newman's property, east of McBride's Hill, seems also to have been called the Fox Estate at one time. The west corner of the hill, William Newman's property, figured in the destructive fire of 1819. Dinah Eliott lived there. The easterly progress of the fire was stopped at Mrs. Eliott's because the cliff, on the east side of McBride's Hill, jutted out into the Lower Path. There was a space of sixty feet between her house and the next building.

This corner again figured in a fire in 1853 when the place was occupied by Captain William Woodford. He had three sailing ships, *Swift, Rainbow,* and *Margaret Ann.* On the night of 16 November, in the house, a lighted candle fell into a magazine containing two kegs of powder. The resulting explosion blew the roof off the dwelling and a man named Archibald was burnt to death in the fire which followed. Captain Woodford's son died of injuries a few days later.

After Woodford's fire the corner was occupied by a Mr. Kitchen. It was still not spared its anxious moments. In the election riots of 1861 Kitchen's was one of the stores broken into by looters. A son of the owner became Monsignor Kitchen, who built St. Joseph's Church in Hoylestown. A daughter married the Hon. Maurice Fenelon, a man born in Carlow, Ireland, in 1834, who became prominent in Newfoundland political life.

Fenelon came to the colony in 1856 to take charge of the mathematics and English departments of St. Bonaventure's College. In 1870 he was M.H.A. for St. John's West. In 1886 he became Colonial Secretary, and served for many years on the Legislative Council. On his resignation from St. Bonaventure's, Fenelon took over Duffy's Bookstore near Beck's Cove. He later occupied the shop on Kitchen's corner until he was wiped out by the fire of '92. Fenelon died 31 January 1897.

Following the '92 fire the Exchange Building was on this corner, with an entrance from McBride's Hill. The Exchange provided offices for lawyers and commission agents. The Bank of Nova Scotia occupied the Water Street level and this was the first branch of a Canadian bank to be established in Newfoundland. It opened 21 December 1894. Anglo-American Telegraphs took over when the bank vacated the premises.

After Anglo crossed to the opposite corner on the south side of the street, Commercial Cables, formerly located in the middle of the block, moved into the space vacated by Anglo. The Exchange became known as the Pope Building when Pope's Furniture Factory acquired the property. For many years the top floor housed radio station VOCM. The structure was pulled down in 1972. The first radio station in Newfoundland, VOS, gave its first official broadcast here 9 July 1922.

The next shop was occupied by Blackwood & Blair. Dan Blackwood and his sons, Andrew and Robert, had a toy emporium and barber shop in the 1860s and '70s. His daughter married H. Blair and the firm was renovated as a drygoods store, under the name of Blackwood & Blair. After the '92 fire, P. J. O'Neill, the noted Total Abstinence Society actor and director, who worked in the Customs House until his death, had a barber shop on Blackwood's site. It was operated for him by a Mr. Wheatley from England.

The ill-fated Moran premises, next to Blackwood's, was occupied by two spinsters, the Misses Moran. One of them woke up one night to find their small shop in flames and her sister dead of suffocation. The place was subsequently acquired by Patrick Buckmaster, a butcher who had earlier opened his first shop just west of Telegram Lane and who became a substantial property owner on LeMarchant Road. Buckmaster had come out from Ireland as a young man to work for M. Connors in his Butcher Shop. Mr. Connors used to supply the warships with freshly killed beef. One day he sent young Buckmaster, and the mate of one of the ships, out to the vessel with several sides of beef. One of the quarters slipped off the hook, when being hauled on board, and went to the bottom. Buckmaster hurried ashore to tell Connors the news. "Oh, sir. We had a terrible misfortune," he gasped. "We lost the meat overboard." His Irish brogue turned "meat" to "mate" and there was much consternation until Mr. Connors realized it was not the mate but the meat that was lost.[11] Patrick Buckmaster died 1 December 1913, aged seventy-two.

In the middle of this block was Roper's Jewellery Store which figures in Cassie Brown's gripping book, *Death on the Ice*, a harrowing tale of Newfoundland's seal hunt. Roper's was later Roper and Thompson, now Thompson's Jewellery. William Cook, father of Mayor Sir Tasker Cook, had a butcher shop near Roper's. William was succeeded by his famous son who was more interested in municipal politics and being consul for such nations as Norway and Denmark. Sir Tasker enjoyed gathering honours from around the world. Part of the site was later Bon Marché, a store which closed in 1971. This was also the location of Goudie and Diamond, the tinsmiths, who had the sign of the kettle.

Bernard Duffy, a bookseller who had figured in the capture of the Bank of England Robbers, Brady and Naughton, and who died Christmas Eve 1862, was three doors east of Beck's Cove. He was supposedly a relative of the famous Dublin firm of Duffy's. Upstairs, over the bookstore, J.W. Manley began publishing the newspaper, the *Pilot*, in 1852. Maurice Fenelon took over the building from Duffy and was in turn followed by James Graham, a Scotsman, who also kept a bookshop. Graham lived in a semi-attached stone house next to Fenelon on Queen's Road. These houses, Nos. 32 and 34, are the only stone houses on Queen's Road to have survived the 1892 fire. Their stonework can best be viewed at the back, from Military Road.

Richard Neyle opened his hardware store in the second building east of the corner of Beck's Cove in 1849. Born at Newton Abbott, Devonshire, in 1828, he came to Newfoundland in 1849 and began a business which continues today two doors east of the original site. Neyle was located in the Exchange Building, for a time, following the '92 fire. He was afterwards united in partnership with James Soper, a young man in his employ. Neyle retired and died in 1917. Soon afterwards Jim Soper was drowned in an accident at Paradise and his brother, William, took over the firm. He was joined by another brother, George. Neyle-Soper, as it is now known, still manufactures the famous squid and cod jiggers of its invention on the premises.

We now come to Yellow-Belly Corner. There exists a description of it in Prowse which says this was "The spot where the wounded in the melee washed in the little brook flowing into Beck's Cove. The Tipperary 'Clear airs', the Waterford 'Whey-bellies', and the Cork 'Dadyeens' were arrayed against . . . the 'Doones' or Kilkenny boys and the Wexford 'Yellow-bellies.' " They fought each other "out of pure devilment and diварsion." The word Yellow-Belly came from the fact that the Wexford men wore yellow sashes to athletic events, and was no reflection on their courage.[12] Beck's Cove corner was their meeting place in immigrant days.

Edward Brennan, who held the corner house, later gave his name to the site. After that it was called McCourt's Corner, in honour of the next tenant, Phil McCourt. There was a hardware supply store there in the 1880s. Yellow-Belly Corner marks the western boundary of the Great Fire of 1892 on Water Street. Here the destruction ended.

In the second building up Beck's Cove, J. Forbes Chisholm, born in Nova Scotia in 1831, ran a photography supply store. He arrived in St. John's as a bookseller in December 1857, and Chisholm's Book Store became the foremost of its day. Everyone who owned that marvel of photographic ingenuity, the stereoscope, went to Chisholm's to choose view cards from the large collection he always kept on hand, including the ever popular Niagara Falls. For a time, in the 1860s, the firm was known as Smith & Chisholm.

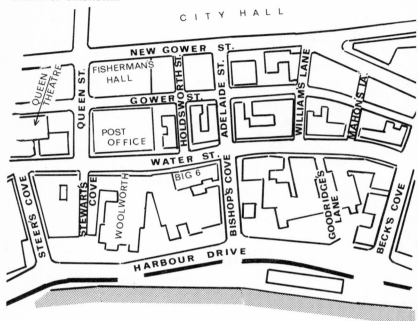

MAP 5 - BECK'S COVE TO QUEEN ST.

Opposite Chisholm's was the office and printing plant where James Seaton published the *Newfoundland Express* every Tuesday, Thursday, and Saturday morning. This was torn down in 1905 to make way for George Street, which was extended to Beck's Cove as a firebreak. The lower corner here was known as Rankin's Corner, and the block between Beck's Cove and Mahon's Lane is the best preserved nineteenth-century block of buildings on Water Street today. They were rebuilt in 1846, inside gutted ruins, immediately after the Great Fire of that year, and are virtually unchanged. The corner building has been commendably restored in recent years by Johnston's Insurance Company. Early in the 1800s Rankin's Corner was known as Strickland's Corner. It later came to be called Stead's. Mr. Stead, who located on the site in the 1860s, married the daughter of Edwin Duder. When Stead passed away Charles R. Rankin took over the store and he was followed by his son. Mrs. Rankin, who had been a Miss McConnan, sold out in 1918. Another tenant in the corner building was Albert Peace, a tinsmith, who sailed with his family to New Zealand in

838

1864 along with Valentine Merchants' son, James and W.E. Cormack, the first white man to cross Newfoundland on foot. Robert Peace, another tinsmith, was at 199 Water Street. John Clouston was an apprentice with Albert Peace before joining his uncle at Market House Hill.

James O'Donnel, an old Irish bachelor, who was in the wine and spirits business had the second store west of the corner. He returned to his homeland and joined a monastery in later life. Father O'Donnell, shot near the Market House in the 1861 election riot, was a member of this family. John O'Connor who occupied the fourth building west of Beck's Cove, created a sensation at the Roman Catholic cathedral one Sunday in 1872 by dropping dead just as he entered his pew to attend mass.

Mahon's Lane at the end of the block gets its name from Mr. Mahon, who had a blockmaker's shop in the lane. It has also been called Block-maker's Lane. Mahon was burned out in a fire on 16 April 1861.

The second building west of Mahon's Lane was for many years the premises of George Langmead, a very well-known jeweller who had come to St. John's early in the century and died in 1892. After the 1846 fire he moved two doors east of the lane. The name of Langmead was on Water Street for eighty years but, even though he had a large family, it quickly died out. The first Langmead site became the home of Acadia Gas Engines, a firm managed by Robert Ritcey, whose wife Muriel was the daughter of the famous historian and clergyman, the Reverend Moses Harvey.

The most important tenant in this block, from a historical point of view, was the man who had the upstairs rooms over R.L. Sleater's Jewellery store in the third building east of Willam's Lane, Simeon H. Parsons. This was the location of the Photo Studio and Fine Arts Emporium of the greatest of all Newfoundland photographers. Parsons's work spanned the era from tintypes to contact prints. In the almost forgotten days of gracious living the great and the lowly of the town got gussied up in their best bibs and tuckers to stare in frozen grace from among potted ferns and painted backdrops into S.H. Parson's camera. After 1892, with his son, he opened a studio at the foot of Prescott Street but it was in the Water Street west building that he worked on the great pre-and-post fire photos of St. John's that are such a priceless legacy today.

David Smallwood, the bootmaker, was next door. His parents left Chester, England, in the 1770s and settled in Prince Edward Island where David was born in 1828. Having learned his trade as a carpenter, he moved to Newfoundland in 1861, where he branched into bootmaking and opened the shop on Water Street. His handbills claimed:

> . . . Smallwood's boots they are so grand,
> they are the best in Newfoundland.

The short, thin man with the long, flowing beard, died in 1928, but not before having an effect on his grandson, Joseph, who says of David, "no man influenced me more."[13] Little did the old man dream of the revolutionary changes little Joey would one day bring to Newfoundland.

William's Lane is a very old name. It was in use early in the 1800s and the street may have been named to commemorate the summer Prince William (William IV) spent in Newfoundland. In 1822 the procession for the laying of the cornerstone of the Amateur Theatre proceeded from Water Street, up William's Lane to the Duckworth Street site.

In the middle of the last century, in a true Dickensian atmosphere, an old gentleman known as Fox kept a snuff shop three doors east of Adelaide Street. In a back room he manufactured the aromas which brought about sneezes of delight by inhaling through the nostrils finely powdered tobacco. When the ladies began to take a pinch, musical snuff boxes became the rage. These elegant works of art are now mostly in museums. When Edward Albert, Prince of Wales, made smoking in public fashionable, to the great disgust of Queen Victoria, the writing was on the wall for poor Mr. Fox. His successor closed down the business, and Dennis Galway, the tailor, took over the store. Next to it Lash's had a bakery which was later moved to the opposite side of the street.

In the mid 1800s the east corner of Adelaide Street was known as Rawlins' Corner after John Rawlins who occupied the site and whose brother, Patrick, found more enduring fame by starting a business on Military Road, and giving his name to a nearby crossroads. When John Rawlins removed to the United States after the American Civil War, a new tenant, Tim Phelan, took over and the place was known for many years as Phelan's Corner. In earlier days this area was the Twisden Estate.

West of Adelaide Street Patrick Laracy had the premises on the corner, across the street from where he was to build the Crescent Movie Theatre, around the beginning of World War I. He was drowned in the wreck of the *Florizel*. The Laracy firm is still in business selling cards, toys and souvenirs in the next block to the east, near the site of Fox's snuff shop. John Reid, the stonemason who built the Arcade for W.R. Firth, was next to Patrick Laracy. On the corner of Holdsworth Steet, Francis Winton published the *Morning Chronicle,* and Antonio Tadini, an Italian artist who painted, sold, and framed pictures, rented quarters beside him.

The next building west of Holdsworth Street was a massive stone structure of four storeys that jutted thirty feet out into Water Street so that all traffic had to go around it. This was the the property of Henry Radford, rented as a supply store by William Cullen, who lived with his family upstairs. Around the corner in Queen Street lived a brother, James Cullen, who was the father of the great Canadian painter, Maurice Cullen. William Cullen imported and sold flour, beef, pork, and other supplies in large quantities. The old man, who had his own vessels, called "pink sterns," used to go to New York to buy the provisions he sold and to personally supervise the loading of his ships. Cullen's great stone house came down in

1900, when Water Street was being prepared for paving by the Reid Company.

The turreted building that replaced it was occupied in the east by Woods West End Candy Store and Dining Rooms. These were later taken over and run with much success by Rex Sterling, father of Geoff Sterling, the radio and television czar who built CJON. On the ground floor there was a candy shop, a bake shop, and soda fountain. Upstairs, stiffly starched maids hovered concernedly over tables spread with white linen tablecloths or moved daintily past potted plants and lace-curtained windows. The Rotary Club first met here early in the 1900s. There were many who mourned the passing of this type of elegant Edwardian dining room.

The General Post Office stands today on what was an open lot called Bennett's Yard, enclosed by a high board fence that bulged out into Water Street. Several vessels were built in a shipyard on the lot. The last of them was the *Ida*, constructed by the famous shipbuilder, Michael Kearney. In 1886 a massive Victorian Post Office was erected on the site, which was replaced in 1958 by the present functional edifice.

The building next to Bennett's Yard was another solid stone structure like Cullen's. In it Prime Minister Sir Michael Cashin conducted his business. In 1888 Sir Michael, then twenty-four-year old, took over the firm of his late grandfather, Richard Cashin, at Cape Broyle. A son, Laurence, joined him in 1909 and another son, Richard, in 1915. Richard met his death in a horse-and-carriage accident near Cape Broyle in 1917. When elected to the Morris government, in 1909, Sir Michael moved to St. John's and opened a business on the McDougall and Templeton site on the west side of Bishop's Cove. In 1924 the firm went into the coal trade and in 1925 a limited liability company was formed. In 1924 Sir Michael bought the stone building next to the Post Office from the government. Cashin & Co. continued to occupy the structure until it was torn down in 1959 to make room for the enlarged Post Office. In the adjoining stone building, on the corner of Queen Street, the Hon. James J. Rogerson carried on his business.

Born at Harbour Grace in 1820, Rogerson was a prominent citizen of his era. At various times he was an M.H.A. for Burin and for Bay de Verde, a member of the Legislative Council, and of the Executive Council. In 1882 he had the title "Honourable" conferred on him for life. His white beard and steel-rimmed spectacles gave him the look of the philanthropist he was. Rogerson was a founder of the Sons of Temperance, the Protestant Industrial Society, the Newfoundland Historical Society, and the Fishermen's and Seamen's Home on Duckworth Street. It is said his hand and heart were ever ready to help some "fallen brother pulling hard against the stream." The genial humanitarian died in 1907, at eighty-seven years of age.

Michael Connors, son of the butcher, founded a drugstore in 1880 in the corner building which he rented from Rogerson. When the fire of 1892 wiped out most of his competitors, Connors found himself with a threefold increase in business and in 1896 he moved to a new location two doors east of Adelaide Street. He died in 1927 and the firm passed to his brother Frank. Thomas O'Neill, a noted amateur actor and stage director, and father of Magistrate Hugh O'Neill, became managing director of Connors.

Behind Rogersons' were two stone residences owned by William Cullen. The famous Dr. McKen and his son lived in the first of these. In the early 1840s the building on the corner of Queen and George Streets was the shop of Hamlin, the cabinetmaker, and it was here that the Great Fire of 1846 began.

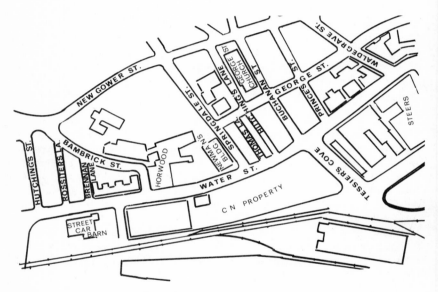

MAP 6 - QUEEN ST. TO HUTCHINGS ST.

In the middle of the next block, almost opposite Steer's Cove, Peter and James Duchemin had a ship's pump and blockmaker's shop where roller cogged blocks were made. Along with David Sclater's, in the east end, Duchemin's was one of the most unique pre-1892 buildings on Water Street. It was distinguished by a fancy front and a balcony on the gable, facing the street. The building next door was taken over in the 1880s by Captain Neilson who was remarkable for outliving three wives. The first was a daughter of John Reid, the stonemason, the second was the daughter of Sergeant Kenna, of Kenna's Hill fame, and the third was a daughter of Mr. Ruby, the farmer who gave his name to the Ruby Line. Having outlived his women, Captain Neilson sold his property to John Duff and emigrated to California where he died.

The Duchemin and Neilson properties were replaced in 1926 by the Duff Building which provided an entrance from Water Street to the Queen Theatre on George Street. The Queen afterwards became the York Theatre and finally a warehouse for Steer's Limited.

John Duff lived at Thornlea Cottage, a large house at the start of Waterford Bridge Road, built by R. Vail. When Vail left Newfoundland the house was acquired by John Bray Ayre who died in 1915 after having been organist at George Street Methodist Church for forty-two years. He was also M.H.A. for Bay de Verde, and had charge of the music department in the firm of Ayre & Sons. Following Ayre's death, Duff purchased Thornlea and the property was in his family until it was torn down in recent years to make room for an office and warehouse building.

John Power lived in the building on the corner of Waldegrave Street, and the area became Power's Corner. The Cathedral Fire Brigade was at the back of Power's in a structure hauled there from Boggan's Lane. The southeast corner of Waldegrave and George Streets was the property of Janet Cormack, believed to be the mother of W.E. Cormack, who is said to have been born on Waldegrave Street. Land on Sudbury Street, where the Poor House once stood, also belonged to Janet Cormack.

On the west corner of Waldegrave Street, Judge Des Barres had some property that was later occupied by Alexander Candow as the Victoria Hotel. The judge also owned land on the opposite side of the street. The same was true of his next-door neighbour, a man named Rennie, who was tied in with Stewart, in the firm Rennie & Stewart. At one time Patrick Morris was at the corner of Prince's Street.

In early days this area was known as Pye Corner and was part of the estate of Samuel Churchill of Dartmouth, England. It is mentioned in an old Churchill will at Somerset House, London. John Widdecombe had a tavern here late in the 1700s. The Widdecombe family is thought to have come to St. John's in 1667, after being turned out of Bay Bulls by Sir David Kirke.

The west corner of Prince's Street, said to have been named to commemorate King William IV's summer in St. John's, was considered the town limits in the middle of the last century. It was here that the Kent Inn was located. A sketch of the inn, done in 1850, shows a three-storey, gable-roof structure with dormers on the third floor, and two very large windows on each side of the front door.[14] Persons leaving town on foot, or by horse, fortified themselves for the trip at Kent's. Travellers reaching St. John's after a long journey refreshed themselves at the inn and washed the dusty germs from their throats with purifying spirits. We are told the "cosy parlor with fires in old-fashioned grates diffused warmth and cheer which were considerably enhanced by mine host Kent." Kent, who was from Ireland, had only one child and she was a nun. After his time the inn was conducted by a niece. During World War I the old inn was still in business, although much modernizd by Thomas Wall, who "determined that no

843

man shall forget himself on the premises." The Gaze Seed Company was afterwards built on the site and remained there until 1972.

Between Prince's Street and Buchanan Street lived the great sealing Captain, Pierre Mullowney, of Witless Bay. His daughter was Gertrude Cashin, the wife of the Prime Minister. Crossing Buchanan Street there were three shops in a substantial old stone building which is still standing although altered in appearance by restoration.

The easternmost shop, in the 1860s, was occupied by Matt McGuire, an Irishman who conducted a provisions trade with Waterford, Ireland, in his own vessel. The western store was occupied by O'Flannigan & Fitzgibbon. O'Flannigan retired from business at the end of the last century and became a lay brother at Mount Cashel where he ended his days. The small block was known as the Dwyer Buildings after the owner, T.S. Dwyer, one-time M.H.A. for St. John's West, and afterward an employee of the General Post Office. It passed into the possession of Mrs. Thomas Fitzgibbon through her first husband, Thomas Farrell, who had bought it from Dwyer. Mr. T. McCarthy, a brother of Professor McCarthy, who played the piano for the silent films at the Nickle, had a grocery business in this block at the turn of the century.

It was opposite the Dwyer Buildings that the first paving stone was laid on Water Street, 12 August 1899. Some two thousand citizens gathered to see the Honourable James McLouglin do the honours. The cobblestones were put down by the Reid Company as part of a deal with the government of the country to lay street railway tracks and operate a streetcar service. The eventual paving cost of nearly $140,000 was charged to the city debt in 1904.[15]

The first sidewalks on Water Street were laid at the same time as the paving. Until then there were wooden boardwalks or paving stones in front of most Water Street stores. It was not until 1930 that Duckworth Street became the second paved street in the city. From Springdale Street west to Alexander Street the roadway along Water Street varied in width from eight to fifteen feet. All the old buildings in this section were torn down at the time of paving and the north side of the street was considerably moved back.

Electric light poles began to appear a little before this time and gradually a maze of ugly wires webbed the downtown area. The first traffic lights went into operation on Water Street 11 September 1952. The overhead wires finally disappeared underground in 1966, vastly improving the look of the street.

Hutchings Lane, west of the Dwyer Buildings, takes its name from the owner of a vast plantation in the area. George Hutchings Jr., the son of a New Englander who had settled in St. John's early in the 1700s. Hutchings Street, further west, was also named for George Jr. who was on the list of Grand Jurors in 1750. It is said Hutchings received this large grant of land for keeping a watch on Admiral de Ternay's fleet, which was thought to be coming to attack St. John's in 1762. George Hutchings made history of a kind when he became the first person in St. John's to defy the laws of the land and erect a house with an attached chimney. His brother-in-law, Peter LeMessurier, who came from Guernsey, later followed suit. In an effort to discourage permanent sellers a law had been enacted forbidding the erection of houses with indoor chimneys, the pretence being that sparks might catch fire to the flakes which were numerous in St. John's in the eighteenth century. It is difficult to imagine the discomfort of people who had no indoor cooking facilities and no heat in their homes during the bitter cold winters. In view of such hardships it is surprising that St. John's had any permanent population. In 1790 Governor Milbanke ordered Hutchings' house and that of Newman Hoyles, which also had a chimney, to be torn down. Both were men of influence in high places. Hutchings entered into litigation which delayed the carrying out of the order until after the governor was recalled to England. Under the new governor, Admiral Richard King, the law was relaxed and houses with chimneys became commonplace throughout the town.

At a time when immigrants were forbidden, and settlers could get no land, the codfish aristocracy were claiming large tracts of St. John's for the most trivial of reasons. Prowse tells us valuable properties on both sides of Water Street sometimes were purchased for a winter's provisions. A profitable building lot on the north side of Water Street, west of McBride's Hill, was given to one large firm for a cook's passage to England.

Hutchings owned most of the land from Springdale Street almost to Patrick Street. A section of this land was leased to Robert Job; and another portion, sold to Robert Brine—a farmer, butcher, and publican—for two hundred pounds and a quarter of beef, became the Brine Estate of our day.

Between Hutchings' Lane and Springdale Street there was a small lane named Thomas's, upon which a concrete block corner structure was built by Vail and later occupied by F. Hue, C.L. March, a Mr. Fearn, and finally Wm. Dawe & Sons. The lane disappeared when the block was torn down in the 1960s to be replaced by the present office building. On this corner the westward progress of the Great Fire of 1846 was finally halted.

Crossing Springdale Street we come to what P.K. Devine has described as "the wonder building of the west end when it was first erected.[16] The firm of Robert & Thomas Newman, an old English company of wine merchants, with interests in London, Dartmouth, and Oporto, followed the Elizabethan taste for port wine to Newfoundland and opened a branch of the firm at St. John's, early in the eighteenth century. It was granted fishing rights in Newfoundland in 1601. The whaling business of Peter LeMessurier, in Hermitage Bay, was acquired as the Newman operations expanded. One year ships of this Devonshire firm brought a winter's supply of port wine from Oporto to St. John's in a salt-cargo. When it was opened the taste of the wine was found to have improved greatly. At first it was thought that the salt-cargo was responsible for the improvement. By accident, some casks of the wine were left on the ship and sent back to London. When these casks were sampled the contents were found to be still further improved. It was deduced that the rolling motion of the Atlantic voyage and something in the air, or climate of Newfoundland, had matured the wine to a high degree of perfection.

In Portugal there are two types of port wine: port from the wood—a blend of different years—and port of a vintage year. Older vintages of port from the wood are refreshed in a cask with a younger wine to give the older wine body. A fifteen-year-old wine is refreshed with a fourteen-year-old wine, a twelve-year-old with an eleven-year-old and so on. Old wine is never refreshed with a very young wine. This blending of wines is called "marrying." The Newman firm, after discovering that the rolling ocean voyage made the different blends marry into one excellent wine, and also that the effect of the Newfoundland climate on this wine gave it a special character, developed a busy trade between Oporto, St. John's, and London.[17] The wine which was shipped from Newfoundland to England became very popular as a high quality wine in English pubs and amongst the aristocracy. It was labelled HUNT'S PORT—MATURED IN NEWFOUND-LAND. The trade is still carried on under the name of NEWMAN'S CELE-BRATED NEWFOUNDLAND PORT.

Wine from Oporto is shipped from Portugal to St. John's where it stays embalmed for four years. It is then sent to England for bottling and enjoys great popularity. Newman's liquor labels have been found in Devonshire dating back to 1650. The firm, after going through many changes of names, sold out its Newfoundland interests in 1907.

The Newman family held considerable plantations in St. John's on Duckworth Street east, at the foot of McBride's Hill, and in the area of Springdale Street. All that remains of the firm today is the house on the corner of Springdale and Water Streets which is now leased from the estate. Set in the sidewalk a few yards west of the house can be seen one of Newman's metal boundary markers containing the initials "R.L.N." for Robert Lydston Newman. There is another on Duckworth Street east of Devon Row. Behind the Springdale Street residence is the warehouse where Newman's Celebrated Port has been stored for over a hundred and fifty years. The first tenant in the house was a Mr. Morey, the company agent.

At a meeting of the trustees and directors of the Phoenix Fire Office, Lombard Street, London, Thurdsay, 28 November 1782, a motion was made and seconded "That the order of Messrs Newman & Roope, of Dartmouth, for insurance at St. John's, Newfoundland, be complied with, to the extent of three thousand pounds only, and that the rate for the same be forty shillings per thousand."[18] It passed unanimously and was the first insurance policy issued on any property in Newfoundland. It was the second for the Phoenix Company outside Britain. The first, a month earlier, was on a sugar mill in Russia.

For over three hundred years Newman's have had an interest in St. John's. The firm purchased everything from train oil to seal skins and supplied everything from wine to a fire engine. It was because of the services of some of Newman's apprentice boys, who happened to be on board H.M.S. *Shannon* at the time of her celebrated victory over U.S.S. *Chesapeake* in Boston Harbour in 1813, that the company was granted the signal honour of henceforth being permitted to fly the white ensign from its Newfoundland premises.

In 1972 Baine, Johnston & Co., agents for Newman's in Newfoundland since 1907, sold the firm's property opposite the foot of McBride's Hill to the Crosbie interests for the erection of Atlantic Place. For many years this land was rented by Ayre & Sons.

In the 1760s William Newman lived in a house underneath Fort William. Governor Palliser felt the place would interfere with the defence of the fort, and on 2 September 1766 Newman was ordered to take it down, along with a number of other private dwellings in the area. He was permitted to dispose of the materials in his own way. The site probably became Robert Newman's Duckworth Street property.

The Newman firm is thought to have been the last in St. John's to abandon the old practice of serving a tot of rum to its employees daily between eleven o'clock and noon, and between three and four in the afternoon. Judge Prowse says it was still done at Newman's in his time. The first man to take a firm stand against this practice was Robert Job. Baine, Johnston & Co.'s attempt at watering the grog nearly brought on a mutiny among its workers.

Following the passing of Morey, the residence on Springdale Street was sold to Lewis Tessier of Newton Abbott, Devonshire, who became M.H.A. for St. John's West in 1873 and represented the district for some years. After his death on 30 April 1854 at the age of sixty-four, the house served many purposes. At one time it was the the office of W.J. O'Neil's newspaper, the *Plaindealer*. It also became the West End Club, a hotel, a liquor package store, and in the 1960s and early '70s the Newfoundland & Labrador Press Club. By a superhuman effort it was saved from destruction when the '46 fire was stopped at Springdale Street. A change of wind direction helped.

At the far corner of the next block Bambrick's Butcher Shop was located. Mr. Bambrick gave his name to the lane which connected Water Street to the foot of Hamilton Avenue, west of his store, and which was widened to become a proper street when Water Street was paved. In the present century the Horwood Lumber Company has covered a considerable portion of the east side of Bambrick Street. R.F. Horwood, who was born at Carbonear in 1867, opened for business at St. John's in 1893. The company passed out of family ownership a few year ago.

Individual fires, some of them fatal, have devastated much of the next block to the west. Peter O'Mara's drugstore has been on the east corner of Brennan's Lane almost from the beginning of the century.

847

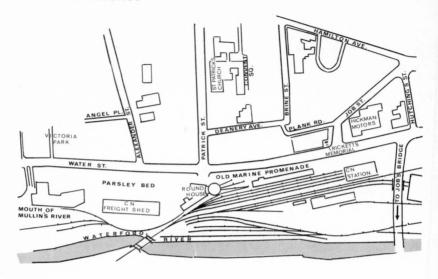

MAP 7 - HUTCHINGS ST. TO VICTORIA PARK

A range of old houses on Water Street, west of the foot of Hutchings Street, was torn down around 1900 opening up the view into the garden next door. It was here that Robert Job lived in a cottage-style house set back in a bower of trees and flowers. Job's Lane, which ran along the back of the property became Job Street. This prominent merchant was also instrumental in having Job's Bridge built, opposite his house, replacing an old wooden structure which linked Water Street to the Southside. It is now called Long Bridge. On 8 July 1860 the cottage was sold by auction for £1,505 to the Honourable James McLoughlan. When it burned down he built a substantial residence on the site.

According to P.K. Devine, an uncle of the Honourable gentleman was the first of the family to come out to Newfoundland from Ireland. This man, also called James, made about ten thousand pounds in his vessels at the seal hunt. He was a bachelor, but wanted an heir, so he sent for his nephew James, who was born in 1820. He made him skipper of one of his vessels and on the old man's death the nephew inherited the business. He increased the fortune by investments in real estate.[19] He was M.H.A. for St. John's West in 1879 and appointed to the Legislative Council in 1882. He died in 1913 at the age of ninety-three years. His son, another James, a medical doctor, inherited his estate. In the late 1940s the house was torn down and Hickman Motors built a modern garage on the site, moving there from opposite Springdale Street.

A bronze plaque in a small park on the west corner of Job Street tells the story of the tenant of the corner building. Placed there 10 June 1972, the inscription beneath a druggist's mixing bowl reads: "Memorial to Sgt. Thomas Ricketts, V.C., Croix de Guerre, D.C.M., 1901-1967, Soldier -

848

Pharmacist - Citizen." The story of Tommy Ricketts, the youngest winner of the Victoria Cross in World War I, is told in the final chapter of Volume I of this work.

In the middle of the block between Job Street and Patrick Street there was another floral garden with tall trees and a large cottage. This was probably part of the land granted to Bishop O'Donel, and known as the Bishop's Garden. Dr. Edward Kielley, the eminent medical man who left his mark on the political history of the British Empire, lived here at Weston Cottage. He died in 1855, and the property came into the possession of Peter Germon Tessier who called it Tessier's Cottage. Peter, a brother of Lewis, died at St. John's 24 April 1886, age sixty-seven.

The cottage was sold to Kaleem Noah around 1916. Noah, a prominent businessman who came to Newfoundland from Lebanon by way of the United States, started in the drygoods business in 1896, on the corner of Water and Buchanan Streets. In 1920 he built the Noah Building, until recently T. Eaton & Co., a few doors west of William's Lane on Water Street, as well as several other properties, including the Bacille Building on the corner of Springdale and New Gower Streets. The man's name was originally Kaleem Noah Bacille, but the surname was dropped when the family settled in Newfoundland. A daughter of Mr. Noah married Senator Mike Basha of Corner Brook.

Built sometime around 1800, the corner building on the west side of Patrick Street is an attractive stone structure of uncertain age. A sketch of the area, at a time when the waters of the harbour came up almost to the door, shows it as the only building in that section of what is now Water Street. It has traditionally been a tavern or public house. A tenant here in the 1940s was Eugene Kennedy, son of Captain Nicholas Kennedy of S.S. *Terra Nova* fame.

A group of tenements west of Alexander Street to Victoria Park took their name from the man who built them, Patrick Gallagher, who died in 1882 at the age of eighty-one years. They were called Gallagher's Range, later Galgay's. At the time they were torn down, in January and February 1960, some eighty people were still living there. The three-storey wooden dwellings with dormer attic windows were then a dilapidated slum, well over two hundred years old. They appear to have deteriorated much earlier, for in the last century the owner, Thomas Raftus, a powerfully built Irishman, was twice assaulted by an Irish tenant who felt he was being overcharged for the miserable quarters. The man was finally taken to court by Raftus.

Next to Gallagher's Range, in what is now Victoria Park, was the St. John's Hospital. The story of this building is told in Chapter 6 of Volume I. Adjoining the hospital was the Bennett Brewery which has been in operation on the site since 1827, making it the oldest manufacturing firm in Newfoundland. Built on the banks of Mullins River by Charles Fox Bennett, the 1869 anti-confederate Prime Minister, the complex included,

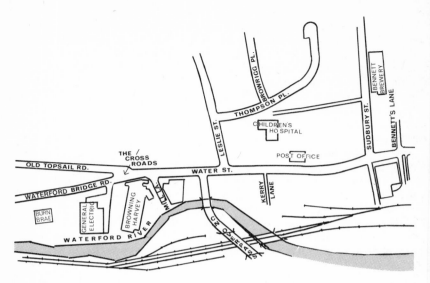

MAP 8 - VICTORIA PARK TO THE CROSSROADS

besides the brewery, a sawmill, a foundry, a forge, a flour mill, and a whiskey distillery where the first whiskey was distilled, 7 May 1860.

Born in Shaftsbury, Dorset, 11 June 1793, Bennett came to Newfoundland as a boy. At the age of twenty-nine he planned to go across the island with W.E. Cormack and a Micmac guide, on the famous trip of exploration, but the government refused him permission, on the grounds that he was a stipendiary magistrate. Bennett's shipyard, formerly on the site of the General Post Office, was established by him. He was also active in mining, especially in the development of Tilt Cove.

Charles Fox Bennett, a Protestant, was elected M.H.A. for Placentia-St. Mary's, a totally Catholic district, and became Prime Minister in 1870. His very able administration was defeated in three years by a series of intrigues. The old man, in his eighties, retired from political life and died at the age of ninety years, 5 December, 1883.

The dwelling house of Charles Fox Bennett was on the south side of Water Street, just east of the foot of Hill o' Chips, probably T.H. Brooking's stone dwelling which was offered for sale when Brookings went out of business. Following Bennett's death, Edward W. Bennett (no relation) obtained an assignment of the Riverhead Brewery in 1884. He died in 1902 and his brother, Sir John Bennett, converted the firm into a limited liability company. During prohibition it closed for two years, reopening in 1918 for the manufacture of "near-beer." In 1962 the company was purchased by Canadian Breweries Limited.[20] Mullins River is now underground except at the top of Victoria Park where a waterfall can still be seen.

There was a private house on the corner of Sudbury Street, once called Poorhouse Lane, which was turned into a club for the Railway Clerks Union. At one time it was the home of J.M. Devine, founder and proprietor of the Big 6 drygoods store.

In the middle of the next block, just west of the West End Post Office stood Sudbury Hall, a building believed to date back to the 1700s. In 1810 it was occupied by Captain Blamey, R.N., of H.M.S. *Comet*, a naval vessel of twenty guns doing patrol duty in the North Atlantic. He is thought to have named the house for Sudbury, near Wembley, England. His wife was Eunice Pearl, sister of Sir James Pearl, and it may have been from hearing of St. John's from Eunice that the founder of Mount Pearl later made his way to Newfoundland where he settled and died.

Blamey was a descendant of Baron Blaney of Ireland, who was created a peer by James I, 29 July 1621. The family later fled to England, the Barony became extinct, and the name was changed to Blamey. The Captain, who settled in Newfoundland, joined H.M.S. *Nonsuch* when he was a child of eight years.

The residence was known as Exmouth Cottage when Edward L. Moore, surveyor of shipping, took it over later in the century. Edward Moore and his brother Lorenzo, direct descendants of the Earl of Droheda, came out to Newfoundland from Newtown, Waterford. Edward married Ruth Blamey, a niece of the Captain, and in this manner the property came into his possession. His son, James Pearl Moore, was the original tenant of Tor Cottage, which stands on high ground just east of the General Protestant Cemetery on Waterford Bridge Road and was, at one time, known as the Torringon Hotel. The cottage was built by his wife's grandfather, Mr Palk of Torquay, Devon, who gave his name to Palk's Hill, at the rear of the property. Palk's Farm was on the present site of Waterford Hospital. It was Edward Moore's daughter, Fanny, who married Thomas McConnan and became the trendsetter who first skated with the boys at the rink.

Exmouth Cottage, was torn down late in the nineteenth century, and the present impressive Victorian structure was erected on the site by C.R. Thompson, manager of the Newfoundland Boot and Shoe Factory. The large field at the back, once known as Stevenson's Field, became Thompsons' Field. In the late 1960s this land was sold for thirty-five thousand dollars and turned into a housing development.

The Thompson house was taken over by Dr. N.S. Fraser as a Children's Hospital, the first in Newfoundland. After that it became a convalescent home for World War I veterans, and in World War II the Merchant Navy Hospital was moved there from the basement of the King George V Institute under the direction of Elizabeth Moore, R.N. Today the place is a custodial home for seriously retarded children.

Next door to this institution, in the second house east of Leslie Street,

A.B. Perlin lived from 1937. Editor of the *Daily News* for many years, as well as a reputable historian, Dr. Perlin is rightly known as the Dean of Newfoundland journalists. His unique contribution to the literary life of Newfoundland was recognized by an honourary doctorate from Memorial University in 1973.

In the long ago, John Brien had a stable on the corner of Leslie Street and worked truck carts. His son, Patrick, is known as "the last of the cabmen." Long after the streetcar and automobile had driven the horses and carriage from the streets of St. John's, Patrick Brien could be seen standing forlornly, beside his sagging nag and ancient victoria, in front of the General Post Office, waiting for fares who preferred the new "taxis."

On the west side of Leslie Street, Carroll's Meadow was occupied by a few cottages. In one of them lived Captain Day, from Nova Scotia, who commanded vessels for Tessier's and was later an M.H.A. for St. John's West. One of his brothers, John, is said to have been the first native-born male to obtain a job as a clerk on Water Street. Before his victory in obtaining his employment, all such persons were imported from the British Isles.

The locality where Waterford Bridge Road and Topsail Road meet Water Street has always been known as the Crossroads. In the nineteenth century Waterford Bridge Road was Blockmaker's Hall Road, and Topsail Road was Cockpit Road and also Palk's Hill. Just west of the Crossroads on what is now Topsail Road, William Best had his tavern, Bunch of Grapes, and it possibly held a cockpit. Until recent years a grocery store that had once been a public house stood at the intersection facing Water Street. It was owned by John Brown and later by one of his clerks, Leo Healey. The wooden building was torn down to open the area to traffic, and a small park replaced the structure.

A short distance from the Crossroads, at No. 10 Waterford Bridge Road, on the west side of a short street that connects Waterford Bridge and Topsail Roads, the noted sealing skipper, Captain Abram Kean, had his home. The front of the house has been altered by recent renovations which removed a large verandah. The legendary captain, whose conviction in his inability to err has been blamed for the tragic S.S. *Newfoundland* disaster that claimed the lives of seventy-eight sealers in 1914, died 18 May 1945 at ninety years of age.

THE CROSSROADS TO MULLINS RIVER
(See Map 8 — Page 850)

At the end of Water Street, on the south side, the firm of Browning-Harvey erected a shelter for streetcar patrons known as Rest-a-While. Somewhat like a small way station on a country railroad in Britain, it had seats built along three walls and a display of company products in a glass showcase in the centre of the shelter.

Behind Rest-a-While, at the bottom of Mill Lane, was a bakery built

852

by R. Vail who had, early in the 1850s, come to St. John's from the United States and started a small bakery on Water Street where he sold ordinary bread. He soon noticed that there was an enormous trade being done in the very hard Hamburg bread, imported from Germany. It lasted fishermen and sailors for years without going bad and was called "hard tack." By trying various mixtures, Vail eventually invented a hard bread of his own, not quite so tasty as the German product, but much cheaper than the imported bread. The American soon had 75 per cent of the hard-bread business and within five years Hamburg bread was driven from the Newfoundland market.

The need for larger premises and a water wheel to provide power caused Vail to build a new bakery on the banks of the Waterford, at the Crossroads. So sensational were the sales of his hard bread that he was able to retire a wealthy man within ten years. He later made his way to California for his health but it turned out to be the death of him. He was drowned while bathing at Catalina Island.

Vail's Bakery was purchased by Gilbert Browning, a white-bearded gentleman, born at New Milus, Ayrshire, Scotland, 19 October 1821. He had come to St. John's after the 1846 fire as a builder engaged to reconstruct the premises of Baine, Johnston & Co. Browning also built a residence for himself in the west end known as "Richmond." This house still stands on a knoll, set back in a grove of tall trees, on the east side of the foot of Shaw Street. Browning became the owner of a sawmill, a cod-liver oil refinery, a boot factory, and eventually a biscuit factory. In 1863 he opened a bakery at the foot of Barter's Hill. This building was destroyed by fire and a new one built at Alsop's Wharf, on the east side of Steer's Cove. When Vail retired, in 1869, Browning bought out his premises at the Crossroads.

Shortly after purchase, it too was destroyed by fire. The place was rebuilt in stone and brick, and the building still stands behind the office of Creative Printers which is the site of Rest-a-While. A water wheel on the Waterford River supplied electric power to the bakery. As the river shrank and electricity became available throughout the city, the old wheel fell into disuse and decay. Gilbert Browning died in September 1882, at Glasgow, while on a visit home to Scotland for his health.

As was mentioned at the beginning of this chapter, Alexander Harvey established a bakery at the foot of Temperance Street in 1870. He was burnt out on 27 November 1879 in a fire that was covered by £3,500 insurance. He later moved to a substantial brick edifice opposite the foot of Hill o' Chips. This structure was torn down in 1972. For many years the Browning and Harvey bakeries were rivals for the biscuit and jams trade. In 1931 the two firms amalgamated and became Browning-Harvey. Today the company bottles Pepsi-Cola and other soft drinks and is located in a modern plant on Rope Walk Lane. The abandoned Browning-Harvey bakery at the Crossroads is now a warehouse.

853

Nearly opposite the West End Post Office a cluster of attached cottages ran down a narrow pathway to what was then the shore of the harbour. This path was known as Kerry Lane. In the small houses lived settlers from Kerry who spoke only the Gaelic tongue. One of them, Mrs. Sheehan, officiated at all the traditional Irish wakes in St. John's. She was an expert at the art of keening, a lamentation in which the good deeds of the deceased are uttered in a loud, wailing voice. Her son Richard was lost with all hands on Tessier's vessel, *Camelia*, a few years before the 1892 fire.

Opposite Mrs. Sheehan, in Kerry Lane, lived John Menchenton, who has long been celebrated in the song "Petty Harbour Bait Skiff." The line, "The lord preserved young Mention's life," refers to John Menchenton, who was the only survivor of the bait skiff tragedy.

Marshall Motors, which was founded as a partnership in 1918, was opposite Sudbury Street and known as Marshall's Garage. The senior partner was Francis W. Marshall, a former manager of the Angel Garage. Marshall's were appointed distributors for the Chalmers and Maxwell Motor Car companies in 1920. In 1924, when these plants were acquired by Walter Chrysler, Marshalls' became the first Chrysler Motors dealers in Newfoundland. In July 1933 the business premises was destroyed by fire. The new building opened in March 1934, under the name of Marshall Motors Ltd. In 1958 Canadian National Railways announced its intention of expropriating over half the firm's property on Water Street, so in December 1961 the company moved to a new building on Kenmount Road. Frank Marshall, the founder, passed away in February 1973, at eighty-three years of age.[21]

MULLINS RIVER TO LONG (JOB'S) BRIDGE
(See Map 7 — Page 848)

At the mouth of Mullins River, now underground, Charles Fox Bennett had the St. John's Mills, opposite his brewery, consisting of timber, sawing, and flour mills and a foundry stretching to the shore. East of Bennett's property, opposite the foot of Alexander Street, the gasworks erected storage tanks on the Parsley Bed which supplied the city. These large wooden cylinders, resembling modern oil-storage tanks, were not removed until the 1940s, when propane gas replaced the underground mains. The Y.M.C.A. of Canada built a hostel for servicemen between Water Street and the tanks early in World War II. There were complaints from citizens that a fire in the hostel could ignite the gas tanks and blow up the town. The long, two-storey Y.M.C.A. building was opened 9 January 1942 by the High Commissioner for Canada. A hostel for United States servicemen, the U.S.O., had opened two days earlier, on the southwest corner of Merrymeeting Road and Bonaventure Avenue.

The Marine Promenade extended from the foot of Alexander Street to the foot of Hutchings Street and on moonlit winter nights in the nineteenth century the area of the present railway station was alive with hundreds of skaters who, like Mr. Pickwick, frolicked with their friends on the ice.

The statue of a woman standing in front of the station is the work of a stonemason from Scotland, named Henderson, who was living in St. John's. The work was commissioned by Sir Robert Reid and is named "Industry." The model for the statue was a Miss Croft from Aquaforte, a beautiful young woman employed as a housemaid by Lady Reid, who at the time of her employment had no formal education. Lady Reid is said to have arranged for the girl to be educated and sent to a finishing school in Britain, whence she returned to become a governess for the Reid children and remained with the family for the rest of her life.

LONG (JOB'S) BRIDGE TO STEER'S COVE
(See Map 6 — Page 842)

Opposite Hutchings Street, in the area east of Long Bridge, Thomas Raftus had his fishing premises of stages and flakes. He is said to have started outside on a mussel bank and gradually extended to the bridge. Devine tells us in one article that Raftus had three hundred green-painted, clinkerbuilt whale boats on the fishing grounds outside the Narrows. In another article he said Raftus had a fleet of eighty boats of all sizes, bully boats, whale boats, and punts. Whatever the truth, he did conduct a large fishery business. Besides what he caught in his own boats, Raftus bought fresh fish from the fishermen and cured it himself. It was so well salted, cured, and dried that merchants vied with each other in the fall to buy the fish of Thomas Raftus. His son Richard was a brilliant scholar at St. Bonaventure's College, who became an actor, poet, and lawyer and later M.H.A. for Ferryland District. As an actor he was last seen on stage in 1875, as Margaroni, in the "The Brigands." His poetry included the ode, "Ye Topsail Stages and Flakes Umbrageous."

From the Raftus property to that of Newman's wharves, opposite Springdale Street, was located Morey's Coal Company, Captain Cole's premises, McLoughlan's, Angel's, and Hickman's. M. Morey & Co. was leading supplier of coal to the town when every house had its hard and soft coal bins. The Managing Director was Herbert J. Wyatt who spent twenty-eight years with the firm. When Mr. Morey withdrew from the coal business after forty-two years Wyatt started the Wyatt Coal and Salt Co. Ltd. with his son Herbert K. Wyatt. The firm was incorporated 6 December 1933 and operated next to Morey's on what had been the site of the Union Coal Co. A bunkering plant was opened by the firm on the Monroe Export Co. property on the south side. The Wyatt property was expropriated by the federal government for the harbour development and Herbert K. Wyatt purchased and operated the Candlelight Restaurant. His daughter-in-law, Dorothy, became mayor of St. John's.

Captain Cole had ships which ranged all over the world. One of his skippers, Captain Prior, died on a voyage to Egypt and was buried in

Alexandria. Cole himself died of a fever on a voyage from Brazil to St. John's and was buried at sea. His wharf was taken over by James Angel in 1870.

Angel, born at Halifax on 12 January 1838, came to St. John's in 1850 to learn his trade as a machinist at Bennett's foundry, where his father John Angel, a native of Bridport, Dorset, was manager. In 1857, with his father, he started a small machine shop on Hamilton Avenue, at the east corner of Alexander Street, for the manufacture of stoves and nails.

The first nails made in St. John's came from this factory. A horse, attached to a long lever and slowly walking round and round, produced the motive power. Angel's soon absorbed Bennett's Mill, and for several years this was the only foundry and machine shop in Newfoundland. In 1885 a machine and boiler shop was opened on the Water Street property. It was around this time that the founding father died and his son James developed Newfoundland's first water-wheel, its first steam engine and boiler, and build the first steel steamship.

Early in the 1890s, Angel, along with Messrs. Harvey and Brown, took over the operation of the drydock, which then passed into the hands of the Reid-Newfoundland Company as part of the railway deal of 1898. Eventually the Angel property on Water Street was disposed of and the company consolidated on Hamilton Avenue as the United Nail and Foundry Company Limited. Much of this property was destroyed by fire in October 1973.

The wharves of A.E. Hickman & Co. were originally those of Newman & Co., the English firm which owned considerable property on the north side of Water Street. Newman's business went through many name changes after starting in Newfoundland in 1701 as Taylor & Newman. Next came Thomas Newman & Co.; then Holdsworth, Olive & Newman; Newman & Roope; Newman, Land & Hunt; Newman & Hunt; Newman, Roope & Co. (1812-1834); Hunt, Roope, Teage & Co. (1835-1907); and finally, Hunt, Roope & Co. Thomas Newman Hunt was a governor of the Bank of England. The firm's waterfront premises was leased to Ewan Stabb who had a fleet of sturdy vessels that carried on a mercantile trade between St. John's and Bristol. When Mr. Hickman took over the property he rebuilt the sheds and wharves.

Early in 1920 Albert Hickman obtained the Ford automobile agency and erected a garage on the property opposite Springdale Street that he had acquired in 1919. By 1947 Hickman's repair shop and showrooms proved too small and the firm erected a modern garage on the McLoughlan-Job property west of Hutchings Street. Hickman Motors was formed in 1948, and in 1951 switched from Ford to the General Motors dealership, formerly held by E.O'D. Kelly, in a garage on the western corner of Hill o' Chips and Duckworth Street.

In the seventeenth century the waterfront east of Springdale Street was in the possession of Mrs. Furzey. Next to her was the property of the

Oxford family. In 1675 Thomas Oxford returned to England with his wife and children, when western adventurers destroyed his holdings which "fifteen hundred men would not in three weeks repair."[22] He claimed that his family had possessed land and houses in the area for seventy years.

Directly opposite the foot of Springdale Street, Patrick Morris had his business premises, and one can be sure many a clandestine meeting took place there when he and Dr. Carson were waging their great fight for self-government. Morris's father is said to have lost a fortune of thirty thousand pounds in the Newfoundland trade. Hounsell, Schank & Hounsell did business on the site for a time and were followed in the 1850s by John Bond, father of the great Prime Minister, Sir Robert Bond. Bond occupied part of the building as a dwelling house and it was probably here that the future Prime Minister was born, 25 February 1857.

The waterfront from Newman's Wharf east to a point opposite Buchanan Street became the premises of Peter and Lewis Tessier. They were Englishmen from Newton Abbot, Devonshire, descended from a Baron de Tessier who had fled the excesses of the French Revolution and who is remembered for having undertaken the care and maintenance of six Roman Catholic priests who fled with him from France to England. The family donated a hundred pounds toward the erection of St. Patrick's Church on Patrick Street.

As noted previously Peter lived west of Job Street, and Lewis in the Newman house at the foot of Springdale Street. At one time the shipping and supply business of this firm was the largest in Newfoundland, with 54,000 tons of ships and 325 employees. When quitting time came the flow of workers blocking traffic in Water Street was known as Tessier's Army.

In time the family became immensely wealthy. This fact may well have contributed to its demise. A great family seat, Germondale, was erected by Peter Tessier's son Charles on Waterford Bridge Road. The long abandoned manor was demolished in the late sixties after being plundered and destroyed by vandals, and in 1973 the grounds became Nottingham and Sherwood Drives.

Before the 1846 fire Tessier's firm was located opposite William's Lane, site of Tooton's photographic supply store. When burnt out they rented a portion of Alsop's Wharf and used it until the premises in the west end was built.

Peter Tessier married a daughter of Robert Carter of Ferryland, a family believed to be the oldest still living in Newfoundland. The first Carter came to the country a year after its discovery by John Cabot. In the records of the Bristol and London merchants there is a notation which reads: "April 1st, 1498, a reward of £2 to James Carter for going to the new isle." Charles Tessier married Miss Rogerson whose ancestors included Patterson, founder of the Bank of England, and Sir Hans Sloane, father of the British Museum.

The Honourable James J. Rogerson had his premises between Tessier's and Stewart & Rennie. David Rennie's office was opposite Prince's Street, on property that had once been Darkuse's Room. Rogerson had several daughters besides the one who married Charles Tessier; another was Mrs. John Bulley Ayre and a third, was Mrs. J.W. McNeilly. Old J.J. was himself twice blessed. His first wife was a daughter of Sheriff Blackie. The second lady was a daughter of James Whiteford, the jeweller. Rogerson's offices were later taken over by George M. Barr, an Englishman, who was a fish exporter and is credited with starting the Newfoundland Lobster industry. Miss Mary Skinner, a sister of the Roman Catholic Archbishop of St. John's, served as Barr's secretary for many years.

East of the Stewart & Rennie property, George Knowling erected three buildings, when he was burned out in the east end in the 1892 fire, and opened them as the West End Stores. The Stores were sold by his heirs about the same time as his rebuilt premises downtown became insolvent and was taken over by Ayre's.

Charles Fox Bennett operated from a stone building erected early in the 1800s, three or four doors west of Steer's Cove. A.E. Hickman took over this structure, tore it down, and used the stone to erect the Hickman building which was occupied on the site by the firm until April 1976, when it moved to Topsail Road.

The west side of Steer's Cove used to be known as McLea's Corner, for a family who had come to Newfoundland from Greenock, Scotland. The McLeas seem to have been doomed to violence. John McLea was stabbed to death by two ruffians who had robbed him while he was on a holiday in Buenos Aires, on 21 January 1833. Kenneth McLea, the owner of the firm, was a candidate for St. John's West in the 1861 election. His campaign was marred by riots in which the military shot and killed several people in the streets of St. John's. It became known as the "McLea election." In 1862 this controversial man was appointed to the Legislative Council, but he died on 27 June of that year, while visiting Richmond Hill, England. McLea is buried in the General Protestant Cemetery, Waterford Bridge Road, and there is an elaborate description of his life and deeds carved on his tombstone. In 1867 the firm was declared insolvent, and the building became the Worrington Hotel. When the hotel closed, late in the seventies, John Steer moved to the site.

Steer carried on a drygoods business that later became a wholesale supply house and insurance firm. Born at Torquay, Devon, 9 October 1824, John Steer was brought out to Newfoundland at the age of three. After completing his schooling, he was apprenticed to the drygoods business of Job Brothers & Co. A prominent Methodist, he married the daughter of another prominent Methodist, Charles R. Ayre, founder of Ayre & Sons. The two were in business together from 1844 to 1858. Steer lived at Hope Cottage, formerly Arundel Cottage, on Allandale Road, where the Arts & Culture Centre now stands. As a buyer for his own firm, Steer crossed the

Atlantic about one hundred times, no mean feat for his day and age.

STEER'S COVE TO BISHOP'S COVE
(See Map 5 — Page 838)

The Honourable Robert Alsop, M.H.A. for Trinity in 1869, Colonial Secretary in 1870, died 25 March 1871, at the age of fifty-seven. His business was located at 371 Water Street, on the east side of Steer's Cove, earlier known as Rennie's Cove. It was also called Alsop's Cove. In 1844 Robert Alsop & Co. had seven vessels at the ice taking part in the seal hunt. The firm did not long survive its founder's death. Simpsons-Sears has occupied the property from the middle of this century.

The site on the east corner of Steer's Cove and Water Street, known as Mudge's Block, has been occupied by a large number of firms throughout the centuries. At one time, Rennie & Stewart had an office there. John Anderson, whose main store was at Beck's Cove, had a branch on the corner, adjoining a building in the cove, next to Alsop's, where Gilbert Browning operated a bakery and lived in the upstairs quarters with his family.

The corner tenant at one time was John Barron who was reputed to have made a fortune of sixty thousand pounds (three hundred thousand dollars) as a seal killer in his vessel the *Dash*. He was the father of Pierce Barron who was elected M.H.A. for Placentia in 1865 and served as Secretary of the General Water Company before joining the Customs House. Earlier in his career he operated a wine and spirit shop a few doors east of his father's dwelling. Another Barron, Laurence, who had a cooperage at the rear of the block, was first President of the Mechanics' Society. He was formerly a master cooper with W.H. Thomas.

The rest of Mudge's Block, during the latter years of the nineteenth century, was occupied by Mrs. Tobin's Hotel, the London Cafe and European Jewellery Store. From 1865 to 1869 schools for the poor were organized by the Honourable J.J. Rogerson upstairs in these buildings. Known as the Ragged Schools, they were a copy of the poor schools then trying to bring education to the totally neglected children of the lower classes in England. The St. John's schools were in the charge of Patrick Meehan.

East of these premises was Pierce Barron's spirits shop. In 1934 it became the publishing office for George Andrews' newspaper, *Watchman*. He also printed the *Co-operative News*, a monthy magazine called *Talk*, and other publications including the *Newfoundland Directory*. It was here that Andrews printed P.K. Devine's *Ye Olde St. John's*.

Opposite Queen Street, Stewart's Cove ran down to the waterfront. Today this cove is a small alleyway separating Parker & Monroe from Woolworth's. Although they are greatly altered both externally and internally Parker's two buildings are the only eighteenth-century stores left between Steer's Cove and Bishop's Cove.

The corner structure was occupied for a time by Charles Rankin and then by Coleman's book and music store. It became known as Sclater's Corner when a Mr. Sclater opened a draper's store there. The property was acquired by Peter Brennan, a celebrated bonesetter, who was elected M.H.A. for St. John's West in 1866. His success at bonesetting was due to his deft use of block and tackle. Before the "operation" the patient was fortified for the ordeal by a glass of strong, black rum for which he was required to pay.

Besides setting bones and his legislative chores as a staunch anti-confederate, Brennan had a small mercantile fleet which he sent to the seal hunt from a wharf behind his premises. It is said he was so economy-minded that the stingy Scot of popular legend was thought "to have nothing on him." However, he was generous with his proficiency on the flute and would often serenade the nuns outside their convent on summer mornings. His house on Hamilton Avenue, opposite Alexander Street, was called "Thrush's Nest" and his tombstone in Belvedere, directly behind Archbishop Flynn, bears the unique inscription "Peter Brennan, born County Kilkenny, a centenarian and a celibate. April 15, 1887. An expert in bone setting and generous benefactor to his country and his church."

Brennan left his property on the corner of Stewart's Cove to the Roman Catholic Church. It was unoccupied for a time until T. Bearns opened a furniture store in the building. He was the father of the well-known King's Beach grocer, W.E. (Billy) Bearns.

The next building to the west, which was Parker & Monroe's original store, was owned by another member of the Barron family, Eugene, a furniture maker and wood-turner. A brother of Dr. J.J. Dearin operated a chemist's shop there for a time and he was followed in the early 1860s by Felix Dowsley who was also a druggist. Dowsley accepted the post of winter doctor for the new copper mine at Tilt Cove in 1867 and this involved him in one of the most tragic stories of shipwreck in Newfoundland history. In began on the evening of Tuesday, 6 December, when the squarerigger *Queen*, out of Swansea, Wales, sailed from St. John's for Tilt Cove in Notre Dame Bay with a cargo of mail and fifteen passengers and crew from St. John's and Swansea.

Among those on board were the young son and daughter of the mine manager, a female schoolteacher who boarded the ship in Wales, and Felix Dowsley, an apothecary who was called doctor. The first night out the ship was caught in a terrible gale and driven 160 miles to sea. After seven days of great hardship the storm-tossed vessel finally reached Notre Dame Bay, only to be driven upon the rocks of Gull Island in a blizzard.

All of the crew and passengers landed safely on the barren shore. Three of the crew and one passenger went back on board to try and procure some clothing and provisions. While they were on the ship she was suddenly swept off the rocks and foundered. The four men drowned. As it turned out they were the fortunate ones. The others huddled for days on the treeless island almost in sight of the lights of Shoe Cove, only eight miles away, and the next village to Tilt Cove.

The shipwrecked voyagers lit fires with their few matches in the sparse tufts of grass. These small flames were seen by the people of Shoe Cove who decided they were Jack o' Lanterns, and fearing to go near the evil spirits, made no attempt to reach the island.

Dowsley kept a diary of the events in heart-rending letters to his wife which describe their sufferings, as frostbite and starvation began to take their toll. He wrote: "I am famishing with thirst. I would give the money I took . . . for one drink of water." The following day, 8 December, he noted: "I am almost mad with thirst; I would give all I ever saw for one drink of water, but I shall never get it. We are all wet and frozen. I am now going under the canvas to lie down and die."

It was finally decided one of their number would have to be sacrificed as food. Lots were drawn and the choice fell on one of the two female passengers, the daughter of the mine manager. Her brother instantly offered himself in her stead. Dowsley makes no mention of actually eating his fellow passenger.

On Christmas Eve, Felix Dowsley wrote:

We have not tasted a bit of food of any kind with the exception of the dirty snow water that melts around and under our feet . . . Oh! What a sad Christmas-eve and Christmas-day it is for me! I think I can see you making the sweetbread and preparing everything comfortable for tomorrow. . . . I had no idea we should have lasted so long. . . . My suffering has been beyond description since we landed on this barren rock. . . .[23]

The following April, according to historian Moses Harvey, a man and boy were shooting birds near the mouth of the bay. They noticed a seagull that kept flying from the island toward them and back to the island. When it came within gunshot the man fired, hitting the bird. Strangely, it flew back to the island and fell among the rocks. When the hunters landed they were horrified to find the gnawed remains of two human beings; nearby, under a piece of old canvas, locked in each other's arms, were the bodies of the rest of the party. The letters and notebooks told the awful story. A monument to the memory of the lost was erected on Gull Island.

After Dowsley, a man named Archibald had what is probably St. John's first boot and shoe factory upstairs in the second building west of Sclater's corner. In 1879 James Parker, who had been in the employ of Goodfellow & Co., and Daniel Monroe, a brother of Moses Monroe, bought out Archibald and were soon manufacturing as many as two hundred pairs of fishermen's boots per day. They took over the Brennan building next door which was then in the possession of the Barron family and in 1889 opened an east end branch. In 1909 a modern factory was put in operation on Alexander Street and it was soon turning out a hundred thousand pairs of boots and shoes per year. In 1924 James Parker died and was succeeded by his son John. Monroe's share of the business had been acquired by the Parkers long before that. Confederation in 1949 meant elimination of protective tariffs and the Alexander Street factory was closed because it could not meet the Canadian competition. Parker & Monroe still occupies the original two buildings opposite Queen Street.

The area of Woolworth's, which from the store opening in 1966 to the present time is the largest of the chain in Canada, was occupied in the west by Stewart's attractive old stone buildings. Sir John Crosbie's interesting structure was in the middle of the block, and to the east Edwin Duder had a handsome range occupied by shops and hotels.

J. & W. Stewart was an old firm dating from early in the nineteenth century. Stewart's operated passenger ships to and from Canada and were pioneers in the use of steamships. In the early days of steam they brought out S.S. *Ranger*, S.S. *Proteus*, and S.S. *Walrus* from England and sent them to the seal fishery with captains from Greenspond where Stewart's had a branch. James Stewart died in Greenock, Scotland, 8 November 1836, and his brother soon followed after him as the firm passed to the control of English shareholders.

John Syme, who became an M.H.A., was Stewart's manager late in the century. An earlier company manager, Mr. Alexander, gave his name to a Newfoundland community. When it was decided to rename Bloody Bay, the manager of Stewart's was honoured by having it called Alexander Bay, after him. A man of bountiful charity, Alexander contributed generously to the Seamen's Home, built on Duckworth Street in 1885. In this venture he was assisted by his wife who used her funds to enable the General Hospital to open Alexander Ward. Edward Morris, the father of the Newfoundland Prime Minister, Sir Edward Morris, was a master cooper at Stewart's.

By the late 1880s J. & W. Stewart was in decline, more from bad management than from anything else. The directors in Britain sent out an actuary to investigate irregularities and he recommended that the business be wound up. The once great firm of J. & W. Stewart closed its doors in 1892, and the premises was taken over by R.G. Rendell. Colonel Rendell had his home at "Northbank," on the shores of Long Pond. His wife was a daughter of Alexander Mackay, of telegraph fame, and their daughter Joan became a noted singer in Charles Hutton musicals. Another daughter married the brother of Prime Minister Alderdice.

Stewart's Block and the stone houses opposite on Queen Street were fashionable residential addresses in the early years of the nineteenth century, occupied by architects, doctors, and businessmen. The house next to Stewart's shop was at one time the surgery of Dr. Edward Kielley. On 10 November 1886 Garrett Byrne opened a bookstore at the eastern end of the buildings, which prospered until his death in the early years of the present century.

Before starting in business for himself, Sir John Crosbie helped his widowed mother operate the Crosbie Hotel. In 1910 he moved into the distinctive building in the centre of what is now Woolworth's store. This edifice owned its stylish architecture to the pretentions of Sir William Coaker who built the place as a headquarters for his Fishermen's Protective Union. Sir William, who was given a knighthood after a stint as Acting Prime Minister in 1918, is buried at Port Union. His hilltop tomb, which includes a bust of him carved in Italy, shows his penchant for the extreme.

The vast Crosbie empire of our day grew from the foundation which the popular Sir John laid in the former F.P.U. building on Water Street. His father George, who came from Dumfries, died when the boy was sixteen years old. At the age of twenty-four young Crosbie went into business for himself and in 1900 formed Crosbie & Company. In 1909 he was elected M.H.A. for Bay de Verde, and in 1925 he opened a margarine factory on LeMarchant Road. Death came to Sir John on 5 October 1932, when he was fifty-six years of age.

The name of Duder has been long gone from the business life of St. John's. In the 1860s it belonged to the largest firm of shipowners in Newfoundland with branches at Twillingate, Fogo, Herring Neck, Change Islands, Barred Islands, and Greenspond. In 1871 Edwin Duder, Jr., entered the firm founded by his father, which by that time owned over two hundred sail of fishing and foreign-going vessels, besides a large number of boats and skiffs, and was said to have grown, numerically speaking, to be the largest firm of shipowners in the world at the time. Edwin Duder lived upstairs until he moved to Circular Road.

The death knell for the firm was sounded in 1895 when the outport branches were offered for sale. Within a few years Duder's had vanished completely from the scene and their premises were taken over by others. Miss Ellie O'Niell had a fruit store in one of them.

S.G. Garland opened his first bookstore in one of Duder's shops. In 1893, the year after the Great Fire, Sammy Garland erected the Garland Building on the south side of Water Street, two doors east of Clift's-Baird's Cove. Garland was for years a leading bookseller and stationer in St. John's. A business decline forced him to sell his building to Baird's. He later opened a small bookstore on Duckworth Street, opposite the War Memorial, where he continued in business until his death in 1954 at the age of eighty-nine.

A series of upstairs hotels, with proper Victorian names, occupied the dwellings above Duder's shops. Wallace Goobie finally took over the group of buildings and was there until shortly before Woolworth's occupied the place in 1956. The chain store acquired Stewart's buildings later, tore down the whole section, and opened the present store 31 March 1966. It is faced with marble especially imported from Italy.

At the end of the last century there was an open lot east of Duder's. Ships built in Bennett's yard, across the street, were pulled through this lot to be launched. The last vessel to be built at Bennett's was of such a size that bets were made as to whether she would be able to pass between the buildings. Michael Kearney, the builder, demonstrated his faith in his judgement by hanging his valuable gold watch over the side. It went very close to the wall but it did not touch.

East of the launchway was Patrick Laracy's Crescent Theatre, now part of the Arcade Stores. A gable roof building, next to the vacant lot and facing Water Street, was the grocery store of H.V. Seymour.

E.M. Jackman, known as "Jackman the Tailor," opened a shop next to Seymour on 1 April 1889. He was burned out in 1893 and his premises was replaced by a single-storey structure. Jackman later moved to a new building which he erected on Water Street west, opposite Brennan's Lane, now occupied by the Newfoundland Light & Power Company. From 1900 to 1908 E.M. Jackman was M.H.A. for Placentia St. Mary's and Minister of Finance. His impressive mansion on the corner of LeMarchant Road and St. Clare Avenue, the White House, became the first St. Clare's Hospital. It is still standing.

W.R. Firth married Margaret Baird, a daughter of David Baird, and left his father-in-law's employ to go in business for himself. With the backing of some friends, he opened the Arcade Building in a store located three doors west of Bishop's Cove. Firth was a great-grandfather of city Councillor Ray O'Neill whose mother was Mary Firth.

Firth's Arcade eventually became insolvent and disappeared for a time from the business life of the city. The name was revived in 1938 by Patrick Halley, whose father, William, came to Newfoundland from Clonmel, Tipperary, and married a daughter of Thomas Haw, who had a grocery and liquor shop at 28 New Gower Street and was a partner in Firth's Arcade. Born in 1844, Halley reached Newfoundland in the 1890s and went to work for the firm of J.J. & L. Furlong. He moved from there to James Baird's and in 1900 founded Halley & Co. in Haw's old store on New Gower Street. This was replaced by a modern concrete structure in 1917. The premises stood opposite the corner of Adelaide and New Gower Streets, where City Hall is located today.

In 1939, a year before William Halley's death, his son Patrick opened a store which he called the Arcade, in Sillars & Cairns former shop, just west of the main branch of the Bank of Nova Scotia. It later moved to its present site opposite the General Post Office. In 1932 Halley was elected M.H.A. for St. John's West. Among various honours he received was a Papal knighthood at the time of the centenary of the Roman Catholic Cathedral. After his death Patrick Halley was followed in the management of the Arcade by his son-in-law, John Murphy, who began his career as a radio announcer on VOCM. Under Murphy's progressive policies the firm underwent a program of expansion so that by 1970 there were nine Arcade Stores serving St. John's and the suburbs. The Crosbie Hotel was later acquired by Mr. Murphy who changed the name to Welcome Hotel.

At the beginning of the nineteenth century Bishop's Cove was known as Codner's Cove, named for the firm of Codner & Tracey which was located on the corner. Samuel Codner, a native of Devonshire, carried on a business in St. John's for twenty-five years from 1819 and formed the Newfoundland School Society, in England, in 1823. The Society's first local institution, the Central School, was founded at St. John's the following year. Codner died in England in 1858 at the age of fifty-two, and his business was carried on by Wilson & Meynell.

Warren & Kelligrew, general merchants in the business of fishery supplies, were also on Codner's corner for some time. The senior partner was William Warren, who had come to the island at the age of fifteen, and died on 17 May 1856 at eighty-five. His grandson, also William, was sixteenth Prime Minister of Newfoundland, born at St. John's on 9 October 1879. He began his political career as M.H.A. for Trinity in 1902 and was Prime Minister from July 1923 to April 1924. He died on 31 December 1927 in his forty-ninth year and was buried with a state funeral. Warren's home at 3 Barnes Road later became the Balsam Hotel Annex.

In 1919 Gerald S. Doyle began a small business upstairs in a building on the present site of Tooton's, opposite Williams Lane, dealing exclusively in patent medicine and allied products, such as soap and toothpaste. He moved to Warren's premises and was incorporated in 1929. Mr. Doyle earned himself the gratitude of unborn generations of Newfoundlanders by being the first person to seriously gather and publish the folk music of Newfoundland. To date, his firm has issued four collections of *Old Time Songs and Poetry of Newfoundland*. He was also famous for the *Doyle Bulletin* a news programme on station VONF.

J.M. Devine, who eventually took over Doyle's premises, founded a small shop at 6 Adelaide Street in 1931. Four years later he moved to 339 Water Street, next door to Gerald S. Doyle, on the site of the old Arcade Building. Devine called his store the Big 6. The Little 6 was the shop on Adelaide Street. In 1961 the Doyle firm moved to the Blackmarsh Road industrial park, and the Big 6 acquired the building to the corner of the Cove. Devine's closed its doors in 1974.

Early in the present century the three stores eventually occupied by the Big 6 were the premises of Bishop, Sons & Co. The corner shop was a hardware store, west of it was a grocery, and in the third building drygoods were sold. At the back of these buildings, on the west side of what was then known as Bishop's Cove, the firm of Bishop & Monroe was located. Moses Monroe's wholesale and retail business had occupied two buildings in the next block, on Water Street, opposite William's Lane. Born in Moira, Ireland, Monroe came to Newfoundland in 1861, as a buyer for Goodfellow & Company. Before his death on 19 May 1895, he was a member of the Legislative Council. On 1 January 1898 the business was combined with another to form Bishop & Monroe. This firm went into liquidation in

1922. A monument to the philanthropies of Moses Monroe stands in Victoria Park.

In 1711 Captain Arthur Holdsworth had a house built on stilts in the area of Adelaide Street and Bishop's Cove which was then a river. Holdsworth Street was named for the pioneer sea captain and plantation owner.

BISHOP'S COVE TO BECK'S COVE

(See Map 5 - Page 838)

Across the cove to the east was Thomas Meagher, a farmer in Tipperary, who emigrated to Newfoundland early in the 1790s and became a trader, merchant, and shipowner, carrying on a prosperous business between St. John's and Waterford. He sent his eldest son, Thomas, to Ireland to establish a branch of the business in Waterford and represent him there. The younger Meagher married a Miss Quan, in the private residence of the bride's family on the Quay which was afterwards Commin's Hotel. In this house his son, Thomas Francis Meagher, was born 23 August 1823. The boy was destined for fame in America. St. John's tradition has it that the lad spent part of his youth in Newfoundland visiting on ships out of Waterford.

The Great Fire of 1817, which ended its western trek at Meagher's wiped out the premises and the firm was never able to recover from the loss. It was declared insolvent and dissolved 31 August 1820. The Meagher family returned to Ireland where young Thomas Francis became a leader of the Young Ireland Party of 1848 and was deported by the British to Tasmania. He escaped to the United States where he headed the Irish Brigade in the American Civil War and fought with the army of the Potomac at Bull Run, Antietam, Fredericksburg, and Chancellorsville. In 1864 he was made Brigidier General and the following year became acting Governor of Montana.

For many years after leaving St. John's old Mrs. Meagher would send for the captains of the Newfoundland vessels, arriving in Waterford, to learn news of her friends in St. John's. She sat imperiously in an old armchair repeating tales of her young days in Newfoundland, a checkered apron covering her dress, a white cap on her head, and spectacles on her nose.

The east corner of Water Street and Bishop's Cove was occupied at one time by the considerable premises of Boyd & McDougall. This firm was the first to give employment to a young St. John's lad fresh from school, named Bill Coaker, later the politically powerful Sir William. Old man McDougall lived upstairs over the premises. Little is known of his partner. The Broadway House of Fashion, which later stood on the site, was destroyed by fire early in the 1930s. The corner was not rebuilt until the present Great Eastern Oil building was erected in 1953.

The very old firm of Huie & Reed was just east of Bishop's Cove at the turn of the nineteenth century. It was on Huie & Reed's property that the second half of the Great Fire of 1817 broke out, spreading west to Meagher's and east as far as the site of the present Court House. The Huie & Reed property was once occupied by Ayre & Marshall, and also by the firm of Shirran & Pippy.

The passageway which leads towards the waterfront, opposite William's Lane, seems always to have existed. In the middle of the latter part of the last century it led from Moses Monroe's on the corner to a cluster of business offices, the most prominent of which was Stabb, Rowe & Holmwood.

Alan Goodridge & Sons moved from the Southern Shore into the Stabb, Rowe & Holmwood premises in 1857. The first Goodridge to come out from England to Renews was Alan, who began a fishery supply business there in 1828. His son Augustus, born at Paignton, Devonshire, on 9 August 1839, joined his father at Renews when he was thirteen. In 1862 he became a partner in the St. John's branch of the firm.

In 1880 Augustus, a Protestant, was elected M.H.A. for the overwhelmingly Catholic district of Ferryland. It was a time of great political turmoil. A number of M.H.A.s, including Robert Bond, and the Prime Minister, Sir William Whiteway, were unseated by the courts, and Goodridge found himself Prime Minister of Newfoundland. His attempts at reform were doomed by a major disaster which brought down the Goodridge administration and ruin to many in the colony.

On 10 December 1894, known in Newfoundland history as "Black Monday," the Union and Commercial Banks in St. John's suspended payment. This action not only brought about financial chaos, but the political survival of the colony looked very bleak.

The immediate cause of the bank crash was the death in England of Mr. Hall, a partner in the London fish exporting firm of Prowse, Hall & Morris. On his death it was decided to investigate the affairs of the company. Its bills were protested and the English banks made immediate demands on the Commercial Bank of St. John's, the drawer of the bills. Unable to meet this sudden request, the Commercial Bank fell back on its mercantile customers, but they were also unable to respond because of the large advances made by them to the fishermen until the end of the fishing season. A month or two later and the crash might never have taken place.

Unable to find funds to meet the demands of the English creditors, the Commercial Bank was forced to suspend operations. When word of this got out it led to a run on the Union Bank, and finally on the Newfoundland Savings Bank. The latter was not involved in the complications which affected the other two banks. However, all three were forced to lock their doors on 10 December 1894, because there was no money to be had. The notes of the Newfoundland banks were valueless, and trade was brought to a standstill. A large number of workers were dismissed from their jobs. A few Water Street firms issued their own money with which to pay their employees, and this scrip was the only form of negotiable currency available.

Bread riots soon broke out among the distressed populace of St. John's and supply stores were looted. Sailors and marines were landed to protect property and public buildings. An anguished Prime Minister Goodridge telegraphed the Imperial authorities in London for assistance in raising an immediate million-dollar loan, and asked that a warship be sent to safeguard the colony from rioters. With that he resigned from office, a broken and dispirited man. The new Prime Minister, Daniel Greene, was to control the government for just over fifty days.

Greene had been born at St. John's in 1850. He was M.H.A. for Ferryland in 1874, and became Leader of the Loyal Opposition at the age of thirty-seven. His grand-nephew, James, accomplished the feat of becoming Opposition Leader in the local Legislature at thirty-one. Daniel Greene, who was childless, lived at 34 Queen's Road. He left the house to his wife Ethel Fox, who in turn, willed it to her nephew, Judge Cyril Fox. It escaped the 1892 fire and is still standing.

Mr. Greene had great powers as an orator. A story is told of the heirless Prime Minister, that one afternoon he held the floor of the House while he talked at great length about agriculture and the wonderful future there was in Newfoundland for potatoes, cabbages, and turnips. After some hours, when he had exhausted himself, as well as the topic and his hearers, the Prime Minister sat down, well satisfied. Only a few minutes remained before adjournment, hardly time for anyone to reply. However, T. J. Murphy, a St. John's M.H.A., rose to his feet and wondered aloud what made the Honourable gentleman such an expert on agriculture when it was obvious that he couln't even raise Greenes.

When sworn in as Prime Minister, 13 December 1894, Daniel Greene followed his predecessor's attempt at obtaining financial assistance from a reluctant British government. After passing the Disabilities Bill, which enabled the disqualified members, such as Bond and Whiteway, to return to the House, Greene stepped down on 8 February 1895, and Sir William Whiteway, a man he supported, resumed his role as Prime Minister.[24]

As a way out of the financial disaster, the Governor, Sir Terence O'Brien, sent a message to the Governor General of Canada, suggesting a reopening of negotiations for a union of the two countries. Robert Bond, Edward Morris, George Emerson, and William Horwood were sent to Ottawa for fruitless discussions that were finally abandoned.

The bank crash gave Robert Bond his moment of glory and he was ready for it. Like a determined Disraeli fighting for the Suez Canal he took his cause to the leading bankers. In spite of the pledge of his own personal credit he failed to raise financial backing in Montreal and New York. He sailed for England, and in London his efforts met with immediate success. Thanks to Bond's courage and determination he obtained a long-term loan of $2,775,000 on the London market. His single-handed efforts had saved the colony and earned for him a place as one of the great men of New-foundland history.

The lack of negotiable currency was relieved shortly afterwards when the Bank of Nova Scotia became the first Canadian Bank to open a branch in Newfoundland. This brought Canadian money into the colony. The Bank of Montreal and the Merchants Bank of Halifax (now the Royal Bank of Canada), quickly followed. The Newfoundland Savings Bank somehow survived the crash, reopened, and continued in business until after Confederation in 1949. For many years it occupied the old Com-mercial Bank building, which still stands on Duckworth Street, a few doors west of Victoria Street. The Union Bank building was taken over for government offices and is now in use as a law court.

Tooton's Kodak Store has been on the east of Goodridge's passage-way since shortly after World War I. When P. & L. Tessier occupied the site, Mr. Grey, the father of the senior partner in the firm of Grey & Goodland, had his home upstairs here. His rooms were later occupied by Gerald S. Doyle. The building was replaced by Anthony Tooton in the late 1920s. Mr. Tooton had another commission agent as an upstairs tenant. He was Chesley A. Pippy, who was destined to become one of the wealthiest men in Newfoundland.

Next door to Tooton's, Alfred McNamara had his jeweller's shop. The young ladies who worked for Mr. McNamara and other merchants along Water Street performed their duties six days a week for a salary of seven dollars. Many female clerks in St. John's were still earning little more than that at the beginning of World War II. Elmsley & Shaw had one of their grocery stores on the McNamara site during the latter part of the nineteenth century.

The third building east of the passageway was the bakery of J. & G. Lash, the leading caterers of their day. This business was founded in 1842 on the north side of Water Street, two doors east of Adelaide, by Jeffrey Lash, who acquired his knowledge of baking in England. He took over a shop formerly occupied by Mrs. Shears. Later the brothers moved to the site on the south side of the street where they remained for half a century. Ustairs, over their bake shop, they operated the Railway Hotel. The McNamara and Lash buildings are now occupied by Thompson's Jewellery Store.

William D. Morison, commission merchant, express agent, and whole-sale grocer was east of Lash's. Morison had a house in the west end called "Springdale" and the property gave its name to Springdale Street, when residents of the area objected to the original name, Flower Hill Firebreak.

Next to Morison, in the 1880s, was Rutherford's begun as R. & I.S. Rutherford. There was a branch, Rutherford Brothers, at Harbour Grace. In the middle of the nineteenth century Robert Rutherford, who was then located a few doors west of the Market House, was one of the few St. John's merchants prominent enough to issue his own coins. They were so numerous that Rutherford's 1841 penny tokens are still only worth about five dollars each. They bore the symbol of the firm, the golden fleece. On the other hand, Peter McAuslane's penny tokens today bring about two hundred and fifty dollars each.[25] McAuslane who was in business at St. John's from about 1800, advised on his tokens that he "sells all sorts of shop and store goods." According to the Colonial Records McAuslane was given permission in 1804 to build a fireplace in his countinghouse, a rare luxury his clerks must have appreciated.

Next to Rutherford's, in the third and fourth buildings to the west of Beck's Cove, Ayre & Marshall located their business when the old Huie & Reed site to the west became too small. They moved again in 1867. Rutherford's was taken over by Sillars & Cairnes, who traded under the sign of the golden codfish. Following the decease of Cairnes this firm was sold by the terrible-tempered Sillars to an employee named Parnell. When the new owner proved unable to meet the payments Sillars returned and repossessed the business, which he ran with an iron fist. One night he goaded the browbeaten Parnell into murdering him in the basement of the shop. The story is told in Chapter 3 of this volume.

The first five buildings in this area, starting at Beck's Cove and running west, were known as the O'Dwyer Block. As a unit they presented a handsome, if simple, Victorian façade with gothic roofs imported from Wales. The line of the block was ruined in 1916 when the Bank of Nova Scotia tore down the two end buildings in order to erect a new bank building along modified neo-classical lines. As it turned out the new Bank of Nova Scotia, with its corner entrance, was among the more attractive structures on Water Street. It was unfortunate that its erection was at the sacrifice of the O'Dwyer Block. This rather interesting bank headquarters was torn down in 1964 to make way for the present functional, if undistinguished, edifice.

The brothers Richard and John O'Dwyer came to Newfoundland from Ireland. Following the Great Fire of 1846 their firm was one of the ten largest on the island. It occupied all the stores in the newly built O'Dwyer Block and had large mercantile interests as well. Richard O'Dwyer, a member of the Legislative Council in 1861, retired to Liverpool where he died at Dirleton House, Prince's Park, on 16 March 1875, at the age of seventy-three. John carried on the business for a few more years until his death on 28 November 1878. Both brothers are buried at Belvedere. As with most commercial firms in those days, O'Dwyer's unmarried clerks and apprentices lived upstairs on the premises. One of them was to win immortality as a satirist. He was Johnny Burke, who gave us "The Kelligrew's Soiree," and other famous songs.

O'Dwyer's firm was involved in a political scandal in 1895 when a customs' raid produced ten cases of contraband liquor hidden in the basement, containing 330 gallons. Various officials were implicated in the revelations that followed. The next year the Water Street stores were let to sundry firms. Michael Dyer, the clothier, took the corner shop when he began his business in 1896. Another tenant, after the 1892 fire, was Harry Blair of Blackwood & Blair.

BECK'S COVE TO AYRE'S COVE
(See Map 4 - Page 832)

The westward sweep of the Great Fire of 1892 was stopped on the east corner of Beck's Cove, a peculiar, wedge-shaped piece of property occupied by James Bryden. After the fire, Pierce Grace erected the Grace Building on the site. This was later taken over by John Anderson, who was born at Saltcoats, Scotland. Anderson, as M.H.A. for St. John's West, introduced daylight saving, or summer time, to the colony in 1916 just before Britain adopted it, making Newfoundland the first country in the world to have daylight saving time. He was also responsible for building the ranges of houses on Merrymeeting Road. Broadway's great producer, John Muray Anderson, was his son. Harris and Joe Goldstone's London, New York and Paris was started in the Grace Building in April 1917. It moved east to James Baird's property in 1952.

Next to Bryden's was Sharp & Kelly, Berney & Fitzgibbon, a mercantile firm, with a coal wharf at the back, and Jabez Finlay, who later moved east of Clift's Cove. Benjamin Bowring had his shop on the adjoining lot to the east. This firm became Bowring Brothers in 1841 and took over Finlay's. It gradually acquired all the stores as far west as Bryden's.

On 30 January 1963 a million-dollar fire swept through Bowring's collection of old buildings and a modern store was erected on the ruins the following year where signal flags now spell out the name of the firm.

Following the 1892 fire, the Honourable J.D. Ryan, M.H.A. for Ferryland and eventually President of the Legislative Council, had his shop in the building east of Anderson's, which he also owned. After the turn of the century Ryan moved to Lash's bakeshop in the next block. Born at Kedra, Tipperary, Ireland, 6 September 1846, J.D. Ryan started his business in Newfoundland in 1880, three doors west of Ayre's Cove. He soon became a wealthy man, was President of the B.I.S. and received a Papal knighthood. He owned what is still one of the most imposing private residences in St. John's, at 28 Circular Road, named "Kedra" for his birthplace.

Next door to Bowring's, at the sign of the book, Dicks & Co. was located for a time before moving to the present site three doors west of Ayre's Cove more than half a century ago. Now the oldest stationery and bookstore in St. John's, the firm was begun by Robert McIver, a bookbinder for government records. He had a bookroom on the Water Street premises of William Dicks, a sailmaker, a few doors east of McMurdo's Lane. Around 1840 McIver retired and sold his equipment to Dicks's son, Robert, who had learned the bookbinding and printing trade under McIver. Robert's wife added a stationery department in 1846.

For a period before the 1892 fire there was a partner and the firm was

871

known as McKenny & Dicks. The partnership did not survive and Dicks & Co. started in business 22 August 1890. In the reconstruction period of the late 90s it occupied the fourth building east of the lane before moving next to Bowring's. In 1910 printing was added to the business and, in 1913, the press was moved to a large four-storey building, occupied by J. Daymond, at the east corner of Bell and Duckworth Streets. The company had been incorporated the previous year. Early in the 1890s, John Leamon, who married Robert Dicks's daughter, Maude, entered the business and soon assumed control. After Leamon's death the firm passed to D. Rogers and, after his retirement in 1955, to James Austin, who started with the company in 1943 as an accountant and died suddenly in 1976, vacationing in Florida.

Dicks's old location was for a time the Canada Permanent Trust Co., at the west corner of the Pitts Building, an impressive structure now wholly occupied by Ayre's Ltd. James and William Pitts were two of the recipients of Benjamin Bowring's famous grandfather clocks. Born at St. John's, William Pitts conducted a large trade in meat and farm products with the Maritime Provinces of Canada. His son was the Hon. James S. Pitts.

The first cable from Newfoundland was sent by J. & W. Pitts, October 1856, to A. & M. Cameron, Baddeck, Nova Scotia. The father of the two St. John's merchants was an Englishman of considerable means with much property on Bell Island.

Early in the nineteenth century the west corner of Ayre's Cove was occupied by the old firm of McBride & Kerr. The cove was known as McBride's Cove, and the hill opposite as McBride's Hill. Before that the area was called Maddock's Lane after Luke Maddock who lived nearby.

Peter and Robert McBride had come out from Scotland. Little or nothing is known about Kerr. He appears to have died or left the firm early in its history. McBride's had a large building-supplies yard at the back of their stores and the lumber stored here became a huge bonfire in the 1846 disaster.

After the fire the rebuilt corner buildings were taken over by Goodfellow & Co. The Honourable James Goodfellow who was born at Tranent, Scotland, in 1830, came to St. John's in his twenties and died in 1898. The business did not long survive him. Goodfellow's west store, with its agency for the lines and twines of Hounsell & Co., was taken over by the firm of John Barron in 1900. At one time the Anglo Telegraph and Cable office was located in the corner building. The place changed hands several times before becoming the first Newfoundland Branch of the Toronto Dominion Bank. Early in the present century it was occupied by the first St. John's branch of the Merchant's Bank of Halifax, now the Royal Bank of Canada.

AYRE'S COVE TO CLIFT'S-BAIRD'S COVE
(See Map 4 - Page 832)

Charles Robert Ayre, the son of a carpenter, was born at Exeter,

Devon, in 1819. His father died when he was quite young, and the boy, having no means to support himself, set out on his own to make his fortune. In 1832, at the age of thirteen years, he became an apprentice clerk in the Exeter firm of Benjamin Bowring and was shipped out to the St. John's branch of Bowring's jewellery business on board Warren's ship, *Freedom*. In 1844, when he was twenty-five years old, Ayre left Bowring and formed a partnership with John Steer. The two young men opened a store a few doors west of Clift's Cove, nearly opposite the Market House.

This union was dissolved in 1858 when Ayre decided to go in business for himself. He began on what was later the Shirran & Pippy site, at the west corner of what we might identify as Goodridge's Lane on 1 January 1859. In 1862 he formed a new partnership with Alexander Marshall. A sister of Charles Ayre, who was a milliner, came out to join her brother and married Sandy Marshall. With the formation of Ayre & Marshall, the firm moved to a larger premises a few doors west of Beck's Cove.

In 1867 Wilson & Co. vacated a building on the site of Atlantic Place at the east corner of what is now Ayre's Cove. Ayre & Marshall took over this premises and in December of that year their former stores passed to Sillars and Cairns. Ayre & Marshall added the adjoining buildings of George Badcock, and a man named Gilliard, to their corner property until the firm occupied all the block east of the cove, to Prowse's archway separating Philip Hutchings property.

The partnership was dissolved in 1884 with the retirement of Alexander Marshall. Charles Ayre, who had married a Miss Bray, took his sons into the business, became M.H.A. for Burin, and was appointed to the Legislative Council in 1879. He died 13 April 1889.

Charles Pascoe Ayre, who took control of the business when his father died, acquired vacant land west of the Crossroads on Waterford Bridge Road and erected his residence, Burn Brae, in 1890. His descendants lived on the property until 1969. Charles Pascoe married twice. His first wife was a Scottish lady, Diana Stevenson, which accounts for the name Burn Brae. When she died he married an English widow, Carlotta Greene.

The Ayre family achieved an unenviable distinction in Newfoundland history, on 1 July 1916, when four of its sons were killed in the ill-fated July Drive that saw so many young men of Newfoundland slaughtered in one of the great military blunders of World War I.

The first supermarket in St. John's was opened in 1952 by Ayre's on the sourtheast corner of Parade Street. Others followed, and the chain was eventually sold to Dominion Stores. Today Ayre's have stores at five locations in St. John's and others around the Province. In 1972 the first branch was opened in Ontario and in 1973 the firm bought out Max-Max, a chain of Ontario shops.

The company's main retail department store, on Water Street east of Ayre's Cove, was closed in 1972 and the property sold by the Newman

Estate to the Crosbie interests for the development of Atlantic Place, proposed as a twenty-storey high-rise hotel, shop, and office complex. Begun in the spring of 1973 it opened in June, 1976. This left Ayre's with The Pitts Building as the only downtown outlet.

Knowling's was once a great name on Water Street. This drygoods firm had the premises east of Ayre's, as well as the previously discussed West End Stores. The Honourable George Knowling was born at Exeter, England, 15 September 1841 and came to Newfoundland in 1857 as a clerk to his uncle, Philip Hutchings. Knowling left Newfoundland in 1859, but returned to his uncle's business nine years later. On the death of Philip Hutchings in 1886 he took over the Hutchings firm and established G. Knowling.

Appointed to the Legislative Council in 1894, Knowling built himself a Victorian three-storey country residence, "Silverton," on the slope of a hill, on the south side of the Bay Bulls Road, about a quarter of a mile beyond Waterford Bridge. It was torn down in 1975 to make way for the St. John's Arterial Road. With his death the business collapsed and the downtown store was annexed by Ayre's.

In earlier times the east corner of Atlantic Place was the location of the St. John's Library Society which eventually gave way to the Athenaeum. It is difficult to ascertain when or where the first library opened in St. John's because the newspapers for the first three years of the *Royal Gazette*, 1807 to 1809, are missing. A notice for 15 November 1810, under the heading LIBRARY, states: "The subscribers to the St. John's Library are requested to send in books in their possession." Since there is no news of its founding in any of the 1810 papers it must have been before that year. It is impossible to establish the location.

There is a mention of the reading room in Lt. Edward Chappell's book, written after visiting St. John's, on board H.M.S. *Rosamund,* in 1813. Chappell writes:

> There is a reading room in St. John's to which any subscriber may introduce the non-resident officers of the army or navy, who from thenceforth are considered as honorary members of the Society. The whole of English Daily Papers, the St. John's Gazette, and most of the British Monthly publications are here to be met with.

In 1820 the town was being served by a library on the premises of J. Slater. On April 20, that year, a meeting was called with the intention of organizing a St. John's Library Society "to be formed for the purpose of forming a library." Newman Hoyles was called to the chair and others on the founding committee were D. H. M'Calman, Benjamin Bowring, and William Carson. On 23 November 1820 a meeting was called to elect a librarian. The job went to Edward B. Moore. The library opened on the south side of Water Street on the site of the east half of Atlantic Place.

Dr. Carson was Chairman in 1821, and at the annual meeting of the St. John's Library Society, held in the Navy and Commercial Hotel on January 21, he relinquished his post to Thomas Brooking while Francis Forbes, the Chief Justice who according to Prowse, "won golden opinions from all classes,"[26] was re-elected president. In 1831, as we have already seen, Thomas Brooking, along with William Thomas and John Bland, was requesting permission to erect a billiards and reading room on the west side of Hill o' Chips for the use of members.

There were soon a number of privately owned rental libraries. Simon Solomon, the Postmaster, had one in a pub he operated, and in 1845 there was one at J. Rendell's on Water Street and another in McMurdo's chemist shop.

By 1842 the St. John's Reading Room and Library, as it was then called, had 1,080 volumes and was contemplating a museum. It moved to an upstairs location in Merchant's Block, just east of McMurdo's Lane. Here, the first Newfoundland museum was begun. In 1855 a start was made on a proposed Athenaeum, which opened 23 March 1861 in a converted building on Water Street, opposite the foot of McMurdo's Lane (possibly on the old library site). The Athenaeum housed a reading room and library, and in 1861 the full-time post of Librarian was advertised at eighty pounds per year (about four hundred dollars).

The foundation stone for an new Athenaeum building was laid by Sir Hugh Hoyles, 4 November 1875, on Duckworth Street, directly opposite the foot of Cathedral Street. It was completed and opened in 1877, at a cost of fifty-eight thousand dollars. This handsome structure included a concert hall in which concerts, lectures, and public meetings took place. The reading room and library were rented by the Athenaeum Literary Institute. The place was gutted in the Great Fire of 1892 and eventually torn down. Another library, gutted in the same fire, was that of the Academia at the foot of Prescott Street.

The Gosling Memorial Library was officially opened on the site of the Athenaeum, 9 January 1936, by Governor Anderson. It was called Gosling Memorial, because Armine Nutting, the widow of William Gilbert Gosling, who had been an author, director of Harvey & Co. Ltd., and mayor of St. John's, donated her husband's library as the nucleus of a new library. Armine Gosling's sister, Mary Adelaide Nutting, who once taught music in St. John's, was the pioneer of modern nursing in the United States.

With the opening of the Arts & Culture Centre, the days of the old Gosling Library were numbered. Its quarters had become cramped and overcrowded. On 16 January 1969 a modern outlet, which became known as the Hunter and Newfoundland Reference Library, named for Dr. Alfred Hunter—a beloved Memorial University professor and long-time member of the Public Libraries Board—was opened by Premier Smallwood in the Arts & Culture Centre complex. The Gosling moved to the new City Hall on New Gower Street. By 1972 there were four public libraries in St.

John's and seventy-five in other Newfoundland communities.

The east corner building on the Atlantic Place site was occupied by Milley's ladies' hat shop, which supplied new hats for spring or fall, "priced to suit the thrifty shopper," until February 1973 when it closed its doors to make room for the modern complex. Founded by the Honourable Samuel Milley, the store was begun in 1890 further east on Water Street, where it remained until it was burned out in 1892. In 1893 Milley went into partnership with McIntosh on the east corner of McMurdo's Lane. In 1897 the partnership was dissolved and he moved across the street to the site where the firm stayed for nearly seventy years.

Baine, Johnston was at one time located on each side of Studdy's Lane which ran down to the waterfront between Atlantic Place and the former Canadian Bank of Commerce building, opposite McMurdo's Lane. The Studdys were connected with the famous Holdsworth and Brooking families. Their business was operated by John Studdy, M.H.A. for Fortune Bay, and Financial Secretary in 1889-93. He died in London in 1908.

The Canadian Bank of Commerce, probably the most architecturally pleasing older building on Water Street, opened on part of the old Baine, Johnston property, 28 February 1921. The bank moved into Atlantic Place in June, 1976. Next door to it the first dime store in St. John's was begun by John and Francis Kelly in 1931, and was popularly known as the "Five and Ten." The building later became a part of the Arcade chain of stores.

The Kelly store was formerly occupied as a grocery by William Ellis who started in business in 1890. In the eighteenth century the Ellis family had a large estate in St. John's which, according to Prowse, Ann Ellis acquired in a curious way. Her brother died leaving it to a woman who was not his wife. Around 1772 Ann, who was probably an unmarried daughter of the Ann Ellis involved in a French spy case at Fort William around 1700, obtained an opinion in her favour from Dunning, a celebrated English lawyer. By the simple method of showing this *ex parte* opinion to Governor Shuldham she obtained the grant of the estate.

Next to the Five and Ten Cent Store was I. F. Perlin. This firm should have been I. & F. Perlin, but a sign painter's mistake was left uncorrected. Israel and Frank Perlin started in business at Bay du Nord, Fortune Bay, in 1891. They were born in eastern Russia, near the Polish frontier, where their father was a revered Talmudic scholar, who was frequently called upon by the people of the region to settle legal problems. It is said legal disputants in the area preferred to have Mr. Perlin settle their arguments rather than the law courts of the Czar. When Israel was sixteen or seventeen years of age he emigrated to New York where somebody told him about the quiet life of Newfoundland. Anxious to get away from the turmoil of the cities of the world, he and his brother reached the island from the United States in 1891. Two years later, in August 1893, they opened a wholesale and retail firm on Water Street, gradually converting entirely to the wholesale trade.

Israel Perlin died in 1945 at the age of seventy-five years. He is remembered for having founded the Jewish community at St. John's. The first meetings of the congregation were held in the store of I. F. Perlin & Co., on Water Street, three doors east of Studdy's Lane. The first synogogue was in a building on the south side of Henry Street, a few doors west of Bell Street, where Mr. Perlin had operated a clothing factory. He was followed in the wholesale business by his sons Albert, William, and Edward. Albert Perlin has been Associate Editor of the *Daily News* since 1934. His son, John Perlin, was first Director of the Provincial Arts & Culture Centre at St. John's.

Until the present decade the firm of W.H. Ewing & Son operated a retail shop east of Perlin's. William Ewing was born 5 March 1860, at Forteau, Labrador, to a father from Seldom and a mother who was an Englishwoman. In his twenties he met and married Sarah Reid of Hare Bay. The couple moved to St. John's and had nine children.

After spending much of his early life as a shoemaker William took up taxidermy as a hobby. Demands for his services were such that in 1896 he started his own business turning out high-quality stuffed birds, caribou heads, rugs, coachman's caps and gloves. In 1906 his son, James Reid Ewing, born 17 May 1887, began the purchase of raw furs and did such outstanding work in the manufacture of fur coats, in a factory on the southwest corner of Pleasant Street at Springdale Street, that it soon became a mark of elegance and good taste to own a Ewing fur. It was said James Ewing "was an amazing craftsman who transferred a seal into a thing of beauty."

The firm achieved international recognition when it mounted two caribou heads for the Duke of Cornwall and York (later King George v). In 1951 it made a fur otter cape for presentation to Princess (later Queen) Elizabeth by the Government of Newfoundland on her visit to the province.

William Ewing died 11 February 1951. One newspaper declared: "St. John's has lost one of its most respected and esteemed citizens." Another added that "as a skilled craftsman, and as a furrier and taxidermist, he had few equals in Newfoundland." His son James, besides being an ingenious artisan in furs, was a noted artist and his paintings of Newfoundland birds were published in the first volumes of the *Book of Newfoundland*. He donated the originals to Memorial University in 1970. The firm of W.H. Ewing & Son folded in 1971.

William Frew, a bearded Scot, born at Saltcoats, Ayreshire, in 1843, had his business three doors west of Clift's-Baird's Cove. He came to St. John's in 1860 to work for Baird Brothers. Frew was afterwards in the employ of James Baird until 1881, when he opened his own drygoods firm. After the Great Fire he operated from a shed he had erected at the foot of

Market House Hill until his new store, in the Baird Building, was made ready. East of Frew was a hotel known as Globe House.

The lot on the west corner of Clift's-Baird's Cove was occupied in 1853 by Baird Brothers. This stone building jutted twelve or fifteen feet out into Water Street from the line of buildings on the east side of the Cove. James Baird was born at Saltcoats, Ayrshire, Scotland, 30 November 1828. He came to Newfoundland in 1844 to work for McBride & Kerr. In 1853 he entered partnership with his brother David and they formed Baird Brothers, under the sign of the Beehive. This lasted until 1872 when James went into business for himself on or near the Perlin site. In 1894 he took over the premises of Thorburn & Tessier, on the east side of the Cove.

The firm became Baird, Gordon & Company in 1898, when James Baird took his nephew, James Gordon, as a partner. Gordon died in 1908, and the following year, James Baird became a limited liability company. It claimed to be "The busiest store on the city's busiest thoroughfare, serving all the people—all the time and serving them well." Various Baird premises were destroyed by fire in 1846, 1892, and 1908. James Baird was appointed to the Legislative Council in 1908. He died 30 May 1915. Following World War II the business went into a decline and was finally liquidated in 1950. The stores were taken over by the London, New York, and Paris Association of Harris and Joe Goldstone.

After the 1892 destruction of Baird Brothers' old premises the two upstairs floors of the new building on the west side of the cove, were occupied by the St. John's City Club. The Light & Power Co. had its offices downstairs. Next door, where John Steer and Charles Ayre started their drygoods and millinery business, T. A. MacNab established an agency in 1907. West of MacNab's, Parker & Monroe took over the site once occupied by Elmsley & Thompson, formerly Elmsley & Shaw's tea and coffee warehouse. James Stott, the well-known grocer, worked for Elmsley & Thompson, as did Thomas Coady, the man who was a partner with Tom O'Neill in building the Majestic Theatre.

In its day, the City Club was to St. John's businessmen what the Lamb's was to New York theatre folk. To gain membership one had to pass a blackball test, and one blackball (actually a bean) slipped into the pot by some anonymous enemy who was a member was enough to cause a rejection. Once in, you could dine, drink, doze, read, and play cards or billiards. With the end of World War II and the emergence of such service clubs as Lions, Elks, and Kiwanis, the City Club began to decline in membership. Even abolition of the blackball system didn't help, and by the late 1960s the handwriting was on the wall. The club expired in 1972 when it was closed and the rooms converted into a steakhouse and bar. In 1974 it became Sergio's, St. John's first Italian restaurant.

Down the west side of the cove the auction house of Clift, Wood & Co. occupied the wharf area. In earlier times this cove was the Government Wharf. The firm of Clift, Wood & Co. consisted of James and Thomas Clift and James Wood. They were commission merchants. The Great Fire of 1817 was halted on the east side of this cove on November 7 after burning its way west from King's Beach, where the War Memorial stands. It was on Clift's side of the cove that the second half of the fire was finally extinguished, two weeks later, after destroying everything from Huie & Reed's premises, in the west at Bishop's Cove, to Clift's Cove.

On the east side of the cove James Baird gradually extended his holdings from the wharves of Thorburn & Tessier, up to Water Street, where he finally took over the corner building of W. H. Mare & Sons. The second building east of the corner had been occupied by Jabez Finlay, formerly Finlay, Fraser & Co. The firm disappeared when J. M. Finlay died suddenly, on a visit to Derbyshire, England, in Janary 1883.

CLIFT'S-BAIRD'S COVE TO HUNTER'S COVE
(See Map 3 - Page 828)

Walter Grieve had the double stores in the third building east of Clift's Cove. He came to Newfoundland from Scotland around 1820 and went to work with Baine, Johnston & Co. He severed his connection with that firm in the early seventies and formed Walter Grieve & Co. He later entered a partnership with the firm of Sir Robert Thorburn. In 1858 Grieve created some excitement when he was fined in court, at the insistence of the Spanish Consul, for speaking disrespectfully of the Queen of Spain.

Grieve made sizable contributions to the building of both the Roman Catholic and Church of England cathedrals. He is said to have made a free gift to Bishop Fleming of all the ropes and scaffolding used in erecting the Basilica. His home was "Carpasia" on Carpasian Road. Originally a country residence of Dr. Fleming, whose co-adjuster title was Bishop of Carpasia in Partibus, the estate was either given or sold to Grieve by the Bishop for a nominal sum. When he retired to Scotland, 11 December 1879, Walter Grieve sold "Carpasia" to John Duder. Gerald S. Doyle later built a fashionable residence on the grounds, and the Doyle dwelling is now a House of Prayer for the Presentation Sisters.

On 6 January 1882 one of Grieve's vessels, the S.S. *Lion* left St. John's for Trinity. Among the passengers was a Church of England clergyman, the Reverend C.H. Foster, and his bride. The ship appears to have been lost near Baccalieu Tickle, off Bay de Verde. The tragedy remains a great mystery, for the night was lit by a beautiful full moon and the sea was calm. The body of one woman passenger, Mrs. Cross of Trinity, was picked up by fishermen the next day. No trace of the others, or the ship, was ever found. Grieve died at Greenock, Scotland, 16 March 1887. After the 1892 fire James Baird and Samuel Garland occupied these sites.

East of Walter Grieve's was the shop of George Gear who sold cooking, parlour, and church stoves, as well as a large assortment of iron things and tinware. He once had a west end branch at 349 Water Street, near Bishop's Cove. Next, Mathias Morey dealt in tea, coffee, and liquors. He was afterwards a partner in the firm of (J.D.) Ryan & Morey. Upstairs, over Morey's, in 1852, Samuel Knight opened a hotel which he called Knight's Home. When he sold out to George Crosbie, father of Sir John, the name became the Central Hotel. After being burned out in the 1892 fire, Crosbie erected the present Welcome Hotel on Duckworth Street.

John Lindberg, watchmaker, optician and jeweller, was in the building adjoining the Central Hotel. The first telephone exchange in St. John's was opened in a room over Lindberg's store. J. Lindberg, Sr., lived at "Rosamond Cottage" on Mt. Scio Road, near the present Pippy Park administration building, southwest of the elbow on the hill. This wooden structure was turreted and known to the people of the town as Lindberg Castle. The family entered the beer business with a large brewery on Signal Hill Road, where St. Joseph's School now stands. At the back of the brewery was the former Castle Rennie, the academy school where John Valentine Nugent was in charge of the scholars. All these buildings were destroyed in the 1982 fire. Castle Rennie is said to have been rebuilt inside the shell by old John Lindberg. After his death it became a convent for the Sisters of Mercy who taught in the new school erected where the Lindbergs, father and son, had brewed Klondike and Jubilee beer. Rosamund Cottage was let in 1896 and eventually fell into ruin. Lindberg had another jewellery store, just east of Prescott Street, operated with a partner and called Lindberg & Lamb.

Next to Lindberg's, W. R. Firth, the man who was later to erect the Arcade Buildings in the west end, had a drygoods shop under the sign of the Newfoundland dog. His motto was "He barks but he won't bite." As has been noted, Firth began with Baird Brothers and later went into business on his own. J. Forbes Chisholm had a bookstore next to Firth's before moving to Beck's Cove.

Doubtlessly the most impressive structure on Water Street, between the 1846 and 1892 fires, was the tall building David Sclater erected in the middle of the block, between Clift's and Hunter's Coves. No other downtown façade could rival its architectural pretensions, not even the General Post Office. An ornate, Grecian style building, complete with pilasters, balcony, and urns, it stood out majestically against it plain, gable-roofed neighbours. Born in Saltcoats, Ayrshire, Scotland, 14 May 1814, David Sclater began his career as a draper. He came to St. John's as manager for Robert Alsop & Co. when he was twenty-two years of age. In three years he was manager for William Thomas. In 1857, he formed David Sclater & Co. and opened a shop on the old Thomas Property with William Thomas as partner. He was one of the seven founders of the Presbyterian Church in Newfoundland and helped organize the Athenaeum. On 5 August 1894 he died at the age of eighty years.

After the 1892 fire, the Thomas-Sclater site was covered by the Delgado Building. Andrew Delgado was born at Seville, Spain, in 1848. As a young man he found his way to Newfoundland where he entered business at Tilt Cove. When the mines were sold in 1880 he came to St. John's and was associated with Lazo & Co. until the late eighties, when he started a fruit store on Water Street, west of Prince's Street. He built Waterford Hall, on the east corner of Waterford Bridge Road and Waterford Lane, once the home of Major Peter Cashin, and now used as a juvenile training home. Following the 1892 fire he erected the Delgado Building and it housed Delgado's Candy and Fruit Emporium. The tea which was sold from three or four large bins in the store ranged in price from moderate to expensive. Many society matrons of the day insisted on drinking nothing but Delgado's best blend. What they did not know was that he filled all the bins from the same tea chest. For a number of years the family, consisting of six daughters and one son, lived upstairs over the Emporium. The charming old gentleman died 15 March 1932 at the age of eighty-four. The building became the British Import Company.

East of the lane which separates the Delgado Building from Harris & Hiscock (a firm incorporated in 1928), LeMessuriers once had an office over a shop operated by Thomas the barber. In the 1880s Horwood's Bakery was next to the barber shop. Thomas Horwood manufactured fancy baked goods and had what was certainly one of the first soda fountains in St. John's. The 1892 fire ended the enterprise. His son became Sir William Horwood, Chief Justice of the Supreme Court of Newfoundland, knighted in 1904. Sir William and his wife, Julia Hutchinson, lived at 12 Church Hill.

John Eden's grocery and provisions store adjoined Horwood's Bakery. After the 1893 holocaust, Edens moved to the southeast corner of Duckworth and Prescott Streets. His Water Street site was built on by J. H. Martin whose firm afterwards became the Martin-Royal Stores. Martin had worked as a wharfinger and general outside man with Job's, while his wife ran a crockeryware shop that was taken over by S. O. Steele in 1899. She made a lot of money, which enabled Martin to purchase Job's hardware store in the third building west of Hunter's Cove. He then brought out two nephews from England, William and Frank Martin, and they took charge of the business. After the Great Fire, Martin Brothers moved three or four doors west of the old site, and erected a new store almost opposite Telegram Lane. William died and, after a few years, Frank Martin sold out to the Royal Stores. He returned to England where he passed away soon afterwards.

John O'Mara, Jr., had drugstores at several locations along Water Street at various times. Just before the 1892 fire his chemist's shop was east of Horwood's Bakery. His father, John, Sr., came to Newfoundland from Waterford, Ireland, in the 1820s. In 1830 he married a daughter of Michael Allan, owner of "Allandale," and built a cottage for himself and his wife on a piece of land given him by his father-in-law. The fireplace and other furnishings for the cottage were brought out from Ireland by

O'Mara, on board one of his own vessels. The estate, which is at 70 Circular Road, eventually passed into the hands of the Murray family. The original cottage was extended into the present rambling house called "Sunnyside."

John, Jr., started his first drugstore on Water Street in 1874. It was located opposite St. John's Lane, very near his father's mercantile premises. Leo, a grandson of the founding father, opened a drugstore later known as O'Mara-Martin, on the southeast corner of Rawlins' Cross. A great-grandson is a druggist with this firm. Peter O'Mara, a cousin of Leo, started a drug business which is still operated by his son, on Water Street, at the east corner of Brennan's Lane. Peter's father, David, was a magistrate on the Southern Shore.

The property adjoining O'Mara's, two doors east of Horwood's Bakery, was formerly occupied by the Barnes family as a house and shop. J.B. Barnes & Co., at 147 Water Street, was founded by Richard Barnes who came from Waterford, Ireland, in 1780, and died in 1804. His only daughter married a Branscombe. His son, Richard, was the founder of the Native's Society and, as M.H.A. for Trinity, introduced the first Bill for the Encouragement of Education in Newfoundland in 1843. Richard, Jr., died in 1846. The firm went insolvent in 1860. The building burned down and was replaced by a single-storey structure. Perhaps the fire, and insufficient insurance, delivered the coup-de-grace. The O'Mara-Barnes lots became the site of the Board of Trade Building in the reconstruction after 1892.

The St. John's Board of Trade was organized in 1852 as the Chamber of Commerce. All records of its early years were burned in the Great Fire, which seems to have been fatal to the organization as well. In 1909, at the instigation of Sir Edward Morris, it was revived, and the present Board of Trade struggled into being. Ever since, it has played a leading role in the civic, marine, and commercial life of Newfoundland. There was a move in the 1960s to revert to the title "Chamber of Commerce" but the suggestion was outvoted. The building stands on or near the traditional site of the tavern from which, in 1786, the future King William IV of England is said to have rushed into the Lower Path and physically attacked Bishop O'Donel. In the seventeenth century the area east of here, at the foot of Prescott Street, was known as Bennett's Plantation. A Colonel Bennett is mentioned in Treworgie's instructions for handling the affairs of Newfoundland on 1 July 1653. He was, in all likelihood, the original plantation owner. By 1712 William Bennett was deceased and a tenant, Mrs. James Benger, was to pay ten pounds per annum to his heir, Tomson Reeve.[27] Madam Benger figured prominently in the Jackson-Lloyd affair at Fort William in 1705 (Volume 1, page 86).

Next to the Barnes property, in the Victorian era, Edward Smith had a drygoods and grocery establishment. An archway, separating him from the grocery shop of W.P. Walsh, led to Job's western wharf. The buildings from Walsh's to the corner of Hunter's Cove were owned by Job's. As stated, J.H. Martin rented one of these as a hardware store. East of him were two residences and offices, and on the corner Job's had their retail outlet. The story of the great firm of Job Brothers is told in Chapter 9.

After 1892 the whole of the block east of the Board of Trade Building to Hunter's Cove was occupied by the Macpherson's and Job's department store, the Royal Stores. Much of the site is today covered by the Royal Trust Building.

The first Macpherson to come to Newfoundland from Scotland settled at Port de Grave where he is buried. The family later moved to St. John's where Campbell Macpherson was born, 31 January 1851. His father had a small business as a general merchant, and the young man intended entering one of the professions. However, the death of his father changed his plans and he became a businessman. His enterprise resulted in the development of a flourishing drygoods establishment. He married Emma Duder and their son Cluny, who was to distinguish himself as a medical doctor, was born on 18 March 1879. Another son, Harold, is credited with saving the Newfoundland dog, almost from extinction, by breeding the animals at Westerland, on Westerland Road, when there were few pure-breds left in the world. A son of Dr. Cluny, another Campbell, who died in July 1973, became Lieutenant-Governor of Newfoundland.

In 1895 an agreement was consummated between Campbell Macpherson, Archibald Macpherson, and William Carson Job to combine the Macpherson and Job retail businesses. As a result of the merger, the Royal Stores came into being on the west corner of Hunter's Cove. The six adjoining buildings, which were erected on Job's pre-fire site, made the new company the largest retail firm on Water Street. By 1899 the Royal Stores Clothing Factory was producing three hundred suits a week. A furniture store was built on the southwest corner of Duckworth and Prescott Streets in 1905, and the following year Riverside Woolen Mills opened at Mackinson's in Conception Bay. In 1911 branch stores were opened at Grand Falls and Millertown. Another was added at Buchans.

Late in 1916 the Royal Stores acquired the Martin Hardware Company and it became the Martin-Royal Stores. In 1922 a concrete extension was added to the west side of the furniture store and clothing factory on Duckworth Street. The future Lieutenant-Governor joined the firm, as a member of the Board of Directors, in 1929.

Campbell Macpherson, Sr., died at Cannes, France, 24 April 1908. On his passing his brother, Archibald, was elected President of the Royal Stores. He died in 1921 and Harold, the son of the founder, became President. In the 1960s the Water Street buildings were sold and torn down, and the Royal Trust structure, the first downtown highrise, was erected on the site. The Royal Stores were relocated in Avalon Mall.

After Bennett's time, in the 1700s, the property around Hunter's Cove was in the hands of the Keen family. Near the turn of the century it became the business premises of Parker & Knight. In 1808 Stephen Knight retired and Parker entered into a partnership with his waterfront neighbour, Bulley & Job, and Parker, Bulley, Job & Co. was formed. This story is told in the next chapter. Following the fires of 1817 to 1820 the governor ordered the cove widened as a firebreak. At the time, Archibald Chambers was renting the corner building.

In the 1700s the property adjoining Keen's Wharf to the east was known as the Clapp Estate. In 1712 there was a Widow Clapp living in Sir William Hopkins's house at Ferryland.[28] She is thought to have acquired possession of the property in some manner and passed the plantation eventually to Peter Weston, a Justice of the Peace at Ferryland and an ancestor of Sir Frederick Carter. Before the 1846 fire, a Gilbert Clapp had a store on the site of O'Mara's drugstore, west of J.B. Barnes. It is not known if he was related to the former estate owners.

HUNTER'S COVE TO HARVEY'S LANE
(See Map 3 - Page 828 and Map 2 - Page 824)

Some historians believe the name Hudson's Cove, as Hunter's Cove was earlier called, commemorates two visits to St. John's by the explorer Henry Hudson. The first was on his voyage to North America in 1607-08. The second took place in 1610, soon after exploring the great river in New York which bears his name. After wintering in James Bay in 1611 mutineers took over Hudson's ships *Discovery* in which he was attempting to find the Northwest Passage. With his son, and six loyal crewman, he was set adrift in a small boat and never heard of again. While in St. John's Henry Hudson is said to have replenished his water supplies from a brook that ran down what is now Prescott Street from the marsh on the Barrens (Military Road).

Widow Bevil's Bridge over the Prescott Street River, linked the Clapp and Keen plantations, in the 1770s. Between the widow's bridge and the Government Wharf (Clift's-Baird's Cove) were the homes of such well-known persons as Richard Barnes, William Thomas, John Noble, Dr. Thomas Dodd, and Dr. King Brown. East of the bridge Benjamin Jenkins, Olive Gaden, John Livingston, and Doctor Rowe had their houses.[29]

Soon after 1800 the Clapp estate was taken over by Hunter & Co. In 1814 this firm wrote the governor of Newfoundland for permission to export flour, stating: "that the market is now so glutted that it is impossible to sell it, and that if not allowed to send it away it will be spoiled." Hunter's were among the earliest adventurers in the Labrador trade. Their premises was destroyed in the 1846 fire and rebuilt, but the company had been dealt a death blow. In June 1861 it was sold by private bargain to Parker & Knight. In the early part of the present century the site was occupied by Hearn & Co., a gorcery concern.

Before 1892 the building on the eastern corner of Hunter's Cove was John D. Martin's boot and shoe store. There is an excellent photograph of this firm showing what appears to be a privy on the cove side of the shop. Next to Martin was George E. Barnes, and then William R. Parnell & Co.

This premises was followed by an archway leading to John Fox & Sons wharf. In mid-century John Tarehin (sic) had a grocer's shop east of Fox's arch, which later was Richard Harvey's drygoods store.

With few exceptions most of the enterprises from here to Maggoty Cove were mercantile firms and their story is told in some detail in the following chapter. The building which was erected on the eastern corner of Hunter's Cove, after the 1892 fire, was torn down in the late 1960s to widen the cove as an access street to and from Harbour Drive. At the time of its demolition it was occupied by Charles R. Bell, whose parents had operated the Crosbie Hotel on Duckworth Street. His mother was a daughter of George Crosbie and sister of Sir John. Charles R. began in business in 1933, with two employees, in a small place on Duckworth Street, near the old City Hall. The business was incorporated in 1936 and moved to Water Street. At the time Bell vacated that premises and moved to Kenmount Road in 1966 he had over fifty employees.

When Bell's was torn down the Marshall Building next door became the corner. This structure was erected after 1891 by the sons of Alexander Marshall on the site where he carried on business after his partnership with Charles Ayre was dissolved. During the 1960s the ground floor of the Marshall Building was occupied by the East End Post Office. For many years prior to that the Post Office had been in the Stott Building, the next structure east of Marshall's.

James Stott, born in Fyvie, Aberdeenshire, Scotland, on 1 May 1845, came to St. John's at the age of fifteen years to work for Elmsley & Shaw. He went from there to James Baird and, in 1877, commenced a grocery business on his own. He married a daughter of Thomas McMurdo, the druggist. A brother, David, also settled in St. John's, and became the Superintendent of Telegraphs in 1892.

Stott lost heavily in the Great Fire of 1892 but he was one of the first merchants to reconstruct. The Stott Building, still standing on Water Street, was the result. During the 1930s and '40s, until a few years after Confederation, the Department of Education was on the second floor. It eventually moved into some abandoned World War II military structures off Plymouth Road, behind Hotel Newfoundland. Before Stott moved to the site opposite Prescott Street the old firm of Rankin & McMillan occupied three stores on the property, then known as Hunter & Co's. range. This partnership was dissolved long before the 1892 fire and Rankin moved west on Water Street and went into business for himself. He gave his name to Rankin's Corner.

Part of the Rankin & McMillan holdings passed into the possession of a man named James Baird. In 1932 he erected a concrete building on the lot which had been left vacant since the Great Fire. The property next door still has not been built upon after nearly a century. Baird, a grandson of the Honourable James Baird, began in business for himself in 1915, on the corner of Water Street east of the War Memorial.

Javelin House, directly opposite St. John's Lane, is an architecturally impressive building erected to house Commercial Cables. It was taken over in recent years as the Newfoundland headquarters for Canadian Javelin. John O'Mara at one time had his business on the site. Between the 1846 and 1892 fires much of the property was also occupied by James Gleeson's Porto Bello House, a large shop with an exceedingly steep gable roof that sloped towards the street. Patrick Gleeson had come from Ireland in 1803 and settled at Placentia, whence he moved to St. John's where he opened a forge on the west side of Prince's Street. This was later transferred to a more convenient site on the west side of Holloway Street, halfway up the hill leading to Duckworth Street. His son James opened the Porto Bello House and for many years it did the largest volume of hardware trade in St. John's. We are told that it was a leading commercial establishment for eighty years. In 1891, through some oversight, the Gleeson family let the firm's fire policies lapse, and a hundred thousand dollars was lost in the blaze that destroyed the city the following year.

Patrick Gleeson tried to recoup his fortune by opening a fruit store on the west corner of Holloway Street, just below the place where his grandfather's forge was located. He failed, and died, leaving two daughters to settle his debts. One of them, married to a Greene, inherited the Water Street building, which was sold to Mrs. Ellen Stewart, who opened a bakery shop and tearooms on the premises. The other daughter, married to a Parker, inherited a useless bog in the Torbay Road area, known as Gleeson's Marsh. In 1973 it was reported that the St. John's Housing Corporation was offering her heirs in the vicinity of a half-million dollars for the marsh which was part of the next phase in the suburban development of eastern St. John's. James Greene, ex-M.H.A. and former leader of the opposition in the Newfoundland Legislature, is a grandson of the second Patrick Gleeson. Jay Parker, head of the firm of Parker & Monroe and former president of the Board of Trade, is another.

Opposite Holloway Street a relative of Patrick Nowlan had a shop. During the 1861 Hogsett-Furey election riots, a mob broke all the windows in the building, looted the store, and scattered the furnishings about Water Street. Tarehin & Noble, a firm of grocers, was in the locality when the place was gutted by fire in 1890, and the Honourable Samuel Milley took over the site. Two years later, in the 1892 disaster, Milley was himself burned out. As we have seen he built a new shop opposite McMurdo's Lane.

Early in the nineteenth century the Honourable Laurence O'Brien conducted a great mercantile business in this area, and had his home on the premises. O'Brien had come to Newfoundland from Ireland in 1793. Beginning as a very poor cooper's apprentice, he rose to a position of wealth and political importance in the colony. From 1855 until his death on 28 June 1870 he was President of the Legislative Council and a man responsible for the development of many of the island's roads. When the exodus of merchants began from their Water Street homes to fashionable estates in the suburbs, O'Brien took over Dr. William Carson's "Billies," on the banks of Rennie's River, and renamed it "Rostellan." The house still stands at the top of Rostellan Street, although its external appearance has been drastically altered.

Adjoining O'Brien's Water Street property were the stores and wharves of the Honourable James Tobin, another Irish lad who made his fortune after settling in Newfoundland from Dublin. Tobin's house and stores were leased from the old James Brine Estate. He later moved his residence to Rawlins' Cross where he built his own mansion, "Monkstown."

HARVEY'S LANE TO WATER ST. EAST
(See Map 1 - Page 823)

Admiral Richard Edwards was appointed Governor of Newfoundland in 1779. When he arrived in the colony that year he is said to have had with him on board his ship two of his daughters. One of the Admiral's daughters, an accomplished artist, is credited with having drawn a sketch identified as "St. John's - 1770," but which must be 1779 or 1780 since Miss Edwards did not arrive in Newfoundland until 1779. The work is discussed and reproduced elsewhere in this volume.

Our interest in the sketch derives not only from the fact that it depicts King's Beach and the famous Ship Tavern but in that it also shows the first Customs House on shore next to the Ordnance shed. It was located in Gill's Cove and it is here at the property of old Michael Gill the story of Water Street ends. The remaining blocks are dealt with in the next chapter.

The life of a customs official in Newfoundland in the old days was obviously not a happy one according to Charles Carmer who wrote to Governor Gower 20 August 1804: "The Custom House in this island has always been a great sore, and provoked hatred. It drew upon me at once extraordinary odium . . . ."[31] Carmen goes on to relate how, when he went to Labrador in 1789 to establish a post, even "the creatures of prey" fell upon him and nearly destroyed him.

The Great Fire of 1846 ravaged the early wharves and premises of O'Brien, Tobin and other famous merchants of the past. A new Customs House was erected on the site of the War Memorial and that was gutted in 1892. The only views of this area of Water Street known to exist are a drawing by William Gosse around 1837, which was published in Volume 1, Page 7 and a photograph of the Customs House by S.H. Parsons around 1885 which appears in this volume.

The year 1969 saw Water Street closed to traffic, from the Court House to Beck's Cove, and turned into a shopping mall with ornamental trees and pots of colourful flowers spread about the sidewalks and pavement to lure shoppers from the suburban malls that were drawing the customers. Its success was a matter of opinion. Some businessmen praised it as a great success while others condemned the venture as hopeless failure. Its success was marred by the fact that a passageway had to be left open for fire trucks, ambulances, and the delivery of goods to stores on the north side of the street which could not be reached in any other way.

The removal of the tangled web of overhead electric wires that went underground in the late fall of 1967 certainly helped give the oldest business street used by the white man in North America a much needed face lift. When John Smith surveyed the coast of New England in 1614 he reported there were no settlements, only Indian villages. By then the Lower Path along the St. John's waterfront was already a busy centre of trade and commerce visited yearly by thousands of merchants, shipowners, sailors and fishermen from many lands.

The first permanent settler in Newfoundland of whom there is any evidence would appear to be a resident of Bristol's Hope, William Wells. Captain Henry Thomey, a veteran seal killer at the turn-of-the-century, said that while he and his father were digging a foundation for their house at Bristol's Hope he found an old stone cellar containing a lot of axes and a hammer on which had been inscribed "Wm. Wells Bristol 1578."[32] Since St. John's is generally acknowledged to be the first place settled in Newfoundland we can be quite sure its beach was engaged in commerce when William Wells of Bristol was building his stone cellar in Conception Bay sometime after 1578.

9

Their Name is on Your Waters

The Narrows as seen from Maggoty Cove at the foot of Temperance Street by Oldfield in 1831. From the stages on the waterfront at the left, fish flakes climb the shore of the Battery. Fort Amherst, to the right of the Narrows, is flying a flag. (Courtesy St. John's City Hall.)

St. John's as it looked to Oldfield from the grounds of Castle Rennie on Signal Hill in 1831. On the left a soldier on horseback rides up Signal Hill Road. Fort Townshend is on the horizon. (Courtesy St. John's City Hall.)

Women are seen spreading salted codfish to dry on the flakes at St. John's in this view of the Battery sketched by an officer on the fish commission steamer *Albatross* late in the nineteenth century. As usual in such pictures the Basilica towers dominate the skyline. (Courtesy Public Archives of Canada.)

893

Ships from Blacksod Bay, Galway, docked every week at Sir Ambrose Shea's wharf here decorated with a bough arch to welcome H.R.H. The Prince of Wales (later Edward VII) seen standing in the carriage while the gentlemen behind him give three rousing cheers for the heir to the throne. (Courtesy Newfoundland Provincial Archives.)

Samuel Bulley, the pioneer senior partner of Bulley & Job for many years, was born in 1739
and died in 1821. In 1780 he established a partnership with his son-in-law John Job.
(Courtesy Ian Reid.)

Shanadithit is thought to have been the last of the Beothuck Indians of Newfoundland.
When she was captured with her mother and sister in 1824 she said the tribe was reduced to
fourteen. She died at St. John's in 1829 at the age of twenty-nine years.

The cull was one of the most important parts of salt fish buying. Here a venerable culler at Job's gives the dry cod the once over as a youth in the foreground yaffles fish to bring to the culling board. The lady on the right is probably boarding a schooner for one of the outports. (Courtesy Ian Reid.)

This range of fine stone buildings on Water Street opposite Queen Street belonging to the great firm of Stewarts was pulled down in recent years to clear the site for Woolworth's department store. Byrne's bookstore is on the left. The men and boys are gathered in front of what was Dr. Edward Kielley's surgery. (Courtesy CBC Newfoundland Region.)

Schooners fill the port of St. John's at the beginning of the century. In the spring and autumn the harbour stream was often chocked with coastal vessels bringing fish and codliver oil to the city mercantile houses and carrying home supplies to outport merchant firms along the coasts. (Courtesy Newfoundland Provincial Archives.)

The wooden drydock constructed by J. E. Simpson and Co. of New York in 1884 was sold to the Reid-Newfoundland Company in 1900 and here it is being replaced by a modern concrete structure in 1925 at a cost of nearly two million dollars. (Courtesy Newfoundland Provincial Archives.)

The deck of the S.S. *Beothic* during the great years of the now nearly defunct seal hunt. In conditions that were frequently appalling, fearless men averted poverty by working and dying for a handful of the millions of dollars their labour earned. (Courtesy Newfoundland Provincial Archives.)

Seals are never skinned at the ice fields. They are "sculped," meaning that the pelt, fat, and hide are taken off in one piece by the swilers. They are later skinned by professionals with two swipes of their knives as is being done here in front of Bowring's southside premises in the early years of the century. (Courtesy Newfoundland Provincial Archives.)

Sealhunters rarely resembled these well-dressed Hollywood actors in the Motion picture *The Viking*. This still shows the hero (Charles Starrett on the right) and the villain facing each other in front of the S.S. *Ungava*. While the acting was generally amateurish the scenes of the actual hunt at the ice raised the picture to the level of an outstanding documentary. (Courtesy Sterling Film Co. Ltd.)

902

The mercantile district of St. John's as seen from Hotel Newfoundland around 1970. The grim Sir Humphrey Gilbert Building in the centre stands on the site of the Atlantic Hotel. Behind it are the spars of ships of the Portuguese fishing fleet. (Courtesy Newfoundland Department of Tourism.)

The old finger piers along Water Street at the time of Confederation in 1949. Atlantic Place and a parking garage now fill this area from Ayre's Cove to Clift's-Baird's Cove. The finger piers have been replaced by Harbour Drive. Left centre the Total Abstinence Building, housing the Capitol Theatre, is seen under construction. (Courtesy Public Archives of Canada.)

Their Name is on Your Waters

Ye say that all have passed away . . .
But their name is on your waters—
Ye may not wash it out.

LYDIA HUNTLEY SIGOURNEY *Indian Names*

Without its almost landlocked harbour of deep water, there would be no St. John's as we know it today. Bay Bulls, Harbour Grace, Fermuse, or some other east settlement would have become the capital of Newfoundland. The fabric of the city is interwoven with the commercial interests of west country fish merchants, British naval superiority, and the grim determination of a boisterous rabble not to be uprooted from their new homeland by English law or French invasion.

The port city that was the cornerstone of the British Empire began as a series of small communities huddled on the harbour shore or in the river valleys to the west and north. It was to these habitations with such names as Maggoty Cove, Freshwater, Riverhead, Southside, and Quidi Vidi that people came from Bideford and Appledore, Topsham and Devonport, Waterford and Cork, from the early days of the sixteenth century and gradually put down permanent roots.

If these early settlers were backward and uneducated they were also industrious and unafraid of the squalor and violence they met as they scratched a living from the soil or wrested one from the sea. They were individuals who excelled in self-reliance to the point where they were able to defy the harsh excesses of early colonial rule. Nothing survives of the community they built. Even the names of such localities as Maggoty Cove, Georgestown, and Riverhead are gone. New features have blurred the old town and modern developments have changed the face of the surrounding hills. All that remains the same is the pride, wit, and hospitality to be found in the gaily painted clapboard houses that lean upon each other's shoulders as they stagger up the steep streets to where the Basilica flaunts twin crosses against the open sky.

St. John's is a remarkable example of man's tenacity. It grew together haphazardly over the decades, menaced by fire and numerous enemies, because it had one great natural advantage that made people return to it as a place of permanent habitation. That great advantage was its large harbour around which rickety timber structures first clustered amidst the dirt and stench of a great fishing industry because it was a place of trade, of buying and selling, where fortunes could be made by poor immigrant planters unafraid of long hours or backbreaking toil. Orderly growth never occurred to them. The place was nothing more than an unruly supply house and trans-shipment base for English fishing interests in the west Atlantic, but for many it also became home.

In time the flimsy dwellings and seasonal business premises gave way to more permanent houses and shops with some architectural pretense and the prospering citizens made the inevitable demands for a voice in their own affairs. None of this would have come about in St. John's without the harbour, the chrysalis from which the city slowly emerged. The place was born out of the needs of commerce, and commerce has dominated its life to this day. While boys and girls in England were playing at being Robin Hood and Maid Marian, Newfoundland children were absorbed in the game of "shop," learning to buy and sell and trade.

The harbour begins inside Chain Rock on the north side and stretches in an oval pattern four miles (five miles before the drydock was built) to Pancake Rock on the south side. In early times the area between Chain Rock and Temperance Street was known as Maggots Cove (later Maggoty Cove). In the late 1700s Studdy and Batten were planters in the locale. During the seventeenth and eighteenth centuries the shore of the cove was covered with fishing stages and behind them were the flakes on which the wet, salted cod was dried. These flakes were platforms of rough cut wood, or longers, eight or ten feet high and covered with boughs of spruce or fir. Wet fish frequently fell through these loosely constructed flakes and in the damp shade underneath soon bred maggots. So offensive was the odour of Maggoty Cove by the 1860s that the residents living nearby complained to the governor. His Excellency ordered the flakes torn down and the cleaned-up area was renamed Hoylestown after Newman Hoyles who owned property there and was the father of a former prime minister, Sir Hugh Hoyles, then serving as Chief Justice.

During World War II the United States built a dock east of Temperance Street to supply Fort Pepperrell, the army base on the north shore of Quidi Vidi Lake. The story of how this base came into being is told in Volume I of this work. In 1941, the Americans realized they would need a dock where supplies could be landed with maximum military security. The shoreline of the Battery, an area of Hoylestown that was once the terminus for the Newfoundland railway, was acquired by the United States government and the American dock was built. It was the first modern pier in the city as all the other wharves of the time were wooden structures or small finger piers behind mercantile premises. The American dock remained in the possession of the United States government until Fort Pepperrell was closed in 1961. At that time it reverted to Canadian ownership and is now operated by the National Harbours Board of Canada.

Before construction of the railway station at the mouth of the Waterford River in the west end of the harbour, the Newfoundland Railway used as a terminal an old stone building that was once part of Fort William. Railway coastal steamers docked at the foot of Temperance Street. A rail spur ran down a steep incline to just below Fort Waldegrave, and trains were able to back up to the pier. Once known as Parker's & Gleeson's Wharf, the property was occupied by the Newfoundland Coastal Co. Ltd., operators of the steamers S.S. *Grand Lake* and S.S. *Virginia Lake*.

Until recent years E.F. Barnes Ltd. operated a small shipyard for the construction of iron vessels on the site of the old railway pier. Almost in the same place John Woods, a shipowner who did a flourishing business in lumber and coal, had a shipbuilding premises and operated the first commercial drydock in St. John's where he cleaned and repaired vessels. Woods, who was known as Gentleman John, started the business around 1845 when he was in his mid-thirties, handled brigs, barques, and brigantines to over one hundred tons for more than fifty years. The sailing ships he serviced were hauled up by a capstan and thirty men on each side. One son was Sydney Woods, the prominent hardware merchant and another was the Hon. H.J.B. Woods, M.H.A. for Bay de Verde and Postmaster General. His daughter Mabel married Arthur Mews and their son Harry was mayor of St. John's. The Wood's property is now occupied by the Fisheries Research Board of Canada Biological Station.

The area of the cove between Barnes's and Woods's dock was once used for a soup kitchen. Able-bodied men, with their wives and broods of children, went there daily for food during the hard times from 1864 to 1868, when the poor constituted half the population. People came from all over St. John's to this soup kitchen for a daily ration of Indian meal and molasses. Times began to improve considerably in 1869 and Archibald's Cove, as it was then called, reverted to being a swimming hole for the men and boys of the town. In those far-off, skinny-dipping days, young ladies dared not go near the water.

Adjoining Woods's, where Charles Fox once had a cod-oil factory, was Wm. Campbell & Co.'s tannery. William Campbell, a native of Bonavista born in 1843, was a contractor in the business of building supplies. He built St. Andrew's Kirk, George Street Methodist Church, and the St. John's Penitentiary, as well as a large number of government buildings. He married an English girl, Jane Herder of Devon, and his son Colin carried on his father's business.

In 1875 Messrs. McTaggert and Germmell started the Terra Nova Foundry west of Campbell's. It serviced many steamer wrecks including the S.S. *Arizona* in 1879. Next to the foundry wharf was McKay's Wharf and then that of the Pitts family, owners of considerable property on the waterfront just east of Hill o' Chips, an area occupied in the late

907

eighteenth century by such planters as Boden, Lang, John Stripling and William Newman.

William Pitts was born at St. John's in 1819. Married to Ann Cochrane of Devonshire, he was an ardent anti-Confederate, and a staunch Methodist. Pitts Memorial Hall on Harvey Road was named for him, after his donation of two thousand dollars to the Methodist College building fund. He was also a leading promoter of the Athenaeum. Probably the largest sufferer in the fire of 1892 was James Pitts. Born in St. John's in 1847, he was proprietor of the Victoria Tobacco Works and Albert Soap and Candle Works, opposite Hill o' Chips, and had a large mercantile premises east of Beck's Cove. He was shareholder and agent for the Canada & Newfoundland Steamship Company and served in both the legislative and executive councils. Pitts was also prominent in the Methodist denomination.

In this century, the property from Campbell's to Pitts' has been covered by the docks and sheds of Furness, Withy and Co., Ltd. In 1833 Sir Christopher (later Lord) Furness, purchased the ships of Edgar Withy, a shipbuilder of Hartlepool, England, when the latter gentleman emigrated to New Zealand. Sir Christopher's new line opened branches at St. John's and Halifax in 1891. As the company expanded it bought out both the Johnson and Warren Lines. Johnson was engaged in cargo trade between Liverpool and Baltimore as well as Greece, Turkey, and the Black Sea. The Warren Line was an inheritor of Enoch Train's White Diamond Line of American sailing packets, founded in Boston in 1839. In the 1870s George Warren replaced the famous sailing clippers with steamers and in 1914 sold a half-interest to Furness, Withy and Co. Ltd. Furness completed the takeover in 1919. At the turn of the century the Liverpool-Halifax return fare was ninety dollars on ships of the Johnson-Warren Line. The crossing took twelve days and there was a call at St. John's.[2]

The Furness property, and that of Harvey & Co., covers much of the ground once occupied by the great firm of Robinson, Brooking's & Co. The Brooking family had a freestone dwelling almost opposite Hill o' Chips. This was one of the grandest homes in St. John's in the early 1800s. Thomas Holdsworth Brooking was related to the famous Capt. Arthur Holdsworth. His wharf was among the most important in the island. The company is reported to have two hundred vessels under sail at various times, and there were branches of the firm in Trinity, Greenspond, and other places. Besides an island trade these ships also carried goods to and from foreign ports and prosecuted the seal fishery. Brooking, who came to Newfoundland to work for Hunt, Stabb & Preston, died in London, England, 13 January, 1869. On the site of the Brooking family home, Harvey's built a bakery which was torn down in 1971.

James Murray took over the wharves and made a vain attempt to keep the name alive by always referring to them as "Down to Brooking's."[3] Mr. Anthony, the storekeeper at Brooking's, was somewhat of a celebrity in his day because he wore gold rings in his ears. The western part of Brooking's was taken over in the 1860s by H.J. Stabb, known as "Major" because of his post in the Newfoundland Volunteers. The firm has been in business on the site ever since.

Shea and Company was located opposite the foot of Cochrane Street, on Clapp's old estate. This was the home of the Galway Line of packet boats that operated between Halifax, St. John's, and Ireland, and the pier became known as the Galway Wharf. Sir Ambrose Shea was a young man when he started the firm, having been born in St. John's in 1817.

In 1874 the British government contracted with the Allan line of packet steamers for the regular conveyance of European mails to and from St. John's. Up to that time all overseas Newfoundland mail passed through Halifax. Sir Ambrose Shea was appointed local agent for the Allan Line and such ships as the *Hibernian* and *Nestorian* called regularly at his wharf. When Sir Ambrose retired from the business in the mid-1800s his nephew George Shea, who was subsequently mayor of St. John's and later a cabinet minister, operated as the agent of the Allan Line until the line was purchased by Furness Withy & Co. who operated from premises to the east of Shea's Wharf. In 1919 the Honourable George Shea retired and the premises was purchased by Harvey & Co. Ltd. During the middle years of the eighteenth century, when the immigrant-laden vessels of the Galway Line called at St. John's, the ancestors of many thousands of Newfoundlanders first set foot on the shores of North America at Shea's Wharf. Early settlers in this locality were Wyatt, Willock, Perryman, and James Winter.

Harvey's firm, which has been conducting business in St. John's since 1763, is one of the few early Newfoundland mercantile firms that was not a branch of an English company.[4] It grew out of the Bermuda Trading Company which acquired the property opposite the War Memorial from Samuel Hill in 1699 and was dissolved in the mid-1700s. The Harvey and Outerbridge families, who control the firm, came from Bermuda where they were related by marriage. At his father's request, Sir Leonard Outerbridge forsook law and entered the firm in 1920, eventually becoming president of the company. Sir Leonard (the last Newfoundland knight) was the province's first full-term lieutenant-governor from 1949 to 1957.

Harvey's firm operated the first scheduled steamship line from St. John's to Halifax and New York. Today the company, which has become the province's leading travel agency, acts as Newfoundland agents for Canada Steamships and Clark Steamships.

West along Water Street, from Harvey's eastern pier, was the People's Exchange, where later W. & G. Rendell had a waterfront lumberyard. Next to this was the famous auctioneering firm of Theodore Clift. Much of the harbour-side property from Maggoty Cove to Cochrane Street was the early plantation of the outstanding eighteenth-century Newfoundlander, John Downing, who is dealt with elsewhere in these volumes. The westermost part of Downing's plantation, almost to Queen's Wharf, became the property of the famous Gill family. Michael Gill, the first colonel of militia,

909

and his brother Nicholas, Chief Magistrate in St. John's, were leading merchants who came to Newfoundland from New England. Their father had won enduring fame by saving Bonavista from French invasion, 18 August 1704. Gill's Wharf, at St. John's, was later McDougall & Templeton's.

Opposite the Newfoundland War Memorial, a roadway leads down Gill's Cove to Queen's Wharf (or King's, depending on the sex of the reigning monarch). Called Admiral's Beach in 1783, this has been a traditional landing place, or point of departure, for over four hundred years. Many famous planters lived in the locale in the late 1700s including Michael Gill, D'Ewes Coke, Jonathan Ogden as well as Mr. Binland, Mrs. Sawer, John Williams and Dr. Rowe. McGlashan, Robinson & Company's flake was also here.

In the early part of the eighteenth century Queen's Wharf was farther east, near the foot of Hill o' Chips, the shortest supply route between the waterfront and Fort William. When Queen's Wharf moved to the Beach, the old landing opposite Hill o' Chips became known as Ordnance Wharf. The third official pier, known as Governor's Wharf, was opposite the present Court House in Clift's-Baird's Cove.

Tradition has Sir Humphrey Gilbert coming ashore at Queen's Beach, when, in 1583, he proclaimed Newfoundland the exclusive property of his sovereign, Elizabeth I, and thereby began the glorious adventure that history was to know as the British Empire. Since most of Admiral's Beach from Gill's Cove, then a river, to Hunter's Cove, also a river, was covered by a marsh it is more probable that Sir Humphrey landed on the dry shore east of Gill's Cove and performed his proclamation routine at the top of the nearby Hill o' Chips.

In any case the area around Queen's Beach can claim to have welcomed or waved farewell to some illustrious persons over the years, including Admiral Lord Nelson, of Trafalgar and Emma Hamilton fame; the American traitor who attempted to betray West Point to the British, Benedict Arnold; Captain William Bligh of H.M.S. *Bounty;* and a cluster of royalties including the future King William IV, the future King Edward VII, the future King George V and Queen Mary, the future King Edward VIII, and the reigning King George VI and Queen Elizabeth. Their daughter, Elizabeth II, and her consort are also no strangers to Queen's Beach.

Today the jetty at Queen's Wharf is mainly used by the St. John's harbour pilot boats. Harbour pilots are men qualified to conduct a ship in or out of port. Navigation of the Narrows, by incoming or outgoing vessels, can be an intricate business. A day mark for ships entering port was established in the nineteenth century by lining up the Customs House flagstaff with the east side of the old Congregational chapel. On 1 September 1863 leading lights were established in a line on both buildings. After the 1892 fire, the one on the Congregational chapel was replaced by a miniature lighthouse erected in Queen's Road, at the top of Chapel Street.

Today there is a leading light in the steeple of the present church and a large red diamond at the back of the spire which, in daylight, is lined up with another diamond at Queen's Wharf. There are fixed fees for the pilot service, which is provided at all hours and in all sorts of weather.

It is recorded that early one July morning, in the year 1610, "in St. John's Harbour Captain Whitbourne saw a marmayde." During Sir Richard's time mermaids were not unusual. For example, four years after his sighting, Captain John (Pocohontas) Smith, on the voyage in which he discovered Maine, also spotted one of the creatures "swimming about with all possible grace." Both gentlemen probably mistook a seal for the legendary sea siren. Maxwell, in *Wild Sports of the West*, says: "To these animals, the submarine beings who have for ages delighted the lovers of the marvellous, may without much difficulty be traced, and many a wonderstricken fisherman imagined himself watching the movements of a mermaid while all the time he was only staring at a sea calf."

West of Queen's Wharf the great Patrick Morris had a wharf at one time where he operated a passenger service, to and from Waterford, in the early nineteenth century. In the same area Stephen March & Son later had offices. March, who was M.H.A. for Trinity in 1865, lived over the store. His later house on Circular Road, at the east corner of Fraser's Lane, was burnt in December 1873 and replaced by the present double house which, along with the one on the west side of Fraser's Lane, are two of the three oldest houses in that section of Circular Road. The third is the house on the east corner of Rennie's Mill Road which is dated in 1849 on the chimney.

During much of the present century the firm of F.M. O'Leary, Ltd. was on the Morris-March site, opposite the War Memorial. Francis Martin O'Leary was a commission merchant who began in 1922 in partnership with Gerald S. Doyle. The relationship did not last, and in the breakup the agencies were divided. O'Leary's father was a captain of banking schooners. In 1937 he began sponsoring a daily radio broadcast, called "The Barrelman," to make Newfoundland better known to Newfoundlanders. The program was filled with yarns, legends, and folk stories sent in from all over the island. The host, who sold the program idea to O'Leary, was a former journalist named Joey Smallwood. Whether Newfoundland became better known to Newfoundlanders is immaterial. Joey certainly did and his name was soon a household word. The O'Leary firm published a monthly newspaper and it sponsored an annual O'Leary Newfoundland Poetry Award, until the Provincial Arts and Letters competition came into being.[5]

Active in public affairs, F.M. O'Leary assumed the leadership of the Responsible Government League during the battle for Confederation. His opponent, as leader of the Confederates, was the erstwhile Barrelman, Joey Smallwood. When introducing O'Leary to a friend years afterwards Joey said "I made him a millionaire" to which F.M. added, "And I made him Premier." Frank O'Leary served as president of the committee which raised the funds for construction of the St. John's Memorial Stadium. He was given the papal knighthood of St. Gregory for his work on behalf of the archdiocese.

Across the laneway from O'Leary's is the western premises of Harvey & Co., property purchased from Samuel Hill and still in use by the second oldest firm in St. John's. It was from the docks behind Harvey's that the popular passenger liners, S.S. *Fort Townshend* and S.S. *Fort Amherst*, operated to and from Halifax and New York until 1950. The history of Harvey's is told elsewhere in this volume.

Next to Harvey's was the mercantile premises of the Honourable James Tobin, leased from the estate of James Brine. Tobin came out to Newfoundland from Dublin as a youth and made his fortune. Ships from Ireland used his wharf. Tobin, who was appointed to the Amalgamated Legislature in 1843, returned to Ireland after 1860 but was sent out by the British government to the colony again, with a Mr. Cole, in connection with attempts to pre-empt the New York, Newfoundland, and London Telegraph Company's rights and plant in 1872-73, a political farce that was the most celebrated subject of the period after the question of Confederation.

Adjoining Tobin's were the wharf, offices, house, and other premises of the Honourable Lawrence O'Brien. He was probably the Horatio Alger of Newfoundland, having emigrated to the colony from Ireland in 1793 as a penniless youth of seventeen or eighteen years. Beginning as a carpenter's apprentice, he rose to a position of great wealth and political authority. For fifteen years, from 1855 until his death on 28 June 1870, he was President of the Legislative Council and the person responsible for the development of many of the island's roads. He was, in fact, known as "The Colossus of Roads."

So impressive a man was he that Bishop Fleming once suggested, when O'Brien and John Valentine Nugent were sent as a delegation to the Colonial Office in London, that O'Brien should enter first but when it came to speaking the work should be left to the scholarly Nugent. During the interval between the departure of Governor Bannerman in 1863 and the arrival of Governor Musgrave in 1864, O'Brien is said by Judge Prowse to have "administered the government with dignity and efficiency."

The wharves of John Fox and the Honourable Nicholas Stabb were west of those of Tobin and O'Brien. Fox, who was in the supply trade, was M.H.A. for St. John's West in the 1855 House of Assembly. Two years later he was appointed to the Legislative Council. The firm burned in the 1846 fire and was rebuilt. A son, James, took a position with Walter Grieve until, having learned what there was to know about business, he joined his father's firm in 1882 at the age of twenty-two years. James Fox, Jr., won a place in Newfoundland history in 1890 by becoming the first person elected to the House of Assembly under the newly proclaimed Manhood Suffrage Act. He was Receiver General in the Whiteway administration of

1893. John Fox died on 23 September 1883, age sixty-six years. James died on 28 February 1899 in his thirty-ninth year. A brother, John Francis, was the father of Justice Cyril Fox.

Nicholas Stabb was one of the principals of the old firm of Stabb, Row & Holmwood. His father Thomas Stabb was resident partner in the firm of Hunt, Stabb, Preston & Co., prize agents during the War of 1812. It is said that clerks in their employ at the time spent Sunday afternoons shooting at champagne bottles taken from some thirty captured American vessels and placed at the end of the wharf. Any clerk who knocked the head off a bottle won a case and whoever missed had to pay for one.

Nicholas and his older brother, Ewan Stabb, had a business on the southwest corner of Beck's Cove, E. & N. Stabb, until it was wiped out in 1846. N. Stabb & Sons was then located east of Hunter's Cove. Appointed to the Legislative Council in 1859, Nicholas Stabb died on 18 June 1876. His wife, Rachel Chancey, a great aunt of Lady Winter, died in 1894 at the age of eighty-nine after dictating telegrams on her death bed to her two absent sons, Thomas and Nicholas, saying that she was dying and sending them her love.

Between Stabb's wharf and the cove was the head office of the oldest business firm in Newfoundland, Job Brothers & Co. Ltd., which still occupies the site. Job's is said to have been founded in 1730, nearly fifty years before the American Revolution, when John Bulley emigrated to Newfoundland from England and commenced a business on the south side of St. John's harbour in an area once know as Prosser's Plantation.

John's son, Samuel who was born in Devonshire the year his father emigrated to Newfoundland, took over the business in 1758 and was soon a prominent citizen. Like most well-to-do merchants of the time he wintered in England where he married a Devonshire girl named Joanna Wood who became the mother of his eight children.

In 1764 an officer of the Royal Navy, John Job, died in the Devon village of Combeinteinehead leaving a pregnant widow. The child, John, was born at Haccombe on December 7 and made a ward of Samuel Bulley who apprenticed him to his planter's business in St. John's when the lad was sixteen years old. In 1789 John Job was taken into partnership as Bulley & Job. Like many a young man before and since with an eye to opportunity he married the boss's daughter, Sarah Bulley. In 1808, two years before Samuel died, the firm took a new partner in Nathan Parker and became Parker, Bulley & Job. Bulley's son, Samuel, married Parker's daughter, Anna. John Job took up residence in Liverpool, England, in 1809.

Nathan Parker, who was born in New England in 1755, came to St. John's in his late teens as a glazier with Wallis Lang, a carpenter. He later formed a partnership with Stephen Knight, a long-time resident of the island, and became a very wealthy merchant. In 1808 old man Knight retired and the two firms on either side of Knight's (Hunter's) Cove united to form Parker, Bulley & Job. Knight died in 1813, and in 1816

913

Parker returned to live in Boston with his wife who was a daughter of
Andrew Barnes whose land became the site of the Congregational Church on
Meeting House Hill.

Parker, Bulley & Job was dissolved in 1819 and the firm took John
Cross as its new partner. Bulleys, Job & Cross (note the plural) did not last
long, for Cross is believed to have perished while on a transatlantic
crossing around 1820 at which time the business became Bulleys, Job & Co.
The present name, Job Brothers & Co., was adopted 12 January 1839.

John Job died on 14 May 1845 and was buried in Newington Chapel
near the grave of the great poet, Edmund Spenser. He left five sons and
one of these, Robert, built Hope Cottage at the west corner of Water and
Hutchings Streets, giving his family name to Job's Bridge, opposite the
cottage and Job Street, a road at the back of the property. On 8 July 1834 a
brother, Thomas, married Jessy Carson, youngest child of Dr. William
Coffinswell, Devon, started at a salary of twenty pounds per year and in
time he became the manager of the firm. He was elected M.H.A. for Trinity

On 1 November 1834 fifteen-year-old Stephen Rendell was Inden-
tured to Job Brothers & Co. as an apprentice. This young lad from
Coffinswell, Devon, started at a salary of twenty pounds per year and in
time he became the manager of the firm. He was elected M.H.A. for Trinity
in 1859 and appointed to the Legislative Council in 1874. His days in
government are remembered for his having introduced rabbits, actually
hares from Nova Scotia, into Newfoundland to delight the taste buds of
countless generations. Rendell returned to England and died in his birthplace on 4 April 1893.

Before 1892 Job's operated a retail store on the old Parker & Knight
property at the west corner of Hunter's Cove and Water Street. After the
Great Fire they quickly erected two small temporary buildings. These were
eventually replaced by Campbell Macpherson's Royal Stores when the two
firms worked out an amalgamation in 1895. Today the Royal Trust
Building occupies the site which in the 1750s was Magistrate William Keen's
wharf. In November 1927 the Hudson's Bay Company purchased a large
portion of the shares of Job Brothers. Ayre & Sons Ltd. holds the remaining shares. After nearly two hundred and fifty years the firm established by
John Bulley is still in business along the St. John's waterfront.

Job Brothers was active in the salt fish trade probably from the
beginning. In 1817 the firm shipped a cargo of fish from St. John's to feed
slaves on the Gladstone plantation in British Guiana, despite the fact that
slavery had been formally condemned by Britain and other nations at the
Congress of Vienna two years previously. A son of the estate owner
became England's Prime Minister under Queen Victoria.

While Bowring's named many of their ships for Shakespeare characters and Sir Robert Reid called most of his vessels after places in Scotland,
the early Job fleet used a series of feminine names such as Flora, Ethel,
Blanche, Dora, Mildred, and Jessie. Two of Samuel Bulley's sons and John

Job were on board the *Flora* when she was captured by the French during the Napoleonic War and taken to LaRochelle. For six months Job received harsh treatment in the prison of Saumur.

The greatest contribution made by Job Brothers to the mercantile history of Newfoundland was probably in the seal fishery. Having started in the early days with sail, the firm turned to steam in 1863. Because of its involvement in the fishing and sealing industries Job's expanded to the point where there were 150 year-round employees on the payroll, as well as many hundreds of sealers each spring. One year alone the firm handled 180,000 seal pelts. Today its only mercantile link is an involvement with the Blue Peter Steamship line which operates a freight service between St. John's and Montreal.

On the waterfront between Hunter's and Clift's Coves were located West & Rendell, and Thorburn & Tessier. James Tessier was born in London in 1842. In 1853 he entered the employ of P. & L. Tessier in Newfoundland. Thirty-eight years later he formed a partnership with Sir Robert Thorburn, and became an M.H.A. for St. John's West. Sir Robert Thorburn, born at Jumper Bank, Pebbleshire, Scotland, in 1836, came to St. John's in 1852 to work for Baine, Johnston & Co., then managed by his uncle James Grieve. He was Prime Minister of Newfoundland from 1885 to 1889 during which time he opened up Thorburn Road. The Thorburn & Tessier property was once occupied by the great firm of W. & H. Thomas & Co.

Just west of the Royal Trust Building two archways still lead underneath buildings towards the harbour. In the days when the waterfront consisted of finger piers there were many such archways leading from Water Street to the docks, but these openings are all that are left. They remain as an important historic curiosity of the days when horses plodded through them pulling longcarts laden with the merchandise of the world.

Clift's-Baird's Cove, once called Man of War Lane, was where the governor's ship always moored. Eventually it became the site of Governor's Wharf. West of this cove, in the area now covered by the municipal parking garage, were found the shop, offices, and wharves of Clift, Wood & Co. According to P.K. Devine, this firm was established in 1790. James Clift joined it soon after 1800 when he came to Newfoundland as a young man in his mid-twenties from his birthplace near Birmingham, England. He died at St. John's 21 January 1860 when he was eighty-four years of age, having established an extensive business as an auctioneer, commission merchant, and mercantile trader. His auction house, on the west side of the cove, should not be confused with Theodore Clift's auction rooms east of Gill's Cove. James Shannon Clift, who became senior partner in the firm of Clift, Wood & Co. and was a member of the Legislative Council, died at the age of sixty-three, 16 July 1877.

The firm of Baine, Johnston & Co., which covered an area on Water Street opposite McMurdo's Lane, was begun at Port de Grave in 1870 by

915

Archibald, Robert, and Walter Baine. When Thomas Lang entered the partnership the name changed to Lang, Baine & Co. In 1801 the business moved to St. John's and took over part of Horton's Plantation, which grant dated from 1752. When Lang retired in 1832 he was replaced by William Johnston and the firm became Baine & Johnston. The male Baines died out and control of the firm passed through the female line to the Grieve family.

James Grieve, who was a member of the Legislative Council in 1850, retired to Scotland where he became M.P. for Greenock in 1868. Walter Grieve, who withdrew from the partnership, formed his own business, Walter Grieve & Co. In 1879 he also retired to Greenock where he died eight years later. A namesake, Walter Baine Grieve, born at St. John's on 19 August 1850, was for many years the head of Baine, Johnston & Co. Elected M.H.A. for Bonavista in 1882, he led the Grieve-Monroe party the following year. Appointed to the Legislative Council in 1919, he died on 3 February 1921. After his death the company was incorporated and passed into the hands of the Collingwood family.

Walter Baine Grieve was arrested on 22 April 1909, on a charge of criminal libel laid by Sir Edward Morris. The charge was based on a message Grieve sent to someone on the Cape Shore in which he alleged that Sir Edward was a spy in the pay of the Canadian government and working for Confederation.

William Collingwood was head clerk with the old Poole firm of Thomas & David Slade of Twillingate and Fogo. Born at Poole in 1842, he came out to work for Slade's at the age of thirteen years. From 1885 he served with the Labrador branch, established in 1698 at Battle Harbour. Baine, Johnston & Co. bought out Slade's Battle Harbour Station in 1872. Collingwood who came to St. John's in 1883, continued to serve the company for another forty years, while his son Thomas joined in 1895. Thomas eventually became president and, together with his own son, Henry, joint managing director.[7]

Baine, Johnston & Co. brought the first steamship, *Bloodhound,* to Newfoundland, 27 February 1863. The *Bloodhound* was the first steam vessel to take part in the seal fishery when she sailed to the ice in 1863. She was lost in 1872, and the following year a second *Bloodhound* was built. She was lost on 15 July 1917 off Point La Haye. In 1867 the company had the *Panther* built at Miramichi, Canada. She was sailed to Greenock where an engine was installed, and returned to Newfoundland to become a noted sealer. The *Panther* was lost at the ice fields, 22 March 1908.

The firm became agents for Cunard in 1868 when that Nova Scotia concern got the contract, from the Newfoundland government, for the mail service between Halifax and St. John's. The S.S. *City of Halifax* was placed on the route. In 1873 she became Baine, Johnston's sealing steamer *Micmac,* and was lost in 1888. The *Hope,* added to the fleet in 1892, was lost in 1901. Following the bank crash in 1895, the company bought out

Munn's sealers: *Vanguard, Mastiff, Greenland*, and *Iceland*. At one time it had seven steamers, with fourteen hundred men, at the ice and sent its last vessel to the seal hunt in 1926, when it chartered the S.S. *Sagona*.

In 1955 the firm of Baine, Johnston's, which at its peak exported a hundred thousand cwts of fish in a year, went out of the mercantile and fish export business, and the company moved to new premises on Kenmount Road. A retail store on Water Street, two doors west of Ayre's Cove, all that remained of the famous business in the downtown area, closed in 1975.

When Newman & Co., mercantile and wine merchants of England, closed down their St. John's operations, Baine, Johnston & Co. became Newman's property agents and took over responsibility for maturing Newman's "celebrated Newfoundland port."

Next to Baine, Johnston's were the wharves of R.H. Prowse, which had been Knight's and before that, part of the estate of John Flood. In 1824 the firm was established by Robert Prowse, grandfather of the famous judge and historian. His son, Robert Henry Prowse, an uncle of the Judge, later took over the firm, and married Catherine, daughter of Kenneth McLea. They lived in a large stone house on Duckworth Street, just west of Victoria Street. The western end of his semi-detached dwelling, next to the Bank of British North America, was rented to Dr. Samuel Carson.

Until the reconstruction of the waterfront in the 1950s Ayre & Sons Wharf occupied the site of Atlantic Place. The firm dates from 1 January 1859 when Charles Ayre, who came to Newfoundland from Devon as an apprentice with Benjamin Bowring, went into business for himself. Though Ayre's never owned any vessels, its wharves were among the busiest in St. John's, catering to thousands of coastal schooners every year.

During both World Wars the port of St. John's was extremely important to the cause of the Allies. This was especially true in World War II when the place became a valuable base for Royal Navy and Royal Canadian Navy vessels responsible for the safe conduct of convoys carrying troops and supplies between North America and Europe. Frequently, in World War II, citizens of the town would go to bed at night with the harbour almost blocked with ships. These vessels were often moored five or six abreast in the stream. Next morning early risers would find the place empty, the convoy having crept out into the Atlantic during the darkness. Sometimes within hours the shattered hulls of ships would limp back into port after having been ravished by U-boats. Often it was possible to row a small boat through a hole on either or both sides of a ship.

St. John's is a year-round port that is rarely frozen over but is sometimes blocked by Arctic ice in late spring. In 1834 the House of Assembly passed the Ice Cutting Act, to regulate the cutting of channels through the ice to enable vessels to proceed on the sealing voyage at the proper season. A meeting was ordered held in each and every port and harbour where sealing ships were fitted out, to choose the Ice Committee,

917

which was formed to make and frame the rules and regulations for cutting the channels. These committees were to meet on the first of January annually.

St. John's did not get around to organizing its Ice Committee until 1837. The *Newfoundlander* for March noted:

> . . . the ice committee, though only formed yesterday, (for the very first time under the Ice Cutting Act), were prepared to enter upon their duties after dinner-hour, and owing to their well-directed exertions, and the personal attendance of the gentlemen caught composing the committee had, by last evening, cut a spacious channel fully half way towards Messrs Newman & Co., which we have no doubt will be completed betimes today . . . the whole fleet will probably have sailed before this day week.

The chairman of the St. John's Ice Committee was William Thomas, with Charles Fox Bennett as treasurer and Ambrose Shea as secretary. It ordered that a channel be cut in the harbour ice not less than sixty feet wide, as near as convenient to the most prominent wharves. Any person obstructing the committee in their duty was to forfeit five pounds. A rate was levied on all sealing vessels of one shilling per man per diem. That year thirty-six firms sent 121 vessels to the ice, carrying 2,940 men.

The port of St. John's is a traditional haven for foreign fishing fleets working on the Grand Banks and in Greenland waters. They use it to take on bunker fuel, water, food, and other supplies. The flags of the world are a common sight along the waterfront. There is 15,200 feet of berthing, offering eleven shedded berths and twenty-six open. Seven transit sheds and four railway transit sheds serve the port. Oil is delivered by pipelines, strewn in unsightly profusion, to eight berths, from tanks which disfigure the crest of the Southside Hills. Two leg cranes of eighty-five tons and fifty tons are supplemented by one crawler-type crane with a capacity of seventy tons. A drydock offers repair facilities.

There was an attempt to turn St. John's into an important harbour in the 1850s but nothing came of it. Cyrus Field wrote from London in February 1856: ". . . during the present year a wharf will be constructed and machinery erected for the express purpose of coaling ocean steamers in the most rapid manner. There is also an 18-pounder gun fired every half hour at the harbour's mouth when weather is foggy."[3] He says coal cost sixteen shillings per ton. Sanford Fleming saw the port as the eastern terminus for the North American railways, a dream that was to die for reasons of politics.

In 1956 the Department of Public Works, in Ottawa, began preliminary work on the modernization of the harbour. Finger piers were demolished between Job's property at the foot of Prescott Street, in the east, and the C.N. dockyard, in the west. Old mercantile houses and warehouse premises were torn down and a new roadway was constructed along the waterfront. Millions of tons of rock and fill were obtained, mostly by defacing the lower section out of the Southside Hills. The unsightly scar remains, as offensive as a festering wound. In 1963 the roadway was completed along the north shore of the waterfront, and by 1964 the vast project was virtually finished, at a total cost of twenty million dollars.

In response to the request of the Newfoundland government and local interests, the Government of Canada placed the port of St. John's under the jurisdiction of the National Harbours Board of Canada, and on 1 January 1965 it became a National Harbour.[9]

The port of St. John's was officially opened on 8 September 1965. These new facilities were soon taxed to full capacity, and harbour pilots were handling nearly two thousand ships a year.

Early in the nineteenth century the port was a haven for deserters who fled from their masters or from numerous ships. Newspapers were full of ads for their recapture. For example the *Mercantile Journal,* 8 June 1820, offered five guineas reward for the capture of any of the following deserters: "a youngster - Robert Canday, about 23 years of age, by trade a mason . . . a native of Plymouth, Devonshire." Another was "Richard Keefe, a native of Kilkenny, about 30 years of age . . . came from Ireland this spring." A third deserter must have found disguise difficult in the town of 1820. He was "Will Green, a black man . . . very stout, from 35 to 40 years . . . Brig St. Vincent of Bermuda."

In the old days, and up until World War II, St. John's harbour was a forest of schooner masts, especially in the autumn when coastal vessels and banking schooners filled the port. By 1970 only a few of schooners could still be seen tied up along the waterfront, all equipped with engines, for the diesel had long vanquished canvas. Radio announcers no longer read such terse messages for listeners at home as, *"Bessie Marie* discharging at Ayre's Wharf," or *"Pauline Winters* departing for home today with a full load."

Between Ayre's Cove and Beck's Cove (formerly Kent's Cove) were the wharves of Goodfellow & Co., J. and William W. Pitts' western premises, and Bowring Brothers. This was once the estate of Joshua Brooks, and in the late eighteenth century of his widow, Edith. Bowring's mercantile and retail firm needs a whole book to properly tell its story. In fact, there is very readable book, *The Bowring Story* by David Kerr (The Bodley Head, London, 1962), which will afford those interested some hours of pleasure.

In 1809 a man named Benjamin Bowring, who was born thirty-one years earlier in the Devonshire village of Mortonhemstead, opened a watchmaker's shop, at 199 Foe Street, in the city of Exeter. The Bowring family were descendents of William Bourynge of Tiverton, who appears in the Devon records of 1436.

919

One day, late in 1810 or early in 1811, a Mr. Pitts, who owned considerable property at Bell Island, is said to have walked into Bowring's shop. He wanted to purchase three grandfather clocks as gifts for his sons in Newfoundland. During the sale Pitts remarked on the lack of watch-makers in St. John's and Bowring made a mental note. Of the three clocks purchased by Pitts, two are still keeping time. One was brought back from the American mid-west by the Bowring family. The other is in the possession of the widow of a former lieutenant-governor, Campbell Mac-pherson, at "Westerland," and it has an account of its origin pasted on the pendulum.[10]

In 1811 Benjamin Bowring decided to come out to Newfoundland and investigate the prospects for himself. The ship on which he was a pas-senger was raided by an American privateer, near St. John's, and the boarding party carried off Bowring's stock of new watches. For the next couple of years he appears to have divided his time between Exeter and St. John's. On 14 September 1815 he announced in the *Royal Gazette:*

> Benjamin Bowring,
> *Working Watch-maker, Silversmith, and Jeweller—From Exeter,*
> Most respectfully begs leave to inform the inhabitants of St. John's and its vicinity, that he has commenced Business in the above branches, and having been regularly educated for them, and hav-ing had great experience in them, he presumes to hope, that by assiduity and moderate charges, he shall merit and obtain their patronage and continued support.
>
> He has taken a House in *Duckworth* Street, belonging to Mr. W. B. Thomas, into which he expects soon to enter; and in the mean time, he has lodgings at Mr. Andrews, over Mr. Stanteford's, near the Lower Street, where he has for Sale an excellent assort-ment of Silver, and some Gold WATCHES, and where their commands will be thankfully received.
>
> Should he experience that support which he has been taught to hope for, it is his intention in the ensuing Spring, to enlarge his stock very generally; and he pledges himself that the Articles he may have to dispose of, shall be selected from the best markets, and be of the first quality—*Cyphers, &c. engraved.*

On December 28 he informed the public he was returning to England for the purpose of removing his family to St. John's, and to select a new and excellent assortment of gold, and silver watches, plate, and jewellery.

The family arrived in the spring of 1816. It was at the suggestion of his wife that he added laces and drygoods to his offerings. These small beginnings grew into a great international mercantile firm with branch stores in St. John's, Grand Falls, Montreal, Toronto, New York, Liver-pool, and London, as well as at the airports of Gander, Halifax, Montreal, and Toronto.

The firm of Bowring Brothers was formed in 1841 by the sons of Benjamin Bowring. The operations in England and Newfoundland became limited liability companies in 1900. Of the directors, one was created a baronet, four have been knighted, two became lord mayors of Liverpool, and Sir Edgar Bowring, who donated Bowring Park to the city of St. John's, was High Commissioner for Newfoundland in London. Bowring Brothers occupied the fifth building east of Beck's Cove on the south side of Water Street.

Robert Kent had his mercantile offices in Beck's Cove. In the 1840s Kent's ships brought thousands of Irish immigrants to Newfoundland from Waterford where another brother, James, became mayor. A third brother, John, came out to Newfoundland from Waterford at the age of twenty years.

There exists correspondence between Robert Kent and Patrick Morris, on the number of cubic feet of ship space immigrant passengers should be allowed. According to Morris, it was precious little. As many as five hundred people would be crowded into a sailing vessel.

John Kent was elected to the first Representative Assembly, in 1832, at the age of twenty-seven. In 1858 he became Prime Minister after the decease of his brother-in-law Bishop Fleming who boosted him into the Legislature. Dr. Fleming's successor was not among Kent's admirers. In fact, Bishop Mullock denounced his administration in a famous letter to the press as "legalized robbery."[11] John Kent, who lived at 2 Gower Street, died on 1 September 1872. His grave at Belvedere is just inside the Newtown Road fence, opposite Calver Avenue. The tombstone bears his likeness carved in marble.

Opposite Kent's shipping offices and coalyard two other Irishmen, Richard and John O'Dwyer, had considerable waterfront premises which included shops along Water Street, west of the cove. The O'Dwyer firm was burnt out in 1846, but it rebuilt the Water Street block. The stone buildings now occupied by A.H. Murray & Co. Ltd., spared in 1892, are thought to have been rebuilt by O'Dwyer's after the 1846 fire inside the original walls. They have been occupied by the Murray firm since the end of the last century.

In 1839 James Murray Sr. emigrated to Newfoundland from Murrayshill, Perthshire, Scotland, where he was born twenty-nine years earlier. A miller and baker, he started a business on the banks of Rennie's River in a building that became Rennie's mill. His hard bread, locally called hard tack, was so hard that a hammer was packed with each barrel sold. The founding father died intestate in 1854. His son, James, who was twenty-two years old when his father died, started from scratch and built up a successful business. In 1889 he became M.H.A. for Burgeo. Young James lived for a time in his father's house, "Bellevue," afterwards the Whiteway residence, on Riverview Avenue, and later purchased John O'Mara's house on Circular Road, which he named "Sunnyside," James Murray lost all he had in the 1894 bank crash and died a ruined man in 1900.

His son Andrew, who was born 31 October 1877, went to work at Bowring's as a clerk. In 1898 he started his own business which included salt, coal, and general supplies, in addition to a schooner fleet which took part in the Labrador fishery. It was as a storage hulk for its salt and coal business that Murray's acquired H.M.S. *Calypso*, or H.M.S. *Briton,* as she was later called. David Murray, a younger brother of Andrew, joined him, and the firm continues in Beck's Cove to this day.

A.H. Murray & Company eventually acquired all the water front property between Beck's and Bishop's coves. In 1689 this area was the Bennett and Pxon (Pollexfen) plantations. In the middle of the nineteenth century the wharves belonged to the previously mentioned R. & J. O'Dwyer, as well as to Stabb, Rowe & Holmwood, P. & L. Tessier, Alan Goodridge & Sons, Boyd & McDougal, and P. Templeman.

Francis McDougal came to St. John's as a cooper in 1833, from his native Ayreshire, Scotland, to work for J. & W. Stewart. He afterwards entered a general dealership with Thomas Boyd as partner. McDougal, who lived above his shop at the west corner of Bishop's Cove and Water Street, died 18 January 1891, at the age of eight-four. The Honourable P. Templeman started his business in 1881, opened a branch at Catalina in 1890, and became a member of the Legislative Council in 1913.

Bishop's Cove was formerly known as Warren's Cove and, early in the 1800s, as Codner's Cove. Samuel Codner, a well-to-do English merchant, was located on the west corner. Between Bishop's Cove and Stewart's Cove, opposite Queen Street (now just an alleyway between Woolworth's and Parker's), were the wharves of the great firm of Edwin Duder, as well as those of Moses Monroe and J. & W. Stewart.

In Steer's Cove is said to lurk the ghost of Lieutenant Lawrey, the naval officer who was supposedly beaten to death on this very spot on 25 October 1794. He has been mentioned several times in both volumes of this work.

The eighteenth century was a time when men were pressed or shanghaied into the navy to take the place of dead or deserted crew members. A few months earlier on May 23, H.M.S. *Boston*, under the command of Captain Morris, dropped anchor in St. John's after a voyage of nearly two months from England. Five months later, October 18, the ship was still at St. John's when orders came for her to join a convoy bound for Spain. At the time her crew was short fourteen members. Captain Morris asked the governor, Sir Richard King, for permission to put up a poster asking for volunteers. The Governor scoffed at the idea and reminded the captain that he could get seamen by any means in his power. The officer was sure the Governor meant impressment. This was a system whereby a young man could be legally pulled off the street and sent sailing around the world without anybody knowing what happened to him.

Captain Morris reluctantly ordered two lieutenants and a boat's crew to put ashore as a press gang. In charge was a young lieutenant, Mr. Lawrey. Several fishermen and layabouts were seized and brought to the ship. Next day some apprentices, and a few others, were claimed by their employers and sent back on land. Eight men remained and all of them agreed to joining the navy. Two of the fishermen, Irishmen named Farrell and Power, wanted to go ashore to get some wages due them from Payne Noble and pick up their belongings. Lieutenant Lawrey and four sailors are said to have rowed to Steer's Cove, then covered with fish flakes about ten feet high. As the group walked under the flakes towards Lower Path (Water Street), Lawrey and two of the four sailors were set upon and beaten unconscious. The other two sailors managed to escape to their boats unharmed. When the attackers and impressed men had fled, the two sailors returned, and carried Lieutenant Lawrey and their badly beaten companions back to the *Boston*, where Lawrey died early next morning. The Governor, who was on board H.M.S. *Monarch* ready to sail for England, went back ashore and ordered the marines to search the town. Hundreds were questioned until finally one man, fearful of his life, turned King's evidence. He swore that Garrett Farrell and Richard Power had beaten the lieutenant to death. The two were arrested in a tavern on the Upper Path (Duckworth Street) on Wednesday, October 29. Next day they appeared before the Supreme Court of Chief Justice D'Ewes Coke, where they were found guilty and sentenced to be hanged and delivered to the surgeon to be dissected and anatomized. On Friday morning, less than a week after the attack, the condemned men were taken from the old jail, on Signal Hill, to the public gallows, on the barrens near Fort Townshend, where they were hanged, "without visible emotion."

The Irish rabble was aroused when news of the affair got about. It is recorded that "persons assembled in a riotous and tumultuous manner on the 25th." Governor King determined to stamp out such goings on and offered a reward of fifty pounds for the capture of the mob's ringleader, William Burrows. As far as is known he was never apprehended and the incident gradually faded into history.

The last press gang action in St. John's, of which there is any record, took place during the War of 1812 when men of H.M.S. *Sabine* tried to impress thirteen crew members of the brigantine *Swiftsure*. The crew jumped overboard to escape the press-boat gang. All made it to shore but one man, Adam Ross, who drowned.[12]

Just west of Steer's Cove (Hoppingly's Plantation of 1689) were the wharves of another well-known Newfoundland mercantile firm, A.E. Hickman and Company. Formed in 1905, as a branch of the Halifax firm of N. & M. Smith by Albert E. Hickman, the company was reincorporated under his name in 1917. In the 1920s Mr. Hickman obtained the premises of the great Newman & Company of Dartmouth, Devonshire. New piers and sheds were constructed on the site and the company was appointed agents for the American firm of Munson Steamships. Munson carried passengers and freight from these piers to Boston and return. When that contract ended, Hickman's operated as agents for the Farquhar Steamship Line of Halifax. In 1928 that contract was terminated and the firm chartered its own steamers for a line between St. John's and Montreal.[13] With the passing years, A.E. Hickman & Co. entered other business ventures and the mercantile interests of the firm declined. They disappeared completely when the old waterfront premises was torn down to make way for the redevelopment of St. John's harbour.

In the eighteenth century the area west of Steer's Cove was George Hutching's plantation which was divided in the nineteenth century. John Steer had his wharves in the Cove. Next to him was Charles Fox Bennett and then Edwin Duder had another wharf. P. Rogerson & Son was located on land that was once the property of Judge Des Barres. There was a public cove opposite Prince's Street, and beyond that the huge premises of P. & L. Tessier. West of Tessiers', at the foot of Springdale Street, were Newman's Wharves, which was Mrs. Furzey's Plantation on Thornton's 1689 map.[14] Before 1890 the property was occupied by J. & W. Stewart, and by Johnson & West.

At the end of Harbour Drive, in the middle of a traffic circle, there was a massive ship's anchor until 1972 when it vanished. Set in the rock below the anchor was a bronze plaque containing the inscription: : "To commemorate St. John's Harbour Development 1959-1964. Department of Public Works, Canada."

The anchor was found in the mud and silt of the harbour when the C.N. dock area was being dredged for the development project. How it got there is not known. It was thought to have come from the S.S. *Desola,* which sank about 1920 and was used as a foundation for one of the old harbour piers. The remains of the hull were blasted apart on 17 February 1960.

Opposite the road from Water Street (Tessier's Cove) there is a large finger pier containing the sheds of Newfoundland Steamships, which operates side loaders between St. John's and Montreal. On the south side of the Newfoundland Steamships warehouse, Canadian National coastal steamers load and discharge passengers and freight, for ports around the island, and as far north as Nain in Labrador. This was the area of the Royal Canadian Navy dockyards of World War II.

The north side of the harbour ends at Riverhead. Once a large body of water, this space is now filled in and occupied by the railway. On the east corner of Water Street and the road leading to Long Bridge the streetcar barn was located. Across the tracks, going south from the former car barn, is the C.N. repair shop where ailing railway engines are put back in working order. Beyond the C.N. repair shop are the gates to the C.N. drydock. Located in what was once the middle of the mouth of the Waterford River, the drydock was commenced on 28 May 1883 and completed in December

924

of the following year. It was built of pine, by the patentees, J.E. Simpson & Co., New York, and was 570 feet long by 76.5 feet wide with a depth of water over the sill of 27 feet. The official opening was set for 9 December 1884, when a visiting warship, H.M.S. *Tenedos* was to lead the celebrations by entering the dock, then said to be the largest drydock in the world. As H.M.S. *Tenedos* moved towards the gates she grounded on some sunken gravel and the opening had to be put off until the following day while the obstruction was removed. One newspaper, unaware that an accident had postponed the opening, was on the street with a complete description of the celebrations, twenty-four hours before they took place.

The cost of the drydock construction was $550,000. In 1925, at an additional cost of $1,940,225, it was rebuilt in concrete, and is now equipped to execute major repairs to hulls and machinery.

The patentees agreed to lease the dock at fifteen thousand dollars per annum, for ten years. Owing to a dispute they had with the Government, over dredging costs, and the non-payment of rent, the dock was taken from Simpson's and leased to Harvey & Angel for eleven thousand dollars per year.[15] It was eventually taken over by the Reid interests, the Newfoundland Railway and, finally, Canadian National.

The largest ship ever to be repaired on the dock was the S.S. *San Felix*, in World War II. So tight was the squeeze that there was one-inch clearance between each side of the dock and the sides of the fourteen-thousand-ton ship.

In 1781 H.M.S. *Pluto*, under the command of Captain Edgell, was lying at anchor in St. John's harbour, with her guns dismantled, when some fishermen brought word that two American pirate ships were operating off Bay Bulls and capturing fishing vessels. The warship was quickly made ready and had sailed by eight o'clock next morning. Before sundown she returned with the captured American privateers in tow.[16] Nothing more was known of them for over a hundred years. Then, in 1882, when dredging for the drydock was begun, the *George,* one of the captured American ships, was found on the bottom of the harbour at the drydock site.

Until the construction of the new finger pier C.N. coastal steamers picked up and discharged passengers and freight on the Waterford River side of the pier that juts out south of the drydock.

Long Bridge spans the Waterford River. Before construction of the drydock the river mouth stretched from the Southside Hills to Job's Cottage on Water Street so that the bridge was truly a long bridge.

The original bridge, which eventually became known as Job's Bridge, was built in 1828. A later construction was destroyed by rafting ice on 16 March 1913. The present structure was erected in 1927 at a cost of eighteen thousand dollars. Six iron lamps were installed at the time on the bridge for a cost of eighty-five dollars. The only one not vandalized is in City Hall. On 25 September 1874 Samuel Prefect, a stonemason, committed

925

suicide by leaping off the bridge. All that remains of the once beautiful Waterford River is an offensive, polluted stream flowing under Long Bridge into the harbour.

On the south side of the Southside Road, after crossing the bridge, one comes upon a graded mound with a monument in the centre. Here, in what was once the yard of St. Mary's Church, lie the bones of Shanadithit, the last of the Beothucks, a once proud tribe of indigenous Newfoundland Indians. The Beothucks may have greeted Leif Erickson if and when he landed in Newfoundland. According to the Icelandic sagas, it was the warlike attitude of these natives toward the Vikings that put an end to the Vinland settlements. When other explorers arrived from Europe in the late 1400s the Beothucks were also standing on shore waiting to greet them. Because they painted their hair and bodies red with ochre they were dubbed Red Men by the Europeans, and it was this small Newfoundland tribe that gave the name of red men to all the Indians of North America. They were, in fact, the only Indian tribe that could claim to be red in any sense.

In 1823 Shanadithit was captured with her mother and sister and brought to St. John's. The sister, and then the mother, died. Several attempts were made to return the girl to her people but they had vanished. This tribe of between three hundred and one thousand people was wiped out by disease and slaughtered by white settlers until only one Shanadithit remained. She died of tuberculosis in St. John's in 1829, at the age of twenty-eight. Dr. William Carson who was caring for her knew she was the last of her race, so he removed the girl's skull and sent it to Sir Thomas Cochrane, of the Royal College of Physicians, London, where it arrived in 1831. It is thought to have been lost when the College of Physicians and Surgeons Museum was destroyed by German bombs in a World War II air raid.

The inscription on the stone near the unmarked grave reads:

> This monument marks the site of the parish church of St. Mary the Virgin. During the period 1869-1963 fishermen and sailors from many ports found spiritual haven within its hallowed walls. Near this spot is the burying place of Nancy Shanadithit very probably the last of the Beothucks who died on June 6, 1829.

The old stone church of St. Mary the Virgin was supposedly torn down to widen the Southside Road during the harbour redevelopment of 1959-1964. The story of Shanadithit and her lost tribe is as heartbreaking as the plight of Evangeline and the Acadians.

Across the road from St. Mary's Church Job's had a small wharf, as did Nicholas Mudge. The Mudge premises was destroyed in a big fire on 26 December 1847 and rebuilt. Old man Mudge, who was highly thought of, went blind and died in Montreal, 16 September 1876. His wharf was taken over by Bowring's and the Mudge warehouse was again destroyed by fire around 1970.

East of Mudge was Charles Fox Bennett and, next to him, a firm of Dundee sealers and whalers. Their store earned a footnote in the island's history when, on 11 April 1911, the sealing vessel *Newfoundland,* under Captain Wesley Kean, arrived back in St. John's from the seal hunt with eleven sick men on board. On the way home from the front the ship put into Trinity and a doctor came aboard to examine the sick men. He found them to be suffering from smallpox. When she reached St. John's about 9:00 p.m. on April 11, the vessel was moored near the present Furness, Withy pier, and the eleven men found suffering from the disease were taken to a hospital on Signal Hill, near Cabot Tower. Sixty-eight others were taken to a warehouse where they were scrubbed clean in big iron tubs of hot water after which they were made to dress in fresh clothing supplied by friends and relatives. When the ship was fumigated she discharged her unfumigated pelts at the south side.

It appears the men were kept in the storehouse overnight. Next day, Sunday, a shed was erected in Connor's Field on Forest Road, to serve as a quarantine station. Measuring one hundred and fifty feet by fifty feet, we are told construction of this building was started and completed in twenty-four hours by a Mr. M. Kennedy, a most remarkable feat in any age.

In the area of the Dundee whalers' storehouse, where the sealers were scrubbed in iron tubs, there was a historic marker which read:

ROYAL NAVY HOSPITAL

A small hospital for the treatment of sick and infirm seamen from ships of the Royal Navy serving in the Newfoundland squadron was built near this site about 1725. Originally designed for use during the summer when the squadron was on station this building was found inadequate for the increased number of patients from the large squadrons stationed here throughout the American Revolutionary War and was replaced by a larger building erected nearby in 1779. The old hospital was maintained until Newfoundland ceased to be a separate naval command in 1825. A brewhouse for the brewing of spruce beer to combat scurvy amongst the ships crews was maintained near this site during much of the 18th century.

In colonial times the King's Watering Place, for the use of naval vessels, was next to the hospital site. From this property, east along the waterfront on what appears to have been Dennis Loney's plantation in 1689, were the firms of T.P. Whitycombe, P. & L. Tessier, and Boyd & McDougal. Strangely enough a skittle alley was located near the present Department of Transport edifice.

The large brick building of the Department of Transport now lining the waterfront is the Newfoundland headquarters fo the Department of Transport Marine Services, one of which is icebreaking. Red painted ships tie up at the dock in front of this premises: a part of Canada's famous fleet of icebreakers, such as *D'Iberville* and *Sir Humphrey Gilbert*. The *D'Iberville* gained international attention when she accompanied the giant United States-owned tanker *Manhattan* on her historic crossing of the Northwest Passage from the Atlantic, through the Arctic, to the Pacific in 1969. Several times, when the *Manhattan* was hopelessly caught up in the ice, it was the *D'Iberville* that freed her.

Ship-to-shore communications are also maintained here by the D.O.T. through marine radio VON on various frequencies. Messages are conveyed, weather information passed on, and distress calls are answered. Conversations are held with passing ships as well as inbound and outbound traffic.

East of the D.O.T. building and the cove leading to the docks, is the premises of the Canadian Overseas Telecommunications Corporation. This building is a supply depot for the C.O.T.C. ship, *John Cabot*. The historic Newfoundland cable stations at Heart's Content, Harbour Grace, Bay Roberts, and St. John's, that once linked North America and Europe, have been replaced by automation. Terminal stations in Deer Lake, Corner Brook, and Clarenville now route and relay passing traffic by computer. The C.O.T.C. maintains the *John Cabot* on permanent station in St. John's for the maintenance and repair of overseas cables damaged in Newfoundland waters. British and French cable ships, such as *Ampere* and *Alert* share the responsibility for maintaining and repairing cables in the Atlantic. Eleven cables link Newfoundland to Nova Scotia, Quebec, Greenland, Great Britain, and France. The building is able to supply all the needs of the repair ships stationed at St. John's.

In the summer of 1973 the *John Cabot* made international headlines when she performed the world's deepest sea rescue by hauling the midget submarine *Pisces* III to the surface, saving her two-man crew, after they were stranded three days at the bottom of the Atlantic off the Irish coast.

Along this section of the waterfront are the rotting remains of docks that saw the great sealing fleets of the past unload hundreds of thousands of pelts each spring for over two hundred years. Their silence echoes with the names of the great skippers, some loved, some feared, some hated: Kean, Knee, Blandford, Bartlett, and a hundred others.

The rotting piers once belonged to N. Stabb & Co., Captain E. White, J. & W. Stewart, P. & L. Tessier, Bowring Brothers. It was also the location of the St. John's Floating Dry Dock. With the exception of Bowring's all these premises have been taken over by John Leckie Ltd., a Canadian firm supplying fish nets, twines, etc., who established a St. John's branch in 1957, Texaco Canada Ltd., and Irving Oil. Imperial Esso has its wharf where the drydock floated.

A steep hill runs down to Bowring's Wharves. The building east of the foot of this hill, once the Bulley & Job property, is now a branch of the world-renowned College of Fisheries. Here students learn the practical application of what they are taught at the College of Fisheries building on

Parade Street. The southside premises contains a special plate-fitters and boat-building shop. Tied up at the pier in front of the building are the *Zelik* and *Beinir*. These two training ships are used to give students practical experience and training at sea. The *Zelik*, a gift to the college from Fishery Products of St. John's, is a 79-ton, 83-foot commercial longliner. The *Beinir* was presented to the college by the Department of Fisheries of the Newfoundland government who used her as an experimental fishing ship in the work of the Newfoundland Fisheries Development Authority. She is a 200-ton, 120-foot ship adapted for multi-purpose training in modern methods of fishing.

From the Imperial Oil dock to the Narrows, Goodfellow & Co. once had a pier, followed by another part of Job Brothers' southside premises. This is thought to be the area where John Bulley established his business in 1730. The day after the Great Fire of 1892, William Carson Job married Edith Harvey Warren, and as there were few houses left to inhabit on the north side of the harbour, took his bride across in a rowboat to live in a dwelling at Job's premises on the south side.[17] Next to Job's was William Stephen & Co., Walter Grieve & Co., and finally Baine, Johnston & Co. near the harbour mouth.

Where these firms were once located a long pier runs almost to the Narrows. This was a wartime dock for the Royal Canadian Navy, now covered with military warehouses which have been mostly removed. The eastern extremity is occupied by the National Sea Products, Ltd. plant for processing frozen fish for the supermarkets of the world.

Behind the docks a narrow road runs beneath the overhanging rock of the Southside Hills. Spaced along this road are rusting iron doors set in the rock face. These doors lead to large underground caverns which were used, during World War II, for the storage of ammunition unloaded at the dock and later reloaded on warships in need of supplies of bullets, shells, depth charges, and so on. Some of the tunnels go back several hundred feet. Today they are abandoned, but for a time, after the war, they were used by the government as bonded liquor warehouses.

A power plant of repulsive aspect squats like a bloated frog on the south side of the Narrows. This steam plant is operated by the Newfoundland Light & Power Company and is an auxiliary source of power for St. John's. When the plant was first put into operation the Power Company hoped to string an overhead cable across the Narrows, to the north side of the city, but a public protest erupted and the cable was finally routed around the harbour. Construction of this steam plant, which all but ruined the natural beauty of the Narrows, was finished in 1956, with a ten-thousand-watt capacity. In March 1958 it proved of benefit when a sudden drop in temperature caused falling rain to turn into a great sleet storm that seriously disrupted electric services in St. John's for several weeks.[18]

A short distance beyond the steam plant is a retaining wall, all that remains of Fort Frederick, site of the famous defence known as the Castle during French invasions of the sixteen hundreds. Below Fort Frederick the harbour of St. John's ends at Pancake Rock. A narrow footpath leads beyond to Fort Amherst where again nothing at all remains of the military post built in 1763 to protect St. John's from enemy invasion and named for Colonel William Amherst.

10

Its Long-Lost Multitude of Ships

One O'Clock was the name of a fishing room which was given up by Edward Haswell to the military in 1698. A fort was then built at one O'Clock which became Chain Rock battery fortified with cannon around the middle of the nineteenth century. Note Chain Rock itself in the Narrows. (Courtesy Public Archives of Canada.)

The loss of the steamship *Argo* eight miles from Trepassey 29 June 1859, on her way from New York to Galway via St. John's, involved Bishop Mullock and Governor Bannerman in the controversy which followed her sinking. (Courtesy the Mariner's Museum, Newport News, Virginia.)

The Atlantic Royal Mail liner *Connaught* was a familiar sight at Sir Ambrose Shea's Galway Wharf. On 3 October 1860 she sailed from St. John's for Boston with 591 passengers. Three days later, buffeted by gales, she caught fire and sank without the loss of a single life. (Courtesy the Mariner's Museum, Newport News, Virginia.)

The S.S. *Adriatic* was built at New York in 1865. After the collapse of the Collins Line in 1858 she was laid up until sold to the Galway Line in 1861. Sold again in 1873 she eventually rotted and fell to pieces in Bonny, Nigeria. On 8 September 1863 she was the centre of attention in the most bizarre stowaway story in St. John's history. (Courtesy the Mariner's Museum, Newport News, Virginia.)

Cabot Tower atop Signal Hill was erected on the site of the old blockhouse where flag signals were transmitted to and from the town and ships at sea. Erected to commemorate Queen Victoria's Jubilee and Cabot's discovery of Newfoundland, it opened in 1900.

In 1762 Sir Hugh Palliser became Governor of Newfoundland. It was Sir Hugh who recognized the talents of one of his crew, James Cook, and started the young surveyor of Newfoundland waters on a career that ended with his death on the shores of Hawaii.

The marvellous misadventure of Louisa Journeaux began in Jersey, Channel Islands, 18 April 1886 and ended in Bay St. George, Newfoundland. She reached St. John's May 24 on her way home. (Courtesy Société Jersiaise.)

The S.S. *Ethie*, seen here at the St. John's drydock, was built by A. and J. Inglis, Glasgow, around 1900 for the Reid-Newfoundland Railway. Her sisters were the *Argyle, Clyde, Dundee, Fife*, and *Home*. The famous wreck of the *Ethie* 10 December 1919 has been immortalized in song and story. (Courtesy St. John's City Hall.)

This photograph of the S.S. *Terra Nova* in the ice of the Antarctic, where she took Captain Robert Scott on his ill-fated attempt to reach the South Pole, has become the logo of her owners, Bowring Brothers. The historic vessel sank on her way from Greenland to St. John's in World War II. (Courtesy British Broadcasting Corporation.)

942

Job's great sealing fleet began with the arrival in St. John's of the S.S. *Nimrod* 26 February 1867. Here she lies off Job's Wharf waiting to go to the ice as she did every spring until she was sold to Sir Ernest Shackleton. She left her home port for the last time 20 May 1907. (Courtesy Ian Reid.)

Walter Grieve's famous sealing vessel S.S. *Bear* is shown here in unfamiliar California waters playing the role of Wolf Larsen's ship in the 1930 Fox film version of *The Sea Wolf*. All that remains of the great sealing vessel is her figurehead in the Mariners Museum, Newport News, Virginia. (Courtesy Fox Film Corporation.)

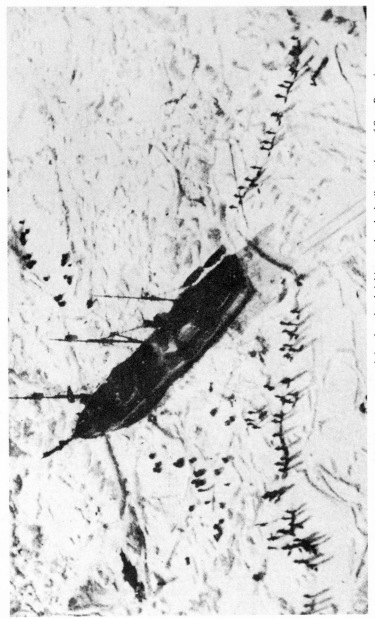

On 27 March 1922 the S.S. *Diana* was reported abandoned and sinking one hundred miles southeast of Cape Bonavista. It was afterwards discovered that the ship was deliberately set on fire by some of her crew. In this unusual photo the mutineers can be seen standing on the ice near the doomed ship. (Courtesy Aerial Survey Co.)

The S.S. *Eagle*, last of the wooden wall fleet of noble sealers, sails past Cabot Tower with flags flying on her way to her scuttling off St. John's 24 July 1950. This wanton destruction enraged a small portion of the public but most citizens were, as usual, apathetic. (Courtesy Rev. James Hickey.)

946

The S.S. *Proteus* with some of her sealers on the ice in St. John's harbour around 1880. She brought the Greeley expedition to the Arctic in 1881. Its members became stranded when the vessel sank 23 July 1883. (Courtesy Public Archives of Canada.)

The great Newfoundland-born Arctic explorer, Captain Bob Bartlett, as he appeared in the role of the captain in Varrick Frizell's Hollywood version of the seal hunt, *The Viking*. Captain Bob led Admiral Peary to the North Pole. (Courtesy Sterling Film Co. Ltd.)

The new St. John's harbour pilot boat in 1910. For generations the pilots were a close guild of Vinnicombes, Lewises, Gallishaws, and Ryans. In the nineteenth century each of the four Master Pilots had a boat and crew of his own and the rivalry was very keen. (Courtesy Newfoundland Centre, MUN.)

The Royal Main Ships *Newfoundland* and *Nova Scotia* linked St. John's and Liverpool from 1925 until they were requisitioned by the British government in World War II. The *Newfoundland*, seen here on her trial runs, was converted to a hospital ship and sunk off Salerno in 1942. (Courtesy Furness Withy & Co. Ltd.)

The Cabot Straight ferry S.S. *Caribou* was sunk by enemy action 14 October 1942 with the loss of 137 lives including the thirty-one crew members shown here. Captain Ben Tavernor is in the centre. His two officer sons are at the top of the left column. The woman is stewardess Bride Fitzpatrick. (Courtesy Newfoundland Historical Society.)

951

This wartime photo of the Narrows shows three anti-submarine and torpedo nets in the harbour mouth. On 14 May 1942 the German submarine U-213 laid fifteen mines near the port entrance but they caused no damage. On 9 October 1943 the U-220 laid sixty-six mines off St. John's. The U.S. freighter *Delisle* and British ore carrier *Penoluer* struck the mines with the loss of twenty-seven lives. (Courtesy Public Archives of Canada.)

952

Its Long-Lost Multitude of Ships

The old, old sea, as one in tears,
Comes murmuring with its foamy lips,
And knocking at its vacant piers,
Calls for its long-lost multitude of ships.
                    THOMAS BUCHANAN READ *Come, Gentle Trembler*

The old, old sea that murmurs with foamy lips around St. John's can no longer knock at its vacant piers. Like its long-lost multitude of ships they, too, have disappeared, having been swallowed up in the federal government's redevelopment of the waterfront in the 1960s. For centuries the long wooden finger piers of such firms as Brooking's, Pitts', Duder's, Tessier's, Bowring's, Job's, Ayre's, Bennett's, Stewart's, Newman's, and others reached out into the sluggish stream and clutched the hawsers of ships great and small. It is important before ending the story of St. John's to recall some of the vessels that used the ancient port and its piers.

One of the first regular passenger lines to service Newfoundland was the Galway Line which operated between Ireland, St. John's, Halifax, and United States ports. Its squarerigged steamers, such as the S.S. *Argo* and the S.S. *Connaught,* were a familiar sight passing in or out the Narrows. They docked at Ambrose Shea's Wharf, near the foot of Cochrane Street, where hundreds greeted each vessel that arrived, anxious for the latest news of the British Isles or America.

The loss of the S.S. *Argo* at Freshwater Point, about eight miles from Trepassey on 29 June 1859 on a passage from New York to Ireland via St. John's, involved both Bishop Mullock and Governor Bannerman. The *Argo* was expected in St. John's on the night of June 27, and a large number of passengers were waiting to join the two hundred, already on board, for the voyage to Ireland. On the twenty-eighth, as she was nearing Cape Race, the ship struck Freshwater Point, between three and four o'clock in the morning. Somebody walked to Trepassey and telegraphed to St. John's for assistance. Ambrose Shea, the local agent, sent the steam tugs *Dauntless* and *Blue Jacket* to the rescue.

Early in the afternoon the passengers were taken on shore where they spent the night huddled in canvas tents, made from the steamship's sails. Late that afternoon the vessel had rolled over on her side, and gradually settled to the bottom. The fishermen of the area were later accused of having plundered the ship. It was said they cut away her masts and completely skinned her, and some of the shipwrecked passengers complained of being robbed of their possessions. A few days later a defence of the men of Trepassey was made by Bishop Mullock, who had visited the community on pastoral duty and investigated the charges. According to the Bishop there was no plunder but it seems the fishermen were reluctant to turn over belongings they had taken from the water without a modest salvage fee being paid. His Lordship preached a sermon about the matter and many of the goods were brought to the church. Shea promised to pay salvage fees, and some of the shipwrecked wrote to the local press to defend the maligned fishermen. One of them was the internationally celebrated English operatic contralto, Agnes Heywood, who gave several concerts in the Colonial Building to replace her lost belongings.

Governor Bannerman became involved in the *Argo* affair when it was found out that four of the passengers were "female maniacs." These unfortunates were not discovered until the ship was two days at sea. Nobody knew how they got on board unnoticed. It was suggested they had been drugged into torpor so that their insanity was not apparent until the effects of the drugs wore off. Two of them were among the rescued passengers brought to St. John's. Another was discovered, a few days afterwards, wandering along the shore near Cape Race, living on wild berries. The fourth was presumed to have drowned, as she was never seen again.

His Excellency was somewhat upset at having to assume responsibility for these unwanted transients. He contacted the British Consul at New York in the hope of discovering the identity of each woman, as well as finding out to whom they had been consigned in Ireland. He wrote:

> You will observe that these three women have been thrown on this colony at an expense of about £100 a year, and placed in an asylum which, I regret to say, was already too full of our own unfortunates afflicted with insanity, and if we cannot get a clue to the parties engaged in such a transaction, I trust we shall be able to make them responsible for the maintenance and support of of the three poor women.

The Duke of Newcastle, then Secretary of State for the Colonies, directed that some investigation be made in Ireland, but without success. The efforts of the Consul in New York were, likewise, fruitless. He wrote to Bannerman:

> I received a communication from the Superintendent of Out Door Poor, stating that he had made all inquiries respecting the lunatics in question and could not find any trace of them, wither in the Alms House or in the institutions under the care of the Commissioners of immigration; and that it was supposed by the secretary at the

Immigration Office, that they were sent from Boston, or some
other place East.

The unfortunate Irish lunitics ended their days in Newfoundland among
strangers.

The following year, 1860, the S.S. *Connaught* set out from St. John's
for Boston on October 3 laden with cargo and a full complement of 591
passengers including many Newfoundlanders. For three days after sailing,
she was buffeted by gales until she began to leak in the engine room.
Pumps were ordered started but they failed to keep out the sea. The
following morning, Sunday, October 7, smoke was seen coming from the
after stokehold. The engineer reported to the captain that he thought the
steamer was on fire, and orders were given to reverse the pumps and pour
water back into the ship. This action was of no avail, for the fire continued
to rage unchecked below decks. Then the burning vessel began to settle
because of the weight of water in her.

At three o'clock on Sunday afternoon the lifeboats were launched and
distress signals raised. A nearby ship, the brigantine *Minnie Schiffer*, took
on board forty-five women and children. The liner's decks were soon too
hot to stand on, and the remaining Irish and St. John's passengers, as well
as the crew, took to the lifeboats and rowed to the brigantine. By ten
o'clock that evening the captain was forced to abandon the blazing ship,
and she soon exploded in a fiery inferno. The last anyone saw of the pride of
the Galway Line was a blazing wreck drifting out of sight on the horizon.

There were other transatlantic lines which serviced St. John's in the
century during which steamer travel lasted. Foremost of these was the
Furness-Warren Line, which operated the Royal Mail Ships *Newfoundland*
and *Nova Scotia*. The first of the Furness-Warren ships to bear these
names were built and put in use in 1925 and 1926 respectively. The
Newfoundland government presented a silver caribou to the R.M.S. *Newfoundland* in 1928, and the province of Nova Scotia gave a silk provincial
flag to the R.M.S. *Nova Scotia*. Requisitioned by the British government in
World War II, both ships had distinguished war records before being sunk
by enemy action.

By September 1941 the *Newfoundland* had been converted into a
hospital ship. She took part in both the North African and Italian cam-
paigns and, despite her Red Cross markings, was bombed and sunk off
Salerno in 1943. Her sister ship was fitted out as a troop carrier in January
1941. She was torpedoed 1 December 1942 off Laurenco Marques, in
Portuguese East Africa, while transporting seven hundred Italian prisoners of war. There was a heavy loss of life, with only 192 survivors.[1]

The second R.M.S. *Newfoundland* and R.M.S. *Nova Scotia* were each
seventy-five hundred tons and built in 1947 at Newcastle-upon-Tyne,
England. They were turbine ships rather than steamers and carried 152
passengers, along with much cargo. Their service came to an end in 1962

when they were sold to a line in Australia. The Dominion Far East Lines had them painted pale olive green with dark brown masts and black-topped red funnels. Swimming pools and sun decks were added and they cruised between Australia, Hong Kong, the Philippines, and islands of the Pacific until 1970 when the *Newfoundland* (alias S.S. *George Anson*) and the *Nova Scotia* (alias S.S. *Francis Drake*) were sold for scrap to a yard in Kachsiung, Taiwan, and slated for Japanese steel mills.[2]

With their passing from the Atlantic run in 1962, the passenger service between Europe, Newfoundland, and the United States came to a lamented end. People were flying the five or six-day route in five or six hours. The third ships of the line to bear the two distinguished names were the *Newfoundland* and *Nova Scotia*, built at Burntisland, Scotland, in 1964. These 6,600-ton cargo boats carried freight only. During the two years lapse before they went into service, Newfoundland cargo (and some passengers) was carried by the *Sycamore* and *Beechmore*.

Two beloved vessels of Furness Withy & Co. have earned themselves a nostalgic place in the waterfront history of St. John's. They are the *Fort Townshend* and the *Fort Amherst*. These ships were built in 1936 for the Red Cross Line which Furness purchased from Bowring's in 1929, along with the *Nerissa*, the *Silvia*, and the Rosalind.

The *Fort Townshend* and *Fort Amherst* carried many thousands of passengers, and hundreds of thousands of tons of cargo in the years they plied between St. John's, Halifax, and New York. The *Fort Amherst*, whose maiden voyage was begun on 20 February 1936, ran aground on June 4 of that year, in a dense fog off the Each Chop of Martha's Vineyard. The U.S. Coastguard cutter *Argo* rescued twenty-six passengers and took them to Woods Hole, Massachusetts.

During the dangerous years of World War II, both vessels continued in the St. John's-New York run, making over a hundred trips through U-boat-infested waters, while carrying a total of 24,834 passengers and 431,577 tons of cargo, without a mishap. The end came for these popular vessels in 1950, when the *Fort Townshend* was sold to a middle-east potentate who converted her into one of the world's largest and most luxurious private yachts. The ending of the *Fort Amherst* that same year was far less exotic. She was sold, to the British government as a munitions carrier.

Another famous shipping service for which Harvey & Co. were the agents was that of the Allan Line which operated between St. John's, Halifax, and Philadelphia. In August 1915 it began to operate instead to Montreal. This left only three small freighters sailing between Liverpool, Newfoundland, and Halifax. Bowring's stepped into the breach to Halifax with the *Stephano* and *Florizel*.

In 1823 Benjamin Bowring & Son acquired a small schooner of forty-four tons, called the *Charlotte*. This purchase was to grow into a great fleet of mercantile vessels. By 1846 the company was seriously pursuing the sealing industry with its own ships, and by 1861 there were seven sealers carrying 370 men to the ice. In 1865 the firm converted a gunboat, H.M.S. *Plover*, into its first local steamship, S.S. *Hawk*.³ She carried the Bowring family to Heart's Content in 1866 to watch the mighty *Great Eastern* successfully land the transatlantic cable.

By 1870 the Liverpool and Newfoundland branches of the firm were operating thirty-six ships. In 1876 Bowring's was awarded the mail contract for the Newfoundland coast, and the *Curlew* and *Plover* are said to have sailed with the pink, white, and green flag of Newfoundland at the masthead. Shortly after the *Plover* reached St. John's that year, she collided with another ship and several passengers were drowned. She was later wrecked again and finally lost at sea. Between them these vessels carried passengers and freight on the mail run for twenty years, until the coming of the *Portia* and the *Prospero*. Bowring's involvement in the coastal service continued until 1921.

The *Curlew* was to bring St. John's one of its most unusual visitors, Louisa Journeaux of the Channel Islands. Her strange tale had its beginning on a lovely spring evening, 18 April 1866. Miss Journeaux, of Elder Cottage, St. Clement's Road, in the Parish of St. Clement on the island of Jersey, decided to attend Evensong at the Anglican Church of St. Helier. She was joined in this pious intent by her cousin, Julia Wiltshire.

At 8:15 p.m., after the hymn singing and a sermon in French by Rev. P.A. Lefevre, the girls walked out into Mulcaster Street where they met Jules Farné, a Frenchman who was in the employ of Mr. Proust's hairdressing firm on Beresford Street. With him was a companion named M.G. Radiguet. Farné invited the two young ladies to join him and his friend in a row to the end of Victoria Pier.

They tried to hire a boat for four from Mr. du Feu, but the only rowboats available were skiffs for two. Miss Journeaux and Jules Farné took one, while Radiguet and Miss Wiltshire took another. A bright moon was rising as the couples rowed beyond the pier, as far as Elizabeth Castle on an island in the harbour. All went well until they circled the inner roads on the way back.

Farné let one of the oars slip from his hand. The shouts of the couple attracted the attention of Radiguet and Miss Wiltshire but, instead of rowing back, the friends went on to shore to report some mishap to the other rowboat. Mr. du Feu went at once to see what was the trouble, but the rowboat was nowhere in sight. To his amazement, he found Farné clinging to a chain, at the pierhead. When he hauled the Frenchman on board, Farné claimed to have lost an oar and, seeing it float away, jumped overboard to recover it. As he climbed back into the skiff, he accidentally knocked both oars into the water. Before he could get them out, they were carried away on the tide. Not knowing if Radiguet had understood the emergency, he decided to swim to shore to get assistance, leaving Julia seated in the boat.

957

When the news spread through St. Helier that a girl was adrift in a rowboat, alone in the darkness, the harbour master, Captain Bichard, and a Captain Allix went out in rowboats to try to locate the small craft. Their search and shouts brought no results. Around midnight clouds blacked out the moon and no further attempts seem to have been made at rescuing Miss Journeaux that night.

Next morning, April 19, a general alarm was raised and the tugboat *Duke* set out in search of Louisa. It returned to port without the girl. That afternoon Jules Farné was arrested by Centenier Le Gros and placed in the cells of the Police Station.

On Thursday, Jules was charged in court, before Judge Gibaut, with "having, by his neglect and imprudence, caused the death or disappearance of Louisa Journeaux." The young hairdresser availed himself of the occasion to repeat his version of what had happened. Mr. du Feu, the owner of the skiff, said in his evidence that he doubted Farné could have done what he alleged he did. Many in the court were of the opinion that the young lady met her death at his hands, probably defending her virtue. Judge Gibaut found that there was insufficient evidence to convict Farné of anything and he was released.

On Thursday, the twenty-third, a momentary excitement gripped the town when a rumour spread through St. Helier that the boat, with the missing body clutching to it by the fingers, was washed ashore at Rozel. This was soon denied by officials. Farné, sensing the hostility of the islanders, decided to clear out before a battered corpse turned up. He left for Paris on Saturday morning. As the days went by, with many rumours but no corpse, the family went into deep mourning and received the sorrowful sympathy of friends.

All of Jersey was electrified on 10 May 1886, when a telegram reached Mr. F. Journeaux, at Elder Cottage, from the Colonial Secretary for the government of Newfoundland. It read: "Daughter Louisa picked up near England and landed at St. George's Bay. Quite well." It was incredible that the girl could be alive and well in such a remote place, thousands of miles across the Atlantic from home. How had she got there? The story is best told in her own words.

> We had returned to a point between the two pierheads, Victoria and Albert, when Jules Farné, who was still rowing, lost an oar; in order to recover it, he turned the boat with the other, and, in so doing, that oar also slipped from his hands. At this time the tide was running out very fast, and the two oars were soon swept away from the boat.
>
> Jules Farné then jumped out of the boat to swim after them, telling me he was a good swimmer. In the course of a minute or so, he got into the boat again, nearly turning her over in doing so; he got in at the side and took off his hat, deposited it in the boat, and jumped into the sea a second time.

He then struck out towards the Pier to get the oars . . . in a short space of one or two minutes. I had lost sight of the swimmer. . . . When I heard his first cry for help I was greatly alarmed. I cried for help myself, shrieking as loudly as I could. I continued shrieking until I became quite fatigued . . . About midnight it grew cloudy and rather dark. . . . An hour or so after it began to rain heavily, and continued raining until about daylight. . . . I was quickly wet through.

Sometime early on Monday morning I found that the boat had a considerable quantity of water in it. I baled it out with Farné's hat, made of hard felt, and this I did until I was rescued. . . . About 7:30 or 8 on Monday morning, I saw a steamer which I took to be a Southhampton boat from Jersey, and going in an opposite direction to me. . . . On Monday night there were a few showers of rain.

Early on Tuesday morning I saw a sail coming towards me as from France. . . . and my spirits began to revive: at length I was, as I hoped, near enough for the sailors to see my signal, and so I made one with my pocket handkerchief, waving it to and fro. . . . She turned out to be the *Tombola* of St. Malo, commanded by Captain Edouard Landgren. . . . I remained in this hospitable ship for 26 days, when the captain landed me at St. George's Bay, Newfoundland, 2,300 miles from Jersey.

They tried to land me first at St. Pierre-Miquelon, but the fog being too thick to permit them doing so, they went some distance out of their way and landed me at St. George's. . . . I arrived at St. John's, Newfoundland, by steamer *Curlew* after a run of four days from St. George's. . . . At St. Mary's church in St. John's, I had the happy opportunity of returning my thanks to Almighty God. . .and my gratitude to Him was and is all the warmer from the fact that some hours after my rescue the weather became very stormy, and three weeks afterwards during a storm a seaman slipped from a yard into the sea and was lost.[4]

On the arrival of Bowring's ship *Curlew*, at St. John's on Sunday, Louisa was delivered into the care of Archdeacon Botwood, who from 1867 to 1900 was rector of the Church of St. Mary the Virgin, Southside. He hastened to Bowring's Wharf to greet the arrival of the steamer and guard the young lady against any and all improprieties. On Monday she was given the freedom of Bowring's store, and when outfitted to her liking was interviewed by two members of the press, carefully chosen by her mentor. They were Mr. Gleeson and John Ferneaux. The Archdeacon insisted that both gentlemen be attired in their finest for the occasion.

Later that day, the young woman was taken to Government House, to be received by His Excellency Sir. G.W. Des Voeux and his lady. Hers was a tale on which she probably dined out for many years afterwards.

On 2 June 1866 a crowd gathered on the St. John's waterfront to watch Louisa climb the gangplank of the Allan line ship, *Siberian*, followed close behind by Rev. Mr. Werry. During the first four days of the voyage, fog and ice on the Atlantic delayed the steamer on its crossing to Liverpool.

The girl's parents had left Jersey, by the Southampton steamer, on May 31, so as to be in Liverpool to meet their daughter when the *Siberian* docked. Immense crowds greeted the arrival of the ship, and Louisa found herself an international celebrity.

With a view to avoiding the excitement of a public reception at home, her intended arrival at St. Helier, on the *Brittany*, on June 12 was kept secret by those who knew. News that she was on board the Southampton steamer, however, got about in the morning.

Her presence on the vessel was not generally known until the steward went his rounds of the cabins before the *Brittany*'s arrival at Guernsey. Hundreds of people crowded the Guernsey dockside to view the celebrity. She came out on deck and was presented with numerous bouquets of flowers and, as the ship left St. Peter's Port on the last stage of the eventful journey, she was loudly cheered.

When the *Brittany* neared St. Helier Harbour the sight of the heroine, standing on the deck, caused considerable excitement among the throng assembled on shore. According to the *British Press and Jersey Times*, "the feelings of many of the ladies present being manifestly acted upon by the hysterical weeping of Miss Journeaux's sister who was anxiously waiting to greet the recovered one."

As Louisa crossed the gangplank and set her foot on native soil again, three hearty cheers rent the air. She was pale and nervous with excitement. After embracing her sister, in a flood of tears, she was escorted to a closed carriage, held in waiting by the Reverend P.R. Braithwaite. She drove off accompanied by her mother, her sister, and an unnamed lady, but not before another handsome bouquet of flowers was thrust into her arms. It was fifty-five days since she had left that same pier for a leisurely row in the harbour.

A few years after these celebrated events had occurred, Louisa left the Channel Islands for London where she married a Mr. Wyse, a clerk in the War Office. She died on the eve of World War II, in 1939. Her saviour Captain Landgren, having been honoured by the people of Jersey with a gold medal, decided to retire to the island, where he lived out his days in a house at La Grand Rue, in St. Martin, with a local wife.

As late as 1954, one of the characters in this story was still alive and living at La Retaite, Ouaisne, St. Brelade, Jersey, as Mrs. J. Kadrewell. She was Julia Wiltshire, the cousin who had gone rowing with Louisa that fateful Sunday night. The eighty-seven-year-old lady told a reporter she clearly remembered the fine spring evening when the two girls met their male companions after church and, without their parent's knowledge, set out in the two skiffs to row to the end of Victoria Pier. She also recalled waiting until one o'clock next morning, by the quay side, for the rowboat that never came back. Farné was never seen or heard of again after he fled to

Paris.[5] Today, with telegraphy and radio, as well as sea and air search and rescue, such an adventure would be virtually impossible.

Unlike the *Curlew*, many of the ships of Bowring's fleet were named for characters in plays by Shakespeare, and they were known as the Shakespeare fleet. This seems to have begun with the *Titania*, which was acquired early in the 1880s to operate a line between St. John's, Halifax, and New York. She was lost soon afterwards without a trace, but the operation she had started continued. Harvey & Co. had chartered ships and was the sole owner of the original steamship line running between St. John's, Halifax, and New York. Subsequently the Bowring branch in Liverpool, England, joined Harvey's on a fifty-fifty basis, and the line was named the Red Cross Line. It was registered in 1884 and carried passengers and freight on the run for the next forty years. When the new steamers such as the *Stephano* and *Florizel* were built, Harvey's became minority shareholders and eventually Bowring Brothers of Liverpool bought out the line. When Bowring's acquired the *Fort Townshend* and *For Amherst* around 1930 Harvey's took over their operation and this continued until Furness Withy bought out the Red Cross Line in 1950.

Vessels of Bowring's Shakespeare fleet were named for such characters as Benedict, Capulet, Cordelia, Desdemona, Hamlet, Imogene, Jessica, Juliet, Miranda, Oberon, Ophelia, Orlando, Othello, Portia, Prospero, Romeo, Rosalind, Silvia, Stephano, Titania, Trinculo, and Viola. In connection with the *Rosalind*, it is interesting to note that the internationally acclaimed film and stage star, Rosalind Russell, was born after her Connecticut parents made a return cruise from New York to St. John's on board the ship. So enchanted were the Russells with the voyage that they named their daughter for the S.S. *Rosalind*. Miss Russell treasures a photo of the ship.

After joining the company fleet in 1909, the three-thousand-ton *Florizel* soon became one of the most popular passenger liners on the West Atlantic service. She broke records at the seal fishery under command of the legendary Captain Abram Kean, a fearsome immortal in the story of the hunt. On the most remarkable of her voyages to the ice fields, the *Florizel* accounted for more than forty-three thousand seals taken at a net value of over ninety thousand dollars.

With the outbreak of war in 1914, Newfoundlanders rushed to join the fighting services. In no time at all the first contingent of the Newfoundland Regiment was ready to embark for England. These 540 men, known as the First Five Hundred, were called the Blue Puttees, after the colour of their leg wrappings. On October 4 this contingent of the land force set out for England on the *Florizel*. The event was one of great military importance to the country and signalled a giant demonstration of national patriotism. The ship was decked in flags as thousands lined the piers and hillsides to cheer the departing soldiers. Twelve days later they landed at Devonport, England, from where they were sent to their train-

961

ing camp on Salisbury Plain. The Blue Puttees went to death and glory when most of them were slaughtered in the bloody battles of No Man's Land.

The *Florizel* ended her days in tragedy. She sailed from St. John's on the evening of Saturday, 12 February 1917, carrying 138 passengers and crew bound for Halifax and New York. It was a dark and threatening winter night when the vessel put out through the Narrows, and as she turned her course south she ran into a snowstorm. Many travellers became sick in the heavy seas and retired early to their cabins. A few sat up in the saloon playing cards and drinking. During the night, as the ship ploughed through the blinding snow and raging waters, she suddenly struck a reef, off Cappahayden on the Southern Shore. The relentless seas pounded the decks, broke her back, and submerged her to the smokestack. For many hours those on shore watched helplessly as giant seas rolled over the wreck. Bowring's immediately dispatched the *Terra Nova*, under Captain Nicholas Kennedy, to the rescue. When the seas abated enough to get the survivors ashore, it was found that ninety-four people had lost their lives on the awful night, including many men prominent in the St. John's business community. Their deaths were a severe blow to the life of the city. The sad tale of one of the drowned passengers, a little girl called Betty Munn, is told in the story of Bowring Park. Bits of wreckage from the *Florizel*, such as brass and crockeryware, may be seen to this day in homes along the Sourthern Shore.

There is a monument to those lost in the sinking about a hundred feet from the southeast corner of the chapel in Mt. Carmel Cemetery. The inscription reads: "Erected by the citizens of St. John's to the sacred memory of those who died when the *Florizel* was wrecked near Cappahayden on February 24, 1918."

On the back it says: "The following members of the crew, Spanish firemen, are interred in this plot." The names of eleven Spaniards follow, only one of whom has a small individual headstone in the plot. The south side of this monument contains the names of seven victims who are buried in family plots elsewhere in the cemetery. On the opposite side there is a cloyingly sentimental verse in Archbishop Howley's worst style.

A sistership of the *Florizel* was the *Stephano* which, under the command of Captain Smith, an American married to a Newfoundlander, had earlier met with disaster, although no personal tragedy was involved. On the afternoon of 8 October 1916 she was steaming past the Nantucket lightship on her way from St. John's and Halifax to New York, with a $250,000 cargo consisting mainly of salt codfish for South American markets, when she was attacked by a German submarine, cruising on the surface.

The U-53 was outside the three-mile limit of the neutral United States when at 3:30 p.m. she fired some shots into the Newfoundland vessel. The U-boat commander gave the one hundred and forty passengers and crew eight minutes to evacuate the liner before the next shots were fired.

A nearby ship, the *Kingstonian*, was also attacked when abandoned and went to the bottom almost immediately. The *Stephano* refused to sink even after having been hit by thirty-six shells. She was finally disposed of by a torpedo, but even then she went slowly, and was still afloat that evening.[6]

The passengers and crew were rescued from their lifeboats by American naval ships and taken to Newport, Rhode Island. President Wilson decided not to protest the attack since the rules of war had been carefully observed by the U-boat. The loss of both *Florizel* and *Stephano* was a severe blow to the Red Cross Line and it became very difficult for Bowring's to maintain the service afterwards.

Between 1866 and 1872 three wooden-hull sealing ships were constructed in Dundee, Scotland, for Job's firm in St. John's. The first of these oak vessels, S.S. *Nimrod*, taken over by Job Brothers in 1867, was to earn a place in world history. It all began in 1902 when Robert Falcon Scott led his first expedition to Antarctica. His party was within three hundred miles of the South Pole before having to turn back. One of those with Scott was a twenty-nine year old physician, Ernest Shackleton. Although he had been a school dropout, he had a quick mind and forceful personality and held a master's certificate in the merchant marine and was a competent navigator. Because he was rather ill with scurvy, Shackleton was returned to England by Scott, on the relief ship *Morning*. This angered the young man who vowed to outlive his leader and someday return to conquer the Pole.

Back in England he set out to raise seventeen thousand pounds for his expedition by using his considerable powers as an orator. To his chagrin he found out that Scott was also planning another Antarctic expedition. Shackleton needed a stout ship for the venture and tried to obtain the Norwegian vessel *Bjorn*, but she proved too expensive and he continued his search. Somebody told him about a wooden sealing ship that the firm of Job's, in Newfoundland, was offering for sale. This was the *Nimrod*. Shackleton got in touch with Job's and purchased the three hundred and thirty three-ton vessel, sight unseen. On 20 May 1907 she sailed from her home port of St. John's for the last time, after forty years of service.

We are led to believe that the explorer's heart sank when he first set eyes on the little sealer in the Thames. Her decks were stinking and still covered with the remains of seal blood and blubber from the recent hunt. Her masts were rotten and her sails were in such poor condition they were useless. Shackleton set to work at once and, under his supervision, she was turned into a trim, attractive craft of which he eventually became quite proud.

The young Englishman was prepared to sail long before Captain Scott was able to get ready his second expedition. By the summer the

Nimrod was at Cowes, Isle of Wight, where she was boarded by King Edward VII, Queen Alexandra, and assorted princelings and royal persons who posed on deck for photographs. Then, with flags flying and the cheers of thousands rending the quiet of Cowes, she set sail for New Zealand via the Cape of Good Hope, under Captain R.G. England, who had been chief officer on the *Morning*.

Ernest Shackleton who was still busy fund-raising and arranging final details, was unable to sail until later, when he went overland, taking a fast ship from Marseilles to Australia via the Suez Canal. His lectures in Australia and New Zealand, while awaiting the arrival of the *Nimrod*, brought him much-needed monetary donations.

When all the animals and supplies were put on board in the New Zealand port of Lyttleton it was seen that the small Newfoundland sealer was seriously overloaded. The Union Steamship Company offered the steamer *Koonya*, as a tow ship. She turned back, 15 January 1908, when the first pack ice was reached. Eight days later the *Nimrod* came in sight of Ross Ice Shelf. Because of a disagreement between Shackleton and Captain England, about the handling of the vessel, it was not until February 11 that the men, animals, coal, and supplies were deposited on the snowy wastes of Antarctica. Hasty notes to loved ones were scribbled, "Onward Christian Soldiers" was sung, and the *Nimrod* sailed away to the north.[7]

The expedition failed ninety-seven miles from the Pole. It was January 9, nearly one year after arriving in Antarctica. By February 26 the exhausted explorers were back at the base hut, where the returned *Nimrod* was waiting for them, having seen a signal with an oil lamp from the crow's nest. She was scheduled to sail next day if they had not returned. When Shackleton reached England he found himself acclaimed, but faced with serious debts. He had to decide if he should sell the ship or keep her for another try at reaching the Pole. The old sealer was refurbished, fitted out as a floating Antarctic museum, and put on display in the port cities of England. She brought in about three thousand pounds but her days were not to end in glory. Shackleton was forced to sell his vessel and she was lost on 29 January 1919 off Caister, Norfolk, carrying a cargo of coal.

When Captain Scott was preparing for this return trip to the Pole in 1909, he recalled the ship that had been sent by the British Admiralty to rescue him when he failed to return on the *Discovery* in 1903. She was the S.S. *Terra Nova*, known as the "roughest and toughest icebreaker to be had."

Built at Dundee, Scotland, in 1884, she joined Bowring's Newfoundland fleet the following year. In 1898 she was acquired by the Liverpool branch of the firm and was attached to that office until a few years after the 1903 venture for the Admiralty. In 1905 she visited Franz Joseph Land with the North Polar Expedition, and then returned to the Newfoundland firm. In September 1909 the Admiralty negotiated with the company for the purchase of the ship to take Scott to the Antarctic. The explorer would have no other, and Bowring's would have an option for repurchase after the expedition was over. She changed hands for the sum of £12,500, and was handed over at the London West India Dock in November 1909. The ship was brought back by Bowring's late in 1912, or early 1913, for approximately the same price as that which was paid for her by the Admiralty, and returned to Newfoundland waters.

On 15 June 1910 Robert Scott sailed in the *Terra Nova* from Cardiff, Wales, on the start of his heroic, but ill-fated, expedition. Of the passage from England to the Antarctic the explorer wrote:

> The Terra Nova proved a wonderfully fine ship . . . [she] behaved splendidly—no other ship would have come through so well. As a result I have become strongly attached to the Terra Nova. As she bumped the flows with mighty shocks crashing and grinding a way through some, twisting and turning to avoid others she seemed like a living thing fighting a great fight.[8]

Captain Scott had not reached New Zealand when he heard that Roald Amundsen had a change of plans. The dour Norwegian had been on his way to the Arctic to find the North Pole when word reached him that it had been discovered by Admiral Peary. Disheartened, he decided to turn about his ship *Fram* and try instead for the South Pole. The news plunged Scott, who was already irritable and depressed, into deep gloom. On the voyage from Australia to New Zealand his spirits sank even lower when the *Terra Nova* was caught in a savage storm. Time and again she was tossed on her beam ends.[9] Her cargo shifted and the pumps broke down. Several of the ponies and dogs she carried on her decks were washed overboard before she finally got to Wellington.

When Scott's expedition reached the South Pole, on 17 January 1912, it was only to see the flag of Norway flapping in the breeze. Amundsen and four others had been there a month earlier, on December 14, to claim the victory. Robert Falcon Scott and his men started to stumble back to their ship, but the hardships and blizzards were too much for them.

On March 29, as the *Terra Nova* awaited his return, Captain Scott, the last survivor, wrote in his diary, "For God's sake, look after our people," and died, a dozen miles from the ship. When the bodies of the party were discovered, and brought on board the waiting vessel seven months later, they were in a state of perfect preservation. Instead of a conquering hero, the Newfoundland sealer carried away from the icy vastness of the Antarctic the frozen corpse of a dead explorer.

It is to be greatly lamented that the old *Terra Nova* was a casualty of World War II. In 1943 she was chartered to carry supplies and equipment between Newfoundland and United States bases in Greenland. She left St. John's on May 28 of that year, with a mixed cargo of cement and lumber and a Newfoundland crew. Slob ice and icebergs presented a problem all along the coast of Greenland, and in trying to avoid the heavy Arctic ice

Captain Llewellyn Lush twisted her stern out below the water line. She started to leak, but the pumps kept the water out so that she reached the island capital, Julianehaab. Divers reported that the stem was gone to the main keel. A patch job was done and she was ordered to St. John's for full repairs.

The old ship left Greenland at eight on the morning of September 13 in a moderate breeze. As the day wore on the breeze stiffened and the vessel began to leak badly. By nine o'clock that night it was necessary to send out an SOS signal. Around midnight an American naval ship came alongside, but it was too rough for the crew of the stricken vessel to be taken off. At daylight they got away in a dory. By then the decks were awash. The rescue ship stood by until the irreplaceable historic hulk went to the bottom shortly afterwards.[10] All that remains today of the *Terra Nova* is her figurehead, a draped female, which was removed from the ship in Cardiff in 1913, and is in the National Museum of Wales. The silhouette of the ship is used as the firm's symbol in Bowring's stores across Canada.

In January 1874 the St. John's merchant Walter Grieve and his family stood on a platform in the town of Dundee, Scotland, and cracked a bottle of champagne against the stem of his new steam barkentine, the *Bear*. The sealing vessel was 190 feet long with fore, top, and mizzenmasts of Norwegian pine. She was 29 feet, 9 inches in beam with a displacement of 1675 tons. Work on the ship was rushed to completion soon after launching and she reached St. John's for the first time on 10 March 1874, just in time for the spring sealing voyage. Captain Graham signed on over 250 hands, and Walter Grieve watched her depart for the ice. When she returned to St. John's she had on board 12,635 seal pelts, a respectable catch.

Every year after that the *Bear* went north to the seal hunt in the spring. In 1883 she was to play a more important role. Her sister ship, the *Proteus*, brought the Greeley expedition to Lady Franklin Bay in August of 1881 to carry out scientific studies of the Arctic. The expedition of Lt. Adolphus Greeley became stranded the following year when the *Proteus* sank. For two years attempts were made to rescue the party, until finally the United States government purchased the *Bear* from Walter Grieve for a hundred thousand dollars and she was fitted out in the Brooklyn Navy Yard in 1883 to go to the rescue of the expedition. At first only dead men were found, but later some survivors were discovered living in nightmare conditions. When the *Bear* returned to New York she was greeted with bands playing and flags flying everywhere.

After the rescue of the Greeley party the ship had a varied career ending up as a floating museum in Oakland, California. In 1930 the Fox Film Corporation borrowed her to play the part of Death Larsen's ship, the *Macedonia*, in the film of Jack London's novel, *The Sea Wolf*, starring Milton Sills and Raymond Hackett. After this, Admiral Byrd bought her and she went to Antarctica on his second expedition. By 1963 she was a rotting hulk in the Halifax harbour when an American bought her for a restaurant and museum. On March 19, on a tow to Philadelphia, she broke adrift in a storm and sank ninety miles south of Cape Sable.

As incredible as it may seem, the last of the great fleet of Newfoundland woodenwalls, Bowring's vessel the *Eagle*, was deliberately sunk in 1950 almost bringing to an end what has been termed the greatest hunt in the world. Built in Norway in 1902, she was the third ship to bear the name. The *Eagle*'s career of forty-five seasons at the ice ended when she was towed through the Narrows to the Cordelia Deeps, 25 July 1950. The sirens and whistles of ships in St. John's harbour sounded a farewell as the vessel sailed out of the port for the last time decked in flags and bunting. Crowds watched from the waterfront and Signal Hill as swarms of small boats followed in her wake.

When she reached the Deeps a small crew set the *Eagle* on fire, her seacocks were opened, and the coverings knocked from scuttling holes that had been cut in the hull. The crew were taken off by the pilot boat, and the vessel burned and settled to the bottom of the Atlantic. Another irreplaceable element in Newfoundland history was irrevocably lost.

James Baird's sealing ship, S.S. *Diana*, was also set on fire and sent to the bottom. That happened in 1922, not as a result of decision by the owners, but because of a mutiny by the crew. Built in Dundee in 1870, she began life as the *Hector* in the service of Job's. In 1889 she became the *Diana*, and was sold to Baird's in 1918.

On 16 March 1922 the vessel was a hundred miles southeast of Cape Bonavista, jammed in ice with seven thousand seals on the pans and nearly five thousand on board. According to the official account, the ship was jammed all day and while trying to get clear, lost her tail shaft. She was abandoned on March 27 when the crew of 125 men were taken off her by the *Sagona* and landed at Bay de Verde, where they were taken on board the *Watchful* and brought to St. John's.

Within days rumours began circulating and newspapers were asking for the true facts. These did not emerge until long afterwards. It seems the ship broke her shaft in clear water, and was soon after caught in the ice, where she remained for twelve days. The sealers were not happy with the situation and wanted to be taken off. Some World War veterans on board got hold of five rifles that were forward, and under the leadership of these veterans about forty men, in an ugly mood, broke into the Marconi house and threatened to throw the captain and the wireless operator overboard if they did not send an SOS. The mutineers were said to have been led by a master watch. At the time, according to one of the officers, the *Diana* was only leaking six inches in four hours and could have been kept afloat.

The captain finally gave in to the demands of the mutineers. The *Sagona* heard the distress signal and went to the rescue. While the sealers were removing the powder and provisions, a fire was started forward by some person or persons unknown, and as the crew sailed away in the

967

Sagona, they watched the burning *Diana* until they were out of sight.[11] She sank later, ending a career in which she brought six hundred thousand seals to port.

Another famous name among St. John's sealing ships is that of the S.S. *Viking*. Built at Arendal, Norway, in 1881, she was used continually from 1904 by the firm of Bowring Brothers in the seal fishery. The *Viking* weathered many a sleet storm and northern gale as she went in search of the patches.

In the spring of 1930 an American film producer, Varick Frissel, a young man who had learned his trade from the great Robert Flaherty, sailed for the ice fields, on the S.S. *Ungava*, to make a semi-documentary feature film about the Newfoundland seal hunt. The leading role was played by Charles Starrett, who was afterwards to know fame as a star of cowboy movies. Later that same spring Frissel chartered the *Viking*, after her return from the ice, for story shots. She was under command of Captain Robert Bartlett, who played himself in the movie. Thus we have preserved on film the person and voice of the famous Arctic explorer who helped Peary discover the North Pole.

When the picture called *Northern Knight*, later *White Thunder*, was assembled in New York, the studio bosses felt the climax was not exciting enough. Frissel was asked to return to St. John's in the spring of 1931 and shoot some additional scenes of icebergs rolling over in the sea. At four o'clock on March 9 the *Viking* sailed from her home port, commanded by Captain Abram Kean Jr. with Capt. Will Kennedy as Navigator. She had on board, her crew, the seal hunters, the movie men, and a large stock of dynamite which was to be used in making the icebergs roll. Just before the vessel left the wharf, twelve boy stowaways were discovered and removed. Another nine lads were found while she was in the stream waiting to sail. The usual number of youthful stowaways found on a sealing vessel was seven or eight.

On Sunday, March 15, the ship was steaming off White Bay, on the Northeast coast, when the dynamite suddenly exploded, tearing her apart. The precise cause has never been determined. In the explosion twenty-seven persons died including Frissel and all but one of his film crew. An undiscovered stowaway, an eleven-year-old boy, Edward Cronan, a first cousin of the author, was among the victims. Some of the maimed and wounded died on the way back to St. John's including Capt. Will Kennedy, a brother of Capt. Nicholas Kennedy.

The film was completed in Hollywood and released as *The Viking*. It has a place in history as the first feature film, using sound, to be shot in Canada. It is also the first American sound feature shot on location outside the United States. *The Viking* is again of interest to historians because of a filmed introduction to the picture featuring Sir Wilfred Grenfell. In it, the great autocratic humanitarian of Labrador pays tribute to his friend, Frissel, and to the film crew, and vouches for the authenticity of the seal hunt as depicted in the movie. This is the ony sound recording of the immortal doctor in existence.

Over the years all prints of the picture disappeared and it lived only in memory. Then in 1950, when one of Job's old fish storage buildings was being torn down to make way for the harbour development, a print was found buried in the dust of a shelf. The highly flammable nitrate film was transferred to modern film, and prints are stored in several places, including the Canadian Public Archives national film collection in Ottawa. While the acting is pathetic by modern standards, the documentary aspect is visually a stunning tribute to Newfoundland's heroes of the ice fields.

As far as recorded history is concerned, the Newfoundland seal hunt, by far the most supervised hunt of all time, began in 1585 when a thirty-five-year-old Englishman, Capt. John Davis, touched at Newfoundland after a vain attempt to discover the Northwest Passage. During his voyage he picked up over a hundred seals, the skins of which he carried to London for the good of the voyage and the owner of his vessel, one Master William Saunderson of London. Davis later discovered the Falkland Islands. He was killed in the East Indies, fighting Japanese pirates in 1605.

The sailing of the sealing fleet to the ice was always one of the great public events of the year in St. John's. Toward the end of the nineteenth century as may as sixty, seventy, or even eighty vessels would crowd the harbour in early March waiting for the signal to sail. The sea wind would howl through the masts of such ships as the *Ranger*, *Diana*, *Vanguard*, *Iceland*, *Leopard*, and *Neptune*. The intense frost could be heard cracking in the deck boards like muted rifle shots. From hundreds of homes all over the island thousands of men would stream into the old port by horse and sleigh, by foot, by special trains, and even by dogsled to try to get a "berth" to the ice.

Those who were fortunate in this quest knew they would have to face incredible hardships for nearly two months. If the voyage was successful, they could hope to take home, at most, seventy or eighty dollars as their share. Many earned far less. The lucky ones who managed to get a berth would go aboard the dozens of ships, taking on supplies and provisions at the numerous piers. Besides a bundle of clothing, each man carried a stout stick called a "gaff." This pole, six to eight feet long with a metal hook at the top, was used to stun the seals before killing them. The gaff was frequently a life saver when a man fell through the ice, into the freezing waters, between the pans. Goggles were a necessity against snow blindness, and heavy home-knit mittens and socks protected the men against frostbite.

The discomfort of their overcrowded quarters was nothing compared to the slime and odours that were to come when the decks ran red with blood and the whole vessel stank of blubber. However, such thoughts were seldom in the sealers' minds as they lined the rails on the day of sailing. Every ship and mercantile firm in St. John's would be a mass of fluttering flags and bunting. Then as hawsers were thrown on the decks, and the sealing armada started downstream towards the Narrows, the bells of every church in the community would ring out, guns would fire on land and on the water, and every steamer in the port would hoot its whistle in a great chorus of farewell.

The story of the men who sailed in and out of St. John's, and other island ports, on the seal hunt is the story of the real folk heroes of Newfoundland. It is a tragic, bloody, and heroic legend, as noble as that of any country which looks for its inspiration to dead revolutionaries. The tale of the seal hunt is, of necessity, one of slaughter and, at times, brutality, but neither as wilful as in the carnage of war. In recent years propagandists have manipulated an uninformed public around the world into thinking of the dying seal hunt as ecological carnage. To do this is to ignore the facts and do a great injustice to the history of Newfoundland. Few of the bloodstained, weary men, living on the raw edge of hunger, if not actual starvation, working for fantastically low wages, daily testing their courage against merciless ice floes and sudden blizzards, ever killed for fun. The same sort of economic necessity drove them as drives men wherever animals or fowl are slain to satisfy a need for money or food.

Many of the fearless men who braved the elemental existence of "swilers," as seal hunters were called, were never seen or heard of after they left home for the ice fields. To list the legion of disasters that claimed the lives of these simple Newfoundlanders would be a chore far beyond the scope of this book. Some samples from the many tragedies will suffice.

In 1830 the *True Blue* went down at Petty Harbour Motion, with thirty men, while returning from the hunt. The Carbonear ship, *Mary*, lost twenty-four of her men, including the captain's fourteen-year-old son, when overtaken by a sudden snowstorm in 1834. The death toll was again thirty in the year 1837. The following season over three hundred are said to have perished, when the great hurricane of 1838 sank fourteen vessels with all their crews. The mournful cry of the starving widow and her orphan was a familiar one throughout the island.

The *Margaret* of Harbour Grace went to the bottom in 1847, taking with her twenty-one men. Of the ninety-six vessels that left St. John's for the ice in 1853, the ill-fated Spring of the Waddhams, nearly fifty were lost. That year the *Georgina* reported the drowning of her captain and six of her men. Another ship told of the deaths of her captain and three of her crew at Funk Island. In spite of the heavy loss of shipping that year, most of the swilers seem to have been saved. In 1857 one man and a boy were the only survivors, in a crew of twenty-six, on board the *John and Maria* when she went down near Brigus. Ten women and two men died in 1867, sealhunting from the land off Catalina. The following year, the loss of four boat crews from the brigantine *Deerhound* accounted for twenty-eight deaths.

The *Village Belle* sailed to the ice in 1872, with eighteen men on board. They were never seen again. Later that year the *Huntsman* was smashed by a hurricane and sank with the loss of forty-three lives, including the captain and his second son. Of eighteen who were rescued, only three did not have badly broken arms, legs, and ribs.

An explosion of the boiler killed twenty-one men of the crew of the *Tigress* in 1874. In 1880 the *Bloodhound* struck an ice island and began to founder. Her crew made their way over two miles of ice to the *Retriever*, only to find that she had also struck the ice and was sinking. All 308 men leaped over the shifting pans to the village of Battle Harbour, Labrador, where they where soon joined by the crews of two more wrecked vessels. The shipless men were eventually rescued by the *Nimrod* and *Mastiff*.

In 1892 a clergyman, Rev. P.A. Carolan, sent the following dispatch from Trinity Bay: "Woe, woe, unutterable woe, crushes us today. Sobs and lamentations rend the air and corpses are strewn along the shore . . . victims of Saturday's gale which crushed the bight and swept off the men . . . who were out in punts seal hunting; some drifted back dead, some dying. . . ." This calamity, known as the Trinity Bay Disaster, claimed the lives of twenty-four who perished amidst the ice floes.

In 1898 there were no wireless sets on any ships. Marconi was still three years away from his historic activities on Signal Hill. The first intimation St. John's had of another shocking disaster at the ice fields was at 7:30, on Saturday evening, when word was flashed along the wires from Bay de Verde that the S.S. *Greenland* had arrived at that Conception Bay port with twenty-five men of her crew dead and twenty-three missing and presumed dead on the pans.[12]

At the time of the disaster the sealer was picking up pelts some seventy miles north of the Funk Islands. The crew had killed and panned enough seals to load the ship, but their catch was plundered by the men of another steamer. On Monday, March 21, Captain George Barbour was anxious to retrieve the loss he had suffered, so he decided to put out all his men. The morning was fine and clear as he sailed to the northeast of a lake, dropping four watches on the way. Then he steamed back along the three-mile path, to the first watch, and began taking on seals until six o'clock. A wind, accompanied by blinding snowdrifts, suddenly arose. The men of the first watch were hastily taken aboard and preparations were made to go at once and pick up the other sealers. However, it was found that the wind had closed the leads in the water and the vessel was jammed tight.

As darkness came on and the storm grew intense, the men on the ice suffered terribly from cold and hunger. Unfortunately, there were few seals that day so there was no fat with which to make a fire. The stranded watches waited in vain for their ship, all through the night. Daylight brought no relief. The blizzard continued into the afternoon. Some men had died of exposure during the darkness and others wandered off, in search of their vessel, never be be seen again. Several men, blinded by the snow, had fallen into holes of water and drowned.

At four o'clock that afternoon the weather cleared a little and the ship's whistle could be heard constantly blowing. It was Wednesday morning before she was able to get clear of the ice. Of the fifty-four men caught by the storm, the captain found only six survivors and twenty-four dead bodies. The corpses were stripped naked and buried in ice on the port side of the ship. When the *Greenland* reached St. John's they were dug from the ice, wrapped in quilts, and taken by horse and sleigh to the Seamen's Home on Duckworth Street, which served as a morgue.

Thousands had lined the waterfront on Sunday afternoon to watch the *Greenland* emerge from a thick fog and sail through the Narrows at four o'clock, with her tragic burden. Funeral services took place on Tuesday, March 29, with more thousands of citizens lining the route. Two mounted policemen led a procession of nineteen hearses that headed for the Church of England Cathedral. By thirty minutes past noon they were back at the Seamen's Home ready to start the procession of coffins to Gower Street Methodist Church. That afternoon the sealing ship sailed for Harbour Grace with the Conception Bay dead. The funeral of the Roman Catholic victims was held the next afternoon at four o'clock, and the procession to the cathedral stretched from Rawlin's Cross, the full length of Prescott Street, to Duckworth Street. Forty-eight men had perished on the tragic hunt.

The first *Greenland* was brought to the country in 1872. She was purchased by John Munn & Co. of Harbour Grace in 1880 and was finally burned at that town in 1884. The next *Greenland* was involved in the sealing disaster. Owned by Baine, Johnston's she ended her days when her main shaft broke during a heavy gale in March 1907 and she was driven 215 miles to sea, where she foundered. Her crew was rescued by the *Newfoundland*, a ship soon to be the focus of another heartbreaking tragedy at the ice.

Although there was little loss of life in 1908, it was one of the worst years on record for mishaps to vessels since the introduction of steam. Three ships went to the bottom and a number of others just made it back into port. The *Walrus*, *Panther*, and the well-known coastal steamer *Grand Lake* all sank with the loss of only one life. The *Grand Lake* went under almost without warning, but her 203 men were rescued by the *Vanguard*. Her sister ship, *Virginia Lake*, had her bows stove in and had to remain at the ice until repairs could be made. The casualty list that season also included the *Eagle*, *Neptune*, *Diana*, *Ranger*, *Newfoundland*, *Vanguard*, *Aurora*, *Eric*, *Labrador*, *Algerine*, *Iceland*, and *Terra Nova*. The *Ranger* made it back to the capital, leaking badly. The *Newfoundland* had perhaps the worst time in trying to reach St. John's. The *Daily News* carried the following details:

> When 85 miles ENE of Baccalieu she ran into a storm and began

to leak freely. . . . The night was one of horror. Mountainous seas broke over her and she began to strain. The stem seams opened and she began to fill with water. Hand buckets and Kerosene casks, sawed off, were requisitioned and every man was at work. . . . At 4:00 p.m. the next day Baccalieu was sighted and course was shaped for St. John's and hopes were high. But off Cape St. Francis another storm with blinding snow squalls was met with and she was again forced to lay-to, for the second night in succession. At 8:25 the following morning (Sunday) she dropped anchor in St. John's after the worst sea trip of all on board.

The value of the catch that season was $375,442, of which the men, who had endured terrible hardships at the risk of their lives, took home between a low of $2.26 and a high of $79.79.

There had been a number of sealers' strikes for better wages and conditions, the most notable of which were in 1838, 1842, 1843, and 1845. Improvement was gradual and grudging. The episode known as the Great Sealers' Strike took place on 8 March 1902, beginning with a group of disgruntled men who, led by a fellow named Colloway, started to air their grievances in Ayre's Cove. By mid-morning the crews of thirteen ships swelled the crowd to three thousand, and the strike was on.

An angry horde had two demands: First, abolition of the merchant shipowners' fee of three dollars, charged every man against the cost of his provisions, and second, increase of the merchant combines set price of $2.40 per quintal of seal fat to the men, when the market value was $6.50. Soon the vast assemblage was led on an orderly march to Government House, where Sir Cavendish Boyle received them cordially and advised them to appoint delegates to talk to the merchants on their behalf. The Governor was cheered, much as an earlier group of striking sealers had cheered Governor Harvey and Queen Victoria.

A.B. Morine, a lawyer who was to make a controversial contribution to the political life of Newfoundland, became their delegate and counsel. They offered to pay him ten cents per man but Morine declined any fee. His attempts to meet with the merchants, Job, Baird, and W.B. Grieve, proved a failure, and the strike dragged on into its fourth day. The hungry men huddled in what temporary shelter they could find from the winter cold, in Ayre's Cove, and were kept from starvation by the food offerings of sympathetic townspeople. Two ships escaped from the harbour but a third was caught by the sealers and held to the cove by a tow rope. The captain cut the rope but the crew launched a boat and rowed ashore, to join the strikers amidst much shouting and cheering.

On the fourth day Morine finally saw the merchants and brought their offer to the strikers. Standing with a megaphone on the top of a police wagon in Water Street, he told the men of an offer of $1.00 berth money and $3.25 per quintal of seal fat. He asked those in favour of accepting to go down Ayre's Cove, and those opposed, to head up McBride's

Hill. Most of the three thousand sealers swarmed up the hillside and Morine returned to tell the merchants their offer was rejected. By five o'clock that afternoon he was back on the police wagon, at the corner of Ayre's Cove, with a new offer: free berths and $3.50 for fat. Cheering proclaimed the lawyer the hero of the hour. His closing words were "To your ships, O sealers." Three thousand men heeded this cry and at 6:40 that evening the fleet began its delayed voyage to the "front," the place of the seal herds.[13]

The *Portia* was bound for western ports of the south coast on 31 March 1914 when she met the *Southern Cross* on her way home to St. John's from the Gulf with seventeen thousand seals and 175 men on board. A dreadful storm was brewing and it was beginning to snow. Thinking the sealer was headed for the shelter of St. Mary's Bay, the *Portia* signalled a greeting and steamed on to her own haven. The captain obviously had other ideas and ignored the portents of disaster. Being the first one home with a load was an obsession with most of the sealing captains. The *Southern Cross* vanished in the blizzard that roared out of the darkness, and nothing was ever again seen or heard of the vessel, or her crew, although the *Kyle* searched from Cape Race to Cape Pine for some trace or clue.

Meanwhile, on the morning the *Portia* passed the *Southern Cross* the weather on the northeast coast was such that Captain Wesley Kean, son of Abram Kean and master of the *Newfoundland*, thought it a good day to put out his seal hunters. By seven o'clock they were on the ice with instructions, if the weather changed, to stay the night on Captain Abram's ship, the *Stephano*. During the forenoon the lack of seals led a group to the *Stephano*, four miles away. They went on board for a "mug up," their own ship then having sailed almost out of sight. Around 10:30 there were signs bad weather might be on the way. Earlier that morning one grizzled, old sealer had foretold that there was a storm coming on. "Boys," he is reputed to have said, "there's a disaster coming out of this seal [hunt]."[14] When the weather began deteriorating, Captain Abram put his son's men out on the ice and sailed off to pick up his own crew. None dared tell him of Capt. Wesley's instructions to stay on the *Stephano*. As the sealers from the *Newfoundland* made their way back in the direction of their ship, the storm suddenly roared down over them, in a vicious blizzard that was to last for nearly twenty-four hours.

About nine o'clock that evening the wind changed to the north and the temperature dropped to zero. Some of the trapped men stumbled into the frigid water and quickly died. Others lay down to await death quietly, while some huddled in groups, and stamped and sang hymns, in an effort to keep alive. By ten o'clock Wednesday morning the storm abated and around two o'clock it stopped snowing. However, drifting continued and the men were unable to find their ship. They had to spend a second harrowing night on the ice. After daylight on Thursday the lookout on board the *Bellaventure* reported a patch of seals ahead. As the ship drew nearer, the excitement of Captain Robert Randell's crew turned to horror, when it was discovered that the seals were actually the dead bodies of fellow swilers, from the *Newfoundland*. Out of 136 men caught in the blizzard, 78 had perished. The corpses had to be hacked from the ice with axes. The story is vividly told by Cassie Brown in her moving book *Death on the Ice*.

The familiar silent crowds lined the dockside of St. John's when the survivors and the dead reached port. The bodies could be seen stacked on deck and those injured by frost and exposure leaning mournfully against the rails. Some were terribly scarred and amputations were necessary on fingers, toes, hands, and feet. Many of the dead were still in the postures in which they had died. Some bodies were unloaded in a kneeling position as if in prayer. Others were in groups of two, three, or four, their arms frozen about their comrades, and they could not be separated until they were landed on the pier and thawed in vats of hot water in Harvey's shed, behind the King George v Institute, which served as a morgue.[15] Each corpse was shaved, dressed in a white shirt, and placed in a coffin for the journey home. Two wards at the General Hospital were taken over for the treatment of those wounded by frost.

The calamities at the ice fields did not end in 1914. Each year lives are still being lost, but no modern sealing disaster has matched the twin catastrophies that befell the *Southern Cross* and the *Newfoundland* when 253 men died in a single storm in March 1914. By the 1970s, as far as the people of St. John's were concerned, the seal hunt had all but faded into the dim mists of past history.

The H.M.S. *Calypso* (renamed H.M.S. *Briton* in 1916 to make the former name available to a new curiser of the Royal Navy), and her sister ship, H.M.S. *Calliope*, were the last of the navy's sailing corvettes. The *Calypso* had been rigged as a three-master barque and fitted with horizontal engines that gave her a speed of fifteen knots. Heavily armed for a ship of the 1890s, she had some sixteen guns, two torpedo tubes, and half a dozen machine guns. All her active sea-going days were spent with the Sailing Training Squadron in the West Indies. She was sent to St. John's in 1898 to be used by the Newfoundland government as a drill ship and depot for the Royal Newfoundland Naval Reserve. She was stripped of her masts and yards and roofed over, so that she could serve as a winter training area. This she did from 1902 until 1919 when her decline began. In 1922 she was purchased by the firm of A.H. Murray and became a begrimed storage hulk for salt and coal. In 1952 she was towed from St. John's to Lewisporte where she served as a salt-storage depot and ended her days a derelict, in spite of the best efforts of those interested in preserving the last of the sail-rigged warships for the pleasure of present and future generations.[16]

The *Calypso*'s last gun has been mounted outside the Legion Club in

Grand Falls. One of her steering wheels is on display in the Military Museum in the Confederation Building at St. John's. Her log book for 1893-1894 is in the Newfoundland Museum on Duckworth Street. In the H.M.S. *Briton* room at the Colonial Inn, an eating place near Topsail, are to be found pictures of her in full sail, the original blueprints, and a stove said to have come from the officers' ward room, discovered in a St. John's second-hand store.

Of all the multitude of ships that have claimed St. John's as a home port few equalled the popularity and fame of the Alphabet Fleet. These were mainly coastal vessels, carrying passengers and freight around the island and north to Labrador, and all were owned by the Reid-Newfoundland Railway. In their day they even brought down the government of Newfoundland. The first eight were built in Scotland in 1898. They were named for the first eight letters of the alphabet and each was given a name associated with Scotland: Argyle, Bruce, Clyde, Dundee, Ethie, Fife, Glencoe, and Home. So graceful were these ships that they became known as Reid's yachts.

In subsequent years the fleet was increased by the addition of new vessels with such other Scottish names as Invermore, Kyle, Lintrose, and Meigle. For some reason J was not used. The *Meigle* originally called the *Solway*, became for a time a prison ship in St. John's harbour. Others were lost in marine disasters, a fate more fitting, if not ideal. The *Fife* was a total wreck, when she ran ashore in the Straight of Belle Isle in 1901. The *Bruce* foundered on the rocks near Louisburg, Nova Scotia, 24 March 1911. In fond rememberance, her likeness appeared on the labels of the whiskey, Old Bruce, sold in government liquor stores. The *Home* struck Flat Island, Placentia Bay, and was abandoned on the beach at Rushoon, but later salvaged. In 1944, when she was on drydock at St. John's, an explosion on board killed two mechanics and injured others by live steam. She was finally wrecked in a gale on the south coast. The *Argyle* arrived in St. John's for the first time 19 February 1900 and was lost when she ran aground in Cuba.

A famous wreck was that of the *Ethie*, 10 December 1919. She had left Daniel's Harbour on the west coast around four o'clock that afternoon. As she steamed for Cow Head a stiffening breeze from the south indicated a storm. By nine o'clock in the evening a heavy sea was raging and the captain gave orders to steer for Bonne Bay. It soon became apparent that the vessel was breaking up under the pounding of the waves. In an effort to try to save the passengers and crew, Captain English drove her on shore, where she struck off Martin's Point about one o'clock the next morning. A mongrel dog, often wrongly referred to as a Newfoundland dog, grabbed a rope that was thrown to shore and held it in his teeth. This is said to have enabled the watchers on land to string up a rude boatswain's chair so that everybody on board was saved, including a newly born infant sent ashore in a mailbag.

The *Invermore* was lost on 10 June 1914 at Brig Harbour Point, Labrador. The *Dundee* was a Boxing Day casualty when she went aground on Noggin Island, Gander Bay, in 1919. And so the story goes. Through grounding, foundering, and sale, the Alphabet Fleet gradually disappeared from Newfoundland waters. By the 1970s the *Kyle* was the only one still around. She lay beached at Riverhead, Harbour Grace, where she was finally purchased by the provincial government for five thousand dollars. The *Kyle* was the vessel chartered by William Randolph Hearst to take part in a search of the Atlantic for the American plane *Old Glory*, and she returned to St. John's with part of the wreckage. In this she was more successful than her search had been for the *Southern Cross*. In world War I she saw service as an icebreaker in the employ of the Tzar of Russia.

One of the Newfoundland Railway boats that joined the immortals of the island's maritime history was the Gulf ferry, *Caribou*. Built by the new Waterway Shipbuilding Company of Schiedam, Holland, she was launched on 9 June 1925. When the sleek, modern vessel reached St. John's, after completing her maiden voyage across the Atlantic, she was a gleaming and luxurious addition to the railway fleet. For seventeen years she was to operate on the Port Aux Basques — North Sydney run, across Cabot Strait, returning to her home port once a year for an overhaul and refit.

The story of the *Caribou* ended in disaster and death in the early hours of the morning of 14 October 1940, the dark days of World War II. She sailed from North Sydney, Nova Scotia, the previous evening, on her scheduled run to Port Aux Basques, Newfoundland, carrying seventy-three civilians, 118 servicemen, and a crew of forty-six for a total of 237 persons. Because it was wartime there was an escort vessel during the whole of the passage. At 2:45 a.m., as the steamer neared the Newfoundland coast, she was torpedoed without warning by a German submarine while most of her passengers were asleep in their cabins.

The torpedo, which hit amidships on the starboard side, plunged the ferry into immediate darkness. The explosion ripped apart some of the lifeboats. The ship sank within minutes as Captain Benjamin Tavernor steered the settling vessel at the surfaced submarine, in an attempt to ram the enemy, but the *Caribou* slid beneath the waves before this could be accomplished. It was reported that the submarine caused a further loss of life by surfacing in the midst of a group of survivors, where she is said to have smashed a lifeboat and upset several rafts. Rescue operations took nearly five hours because the escort was employed in making an unsuccessful try at tracking down the U-boat.

At six o'clock that morning word of the sinking was received at the Newfoundland Railway headquarters in St. John's. The message stated that the S.S. *Caribou* had been torpedoed two hours previously. Within an hour a small fleet of six boats was sent out from Port Aux Basques to search for survivors while a special train was made ready to carry them to St. John's. The ship was nearly fifty persons short of capacity on the fatal voyage, but because of the darkness and the speed of the sinking, life-saving operations on board were difficult. The officers and crew were praised for the manner in which they tried to avert panic.

When the rescue operations were over, it was found that 137 lives were lost, including Captain Tavernor and his two sons who were both serving as officers. Of the survivors, thirty were injured and eight were hospital cases.[17] The slogan "Remember the *Caribou*" was to inspire patriotic zeal in Newfoundlanders for the remainder of the war.

The *Caribou* was not the first vessel out of St. John's to be sunk by submarine action in Newfoundland waters. During World War I, the S.S. *Eric* met a similar fate. This three-masted, 582-ton sealing steamer made her first trip to the ice in 1902. On 23 August 1918, she was about seventy-five miles from St. Pierre, on a voyage from St. John's to Sydney for a load of coal, when sighted by an enemy U-boat that was operating on the surface.

It was 1:30 on Sunday morning when a shell came out of the darkness and blew a hole in the side of the funnel. The watch rang the telegraph to stop engines as Captain William Lane came out of the Marconi Room. When the shelling ended, the ship was a wreck. All the woodwork around the bridge was shot away, and the main rigging had fallen over the deck. The metal lifeboat was blown to bits and the port side of the deck full of holes.

An attempt was made to launch a small boat. Because of damage, she filled with water as soon as she went over the side. She was bailed out with difficulty and some of the crew boarded her. By then the submarine was under the stern of the *Eric*. The U-boat commander asked how many had been killed. When he was told none but that some had been wounded, he said, "Ah, you were lucky." The wounded were taken aboard the submarine to have their wounds dressed by a jovial doctor, while three German sailors boarded the *Eric* and placed charges about, to blow her to the bottom.

When it became apparent that the longboat wasn't seaworthy, the crew of about thirty men were taken into the U-boat. Later, the Germans signalled a French schooner to stop, and transferred the Newfoundlanders on board. They were landed at St. Pierre, carried to Lawn, and then to Placentia, from where they made their way back to St. John's by train. Captain Lane died in 1948, at the age of ninety-one, a victim of the tragic Hull Home fire, which took the lives of many old people in St. John's.

A number of ships that used the port during World War II were lost to enemy action. The story of one wartime casualty deserves telling because the effects of its encounter with a U-boat were to bother the city for twenty-seven years.

The seven-thousand-ton British freighter, *Kelmscott*, was steaming towards Europe about fifty miles off St. John's on 6 February 1944, when she was struck by a torpedo from the U-845 of Korvette Kapitan Werner Weber. The crippled ship was escorted into St. John's by a naval tug because her steering gear was out of order. Two torpedoes had gone through the freighter. No. 2 hold and No. 3 hold, the crossbunker, the engine room, and the stokehold were flooded to sea level, and it is probable that the ship would have sunk except that she was loaded with newsprint. If she had been farther out at sea she would certainly have foundered.[18]

After entering port the freighter was berthed at Harvey's pier and an attempt was made to remove the cargo. On February 20 the *Kelmscott* entered drydock, and here dynamite was used to loosen some of the paper which had swollen to a solid mass. It was taken in trucks to be dumped at Cape Spear, until that road became impassable. After that the sodden rolls were dumped on Waterford Bridge Road, almost opposite Sherwood Drive, but most of it went over the cliff face at the summit of Signal Hill, into Ross's valley. Over the years this eyesore, near Cabot Tower, was constantly on fire due to spontaneous combustion. It took twenty-seven years before the waste was finally removed in 1971. When it was removed the ruins of the old hospital used by Marconi were discovered underneath.

The *Kelmscott* was repaired at a cost of one million dollars. She sailed from St. John's 9 August 1944, for Baltimore but was rammed by a liberty ship on the way. She finally reached her destination in the tow of a tug.

A familiar sight in the harbour of St. John's was the schooner *Effie M. Morrissey* of Brigus, whose master was the great Arctic explorer, Bob Bartlett.

Captain Bartlett had begun his Arctic explorations with Robert E. Peary, in 1897. He was with Peary in Hudson Bay in 1901, and was master of Peary's ship *Roosevelt* from 1905 to 1909, during which time he played a leading part in the famous expedition to the Pole. With two Eskimo assistants, Bartlett blazed the trail which Peary followed across the frozen wastes of the north. In this way the American travelled in ease, after the Newfoundlander carried the burden and the risks.

On the last day of March and the first day of April 1906, Captain Bob reached a point forty-four miles farther north than any white man had ever been, to 87° 47′. He could have gone on to the Pole with little difficulty and claimed the glory for himself, but he stopped just short of the 88th parallel and waited for Peary to catch up. Instead of allowing him to share in the final reward, Peary ordered Bartlett to stay behind because he was not an American, telling him that the victory had to be for America and he could not let any country but his own have the prize. Peary went on to the Pole accompanied by an American negro while promising Bartlett to make it up, but how could he?

Others did take note of Robert Bartlett's accomplishments and he was honoured with medals from the National Geographic Society, the English Geographic Society, the Italian Geographic Society, the Royal Geographic Society, the Harvard Club, the Explorers Club, and many more groups.

In January 1914, Bartlett was captain of the *Karluk*, with Stefansson's

Canadian Government Arctic Expedition, when he was caught in the ice of the Bering Strait and his ship crushed. With an Eskimo companion he spent seventeen days crossing the ice to a village in Siberia and returned with a rescue party.

The *Effie M. Morrissey,* which had been built at Essex, Massachusetts, in 1894, was a derelict banker moored in Halifax harbour in 1925 when the Captain purchased her from a cousin, for six thousand dollars. In the years that followed her refit, he sailed her to the banks, and later, under charter, to the Arctic for George Palmer Putnam, the newspaper magnate whose wife, Amelia Earhart, twice made history by flying the Atlantic from Newfoundland towns. The trim schooner roamed the Panama Canal and the Pacific to Alaska. She wandered the North Atlantic to Greenland and Iceland.

When Bartlett found himself short of funds he wrote of his voyage in the *Morrissey,* in a book called *Sails Over the Ice,* which proved a publishing flop. Just before his death in April 1946, Captain Bob said, "My first love is the *Effie M. Morrissey,* my schooner; my second, the Arctic. . . ." Following his decease the estate sold the little banker to a lawyer and doctor in New York, who fitted her out for a luxury cruise to Tahiti, but she was gutted by fire just before sailing. The hulk was left rotting at Rowayton, Connecticut, until Louisa Mendes of Egypt, Mass., spent twenty thousand dollars to put her in the cargo-carrying trade, between New Bedford and the Cape Verde Islands. On 16 December 1948 the schooner was sold to Henriques Mendes of Cape Verde, refitted at the cost of another twenty thousand dollars in 1959, and given Portuguese registry as the *M.V. Ernestina.*[19] In 1970 she was again placed on the auction block. Newfoundlanders agitated for her return to Brigus as a floating museum to the honour of a favourite son, but the provincial government of the time was unwilling to meet the purchase price of around fifty thousand dollars.

Among the most interesting ships in St. John's harbour, over many centuries, have been the vessels of the Portuguese fishing fleet. These began using the port in the first decade of the sixteenth century. The first official record of the export of salt codfish from Newfoundland is found in the custom records of the port of Viana do Castelo for 1506. In 1527 Captain John Rut mentions two Portuguese barques in the harbour of St. John's. With time this fishery declined. A rival was begun in the 1930s under Antonio Salazar's dictatorship.

Until the early 1970s large three- and four-masted schooners came out from Portugal each spring. Their crews were dorymen who fished alone in a dory with tubs of long lines. Kipling immortalized them in his tale of the Newfoundland banks, *Captains Courageous.* After World War II, ships of this Portuguese white fleet were so numerous that they tied up along the St. John's waterfront, two, three, or even four abreast. Until a few years ago, the colourful plaid shirts and knitted caps of these four thousand fishermen on Water Street gave St. John's a modest exotic charm.

Painted white and kept spotlessly clean, many of the trawlers might have been mistaken for yachts, were it not for the fishnets and nests of dories stacked on their decks. Vessels of the Portuguese fleet ranged from 425 to 700 tons, and had such names as *Rio Lima, Santa Izabel, Gazela Primerio, Maria dos Flores,* and *Argus.*

The large white Portuguese hospital ship, *Gil Eanes,* which still serves the fleet, was named for one of Prince Henry the Navigator's captains, who sought the passage to the Indies by way of the Cape of Good Hope. The present *Gil Eanes* is the second vessel to carry the name. The first was a two-thousand-ton cargo ship converted between the decks into a forty-bed hospital. The present ship was built as a floating hospital and she carries a full compliment of doctors and male nurses as well as a chaplain.

Many are the good ships that have come to grief entering or departing St. John's through the Narrows. The chronicle goes all the way back to 1583 when Sir Humphrey Gilbert's *Delight,* of one hundred and twenty Guernsey, soon had reason to rue its decision to avail itself of "that class of men called pilot." A report sent to the firm and dated St. John's, 31 August chants for help in pulling his ship off the rock. Fearful that the half-brother of Sir Walter Raleigh might be the commander of a pirate squadron, at first they refused to render assistance. When the rejected knight asserted his authority and made it clear he was under orders from Queen Elizabeth, the gentlemen of the place hastily sent aid and Gilbert's ship was towed to a safe anchorage.

On 23 July 1812 Governor Duckworth issued an order for "the encouragement of that class of men called pilots" who had recently been charged with assisting vessels in and out of St. John's harbour. Shipowners were instructed to give information on all expected arrivals and departures, and those who refused the use of a pilot did so at their own peril. Later their use was to become mandatory.

The firm of Carteret & Co., a leading house on the Channel Island of Guernsey, soon had reason to rue its decision to avail itself of "that class of men called pilot." A report sent to the firm and dated St. John's 31 August 1812, describes a shipwreck involving one of its vessels.

> I acquaint you with the loss of your schooner *Vulture* . . . in consequence of the pilot's imprudence in attempting to beat through the Narrows into this harbour. In going about he went to the South Side and in consequence thereof lodged upon a point of rock. . . . The Guernsey captains now in this port and about 120 men from H.M.S. *Antelope* succeeded in saving the cargo, and in 30 days and not 'til then in getting the masts and rigging ashore.[20]

The *Antelope* was the flagship of Governor Duckworth.

The schooner *Helen* was wrecked on 26 December 1819 when she was driven on the rocks on the north head of the Narrows. Originally called Wash Ball Rocks on early charts, they are now known as Wash Balls. The *Helen* incident involved Newman Hoyles in a protracted press controversy and investigation, relating to the conduct, in the rescue operations, of the sergeant commanding Fort Amherst.

On 9 August 1821 an old custom involving the Narrows came to an end. Previous to this date there existed a practice known as "Let-pass," first begun in 1776. A Let-pass was a paper signed by the governor and sent to the commanding officer at Fort William. It signified that all customs and port charges had been paid and the vessel concerned was allowed to sail out of the Narrows. If a Let-pass was not received, the artillery would train a gun on the ship and bring her to. In 1784 a man on the brig *St. Vincent* was killed in the Narrows by an artillery shot fired to stop his ship from leaving port without a Let-pass. Following a non-fatal incident in 1821, the firm of John F. Trimingham & Co. took artilleryman, Johnston Gaskin, to court, and Chief Justice Forbes ruled in favour of the plaintiff. The dictum he laid down ended the practice forever.[21]

The voyage from Scotland to Newfoundland was long and dangerous in the winter of 1848. On the night of February 1 the ten-man crew of the brigantine *Avalon*, belonging to William Walsh of St. John's, sighed with relief to see the lights of their home port ahead as they neared shore with a load of coal from Glasgow. Unfortunately, the Narrows was blocked with ice so the ship anchored near the south head. Around 11:30 p.m. a strong breeze blew up and by midnight it had become a raging storm. In spite of the efforts of the captain and crew, the vessel was dashed on the rocks under South Battery. She struck amidships and fell asunder immediately. Because of the violence of the storm and the darkness of the night, watchers on shore were almost helpless. They did manage to save five of the crew, but the other five, who climbed into the rigging, were drowned, including Patrick Walsh, eighteen-year-old son of the owner.

A few minutes before ten o'clock on the evening of Tuesday, 5 June 1866, the U.S. Navy steamer *Augusta*, with the Monitor *Miantonomah* in tow, went out through the Narrows. The double-ended United States warship, *Ashuelot*, was some distance astern of them. These ships had been on an official visit to St. John's. While the *Ashuelot* was going out the north side of the Narrows, the steam tug Dauntless, towing the vessels *Selina, Spracklin*, and one other, appeared from the south heading for the north side of the entrance in accordance with regulations. No action was taken on board the warship to turn her to the south. The tug ran across the path of the *Ashuelot*, but the *Selina* was not so fortunate. She was struck just aft of amidships and was cut through to the hatchways, going down almost immediately. The greater part of the crew got on board the American ship, but one man was drowned, a twenty-one-year-old seaman of

Cupids, named Pomeroy. The tragedy seems to have been caused by the tug's insistence on its right to enter the harbour on the north side.

Three years later, in July 1869, a harbour pilot named Thomas Powers was killed in the Narrows when knocked overboard from a lumber vessel in a freak accident. The following year the Narrows was once more the scene of a collision, when a fore-and-after, a schooner with no square sails belonging to Trinity Bay, was run down by a warship of the Royal Navy. H.M.S. *Niobe*, which was leaving port for Halifax, smashed into the schooner bound inwards from Hant's Harbour, with a load of fish for Job Brothers. The collision damaged the small vessel so badly she went to the bottom almost at once, but the crew was saved.

Of the many sinkings in the Narrows the worst tragedy we know of took place in 1876. The large brigantine, *Julia*, left St. John's about eleven o'clock on the night of October 15, bound for the Mediterranean, carrying three thousand quintals of salt fish and a number of passengers, including women and children. After leaving Labrador, the vessel had called in at the capital to supplement her crew, which was short by two hands. Most of those on board were in their bunks when the ship struck a rock on her way out of port, and began to founder immediately. People on shore could hear the heartrending screams of the injured and drowning as the crushed vessel sank in the darkness. The disaster took the lives of thirteen people, including several of the women and children passengers. The corpses of eight males and one female were laid out in the Seamen's Home on Duckworth Street. The other four were probably taken to their own homes or to those of relatives.

The *Dauntless* was a paddlewheel steam tug that had arrived from Swansea, Wales, in 1857. At 4:00 p.m., on April 5 of the following year, while running to port at full speed after having taken out a vessel, she ran on and over Cahill's Rock, on the south side of the Narrows, and sank immediately, just inside the harbour mouth. Several citizens who were on board for a short pleasure cruise, and the crew, were all rescued. Charles Fox Bennett bought the paddlewheel as she lay on the bottom, and she was raised, repaired, relaunched, and provided a tug service for almost twenty years. She was lost near Dildo in 1877.

The 4,170-ton British freighter, S.S. *Titian*, was on her way from New York to Manchester in 1906, when a fire was discovered in her ten thousand tons of general cargo. At the time, she was four hundred miles southeast of Cape Race, and it was decided to head for St. John's. About ten o'clock on the night of March 25, as she was entering the Narrows, the captain thought his ship was too close to a rock on the starboard bow. The pilot showed little concern and told the captain it was Chain Rock and he would tell him all about it later. With that there was a loud grinding noise as the hull struck some unknown object. "We have struck the rock, pilot!" the captain cried. "No, sir, that was a piece of ice," the pilot replied. By the time the *Titian* was moored in the stream, it was found that she had indeed struck a rock and there was three feet of water in No. 2 hold. By one o'clock in the morning it had risen to ten feet and it was obvious the vessel was sinking. At two o'clock she was beached, at the end of the harbour, beside the Newfoundland Railway docks.

The schooner *Veronia* made history of sorts on 14 October 1909. Having stowed away a full load of general cargo, the captain and crew came ashore early in the evening for some relaxation, before sailing for home next morning at daylight. Around nine o'clock, when the captain rowed back to where the *Veronia* was left moored off Hunter's Cove, he was startled to find his schooner nowhere in sight. The mystery was solved by the captain of a nearby schooner who had just arrived in port. He said the *Veronia* passed him outside the Narrows, an hour earlier, travelling at a good speed.

A search was instituted. The truant was apprehended next day, loitering in the ocean four miles off Cape Spear, without a soul on board. A tug was sent out on the afternoon of the fifteenth to bring the runaway to port. It seems she slipped her anchor while the captain and crew were on shore, and was far enough out in the stream to be carried off by the tide. Where many a ship, manned by skilful mariners, had come to grief on the rocks of the Narrows, the unmanned *Veronia* glided straight through the channel into the freedom of the Atlantic.

About a month later, on November 18, the schooner *Phoebe* was less fortunate, when trying to sail out of the harbour in a growing gale. Dashed on the rocks under Fort Amherst, as the schooner broke apart her crew were drenched to the skin. They barely escaped with their lives, thanks to those on shore who waded into the water to pull the unfortunate men to safety.

On 13 March 1913 seven sealing vessels made their way out of St. John's for the ice fields. The S.S. *Beothic* and the S.S. *Bonaventure* headed for the Narrows at the same time. The excitement was great for the thousands of watchers on land, as the *Bonaventure* hit the *Beothic* and the two headed into the cliffs at Hay Cove, just outside Fort Frederick. The *Bonaventure* soon reversed and sailed away to the north. The crippled *Beothic* sheltered in Freshwater Bay until she was able to crawl back into port for repairs.The event could have been tragic, for the collision had upset the stove in the *Beothic* and set the galley on fire. Thirty kegs of powder were stored close by and several of the crew risked their lives to move it out of the area of danger.

The *Metagama* was a large ocean liner that was involved in a collision off Cape Race in 1924. She arrived in St. John's on June 19 for repairs, and was ready to sail for Montreal by July 11. As she was leaving the harbour she went ashore on Pancake Rock, where she resisted the efforts of three tugs to move her. The *Silvia* finally succeeded in pulling her off the rock at 3:00 a.m. during high tide, with no serious damage done.

The next victim of the Narrows was not so fortunate. The S.S.

Marsland, a seven-thousand-ton freighter bound out from Cadiz with a cargo of salt, arrived off St. John's on 2 July 1933. As she was about to enter port in the first light of dawn, the captain spied a small schooner coming out the Narrows. He ordered full speed astern to avoid a collision. The *Marsland* drifted out of the channel and all was well for the moment. As she attempted to enter the harbour a second time she grounded on the sunken shoal of Ship's Rock, below Fort Amherst lighthouse.

Attempts that day to refloat the listing freighter failed. Her cargo of salt was jettisoned to no avail. The Railway ships, *Meigle* and *Argyle*, tried towing her, but the hawser snapped. On July 8 the seagoing tug, *Foundation Franklyn*, arrived from Nova Scotia and new attempts were made to free the *Marsland*. These efforts were also futile. It was rumoured that a British warship H.M.S. *Norfolk*, due on a visit, would be asked to blow the wreck out of the harbour entrance, but before this could happen the *Marsland* suddenly slipped of the rock of her own accord and slid beneath the waves to her grave under Fort Amherst light.

Seaports are always full of strange tales of ships and men. In the late fall of 1883 a three-masted American schooner, *Nora Bailey*, left St. John's on a voyage to Sydney, Nova Scotia. On Monday, November 12, the day after she sailed, the sky became overcast, the barometer started to fall, and a heavy sea began to roll causing the vessel to heave and plunge dangerously. Toward evening a storm burst, with gale force.

At 9:30 in the evening, the mainsail went out of the ropes with a crack, while waves were pounding the schooner from all sides. The gale began to moderate on Friday evening; then, on Saturday morning, about 250 miles southeast of St. John's, a hurricane suddenly struck the schooner, tossing her on her beam ends, smashing the foregaff, and tearing the sails to ribbons. On Sunday, one week after leaving port, the captain decided to return to St. John's for a new set of sails. They were thirty miles from port when another fierce hurricane slammed into them. This cracked off the foremast and carried away the jibboom. Finally, the mizzen-mast broke and smashed the lifeboat.

The wreck drifted out across the Atlantic where the crew spent a bleak Christmas. On 11 January 1884 a large steamer passed, ignoring their distress signals. Next day a schooner, the *Excelsior*, out of Bristol and bound from St. John's to Gibraltar, took them in tow. The weather grew bad again and the derelict had to be abandoned. Late in January the crew of the *Nora Bailey*, who had set out for Nova Scotia in early December, landed at Gibraltar.

History repeated itself, as late as 1929 when the schooner *Neptune* II, with a crew of five under Captain Job Barbour, left St. John's on November 29 for Newtown, Bonavista Bay. Of the five passengers one was a female, Mrs. Esther Humphries. Instead of reaching Newtown in a few days the *Neptune* II went unreported and was given up for lost. On 14 January 1929 the battered vessel was towed into the harbour of Tobermory on the island of Mull, in Scotland's Inner Hebrides by the steamer *Hesperus*. Soon after leaving St. John's the ship was forced off shore by strong gales. During the next forty-eight days she was driven all the way across the Atlantic Ocean to Scotland. Like the crew of the *Nora Bailey*, twenty-six years earlier, the crew of the *Neptune* II, passed a bleak Christmas at sea. Captain Barbour narrated the gripping adventure in his book, *Forty-Eight Days Adrift*. Mrs. Humphries, who was so seasick they feared she might die, the passengers and crew were returned home and Mrs. Humphries vowed never to leave Newtown again.

The last British ship, sailing from Newfoundland to Europe, is said to have been the *Lady St. John's*. A two-masted vessel of ninety-five tons, she was built in 1898 for service to the city for which she was named. Unfortunately most of her papers were lost in the World War II blitz. It is known that she was carrying cargo from St. John's to Oporto, Portugal, and to Greece and Italy, under sail and without motor power, until she was sold in 1930.

Her last passage from Newfoundland was a serious one in which she lost most of her bulwarks during a gale, which did three hundred pounds damage. Her lifeboat was swept away and a sailor was washed overboard. A second wave washed the man back again and he was left lying on the deck. She was repaired at Oporto where hundreds came to admire her.

In 1930 a French firm bought her for nine hundred pounds, and she was lost on her first voyage for the new owners, with no survivors.[22] The long history of British sail between Europe and Newfoundland, a history that began with John Cabot in 1497, came to a close after 433 years.

The Atlantic Royal Mail steamer *Adriatic* docked in St. John's, from Ireland, on 8 September 1863, carrying such distinguished passengers as Judge Des Barres, Hon. P. Tessier, Hon. (later Sir) F.B. and Mrs. Carter, Mr. and Mrs. Stephen Rendell, and Mr. Samuel Job. She also carried an amazing number of passengers, unknown to the captain and crew. Just before her departure from the port, someone moved a board in one of the holds and discovered there were "strangers" underneath. The alarm was raised and the stowaways were marched out on deck, all sixty-three of them. The captain ordered them arrested. As soon as the unauthorized passengers were landed and made prisoners in the jail, the *Adriatic* sailed away to the United States.

The colony was left with sixty-three unwanted miscreants to house and feed. The populace rose to the defence of the stowaways. One Newspaper cried, "No law could sanction such a violation of personal liberty." Others claimed that the government should not have taken the responsibility from the captain of the steamer for landing them. Eventually they were let go as there was nobody to prefer charges. How sixty-three men and women could be smuggled on board a ship, and spend a number of weeks undetected in the hold, remains a mystery to this day. Their eventual fate is unknown, some probably settling in Newfoundland.

A second stowaway story had no such happy ending. The Allan liner, S.S. *Austriah*, eighteen days out of Liverpool, reached St. John's on 7 April 1904. At seven o'clock in the morning, workmen engaged in unloading the ship found the body of a man, in the hold between decks. He was well dressed and about twenty-five or thirty-years of age. His boots were off and it was obvious that he had used them for knocking to attract attention. The hold held ammunition, and a box of gun caps was found beside the corpse, in the one square yard of space. There was also a postcard with the words, "Emma - Bob." The name "C. Buckly" was on the man's trousers. The unfortunate stowaway had died for want of water. As no food was found, it was obvious he had intended to crawl out of the hold as soon as the ship put to sea. Unfortunately, cargo was loaded on deck just before sailing, covering the hatch, and the man met a horrible death of thirst, starvation, and suffocation. Next day, a package found in the hold identified him as a young Englishman named Robert Lea. His family had no information as to why he stowed away on the ship bound for Newfoundland.

The fact that St. John's was on the shipping lanes to and from Europe brought it a number of notorious, as well as distinguished, visitors. Devine & O'Mara report that the Grand Master of the Fenians, James Stephens, was in port briefly on 26 April 1866, a few weeks before the Fenian invasion of Canada. He was supposed to have been travelling in disguise among the seven hundred emigrants on the steamship, *William Penn,* from London and Havre, that put into St. John's short of coal. We are told there was a five-thousand-dollar reward on his head at the time, and of the four men who knew of his being here only one saw him while he was in port. The story appears to be a fabrication, for James Stephens arrived in New York May 10, on the French Steamer *Napoléon* from Havre, and not on the *William Penn* via St. John's.

Exaggerated myth seems to surround an earlier visit by another Irish hero, William Smith O'Brien. According to legend he arrived in the port on 2 February 1859, on a Cunard steamer short of coal, and was given an ovation by the citizens. It is said that on February 18 he spoke to ten thousand people from the steps of the Roman Catholic Cathedral, and among those around him he recognized a few informers of the past. The facts are that William Smith O'Brien and his son reached St. John's on the evening of Thursday, 17 February 1859, on board the *Prince Albert* of the Galway Line, making her regular call. He was on his way to pay a visit to the United States. The ship, with her 224 passengers, sailed on Sunday for New York. According to the *Patriot* for Monday, February 21, Mr. Smith O'Brien was "celebrated no less for his political struggles for the benefit of his native land than for being the victim of a state trial." The newspaper went on to say: "For the short time the ship remained in port, Mr. O'Brien was the guest of Rt. Rev. Dr. Mullock." There is no mention, in any newspaper, of the gathering of an enormous concourse of ten thousand people. Such a notable event would surely have made the press. The Irish leader, then living in exile in Belgium, might have addressed some remarks to a small group of admirers on the steps of the cathedral after Sunday mass, but even this is unlikely as he was a Protestant.

Captain E.K. Kane brought the American brigantine *Advance* into St. John's on 16 June 1853, on her way to search for Sir John Franklin and his lost party. The brig arrived, just sixteen days out of New York. Next day, previous to his sailing to the Arctic, the St. John's Masonic Body presented an address to the captain. Franklin's expedition, of 129 men, was lost in 1845. Over forty rescue parties sought traces of the group, but it was not until the voyage of the *Advance* that evidence of their tragic fate was finally discovered by the captain. It was his second expedition in search of Franklin, and the one on which he discovered Kane Basin.

Another famous name in Arctic exploration, Robert E. Peary, discoverer of the North Pole, reached St. John's on 12 June 1896, on board the *Portia* from New York. The gentleman's exploring days were almost brought to an abrupt conclusion when the *Portia* had a narrow escape from serious collision with an iceberg, just of Cape Spear, in a heavy fog. Except for the prompt action of the captain, the ship would certainly have struck and possibly foundered. Lieutenant Peary was in town to arrange for the charter of a steamer for a Greenland cruise. He left again on the *Portia* Saturday, June 13, after having chartered the *Hope*, and leaving all matters in the hands of Captain Bob Bartlett, who was to command her.

On 8 November 1858 the North American Line steamer *Pacific* left New York. She reached St. John's on the thirteenth and, having coaled, departed next day for Galway. She carried with her a number of people prominent in the life of St. John's, including Mr. Frederic Gisborne, who was off to Britain on the business of his telegraph, and such social dragons as Mrs. W.H. Mare, Mrs. Hugh Hoyles, and Mrs. David Rennie. Imagine the lift of the ladies' eyebrows when a fellow traveller among the saloon passengers turned out to be none other than the infamous Lola Montez, the scandal of two continents. This Irish dancer and adventuress, who claimed to be the illegitimate daughter of Lord Byron, had made a sensational success due to her ravishing (and ravished) beauty. Louis I, whose mistress she was, made her a countess. His attempts to install her as Queen of Bavaria in 1848 brought about her flight to America. Lola was in California for the Gold Rush, but ended her days saving fallen women on the streets of New York where she died in poverty, a scant three years after her brief visit to St. John's.

The last early visitor to be mentioned here, and certainly one of the most famous, came to Newfoundland as master of Lord Colville's flagship, for the retaking of St. John's from the French in 1762. His name was Captain James Cook. He was afterwards to discover Australia, New Zealand, Tonga (the Friendly Islands), and Hawaii where he was killed by a party of less friendly natives. Cook, who had been with Wolfe at the Battle of the

Plains of Abraham in Quebec, was to spend the next four years in Newfoundland waters.

Born in England of Scottish parents, he went to sea as a lad. Preferring the Royal Navy to the Mercantile Marine he took a berth in H.M.S. *Eagle* under Admiral Hugh Palliser. He rose rapidly and was soon recognized as talented ship's master and surveyor. In 1762 he draughted the harbours of Carbonear and Harbour Grace. The following year, when his former commander Sir Hugh Palliser, became governor of Newfoundland, young Cook's position in the colony was assured. Given the title of Marine Surveyor of Newfoundland and Labrador, he mapped and charted much of the coast and many of the harbours. It was while in Bay of Islands, on the west coast, that he discovered the site of the city of Corner Brook.

When Cook's survey was completed in 1766, Governor Palliser insisted that the young officer embody his work in an atlas set, complete with sailing instructions. These were the first accurate maps of Newfoundland and Labrador. A set of these maps is now in the possession of Memorial University of Newfoundland.

On 3 October 1786 Capt. George Cartwright noted in his famous *Labrador Journal* that he arrived in St. John's after a voyage from Labrador on a man-of-war. He was lavishly entertained on the governor's ship, in the homes of such people as Richard Routh and Jonathan Ogden, and at The London Tavern while trying to procure passage to England. He met General Benedict Arnold, who six years previously had attempted to betray West Point to the British, and together they "hired the cabin of the brig John, belonging to Tinimouth [sic], John Bartlett owner and master." They embarked at two o'clock in the afternoon along with Arnold's manservant, one hundred and eleven discharged fishermen, and a crew of ten. Cartwright says: "We laid in for our own use, two live sheep, several head of poultry, plenty of vegetables, and good store of every other article we thought requisite for our passage to England."[23]

For two weeks all went well until a great gale sprung up which carried away the boltsprit, foremast, mainmast, tiller, and taffrail. The sheep were drowned and the poultry and vegetables, except the potatoes which were in their cabin, were washed overboard. Water ran short and passengers and crew were put on rations. They came upon one abandoned ship with a few casks of water and a full load of salt fish on board. Eventually they reached Devon but not before Arnold once more demonstrated his propensity for perfidy. Cartwright discovered that while he and the General were walking the deck Arnold's servant stole most of their common stock of wine which his master bartered with the crew for part of their rations of water. At the end of the voyage there was but one bottle of wine to be found while Arnold had nine bottles of water left from what he bought with the missing wine.[24]

In June 1860 Stephen March, M.H.A., made the peculiar proposal of erecting a gigantic arch over the Narrows, constructed of wood and

989

boughs, to welcome the Prince of Wales on his visit to Newfoundland. March and the men of H.M.S. *Styx* measured the Narrows, but for what must be obvious reasons the arch never materialized. However, on 20 June 1892 a motto was strung across the Narrows, from head to head, welcoming Dr. Michael Howley, who arrived home from Halifax on the twenty-second, two days before his consecration, in St. John's, as the first Newfoundland-born bishop of a Newfoundland diocese. There are no details of the motto, or how it was suspended.

Almost in the middle of the inner Narrows, at the apex of a triangle with Pancake and Chain Rocks, lies Merlin Rock. This treacherous pinnacle, eighteen feet below the surface, did not cause real trouble until the depth of ships' hulls increased. Work on its removal was begun in 1855 by two engineers, named Husted and Knochl, who were entrusted with the job by the New York, Newfoundland, and London Telegraph Company.

The work was commenced on August 8 and completed by the sixteenth, so that at low tide there was a sounding of twenty-seven feet. The east and west sides were removed first, and these fell into sixty feet of water surrounding the rock. The remaining core was removed by a drag made of iron, so that the Narrows could then accommodate the *Persia,* the largest steamer afloat. She drew twenty-three feet of water.

In September 1880 the crew of H.M.S. *Diana* tried to remove more of Merlin Rock but their efforts were only successful to a minor degree. It was another eighty years before the hazard was finally taken down to thirty-five feet, below water, as part of the 1959 harbour development plan.

The past of St. John's is an important part of the vast panorama of North American history. The city is almost as old as the white man's discovery of the continent. Although greatly altered by the elements, catastrophe, neglect, and modernization the place still retains many of the tastes, the smells, and the sights that have given it life for nearly five hundred years. It is impossible for any book to contain more than an echo of its history. Much that should be written has been unrecorded. No words can bring to life what is only memory - the sound of sails being hoisted on Jacques Cartier's ship, the voice of Humphrey Gilbert proclaiming the British Empire, the shots of French soldiers storming Fort William, guns booming farewell to Governor Pickmore departing in a puncheon of rum, voices singing by candlelight in the London Tavern, Bishop Fleming threatening anathema from the pulpit of the Old Chapel, Carson and Morris in political argument at Sally Dooley's Inn, applause for the celebrated Miss Davenport at the amateur theatre, cheers for the crew from Outer Cove at Quidi Vidi, great merchant houses crashing in flames on Water Street, Marconi's letter S being repeated on Signal Hill, Alcock and Brown's engines fading overhead, or the smash of glass in windows of the Colonial Building.

Today and tomorrow will reshape and do away with many things. Already much is gone—the courthouse where Eleanor Power was tried, the

Meeting House where John Jones preached, the Government House where Lady Hamilton lived, Mary Traver's Inn where the first Legislature met, the Rising Sun Tavern where the Presentation Sisters taught, the Octagon Castle where Professor Danielle displayed his coffin, the Casino Theatre where Jessie Bonstelle performed, and the Prince's Rink where hockey history became legend.

Into the making of St. John's many people poured their lives—noble lords and drunken rowdies, rich merchants and poor fishermen, tireless English masters and diligent Irish servants, righteous lawmakers and unrepentent criminals. If there were decaying shanties there were fashionable mansions, if there was ignominy there was honour, if there were spiritless individuals there were men and women of vision. Amidst privation there was hospitality, amidst repression there was wit, amidst shabbiness there was dignity, and amidst provincialism there was the cheeky grin of an urchin city with a disregard of time and an absence of pretence. What the children of plenty do with the fragments that are left will depend on their respect for their heritage and the depth of their love.

Notes

It is impossible to refer here to all the sources that have been consulted or quoted. This is to be regretted as many of those not given may be important. However, in the circumstances it was not possible to do otherwise. The following abbreviations are used: Prowse refers to *A History of Newfoundland* by D. W. Prowse, Q.C., still the most definitive history of Newfoundland; *D.N.—Daily News; E.T.—Evening Telegram;* M.U.N.—Memorial University of Newfoundland; *N.S.—Newscene: N.Q. —Newfoundland Quarterly,* and N.P.A.—Newfoundland Provincial Archives. Colonial records refers to correspondence in the Governor's letter books in the Newfoundland Provincial Archives.

CHAPTER 1
1. Archives, Merchants Venturers Society, Bristol.
2. M. P. Murphy, *The Story of the Colonial Building,* Newfoundland & Labrador Provincial Archives, 1972, pp. 7-9.
3. *Ibid.,* p. 17.
4. *Ibid.,* pp. 20-21.
5. *Ibid.,* p. 26.
6. *Newfoundlander,* 14 May 1861.
7. Murphy, p. 38.
8. *E. T.,* 3 April 1886.
9. *Ibid.,* 12 August 1887.
10. *Ibid.,* 14 April 1921.
11. *Ibid.,* 6 April 1932.
12. Murphy, p. 59.
13. *Ibid.,* p. 62.
14. *Ibid.,* p. 72.
15. Sir Edward Morris, "Growth of Municipal Government in St. John's," *N. Q.,* July 1907, p. 5.
16. Newfoundland Directories.
17. J. L. Slattery, "Opening of the City Hall," *N. Q.,* October 1911, p. 6.
18. J. R. Smallwood, *Book of Newfoundland, I,* p. 199.
19. S. E. Morrison, *The European Discovery of America.* pp. 446-7.

CHAPTER 2
1. J. M. Murray, *The Journal of Aaron Thomas,* p. 56.
2. *Ibid.*
3. *Ibid.,* p. 57.
4. *Ibid.,* p. 71.

5. *D. N.*, 1 June 1966, p. 8.
6. *Ibid.*
7. *Carbonear Sentinel,* 7 June 1838.
8. *Ibid.*
9. *Ibid.*, 15 November 1838.
10. Prowse, p. 486.
11. J. W. McGrath, "R. E. Reid & The Newfoundland Railway," Paper for Newfoundland Historical Society (8 December 1971), p. 3.
12. H. Clayton, *Atlantic Bridgehead*, p. 98.
13. *D. N.*, 28 April 1966, p. 7.
14. *Ibid.*
15. Devine & O'Mara, *Notable Events in the History of Newfoundland*, p. 103.
16. Archives, Phoenix Fire Office, London.
17. B.J. Wadden, "St. John's Electric Light Co., 1885-1892," *N.Q.* (June 1957), pp. 4-5.
18. *Ibid.*, pp. 39-41.
19. McGrath, p. 19.
20. Clayton, p. 119.
21. Murray, p. 110.
22. Capt. G. Cartwright, *A Journal of Transactions and Events on the Coast of Labrador.*
23. A. M. Lysaght, *Joseph Banks in Newfoundland and Labrador: 1766,* pp. 146-147.
24. *D. N.*, June 1961.
25. M. P. Murphy, pp. 31-32.
26. Devine & O'Mara, p. 235.

CHAPTER 3
1. Inspector Fagan, unpublished paper, 1964.
2. Colonial Records, 1777.
3. *Ibid.,* 1811.
4. *Ibid.,* 1750.
5. J. Reeves, *History of the Government of the Island of Newfoundland*, pp. 52-53.
6. Kempthorne's answers to inquiries. Colonial Office 194: 5, 6.
7. R. G. Lounsbury, *The Bristol Fishery at Newfoundland: 1634-1763*, p. 274.
8. *Ibid.*, p. 297 ff.
9. Rev. Charles Pedley, *The History of Newfoundland,* pp. 89-90.
10. Prowse, pp. 358-359.
11. *Ibid.*, p. 361.
12. *Ibid.*, p. 390.
13. Newfoundland Government Bulletin, March 1971.
14. Colonial Records, 1825.
15. J. R. Smallwood, *Book of Newfoundland,* II, pp. 172-173.
16. Records of H. M. Penitentiary, St. John's.
17. *Ibid.*
18. Murphy, pp. 40-41.
19. Records of H. M. Penitentiary, St. John's.
20. Colonial Records, 1889.

21. *Ibid.*, 1821.
22. A. Fox, *The Newfoundland Constabulary*, p. 22.
23. Colonial Records, 1865.
24. N. P. A., Letters of Sir Stephen Hill to Earl of Kimberly, 1870-1871 (Despatches to Colonial Office).
25. A. R. Brazill, "The Newfoundland Police Force," *N. Q.*
26. Fox, *Constabulary*, p. 140.
27. Colonial Records, 1834, p. 220 ff.
28. Fox, "The Murder of Robert Crocker Bray," *N. S.* (6 February, 1971), p. 10.
29. *The Public Ledger*, 22 July 1834.

CHAPTER 4

1.   Archives, Phoenix Fire Office, London.
2.   Colonial Records, 1817, pp. 107-108.
3.   *Ibid.*
4.   Sir W. Eliot, *Naval Sketch-Book: or Service Afloat and Ashore*, p. 165.
5.   *Ibid.*, pp. 167-169.
6.   *Ibid.*, pp. 171-172.
7.   *Mercantile Journal*, 22 July 1819.
8.   D. Keir, *TheBowring Story*, p. 65.
9.   Archives, Phoenix Fire Office, London.
10. *Ibid.*
11. *Ibid.*
12. *Royal Gazette & Newfoundland Advertiser*, 30 June 1846.
13. Fox, *Constabulary*, p. 93 ff.
14. *Ibid.*, p. 98.
15. M. Harvey and H. O'Meara, *The Great Fire in St. John's, Newfoundland, July 8, 1892*, p. 20.
16. *Ibid.*, "A Bostonian's Description of the Calamity," p. 28.
17. *Ibid.*, p. 29.
18. *Ibid.*, p. 23.
19. Ibid., pp. 30-31.
20. *St. John's Evening Herald,* 10 September 1892.
21. F. Rasky, *Great Canadian Disasters*, p. 46.

CHAPTER 5

1.   Prowse, p. 70.
2.   S. Burrage, *Early English and French Voyages,* p. 198.
3.   D. B. Quinn and N. M. Cheshire, *The New Found Land of Stephen Parmenius*, p. 171.
4.   *Ibid.*
5.   Colonial Records, 1751.
6.   Prowse, pp. 399-400.
7.   Keir, pp. 398-399.
8.   *Ibid.,* p. 398.
9.   *Ibid.,* p. 241.
10. *E. T.*, 23 October 1971.
11. Murray, p. 146.
12. Prowse, pp. 372-374.
13. *Ibid.*, p. 174.

14. Presentation Convent, Galway, *Sesquicentenary Souvenir*, 1965, p. 22.
15. Devine & O'Mara, p. 67.
16. C. A. Lindberg, *The Spirit of St. Louis,* p. 278.
17. *D. N.,* 14 June 1966.
18. H. Halpert and G. Story, *Christmas Mumming in Newfoundland*, pp. 37-38, 110-111.
19. *Ibid.*, p. 45.
20. *Ibid.*, p. 49.
21. *Ibid.*, p. 176 ff.
22. *Ibid.*, p. 59 ff.
23. *Public Ledger*, 2 January 1861.
24. Halpert and Story, p. 179.
25. Colonial Records - 1811, Vol. 21, p. 425.
26. *D. N.,* 21 May 1954.
27. Devine & O'Mara, p. 217.
28. Smallwood, *The Book of Newfoundland,* IV, p. 579.

CHAPTER 6

1. *Tyranny in St. John's: 1705-1706* (Publication of Newfoundland & Labrador Provincial Affairs), 1971, pp. 3-4.
2. Prowse, p. 252.
3. Rev. F. M. Buffett, *The Story of the Church in Newfoundland,* p. 13.
4. Colonial Records, 1825.
5. Buffett, p. 23.
6. *Ibid.*, p. 32.
7. Rev. E. Wix, *Six Months of a Newfoundland Missionary's Journal*, IX,X,XI.
8. Buffet, p. 33.
9. A Sketch of this building appears in the *Newfoundland Government Bulletin,* March 1971.
10. Buffett, pp. 69-70.
11. H. W. LeMessurier, *The History of St. Thomas's Church*, p. 12.
12. *Ibid.*, p. 16.
13. *The Times*, 9 November 1842.
14. *Church of St. Mary the Virgin: 1859-1959*, souvenir publication, p. 14.
15. Prowse, p. 293.
16. *Ibid.*, p. 294
17. Parish records, Old St. Patrick's, Waterford, Ireland.
18. P. O'Connell, "Dr. James Louis O'Donnell," in *Irish Ecclesiastical Record,* May 1964.
19. *Irish Ecclesiastical Record*, II, 511.
20. *Ibid.*
21. Colonial Records, 1790.
22. *Irish Ecclesiastical Record, op.cit.*, p. 513.
23. *Ibid.*, p. 515.
24. *Ibid.*, p. 517.
25. *Ibid.*
26. Colonial Records, 1806.
27. Rev. M. F. Howley, *Ecclesiastical History of Newfoundland.*
28. *Public Ledger,* 8 May 1838.
29. Colonial Records, 30 June 1838.

30. *The Tablet* (Dublin), 2 October 1841, p. 637.
31. *Basilica Centenary Sourvenir Book*, pp. 218-219.
32. *Ibid.*
33. Presentation Convent, Galway, *Sesquicentenary Souvenir*, p. 18.
34. Copy of a letter in Archives of Presentation Convent, Galway.
35. Howley, p. 364.
36. D. G. Pitt, *Windows of Agates*, p. 20.
37. *Ibid.*, p. 24.
38. *The Methodist Magazine*, 1816, p. 878.
39. *Ibid.*
40. *Pitt*, p. 33.
41. Rev. T. W. Smith, *History of the Methodist Church in Eastern British America*, p. 38.
42. *The Mercantile Journal*, 24 February 1820.
43. W. Wilson, *Newfoundland and its Missionaries,* pp.251-252.
44. Pitt, p. 52.
45. *Ibid.*, p. 72.
46. R. Duder, *St. Andrew's Presbyterian Church*, p. 8.
47. Rev. W. M. Moncreiff, "A History of the Presbyterian Church in Newfoundland, 1622-1966," unpublished thesis, p. 25.
48. *Ibid.*
49. *Ibid.*, p. 27.
50. *Ibid.*, p. 30.
51. *Ibid.*, p. 42.
52. *Ibid.*, p. 47.
53. *Newfoundland Government Bulletin,* April 1970, p. 15.
54. Eliot, pp. 172-173.
55. Newfoundland Government Bulletin, p. 15.
56. St. Andrew's Kirk Session Minutes, 24 May 1936, p. 35.
57. Rev. W. M. Moncreiff, "A History of the Presbyterian Church," p. 171.
58. *Ibid.*, p. 175.

CHAPTER 7

1.   F. W. Rowe, *The Development of Education in Newfoundland*, p. 28.
2.   Colonial Records, 1798.
3.   H. M. Mosdell, *When Was That?*, p. 24.
4.   Rowe, p. 40.
5.   *Ibid.*, p. 138.
6.   J. R. Smallwood, *Book of Newfoundland,* I, p. 290.
7.   Howley, *Ecclesiastical History of Newfoundland*.
8.   *Basilica Centenary Souvenir Book*, p. 256.
9.   *Ibid.*
10. *Ibid.*
11. Rowe, p. 108.
12. Howley, *op.cit.*
13. Presentation Convent, Galway, *Sesquicentenary Souvenir,* 1965, p. 12.
14. *Ibid.*, pp 12-13.
15. *Ibid.*, p. 15.
16. *Ibid.*, p. 16.
17. Letter in Archives of Presentation Convent, Galway.

18. *Presentation Sesquicentenary Souvenir*, pp. 18-20.
19. *Ibid.*, p. 19.
20. *Ibid.*, p. 21.
21. Sir R. Bonnycastle, *Newfoundland in 1842*, p. 112.
22. "Annuals of Mercy Order," Mercy Convent Archives, Blackrock, Ireland.
23. "Leaves from the Annals of the Mercy Order."
24. Smallwood, I, p. 405.
25. *Sixtieth Anniversary Review: The Salvation Army St. John's Temple Songsters*, p. 5.
26. M. U. N. *Gazette*, 24 July 1975, p. 5.
27. *Ibid.*, p. 9.
28. *Basilica Centenary Souvenir Book*, p. 193.
29. College of Fisheries, *Calendar: 1970-1971*, pp. 28-29.
30. College of Trades and Technology, *Calendar, pp. 15-16.*

CHAPTER 8

1. Lt. E. Chappell, *Voyage of H. M. S. Rosamund to Newfoundland.*
2. *Ibid.*
3. In private possession of the Honourable Chief Justice, R.S. Furlong.
4. J. Puddester, *The Crow's Nest: 1972: 30th Anniversary Souvenir,* p. 12.
5. S. Leacock, "Atlantic Hideaway" from *Canada's War at Sea.*
6. Colonial Records, Report to Governor Edwards, vol. 9, 1780-1783.
7. *Ibid.*
8. P. K. Devine, *Ye Olde St. John's*, p. 110.
9. J. Hatton and M. Harvey, *Newfoundland*, p. 131.
10. Devine p. 126.
11. *Ibid.*, p. 130.
12. *Prowse*, p. 402.
13. R. Gwyn, *Smallwood: The Unlikely Revolutionary*, p. 4.
14. Sketch in *Commercial Review*, 26 March 1910.
15. B. J. Wadden, "St. John's Street Railway Co.," *N. Q.* (Spring 1965), p. 3; (Autumn 1965), p. 10.
16. Devine, p. 156.
17. C. R. Fay, *Life and Labour in Newfoundland*, pp. 16-17.
18. Archives, Phoenix Fire Office, London, 1782, p. 213.
19. Devine, pp. 82-83 and 159-160.
20. *Songs of Newfoundland*, Bennett Brewing Company booklet, pp. 16-17.
21. *E. T.,* 30 March 1973, p. 40A.
22. Prowse, p. 194.
23. Hatton and Harvey, extracts, p. 418 ff.
24. M. Harrington, *The Prime Ministers of Newfoundland*, p. 30 ff.
25. *Standard Catalogue of Canadian Coins, Tokens and Paper Money* (1973), p. 54.
26. Prowse, p. 402.
27. *Ibid.*, p. 272 (Sect. v-5th)
28. *Ibid.*, (Sect. v-4th)
29. N. P. A. Report to Governor Edwards, Vol. 9. 1780-1793.
30. Prowse, p. 402.
31. Colonial Records Vol. 17, p. 379.
32. Newfoundland Historic Society Minute Book 1905-1909 p. 86.

CHAPTER 9
1. Devine, p. 9.
2. A. J. Henderson, "Eleven Decades of Maritime Service," from *Sea Breezes,* May 1950.
3. Devine, p. 14.
4. A. B. Perlin, *The Story of Newfoundland,* p. 158.
5. *Ibid.,* p. 180.
6. R. B. Job, *John Job's Family: 1730-1953,* p. 47.
7. Perlin, p. 184.
8. State House Library, Boston, Mass.
9. *The Port of St. John's,* National Harbours Board pamphlet.
10. Keir, pp. 25-26.
11. Prowse, pp. 486-487.
12. H. M. Mosdell, p. 110.
13. Perlin, p. 192.
14. Map of St. John's, Prowse, p. 204.
15. J. W. McGrath, "The 1898 Railway Contract," Newfoundland Historical Society paper, 20 March 1973, p. 7.
16. Prowse, p. 351.
17. Job, pp. 52-53.
18. Perlin, p. 224.

CHAPTER 10
1. A.J. Henderson, *op. cit.*
2. *E.T.,* 11 June 1970, p. 89 (4).
3. Keir, p. 121.
4. *British Press and Jersey Times,* 11 June 1886.
5. P. Ahier, *Stories of Jersey Seas, of Jersey's Coast and of Jersey Seaman,* p. 64.
6. *D.N.,* 10 October 1916.
7. D.B. Chidsey, *Shakleton's Voyage,* pp. 50-51.
8. D. Keir, pp. 203-204.
9. Chidsey, p. 82.
10. G.A. England, *The Greatest Hunt in the World,* Introduction, pp. xx-xxi.
11. *Ibid.,* pp. 247, 252-253.
12. *E.T.,* 28 March 1898.
13. Rev. E. Hunt, "The Great Sealers Strike of 1902," *N.S.,* 6 March 1970, p. 3.
14. *N.S.,* "The Newfoundland Disaster," 27 March 1971, p. 8.
15. C. Brown, *Death on the Ice,* p. 246.
16. Col. G.W.L. Nicholson, *More Fighting Newfoundlanders,* pp. 448-449.
17. *D.N.,* 14 October and 17 November 1942.
18. *E.T.,* 29 March 1971.
19. P. Sarnoff, *Ice Pilot: Bob Bartlett,* pp. 179-180.
20. C.R. Fay, *The Channel Islands and Newfoundland,* p. 37.
21. Devine & O'Mara, p. 151.
22. Archives, Merchant Venturers Society, Bristol.
23. C.W. Townsend, *Captain Cartwright and His Labrador Journal,* p. 333.
24. *Ibid.,* p. 337.

Author's Note

This volume concludes the story of St. John's to date as seen through the flawed vision of a lover and not a professional historian. With more erudition, more time, more energy it might have been possible to produce a more polished and accurate work but in the words of the thirteenth century Chinese writer, Tai T'ung, (as quoted by Winthrop Boggs in his postal history of Newfoundland) "Were I to await perfection, my book would never be finished, so I have made shift to collect the fruits of my labours as I find them." When one considers the scope of the subject and the vast panorama of history that has engulfed St. John's in nearly five hundred years the present work can only be a rough draft. Again in the words of Tai T'ung, these two volumes await "the judgement of a master mind; one whose wise and lofty spirit will lead him, without looking down upon the author, to correct where the text is in error, to add where it is defective, and supply new facts where it is altogether silent."

Meanwhile due to small oversights, source misinformation and some printer's errors there are several minor mistakes in Volume I which should be corrected for the benefit of researchers using the book.

P. 34 G.R.F. Prowse was the nephew of Judge Prowse.

P. 50 Line 1. 1775 should be 1755.

P. 80 Line 20. Delete the phrase "and later became the site of Waldegrave Batthery."

P. 85 A recently discovered report shows the incident involved Jackson's eldest daughter, Margrett, not his wife.

P. 105 The Doctor Carson referred to is Samuel Carson.

P. 111 The Dole was six cents a day.

P. 119 The Hamiltons were six years in Newfoundland.

P. 176 Line 29. Delete the phrase "the year the first stamps arrived."

P. 180 Line 24 should read "John Ryan took John Collier Withers as a partner in 1832 and retired soon afterwards. He died at St. John's 30 September 1847."

P. 195 The last line is in error as Sir Patrick returned to St. John's where he died.

P. 206 Paragraph 2 was distorted in printing. From line 3 it should read; "The call letters were 8WMC which later became VOWR, the oldest continuing broadcasting service in Newfoundland. 8LR, for Loyal Reid of the Reid family, who were to operate the station, went on the air 4 November 1924 with a gramaphone production of Gilbert & Sullivan's *The Gondoliers* and broadcast twice weekly."

P. 203 Line 17 should read Fort St. George.

P. 262 There were two fires at Callaghan, Glass & Co. The one referred to here was 11:00 a.m., Sunday, 10 June 1917.

P. 308 Line 27. St. Clare's School of Nursing was started in 1939. The Nurse's residence opened in 1947.

P. 342 Line 28. Byers Road should read Barrows Road.

P. 363 Line 7. Eleanor Mills should be Eleanor Hall.

P. 378 Line 12 should read Mr. James French.

P. 421 Sir Robert Bond himself built the house between 1883 and 1886.

P. 423 The Judge Prowse entry should read "Mary, Queen of Peace rectory site next ot Glenbrook Lodge."

P. 423 Sir Robert Reid lived at "9 Church Hill". His son resided at 3 Forest Road.

Bibliography

The following works were consulted in preparing this book.

AHIER, PHILIP. *Stories of Jersey Seas of Jersey's Coast and of Jersey Seamen.* Hudderfield: The Advertiser Press.

ALCOCK, SIR JOHN, and BROWN, SIR ARTHUR WHITTEN. *Our Transatlantic Flight.* London: William Kimber, 1969.

ANDERSON, HUGH ABERCROMBIE. *Out Without My Rubbers.* New York: Library Publishers, 1954.

ANSPACH, LEWIS AMADEUS. *History of the Island of Newfoundland.* London: Sherwood, Gilbert and Piper, 1819.

ARCHIBALD, RAYMOND CLARE. *Carlyle's First Love.* London: John Lane The Bodley Head, 1910.

AYRE, AGNES MARION. *Newfoundland Names.*

BALBO, AIR-MARSHALL ITALO. *My Air Armada.* London: Hurst & Blackett Ltd., 1934.

BARTLETT, CAPT. ROBERT A. *The Log of Bob Bartlett.* New York: Blue Ribbon Books, 1928.

BAXTER, JAMES PHINNEY. *A Memoir of Jacques Cartier.* New York: Dodd Mead and Co., 1906.

BIGGAR, H. P. *Voyages of Jacques Cartier.* Ottawa: F. A. Acland, 1924.

BLUM, DANIEL. *A Pictorial History of the Silent Screen.* London: Spring Books, 1953.

BOGGS, WINTHROP S. *The Postage Stamps and Postal History of Newfoundland.* Lawrence, Mass.: Quarterman Publications, Inc., 1975 reproduction.

BONNYCASTLE, SIR RICHARD. *Newfoundland in 1842.* London: Henry Colburn, 1842.

BRENT, PETER. *Captain Scott and the Antarctic Tragedy.* New York: Saturday Review Press, 1974.

BROWN, CASSIE. *Death on the Ice.* Toronto: Doubleday Canada Ltd., 1972.

BUFFETT, REV. F. M. *The Story of the Church in Newfoundland.* Toronto: General Board of Religious Education, 1939.

BURRAGE, HENRY S., D.D. *Early English and French Voyages.* New York: Charles Scribner's Sons, 1906.

BURROUGHS, POLLY. *The Great Ice Ship Bear.* Van Nostrand-Reinhold Company, 1970.

BYRNES, JOHN MACLAY. *The Paths to Yesterday.* Boston: Meador Publishing Company, 1931.

CARROLL, SR. MARY TERESA. *Leaves from the Annals of the Sisters of Mercy.* London: Burns and Oates, 1889.

CARSE, ROBERT. *The Seafarers.* Harper and Row, 1964.

CARTWRIGHT, GEORGE. *A Journal of Transactions and Events on the Coast of Labrador.* Newark: 1792.

CAVANAGH, MICHAEL. *Memoirs of Gen. Thomas Francis Meagher.* Worcester, Mass.: The Messenger Press, 1892.

CELL, GILLIAN T. *English Enterprise in Newfoundland: 1577-1660.* Toronto: University of Toronto Press, 1969.

CHADWICK, ST. JOHN. *Newfoundland: Island into Province.* Cambridge: University Press, 1967.

CHAPPELL, LT. EDWARD. *Voyage of H.M.S. Rosamund to Newfoundland.* London: J. Mawman, Ludgate St., 1818.

CHIDSEY, DONALD BARR. *Shackleton's Voyage.* New York: Universal Publishing and Distributing Corporation, 1967.

CLAYTON, HOWARD. *Atlantic Bridgehead.* London: Granstone Press, 1968.

COCHRANE, J. A. *The Story of Newfoundland.* Boston, London, and Montreal: Ginn and Company, 1938.

COLVILLE, LORD, REAR ADMIRAL. Dispatches: 1761-1762. Ed. Instructor Commander C. H. Little, R.C.N. Maritime Museum of Canada, 1959.

CRAMM, RICHARD. *The First Five Hundred.* Albany, New York: C. F. Williams and Son, Inc.

DAVIN, NICHOLAS FLOOD. *The Irishman in Canada.* London: Sampson Low, Marston and Co., 1877.

DAVIS, DAVID J. *St. John's and the Commissariat:* 1810-1820.

DEVINE, P. K. *Ye Olde St John's.* St. John's: Newfoundland Directories, 1936.

DEVINE and O'MARA. *Notable Events in the History of Newfoundland.* St. John's: Newfoundland Trade Review Office, 1900.

DEVOLPI, CHARLES P. *Newfoundland: A Pictorial Record.* Don Mills, Ont.: Longmans Canada Limited, 1972.

DIBNER, BERN. *The Atlantic Cable.* New York, London, and Toronto: Blaisdell Publishing Company, 1964.

DUFF, GORDON. "A Biographical Dictionary of the Governors of Newfoundland. Unpublished thesis, Memorial University, 1964.

DULEY, MARGARET. *The Caribou Hut.* Toronto: Ryerson Press, 1949.

EDEY, MAITLAND A. *The Northeast Coast.* New York: Time-Life Books, 1972.

EGAN, FATHER BARTHOLOMEW. *Franciscan Limerick.* Limerick: Franciscan Fathers, 1971.

ELIOT, CAPT. SIR WILLIAM. *Naval Sketch Book.* London: Henry Colburn, 1826.

ENGLAND, GEORGE ALLAN. *The Greatest Hunt in the World.* Montreal: Tundra Books, 1969.

ENGLISH, L. E. F. *Historic Newfoundland.* St. John's: Department of Economic Development.

—*Outlines of Newfoundland History.* London, Edinburgh, New York, Toronto, and Paris: Thomas Nelson and Sons, Ltd.

FAY, C. R. *Channel Islands and Newfoundland.* Cambridge: W. Heffer & Sons Limited, 1961.
—— *Life and Labour in Newfoundland.* Toronto: University of Toronto Press, 1956.
FIELD, CYRUS. *Statement of Some of the Advantages Attendant upon Making St. John's, Newfoundland as a Port of Call for Transatlantic Steamers.* London: M. Lownds, 1856.
FLEISHER, NAT, and ANDRE, SAM. *A Pictorial History of Boxing.* London: Spring Books, 1959.
FORAN, E. B. *Old St. John's.*
FREEDLEY and REEVES. *A History of the Theatre.* New York: Crown Publishers, 1941.

GOSLING, W. S. *Life of Sir Humphrey Gilbert.* London: Constable and Company, 1911.
GRAVES, CHARLES L. *Hubert Parry: His Life and Works.* London: Macmillan and Co., 1926.
GREENE, MAJOR WILLIAM HOWE. *The Wooden Walls Among the Ice Floes.* London: Hutchinson & Co. (Publishers) Ltd., 1933.
GRENFELL, WILFRED THOMASON. *A Labrador Doctor.* Boston and New York: Houghton Mifflin Company, 1919.
GUNN, GERTRUDE E. *The Political History of Newfoundland: 1832-1864.* Toronto: University of Toronto Press, 1966.
GWYN, RICHARD. *Smallwood: The Unlikely Revolutionary.* Toronto: McClelland and Stewart, 1968.

HAITNOLL, PHYLLIS. *The Oxford Companion to the Theatre.* Oxford: Oxford University Press, 1967.
HALPERT, HERBERT and STORY, G. M. *Christmas Mumming in Newfoundland.* University of Toronto Press, 1969.
HARRINGTON, MICHAEL. *Prime Ministers of Newfoundland.* St. John's: The Evening Telegram, 1962.
HARRIS, LESLIE. *Newfoundland and Labrador: A Brief History.* J. M. Dent and Sons (Canada) Limited, 1968.
HARRISSE, HENRY. *John Cabot and Sabastian His Son.* London: Benjamin Franklin Stevens, 1896.
HARVEY, REV. MOSES. *Newfoundland in 1900.* New York: The South Publishing Company, 1900.
—— and O'MEARA, HENRY. *The Great Fire in St. John's, Newfoundland.* Boston: The Relief Committee, 1892.
HATTON, JOSEPH, and HARVEY, REV. MOSES. *Newfoundland.* Doyle and Whittle, 1883.
HENDERSON, DOROTHY. *The Heart of Newfoundland.* Montreal: Harvest House, 1965.
HIBBS, R. *Who's Who in and from Newfoundland.* St. John's: R. Hibbs, M.H.A., 1927 and 1930.
HILL, KAY. *And Tomorrow the Stars.* New York: Dodd, Mead and Co., 1968.
HORWOOD, HAROLD. *Newfoundland.* Toronto: MacMillan of Canada, 1969.
HOWLEY, JAMES P. *The Beothucks or Red Indians.* Cambridge: University Press, 1915.

HOWLEY, VERY REV. M. F. *Ecclesiastical History of Newfoundland.* Boston: Doyle and Whittle, 1888.

JELKS, EDWARD B. *Archaeological Explorations at Signal Hill, Newfoundland, 1965-1966.* Ottawa: Department of Indian Affairs and Northern Development, 1973.

JOB, ROBERT BROWN. *John Job's Family.* St. John's: Private publication, 1953.

JOHNSON, D. W. *History of Methodism in Eastern North America.* Sackville, N. B.: Tribune Press.

JOLLY, W. P. *Marconi.* New York: Stein and Day, 1972.

JOYCE, R. B. *Sir William MacGregor.* Oxford University Press, 1971.

JUKES, JOSEPH BEETES. *Excursions in and About Newfoundland, During the years 1839-1840.* London: Canadiana House, 1842; Toronto, 1969.

KEIR, DAVID. *The Bowring Story.* London: The Bodley Head, 1962.

KERR, J. LENNOX. *Wilfred Grenfell: His Life and Work.* Toronto: The Ryerson Press, 1959.

KUNSTLER, WILLIAM M. *The Minister and the Choir Singer.* New York: William Morrow and Co.

LEMESURIER, H. W. *History of St. Thomas Church.* St. John's, 1928. As amended and added to by the Centenary Committee, 1936.

LEONARD-STUART and HAGAR. *People's Cyclopedia.* New York: Syndicate Publishing Company, 1911.

LINDBERG, CHARLES A. *The Spirit of St. Louis.* New York: Charles Scribner's Sons, 1953.

LOUNSBURY, RALPH GREENLEE. *The British Fishery at Newfoundland: 1634-1763.* Archon Books, 1969.

LYSAGHT, A. M. *Joseph Banks in Newfoundland and Labrador: 1766.* London: Faber and Faber, 1971.

McALLISTER, R. I. *Newfoundland and Labrador: The First Fifteen Years of Confederation.* St John's: Dicks and Co. Ltd.

McCARTHY, MICHAEL J. The Irish in Newfoundland 1759-1800, *Arts and Letters Competition Winning Entries,* 1974.

McCREA, ROBERT B. *Lost Amid the Fogs: Sketches of Life in Newfoundland.* London, 1869.

McGRATH, J. W. "R. G. Reid and the Newfoundland Railway." Unpublished lecture to Newfoundland Historical Society, 1971.

McGRATH, P. T. *Newfoundland in 1911.* London: Whitehead, Morris and Co. Ltd., 1911.

MacINNES, PROF. C. M. "Plan for Pamphlet on Bristol and Newfoundland: Part 1." Unpublished work.

MAGDELENE, SR. MARY. *Presentation Convent, Galway: 1815-1965 Part I.* Galway: Presentation Order, 1965.

MILLAIS, J. G. *Politics in Newfoundland.* University of Toronto Press, 1971.

MONCRIEFF, REV. W. M. "A History of the Presbyterian Church in Newfoundland: 1622-1966." Thesis, Knox College, Toronto, 1966.

MORISON, SAMUEL ELIOT. *The European Discovery of America.* New York: Oxford University Press, 1971.

MOSDELL, H. M. *When Was That?* St. John's: Trade Printers and Publishers, Ltd., 1923.

MOTT, HENRY YOUMANS. *Newfoundland Men.* Concord, N.H.: TW and JF Cragg, 1894.

MOYLES, R. GORDON. *Complaints Is Many and Various but the Odd Devil Likes It.* Toronto: Peter Martin Associates, 1975.

MURPHY, MICHAEL. *The Story of the Colonial Building.* St. John's: Newfoundland and Labrador Provincial Archives, 1972.

MURRAY, JEAN M. *The Newfoundland Journal of Aaron Thomas.* Don Mills, Ont.: Longmans Canada Limited, 1968.

NEARY, PETER and O'FLAHERTY, PATRICK. *By Great Waters.* University of Toronto Press, 1974.

NICHOLSON, COLONEL G. W. L. *The Fighting Newfoundlander.* Published by the Government of Newfoundland.

____ *More Fighting Newfoundlanders.* Published by the Government of Newfoundland and Labrador, 1969.

NOEL, S. J. R. *Politics in Newfoundland.* University of Toronto Press, 1971.

O'DEA, FABIAN A., Q.C. "Cabot's Landfall—Yet Again." Newfoundland Historical Society Paper, 1971.

O'DEA, SHANE. "St. John's—Development of the City—and its Architecture." Newfoundland Historic Society Paper, 1973.

PARKER, JOHN, M. P. *Newfoundland: 10th Province of Canada.* London: Lincolns-Prager (Publisher) Ltd., 1950.

PEDLEY, REV. CHARLES. *The History of Newfoundland.* London: Longman, Green, Longman, Roberts and Green, 1863.

PERLIN, A. B. *The Story of Newfoundland.* November, 1959.

PILOT, REV. WILLIAM. *History of Newfoundland.* London and Glasgow: Collins, 1908.

PITT, DAVID G. *Windows of Agates.* St. John's: Gower Street United Church, St. John's, Newfoundland, 1966.

POWER, PATRICK. *Waterford and Lismore.* Cork: Cork University Press, 1937.

POYNTER, F. L. N. *The Journal of James Yonge: 1647-1721.* London: Longmans, Green and Co. Ltd., 1963.

PRATT, CLAIRE. *The Silent Ancestors.* McClelland & Stewart, 1971.

PROWSE, D. W. *A History of Newfoundland.* London: Eyre and Spottiswoode, 1896.

____ *The Newfoundland Guide Book - 1905.* London: Bradbury, Agnew & Co. Ltd., 1905.

PUDDESTER, JOHN. *The Crow'a Nest: 30th Anniversary Souvenir.* St. John's: The Crow's Nest, 1972.

QUINN, DAVID B. and CHESHIRE, NEIL M. *The New Found Land of Stephen Parmenius.* Toronto: University of Toronto Press, 1972.

REDMAN, ALVIN. *The House of Hanover,* New York: Funk and Wagnalls, 1968.

REEVES, JOHN. *History of the Government of the Island of Newfoundland.* London: Printed for Sewell, Debrett, Downes, 1793.

SARNOFF, PAUL. *Ice Pilot Bob Bartlett.* New York: Julian Messner, 1966.
SAUNDERS, H. C. *Jersey in the 18th and 19th Centuries.* Jersey: J. T. Bigwood, 1930.
SAVAGE, RONALD BURKE. *Catherine McAuley: The First Sister of Mercy.* Dublin: M. H. Gill and Son, Ltd., 1955.
SEARY, E. R. *Place Names of the Avalon Peninsula of the Island of Newfoundland.* University of Toronto Press, 1971.
SHERSON, ERROLL. *London's Lost Theatres of the Nineteenth Century.* London: John Lane, The Bodley Head, 1925.
SHORTIS, H. F. *Old St. John's Partial Census: 1796-1797.* Reprinted by Provincial Archives from *The Cadet,* 1916.
SMALLWOOD, J. R. *Hand Book Gazetteer and Almanac.* St. John's: Long Brothers, 1940.
——*The Book of Newfoundland,* vols. I and II St. John's: Newfoundland Book Publishers Ltd., 1937.
——*The Book of Newfoundland,* vols. III and IV. St. John's: Newfoundland Book Publishers Ltd., 1967.
——*The New Newfoundland.* New York: The Macmillan Company, 1931.
SMITH, J. HARRY. *Newfoundland Holiday.* Toronto: The Ryerson Press, 1952.
SMITH, REV. T. W. *History of the Methodist Church in British America.* Halifax, N.S.: S. F. Heustis, 1890.
STOREY, GEORGE M. *George Street United Church: 1873-1973.* St. John's: George Street United Church, 1973.

TEMPLE, W. B., and HARNUM, L. J. *Information Booklet of Newfoundland and Labrador.* St. John's: Robinson and Company Ltd., 1946.
THOMPSON, FREDERIC F. *The French Shore Problem in Newfoundland.* Toronto: University of Toronto Press, 1961.
THOMS, JAMES R. *Newfoundland-Labrador Who's Who.* St. John's: E. C. Boone Advertising Limited, 1968.
TOCQUE, REV. PHILIP. *Kaleidoscope Echoes.* Toronto: The Hunter, Rose Company, Ltd., 1895.
——*Newfoundland as It Was and as It Is in 1877.* London: Sampson Low, Marston, Searle and Rivington, 1878.
——*Wandering Thoughts.* London: Thomas Richardson & Son, 1846.
TODD, WILLIAM A. "Reconstructions and Evolution of Mount Pearl Park —Glendale." Unpublished Thesis, M.U.N., 1971.
TOWNSEND, CHARLES WENDELL, M.D. *Captain Cartwright and His Labrador Journal.* Boston: Dana Estes & Co., 1911.
TURNBULL, ROBERT. *The Story of Newfoundland.* Toronto, London, New York, and Sydney: McGraw-Hill Company of Canada, 1966.

VILLIERS, ALAN. *The Quest of the Schooner Argus.* London: Hodder and Stoughton, 1951.

WADDEN, BRIAN J. *The St. John's Electric Light Co.: 1885-1892.*
WALLACE, GRAHAM. *The Flight of Alcock and Brown.* London: Putnam, 1955.
WALSH, T. J. *Nano Nagle and the Presentation Sisters.* Dublin: M. H. Gill and Son Ltd., 1959.

WEBBER, DAVID A. *The St. John's Volunteer Rangers: 1805-1814.*
——*Skinner's Fencibles: The Royal Newfoundland Regiment: 1795-1802.* St. John's 1964.
WHIPPLE, A.B.C. *The Fatal Gift of Beauty.* New York: Harper and Row, 1964.
WHITBOURNE, RICHARD. *Westward Ho for Avalon in Newfoundland: 1622.* London, 1870.
WILKINSON, C.H. *The King of Beggars: Bampfylde-Moors Carew.* Oxford: Claredon Press, 1931.
WILKINSON, GEORGE THEODORE. *The Newgate Calendar (3).* London: Panther Books, 1963.
WILLIAMSON, JAMES A. *The Cabot Voyages and Bristol Discovery Under Henry* VII. Cambridge: The University Press, 1962.
WINTON, HENRY. "A Chapter in the History of Newfoundland for the Year 1861." Unpublished booklet, Provincial Archives.
WIX, REV. EDWARD. *Six Months of a Newfoundland Missionary's Journal.* London: Smith, Elder and Co., Cornhill, 1836.

PERIODICALS AND NEWSPAPERS.

Annals of all Hallows, Dublin, Ireland.
"Annals of the Mount"—Private papers in the Irish Christian Brothers Archives, St. John's.
British Press and Jersey Times. Various issues, 1886.
Centenary Souvenir Book (Basilica of St. John the Baptist). St. John's: Robinson and Company, 1955.
Centenary Volume of the Benevolent Irish Society: 1806-1906. Cork: Guy & Co. Ltd. 1907.
Centennial Souvenir- Sisters of Mercy: 1831-1931.
Compton Castle. London: CountryLife Ltd., 1971.
Daily News. Various issues.
Dublin Builder. Vol. I, 1859. Dublin: Peter Roe, Mabbot St
Evening Telegram. Various issues.
Floes, London: Hutchinson & Co. (Publishers) Ltd., 1933.
Inter Nos. Issues of June 1942; June 1944; June 1947.
Irish Digest. Various issues.
Irish Ecclesiastical Record. Vol. II. Dublin: John F. Fowler, Dame St., 1866; Browne & Nolan, Ltd. Nassau St., 1933.
Journal of the Waterford and South East Ireland Archaeological Society. Vol. VI. Waterford Harvey & Co., 1900.
Maurice Cullen. The National Gallery of Canada, 1956.
Monitor. Various issues.
Newfoundland. Department of External Affairs, 1950.
Newfoundland Quarterly. Numerous old papers.
Newscene. Various issues.
Old Properties: Early Residents. Provincial Archives.
Port of St. John's. The National Harbours Board.
Program of the Presentation of Civic Symbols to the City of St. John's: Friday, October, 1, 1965.
St. Bride's College Annual, Issues of June 1919; June 1947.

St. John's: North America's Oldest City. Newfoundland Board of Trade, 1961.
Story of Newfoundland: The Great Island. 1928.
Tablet. Dublin: 2 October 1841.
Twillingate Sun. 1888.
Tyranny in St. John's: 1705-1706. Provincial Archives.
Where to Go! What to Do! What to see! St. John's, Newfoundland. Newfoundland Tourist and Publicity Commission.

In addition to the newspapers listed above, isolated issues of almost all St. John's, Harbour Grace, and Carbonear Newspapers of the past have been consulted. They are too numerous to list here and are available at the Provincial Archives and the Provincial Reference Library—Newfoundland Section.

Index

Abbott, Eric, 270
Abenaquis Indians, 85
Academia, 253, 254, 829
Acrostic, 152
Actors and actresses, 237, 242, 252, 266-68, 516-17, 682
Adams, D., 209, 833
Adams, Edward, 646
Adams, William G., mayor, 477
Adelaide Street, 44, 518, 622, 632
Admiral's: ship's room, 43
Agriculture, 45, 50, 55, 58, 144, 147
Air Canada, 367
Aircrashes, 363-64, 367-68
Airships, 350, 358, 362
Alcock, John, 351, 352, 355-58, 677; illus., 345, 346, 347
Alderdice, Frederick, 362, 470, 472
Alexander Bay, 359
Alexander, Mr., 862
Alexander, Robert, 478
Alexander Street, 374
Alexandra Players, 266-67
Allan, Dr., 281
Allan, Thomas, 235
Allandale Road, 205
Allen, Alfred H., 151
Allen, G.G., 332
Allworth, Ardis, 255-56
Alsop, Robert, 633, 859
Amateur Athletic Association, 335-36
Amateur dramatics, 241, 242-46, 248-49, 252, 254 passim, 258, 267-70 see also Theatre
Amateur Theatre, 241, 242-46, 262
American football, 329
American Oyster House and Coffee Saloon, 209, 527
American Repertoire Company, 255
American Revolution: and fortifications, 97
American vessels, 982-83
Amey, Robert, 594-95
Amherst, Sir Jeffrey, 90, 91
Amherst, Lt. Col. William, 91, 92, 93, 94, 97 passim, 678, 713, 930
Amulree Royal Commission, 470-71
Anderson, Sir David Murray, gov., 362

Anderson, John Murray, 267, 380-82, 859, 871; illus., 371
Anderson Avenue, 205
Andrews, George, 859
Andrews, William, 39, 40
Angel, James, 856
Angel, John, 856
Angell, Edward, 228
Anglican Cathedral churchyard, 285, 686-87
Anglican Church see Church of England
Anglo-American Telegraph, 198-99, 202, 203 passim, 204, 827, 836
Anglo-Newfoundland Development Company, 364
Anspach, Louis Amadeus, 776
Ansty, Capt. George, 110
Apple Tree Well: fire, 250, 506-17
Arcade Stores, 262
Archery, 322
Archibald, Edward, 457
Archibald, S.G., 320
Archibald, Sir William, 693
Archibald's Furniture Factory, 204
Architecture, 46, 50, 52-53, 54-55, 57, 60, 61
Arctic expeditions, 979-80
Arena Rink Company, 325
Arena see Prince of Wales Skating Rink
Arnold, Gen. Benedict, 989
Argentia Base, 109, 366
Argo Construction Company, 178
Armed Forces Day celebrations, 111
Armstrong's Sail Loft: theatre, 250
Army Street, 111
Arts & Culture Centre, 258, 269-70, 823-25; illus., 222
Arts & Letters Competition, 258
Ashehurst, Thomas, 33
Association of Canadian Television and Radio Artists, 207
Athenaeum, 252, 253, 254, 875; illus., 613
Atlantic Cable, 198-99; illus., 167
Atlantic Films, 112, 328, 390
Atlantic Hotel, 178, 524, 825; illus., 499
Atlantic Place, 530, 847, 873-74
Avalon Athletic Club, 334
Avalon Curling and Skating Rink, 324, 389

Avalon Curling Rink, 325-26
Avalon Green Spring Club, 334
Avalon Hotel, 107, 529-30
Avalon Mall, 211, 374
Avalon Mall Theatre, 266
Avalon Race Course, 319
Avalon Raceway, 320
Avalon Rink *see* Avalon Curling and Skating Rink
Avalon Telephone Company, 204, 206
Avery, William, 108
Aviation, 352-68
Aylward, Mrs., 691
Ayre & Sons Ltd., 206, 335, 640, 917; illus., 810, 815
Ayre, Charles Pascoe, 873
Ayre, Charles Robert, 746, 858, 872-73
Ayre, John Bray, 843
Ayre, John Bulley, 833
Ayre, Mrs. John Bulley, 858

Bacon, Joseph, 747, 776
Baine, Johnston & Co., 242, 268
Baine, Robert, 916
Baine, Walter, 916
Baird, David, 864
Baird, James, 326, 380, 885
Baird, Hon. James, 878-79
Baird, Margaret, 864
Baker, Ted *see* MacDonald, Aubrey
Balbo, Italo, 361-62, 366
Ballads, 375, 384-86
Bally Haly Curling Rink, 325
Bally Haly Golf Club, 336-37
Baltimore, Lord *see* Calvert, Sir George
Bambrick Street, 51
Banishment, 546-47, 725
Bank of British North America, 175
Bank of Commerce, 395
Bank of Montreal, 210, 332
Bank of Nova Scotia, 384
Banks, 867-69; illus., 445
Banks, Sir Joseph, 48-49, 520, 521
Bannerman, Alexander, gov., 148, 321
Bannerman Park, 251, 321, 322, 324, 332, 389, 462, 629, 642, 669-70, 671, 687
Bannerman Road, 289, 332
Bannerman Street, 58
Banting, Sir Frederick, 367
Barbary pirates, 79
Barbers and hairdressers, 51, 242, 282
Barbour, Capt. George, 971
Barbour, Capt. Joe, 985
Bard, Philip, 47
Barnes, Andrew, 914
Barnes, Dr. Arthur, 468
Barnes, Billy, 180
Barnes, James, 753

Barnes, Richard, 687, 689
Barne's Lane, 296
Barr, George M., 403, 858
Barrett, Fred, 594-95
Barrie, Sir James, 672-73
Barron, Capt. John, 525, 859
Barron, Laurence, 859
Barron, Pierce, 477, 859
Barrow's Road, Quidi Vidi, 342
Bartar, Jonas, 250, 612
Barter's Hill, 456
Bartlett, Gordon, 270
Bartlett, Capt. Robert, 690, 968, 979-80, 988; illus., 948
Baseball, 331-32
Basha, Mike, 849
Basketball, 333
Basque, 79, 135
Bates Hill, 43, 210, 243, 292 *see also* Gallows Hill
Bathing, 320 *see also* Swimming
Battle Harbour, Labrador, 108
Bavarian Beer Depot, 318
Bay Bulls, 51, 81, 84, 90, 92, 98, 99, 144
Bay Bulls Arm: Atlantic cable, 198
Bay Bulls Big Pond, 360, 367
Bay de Verde, 301
Bay of Islands, 137
Bay Roberts, 327, 365
Beaconsfield (house), 464
Bearns, T., 860
Bearns, W.E. (Billy), 860
Beauclerk, Amelius, 141
Beauclerk, Lord Vere, gov., 128, 129, 551
Beck, Thomas, 504
Beck's Coffee House, 252
Beck's Cove, 43, 178, 209, 211, 243, 476, 624, 641
Belcombe, Lt., 92
Bell, Alexander Graham, 204, 514
Bell, Charles R., 885
Bell, Rev. John, 744
Bell Island: and telephone, 204
Bell Street, 196, 232
Bell Telephone, 204
Bella Vista Fair Grounds, 320
Belmont Tavern, 264
Belvedere Cemetery, 396, 401, 693-94
Belvedere Monastary, 780
Belvedere Street, 102
Benevolent Irish Society (B.I.S.), 179, 230, 253, 254, 260, 318, 329, 332, 383, 458, 638, 693, 779-83, 829
B.I.S. Dramatic Company, 254
B.I.S. Orphan Asylum, 320, 458, 459, 629, 632, 639, 780-83; illus., 766
Benger, Mrs. James (Mary), 86, 87, 882
Bennett, Col., 882

Bennett, Magistrate, 462
Bennett, Charles Fox P.M., 51, 295, 625, 632, 849-50, 854, 858, 918, 924, 927
Bennett, Edward W., 850
Bennett, Sir John, 358, 850
Bennett, Sydney, 358, 359
Bennett's: plantation, 44, 45
Beothuck Indians, 33, 34, 926
Berry, Sir John, 45, 46
Best, William, 322
Best, W.R., 667, 749, 712
Best's farm, 319
Bevan, Mr., 255
Billiards, 53, 317-18
Bingo, 264
Binland, Mr., 910
Bird-in-Hand, 229
Bishop, Edward see Bishop, George
Bishop, George, 267
Bishop Feild College, 259, 267, 323, 326, 381, 395, 779
Bishop's Cove: and fire, 625
Bishop's House, 55
Black, Harry, 729
Black, James, 204
Black, Rev. James, 151
Blackall, Dr. W.W., 779, 798
Blackie, Sheriff, 858
Blackman, Rev. Charles, 244-45, 720
Blackmarsh Road, 299, 357
Blacksmiths, 51, 232, 830
Blackwood, Eric, 368
Blackwood, R.B., 320
Blackwood's, 320
Blaikie, James, 240, 286
Blamey, Capt., 851
Blamey, Eunice Pearl, 681, 851
Blamey, Ruth, 851
Bland, John, 106, 824
Bligh, Capt. William, 135-36, 519
Blondell, Joan: and the railway, 516-17
Blue Puttees, 112, 307 see also Royal Newfoundland Regiment
Blundon, R., 546
Board of Trade, 882
Board of Trade Building, 196, 205, 318
Boden (planter), 908
Boggan, Frank, 636
Boggan, John, Sr., 512
Boland, Martin, 341
Bolt, Canon, 464
Bonaventure Avenue, 269, 322
Bonavista: and French, 81, 85, 280, 403, 910
Bond, John, 857
Bond, Sir Robert, P.M., 200, 201, 474, 570, 643, 857, 868-69; illus., 444
Bond Street: rebuilt, 249, 267, 643
Bonfoy, gov., 549, 554

Bonnycastle, Sir Richard, 57, 60, 248, 791-92
Boone, John, 571
Bonstelle, Jessie, 150, 259
Bookstores, 196, 209, 287
Boston, 93
Boston Criterion Comedy Company, 256
Boulevard, 354
Boulos, Edward, 262
Boulton, Judge Henry John, 187, 188, 189, 290, 582-83, 584, 585; illus., 537
Bounds, Miss, 252
Bounteous, Mr., 241
Bowker, Capt., 319
Bowcock farm, 299
Bowdin, Caroline, 375
Bowdon, Mr., 199
Bowling, 323
Bowring, Benjamin, 234, 626, 871, 919-21, 956-57
Bowring, Sir Edgar, 393, 475, 512, 671-72, 921; illus., 638
Bowring Park, 322, 323, 671-72
Bowring's, 513, 589, 628, 637, 640, 671, 871, 914, 919-21
Bowring's fleet, 961
Bowring's Mill, 299
Boxing, 333-34, 392
Boyd, Nellie, 251
Boyd, Thomas, 922
Boyle, Sir Cavendish, gov., 150-51, 200, 201, 327, 689-90, 973
Boyle trophy, 151, 327
Brace, Mr., 721
Brace, George, 753, 775
Brace, Richard, 561, 563
Bradshaw, Dr., 281
Brady, 562-63
Brady, Chief Justice, 460, 586
Brady, Lady, 460
Brady, Maj., 678
Brady, Phil, 564-65
Brain, Lord, 308
Bray, Robert Crocker, 581-82
Brazill, Fred, 392
Brennan, Edward, 837
Brennan, Peter, 860
Brenton, R.P., 726
Brewin (child), 671
Brewin, Mr., 340
Brian, James, 671
Brien, John, 852
Brien, Patrick, 852
Bridge, Archdeacon, 687, 716, 721
Bridge, Capt. Timothy, 84, 85-86
Brine, Mr., 138
Brine, Robert, 229, 317, 845
Brine Street, 317
Brine's Bridge, 229

Brine's Tavern, 233, 317
Britannia tavern, 228
British Hall, 249, 252, 254, 260, 263
Brookfield Road, 266, 353, 354, 377
Brooking, Thomas Holdsworth, 234, 338, 824, 850, 908
Brookings dock, 294
Broom, John, 250, 573, 574
Broomfield, J.J., 244, 513, 523, 627, 629-30, 635 see also Phoenix Fire Office
Brouillon, de, 80
Browker, Capt., 141
Brown, Father, 782
Brown, Arthur Whitten, 352, 355-58, 677; illus., 345, 346, 347, 351
Brown, Cassie, 258
Brown, Catherine, 548
Brown, James, 548
Brown, John 852
Brown, Maj. W.C., 797
Brown, King, 279
Browning, Gilbert, 853, 859
Brown's Field: circus, 254
Browne, John, 43
Browne, Capt. Maurice, 39, 41
Browne, Robert, 82
Buchan, Capt. David, 139, 144, 145, 285, 557
Buchanan, James, 198
Buchanan Street, 111
Buckley, Sister Mary Cecilia, 305
Buckmaster, Patrick, 836
Buckmaster's Field, 111, 329, 336
Buildings see esp. chapter 8
Bull-baiting, 317
Bulley, Eliza, 681
Bulley, John, 913, 914
Bulley, Robert, 547
Bulley, Samuel, 913, 914; illus., 895
Bulley & Job, 104
Bulley's Farm, 228
Bunch of Grapes, 228
Bunting, Dr. (Sr.), 281
Bunting, Dr. John, 292, 293
Bunting, Dr. Frederick, 293, 298
Burgess, Elizabeth R., 523, 529
Burin: diptheria, 295
Burke, John, 282
Burke, Capt. John, 384
Burke, Johnny, 253, 358-59, 375, 384-86, 565, 870
Burke, Thomas, 579-80
Burke, Vincent, 798
Burlington, 365
Burnham, Fred, 235
Burrage, Hayward, mayor, 682
Burrows, Mr., 87
Burrows, William, 923
Bursey, Gertrude, 565-66

Bursey, William, 526
Burst Heart Hill, 43
Butchery inn, 229
Bute, (merchant), 32
Butler, (soldier), 285
Butler, (Commander of Raleigh), 38, 39
Butler, Alan, 358
Butler, Clara, 785
Butler, Philip, 557
Butler, Roma, 255, 268
Butt, Grace, 258, 268
Butt, John, 691
Byers Road, Quidi Vidi, 342
Byng, Adm. John, gov., 130-32; illus., 123
Byrne, Garrett, 862
Byrne, Patrick, 282, 283
Byron John, gov., 132-35

CBC, see Canadian Broadcasting Corporation
CBN, 682
CJON, 207, 268, 841
CKZN, 682
CTV, 207
Cabot, John, 31-34, 200
Cabot, Sebastian, 32, 33
Cabot Street, 211
Cabot Tower, 97, 200, 201, 362, 675-76, 677; illus., 939 see also Signal Hill
Caddy, Lt. John, 139
Cahill, (widow), 243
Cahill, John, 228, 547
Cahill, Tom, 258, 270
Callahan, Glass & Company, 262
Calos Youth Orchestra, 270
Calvert, Sir George, 44, 79, 81, 723
Cameron, Arthur Priestman, 263
Camp Alexander, 110
Campbell, Maj. Gen., 107
Campbell, Dr. Alex, 467
Campbell, Colin, 85
Campbell, Capt. John, gov., 135-36, 330, 725, 726, 729
Campbell, William, 907
Campbell Avenue, 395
Canada: Centennial Year, 112; first Canadian governor, 148 see also Federal Government
Canadian Armed Forces, 111, 112, 329
Canadian Broadcasting Corporation, 206, 207, 258, 265, 268, 682, 824, 825
Canadian Expeditionary Force, 399
Canadian Legion Building, 354
Canadian Marconi Office, 205
Canadian National, 206
Canadian National Railway, 530, 854, 925
Canadian National Telegraphs, 204
Canadian Overseas Telecommunication Corporation, 928

Canadian Pacific Railway, 508-9
Candow, Alexander, 843
Canning, Francis, 590-91
Canning, Jack, 205
Cape Breton, 32, 197, 199
Cape of Hope see Cape Spear
Cape Race, 41, 44
Cape Ray: telegraph, 197, 199
Cape St. Francis, 34
Cape Spear, 34, 35, 203
Capitol Movie Theatre, 254, 264-65 see before
  Casino
  Car racing, 320
Carbonear, 100, 189, 191, 198, 204, 248, 503,
  504, 506, 517
Carbonear Sentinel, 688
Card playing, 232-33
Carew, Bampfylde-Moore, 235-36, 377-78
Carew, Archbishop William A. 386-87
Carew, William J., 386
Carew Street School see Bishop Feild College
Carey, Jane, 586
Carey, Michael, 586-87
Caribou Hut, 394
Carmanville, 366
Carmen, Rev. Dr., 747
Carmer, Charles, 887
Carnell, Andrew G., mayor, 320, 477, 830
Carnell, John T., 475, 830
Carolan, Rev. P.A., 971
Carpasia (house): owners, 791
Carpasian Park Ltd., 110
Carpasian Road, 110, 112, 332, 329
Carrington, Rev. Frederick, 687
Carrol, Dan, 262
Carroll, Ellen, 645-46
Carson, Jessy, 914
Carson, Dr. Samuel, 17, 105, 293, 298, 834, 917
Carson, Dr. William: horse racing, 319; and
  hospital, 289, 290, 293, 298; and military,
  104-6 passim; and politics, 184, 187-89
  passim, 284-86, 455, 456, 457, 471, 472, 475,
  557, 684, 687, 688, 734, 786, 834, 914, 926;
  and Turf Club, 522-23; illus., 273, 450
Carter, Sir Frederick, 400, 464; illus., 439
Carter, Sheriff James, 523
Carter, Judge Peter Weston, 577, 671
Carter, Robert, 858
Carter, Weston, 671
Carter's Hills, 43, 243, 292 see also Gallows
  Hill
Cartier, Jacques, 36-37, 480
Cartwright, Mr., 136
Cartwright, Capt. George, 520, 989
Cartwright, Labrador: and aviation 360, 361
Carty, Paul, 575, 635
Casey, John, 235
Casey Street, 264

Casey's Lane, 462
Cashin family, 841, 844
Cashin, Sir Michael, P.M., 465-66, 474, 528, 841
Cashin, Maj. Peter, 467-70, 474; illus., 452
Casino Theatre, 254-56 passim, 259, 261, 264,
  269, 288, 302 see also Capital Movie
  Theatre
Castle, 79, 80, 84, 85, 88, 93, 97, 104-5, 684, 930
Castle Rennie, 778
Cathedral Fire Brigade, 634-36
Cathedral Fire Brigade Hall, 232
Cathedral Square, 304
Cathedral Street, 58, 193, 269
Catherine Street, 175, 296
Catholic Cadet Corps, 108, 303, 333
Catholics: and burial rights, 690-91, 693-94;
  and education, 779 ff; and penal laws, 545,
  725, 775; persecution of, 554, 577-78, 724-
  25; and Protestants, 688, 718, 719, 745, 750
Cavendish Square, 39, 303, 336
Census, 45-46, 48-50, 54 see also Popula-
  tion
Central Hotel, 204, 206, 525-26, 880 see also
  Crosbie's Central Hotel
Chain Rock, 80, 95, 96, 104, 105, 106
Chalker, Tom, 367
Chancey, Lionel, 775, 834
Chancey, Rachel, 913
Channing, Florence, 386
Channing, Lynn, 268
Chapel Street, 58
Chaplin, Mark, 332, 828
Chapman family, 248, 249
Chapman, Rev. John, 145
Chappell, Lt. Edward, 53-54, 60, 230, 820-21,
  822, 874
Charitable organizations, 230, 240, 243, 245
Charles I, 126, 475
Charles II, 127
Charlottetown, 368
Cherry Gardens, Waterford Bridge Road,
  231-32
Chess, 337-38
Children: early 19c 56; hospitals, 301, 307,
  851; and schools, 777-78, 789, 792, 796; and
  theatre, 242
Chinese settlers, 829
Chisholm, J. Forbes, 209, 837-38
Chloroform: first used, 293
Cholera epidemic, 294-95, 796
Christ Church, Quidi Vidi, 91, 721-22, 753
Christmas Bells (magazine), 196
Christmas celebrations, 685-86; mumming
  banned, 686
Chronicle, 193, 750
Church Hill, 43, 287, 288
Church Lads Brigade, 108, 307, 333, 334
Church of England, 47, 57, 84, 108, 185, 186,

711-23, 743, 744; education, 779, 784-85; illus.,760,761,762
Church of England Cathedral, 628, 639, 715, 716-19,723; illus.,611,700,702
Church of England Cemetery, 392, 681, 692-93 *see also* Anglican Cathedral Churchyard
Church of England Men's Bible Class: orchestra,256
Church of England Total Abstinence Society, 231
Church of St. Mary The Virgin, 722-23
Churchill, Emma (teacher), 797-98
Churchill, Winston S., 109
Churchill Square, 332, 403
Churchwarden, Capt., 189-90 *passim*
Cinema,259-66
Circular Road,146,318,319,325,332,403
Circuses, 111,254
City Club, 318
City Council *see* Municipal Government, *and under* St. John's
City Dump,332
City Hall: 1895 fire, 262 *see also* Municipal Government
City Rink, 328
City Terrace, 196, 204
Clapp, Widow, 884
Clare, Sister, of Presentation Convent *see* English, Mary Theresa
Clarenville, 366
Clark, Rev. Dr., 470
Clark, Dr. Raymond, 735-36
Clarke, Benjamin, 644
Clarke, Commodore E.N., 826
Clarke, Richard, 41
Clarke, Walter, 644
Clayton, Bertram, 365-66
Clearview drive-in, 266
Cleary, Thomas, 247
Cliff, William, 83
Clift, Fanny, 395
Clift, James, 106,234,878
Clift, James Shannon, 913
Clift, Theodore, 909,913
Clift, Thomas, 878
Clift's Cove, 337
Climate, 56,139,140,143
Clinch, Dr. John, 280
Clinton, Sir George, gov., 129-30
Clouston, John, 832,839
Clouston, W.S., 514
Clouston, William J., 832
Clubs & Societies, 230, 251, 252-53, 318, 775-76, 785, 878
Cluny, Dr., 883
Coady, John, 546
Coady, Nicholas, 98
Coady, Thomas, 878

Coaker, Sir William, 205, 474, 863, 866
Coastal boats, 196
Cochius, Rudolph H.K., 671, 682; illus., 658
Cochrane, Sir Thomas, gov.: account, 142-45; and churches, 714, 719-20, 745; and golf, 336; Government House, 54, 153; and politics, 186-88 *passim*, 284-85 *passim*, 456, 476, 503, 559-60, 574, 678-81, 732; and religion, 146; and theatre, 245; illus., 115
Cochrane, Sir Thomas (of London), 926
Cochrane Hotel: and aviators, 352, 354, 355, 360; and Lindberghs, 529; and Marconi, 199, 202, 203; illus., 502
Cochrane Pond, 366
Cochrane Street, 43, 44, 45, 57, 137, 143, 148, 206, 229, 400
Cochrane Street Church, 398
Cock, Aaron, 235, 377
Cock-fighting, 317
Cockpit Road *see* Craigmillar Avenue
Codner, Samuel, 776-77, 865, 922; illus., 759
Cody, Tom, 262
Coffee, Philip, 666
Coke, Chief Justice D'Ewes, 101, 279-80, 342, 910, 923
Colclough, Caesar, 555-56, 821
Cole, Capt., 855-56
Coleman, Robert J., 529
College of Fisheries, 319, 801, 928-29
College of Trade and Technology, 802
Collingwood, William, 916
Collins, J.J., 205, 206
Collins, John, gov., 88, 89, 236
Collins, Sister Veronica, 523
Colonial Bookstore, 287
Colonial Broadcasting System, 206
Colonial Building, 177, 252, 289, 457-58, 460, 463, 464, 473, 474, 689; beseiged, 469-70; official opening, 459; riots, 461-62; illus., 440-41, 448-49
Colonial Street, 58, 323
Columbus, Christopher, 31
Colville, Lord, 90-91 *passim*, 93
Commerce and business development, 906-9, 913, 914-15; oldest, 819-20, 888; shipping, 863, 908, 956-57; illus., 903-4; *see esp*. Ch. 8
Commercial airlines, 358-59, 364-68
Commercial Building, 324
Commercial Hotel, 505
Commissariat Building, 60
Committee of Merchants, 54
Commodore, office of, 89, 129 *see also* Governors
Community Concert movement, 266
Conception Bay, 81, 85, 196, 197, 199, 204, 253, 503-8
Condon, Daniel, 51
Condon, Jack, 263, 264

1014
Part II begins on page 433

Confederation: *1867*, 107, 400; *1949*, 152, 153, 263, 472-73, 711, 824, 868
Confederation Building, 475, 684
Congregational Church, 713, 721, 751-55, 914
Congregational Meeting House, 232
Conn, Capt., 524-25
Connell, 463
Connolly family, 375
Connolly, Mrs., 469, 470
Connors, Michael, 820, 836, 841
Conway, Sir William, 43
Cook, Capt. James, 136-37, 988-89
Cook, Michael, 255, 258
Cook, Sir Tasker, mayor, 477, 672, 836-37
Cook, William, 836-37
Cooke, Thomas, 54
Cookstown: development, 54
Coombs, Ellen, 582
Coote, Judge Thomas, 691
Corinne Opera Company, 253
Cormack, Janet, 296
Cormack, W.E., 296, 850
Corner Brook, 137, 327, 401
Cornwall Theatre, 265-66
Corte-Real, Gaspar, 33-34, 504; illus., 435
Costabelle, de, 87-89 *passim*
Costello, Miss, 252
Coster, George, 719
Costley, Darby, 724
Cotton, Major F. Sydney, 358-59, 385
Coughlan, Sgt., 463
Coughlan, Lawrence, 742
Coughlan, Paddy, 565
Coughlan, William, 505
Coughlan's Coaches, 505
Courcy, Count de, 377, 378-79
Courier, 746
Court House, 106, 176-78 *passim*, 234, 249, 264, 283, 457, 462-63, 560, 571, 572, 621, 622, 628, 638-39, 832-33; illus., 542-43
Court House Steps: ship's rooms, 43
Courtney, Rev. Frederick, 719
Covey, Thomas, 49
Cowan, Patrick, 339
Cox, William, 39
Cox Marsh Battery, 97
Coyle, Nancy, 292
Cozens, Samuel, 506
Craigmillar Avenue: history, 317, 319; personalities from, 383
Crane, R., 207
Creedon, Mother Francis (Mary Ann), 792-93, 794-96; illus., 791
Crescent Theatre, 261-62, 840, 864
Crichton, W., 578
Cricket, 112, 330-31
Crime: theft, 286; *see also* Banishment, Executions, Law & Order, Prisons, Rape, Violence

Croke, Bernard, 399
Croke, Dennis, 341
Cromwell, Oliver, 127
Croquet, 322
Crosbie, Chesley A., 368
Crosbie, George, 204, 206, 525-26, 880
Crosbie, Sir John, 465, 526, 863; illus., 811
Crosbie's Central Hotel, 301, 863-64; illus., 160, 526; *see also* Central Hotel
Croscombe, Father, 745
Crossroads, 51, 317, 392
Crow, Capt. Joseph, 47-48, 56
Crowdy, Dr., 298
Crowe, Capt., 550
Crowe, Daniel, 579-80
Crowe, John, 579-80
Crow's Nest Battery, 94
Crow's Nest Club, 825, 826
Crown tavern, 229
Crown & Anchor tavern, 229, 244, 319
Crute, John, 231, 506
Cubit, George, 743-44
Cuckold's Cove, 91
Cuddihy Street *see* Tank Lane
Cullen, James, 250, 387, 840
Cullen, Maurice, 250, 387-89, 397, 840
Cullen, Michael, 256
Cullen, William, 840-41, 842
Cuper's Cove *see* Cupids
Cupids, 42
Curling, 324-26, 328
Currie, J.S., 196
Curtis, Levi, 798
Curtiss-Ried, 364
Customs House, 528, 628, 827, 887; illus., 805
Cycling, 323-24

Daily News: 1869 only, 193
Daily News: 1894- , 194, 196, 242, 578, 591, 690, 852
Dalton, Lawrence, 547
Dancing, 252, 374, 389
Danielle, Prof. Charles Henry, 324, 340, 389-392, 829, 831
Daniels, Cyril, 108
Darrigan, Michael, 579-81
Darkuse's: ship's room, 43
Darley, Sgt. James, 99, 100
Darling, Sir Charles Henry, gov., 148, 295
Darling Street *see* Bond Street
Davenport, Jean M., 246-47
Davids, Walter Charles, 180
Davidson, Lady, 264
Davidson, Sir Walter E., gov., 464; illus., 117
Davis, E. Fredd, 269
Davis, Capt. John, 969
Davis, Robert, 38
Dawe, William, 108, 365, 573, 845

Dawson, Charles (teacher), 797
Dawson, M., 236
Day, Capt., 852
Day, John, 32
Day Book, 193
de Brouillon, St. Ovide, 712
De Forest, George, 527
de la Mare, Edith, 785
de la Rade, Marquis, 79
de la Roque, Jean-François, Sieur de Rober-
   val, 36-37, 480
de la Roque, Marguerite, 480-81
de Ternay, Admiral, 844-45
De Uriarte, Don Hipolito, 524-25
Deakins, John, 336
Dearin, Dr. J.J., 209, 287, 831
Deer Lake: and aviators, 359
Delaney, Dr., 279
Delaney, Mark, 529
Delany, John, 204
Delgado, Andrew, 880-81
Dempsey family, 736-37
Demsey, Patrick, 462
Dental Board, 288
Dentistry, 287-88, 299
Denys, Father Joseph, 724
Derby Place, 320
Des Barres, Judge, 843, 924
Des Barres, Wallet, 558
Des Vouex, gov., 784
Desertion, 100, 102, 127, 919
Deucher, A., 252
Devereux, Joseph, 507
Devine, Brenda, 268
Devine, J.M., 851, 865
Devine, M.A., 199, 464, 676
Devine, P.K., 294, 643, 845
Devon Row, 39, 88, 204, 640-41; illus., 607
di Pazzi, Mother, 791-93
Dickens, Mr. and Mrs. Charles, 562
Dickinson, Ethel, 303; illus., 278
Dicks, Mrs., 830
Dicks, Robert, 871-72
Dicks, William, 871
Dicks & Company, 175
Dickson, William, 573
Diet, 47, 56, 96, 100-101, 241
Dillon, John, 739
Diptheria, 295
Direct United States Cable Company, 199
Dissenters: and marriage ceremony, 284 *see
   also* Protestants
Diteman, Urban, 361
Dixie Line, 379
Dobie, Mr., 286
Dobie's Chemical Establishment, 286
Doctors, 280-86, 299
Dodd,   Mr., 279

Dodd, Dr. Thomas, 547, 580
Dogs, 49, 56, 58, 101, 133-35
Domestic servants, 60-61, 85-86, 145
Dominion Broadcasting Company, 206, 207
Donergan, Dr., 281
Donnelly, William, 507
Dooley, Din, 234-35
Dooley, Garret, 634
Dooley, John M., 331, 529
Dooley, Sally, 522-23
Dooling, Robert, 228
Dooly, Michael, 504
Dorrell, Richard, gov., 724, 725
Dorril, Richard, gov., 49-50
Douglas, Capt., 93
Douglas, Mr., 229
Douglas, James, 747
Downing, John: planter, 44, 45, 46, 47, 127,
   341, 342, 455, 909
Downing, Patrick, 506, 581-83
Downtown, 52
Downtown Development Corporation, 337
Dowsley, Felix, 860-61
Dowsley, John, 693
Doyle, Mr., 229
Doyle, Dicky, 237
Doyle, Gerald S., 865, 911
Doyle, James, 506
Doyle, Maurice, 506
Doyle, Tome, 690
Drake, Sir Francis, 78
Drake, Sir Francis William, gov., 132, 552-53
Drew, William, 81
Driscoll, Daniel, 229
Drive-in Cinemas, 266
Drug Stores, 286-87, 469
Drysdale, Andrew, 506
Duckworth, Sir John Thomas, gov., 52, 55,
   106, 284, 289, 322, 549, 559, 574, 690-91,
   981; illus., 124
Duckworth Street: *mid 19c* 57; clubs, 253;
   Court House, 234, 458; and doctors, 290;
   Fishermen's/Seamen's Home, 478-79; and
   flakes, 52; hotels, 522-29; Market House,
   458; newspaper offices, 184, 193-96 *pas-
   sim*; old street pattern, 137; post office, 175-
   77 *passim*; prison, 559; prostitution, 237;
   public houses, 229, 231, 318; reconstruction, 643-44; rink, 328, 389; ship's rooms,
   43; and telephone, 204, 205; and temper-
   ence, 232; and theatres, 241, 243, 244, 249-
   51 *passim*; 254, 256, 262, 268; War Memorial, 389; illus., 17, 215, 609, 610
Duchemin, James, 842-43
Duder, Edwin, 838, 863, 924
Duder, Edwin Jr., 863
Duelling, 233-35, 241
Duff, J.J., 265, 842-43

1016   *Part II begins on page 433*

Duff Building, 265, 323, 843
Duffy, Bernard, 562-63, 837
Dugdale, Lt., 91
Duggan, David, 106, 280
Duggan, Ken, 802
Duke of York, 229
Duke of York Battery, 97
Duke of York Street, 137, 138, 229, 288
Dunfield, Sir Brian, 647
Dunne, Tom "Dynamite", 334, 335
Dunscomb, Hon. John, 778
Dunscomb, William, 679
Durnford, Elias, 104
Durnford, Isabella, 53, 105-6
Dutch, 35
Dwyer, John, 509
Dwyer, Johnny, 333, 392
Dwyer, T.S., 844
Dyer Building, 211

Eager, William, gov., 230, 560
Earhart, Amelia, 980
Earle, Julia Salter, 466-67, 479
Earle, R.H., 512
Eastern Provincial Airways, 368
Easton, Peter, 79
Eccentrics, 374-79
Economy: prices, *19c* 53, 56; trades, *18c* 50-51;
   and World War II, 111 *see also* Trade
Edens, Mrs. (teacher), 780
Edgell, Capt., 684, 925
Edward VII, 339, 375, 525, 671, 689
Edward VIII, 784
Edwards, Capt. Richard, gov., 137, 138, 279,
   519, 573, 713, 752, 826, 887; illus., 122
Edwards, Kitchener, 566
Elections, 456, 475; and riots, 833, 835, 839,
   886
Electric Light Works, 513
Electrification, 513-15; illus., 493
Electric Street, 513
Eliot, Capt. Sir William, 181-82, 183, 238-40,
   623-26, 753
Eliott, Dinah, 625, 835
Elizabeth I, 38, 39, 40
Elizabeth Avenue, 205, 285, 321
Elliot, Hugh, 33
Ellis, W.G., 572
Ellis, William, 229, 825, 876
Ellis, Rev. William, 743
Ellis, William J., mayor, 477
Elmsly & Shaw, grocers, 209
Emerson, Mr., 362
Emerson, Archibald, 194, 300
Emerson, Sir Edward, Chief Justice, 469
Emerson, George H., 679
Emerson, H.E., 693
Empire Avenue: sport, 329, 331, 332

Empire barracks: hospital, 300
Empire Hospital, 300-301
Empire Woodworking Factory, 300
Employment: demands and unrest, 462, 465-
   67; on railway, 509 *see also* strikes
English, John, 304
English, Margaret, 304
English, Mary Theresa, 304-6
Entertainment, 226-70; Gilbert's expedition,
   39; and governors, 144-45, 150-51; mili-
   tary, 101
Epps, W.J., 503
Era Gardens, 319
Escasoni Hospital, 300
Evans, Thomas, 566
Evening Herald, 194, 195, 259, 260, 391, 669
Evening Mercury, 195, 253, 318, 325, 378-79
Evening Standard, 514
Evening Telegram, 188, 193-95, 199, 261, 298,
   299, 325, 326, 327, 331, 336, 395, 463, 465,
   466, 514, 517, 518, 636, 689
Everson, Capt. Jacob, 79
Ewing, James, 877
Ewing, James Reid, 877
Ewing, William, 877
Examiner, 395
Exchange Building, 204
Executions, 506, 547-50, 554, 580, 581, 582,
   584-86, 589, 590-92; gallows sites, 549, 699,
   923; the last, 594, 666, 693, 923
Exmouth Cottage, 301
Exon, Andrew, 44, 45
Exon House, 304

Facey, Mr. and Mrs. John, 523
Factory, 232, 249, 253, 254, 463
Fagner, Capt. E.J., 306
Famine: *1697,* 82; *early 19c* 54, 139, 140
Famous Players, 255, 264, 265, 266
Fancy-dress balls, 389, 390
Farné, Jules, 957-60
Farrell, Garrett, 692, 736, 923
Farrell, John, 563
Farrell, Mary Lou, 268
Farrell, Thomas, 832, 844
Faulkner, Alex, 327-28
Faulkner, George, 327-28
Fawcett, Maj. Morris J., 462, 575
Fearn, Mr., 845
Feaver's Lane, 39
Federal Department of Agricultural Research,
   Mount Pearl: and aviation, 353, 354
Federal Government: Dept. of Public Works,
   918-19
Federal government: buildings, 111
Feild, Bishop Edward, 692, 693, 717-18, 722,
   749, 778-79, 784
Feildian Hockey team: illus., 314

Fenelon, Hon. Maurice, 835-36, 837
Fenwick, Gillie, 267
Fenwick, Moya, 267
Ferry, David, 268
Ferry lines, 911 see also shipping lines
Ferryland, 79, 81, 90, 127, 231, 355
Ferryland Head: fortifications, 48
Fever hospitals, 298, 301-3
Fewer, Elizabeth, 578
Field, Cyrus, 197, 198-99, 460, 918
Field, Matthew, 197
Fieldian Gardens, 323, 327, 329
Fielding, William, pvt., 550, 666
Finn, Robert, 724
Fire-fighting, 232
Fires, 680; 18c 49-50, 51, 620; 19c 52-53, 59, 140, 264, 281, 389; 1817 54, 140, 175, 231, 240; 1819 744, 835; 1846 55, 57, 146, 184, 249, 296; 1892 61, 137, 138, 176, 178, 181, 196, 204, 209, 232, 254, 264, 323, 328, 348, 390, 392; 1895 262; 20c 195, 325, 337, 749-50; forts, 101, 105; French, 48, 85; Gov't. house, 143; governors, 49-50; hospitals, 298, 300, 301-2; see also chap 4, Great Fires
First Five Hundred, 108, 112, 307
Firth, Mary, 864
Firth, William, 230-31
Firth, W. R., 864, 880
Fisher, Clara, 251, 253
Fishermen's and Seamen's Home, 478-79
Fishermen's Hall, 250-51, 264, 387
Fishery, 43, 45, 46, 47, 59, 79, 104, 107, 136, 180, 393-95, 455, 855, 906; early, 36, 43, 47, 49, 50, 51, 54, 59, 830, 845; foreign, 35, 42, 47, 78-79, 918-81; seal, 915, 916, 917, 961; illus., 893, 896, 900. 901, 902
Fishing: sport, 335
Fishing Admirals, 126-29 passim, 550-52
Fisk Jubilee Singers, 255
Fitzgerald, Rev. Mr., 581
Fitzgerald, Lord Edward, 101, 145
Fitzgerald, John, 51, 228
Fitzgerald, Paddy, 172
Fitzgibbon, Mrs. Thomas, 844
Fitzpatrick, Catherine, 300
Fitzpatrick, Maria, 335
Fitzpatrick, Tommy, 637, 643
Flags, 676, 687-90
Flaherty, J.J., 305
Flavin's Lane see Electric Street
Fleet, William, (teacher), 777
Fleming, Elizabeth, 286
Fleming, Johanna, 741
Fleming, Rev. Martin, 732
Fleming, Dr. Michael Anthony, Bishop, 146-47, 185-88, 191, 231, 563, 582, 584-85, 629, 688-89, 693, 716-17, 732-41, 745, 778, 780, 782-83, 786-96, 921; illus., 162

Fleming, Sir Sandford, 508-9
Flood, John, 505, 586, 831
Flower Hill Racecourse, 319
Flower Pot tavern, 228
Flower shows, 250
Flowers, Jane, 339
Flynn, Edward, 477
Flynn, John, 477
Fogarty, William, 339
Fogo, 145
Foley, Miss, 566
Foley, B., 252
Foley, Thomas, 575
Footwear, 56
Foran, John, 328, 527-28, 825, 830
Foran's City Rink, 323, 389
Forbes, Lady, 556
Forbes, Sir Francis, 556-57
Fordyce, Rev. Mr., 712
Forest Road, 54, 289, 297, 322, 331
Forests, 46, 50, 51-52, 53, 54
Fort Amherst, 94, 96, 98, 105, 106, 930
Fort Charles, 97, 104-5
Fort Frederick, 95, 104-5, 930 see also Castle
Fort Pepperrell, 74, 110-11, 207, 307, 332, 906-7
Fort St. George, 88, 89, 230
Fort Townshend, 98, 100, 102, 104, 107, 137, 138-42, 176, 233, 288, 294, 295-96, 319, 325; building, 39, 54, 95-96, 97, 458, 736; illus., 71, 75
Fort Townshend hollow, 235
Fort Waldegrave see Waldegrave Battery
Fort William, 104, 107, 112, 235, 236, 279, 280, 288, 289, 319, 325, 328, 529-30, 620, 712; history of, 47-48, 78, 80, 81, 82-84, 87-97, 101, 458, 509; and governor, 87, 127-28, 138
Fort William Station, 107, 203
Fortifications: 17c 48, 78-80; late 17c and early 18c 81-83; 18c 88-91, 93-97; early 19c 53, 104-6; withdrawal of garrison, 107-8; World War II installations, 111-12
Fortune, William, 729
Fortune Bay, 195
Forum Rink, 327
Foster, Frances Daisy, 150, 259
Foster, George Paddon, 267
Fowler, C.A., 178
Fowlow, F., 392
Fox, C.J., 401
Fox, Charles, 907
Fox, Judge Cyril, 480, 868, 913
Fox, Ethel, 868
Fox, James, 475, 912-13
Fox, John, 912-13
Fox Trap, 385
Frampton, Sir George, 672-73
Francis I, 480

Franklin, Sir John, 988
Franciscan Brothers, 780-81
Fraser, Allan, 207, 474
Fraser, Rev. Donald, 748-49
Fraser, Douglas, 364-67; illus., 373
Fraser, Dr. N.S., 301, 302, 364, 851
Frederick, Capt. T.L., 105
Frederick Battery *see* Fort Frederick
Free-Mason's tavern, 175
Free Press weekly, 196
Freeling, Francis, 174
Freeman, Edward, 753
Freeman, John, 172
Freemasons, 230, 244
French, 31, 35, 87, 89, 724; *16c* voyages, 36-
   37; settlers, 40; attacks and threats, 48, 49,
   78-80, 80-81, 82, 84-85, 86, 87-89, 90-93,
   97-99, 103-4, 138, 712, 713, 930
French, James, 378
Freshwater, 58, 321
Freshwater Road, 54
Freshwater valley, 58, 96
Frew, William, 514, 877-78
Froude Avenue, 357
Funichon, John, 304
Funny Lane, 287
Furey, Charles, 461
Furlong, Chief Justice, 519, 595
Furlong, Laurence O'Brien, 60, 287, 831
Furlong, Lawrence, 323
Furneaux, Mr., 338
Furneaux, John E., 195
Furness, Christopher, 908
Furzey, Mrs., 44, 45, 250

Gaden, George, 828
Gaden, Olive, 828
Galgay, W.F., 206
Gallagher, Patrick, 849
Gallagher's Range, 375
Gallery, Cornelius, 580
Gallows Hill, 43, 243
Galway, Dennis, 840
Galway Wharf, 400
Gambier, Lord James, gov., 226, 776
Gambier Street: and fire, 621
Gambling, 232-33
Game, Wo Fen, 591-92
Gander, 207
Gander airport, 366-67, 368
Garden City: conception, 682
Gardens and gardeners, 671-72; early, 45, 46,
   51, 54; 665-66, 667-68, 671
Gardiner, Dr., 279
Garland, Charles, 724
Garland, John Bingley, 456
Garland, Sammy, 863
Garrett, George, 292

Garrett, John, 677
Garrett, Samuel, 677
Garrison Hill, 39, 176, 249, 306, 463, 476
Garrison Theatricals, 249
Gas masks, 307
Gas Works: illus., 488
Gaultois: postal service, 177
Gazette Building, 210, 835
Gear, George, 623, 879-80
Geehan, Patrick, 588-89
General Hospital: origins, 288, 289, 293, 295;
   297-8, 301, 302, 303-4, 308
General Protestant Cemetery, 398, 692; illus.,
   654
General Water Company, 477
George III, 520
George IV, 143, 520, 557-58
George V, 572, 671; illus., 542
George VI, 403
George Street, 250, 265, 387
Germany: governor from, 149
Ghosts, 234
Gibbet Hill, 94; illus., 534
Gibbs, Father, 470
Gibbs, Michael, mayor, 477
Gibson, Col., 81
Gibson, Mr., 680-81
Gilbert, Sir Humphrey, 37-42, 43, 665, 910;
   illus., 3, 10
Gill, F. Burnham, 474
Gill House, 780
Gill Michael, 547, 554, 887, 909-910
Gill, Nicholas, 234, 580, 752, 910
Gisborne, Frederick, 168, 169, 197, 198, 199
Gledhell, Samuel, 128
Gleeson, James, 514, 886
Gleeson, Patrick, 827, 886
Glenelg, Lord, 457, 733, 735
Glendenning's Farm, Mount Pearl, 353
Globe Tavern, 229, 242
Glover, Sir John H., gov., 149, 478, 569, 575
Glovertown, 359
Godden, E.J., 469
Godden's property, Harbour Grace, 190
Godfrey, Rev. W.E., 468-69
Golden Grove Farm, 330
Golden Lion inn, 229, 827
Golf, 336-37
Golf Avenue, 111, 329, 336
Goobie, Wallace, 863
Gooderidge, Mrs. T.B., 479
Goodfellow, Hon. James, 475, 872
Goodridge, Alan, 867
Goodridge, Augustus, P.M., 867-68
Gordon, James, 878
Gordon, Margaret, 148
Gordon, Oliver, 267
Gosling, William Gilbert, mayor, 464, 477,
   785

Gosse, Capt. Benjamin, 87
Gosse, Samuel, 340
Goswold, Capt. Bartholomew, 44
Gotta, Basil, 672
Goulds, 320
Government, Commission of, 127, 471-73; illus., 487
Government, Representative, 146, 184, 185, 186, 187, 284-85, 455, 680, 687
Government, Responsible, 148, 285, 471-73, 561, 711, 783, 911 see also Newfoundland Government, House of Assembly and Legislative Council
Government House: Cochrane's building, 54, 142-44, 629, 636, 640, 720, 824; early locations, 137-38; electrification, 514; Fort Townshend, 138-42; as hospital, 288; landscaping, 670; Lieut. governors, 153; and redecoration, 569; visitors to, 144; illus., 116, 437
Governor, office of: lacking, 126; petition for, 80; and military, 81, 87, 89, 127-128; "Fishing Admirals", 126-29 passim, Commodore, office of, 89, 129; 1st civil, 128, 144; winter residence, 101, 140; powers in 18c 99-100, 132; end of office 152-53
Governors, 126-53; 17c 48; 18c 90, 98, 99; 19c 52, 54
Gower, Sir Erasmus, gov., 103, 174, 179-80, 188, 230, 237, 730, 743
Gower, Samuel, 585-86
Gower Street, 54, 137, 230, 287, 355, 396, 548; and fire, 620, 639; illus., 11
Gower Street Church, 256, 742, 747
Grace Hospital, 306-7, 308
Graham, Mr., 242
Graham, Aaron, 554-55
Graham, James, 474, 837
Grand Bank, 398
Grand Falls, 204, 207, 364, 365
Grant, Col., 461, 462
Grant, M.H., 209
Grantham, Rev. Thomas, 141
Graves, Lord Thomas, gov., 48, 90, 92
Gray, Norman, 480
Great Depression, 682
Great Fires: 1817, 520, 621-23, 744, 866-67, 879; 1846, 458, 515, 561, 571, 572, 621, 627-31, 668, 745, 790, 822, 832, 835-36, 838, 842, 887, 916; 1892, 526, 528, 569, 572, 635-36, 637-43, 670, 718, 746, 751, 753, 782, 784, 822, 829, 832, 837, 871, 875, 929; and looting, 622-23, 625, 639; see esp chap. 4, Great Fires; illus., 447
Greatheed, Rev. Samuel, 713
Green, Daniel, P.M., 868
Green, Maj. William Howe, 672, 677
Green Lantern Cafe, 211

Greene, James, 176, 474
Greening, Mr. and Mrs. George, 526
Gregory's Lane, 175, 177
Grenfell, Sir Wilfred, 322, 323, 326, 392-95, 642, 968
Grenfell Avenue, 327
Grenfell Seamen's Institute, 478 see also King George v Institute
Grey, Rev. William, 722
Grey, Sir George, 735
Grey & Goodland, 196, 242, 260
Grierson, Mr., 248
Grieve, Cmdr. see McKenzie-Grieve, Cmdr. K.
Grieve, James, 915, 916
Grieve Walter, 746, 791, 879, 916, 966
Grieve, Walter Baine, 916
Grieve, William, 106
Griquet, 32
Groke, Joseph, 678
Grube, Mr., 173
Gualley, Capt., 93
Guards Athletic Association, 318, 325, 327, 334
Gull Island, 860-61
Guns and cannon, 90, 93, 95-96, 97, 104-5, 108-9
Gushue, Mrs., 287
Guy, John, 42

Hackett, Father, 723
Haddon, William, 143
Haig, Field-Marshal Earl, 826
Hakluyt, Richard, 665
Haley, Capt. William, 103
Halifax, 90, 91, 100, 103, 143, 174, 176, 248, 359
Hall, Rev. Edward, 363
Hall, John, 579
Hall, Canon Wood, 720
Halley, Patrick, 864
Halley, William, 864
Halliday, James, 680
Hallohan, Lawrence, 547
Halluran, Matthew, 553-54
Halpin, Sister Mary Theresa, 305
Haly, Col. William, 336
Hamilton, Lady, 520; illus., 119
Hamilton, Sir Charles, gov., 54, 141-42, 240, 243, 284, 520, 626
Hamilton, Joanna, 588-89
Hamilton, Kerr Bailie, gov., 291, 573, 721
Hamilton Avenue, 58
Hampton, Dr. William, 801
Hanbury, William, 279
Handel & Haydn Society, 252
Handyside, Capt., 82
Hanlen, Michael, 228

Hanlon, Gerald, 567
Hannagan, B., 182, 229, 244
Harbour, 45, 48, 53, 57, 59, 141, 321, 338, 353, 819-20, 905-6, 917-19, 925, 981-82, 990; early, 31, 33, 37, 49, 50, 55, 61, 95, 173; modernization; 918-19, 924, 953; in World War I and World War II, 675, 906-7, 917, 924, 925, 929 see also Ship's rooms, Narrows; illus., 23, 25, 26, 28, 30, 73, 150, 891, 892, 894, 898, 935, 949
Harbour Drive: construction, 375
Harbour Grace, 504-6; and aviation, 352, 355, 358, 361, 362, 366; courts, 285; crime, 189, 190, 191; doctors, 280, 281; insane, 290; photography, 210; railroad to, 509-10; Shipbuilding Company, 262; smallpox, 295; theatre, 247, 248
Harkins, W.S. Theatrical Company, 251, 261
Harper, Dr. R. W., 288, 295
Harries, Mr., 179
Harries, Rev. John, 754, 775
Harris, Sir Charles A., gov., 303
Hart & Robinson, 252
Harvey & Co. Ltd., 908, 909, 912
Harvey, Dr., 256
Harvey, Alexander, 822, 853
Harvey, Frank, 146
Harvey, Sir John, gov., 145-46, 320, 574, 628, 666, 687, 714, 832; and church, 716, 717, 748; and theatre, 247, 248, 249; illus., 601
Harvey, Rev. Moses, 637-41, 749; illus., 601
Harvey, Richard, 722
Harvey & Co. Ltd., 908, 909, 912
Harvey Road, 108, 207, 265, 323, 333, 335
Haussonville, Count de, 90, 92, 97
Haw, Tom, 376
Hawke, Sir Edward, 90
Hawker, Harry, 352-54, 355, 681; illus., 348, 502
Hawkins, Dennis, 553
Hawkins, Jack, 78
Hay, Matthew, 100
Hayden, William, 546
Hayes, James, 580
Hayes, Capt. Edward, 39, 40, 4l, 42, 665
Hayes, Kathleen, 258
Hayes, Thomas, 627
Haymarket Square, 264, 389; illus., 816
Hayward, Ferd, 335, 336, 337
Hayward, J.W., 671, 688, 749, 921
Hayward, William, 573
Hayward Avenue, 102
Healey, Augustus, 234-35
Healy John & Company, 250, 251
Heap & Partners, 263
Hearn family, 249
Hearn, John, 581
Hearn, Mary, 581

Heart's Content, 198, 199, 234
Heath, John, 834
Henderson: sculpted "Industry" statue, 855
Hennessey, Mary, 228
Henry VII, 32
Henry VIII, 32, 35, 173
Henry, Prince of Netherlands, 320
Henry, Michael, 237
Henry Street, 55, 210, 264, 281
Hepburn, Mr., 338
Herder, William J., 193
Herder Memorial Trophy, 327
Hermit, 377, 378
Heywood, Agnes, 252, 954
Hickey, Amy, 204
Hickman, Albert, 856, 858, 923-24
Hickson, Rev. Thomas, 742
Hig, Hong King, 591
Higgins, Judge James, 745
Higgins, John, 204
Higgins, Mrs. William, 527
Higher levels, 54, 235
Hildreth, Miss, 248
Hill, R.D., 561-62
Hill, Samuel, 912
Hill, Sir Stephen, gov., 324, 575
Hill o'Chips, 39-40, 43, 93, 229, 232, 300, 318, 320, 823; illus., 608
Hoare, Richard, 32, 35-36
Hockey, 151, 206, 325, 326-27
Hogan, Timothy, 187
Hogan, William, 623
Hogsett, Aaron, 245
Hogsett, George, 461
Holbrook, George, 679
Holbrook, Hal, 267
Holdsworth, Capt. Arthur, 46-47, 56, 84, 377, 866, 908
Holdsworth Street, 52, 261
Hollis, Mr., 254
Holloway, Elsie, 210-11
Holloway, John, gov., 104, 174, 175
Holloway, Dr. Robert E., 210; illus., 765
Holloway, Lt. Vere, 108, 109
Holloway School, 210
Holloway Street, 184, 208, 229, 252, 323, 459, 517-18, 621
Holmes, John, 269
Holy Cross Field, 232
Holy Cross School, 267
Holy Heart of Mary Auditorium, 255, 269
Holy Name Society, 323
Hood, Mr., 680-81
Hopkins, William, 884
Hoppingly, Richard, 45
Horse racing, 318-20
Horton, Richard, 46
Horton, William, 44-45

Part II begins on page 433   1021

Horwood, Mrs., 91
Horwood, Andrew, 395
Horwood, Harold, 258, 270, 395
Horwood, R. F., 847
Horwood Thomas, 881
Horwood, Sir William, 464-65, 479, 591-92, 672, 881
Horwood, Vina, 395
Horwood Lumber Co., 572, 847
Hospitals, 57, 91, 200, 288-92, 293, 295-302, 304
Hostel, Bishop Jones, 786
Hostels: fishermen's, 393-95; for girls, 305-6; for soldiers, 854
Hotels, 522-30 *see also* Public Houses, *and hotel names;* illus., 499-502
Houlton, Capt., 93
House of Assembly, 186, 187, 195, 282-85, 456, 464-66, 575
Houses: 1st permanent, 31, 40, 42, 43; *17c* 44-47 *passim; 17c* building materials and methods, 50; *18c* 48, 51; *19c* 56; *19c* great houses, 54, 60; *late 19c* poor houses, 60-61; deliberate destruction of, 49-50; exterior paint, 58; oldest standing, 521; over fortifications, 89
Howard, Lord Edward, 173
Howell, Alfred, 567
Howell, J.M., 468
Howlett, Charles J., mayor, 477
Howley, Archbishop, 138, 305, 306, 386, 400, 505, 506, 726
Howley, Archbishop Michael, 588-89, 640, 677, 737, 741, 783, 990; illus., 705
Hoyles, Mr., 338, 461
Hoyles, Sir Hugh, 243, 253, 632, 875, 906, 914
Hoyles, Newman, 243, 635, 845, 874, 906
Hoyles Home, 296, 300
Hoylestown, 44
Hudson, Henry, 44, 884
Hudson's *see* Hunter's Cove
Hue, F., 845
Hughes family, 249
Hughes, Thomas, 100
Hunt, Thomas Newman, 856
Hunter's Cove, 43, 185, 196, 228
Hurley, game of, 53
Hutching's Street, 264
Hutchings, George, 336
Hutchings, George Jr., 844-45
Hutchings, Philip, 874
Hutton, Charles, 254-56, 835, illus., 225
Hypnotism, 256

Iberville, Le Moyne d': illus., 118
Icebreaking, 927-28, 977
Ice Committee, 917-18
Ice-Cutting Act, 917-18
Imperial Aircraft Company, 358, 366

I.O.D.E., 299
Imperial Tobacco Company, 332
Imperial War Cabinet, 464
Influenza outbreaks, 302-3
Inglis, Bishop John, 714, 731
Inns *see* Public Houses
International Woodworkers of America, 576-77
Ireland, 47, 101-2
Irish: *18c* 48, 49; and French in 1762, 90, 92-93; governor, 130; houses burned, 49-50; immigrants, 47, 51, 54, 794, 921; laws against, 136; and political disturbances, 145, 186, 188, 190
Irish Christian Brothers, 781-83; illus., 763, 768
Irvine Station, 390
Isle of Chips: ship's room, 43
Ivey, Solomon, 108

Jackman, E.M., 305, 306, 864
Jackson, Rev. John, 84-86 *passim*, 235, 236, 279, 711-12
Jacobins, 728, 729
Jacobs, Capt. (Jakob Everson), 675
Jago, John, 553
James, King, 675
James Street, 296
Jamieson, Don, 207
Janeway, Charles H., 307
Janeway Hospital, 307
Jensen, Phil, 300; illus., 276
Jerrett, Mrs. Eric, *see* Mews, Eleanor
Jersey Fishermen, 42
Jervis, Capt., 93
Jewish community, 877
Jeynes, Mr. and Mrs. William, 777
Job, Mr., 626
Job, Robert, 513, 845, 847-48, 914
Job, William Carson, 929
Job Brothers & Co. Ltd., 208, 913, 914-15, 929
Job family, 286, 913-14
Job Street, 399
Jocelyn's farm *see* Ross's farm
Johnny's Hill, 329
Johnson, Rev., 470
Johnson, Thomas, 83
Johnston, Ruby, 268
Jolly Fisherman, 228
Jones, Jenkin, 620, 626
Jones, John, (Rev.), 713, 721, 737-38, 775; illus., 759
Jones, John, (soldier), 751-55
Jones, Bishop Ll ewellyn, 638, 639, 643, 718, 719
Jordan, ex-private F., 466
Josie Loane Dramatic Company, 251
Josie Mills Company, 254

Jost, C.H., 178
Journeaux, Louisa, 957-60; illus., 940
Joyce, Rev. J.G., 206, 592
Joyners: *17c* plantation, 44, 45
Juitt, John, 46-47
Jukes, J.B., 246

Katem, Michael, 724
Kavanagh, James, 460
Kean, Capt. Abram, 109, 852, 961, 974
Kean, Capt. Abram Jr., 968
Kean, Capt. E.K., 988
Kean, Capt. Wesley, 927, 974-75
Kearney, Michael, 841, 864
Keating, Mr., 829
Keating, Michael, 457
Keats, Sir Richard, gov., 54, 107, 139, 289, 581, 667, 742-43, 821
Keegan, Dr. Leonard, 304
Keen, William, 88, 89, 553-54, 725
Keith, D.C., 594-95
Kelligrews, Mrs., 640
Kelly, E.O'D., 856
Kelly, Patrick, 336, 693
Kelly, Capt. William, 693
Kemp, Carmel, 268
Kemp, G.S., 199, 201
Kempthorn, Capt., 551
Kenmount Road, 58, 207
Kenna, Sgt., 842
Kenna's Hill, 60, 319
Kennedy, David, 58-59, 60
Kennedy, Edward, 242
Kennedy, Eugene, 849
Kennedy, Ludovic, 267
Kennedy, M., 927
Kennedy, Capt. Nicholas, 849
Kennedy, Capt. William, 968
Kennelly, John, 579-80
Kenny, John, 281
Kenny's Lane *see* Duke of York Street
Kent, James, mayor, 396, 921
Kent, John, 186, 187, 282-83 *passim,* 437, 522, 684, 741, 921; illus., 157
Kent, Robert, 396, 724, 802, 921
Kent Inn, 843-44
Keough, Patrick, *see* Kough
Kerr, Mark, 352, 355, 358
Kickum, Charles, 829
Kielley, Dr. Edward, 188, 242, 281-84, 285, 290, 298, 319, 339, 558, 626, 687, 849, 862, illus., 124
Kiely, J.P., 262
Kilbride, 81
King, Sir Richard, gov., 709, 845, 922-23
King, So Ho, 591
King, W.L. Mackenzie, 473

King George v Institute, 301, 303, 322, 323, 333, 393-95, 851
King George v Park, 329, 330
King William's Fort *see* Fort William
King's Beach, 52, 229, 237, 287, 342, 887, 910, illus., 437
King's Bridge, 330
King's Bridge Road, 54, 60, 326, 330, 335
King's Pinch, 330
King's Place, 436-37
King's Road, 290, 326, 384, 436
Kinsella, P.J., 378
Kinsmen's Club, 255
Kipling, Rudyard, 827, 978
Kirke, Sir David, 127, 843
Kirwan, Mother Bernard, 741, 787-89; illus., 770
Kit, Eng Wing, 592-93
Kitchen, Mr., 835
Kitchen, Monseigneur, 835
Klark-Urban Company, 259
Knight, Surgeon Major, 300
Knight, Fanny, 398
Knight, Frank, 267, 395-96
Knight, Herbert E., 395
Knight, Samuel, 525, 880
Knight, Stephen, 250, 913
Knight, Capt. William, 398
Knight's Speedway, 320
Knights of Columbus, 796-97; illus., 617
Knowlan, Patrick, 547
Knowling, George, 329, 874
Knowling's West End Stores, 211, 329
Kough, Patrick, 62, 187, 458, 574, 720
Krippner, Mr., 151
Kuehnert, Karl, 365

Labour, 82-83, 143, 263
Labrador, 32, 136
Lady's: ship's room, 43
LaFosse, Sam, 333-34
Lahey, William, 667, 669
Laing, Ronald, 576-77
Lakeside Speedway, 320
Lambert, Bishop Patrick, 179, 690-91, 731
Lamley, Lawrence, 553
Land Grants, 679-80, 682, 691-92, 737, 779, 820
Landergan, Mr., 285
Landergan, James, 556-57
Landircan, Michael, 706
Landseer, Sir Edward, 135
Lane, Adelaide, 692
Lang (planter), 908
Lang, Thomas, 916
Lang, Wallis, 753
Langen, Roger, 337-38 *passim*
Langman, Rev. Edward, 547, 713, 752, 754

Langmead, George, 839
Laracy, Patrick, 261, 840
Larkin, George, 572
Lash, Mr., 338
Lash, J. and G., 460, 525, 869
Lash's Railway Hotel, 209, 525
Latham, Lt. Robert, 85, 86
Law, Col., 252, 561, 632, 667
Law and order: *17 c* 47, 126, 127-28; *18 c* 86,
    128-29, 550-554; *19 c* 284; 52, 103-4, 126,
    144, 187, 188, 194, 234, 245, 279-80, 282-84,
    285, 288, 545, 549, 555-56, 557-58
Lawrence, Sandy, 205
Lawrey, Lt. Edward, 692, 718, 736, 922-23
Lawyers, 572, 573, 588, 638
Leamon, Mrs. John, 830
Leamon, John, 872
Leary, Mr., 437
Leary's Bridge, 374
Leary's Brook, 287
LeDrew, Mr., 336-37
Lee, gov. (1735-37), 552
Lee, Donald McPhee, 183
Lee, Hong, 591
Lee, Thomas, 358
Legge, W.G., 718
Legion of Frontiersmen, 108-9 *passim*
Legislative Council, 186, 187
Leigh, Rev. John, 285, 557
LeMarchant, Sir Gaspard, 146-48, 459, 460,
    524, 692-93
LeMarchant Road, 58, 228, 265, 305, 306, 317,
    329, 357, 398
Le Messurier, Peter, 845
Lemon family, 175
LeMoyne, Pierre, Sieur d'Iberville, 80, 81
Lennox, John, 563
Leslie Street, 332, 398
Lester, Mr., 355
Lester, John, 681
Lester, Widow Mary, 828
Lester's field: and aviation, 355, 356, 357, 361
    362-63, 366
Libraries, 874-76
Lieutenant-governorship, 153
Lighthouses, 94, 105
Lilbourne, Lt., 82
Lilly, Christopher, 48
Lilly, Judge George, 104, 283, 573
Lindberg, John, 204, 880
Lindbergh, Charles, 359-61, 367
Lindberg's alley, 323
Linegar, Patrick, 828
Lion's club, 322
Liquor, 83, 227, 228 *see also* Public Houses
Literature, 395 *see also* Ballads, Poetry
Little, Judge, 545, 570, 681
Little, Michael, 229

Little, Philip, P.M., 800; illus., 439
Littledale: illus., 711
Littlefield, 367
Liverpool, Lord; illus., 759
Livingston (merchant), 825
Ljung, Esse W., 258
Llewellyn Grounds, 331
Lloyd, Capt. Thomas, 83-89 *passim*, 100, 128,
    235-36, 279, 308, 712
Lobster fishery, 403
Locke, Eugene, 358
Logy Bay Road, 144, 320, 336, 337
London Tavern, 53, 229-31, 318, 520, 821;
    illus., 217
London Theatre Company, 267, 268, 269
Loney, Dennis, 44, 45, 927
Long, 567
Long, Richard, 691
Long Pond, 82, 321, 337; illus., 651
Long Pond Road, 110
Long's Hill, 54, 108, 287, 335, 476, 691, 693, 733
Longville, Father, 723
Lott, Herman, 190-92
Louis xiv, 724
Louisbourg, 90, 91
Lowman, Joseph, 753
Loyal Volunteers of St. John's, 1805-11: 103-4,
    106-7, 284
Lucas, Arthur, 108
Lundberg's, 324
Lush, Capt. Llewellyn, 966
Lush, Maxwell, 566
Lynch, Sister Mary Xaverius, 55-56, 740-41,
    786-89
Lyon, E.W. 210, 833
Lyttleton, Sir Thomas, 132

Macallastar, Dr., 288
McAuley, Catherine, 792-93
McAuliffe Stock Company, 150, 259
McAuslane, Peter, 870
McBraire (Macbraire), Maj. James, 54, 104,
    106-7 *passim*, 228, 635
McBride, Peter and Robert, 872
McBride's Hill, 44, 205, 206, 207, 251, 461,
    627; illus., 610
McCallum, Sir Henry, gov., 153, 325
McCallum & Coleman, 242
McCallum's Lane *see* McMurdo's Lane
McCalman, Donald H., 106, 241-42
McCarthy, Mr., 261
McCarthy, Prof., 844
McCarthy, Charles, 396
McCarthy, Daniel, 341
McCarthy, Dennis, 341
McCarthy, Sgt. Mike, 396
McCarthy, T., 844; illus., 814
McCarthy, Trotters, 374

Part II begins on page 433

McCarty, Robert, gov., 130
McConnan, Thomas, 834, 851
McCormack, Janet, 843
McCormack, W.E., 843
McCormack Trophy, 332
McCoubrey, Mr., barber, 282
McCoubrey, John, 184, 830
McCoubrey, Richard, 184
McCourby, Alexander, 242
McCourt, Phil, 837
McCowen, John R., 575-76, 636
McCrudden, Mr. and Mrs. Leo, 523
McCurdy, Dr. John, 280
McDermott, Monsignor, 470
MacDonald, Aubrey, 207
MacDonald, Sir Gordon, gov., 151-53, 473
MacDonald, John, 747
MacDonald, Sir John A., 508-9
McDonald, Paul, 553
McDonald, Ronald, 725
MacDonald Drive, 300
McDonnell, Capt., 91
McDougal, Francis, 922
MacFarlane Commission, 308
Macgillivray, Darroch, 266
McGin, Mr., 336-37
McGiver, Robert, 871
McGrath family, 528-29
McGrath, Mr., 683
McGrath, Michael, 738-39, 741
McGrath, Sir Patrick, 195; illus., 170
McGrath, Thomas, 823
McGrath, William, 232, 823
MacGregor, Sir William, gov., 797
McGuire, Matt, 844
MacKay, A.M., 513
Mackay, Alexander, 198, 203, 204, 862
Mackay, Joan, 862
McKay, R.D., 261
McKay, Smith, 324, 325
McKay, W.L., 287
McKen, Dr., 293, 297, 298, 339, 842
McKenny & Dicks, 209, 210
McKenzie, John, 830
McKenzie, Sister Mary Benedict, 306
Mackenzie, William Lyon, 187
McKenzie-Grieve, Lt. Cmdr. K., 352-54, 681; illus., 348
McLaren, Malcolm, 330
McLea, John, 858
McLea, Kenneth, 461, 747, 748, 858, 917
McLoughlan, James, 848
McMillan, John, 694
McMurdo, Thomas, 286-87, 747, 834, 885
McMurdo's Lane, 209, 242, 286, 318
McNamara, Mr., 292
McNamara, Alfred, 869
McNamara, Augustin, 182

McNamara, Frank, 251
McNamara Industries, 392
MacNeil, L.G., 751
McNeil, Mrs. Hector, 479
McNeil, T., 324, 834
McNeilly, J.W. 858
Macpherson, Archibald, 883
Macpherson, Campbell, Lt.-gov., 307, 883, 920
Macpherson, Campbell Sr., 883
Macpherson, Dr. Cluny, 307-8
Macpherson, Harold, 883
Maddock, Luke, 872
Magee, Dickie, 375
Magical shows, 249, 251
Maggoty Cove, 279, 331
Maggoty Cove Bridge, 237
Magott's Cove see Hoylestown
Mahon's Lane, 250, 478-79
Mahoney, James, 579-80
Mahoney, John, 579
Mainguy, V-Adm. Edmund, 825-26
Mainwaring, Mr., 831
Mainwaring, Sir Harry, 79, 675
Majestic Cinema, 262-63
Majestic Theatre, 333, 468
Malone, Patrick, 581-82
Maloney, Sister Mary Nolasco, 801
Mandeville, Tobias, 583-85
Manley, J.W., 837
Manners, Lt. Col., 319
Maps: *16c* 34; Cook, 136-37; harbour, illus., 65; illus., 9, 14, 69; fires, illus., 620; Thornton's, 44; Water Street, 823, 824, 828, 832, 838, 842, 848, 850
Mara, Michael, 229, 231
Marathon, 336
March, C.L., 845
March, Stephen, 989
Marconi, Guglielmo, 199-203, 205, 300; and aviators, 362; illus., 163, 164
Marcus, Mr., 240
Mare, Emily: illus., 219
Mare, R.L., 827
Marine Drive, 337
Marine Parade, 667-68
Maritime Central Airways, 368
Market House, 176-77, 178, 294, 383, 457, 458, 461, 571-72, 639, 832-33; illus., 442, 536
Market House Hill, 177
Marroty, Jeremiah, 51
Mars, Lt.-Cmdr. Alistair, 380
Mars, P.C., 380
Marshall, Alexander, 873, 885
Marshall, Francis W., 854
Martin (child), 671
Martin, Miss, 741
Martin, Christopher, 79

Part II begins on page 433   1025

Martin, J.H., 881
Martin, Mrs. J.H., 827
Martin, John, 340
Martin, John D., 884
Mary, Queen, 572; illus., 542
Marystown, 207
Masonic Club, 318
Masonic Hall, 252
Maternity Hospital, 306-7
Matthews, Mrs., 229
Mawer, W. Moncrieff, 256
Maxse, Sir Henry Fitz-Hardinge, 149
Meaden, Bishop, 785
Meagher, Patrick, 782
Meagher, Thomas Francis, 625, 626, 782, 866
Meaney, John, 529
Mechanics' Fraternal Society, 827
Mechanics's Hall, 250, 264, 283
Medhurst, Dr., 279
Medical Hall, 287
Medical Health Officers, 302
Medical Society, 288
Medicine, 279-308, 365, 366 see also Public
    Health
Meehan, Patrick, 859
Meeker, Howie, 327
Meeting House Hill see Victoria Street
Melis, Hans, 357
Melville, Elizabeth, 550, 666
Memorial Stadium, 326, 327, 334
Memorial University College, 268, 333
Memorial University of Newfoundland
    (M.U.N.), 307-8, 322, 335, 337-38, 475, 798-
    800; illus., 773
M.U.N. Extension, 255, 270
M.U.N. Fisheries Research Laboratory, 337
M.U.N. Glee Club, 255
M.U.N. Little Theatre, 255, 269
Menchenton, John, 854
Mennie, Ian, 270
Mental Health: early treatment, 290-91; hos-
    pitals, 291-92, 300
Mercantile Investment Club's Dramatic Soci-
    ety, 254
Mercantile Journal, 238, 240, 241, 242, 281,
    319, 330, 338, 626, 777, 919
Mercer, Ensign E.N., 797
Mercer, Thomas, 686
Merchant, Barbara, 396-97
Merchant, Valentine, 396-97, 834
Merchant Navy Hospital, 301, 821
Merchants, 47, 54, 147, 174, 775, 822, 973; and
    military, 86-87, 89, 104; see also Trade and
    esp. chapter 9; illus., 813
Merchant's Arch: illus., 829
Merchant's Club, 318, 834
Merrifield, Esther, 550
Merrymeeting Road, 111, 235, 329

Methodist, 721, 742-47, 784 see also United
    Church; illus., 729
Methodist College, 210, 326
Methodist College Hall, 256
Methodist Guards Brigade, 108, 307
Metropolis see Casino
Mews, Arthur, 907
Mews, Eleanor, 255
Mews, Henry, mayor, 477, 907
Mic Mac Curling Club, 325
Middle Arm, White Bay, 399
Middleton, Sir John, gov., 468
Milbanke, Adm. Mark, gov., 133, 135, 554,
    726, 729
Milbanke Street, 133
Military: 16c 78-79; 17c 79-82; 18c 82-101;
    19c 101-7; 20c 107-12; allied bases, 917;
    British Garrison, 107, 127-28, 678; disci-
    pline, 85, 87, 100, 106, 112; and fires, 624-
    26, 628, 635; gameing and duels, 233-35;
    and governorship, 144; hospitals, 288-89,
    297; medicine, 279, 280; political violence,
    185-86; provisions, 96, 100-101; and pub-
    lic houses, 229; and theatre, 249; illus., 681,
    683-84
Military Museum, 234, 307
Military Road, 54, 96, 143, 177, 241, 253, 254,
    289, 459, 719; illus., 70, 652, 699
Milley, Hon. Samuel, 886
Minard's Linament Building, 206
Miners, gov. of Fort William, 81
Minshew, Thomas, 86, 279
Miquelon, 79, 99
Mitchell, Mr., 146
Mitchell, Harold, 470
Mitchell, Mrs. J.B., 479
Mitchell, Maggie, 253
Mitchell, Supt. Timothy, 574-75, 577
M'Ivor, Alexander, 506
Molloy, Dr., 190
Molloy, John, 558
Monitor, 473, 712
Monkstown Field, 296
Monkstown Road, 175, 204, 254, 304
Monroe, Daniel, 861-62
Monroe, James H.: illus., 811
Monroe, Moses, 475, 671, 861, 865-66
Montague, John, gov., 752
Montigny, 84, 85
Montreal: 1st flight to St. John's, 364-65
Monuments and plaques: to aviation, 354,
    355, 357, 360-61; to Grenfell, 394
Moody, Elenor, 546-47
Moody, John, 553
Moody, Capt. John, 84-87 passim, 89, 236
Moore, Ann, 666
Moore, Edward B., 874
Moore, Edward L., 301, 851

Moore, Elizabeth, R.N., 301, 851
Moore, Miss Fanny, 834, 851
Moore, Maj. Gen. Francis, 104, 106
Moore, James Pearl, 851
Mooring, Michael, 724
Moran, Misses, 836
Moravian Missionaries, 136
Morey, Mr., 572, 855
Morey, Mathias, 880
Morgan, Cmdr., 352-55; illus., 349
Morgan, Mr., 255
Morgan, Capt. Henry, 675
Morgue, 292
Morine, A.B., 319, 973
Morison, Judge, 194
Morison, W.D., 475, 869
Morning Chronicle, 375, 634, 840
Morning Courier, 57-58, 291
Morning Post, 506-7
Morrice, George, 233
Morridge, John, 98, 99
Morris, Capt. 922-23
Morris, Father, 670
Morris, Lady: illus., 764
Morris, Miss, librarian, 469-70
Morris, B., 205
Morris, Edward, Sr., 862
Morris, Sir Edward, 108, 253, 456, 474, 654, 670, 916; illus., 444
Morris, Patrick, 106, 144, 184, 187, 285, 455, 458, 471, 472, 522, 557, 734, 777, 857, 911, 921; illus., 436
Morris, Roland, 682
Morris Dancers, 39
Morrissey, Joan, 207
Morton, Thomas, 231
Mosdell, Dr. H.M., 468, 566
Mosquito, 574
Moss, Con. William, 566-67
Mount Carmel Cemetery, 693-94
Mt. Cashel Orphanage, 255, 322
Mount Ken, 58, 287
Mount Pearl, 206, 252, 253, 320, 364; illus., 657
Mount Scio, 337
Mountain, Rev. Jacob, 717-18, 722
Moyne, Alain, 36
Moyne, John, 546
Muddy Hole *see* Musgrave Harbour
Mudge, Nicholas, 580, 903
Muir, Rev. Dr., 714
Mullins, 736
Mullock, Bishop J.T., 58, 196-98 *passim,* 295, 462, 507, 508, 574, 632, 729, 730, 741, 779, 782-83, 787, 792, 796, 797, 916, 953-54; illus., 485
Mullock, Thomas, 524, 791
Mullock Street, 322, 327
Mullowney, Patrick, 506

Mollowney, Capt. Pierre, 844
Mumming: illus., 655; *see* Christmas celebrations
Mundy, John, 173
Mundy Pond, 355
Munhall, John, 553
Municipal Council, 128, 144, 284, 635, 644-45
Municipal Council Board, 195
Municipal Government: City Charter (1966); 477; Council offices, 477-79, 671
Munn, Betty, 672, 962
Munn, John, 507
Murch, Hannibal, 827
Murder cases: sites, illus., 539, 541; *see* violence
Murine, Patrick, 228
Murphy, Canon, 738
Murphy, Father, of Ferryland, 231
Murphy, Hon. Anthony (Ank), 690
Murphy, Bride, 261
Murphy, Clem, 474
Murphy, Dennis, 229
Murphy, Father Edward, 691
Murphy, John, 229, 526, 590
Murphy, R.J., 566
Murphy, T.J., 834
Murphy, William, 376-77
Murray, Capt., 324
Murray, Gen., 179
Murray, Amelia, 380
Murray, Andrew, 380, 922
Murray, David, 380, 922
Murray, Sir Herbert Harley, gov., 194, 195, 557-58, 636, 689
Murray, James, 478, 908, 921-22
Murray, James, Sr., 921
Murray, Jean, 786
Murray, Joseph, 578
Musgrave, Sir Anthony, gov., 148-49, 237, 340, 912
Musgrave Harbour, 149
Musgrave Terrace, 203-4
Music, 53, 236-37, 252, 253, 254-57, 266, 270, 374
Musical Comedy, 255, 380-82, 382-84
Mutiny, 99-103, 280, 673-74, 967-68
Myrick, Patrick, 461-62

Nagle, Nano, 786, 791
NALCO, 569-70
Napoleonic Wars, 97, 103-4
Narrows, 39, 52, 61, 95, 105, 109, 110, 929; fortications, 79, 84, 94; illus., 6, 8, 67, 68, 685, 907, 976; *see also* Harbour
Native Society, 668, 687-89
Naughton, 562-63
Navratil, Zdanek (Stan), 270
Navy: and army, 83-84; and French, 88; and

government, 126-29 *passim;* and hospital, 288,927; and medicine, 279,282; surgeons, 279; and whipping, 548
Navy, Army & Commercial Hotel, 330
Navy Street, 111
Neal, Dr., 375,376
Neilson, Capt., 842
Nelson, Admiral Lord, 519
Neptune Theatre, Halifax, 258
Nesmond, Chev., 80
New England, 32,43-44,82
New Fieldian Club, 318
New Gower Street, 204, 264, 323, 376, 456; illus., 12
New York, Newfoundland & London Tele-graph Company, 197-99
New York Stock Company, 258
Newfie Bullet, 516
Newfoundland: discovery and voyages to, 31-34, 35-42; colonization, 33
Newfoundland Airways, 364
— Amateur Wrestling Champi-onship, 334
— & Labrador Press Club Build-ing, 60
— Appeal to U.K., 471-72
— Archives, 474
— Boot & Shoe Factory, 301
— Coat of Arms, 475
— Chess Association, 337
— Choral & Orchestral Society, 256
— Clothing Company, 195
— Company, 42-43
— Cycle Club, 323-24
— Dog, 49
— Electric Telegraph Company, 197
— *Express,* 287,324,516-17
— Flag, 687-90
— *Gazette,* 181 (formerly the *Royal Gazette*)
— Glass Embossing Company, 478
— Government: health care, 301, 644-45; Dept. of Posts & Tele-graphs, 199, 929; Ministry of Marine & Fisheries, 199,200
— Highlanders, 108
— Historic Trust, 722
— Home Defence, 111,329
— Horseman's Association, 320
— Hotel: and aviators, 361; and celebrities, 530; cricket, 330; monument, 303; and radio, 206; site, 107; tennis, 322, 328; illus., 615
— Law Society, 573

Newfoundland Light and Power Company, 518,929
— Lawn Tennis Association, 322
— Medical Care Commission, 308
— *Mercantile Journal,* 183-84
— Museum, 199
— National Convention 1948, 473
— Nurses Association, 304
— Open Chess Tournament, 337-38
— Open Golf Tournament, 337
— Parliament, 456,471
— Postal Telegraphs, 203
— Public Debt, 681
— Public & Social Services, 471, 528-29
— *Quarterly,* 529
— Railway, 509, 907; illus., 488, 490
— Referendum 1948, 473
— Regiment: 1780-1783, 330
— Regiments: *late 18c and early 19c* 96,97,99-104,106-7,280; *mid 19c* 112,231; World War I, 107-9,961
— Softball Association, 332
Newfoundlander, 184,185,318,396,461,525, 549,585,586,587-88,628,669,831,918
Newman, Robert, 835,845-47
Newman, William, 286,835,845-47,908
Newsmagazine, 196
Newspapers, 172,178-99,829,859
Newtown Road, 111,329
Neyle, Richard, 837
Nichols, J.W., 830
Nickel Theatre, 254,260-61,262-63,265
Nickells, Richard, 548
Night Watchman, 172
Niven, George, 106,241
Noah, George K., 365
Noah, Kaleem, 365,849
Noftall, Frederick, 566
Noonan, Ned, 376
Norris, Adm., 81
Norris, Mr., 748
Norris, William, 108
North Bank Ski Club, 337
North Battery, 80,84,85
Northcliff Drama Club, Grand Falls, 258
Norton, Judge, 523
Noseworthy, Winston, 594
Nova Scotia, 89, 128; Fencibles, 103; Tele-graph Company, 197,198
Nowlan, John, 526
Nowlan, Patrick, 461
Nugent, Agnes, 795

Nugent, John, 341
Nugent, John Valentine, 146, 188, 476, 734, 735, 788, 880, 912; illus., 161
Nugent, Mary, 590, 794; as Sister Mary Joseph, 794-95; illus., 791
Nursing & Nurses, 303-6, 308
Nutting, Armine, 785

O'Brien, Dennis, 267, 382-84; illus., 220
O'Brien, Dennis Francis, 383
O'Brien, Sir John Terence, gov., 188, 253, 642, 751, 827
O'Brien, Josephine, 593
O'Brien, Hon. Lawrence, 286, 558, 886-87, 912; illus., 274
O'Brien, Timothy, 637, 643
O'Brien, Thomas, 833
O'Brien, William Smith, 987
O'Brine, Dennis, 58
O'Connell, Philip, 318
O'Connor, John, 839
O'Dea, Fabian, Lt. Gov., 338
O'Doherty, Kevin, 378
O'Donel, James, Bishop, 101, 102, 138, 179, 230, 280, 289, 318, 711, 775, 849, 882; illus., 717
O'Donel, Rev. Dr. James, 725-31, 754
O'Donnel, James, 839
O'Donnell, Rev. Jeremiah, 461, 833
O'Driscoll, P.C., 320
O'Dwyer, John, 870, 921
O'Dwyer, Richard, 870, 921
O'Dwyer's, 384
O'Leary, F.M. Limited, 207, 911-12
O'Leary Avenue, 196
O'Mara, John Jr., 881-82, 886, 921
O'Mara, Peter, 847, 882
O'Mara's Drug Store, 469, 847
O'Meara, Henry and family, 637, 638-39, 640, 641-42
O'Neil, Issac, 587
O'Neil, W.J., 847
O'Niell, Miss Ellie, 863
O'Neill, Hugh, 842
O'Neill, P.J., actor, 836
O'Neill, Patrick J., Supt. of Police, 468, 469, 576
O'Neill, Paul, 255, 268, 269
O'Neill, Ray, 864
O'Neill, Thomas, actor, 842, 878
O'Neill, Tom, 262
O'Shaughnessy, Joseph, 256
O'Shaughnessy, Sister Magdalene, 675, 786-88, 790
O'Toole, Ron, 336
Oakley, Miss, 248
Octagon Castle Restaurant, 390-91, 392; illus., 216

Octagon Pond, 336
Ode to Newfoundland, 150-51, 259, 690
Ogden, Jonathan, 910
Ogden, Dr. Jonathan, 101, 138, 280, 288
Old Chapel, 231, 264, 281, 728-29, 740; illus., 720
Old Colony Airways, 365-66
Old Factory, 629, 632
Old Garrison Church, 719-20
Old Garrison Hospital, 289
Opera, 252, 253
Operetta, 251, 253, 254-55 see also Musical comedy
Oppelt, Otto, 334
Orchestras, 256, 270
Ordnance Street, 230, 231, 396
Ormsby, James, 237
Ormsby, Mary, 237
Orphanages: Anglican, 304; B.I.S., 320; Mount Cashel, 255, 322
Osborne, Capt. Henry, gov., 128-29, 551-52, 553, 573; illus., 533
Oughtred, Henry, 78
Our Lady of Angels Church, 724
Outerbridge family, 110
Outerbridge, Lady, 825
Outerbridge, Sir Leonard, 558, 825, 909
Oxen Pond Road, 374
Oxenham, Lt., 683
Oxford, Thomas H., 44, 45, 46, 180, 857
Oyez, Mr., 284

Paget, P.W., 199
Palk's Farm, 291
Palliser, Sir Hugh, gov., 100, 136, 520, 846, 989; illus., 940
Pancake Rock, 95, 97, 105
Pankhurst, Emmaline, 466
Parade Grounds, 325
Parade Rink, 265, 325, 335
Parade Street, 206, 207, 268, 333
Paradise, 374
Paramount Theatre, 265, 325
Parisian Photographic Studio, 211
Parker, James, 861
Parker, John, 862
Parker, Nathan, 104, 753, 913-14
Parker, William, 176
Parker, Sir William, 53
Parker & Knight, 250
Parkhurst, Anthony, 34
Parmenius, Stephen, 40, 41, 676
Parnell, William, 589-90, 870
Parsons, Alexander A., 194
Parsons, Robert, 228
Parsons, Robert John, 104, 188, 189, 296, 522, 553
Parsons, Simeon H., 209-10, 840

Part II begins on page 433

Parsons, W.J., 830-31
Paton, John Lewis, 799
Patrick Street, 58, 267, 295, 300, 306, 357; illus., 658
Patriot, 187-89 *passim*, 292, 294, 613, 667, 693, 739, 987
Patterson, Florence, 258, 268
Payne, Philip, 363-64
Payne, William, 43
Peace, Albert, 838-39
Peace, Robert, 838-39
Pearl, Anne, 679, 681
Pearl, Sir James, 184, 679-82
Peary, Robert E., 979-80, 988
Peasley, Rev. Mr., 712-13
Peddle, Tommy, 374-75
Pedley, Rev. Charles: illus., 708
Pellu, M., 726-27, 729
Pennell, Dr. John, 281, 308
Penny postage, 178
Pennywell Road, 327, 374
People's Theatre *see* Casino
Pepperrell, Sir William, 110
Perchard, Richard, 228, 561, 829
Perkin's Hotel, 319
Perlin, John, 269
Perlin family, 876-77
Perrot, Sir John, 78
Perryman (settler), 909
Peter-from-Heaven, 374; illus., 372
Peters, Richard, 678
Petty Harbour, 81, 83
Petty Harbour Motion, 384
Phelan, Nicholas, 319
Phelan, Tim, 840
Phelps, Francis Robinson, Archbishop, 397-98
Phelps, Rev. Joseph, 397
Philco Cup, 336
Phillips, Lt., 89
Phillips, Henry, 753
Philpot, Ens., 233-34
Philpott, Lt., 718
Phipard, William, 574
Phippard, Thomas, 175
Phoenix Fire Office, 619-20, 626, 627, 631, 635, 750, 846
Photographic Studio and Fine Art Emporium, 209
Photography, 208-11
Pickavant, Rev. Mr. John, 732-33, 745; illus., 708
Pickmore, Sir Francis, gov., 139-41, 142, 284, 621-23, 743
Pierce, Mr., 338
Pike, Rev., 470
Pillar boxes: 1st, 177
Pilot, Canon, 388, 396

Pilot, Barbara, 388
Pilot, Edward Frederick, 388, 396
Pilot, Robert Wakeham, 388, 396-97
Pilot, 146, 147
Pilot's Hill, 229, 396
Pindikowsky, Alexander (W.J.), 474, 568-69
Pine Bud Avenue, 112
Pippy, Chesley A., 211, 682
Pippy, Father Joseph, 469
Pippy, Capt. Wilfred, 526
Pippy Park, 682-84
Piracy, 78-79, 675, 925
Pitt, Dr. David, 742-44, 745
Pitt, William, 174
Pitts, Capt., 330
Pitts, Hon. James, 872
Pitts, William, 872, 908
Placentia, 128, 295, 300, 340; British capture, 87, 89; and French, 79, 80, 81, 82, 84, 85, 87-89, 90, 92 *passim*
Plagues and epidemics, 293-95, 302-3, 692, 745-46
Plaindealer, 847
Planters, 42, 44-47, 127, 279, 846, 908, 910, 924, 927; and fishery, 45, 47; and French, 80, 81, 83, 84, 86-87, 90
Playhouse Hill *see* Queen's Road
Plays, locally written, 249, 258
Pleasant Street, 306
Pleasantville: and aviation, 354, 355; sport, 321, 324, 330, 331, 332; after World War II, 111-12
Pleasantville Base *see* Fort Pepperrell
Plimpton, A., 287
Plough, 229
Plymouth Road, 229
Plymouth Tavern, 229
Poetry, 182-83, 229, 245, 386
Pole, Sir Charles M., gov., 280; illus., 120
Police, 107, 573, 575, 576; illus., 535
Ponds, 683-84; illus., 651
Poole, Mr., 392
Poor House, 296
Pope Pius VI, 728
Pope Pius XII, 742
Pope Building, 205, 207
Pope Street, 302
Population: *16c* 37; *17c* 45-46, 46-47; *18c* 48, 49, 50-51, 137; *19c* 51, 54, 58, 145, 714, 715; church going, 711, 713, 721-22; military, 85, 89, 90, 98 *see also* Census
Port Union, 205
Portugal, 33-34, 35, 40, 78, 329
Portugal Cove, 144, 247, 280, 295, 510, 503-7
Portugal Cove Road, 96, 296, 300, 335
Portuguese fishermen: illus., 708
Portuguese fleet, 980-81
Post Office, 175, 176-78, 264; illus., 171

Part II begins on page 433

Postal service, 172-78, 199, 203, 204, 359, 365
Postmaster, 104, 174, 177
Potts, Rev. Dr., 747
Pouch Cove, 320
Pour, Charles, 331
Pour's Bridge see Brine's Bridge
Pour's Hill, 331
Power, Bishop, 232, 251, 253, 464, 782-83
Power, Charles, 229
Power, Eleanor and Robert, 553-54
Power, John, 843
Power, Mother John, 786-87
Power, Johnny (Rhodie), 830
Power, Mogue, 340, 475
Power, Nicolas, 553
Power, Richard, 692, 736, 923
Power, Richard, 547
Power, Tom, 572
Power, Walter, 341
Powers, Thomas, 983
Power's Court, 60
Prato, Albert de, 173
Pratt, Christopher, 397-98
Pratt, Claire, 399
Pratt, Edwin John, 398-99
Pratt, John, 398
Pratt, Mary, 398
Prefect, Samuel, 925
Presbyterian Church, 748-50, 751
Presbyterians, 108, 749-51
Prescott, Lady, 251
Prescott, Capt. Henry, gov., 145, 146, 175, 188, 290, 457, 635, 732-36, 748; illus., 701
Prescott Street, 44, 184, 194, 195, 210, 249, 253, 328, 386, 389
Presentation Convent, 304-5
Presentation Sisters, 55-56, 786-92
Press gangs, 820, 922-23
Preston, H.W., 248-49 passim
Prim, Peter, 547
Prime, Prof., 324
Prince Arthur, Duke of Connaught, 671
Prince Edward Island Railway, 509
Prince of Wales Arena, 327
Prince of Wales College, 395, 397
Prince of Wales Skating Rink, 206, 325-28 passim, 333, 334; illus., 615
Prince of Wales Street, 111, 327, 329
Prince Philip Drive, 308
Prince's Baths, 320-21, 511
Prince's Rink see Prince of Wales Skating Rink
Prince's Street, 43, 44, 111
Pringle, Col., 95, 138, 753
Pringle Place, 229, 233, 329, 558
Pringle's Bridge see Rennie's Bridge
Pringlesdale, 558 see also Littlefield
Prisons, 283, 290, 559-62, 562-68, 594, 782-83

Pritchard, Dr., 365
Pritzler, Theophilus, 50
Professor David Bennett's Band, 464, 510, 735
Property rights, 46, 49-50, 52, 55
Proctor, Dr., 281
Prostitution, 226-27, 235-36, 237
Protestants, 50, 145, 231-32, 714-16; dissenting, 718, 719, 744, 752, 753 see also Religion
Protocol review, 395
Prowse, Judge D.W., 301, 462, 504, 551, 558-59, 643, 665, 677, 917; illus., 540
Prowse family, 917
Public buildings, 54-55, 57-58, 60
Public Health, 52-53, 55, 61, 100-101
Public houses and inns, 136, 176, 227-31, 237, 318, 456, 504, 522-30, 577, 632, 820; early, 53, 58, 175, 226, 519; and transportation, 519-20
Public Ledger, 184-87 passim, 190, 191, 320, 338, 339, 523, 568, 732, 734, 739, 829
Public Parks, 678, 682, 684, 686; illus., 661, 663 see also under individual names
Public transportation: bus system, 519; cabs, 511-12; ferry and rail, 520; omnibus, 511; illus., 494-95; railway history, 515-17; streetcars, 517-19; street railway, 513; street paving, 517-18
Puddester, John, 269
Purcell, James, 458, 459, 716-17, 740
Putnam, George Palmer, 980
Pxons see Exon, Andrew
Pye Corner see Rotten Row

Queen, cinema, 263, 265
Queen Street, 43, 44, 57, 178, 250, 323, 383, 387
Queen's Battery, 94, 96, 106
Queen's College, 388, 396, 397
Queen's Road, 243, 253, 254, 262, 292, 320, 335, 386, 458, 459; illus., 917
Queen's Wharf, 59, 910
Quidi Vidi, 45, 341-42, 390; illus., 24, 66
Quidi Vidi Harbour, 90, 91, 97
Quidi Vidi Lake: airship, 358; and aviation, 354, 355, 359, 366, 367; bull-baiting, 317; common pasture, 330, 642; forest, 52, 54; Fort Pepperrell, 110; Regatta, 339-41 passim, 676; sports, 112, 319, 321, 324, 326, 329, 330; illus., 661
Quirk, Cornelius, 229-31

Radford, Henry, 840
Radio, 205-8, 395, 671
Radio Building, 323
Radio Telegraph see Telegraph, Radio
Raftus, Anastasia, 633
Raftus, Richard, 588, 855
Raftus, Thomas, 849, 855

Railway, 196, 385, 392, 462, 465, 506-10, 515-18; Fort William Station, 107, 108, 203, 328; illus., 487 see also Newfoundland Railway, Reid-Newfoundland Railway
Raleigh, Sir Walter, 38, 42
Rals see Violence
Randell, Capt. Robert, 975
Rankin, Charles R., 838
Rankin Street, 329
Rape, 550, 578, 646, 666 see also Violence
Rau, A.H., 207
Rawlins, John, 840
Rawlins, Patrick, 840
Rawlin's Cross, 512, 629, 637, 646; illus., 616
Raynes, George, 693
Raynham, F.P., 352-55; illus., 349
Reading Rooms, 175
Reardon, Monseigneur, 829
Red Cow, 228
Red Lion, 332
Reddin, John H., 305
Redmond, Patrick, 228
Reeve's Place, 321
Reeves, Judge John, 280, 550, 727; illus., 533
Regal, 264
Regatta, 338-41; illus., 312, 313, 316
Reid, Lady, 855
Reid, John, 840, 842
Reid, Loyal, 206
Reid, Sir Robert, 509, 515-17, 529-30, 855, 914; illus., 486
Reid, Robert, Jr., 512; illus., 497
Reid, W.D., 299, 334
Reid-Newfoundland Railway, 332, 390, 515-17, 529-30, 856, 925, 976; illus., 489, 491
Religion, 47, 146, 725, 753; disturbances, 145, 686, 688; and politics, 184-93
Remmington, John, 742
Rendal, John, 82
Rendell, Dr., 196, 299
Rendell, George, 640
Rendell, Margaret, 303
Rendell, Col. R.G., 684, 862
Rendell, Stephen, 914
Rendell, W. & G., 825, 909
Rendell Place, 112
Rennie, David G., 321
Rennie's Bridge, 234, 238
Rennie's Mill: illus., 311
Rennie's Mill Road, 110, 112, 335
Rennie's River, 321, 323, 337, 340
Renouf, G. Rex, 835
Renouf, J., 626
Renouf Building, 478
Renouf's Academy, 396
Representative Government see Government, Representative
Responsible Government see Government, Responsible

Rice, Rev. Jacob, 712
Rice family, 781
Richard, Adm., gov., 824
Richards, Gladys, 267
Richards, Capt. Michael, 82, 83
Richardson, Joseph, 564
Richery, Adm., 97, 98
Richey, Rev. Matthew, 746
Ricketts, Thomas R., 399-400, 848-51; illus., 76
Ridley, Thomas, 507
Ring, Patty, 261
Rinks, 324-26, 328-29
Riots: illus., 448-49 see also Violence
Rising Sun, 229
Ritcey, Muriel, 839
Ritcey, Robert, 839
Riverdale, 323
Riverhead, 44
Riverhead Hospital see St. John's Hospital
Roads see Streets and roads
Robbins, James, 567
Robe, Maj., 459
Roberval, see De la Roque, Jean-François Sieur de Roberval
Robin Hood Bay, 332
Robinson, J. Alex, 196
Robinson, Chief Justice Bryan, 558, 588
Robinson, Sir Robert, 80
Robinson-Blackmore, 196
Robinson's Hill see Pringle Place
Roche, Archbishop Edward Patrick, 306, 473, 711, 742
Roddick, Sir Thomas, 308
Rodney, 132
Rodney, Mr., 248
Rodney, Capt. George Brydges, gov., 132; illus., 123
Rogers, Capt., 330
Rogers, Dominie, 747
Rogers, John, 726
Rogerson, Miss, 857
Rogerson, J. J., 478, 632, 746, 841, 859
Roleston, Richard, 585-86
Roller-skating, 328-29
Roman Catholic Cathedral, 57, 147, 252, 255, 716, 736-42; illus., 703, 704, 705
Roman Catholic Church, 40, 50, 55-56, 57, 108, 136, 145, 231, 237, 295, 306, 693-94, 711, 723-42; and governors, 141, 144, 146, 147; and politics, 101, 184-93; see also Catholics
Roope, Col. John, 83, 85
Rorke, James, 507
Rose & Crown, 228
Ross, Capt., 301
Ross, Adam, 923
Ross's Farm, 330
Ross's Valley, 301
Rossley, Mr., 263

Part II begins on page 433

Rossley, Bonnie, 264
Rossley's East, cinema, 263-64
Rossley's West, cinema, 263-64
Rostellan Street, 285
Rotary Club, 266, 321
Rotten Row, 43
Routh, Richard, Chief Justice, 775
Routledge, Bennett, 319
Row, William B., 238, 240, 458, 573
Rowe, Dr., 279, 825, 910
Royal Americans: and French, 91
Royal Artillery, 98
Royal Canadian Engineers, 97
Royal Canadian Mounted Police, 576
Royal Canadian Naval Hospital, 299-300
Royal Canadian Navy, 111, 929
Royal Commission: 1966, 477
Royal Commission on Health Services for
    Newfoundland, 308
Royal Dispensary, 287
Royal Engineers, 83, 104, 720
Royal Gazette & Newfoundland Advertiser,
    175, 179-83, 238, 317, 339, 463-64, 476, 485,
    561, 568-69, 627, 634, 643, 667, 675, 684,
    717, 920
Royal Lake Pavilion, 390
Royal Naval Reserve, 108, 109
Royal Newfoundland Companies, 112, 231,
    458, 632, 633
Royal Newfoundland Fencibles, 103
Royal Newfoundland Regiment, 96, 97, 98,
    99-103, 108, 112, 280, 307, 325-26, 394, 395,
    399
Royal Newfoundland Volunteers, 96, 98
Royal Oak Tavern, 228, 829
Royal Restaurant, 390
Royal Standard, 228
Royal Trust Company, 357-58
Ruby, Mr., 842
Rudkin, Capt. Mark, 233-34
Rumbolt, Ignatius, 255
Russell, Sgt. E., 108
Russell, Ted, 258
Russell, Sgt. William, 108
Rusted, Dr. Ian, 308
Rut, John, 34, 35, 172, 173
Rutherford, R. and J. J., 833, 869-70
Rutledge, Burrell, 678
Rutledge, Peter, 331
Rutledge's Brook *see* Virginia River
Ruyter, Adm. de, 79; illus., 121
Ryall family, 470
Ryan, Hon. J. J., 872
Ryan, John, 178-80, 182, 188
Ryan, John D., 545
Ryan, Lewis Kelly, 180-81
Ryan, Mary, 546
Ryann, Michael, 666

Sabine, Rev. James, 744
Sailor, The, 228
St. Andrew's Soccer Team, 329
St. Augustine, Florida, 31
St. Anthony, 365, 366
St. Barbe, 467
St. Bonaventure College, 57, 326, 327, 386,
    395, 736, 782-84, 835; illus., 767, 769
St. Bride's College, 322, 800-801
St. Catherine's, St. Mary's Bay, 397
St. Clare Avenue, 305, 306
St. Clare's Hospital, 300, 306, 308, 357
St. George's Barracks, 297
St. George's Bay, 508
St. George's Field, 329, 331
St. John, Edward, 828
St. John, Frances, 475
St. John, N.B.: fire, 641
St. John's: descriptions, *16c* 35; *17c* 47-48; *18c*
    48-51; *19c* 51-62; founding, 42; geographi-
    cal site, 819-20; Gilbert's proclamation, 39-
    40; growth, 44-48, 48-51, 51-62; naming,
    33-35; "oldest city" controversy, 31; oldest
    commercial street, 819, 888; oldest houses,
    521, 627-28, illus., 604, 605; public trans-
    portation, 503 ff, 519; town council and
    police, 475; illus., 535; *see also* Municipal
    Government
St. John's Agricultural Society, 464
— — Amateur Baseball League, 331-32
— — Ambulance Brigade, 307
— — & Carbonear Electric Telegraph
        Company, 197
— — Athlete of the Year Award, 335
— — Church, 57
— — Cricket Club, 330
— — Cricket Grounds, 330-31
— — Curling & Skating Rink *see* Parade
        Rink
— — Dog, 135
— — Football Club, 329
— — Gas Light Company, 513
— — Historic Trust, 342
— — Hospital, 282, 283, 289-91, 292, 293,
        295, 296-97, 298, 302, 849; and poor
        house, 298
— — Isle, 35
— — Lane, 43, 204, 389
— — Library and Reading Room, 834, 875
— — Players, 267, 268-69
— — Races, 319-20
— — Radio Club, 205
— — School of Music, 253
— — Senior Hockey League, 326
— — Skating Rink Company, 325
— — Symphony Orchestra, 270
— — Theatre, 240-41, 248-49 *see also*
        Amateur Theatre

St. John's Turf Club, 319, 320
— — Volunteer Rangers, 106-7, 284
— — War Services Committee, 394
— — Water Company, 476
St. Joseph's Convent, 60
St. Mary's Bay, 81, 295
St. Ovide, 87, 88, 89
St. Pat's field, 329, 332
St. Patrick's Auditorium, 323
St. Patrick's Church, 251
St. Patrick's Day, 258
St. Patrick's Hall, 253, 260, 262, 383, 782 *see also* Nickel Theatre
St. Patrick's Schoolroom, Riverhead, 232
St. Peter's Chapel, 251
St. Pierre, 79, 99
St. Pius x School, 286, 322
St. Thomas' Church, 60, 245, 336, 721; illus., 712; *see* Old Garrison Church
Salee Rovers, 79
Saltbox houses, 46
Salvation Army, 306-7, 797; illus., 794
Sanatorium, 299-300, 306
Sarnoff, D., 207, 208
Saunders, Mrs. Wix, 681
Sawer, Mrs., 910
Scallan, Rev. Thomas, Bishop, 245, 731-32, 745; illus, 705
Scanlan's Lane, 175
Schmidt, Herr, 737-38
Schools, 144, 251, 326, 329, 333, 775-81, 796, 798, 865 *see esp.* chapter 7
Schuyler, Lt., 91
Sclater, David, 880
Scotland Row, 287, 288
Scott, Rev., 237
Scott, Barbara Ann, 326
Scott, Frank, 676-77
Scott, Sir Giles Gilbert, 717-18, 798
Scott, Robert Falcon, 963-65
Seaborn, R.L., Archbishop, 723, 785
Seal Hunt, 208, 358-59, 966-75; illus., 900, 901, 902; *see esp.* chapter 10; *see also* Commerce and Business Development
Search and Rescue service, 365, 366
Sears, Garrett, 588
Seaton, James, 838
Selby, Margaret, 383
Serjeant, William, 46
Servants *see* Domestic Servants
Settlement, 905-6; *16c* 33, 39-40, 42; *17c* 43-48; *19c* 284
Seven Years War, 90-93, 677
Sewage system, 52, 55
Sexual mores, 235-36, 237
Seymour, Geoff, 255
Seymour, Vice-Admiral Sir George, 460, 524
Shackleton, Ernest, 763-64

Shadforth, Lt. H., 825
Shamrock Cricket Team: illus., 315
Shamrock Field, 111, 329, 332
Shamrock Wrestling Club, 334
Shamrocks (baseball team), 332
Shanadithit, 833, 926; illus., 895
Shang, Que John, 592-93
Shanks, Thomas, 244
Shaw, Joseph, 267
Shea, Dr., 256
Shea, Mr., 282
Shea, Capt. Ambrose, 303
Shea, Sir Ambrose, gov., 104, 400-401, 462, 464, 824, 909, 918; illus., 125
Shea, Edward Dalton, 184, 831
Shea, George, mayor, 303, 476, 909
Shea, Henry, 104
Shea, Mary, 750
Shea, Richard, 557
Shea, William, 528
Sheehan, Mrs., 854
Ship, tavern, 228, 342, 519-20, 825, 887
Ship Assistance, tavern, 228
Ship disasters *see under individual names and also* chapter 10
Ship's rooms, 43, 44, 46, 47, 52, 55, 86, 243, 820 *see also under individual names*
Shipbuilding, 841, 907
Shipping lines, 862, 909, 912, 924, 953 ff.
Ships: largest in port, 1941, 110; plague and epidemics from, 292-93, 294; radio, 207-8
Ships: *Adriatic* 986, illus. 956; *Advance* 998; *Alert* 644, 928, illus. 614; *Algerine* 972; *Ampere* 928; *Antelope* 982; *Argo* 953-54, 956, illus. 936; *Argyle* 976, 985; *Ariel* 506, 508, 787; *Arizona* 907; *Aurora* 637, 972; *Austriah* 987; *Avalon* 982; *Bear* 966, illus. 944; *Bedford* 93; *Beechmore* 956; *Beinir* 802, 929; *Bellaventure* 975; *Beothic* 208, 984, illus. 900; *Bermuda* 460; *Bessie Marie* 919; *Bjorn* 956; *Bloodhound* 916, 971; *Blue Jacket* 953, 955; *Bonaventure* 984; *Boston* 692, 718, 922-23; *Britannia* 562; *Briton* 922 *see also Calypso; Brittania* 105; *Brittany* 960; *Bruce* 302, 516, 976, illus. 492; *Bullfinch* 750; *Buzzard* 460; *Calliope* 975; *Calypso* 72, 108, 676, 922, 975-76; *Camelia* 854; *Canada* 506; *Caribou* 977-78, illus. 951; *Carmenia* 363; *Carthaginian* 400; *Charlotte* 956; *Chesapeake* 847; *City of Halifax* 378, 916; *Cleopatra* 678; *Comet* 851; *Connaught* 953, illus. 937; *Cumberland* 460, 524; *Curlew* 957, 959; *Cygnet* 579-80; *Dash* 859; *Dauntless* 953, 983; *Deerhound* 970; *Delight* 39, 40, 41, 981; *Desola* 924; *Diamond* 293; *Diana* 967, 969, 972, 990, illus. 945; *D'Iberville* 928; *Discovery* 884, 964; *Dover* 641; *Duke* 958; *Dundee* 977; *Eagle*

Part II begins on page 433

Ships (continued)

967, 969, 989, illus. 946; *Edward B. Alexander* 110, 684; *Edward* 294; *Effie M. Morrissey* 979-80; *Egeria* 141; *Endeavour* 137; *Enterprise* 93; *Eric* 972, 978; *Ethel* 641; *Ethie* 976, illus. 941; *Excelsior* 985; *Express* 506; *Favourite* 636; *Fiddell* 89; *Fife* 925; *Fiona* 109, 194, 195; *Flora* 915; *Florizel* 112, 208, 672, 840, 956, 961-63; *Fly* 141; *Fort Amherst* 912, 956, 961; *Fort Townshend* 912, 956, 961; *Foundation Franklyn* 985; *Fram* 965; *Garland* 510, 511; *George* 925; *Georgian* 825; *Georgina* 970; *Gil Eames* 981; *Golden Dawn* 510-11; *Golden Hind* 39, 41; *Gosport* 90, 93; *Grace* 301; *Grand Lake* 529, 907; *Grasshopper* 557; *Gratias Deo* 37; *Great Eastern* 957, illus. 166; *Greenland* 644, 917 972-73; *Greenwich* 829; *Hanovian* 513; *Hawk* 717, 957; *Hazard* 189; *Hector* 967; *Hiberian* 909; *Home* 398, 976; *Hope* 916, 988; *Huntress* 641; *Huntsman* 971; *Hydra* 139; *Iceland* 644, 917, 969, 972; *Ida* 841; *Invermore* 690, 977; *John and Mary* 635, 970; *John Cabot* 928; *Julia* 983; *Karluk* 979; *Kelmscott* 978; *Koonya* 964; *Kyle* 363, 367, 974, 977; *Labrador* 972; *Lady Le Marchant* 507; *Lady St. John* 986; *La Garonne* 91; *La Grande Hermine* 37; *La Jupitor* 97; *La Sicorne* 91; *Latona* 99, 673-74; *Lapland* 363; *L'Emerillon* 37; *Leopard* 969; *L'Eville* 91; *Macedonia* 966; *Manhattan* 928; *Marcia* 546; *Margaret* 970; *Margaret Ann* 835; *Marigold* 341; *Marsland* 985; *Mary* 970; *Mary of Guildford* 35, 172, 173; *Mastiff* 917, 971; *Matthew* 33, 37; *Merlin* 509; *Metagama* 984; *Micmac* 916; *Meigle* 528-29, 976, 985; *Minerva* 100; *Minnie Schiffer* 964; *Miranda* 513; *Monarch* 923; *Moravian* 781; *Morning* 963-65; *M.V. Ernestine* 980; *Native Lass* 506; *Nelly* 641; *Neptune* 208, 969, 972, 985; *Neptune II* 985-86; *Nerissa* 956; *Nestorian* 909; *Newfoundland* 852, 927, 955-56, 972, 974, illus. 950; *Nimrod* 963-64, 971, illus. 943; *Niobe* 983; *Nonsuch* 851; *Nora Bailey* 985; *Nora Creina* 506; *Norfolk* 985; *North American* 176; *Northumberland* 90, 93; *Nova Scotia* 985, illus. 950; *Pacific* 988; *Panther* 644, 972; *Pauline Winters* 919; *Pegasus* 548; *Persia* 990; *Phoebe* 984; *Plover* 957; *Pluto* 684, 925; *Polynesian* 514; *Portia* 178, 302, 957, 974, 988; *Prince Albert* 987; *Prince Le Boo* 641; *Prospero* 957; *Proteus* 862, 966, illus. 947; *Queen* 860; *Rainbow* 132, 835; *Raleigh* 38, 39; *Ranger* 862, 969, 972; *Regulus* 828; *Robuste* 91; *Roosevelt* 979; *Rosalind* 956; *Rosamund* 53, 54, 874; *Rose* 504; *Sabine*

Ships (continued)

923; *Sagona* 917, 967-68; *St. Laurent* 826; *St. Mary St. Vincent* 79; *Samson* 35, 173; *San Felix* 925; *Santa Maria* 37; *Sardinia* 199; *Shannon* 847; *Shark* 101; *Sharpshooter* 641; *Shrewsbury* 93, 100, 136; *Siberian* 959-60; *Silvia* 956, 984; *Sir Francis Drake* 141; *Sir Humphrey Gilbert* 925; *Sir Walter Scott* 793; *Solway* 976; *Southern Cross* 644, 974; *Spikenard* 825; *Squirrel* 39, 40, 41, 128; *Standard* 509; *Star* 587; *Stephano* 956, 961-63, 974; *Styx* 990; *Superb* 93, 100; *Surprise* 99; *Sutherland* 712; *Swallow* 39; *Swifts* 833; *Swiftsure* 923; *Sycamore* 956; *Sylvia* 359; *Syren* 90, 93; *Tamer* 107; *Tenedos* 478, 925; *Terra Nova* 849, 962, 964-66, 972, illus. 942; *Tiger* 508; *Tigress* 971; *Titan* 983; *Titania* 961; *Trincomalee* 292; *Trinity* 36; *True Blue* 970; *Ungava* 968; *Vanguard* 983, illus. 21; *Venus* 546; *Veronica* 983; *Victoria* 507-8; *Victorian* 205; *Viking* 968; *Village Belle* 971; *Virginia Lake* 907, 972; *Walrus* 508, 862, 972; *Watchful* 967; *William* 36; *William Penn* 987; *Zelik* 802, 929

Shoal Harbour, 361, 362

Shop owners *see esp.* chapter 8

Shops, 52, 53, 58-59, 831 *see esp.* chapter 8

Short, Mrs., 235, 236

Shoulder of Mutton, tavern, 228

Sidewalks, 58

Signal Hill, 561-62, 565, 641, 666-67, 673-78, 733; Battle of, 91, 93; fortifications, 90, 96, 97, 106; hospitals, 165, 297, 299, 300-302; and Marconi, 200, 205, 677; Military Tattoo, 112; Regatta gun, 340; stone for Government House, 143; timbered, 52

Signal Hill Road, 60, 230, 245

Sillars, Mr., 589, 870

Sillars and Cairns, 589, 870; illus., 530

Simms, Ann, 145

Simms, Charles, 573

Simms, Henry, 780

Simms, James, 573

Sisters of Mercy: and hostel, 304, 305, 306; nursing, 295; school, 251, 295, 304, 305, 306, 792-95, 796

Sisters of Service: hostel, 176, 306

Skating, 322, 324-26, 328 *see also* Hockey

Skeans, Walter, 443

Skeans, William, 335

Skerret (Skerritt), Brig. Gen. William, 101-4 *passim*, 230, 730

Skiffington, Maurice, 567

Skiing, 322, 337

Skinner, Archbishop, 742

Skinner, Mary, 858

Skinner, Gen. Thomas, 96-97 *passim*, 100-103 *passim*, 179

Slater, David, 747
Slaves, 180, 181
Sleater's Store, 209
Sleighs, 56, 319
Smallpox, 280-81, 292-94, 295, 299, 301-3, 927
Smallwood, David, 839-40
Smallwood, Fred, 834
Smallwood, Joseph R., 152, 178, 207, 270, 327, 395, 472, 474, 569, 576-77, 682, 830, 839-40, 911; illus., 452
Smith, Father, 723
Smith, Alexander, 681
Smith, Flipper 275
Smith, Capt. Thomas, 89, 132
Smith, Dr. W.I., 588
Smith, Dr. Whitney, 690
Smith & Chisholm, 209
Smith Avenue, 327
Smithville, 322-23
Snow, Catherine, 571, 583-85
Snow, John, 594
Soccer, 329-30
Social conditions: *17c* 47; *18c* 51; *early 19c* 53-56; *late 19c* 59, 60-61; of military, 82, 83, 96, 100-101, 102, 103; poorhouse, 296; welfare *19c* 147
Social customs, 83-84, 96, 226 *see also* Entertainment
Social life, 144-45
Society for Improving the Conditions of the Poor, 230, 240, 243
Society of Merchant Venturers of Bristol, 42-43
Softball, 332
Soldiers Meadow: illus., 853
Solomon, Simon, 104, 174-75, 729-30, 831
Solomon, William, 175-76, 177, 831
Solomon's Lane *see* Gregory's Lane
Somers, Bill, 505
Soper, George, 837
Soper, James, 837
Soper, William, 837
Sothoron, Frank, 99
South Battery, 97, 105
South West Street *see* Colonial Street
South West Street Skating Rink, 323, 324
Southcott, John, 304
Southcott, Mary, 303-4
Southcott, Pamela, 304
Southcott Hall, 304
Southside, 288
Southside Hills, 52, 53, 81, 111, 143
Southwest (street), 204
Spain, 38, 40, 78, 329
Sparkes, G.N., 566
Spencer, Dr. Aubrey, Bishop, 687, 714-15, 716, 720, 721; illus., 697
Spence's Speed Bowl *see* Lakeside Speedway

Sports, 53, 112, 151, 317-41
Spratt, Herbert, 594-95
Spratt, James, 594
Spring, Arthur, 583-84
Springdale Street, 44, 51, 52, 60, 228
Squires, Lady Helena, 480
Squires, Sir Richard, 110, 466-70, 480, 570, 671, 673, 798; illus., 473
Stabb, Dr. H.H., 288, 291-92 *passim*, 293, 294, 298, 508, 824
Stabb, H.J., 893
Stabb, Hon. Nicholas, 912, 913
Stabb, Thomas, 913
Stacey, Mr., 252
Stackebald, John, 550
Stages, 45 *see also* Ship's rooms
Stamp, Frank, 333
Stamps, 176, 210
Stanilan, Dr., 281
Stanley, Lord, 285
Star, The, 302
Star Chamber, 126
Star Hall, 254, 264, 281, 318
Star of the Sea Society, 251, 264, 318, 329, 719, 728
Starr, John, 514-15
Starrett, Charles, 722, 968
Stationery shops, 184, 196, 209
Stead, Mr., 838
Steel, Sgt., 88
Steele, S.O., 827
Steer, John, 678, 858-59, 873, 924
Steer's Cove, 43, 265
Stephens, James, 987
Stephenville, 110, 366
Sterling, Geoff, 841
Sterling, Rex, 841
Stevenson, John, 506
Stewart, Andrew and Mrs., 522
Stewart, Ellen, 827
Stewart, James, 106, 244, 862
Stewart & Company, 176
Stilts: houses built on, 56
Stirling, Geoff, 207
Stirling, Georgina, 190, 256-57; illus., 224
Stirling, Dr. W., 190, 583
Stocks, 86
Stone, Marian, 304
Stonemasons, 46, 85
Stott, James, 878, 885
Stourton, Rev. Erasmus, 723
Strachan, Dr., 233, 234
Strawberry Marsh Road, 304
Street rail routes, 517-18, 844; illus., 515; *see also* Public Transportation
Streets and roads, 144, 237, 517-18, 682-83; early, 39, 137, 829; *19c* 52, 55, 57, 58, 59, 61, 678, 680; ship's rooms, 43, 46; *see esp.* chapter 8

Strikes, 576, 973-74
Stripling, John, 137, 547, 551, 824, 908
Stripling, Mary, 138
Stuart, John, 667
Studdy, John, 828, 876
Stuldham, Lord, 96
Subercase, gov., 84-85 *passim*
Submarines, 928; U-boats, 956, 962, 977-79
Sudbury Hospital, 301
Suffragette Movement, 479-80
Sullivan, Inspector Gen., 464
Sullivan, Mrs., 741
Sullivan, Arthur, 364-66
Sullivan, John, 776
Summers, Miss, 304
Summers, Dennis, 587
Summers, George, 401
Summers, P.J., 401
Sun, tavern, 229
Supple, Henry, 379
Supreme Court of Newfoundland, 144, 194
Surrogate Courts, 285
Sutton, Mr., 92
Swimming pools, 320-22
Syme, John, 862
Symons, Mr., 87
Synod Hall, 254

Tabernacle School, 207, 746
Tadini, Antonio, 840
Talbot, Thomas, 57
Tank Lane: water supply, 476
Tarahan, Anastasia, 523
Tarahan, Patrick, 828
Tarahan's Town: fire, 631-32
Tavern for All Weathers, 228
Taverner, Abraham, 86
Taverner, Ben, 367
Taverner, William, 86
Tavernor, Capt. Benjamin, 977-78; illus., 951
Taverns *see* Public Houses
Taylor, Hayward, 108
Taylor, William, 378-80
Teachers, 778, 785-86, 795-96 *see also under*
     schools, colleges
Telegram Lane, 184, 195, 318
Telegraph, Cable, 196-99, 203-4 *see also* At-
     lantic Cable
Telegraph, Radio, 199-203
Telegraph, Radio, 199-203, 912
Telephone, 204-5
Television, 207, 266, 267, 268, 334-35
Temperance Hall, 232
Temperance Hotel, 208
Temperance movement, 231-32
Temperance Saloon, 318, 323
Temperance Street, 229, 232, 237, 279, 320
Templeman, John, 87

Templeman, Hon. P., 922
Templeman's Bonavista, 403
Tennis, 322-23, 328
Terminer, Mr., 284
Terra Nova Curling Club, 324, 325
Terra Nova Foundry, 329
Terra Nova Wrestling Club, 334
Ternay, Adm. de, 90, 92
Tessier, Charles, 857-58
Tessier, Lewis, 847, 858
Tessier, Peter Germon, 849, 858
Theatres, 144, 150-51, 229, 232, 237-52, 253,
     254-59, 261, 266-70, 380-82, 628, 834; illus.,
     659
Theatre Arts Club, 269
Theatre Guild, 267, 268
Theatre Hill *see* Queen's Road
Theatre St. John's, 238-41
Thomas, Aaron, 228, 341-42, 519, 673
Thomas, Henry J., 677
Thomas, William, 104, 187, 238, 240, 667, 745,
     824, 918
Thomas, W. & H. & Company, 287
Thomas' Farm, 319
Thomey, Capt. Henry, 888
Thompson of Fleet, Lord, 195
Thompson, C.R., 301, 851
Thompson, J.B., 626-27
Thompson's Jewellery Race, 336
Thorburn, Sir Robert, 464, 915
Thorne, James, 594
Thorne, Robert, 173
Thorne Bay *see* Torbay
Tilt Cove Copper Mine, 324
Tilt houses, 44, 46, 50
Tilts: illus., 13
Times, 184, 208, 231, 248, 668, 717, 720, 721-
     22
Tobin, Hon. James, 296, 459, 460, 912; illus.,
     275
Tobin, Mr. and Mrs. John, 526
Toe, Tommy *see* Peddle, Tommy
Tonge, Capt. 179
Tonkin, Lady Eliza, 824
Tooton, Anthony, 311
Topsail: road to, 58, 144; railway to, 509-10
Topsail Road, 51, 266, 299-300, 306, 319, 383,
     464
Torbay, 44, 91, 97, 144, 335
Torbay Airport, 322, 366, 367-68
Torbay Road, 144, 320
Toronto, 364-65
Total Abstinence & Benefit Society, 232, 254,
     265, 318, 823, 836
Total Abstinence Hall: building, *1873* 232,
     251; building, *1894* 254; circus, 254; con-
     certs, 253; fires, 254, 265; radio studios, 206;
     theatre, 150, 257; cinema, 259, 261

Tough, George, 546
Toulinguet, Marie see Stirling, Georgina Ann
Toussaint, Mr. and Mrs. John C., 524-25
Toussaint, William, 504, 524
Towill, Christopher, 174
Town crier, 172
Townshend, Lord, 96
Tracey, Miss, 590
Track and field sports, 335-336
Trade: *16c* 35, 37; *17c* 44, 47, 49; *18c* 50-51, 137; retail, *19c* 61; see also Commerce and business development
Trade Review, 199, 464
Trade unions, 827
Traffic, 58
Trans-Canada Airlines see Air Canada
Trans-Canada Highway, 58
Transatlantic flights, 352-58, 681; illus., 657
Transatlantic passenger service see Shipping lines
Transport, 56, 58, 135, 196, 512, 518-20 see also Public transportation, Railways
Travers, Mary, 456-57
Treaty of Utrecht, 89, 508
Tremblett, Capt., 102
Tremblett, Thomas, 555
Tremlett, Chief Justice, 179, 548
Trepassey, 79, 352-53
Trevanion, Sir Nicholas, 89
Treworgie, John, 127
Trinity, 279, 280
Trites, Mr., 261
Trolleys: *early 19c* 56
Troy, Rev., 186, 188, 285, 582
Tuberculosis, 299-300
Tucker, Chief Justice Richard, 234, 558, 559
Tudor, Maj. Gen. Sir Hugh, 401-3
Tuff, Hector, 566
Tullidge, Dr. Henry H., 281, 308
Tulliken, Lt., 92
Tupper, Alvin, 527
Turbid's Town, 296
Twenty Mile Pond see Windsor Lake
Twenty Mile Pond Battery, 96-97
Twillingate, 145, 177, 256, 257, 282
Typhus, 302, 794-95
Tyrell & Landigan Company, 250

U.S.O., 854
Ugly Club, 521-22
Union Bank Building, 478; illus., 445
United Church, 747, 754, 784 see Methodists
United Kingdom: responsibility for Newfoundland's debts, 471-72
United States of America: War against Britain, 106-7; World War II, 109-11, 112, 579, 684; illus., 663
United States Army Transportation Terminal Command Arctic, 111

United States Picture & Portrait Company, 211
United Towns Electric Company, 204
Universal suffrage, 475
Unknown murderer, 587-88, 693
Urquhart, A.A., 253

VOAS, 206
VOCM, 205-6 *passim,* 646, 747, 836
VOGY, 206
VON, 928
VONF, 206, 207, 472
VOS, 205-6 *passim,* 836
VOWN, 472
VOWR, 206
Vail, R., 849
Valdmanis, Dr. Alfred, 569
Valentine & Doane, 208
Vanburgh, gov., 552
Vane, Mr., 89
Vandalism see Violence
Vardy, O.L., 207
Vaudeville, 263-64
Venereal disease, 281
Vera Cruz, 31
Vernon, Hilary, 267
Veterans hospitals, 300-301
Vey, James, 210
Victoria, Queen, 198, 259, 463, 464, 637, 677, 736-37
Victoria Cross, 399
Victoria Hall, 335
Victoria Park, 289, 322
Victoria Rink, 251, 324, 389
Victoria Street, 58, 210, 232, 253, 396
Victorian Era, 60-61
Victorian Rink, 326
Vikings, 31, 235
Vinnicomb, Joan, 230
Vinnicomb's Hill, 230
Violence: *17c* 127; *19c* 146; bread riots, 868; hooliganism, 109; Irish riots, 145; against LeMarchant, 147-48; and liquor, 227, 233-35; medical issues, 283, 285; murder cases, 579-95, 686, 693, 725; political, 185, 189-93, 263, 461, 465-70, 570-71, 576-79; and prostitution, 237; railway employment, 462; "rals", 140, 744, 748; at Regatta, 339; religious riots, 732; and theatre, 240-41
Virginia River, 112, 321, 330, 366
Virginia Water, 45, 54, 144, 678-79
Visual Arts, 387-89, 396-97, 397-98
Voeux, Sir G.W. des, gov., 149
Voluntary Armed Association see Loyal Volunteers of St. John's

Wadden, Brian, 514
Wadden, Wynn Ann, 255
Wagner, Richard, 135

1038   *Part II begins on page 433*

Wakefield, Dr. Arthur, 108
Walbank, Rev. Thomas, 712
Waldegrave, William, gov., 51, 99, 100-101 *passim*, 104,674,713,728
Waldegrave Battery, 80, 104, 107-9 *passim*, 143
Waldegrave Street, 43, 44
Waldron's Farm, 305
Wales: governor from, 151, 152
Walker, Capt., 735
Wall, Thomas, 843-44
Wallace, James, 98
Wallace, W.J. "Billy", 205
Walsh, Bernard, 375-76
Walsh, Mr. and Mrs. George, 529
Walsh, John, 286
Walsh, Margaret, 228
Walsh, Martin, 546
Walsh, Mary: illus., 277
Walsh, Norman, 267
Walsh's Square, 297
Walwyn, Sir Humphrey Thomas, 267, 337, 394
Wanderers: baseball team, 332
War Memorial, 39, 389, 456, 826-27; illus., 77, 662
War of the Austrian Succession, 89-90
Ward, Father, 582
Ward, Rev. Daniel S., 753
Ward, Elizabeth, 546
Ward, Sarah, 387
Warner, Dr., 281, 282, 285, 290, 298
Warner, James, 776
Warren, Edith Harvey, 929
Warren, William, P.M., 570, 865
Warrington, Mr. and Mrs., 527
Watchmakers, 51, 175
Water Street: *19c* development, 51, 52, 53, 57, 58, 59, 61; business 384, 396, 400; characters, 375, 376, 385; cinema, 261, 263, 264, 265; clubs, 318, 352, 353; and doctors, 285; drug stores, 286, 287, 399; and fire, 621-22, 639-40; gas works, 513; and harbour, 250; hospitals, 289, 295, 300, 301, 303; and hotels, 522-23, 525-28, 530; improvements, 389; mall, 337; market house, 294; newspapers, 183, 185, 195, 196; nightwatch, 172; paving and electric light, 518, illus., 442, 495, 496, 897, 904; photographers, 208-11 *passim;* post office, 175, 176, 178; printers, 184; publichouses, 228, 318; radio, 206, 207; railway, 392; reconstruction, 643; restaurant, 390; riots, 461; seamen's institute, 478; sport, 320, 323, 329, 333; telephone, 204; temperance movement, 232; theatre, 241, 244; water supply, 476; World War II installations, 111; illus., 7, 18, 19, 20, 27, 159; *see esp.* chapter 8

Waterford, Ireland, 49, 57
Waterford Bridge Road, 232, 398
Waterford Hospital, 291-92, 300
Waterford River, 34, 322, 323
Waterford Valley, 81
Watson, Thomas, 249
Wayfarers, The, 269
Webber, David, 557
Weedon, Ezra, 568
Wells, William, 888
Welty, Col. Maurice, 110
Wesleyanism, 136, 206, 746 *see* Methodists
West Country merchants: *16c* 33, 37; *17c* 127, 128, 129; and colonists, 45, 46; and French, 82, 87-88; and settlement, 79
West End Fire Hall, 265, 375
West End Post Office, 301
West End Stores, 111
West India Coffee House, 228
Westerland Road, 322
Western Bay, 398
Western Union Commercial Cables, 199, 203, 204
Weston, Peter, 884
Whaling, 845
Wheatsheaf, 229
Whelan, John, 341
Whelan, Michael, 460, 564
Wheyland, Katherine, 666
Whipping post, 86, 548
Whitbourne, Capt. Richard, 42, 126, 549, 911
Whitbourne, 288
White, Edward, 547
White, John, 207
White, Kit, 583-84
White, T.M., 254
Whiteford, Barney, 835
Whiteway, Louise, 252
Whiteway, Sir William, P.M., 390, 464, 570
Whitney, Viola, 399
Whitty, Father, 691
Widdicombe (Widdecombe), John, 228, 843
Wigh, Sylvia, 255, 269
Wigwam Pond, 365
Wilkins, Nigel, 270
William IV, 318, 521, 548, 680, 840, 843, 882
William Street, 296
Williams, Col. John, 330
Williams, John, 910
Williams, Sir Ralph, gov., 151, 325, 393, 529; illus., 446
Williams, Thomas, 238, 240, 604, 726
Williams Lane, 209, 211, 244, 632
Willock, 909
Willoughby, Sir Percival, 43
Wills & Sons, 714
Wilson, Mr., 587
Wilson, Mrs., 248

Wilson, George E., 251
Wilson & Clark Company, 251
Wilson's New Theatre, 251
Wiltshire, Julia, 957, 960
Winchen, Mr., 88
Windsor Lake, 96, 335, 476, 477, 503
Winston, Henry, 732, 734, 739, 829-30
Winter, Mr., 338
Winter, H.A., 468
Winter, Sir James, 558-59, 909
Winter, Sir Marmaduke, 306, 578, 823
Winter, William, 39, 40
Winter Avenue, 60
Winter Garden Rink, 328
Winter of the Rals, 140
Winterton, 60
Winton, Francis, 193, 840
Winton, Henry David, 184-87, 189-90, 191, 193
Winton, Robert, 193
Wireless Telegraphy see Telegraph, Radio
Wishing Well Park, 329, 332
Wishing Well Road, 205
Withers, J.W., 318, 319
Withers, John Collier, 181
Withy, Edgar, 908
Witless Bay, 302
Wix, Archdeacon, 149, 715-16, 719-20, 789
Wolsey, Cardinal, 172
Women: and education, 763, 784-86, 789, 795; and illiteracy, 777; liberation movement, 466, 479-81
W.R.E.N.S., 111
Wood, Canon, 396, 582-83
Wood, Rev. A.C.F., 590
Wood, F. Page, 209
Wood, J.P., 831
Wood, James, 879
Wood Street, 229, 396
Woodford, Capt. William, 835
Woodland, W.C., 797

Woodley, Mary, 823
Woodley, William, 823
Woods, Hon. H.J.B., 907
Woods, John, 907
Woods, Mabel, 907
Woods, Sydney, 907
Woodward - Whitman Dramatic Company, 258-59
World War I, 107-9, 112, 464, 961; chain boom across Narrows, 95; ex-servicemen's hospital, 300-301; heroes of, 399-400; nurse, 303; and radio station, 681-82; and Regatta, 341
World War II, 109-12, 571, 576; American docks, 927; ammunition storage, 929; blackout, 328; and fires, 645; force facilities, 394-95; Fort Amherst, 94-95; hospitals, 299, 301; hostel, 854; military camps, 329, 332; and narrows, 95; officers club, 825-26; police responsibility, 578; and trains, 516; illus., 663
Wrestling, 334-35
Wright, Andrew and Elizabeth, 830
Wyatt, 909
Wyatt, Dorothy, mayor, 480-81, 855; illus., 453
Wyatt, Herbert J., 855
Wyatt, Herbert K., 855
Wynne-Eaton, Maj., 362-363
Wynott, James, 566

Yellow Belly Hill see Bates Hill
Yeo, Leslie, 267
Yonge, James, 50, 279, 341
Yore, Father, 726
York Street, 137, 229
York Theatre see the Queen
Young, Hackenschmidt see Oppelt, Otto
Young, Melvin, 594-95
Y.M.C.A., 322, 394